Computability and Complexity

Computability and Complexity

Hubie Chen

The MIT Press
Cambridge, Massachusetts
London, England

This book was set in Times New Roman by Hubert Chen. Printed and bound in the United States of America.

Library of Congress Cataloging-in-Publication Data

Names: Chen, Hubie, author.
Title: Computability and complexity / Hubie Chen.
Description: Cambridge, Massachusetts : The MIT Press, [2023] | Includes bibliographical references and index.
Identifiers: LCCN 2022054401 | ISBN 9780262048620 (hardcover) | ISBN 9780262376860 (epub) | ISBN 9780262376853 (pdf)
Subjects: LCSH: Computational complexity.
Classification: LCC QA267.7 .C44 2023 | DDC 511.3/52–dc23/eng20230429
LC record available at https://lccn.loc.gov/2022054401

10 9 8 7 6 5 4 3 2 1

Contents

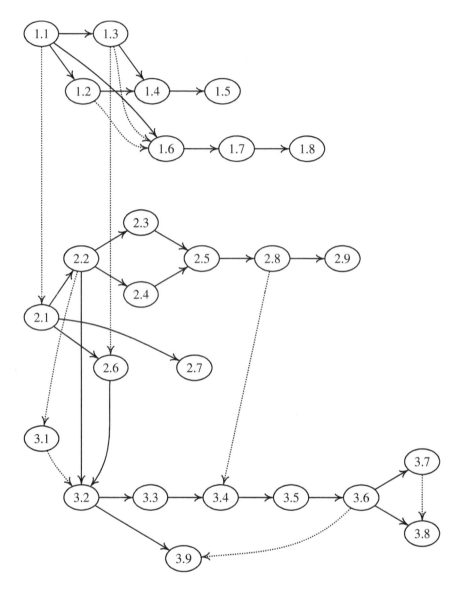

Figure 0.0.1. The dependencies between the sections of Chapters 1, 2, and 3. Each solid arrow indicates a strong dependency; each dotted arrow indicates a weak dependency.

Preface

This textbook is an introduction to the *theory of computation*, viewed here as the study of forms of computation that are abstract in the sense of being defined mathematically, and hence amenable to a mathematical treatment. These forms include general computation as typically associated with the term *algorithm*, time-efficient computation, and space-bounded computation. A key aim of this theory is to understand both the capabilities and limitations of each of these forms of computation; in part, this aim is achieved by comparing the forms to each other.

Audiences

This book is targeted to multiple audiences.

First, this book aspires to be useable in a computer science curriculum at the upper undergraduate level, and above. In particular, it was designed to be accessible to computer science undergraduates having a basic mathematical maturity—namely, comfort working with mathematical notation, definitions, and proofs.

At the same time, this book aims to serve as a thorough, rigorous initiation into the theory of computation which may be used by students, researchers, and workers in disciplines that draw on or depend upon this theory. This initiation should provide its users with the ability to begin engaging with research literature that employs the theory of computation, and a point of departure for learning more about this theory. This book could serve as a primary text or as a reference for both undergraduate-level and graduate-level courses that cover or contact the theory of computation. For all use cases, the crucial background is the aforementioned basic mathematical maturity.

This book's presentation assumes familiarity with basic set-theoretic notions (such as those of *set, subset, power set, intersection,* and *union*), functions, and propositional logic. On the part of the reader, some acquaintance with graph theory and with computer programming would be helpful, but is not strictly required.

Approach

This book attempts to offer a uniform treatment of core concepts and topics in the theory of computation. Throughout, an effort is made to underscore the unity of the subject and its methods of inquiry. A small number of recurrent themes are emphasized: computational models and the comparison of their respective language classes; closure properties of language classes; how determinism and nondeterminism compare in various contexts; and, notions of *reduction* and *completeness*. The treatment strives to sculpt these themes and the covered material into a coherent storyline in the hope of imbuing the reader with a sense of the beauty and mystery held by the subject. Indeed, the desire to maintain an overall narrative influenced not only the approach to the material, but also, to some extent, the choice of which results and topics to include.

Where relevant, the treatment points out alternative ways to approach the material. In addition, numerous remarks, notes, and exercises anticipate and explore ideas that deepen the main presentation. These features were included with the goals of imparting a rounded, robust appreciation of the subject, and of laying a foundation that naturally encourages and leads to further study.

In writing this book, I (the author!) endeavored to provide rigorous proofs of all major results. In fact, there are at least a few points in the book where, in lieu of waving my hands or requesting exercises from the reader, I elected to give arguments in significant detail. I did this with the philosophy that such detailed arguments should, at the minimum, be available to a reader wishing to see them, and with the understanding that a given reader should feel comfortable in skipping such arguments, especially upon initial readings. I have attempted to signal such detailed arguments. (Examples of proofs where such detail occurs include those of Theorem 1.4.1, Theorem 1.4.2, and Theorem 3.6.15; in these cases, I attempted to structure each proof so that the most detail-intensive portions occur in the latter part of the proof.)

Contents and use

A primary axis along which this book is organized is a presented procession of *computational models*, which are mathematical descriptions of computing devices. Following a time-honored tradition, the book begins by considering relatively restricted models called *finite-state automata*, which can process their inputs only by reading and with a finite amount of memory. These models are the subjects of Chapter 1; although restricted, they are well motivated and appealing in their own right, and provide meaningful preparation for the subsequent development. Chapter 2, on *computability theory*, introduces and studies the *Turing machine* model as a formalization of the notion of *algorithm*, and as representative of a fully fledged computational model. *Complexity theory*, the study of resource-bounded computation, is covered in Chapters 3 and 4. Chapter 3 studies time-bounded computation; *polynomial-time deterministic computation* is presented as a formalization of efficient computation, and the framework of *NP-completeness* complements it by offering an avenue for showing negative results. Chapter 4 presents a selection of further topics from complexity theory: space-bounded computation, hierarchy theorems, and parameterized complexity theory.

In writing this book, efforts were made to minimize dependencies between sections, so as to promote modularity and allow for multiple pathways through the material. Some suggestions as to how this book could be used in courses are as follows:

- A course covering automata, computability, and complexity could cover Sections 1.1–1.4 and 1.6; Sections 2.1–2.6 and 2.8; and, Sections 3.1–3.6, along with a selection of the reductions in Sections 3.8. Other sections could be added in optionally.

- A course focused on computability and complexity could cover Sections 2.1–2.8, Sections 3.1–3.7, and a selection of the reductions in Section 3.8. Other sections could be added in optionally.

- A course focused on complexity could cover Sections 2.1, 2.2, and 2.6; all Sections of Chapter 3, with a selection of reductions made from Section 3.8; and, a selection of topics from Chapter 4.

The beginning of Section 3.8 contains guidance on how one might form a selection of reductions, from this section, for study: see Remark 3.8.2.

The dependencies between the sections of Chapters 1 through 3 were shown in Figure 0.0.1 (a few pages ago). Let us describe the ways in which each section of Chapter 4 depends on prior sections. Section 4.1 depends on the same sections as Section 3.2 does—namely, Sections 2.1, 2.2, and 2.6; acquaintance with Section 3.2 is also useful for studying Section 4.1. Section 4.2 depends on Sections 3.2 and 4.1, and also, in a basic way, on Section 2.3. Sections 4.3 and 4.4 are intended to be read in sequence; they mainly depend on Section 3.2, although a general acquaintance with NP-completeness as presented in Chapter 3 is helpful. Section 4.5 depends on Section 3.2, and expects general knowledge of NP-completeness; familiarity with Section 4.3 is also of aid.

For the most part, I believe that this book's mathematical conventions are fairly standard. But there is one deviation from the norm that I wish to directly address here. In this book's treatment of complexity theory, where it would usually be said that a language is *in* $\mathcal{P}$, where $\mathcal{P}$ denotes the class of polynomial-time computable languages, I say adjectivally that the language *is PTIME* or that it is a *PTIME language*. I similarly state that a language *is NP* or *is coNP* where the norm would be to say that the language is *in* $\mathcal{NP}$ or in $\mathrm{co}\mathcal{NP}$, respectively; here, $\mathcal{NP}$ and $\mathrm{co}\mathcal{NP}$ denote the suggested complexity classes. My personal experience from teaching this book's material is that each instance of non-uniformity in presentation forms a potential stumbling block and a potential source of confusion for the student. In my view, the use of class notation in complexity theory forms such a stumbling block, as it is not at all standard to use class notation in automata theory or in computability theory: the tradition is to say adjectivally, for example, that a language *is regular*, as opposed to saying that it *is in* the class of regular languages; indeed, it is atypical to introduce a notation for denoting the class of regular languages. In favor of uniformity and consistency, I opted to maintain the adjectival approach in the treatment of complexity theory. I elected use of the adjective *PTIME* over the shorter alternative *P* due to its higher readability and higher descriptiveness. Despite these adjustments to the norm, due to the prevalence of class notation in complexity theory at large, I often show how statements can be alternatively presented using class notation where it is natural to do so.

Acknowledgments

For their feedback of many forms, I thank Eric Allender, Ilario Bonacina, Ronald de Haan, Montserrat Hermo, Neil Immerman, Bart M. P. Jansen, Jari J. H. de Kroon, Victor Lagerkvist, Benoit Larose, Moritz Müller, George Osipov, Riccardo Pucella, Friedrich Slivovsky, Johan Thapper, and Harry Vinall-Smeeth. I extend special thanks to Moritz Müller for aiding with a wide range of queries, and for discussions on how to approach a number of the covered topics. Curt Alexander, Christine Cuoco, and Joe Halpern provided useful advice for which I am grateful. I thank my editor Elizabeth Swayze for all of her patience and kind help.

I thank all of my teachers, in general; of all of them, I'll explicitly name my doctoral advisor, Dexter Kozen, to whom I'm grateful for sharing with me an abundance of mathematics, computer science, and ideas about exposition.

I thank my mother and my father for their continued support. For their generous and warm hospitality during a crucial stage of writing, I express gratitude to my in-laws Harumi-san, Tsuneo-san, Mika-san, Michio-san, and their family; I'll always fondly remember all of the time that we spent together. I am indebted to my mother-in-law Mariko for her extensive and sustained help during the final years of this project. For their companionship over many of this project's varied phases, I thank my wife Mayumi for her humor and backing, and for extending her decision-making capacities; and I thank my son Noah for all of his instinct, laughter, and curiosity. I thank my daughter Arisa for joining us in this world with a signature energy after this book's final draft was submitted, and for not waiting very long to begin smiling. Ari-chan, Noah-kun, and Mayumi, this book is dedicated to you.

Hubie Chen
London, 2022

Introduction

Just as the natural sciences aim to uncover, abstract out, and understand fundamental laws of nature, the *theory of computation* aims to distill and analyze basic principles governing computational phenomena—in particular, to understand both the capabilities and limitations of computation. This book strives to provide a solid grounding in the core concepts of this theory as it has been developed thus far.

This book's material is motivated by the following two focal questions:

- *What is computable?*
- *What is efficiently computable?*

We will interpret, approach, and answer these questions mathematically. In doing so, we will engage with a beautiful and intricate tapestry of ideas and concepts, which, we will argue, are of a timeless, indelible character. However, in order to initiate our acquaintance with this tapestry, these questions need to be made precise and we need to elucidate a couple of points.

First, we need to qualify the *what* in these questions, by specifying which *things* we will classify as being *computable* or not, and as being *efficiently computable* or not. *Languages* are the objects that we will focus on classifying in this way, where a language is a set of *strings*—fortunately, we will be able to give formal definitions of these notions relatively readily. A language can be alternatively viewed as a so-called *decision problem*, which provides an infinitude of yes-or-no questions: given as input a string x, decide whether or not x belongs to the language. As we will see, the definition of language is sufficiently generic that we will be able to take various sets of objects and encode them as languages— for example, sets of graphs, or sets of natural numbers.

Next, we need to define what it means for a language to be *computable* or *efficiently computable*. Robust definitions of these notions emerged in the first half and second half of the twentieth century, respectively. Presenting these definitions requires some development: to arrive at them, we will present and study so-called *computational models* (also known as *models of computation*), which are abstract, mathematically defined models of computing devices. For example, the first and simplest computational model that we will encounter is the *deterministic finite automaton (DFA)*. Each DFA M renders a judgement of *acceptance* or *rejection* on every input string, and thus has an associated language: its set of accepted strings, denoted by $L(M)$. A language is defined as *regular* when there exists a DFA M such that it is equal to $L(M)$. In this way, the DFA model gives rise to and defines the class of regular languages, the simplest language class with which we will engage. By enriching this model, we will reach a model known as the *Turing machine*, different versions of which will be seen to define the *computable* languages and the languages considered to be efficiently computable.

The interplay between computational models and the language classes that they define is an overarching theme of this book. In particular, for each of the various models, we endeavor to understand the range of its language class, which yields insight into the nature and capabilities of the model. At the same time, we develop tools so that, when confronted with a language of interest, we may attempt to classify it within our taxonomy by trying to understand which classes it does and does not fall into. In essence, performing such classification makes precise what form of computing machinery is needed, or not needed, to cope with the language and its accompanying decision problem.

Agreements

Here, we present some definitions that will be basic for our study; we also set down some of the conventions to be used during our presentation.

Alphabets, strings, and languages

An **alphabet** is a nonempty finite set, typically denoted by capital Greek letters such as Σ and Γ. Here are three examples of alphabets:

- $\Sigma_1 = \{0, 1\}$,
- $\Sigma_2 = \{0, 1, 2, ..., 9\}$,
- $\Sigma_3 = \{a, b, c\}$.

We refer to the elements of an alphabet as **symbols**. We tend to use the term *alphabet* to refer to a set having the specified properties when we form *strings* over the set.

A **string** over an alphabet Σ is a finite-length sequence of symbols from Σ; the **length** of a string x is its length as a sequence, and is denoted by $|x|$. As examples:

- *abbaba* is a string of length 6 over the alphabet $\{a, b\}$,
- 31415926 is a string of length 8 over the alphabet $\{0, 1, 2, ..., 9\}$.

By convention, there is a unique string of length 0 (over any alphabet), which is called the **empty string** and denoted ϵ. It is always assumed that ϵ does not occur as a symbol in an alphabet; that is, for each alphabet Σ, we assume that $\epsilon \notin \Sigma$. Note that we write the symbols of a string contiguously, without any separating marker. When x is a string of length m, we often use $x_1, ..., x_m$ to denote its constituent symbols, so that $x = x_1...x_m$.

When $x = x_1...x_m$ is a string of length m and $y = y_1...y_n$ is a string of length n, the **concatenation** of x and y is the string $x_1...x_m y_1...y_n$ of length $m + n$, and is denoted by xy or $x \cdot y$. Observe that for any string x, it holds that $\epsilon x = x\epsilon = x$. When x is a string and $k \geq 0$, we use the exponentiation notation x^k to denote the concatenation of x with itself k times:

$$x^k = \underbrace{x \cdot x \cdot \cdots \cdot x}_{k}.$$

By a usual and useful convention, for any string x, we consider x^0 to be the empty string ϵ. By default, in working with strings, exponentiation is evaluated prior to other concatenation. So for example, over the alphabet $\Sigma = \{a, b\}$, we have $bab^2a^3a = babbaaaa$.

A string x is a **prefix** of another string y if there exists a string v such that $y = xv$. A string x is a **substring** of another string y if there exist strings u, v such that $y = uxv$. For example, consider the string $abcd$; its prefixes are ϵ, a, ab, abc, and $abcd$, and its length 2 substrings are ab, bc, and cd. Observe that for any string y, it holds that each of the strings ϵ and y is both a prefix and a substring of y, and indeed it holds that each prefix of y is a substring of y.

When x is a string over alphabet Σ and $a \in \Sigma$, we use the notation $\#_a(x)$ to denote the number of occurrences of the symbol a in the string x. Over the alphabet $\Sigma = \{0, 1\}$, for example, we have $\#_0(01101) = 2$, $\#_1(01101) = 3$, $\#_0(10^5 1^6) = 5$, and $\#_1(10^5 1^6) = 7$.

When Σ is an alphabet, we use Σ^* to denote the set of all strings over Σ. As examples:

- For $\Sigma_4 = \{a, b\}$, we have $\Sigma_4^* = \{\epsilon, a, b, aa, ab, ba, bb, aaa, \dots\}$.
- For $\Sigma_5 = \{0\}$, we have $\Sigma_5^* = \{\epsilon, 0, 00, 000, \dots\}$.

In both cases, we have explicitly presented some initial elements of Σ^* according to a length-increasing ordering. We note that, when Σ is an alphabet, the set Σ^* is always countably infinite.

A **language** over an alphabet Σ is a set of strings over Σ; equivalently, a **language** over Σ is a subset of Σ^*. When B is a language over alphabet Σ, its **complement**, denoted by $\overline{B}$, is defined as $\Sigma^* \setminus B$, that is, as the complement of B with respect to Σ^*; whenever we refer to the complement of a language, the alphabet Σ should be clear from the context. A language B over alphabet Σ is **trivial** if $B = \emptyset$ or $B = \Sigma^*$, and is **nontrivial** otherwise. Observe that a language is trivial if and only if its complement is.

Conventions

Here, we present mathematical notions and notation to be used throughout the book.

We use the notation $\mathbb{N}$ to denote the set of **natural numbers** $\{0, 1, 2, \dots\}$. A natural number is **positive** if it is not equal to 0; we use the notation $\mathbb{N}^+$ to denote the set of positive natural numbers $\{1, 2, 3, \dots\}$. By default, we assume all numbers under discussion to be natural numbers, unless mentioned otherwise. By a **unary representation** or a **unary encoding** of a natural number n, we refer to a string c^n containing n occurrences of a symbol c; typically, c is taken to be the symbol 1. For our purposes, a **multiple** of a natural number $d \in \mathbb{N}$ is a natural number that can be expressed in the form $d \cdot k$ where $k \in \mathbb{N}$; here, with $d \cdot k$ we denote the product of d and k. As an example, the five initial multiples of 4 are 0, 4, 8, 16, and 20. When d and n are natural numbers, we say that d is a **divisor** of n if n is a multiple of d, and that d is a **proper divisor** of n if, in addition, it holds that $1 < d < n$. A **prime number** is defined as a natural number that is greater than or equal to 2 and that has no proper divisor.

When B and C are sets, B is a **subset** of C if each element of B is an element of C; B is a **proper subset** of C if, in addition, B is not equal to C. We write $B \subseteq C$ to indicate that B is a subset of C, and $B \subsetneq C$ to indicate that B is a proper subset of C.

The **power set** of a set C is denoted by $\wp(C)$, and is defined as the set containing as elements all subsets of C; that is, $\wp(C) = \{B \mid B \subseteq C\}$. For example, we have

$$\wp(\{1, 2, 3\}) = \{\emptyset, \{1\}, \{2\}, \{3\}, \{1, 2\}, \{1, 3\}, \{2, 3\}, \{1, 2, 3\}\}.$$

Observe that, for any set C, the empty set $\emptyset$ and C itself are both elements of $\wp(C)$. When C is a set, we use $\wp_{\mathrm{fin}}(C)$ to denote $\{B \mid B \subseteq C \text{ and } B \text{ is a finite set}\}$, that is, the subset of $\wp(C)$ whose elements are the finite sets in $\wp(C)$.

The **product** of two sets B and C, denoted $B \times C$, is the set of pairs (b, c) where the first coordinate b is an element of B, and the second coordinate c is an element of C. That is,

$$B \times C = \{(b, c) \mid b \in B, c \in C\}.$$

For example,

$$\{1, 2\} \times \{1, 2, 3\} = \{(1, 1), (1, 2), (1, 3), (2, 1), (2, 2), (2, 3)\}.$$

More generally, the **product** of a finite sequence of sets $B_1, \ldots, B_k$, denoted $B_1 \times \cdots \times B_k$, is the set of tuples

$$B_1 \times \cdots \times B_k = \{(b_1, \ldots, b_k) \mid b_1 \in B_1, \ldots, b_k \in B_k\}.$$

Note that tuples are considered to be ordered; so, for example, $(1, 2)$ and $(2, 1)$ are considered to be distinct tuples.

Let B be a set and let k be a natural number. We use B^k to denote the k-fold product

$$\underbrace{B \times \cdots \times B}_{k}.$$

For any set B, we consider B^0 to be the set containing a single tuple, called the **empty tuple**. A k**-ary relation** on B is defined as a subset of B^k. A 2-ary relation is also called a **binary relation**. When R is a binary relation on B, we will sometimes use the infix notation aRb to indicate that $(a, b) \in R$. Examples of binary relations on a set B include the empty set $\emptyset$; the equality relation on B, which is the set $\{(b, b) \mid b \in B\}$; and, the set $B \times B$.

Let $f\colon A \to B$ be a function. We use $f[c \mapsto d]$ to denote the function that maps c to d, and otherwise behaves as f does, mapping each element $a \in A \setminus \{c\}$ to $f(a)$. On occasion, we extend this notation, by using $f[c_1 \mapsto d_1, \ldots, c_k \mapsto d_k]$ to denote the function that maps each c_i to d_i, and maps each element in $a \in A \setminus \{c_1, \ldots, c_k\}$ to $f(a)$. Whenever this extended notation is used, the values $c_1, \ldots, c_k$ will be pairwise distinct.

1 Automata Theory

One for sorrow,
Two for mirth,
Three for a wedding,
Four for birth . . .
— Traditional nursery rhyme

Our story commences with the study of *finite-state automata*, computational models that are quite restricted in that each *automaton* can only use a bounded amount of memory and processes an input string by reading it once from left to right. Although relatively simple, they will allow us to encounter and explore, in a gentle fashion, a number of the themes that will recur in our study of computation—for instance, they will provide our first exposure to nondeterminism, a concept at the heart of the *P versus NP* question in complexity theory. They also enjoy applications, for example, in text searching and parsing. Moreover, they give rise to a theory that is elegant and appealing in its own right.

1.1 Deterministic finite automata

We begin by presenting our first computational model: the *deterministic finite automaton (DFA)*. A DFA contains a finite set of *states*, which represent its only memory; one state is designated the *start state*. Given an input string, a DFA begins in its start state and reads in one symbol of the string at a time. Each time a symbol is read, the automaton discretely changes state based on its current state and the read symbol; the way in which the state is changed is specified by a *transition function*. After having read all symbols of a string, a DFA accepts or rejects the string based on whether or not its final state is an *accept state*. We proceed to the formal definition of this model.

Definition 1.1.1. A **deterministic finite automaton (DFA)** is a 5-tuple $M = (Q, \Sigma, s, T, \delta)$ where

- Q is a finite set called the **state set**, whose elements are called **states**,
- Σ is an alphabet called the **input alphabet**,
- $s \in Q$ is a state called the **start state** or **initial state**,
- $T \subseteq Q$ is a set of states, where each member is called an **accept state**, and
- $\delta : Q \times \Sigma \to Q$ is a function called the **transition function**.   ◇

To get a feel for this model, we consider some examples.

Example 1.1.2. As a first example of a DFA, take the set of states to be $Q = \{0, 1, 2\}$; the input alphabet to be $\Sigma = \{a, b\}$; the initial state s to be 0; and the set of accept states T to be $\{2\}$. We give the transition function δ by the following table:

δ	a	b
0	0	1
1	1	2
2	2	2

When specifying a DFA, we must specify all five of its parts! We have just done this by giving each of the parts individually. There is another convenient and often intuitive way to specify a DFA, namely, drawing a diagram. The following is a diagram for the example DFA just given, drawn under the conventions we will use:

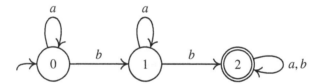

In general, we form the diagram for a DFA as follows. Each state is placed in a circle; the initial state is indicated by an unlabeled arrow that points to it; and each accept state has a double circle placed around it. Each *transition* $\delta(p, c) = q$ is indicated by drawing an arrow from the state p to the state q, with label c. Multiple transitions having the same source and target states are indicated using the same arrow, but with multiple labels; for example, in the diagram above, the transitions $\delta(2, a) = 2$ and $\delta(2, b) = 2$ are indicated by a single arrow from the state 2 to itself having the two labels a and b.

Let us explain how this DFA processes strings. As an opening example, consider the string *bab*. The DFA begins in its start state 0. It reads the initial symbol b, and makes a transition to the state $\delta(0, b) = 1$, that is, the state that the transition function yields when fed the current state with the seen symbol. Once in state 1, the DFA then reads the second symbol a, and makes a transition to the state $\delta(1, a) = 1$, so it effectively stays in the same state. It then reads the final symbol b, and makes a transition from state 1 to the state $\delta(1, b) = 2$. At this point, the DFA has fully processed the string, and has ended up in the state 2, which is an accept state; thus, the string *bab* is said to be *accepted*. As another example, consider the string *aba*. To process this string, the DFA begins in state 0; it reads the initial symbol *a* and remains in state 0; it then reads the second symbol *b* and transitions to state 1; and it then reads the final symbol *a* and terminates in state 1. As state 1 is not an accept state, the string *aba* is said to be *rejected*. Verify further for yourself that the strings *ab* and *ba* are rejected, and that the string *abba* is accepted.

There is a simple description of the strings that are accepted by this DFA; to arrive at it, let us contemplate the transition function. When this DFA reads the symbol *a*, it does not change state. When this DFA reads the symbol *b*, from state 0 or 1, it increments its state by one, proceeding to state 1 or 2, respectively; from state 2, it remains in state 2. In effect, the state of the DFA counts the number of *b* symbols that it has seen so far, up to 2; once it reaches the state 2, it remains there. As this DFA only accepts strings that cause it to terminate in state 2, it accepts precisely each string that contains two or more occurrences of the symbol *b*. ◇

Example 1.1.3. We present a second example of a DFA, where each state is a pair. This DFA has state set
$$Q = \{(E, E), (E, O), (O, E), (O, O)\},$$
input alphabet $\Sigma = \{a, b\}$, initial state $s = (E, E)$, and set of accept states $T = \{(E, E)\}$, so the initial state is the unique accept state. The following table gives the transition function:

δ	a	b
(E, E)	(O, E)	(E, O)
(E, O)	(O, O)	(E, E)
(O, E)	(E, E)	(O, O)
(O, O)	(E, O)	(O, E)

A diagram for this DFA is as follows:

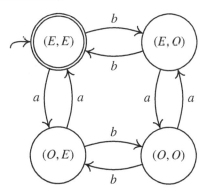

What does this DFA do? Each of its states consists of two components; each of these components can be either E or O. Whenever the symbol a is read, the first component toggles between E and O; similarly, whenever the symbol b is read, the second component toggles between E and O. In effect, the first component keeps track of whether or not the number of a's seen is **even** or **odd**, and the second component keeps track of whether or not the number of b's seen is **even** or **odd**. (The even natural numbers are $0, 2, 4, \ldots$ and the odd natural numbers are $1, 3, 5, \ldots$.) When the DFA has not yet read any symbols, both the number of a's seen and the number of b's seen are equal to 0, an even number; this observation accords with the initial state being (E, E). Since the only accept state is (E, E), a string is accepted by this DFA if and only if its number of occurrences of a and its number of occurrences of b are both even.   ◇

Remark 1.1.4. The particular names given to states in a DFA are, in a sense, immaterial to the DFA's functioning. Suppose that a DFA is modified by renaming its states, and adjusting its other parts correspondingly; in terms of the DFA's diagram, this amounts to just changing the name of each state inside each state's circle. Then, on any input string, the modified DFA makes transitions corresponding to those of the original DFA, and accepts a string if and only if the original DFA does.   ◇

Example 1.1.5. As another example, consider the DFA having state set $Q = \{0, 1, 2\}$, input alphabet $\Sigma = \{a, b\}$, initial state $s = 0$, accept states $T = \{0, 1\}$, and the following transition function:

δ	a	b
0	1	0
1	2	0
2	2	0

The following is a diagram for this DFA:

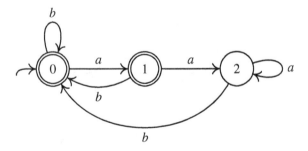

Let us consider how this DFA treats a few example strings. On the string aa, the DFA terminates in state 2, and rejects. On the string aba, the DFA terminates in state 1, and accepts. And on the string $aaaba$, the DFA also terminates in state 1, and accepts.

Which strings are accepted by this DFA? When the symbol a is read in state 0 or 1, this DFA increments its state by 1; when the symbol a is read in state 2, this DFA remains in state 2. When the symbol b is read, however, the DFA always resets its state to 0. Following these observations, it can be seen that the DFA will be in state 2 precisely when the last two symbols read are a, that is, if the string read thus far ends with aa. This DFA, however, accepts if it terminates in state 0 or 1; therefore, it accepts a string if and only if the string does *not* end with aa. ◇

We now introduce the notion of a *configuration* of a DFA, which will be very useful to reason about DFA behavior. In fact, as our study proceeds, we will define a notion of *configuration* for each computational model to be considered. In general, a configuration captures everything about a computation, at a given moment in time, that is relevant to know how the computation will proceed. In the case of a DFA, this amounts to the state that the DFA is in, and the portion of the string that has *not* yet been read.

We also introduce the notion of the *initial configuration* of a DFA on a string, and the *successor configuration* of a configuration of a DFA, which formalizes how the DFA processes a single symbol.

Definition 1.1.6. Let $M = (Q, \Sigma, s, T, \delta)$ be a DFA.

- A **configuration** of M is a pair $[q, y]$ consisting of a state $q \in Q$ and a string $y \in \Sigma^*$.
- The **initial configuration** of M on a string $y \in \Sigma^*$ is the configuration $[s, y]$.
- The **successor configuration** of a configuration $[q, y]$ of M is defined when $|y| \geq 1$ (that is, when y is not the empty string ϵ); in this case, denoting y by ax with $a \in \Sigma$ and $x \in \Sigma^*$, the configuration $[\delta(q, a), x]$ is the successor configuration of $[q, y]$. ◇

So relative to a DFA, when the successor configuration of a configuration $[q, y]$ is defined, it is obtained by removing the string y's leftmost symbol a, and replacing the state q with the state $\delta(q, a)$.

Example 1.1.7. Consider the DFA M from Example 1.1.2. The initial configuration of M on the string bab is $[0, bab]$. The successor configuration of the configuration $[0, bab]$ is $[1, ab]$; the successor of $[1, ab]$ is $[1, b]$; the successor of $[1, b]$ is $[2, \epsilon]$; and the configuration $[2, \epsilon]$ has no successor configuration, as its string is the empty string. ◇

We next introduce notation to discuss configurations of a DFA M; in particular, we introduce binary relations on the set of configurations. However, before proceeding to this, a remark is in order. A configuration of a DFA has at most one successor configuration; we accordingly speak of *the* successor configuration of a configuration of a DFA. In the following definition, however, we speak of *a* successor configuration of a configuration; this is because we will want to reuse this definition, and employ it to discuss other computational models (in particular, *nondeterministic* models) where a configuration may have more than one successor configuration.

Definition 1.1.8. Let α and β be configurations of M.

- We write $\alpha \vdash_M \beta$ if β is a successor configuration of α.
- For each $n \geq 0$, we write $\alpha \vdash_M^n \beta$ if β can be obtained by starting from α and itera-tively taking a successor configuration n times. That is, we write $\alpha \vdash_M^n \beta$ if there exist configurations $\gamma_0, \gamma_1, ..., \gamma_n$ such that $\gamma_0 = \alpha$, $\gamma_n = \beta$, and $\gamma_0 \vdash_M \gamma_1 \vdash_M \cdots \vdash_M \gamma_n$.
- We write $\alpha \vdash_M^* \beta$ if there exists $n \geq 0$ such that $\alpha \vdash_M^n \beta$. (Note that we can view the relation $\vdash_M^*$ as the union $\bigcup_{n \geq 0} \vdash_M^n$ of the relations $\vdash_M^n$.)

In using this notation, we sometimes omit the M subscript when the context allows.   ◇

Remark 1.1.9. In Definition 1.1.8, the relations $\vdash_M^n$ may be equivalently defined by induction, as follows:

- It holds that $\alpha \vdash_M^0 \beta$ if and only if $\alpha = \beta$.
- For each $n > 0$, it holds that $\alpha \vdash_M^n \beta$ if and only if there exists a configuration γ such that both $\alpha \vdash_M \gamma$ and $\gamma \vdash_M^{n-1} \beta$ hold.   ◇

Example 1.1.10. Consider again the DFA M from Example 1.1.2. Let us continue the discussion of Example 1.1.7; from the observations made there, we may write the following:

$$[0, bab] \vdash_M [1, ab] \vdash_M [1, b] \vdash_M [2, \epsilon].$$

Having seen this, we may give the following examples of the notation presented in Definition 1.1.8:

$$[1, ab] \vdash_M^0 [1, ab], \qquad\qquad [0, bab] \vdash_M^3 [2, \epsilon],$$
$$[1, ab] \vdash_M^1 [1, b], \qquad\qquad [1, b] \vdash_M^* [1, b],$$
$$[1, b] \vdash_M^1 [2, \epsilon], \qquad\qquad [1, ab] \vdash_M^* [2, \epsilon],$$
$$[0, bab] \vdash_M^2 [1, b], \qquad\qquad [0, bab] \vdash_M^* [1, b],$$
$$[1, ab] \vdash_M^2 [2, \epsilon], \qquad\qquad [0, bab] \vdash_M^* [2, \epsilon].$$ ◇

We will often refer to a particular realization of a computational model—for example, a particular DFA—as a **machine**. In general, we refer to the process by which a machine operates on an input string as a **computation**. We also use the term **computation** to refer in particular to a sequence containing all configurations that a machine passes through when invoked on an input string; in the case of a DFA, such a sequence begins with an initial configuration, and ends with a configuration having no successor.

Example 1.1.11. Let M again be the DFA from Example 1.1.2. The following are examples of computations of this DFA M:

$$[0, bab] \vdash_M [1, ab] \vdash_M [1, b] \vdash_M [2, \epsilon],$$
$$[0, aba] \vdash_M [0, ba] \vdash_M [1, a] \vdash_M [1, \epsilon].$$ ◇

Let $M = (Q, \Sigma, s, T, \delta)$ be a DFA, let y be a string of length n, and let $q \in Q$ be a state. Starting from the configuration $[q, y]$, we may iteratively take the successor configuration n times; in doing so, each time we take the successor configuration, it is unique, and its string is the string of its predecessor configuration with the first symbol removed. We thus have the following observation, which we will use tacitly throughout our discussion: for each value k with $0 \leq k \leq n$, there is a unique configuration β such that $[s, y] \vdash_M^k \beta$, and the string component of β is equal to y with its first k symbols removed.

We may now define formally what it means for a string to be *accepted* or *rejected* by a DFA. This status is determined by the state that the DFA arrives at after processing the string, when it begins from the respective initial configuration.

Definition 1.1.12. Let $M = (Q, \Sigma, s, T, \delta)$ be a DFA. Let $y \in \Sigma^*$ be a string of length n, and let $q \in Q$ be the unique state such that $[s, y] \vdash_M^n [q, \epsilon]$.

- If $q \in T$, we say that M **accepts** y.
- If $q \notin T$, we say that M **rejects** y.

We define the **language of** M, denoted by $L(M)$, to be $\{y \in \Sigma^* \mid M \text{ accepts } y\}$.   ◇

Although it may seem that we are merely formalizing notions that are intuitively clear, there are at least a couple of reasons why we want to make fully precise and formal the components and behavior of a DFA. First, a true formalization will allow us to rigorously prove theorems and results about DFA, for example, impossibility results demonstrating the limitations of DFA. We would be hard-pressed to prove limitations on a computational model that was not well-defined! Second, the process of formalization that we have carried out for DFA offers us gainful practice and preview for the study that follows, in which we will formalize increasingly complex computational models—not all of which are, by any means, as simple or transparent as the DFA.

As we have just seen, each DFA M gives rise to a language $L(M)$, which we call the **language of** M or the **language decided by** M. We will want to discuss in an aggregate fashion all of the languages thusly arising, and hence give the following name to a language decided by a DFA.

Definition 1.1.13. A language B is **regular** if there exists a DFA M where $B = L(M)$.   ◇

That is, a language is regular if there is *some* DFA that decides it. We have here identified a class of languages: each language is either regular, or it is not. Having been provided this definition, perhaps the most basic question that one could proceed to ask is whether or not there is a language that is *not* regular. (If there is no such language, our definition would be somehow trivial: in this case, the identified class of languages would simply be the class of all languages.) At the risk of quashing the suspense, it can be reported here that there are indeed languages that are not regular. Perhaps the most classic example of a language that is not regular is

$$\{a^n b^n \mid n \geq 0\} = \{\epsilon, ab, aabb, aaabbb, \dots\}.$$

In words, a string is in this language if it begins with some number of a's, followed by the same number of b's. Later in this chapter, we will acquire techniques for proving that this language and others are not regular.[1]

1.2   Closure properties

We just defined the class of regular languages in terms of the DFA computational model. As we encounter further computational models, we will correspondingly define further classes of languages. One basic type of question that we will ask, for each of these various classes of languages, is whether or not they possess certain *closure properties*. For example, in a moment we will ask whether or not the regular languages are *closed under complementation*, that is, whether or not the complement of an arbitrary regular language is always itself regular. Given a class of languages, one can indeed inquire about closure under any operation defined on languages: the class is closed under such an operation if, whenever the operation is applied to a language or languages from the class, the resulting language is also in the class. Understanding the closure properties of a class of languages gives us insight into the internal structure of the class, and can be helpful in identifying whether a particular language is inside or outside of the class.

In this section, to show closure properties of the regular languages, we demonstrate that operations on regular languages can be effected by performing respective operations on DFA. This pattern exemplifies our general approach to showing closure properties of language classes: the typical language class that we study is defined from a group of machines, and so establishing closure properties on the class is naturally performed by defining operations on the machines.

1.2.1   Complementation

We begin by considering the operation of complementation. What would it mean for the regular languages to be closed under complementation? Let us recall that a language is regular if there exists a DFA that decides it. Hence, closure under complementation would mean that for an arbitrary DFA M, it is possible to design a second DFA M' that decides the complement of $L(M)$. By definition of the complement, the DFA M' should reject each string that is accepted by M, and accept each string that is rejected by M: its final judgment should always be the polar opposite of that of M. It is indeed always possible to design such a DFA M', by starting with M, and swapping the acceptance status of each of the states: a state is accepting in M' if and only if it was not accepting in M.

Theorem 1.2.1. *If B is a regular language over the alphabet Σ, then its complement $\overline{B}$ is also a regular language.*

---

1. Intuitively speaking, in order to check if a string is in this language by scanning the string from left to right, it is necessary to first count the number n of a's that occurs, and then ensure that the number of b's that follow is equal to n; a DFA, however, cannot count up to an arbitrary natural number, and hence cannot decide this language.

Proof. Since B is a regular language, there exists a DFA $M = (Q, \Sigma, s, T, \delta)$ such that $L(M) = B$. Define $M' = (Q, \Sigma, s, T', \delta)$ be the DFA that is identical to M except that its set T' of accept states is $Q \setminus T$.

We claim that $L(M') = \overline{B}$. The DFA M and M' have the same set of states and the same transition function; by a review of Definition 1.1.6, one sees that they have the same configurations and also the same notion of successor configuration, that is, the relations $\vdash_M$ and $\vdash_{M'}$ are equal. So, for any string $x \in \Sigma^*$ of length n, if we let $q \in Q$ be the unique state such that $[s, x] \vdash_M^n [q, \epsilon]$, then $[s, x] \vdash_{M'}^n [q, \epsilon]$ also holds. We have that $q \in T$ if and only if $q \notin T'$, so x is accepted by M if and only if x is rejected by M', yielding the claim. □

1.2.2 Intersection and union

We next consider closure under intersection; the regular languages satisfy this closure property, in the following formalization.

Theorem 1.2.2. *If B and C are both regular languages over the same alphabet Σ, then their intersection $B \cap C$ is also a regular language.*

Let $M_B = (Q_B, \Sigma, s_B, T_B, \delta_B)$ be a DFA with $L(M_B) = B$, and let $M_C = (Q_C, \Sigma, s_C, T_C, \delta_C)$ be a DFA with $L(M_C) = C$. To establish the theorem, our mission is to construct a DFA that decides $B \cap C$. How are we to do this? In particular, what should the state set of our new DFA be? A natural idea is the following: as the new DFA processes a string, its state keeps track of both the state that the first DFA M_B would be in, as well as the state that the second DFA M_C would be in. This can be accomplished naturally by taking the state set of the new DFA to be the product $Q_B \times Q_C$ of the state sets of the original two DFA.

In a construction typically referred to as the **product construction**, we use the DFA M_B and M_C to define a DFA $M = (Q, \Sigma, s, T, \delta)$, as follows:

$$Q = Q_B \times Q_C,$$

$$s = (s_B, s_C),$$

$$T = T_B \times T_C,$$

$$\delta((q_B, q_C), a) = (\delta_B(q_B, a), \delta_C(q_C, a)).$$

Why do the definitions of the other parts make sense? The start state s should indicate where each of the original DFA start; hence, we take the pair consisting of the start states of those DFA. The new DFA M should accept a string precisely when both of the original DFA accept the string. Hence, its set of accept states should contain all state pairs such that the first state is accepting in M_B, and the second state is accepting in M_C; this can be expressed as the product $T_B \times T_C$. Finally, when a symbol is read and the new DFA M is in the state (q_B, q_C), the first component q_B should be updated according to the transition function δ_B, and analogously the second component q_C should be updated according to the transition function δ_C. Figure 1.2.1 provides an example of this construction.

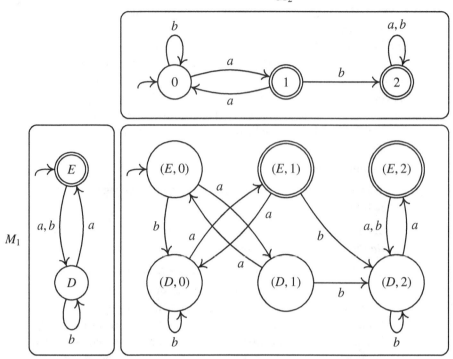

Figure 1.2.1. Example of the product construction on DFA. Here, the construction is applied to the shown DFA $M_1 = (Q_1, \Sigma, s_1, T_1, \delta_1)$ and $M_2 = (Q_2, \Sigma, s_2, T_2, \delta_2)$; each is over the alphabet $\Sigma = \{a, b\}$. The state sets of these two DFA are $Q_1 = \{E, D\}$ and $Q_2 = \{0, 1, 2\}$; the state set of the resulting DFA is $Q_1 \times Q_2$. The start state of the resulting DFA is the pair $(E, 0)$ obtained by pairing the start states of the original two DFA. The set of accept states of the resulting DFA is the product $T_1 \times T_2$, which is equal to $\{E\} \times \{1, 2\} = \{(E, 1), (E, 2)\}$. The transition function δ of the resulting DFA, when applied to a pair and a symbol, is defined to yield the applications of the transition functions δ_1 and δ_2 to the respective pair entries, along with the symbol; as one example transition according to δ, we have $\delta((E, 1), b) = (\delta_1(E, b), \delta_2(1, b)) = (D, 2)$.

In order to prove, as desired, that the language of M is the intersection $B \cap C$, we first establish a lemma showing that M behaves as claimed: from a state (q_B, q_C), after a string y is processed, the resulting state is the pair consisting of

- the state that M_B would end up in after processing y from q_B, and
- the state that M_C would end up in after processing y from q_C.

Lemma 1.2.3. *Let $y \in \Sigma^*$ be a string of length n; let $q_B \in Q_B$ and $q_C \in Q_C$ be arbitrary states; and let $r_B \in Q_B$ and $r_C \in Q_C$ be the unique states where $[q_B, y] \vdash_{M_B}^n [r_B, \epsilon]$ and $[q_C, y] \vdash_{M_C}^n [r_C, \epsilon]$. Then, it holds that $[(q_B, q_C), y] \vdash_M^n [(r_B, r_C), \epsilon]$.*

Proof. We prove this by induction on n.

When $n = 0$, we have $y = \epsilon$, $q_B = r_B$, and $q_C = r_C$, from which the claim can be seen.

When $n > 0$, write $y = ax$ where $a \in \Sigma$ and $x \in \Sigma^*$; Figure 1.2.2 shows a diagram indicating the setup and the result for this case. Define

$$q_B' = \delta_B(q_B, a) \quad \text{and} \quad q_C' = \delta_C(q_C, a).$$

We have

$$[q_B, ax] \vdash_{M_B} [q_B', x] \vdash_{M_B}^{n-1} [r_B, \epsilon] \quad \text{and} \quad [q_C, ax] \vdash_{M_C} [q_C', x] \vdash_{M_C}^{n-1} [r_C, \epsilon].$$

We also have, from the definition of δ, that

$$[(q_B, q_C), ax] \vdash_M [(q_B', q_C'), x].$$

By appeal to induction, we obtain from $[q_B', x] \vdash_{M_B}^{n-1} [r_B, \epsilon]$ and $[q_C', x] \vdash_{M_C}^{n-1} [r_C, \epsilon]$ that

$$[(q_B', q_C'), x] \vdash_M^{n-1} [(r_B, r_C), \epsilon].$$

Combining the previous two results, we obtain $[(q_B, q_C), ax] \vdash_M^n [(r_B, r_C), \epsilon]$. □

Proof of Theorem 1.2.2. Let $x \in \Sigma^*$ be a string of length n. By Lemma 1.2.3, when we define r_B and r_C to be the states such that $[s_B, x] \vdash_{M_B}^n [r_B, \epsilon]$ and $[s_C, x] \vdash_{M_C}^n [r_C, \epsilon]$, we obtain $[(s_B, s_C), x] \vdash_M^n [(r_B, r_C), \epsilon]$. We then have

$$x \in B \cap C \Leftrightarrow x \in L(M_B) \cap L(M_C) \quad \text{(by the choices of } M_B \text{ and } M_C)$$

$$\Leftrightarrow r_B \in T_B \text{ and } r_C \in T_C \quad \text{(by the definition of acceptance for } M_B \text{ and } M_C)$$

$$\Leftrightarrow (r_B, r_C) \in T_B \times T_C \quad \text{(by the definition of the set product } T_B \times T_C)$$

$$\Leftrightarrow (r_B, r_C) \in T \quad \text{(by the definition of } T)$$

$$\Leftrightarrow x \in L(M) \quad \text{(by the definition of acceptance for } M).$$
□

We next consider closure under union; once again, we have that the class of regular languages enjoys this closure property.

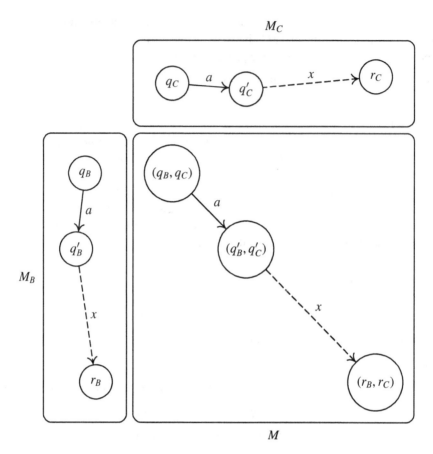

Figure 1.2.2. The setup and desired result of the inductive step in the proof of Lemma 1.2.3. The string y is viewed as the concatenation of a and x, where $a \in \Sigma$ is a single symbol and $x \in \Sigma^*$ is a string. In the DFA M_B, from the state q_B, reading the symbol a leads to the state q_B', and then reading the string x leads to the state r_B. Similarly, in the DFA M_C, from the state q_C, reading the symbol a leads to the state q_C', and then reading the string x leads to the state r_C. It follows that, in the DFA M, from the state (q_B, q_C), reading the symbol a leads to the state (q_B', q_C'), and by induction, subsequently reading the string x leads to the state (r_B, r_C).

Theorem 1.2.4. *If B and C are both regular languages over the same alphabet* Σ, *then their union* $B \cup C$ *is also a regular language.*

At this point, there are a couple of ways that we may prove this theorem.

One way to proceed is to directly present a DFA, as was done for the previous theorem. Namely, we can directly describe, given two DFA M_B and M_C, a DFA M' whose language $L(M')$ is equal to $L(M_B) \cup L(M_C)$. Indeed, such a DFA M' may be defined as identical to the DFA M above, but with the change that its set of accept states is

$$T' = \{(q_B, q_C) \in Q \mid q_B \in T_B \text{ or } q_C \in T_C\}.$$

Note that the accept states of the DFA M, namely $T = T_B \times T_C$, may be equivalently expressed as

$$T = \{(q_B, q_C) \in Q \mid q_B \in T_B \text{ and } q_C \in T_C\}.$$

One can see that, to define T', the *and* in this expression of T has been changed to *or*, reflecting the difference in definition between the intersection and the union. Lemma 1.2.3 holds with M' in place of M, as its statement and its proof do not refer to the set of accept states of M. By adjusting the argumentation in the proof of Theorem 1.2.2, it can be proved that $L(M') = L(M_B) \cup L(M_C)$. (We leave a verification of this to the reader.)

We may alternatively obtain that the regular languages are closed under union by invoking the following versions of De Morgan's laws.

Proposition 1.2.5 (De Morgan's laws, for languages). *For any languages B and C over the same alphabet, the following hold:*

(1) $B \cup C = \overline{(\overline{B} \cap \overline{C})}$,

(2) $B \cap C = \overline{(\overline{B} \cup \overline{C})}$.

We have already established that the regular languages are closed under intersection and complement. So, when B and C are regular languages, the languages $\overline{B}$ and $\overline{C}$ are also regular, implying that $\overline{B} \cap \overline{C}$ is regular, from which we obtain that $\overline{(\overline{B} \cap \overline{C})}$ is regular. By De Morgan's law (1), this immediately implies that $B \cup C$ is regular.

Note that De Morgan's law (1) implies that, in general, *any* class of languages closed under intersection and complement is closed under union. Similarly, the dual De Morgan's law (2) implies that any class of languages closed under union and complement is closed under intersection.

1.3 Nondeterministic finite automata

Nondeterminism in computation is a theoretical construct; it is not intended to faithfully model real computers or any aspect thereof, but rather is an instrument for analysis. In deterministic computation models, such as the DFA, how a computation evolved was uniquely determined at each step: as long as the computation proceeded, each configuration had a unique successor configuration. In nondeterministic computation models, a configuration may have multiple successor configurations, and acceptance is always defined via the notion of *possibility*: a string is accepted by a nondeterministic machine if there *exists* a computation which results in acceptance. This section introduces nondeterministic finite automata (NFA), which are nondeterministic counterparts of the deterministic finite automaton. Whereas a deterministic finite automaton has a transition function that provides a *unique* state, given a state and a symbol, a nondeterministic finite automaton has a transition function that provides a *set* of states, given a state and a symbol.

As a theoretical construct, nondeterminism has been immensely and supremely fruitful in supplying insights into the nature of computation; in particular, it has shed light and perspective on the reach and limitations of deterministic computation. In our study of complexity theory, nondeterministic computation will be used crucially to classify languages of interest. By the end of the current section, we will have compared NFA to DFA formally and will have shown that these two models have the same expressiveness (in a sense made precise). An offshoot of this result is that providing an NFA for a language is an avenue for establishing the language's regularity. Working with NFA has the advantages that they may be more succinct than DFA, and also that they may be easier to comprehend and maintain.

In this section, we present and study two brands of nondeterministic automata: the *nondeterministic finite automaton (NFA)*, and an extension thereof referred to as the ϵ-*NFA*.

1.3.1 NFA

We begin with the definition of NFA.

Definition 1.3.1. A **nondeterministic finite automaton (NFA)** is a 5-tuple $M = (Q, \Sigma, S, T, \Delta)$ where

- Q is a non-empty finite set called the **state set**, whose members are called **states**,
- Σ is an alphabet called the **input alphabet**,
- $S \subseteq Q$ is a set of states, where each member is called a **start state** or an **initial state**,
- $T \subseteq Q$ is a set of states, where each member is called an **accept state**, and
- $\Delta: Q \times \Sigma \to \wp(Q)$ is a function called the **transition function**.   ◇

Remark 1.3.2. This definition is different from the definition of a DFA in two ways. First, there is a *set* of initial states S, as opposed to a single initial state. Second, the transition function Δ, instead of being a mapping to the set of states Q, is a mapping to the *power set* of states $\wp(Q)$. So, when the transition function Δ is given a state and a symbol, it returns a *set* of states, as opposed to a single state.   ◇

Let us achieve a first understanding of this model by examining some examples.

Example 1.3.3. As an initial example, consider the NFA $M = (Q, \Sigma, S, T, \Delta)$ with state set $Q = \{0, 1, 2\}$, input alphabet $\Sigma = \{a, b\}$, initial state set $S = \{0\}$, accept state set $T = \{2\}$, and the following transition function:

Δ	a	b
0	$\{0, 1\}$	$\{0\}$
1	$\{2\}$	$\emptyset$
2	$\emptyset$	$\emptyset$

Observe that the sets $\Delta(2, a)$, $\Delta(1, b)$, and $\Delta(2, b)$ are empty; that each of the sets $\Delta(1, a)$ and $\Delta(0, b)$ contains one element; and that the set $\Delta(0, a)$ contains two elements.

The following is a diagram for this NFA, drawn under the conventions we will use:

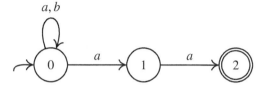

We form the diagram for an NFA in the following fashion. Mimicking our convention for DFA, each state is placed in a circle, each initial state is indicated by an unlabeled arrow, and each accept state is in a double circle. For each state p, each symbol c, and each state $q \in \Delta(p, c)$, the diagram includes an arrow from p to q with label c; as with DFA, multiple labels are placed on a single arrow. Observe that the emptiness of such a set $\Delta(p, c)$ translates to the diagram lacking an arrow coming out of the state p with label c.

Let us consider how this example NFA processes the string *baa*. It starts in state 0, which is the only initial state. After reading the symbol b, the NFA can only transition to state 0, as this state is the lone element in $\Delta(0, b) = \{0\}$. From state 0, after reading in the next symbol, a, the NFA may transition to either state 0 or 1, as $\Delta(0, a) = \{0, 1\}$. After reading in the last symbol a, from state 0, the NFA may transition to either state 0 or 1; from state 1, the NFA may transition to state 2, the lone element in $\Delta(2, a) = \{2\}$. Hence, after reading in *baa*, the NFA may be in state 0, 1, or 2.

As for a DFA, a *configuration* of an NFA is a state paired with a string. While we will formalize the notion of *successor configuration* of an NFA below, we now look at some examples. As is consistent with the notation for DFA, the symbol $\vdash$ is used between two configurations to indicate that the configuration coming after the symbol is a sucessor configuration of the configuration before the symbol. The following diagram shows all of the configurations reachable when this example NFA is invoked on the string *baa*:

$$[0, baa] \vdash [0, aa] \begin{array}{c} [0, a] \begin{array}{c} [0, \epsilon] \\ \\ [1, \epsilon] \end{array} \\ \\ [1, a] \vdash [2, \epsilon] \end{array}$$

How does an NFA cast a judgment of acceptance or rejection on a string? After fully reading in the string *baa*, the example NFA *M* may be in any of its three states. Exactly one of these three states, the state 2, is an accept state. A staunch advocate of democracy might suggest that *baa* ought to be considered rejected, since the majority of these three states are not accept states! Indeed, the fact that an NFA configuration can admit multiple successor configurations may invite the idea of making transitions based on chance. However, for an NFA, acceptance is defined in terms of *possibility*; no real notions of *probability* come into play. In the case of the NFA *M*, a string is considered accepted when, starting from the initial state 0, there *exists* a choice of transitions such that the NFA terminates in an accept state. Thus, the string *baa* is regarded as accepted by the NFA *M*.

Next, let us consider this NFA's behavior on the input string *aba*. The following diagram shows the reachable configurations:

$$[0, aba] \begin{array}{c} \diagup \\ \\ \diagdown \end{array} \begin{array}{c} [0, ba] \vdash [0, a] \begin{array}{c} \diagup \\ \\ \diagdown \end{array} \begin{array}{c} [0, \epsilon] \\ \\ [1, \epsilon] \end{array} \\ \\ [1, ba] \end{array}$$

Note that the configuration $[1, ba]$ has no successor configurations, since $\Delta(1, b)$ is empty; from this configuration, the computation simply terminates. After processing the entire string *aba*, the NFA *M* may be in either state 0 or state 1. As neither of these states are accept states, the string *aba* is regarded as rejected.

Which strings are accepted by this NFA? The only way to transition to the accept state 2 is to read an *a* from state 1, and the only way to transition to state 1 is to read an *a* from state 0. On the other hand, state 0 also permits transitions to itself, on each of the symbols *a* and *b*. Clearly, each string accepted by this NFA must end with *aa*; moreover, any string that ends with *aa* is accepted by this NFA, for the symbols prior to the final *aa* can be processed by staying in state 0, and then the final *aa* can be processed by moving from state 0 to state 2. Hence, the NFA accepts precisely those strings that end with *aa*.

It may be instructive to compare this NFA with the DFA of Example 1.1.5. That DFA's language is the complement of the language accepted by this NFA, but if we modify that DFA so that 2 is its only accept state, its language becomes equal to that of this NFA. This NFA offers a dash of expressional economy over the modified DFA: its diagram contains only 4 arrow labels, in contrast to the DFA diagram's 6 arrow labels!   ◇

The computation of a DFA on a string may be said to proceed in a *linear* fashion: each configuration either has a unique successor configuration, or no successor configuration; and the reachable configurations naturally form a linear sequence. On the other hand, the computation of an NFA on a string may be said to proceed in a *branching* fashion: a configuration may have multiple successor configurations; and the reachable configurations naturally form a tree, as seen in Example 1.3.3.

Example 1.3.4. We consider a second NFA $M' = (Q', \Sigma, S', T', \Delta')$, which is an extension of the example NFA M from Example 1.3.3. The NFA M' has state set $Q' = \{0, 1, 2, 0', 1'\}$, input alphabet $\Sigma = \{a, b\}$, initial state set $S' = \{0, 0'\}$, accept state set $T' = \{2, 0', 1'\}$, and the following transition function:

Δ'	a	b
0	$\{0, 1\}$	$\{0\}$
1	$\{2\}$	$\emptyset$
2	$\emptyset$	$\emptyset$
$0'$	$\{1'\}$	$\{1'\}$
$1'$	$\emptyset$	$\emptyset$

The following is a diagram for the NFA M':

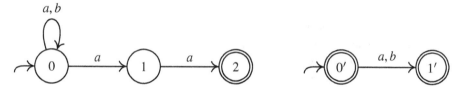

The NFA M' has two initial states, 0 and $0'$. On an input string, an NFA may begin in any of its initial states; if there *exist* a choice of initial state and a choice of transitions from this initial state to one of the accept states, the string is regarded as accepted. For example, the NFA M' accepts the strings a and b, since from the initial state $0'$, both the symbols a and b permit transitions to the state $1'$, which is an accept state. The NFA M' also accepts the empty string ϵ: on this string, it may begin and terminate in the state $0'$, which is both an initial state and an accept state.

It can be seen that when the NFA M' begins in the state $0'$, the strings that can lead to acceptance are precisely ϵ, a, and b. On the other hand, when this NFA begins in the state 0, the strings that can lead to acceptance are exactly the strings accepted by the NFA M of the previous example. Hence, the set of strings accepted by the NFA M' is equal to the union of the set of strings $\{\epsilon, a, b\}$ with the set of strings ending with aa. ◇

Example 1.3.5. We next consider an example NFA that performs a type of substring search. This example NFA has state set $Q = \{0, 1, 2, 3, 4\}$, input alphabet $\Sigma = \{a, b\}$, initial state set $S = \{0\}$, accepting state set $T = \{4\}$, and the following transition function:

Δ	a	b
0	$\{0, 1\}$	$\{0\}$
1	$\emptyset$	$\{2\}$
2	$\emptyset$	$\{3\}$
3	$\{4\}$	$\emptyset$
4	$\{4\}$	$\{4\}$

The following is a diagram for this example NFA:

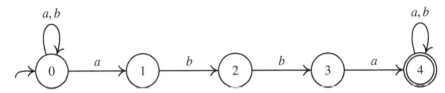

This NFA always begins in state 0, its unique initial state. From that state, the NFA may consume either of the symbols a and b and remain in that state; or it may proceed to state 1 upon reading an a. Once it proceeds to state 1, however, for the computation to stay alive, it must read the symbols b, b, and a, in order, after which it reaches state 4, the only accept state. In state 4, the NFA may consume either of the symbols a and b and remain in that state. From this description, it can be seen that this NFA accepts exactly those strings that contain *abba* as a substring.   ◇

Example 1.3.6. We present our final example of an NFA; whether a string is accepted by this NFA depends on the contents of the end of the string, in particular, on the last few symbols in the string (should they exist). This NFA has state set $Q = \{3, 2, 1, 0\}$, input alphabet $\Sigma = \{a, b\}$, initial state set $S = \{3\}$, accept state set $T = \{0\}$, and the following transition table:

Δ	a	b
3	$\{3, 2\}$	$\{3\}$
2	$\{1\}$	$\{1\}$
1	$\{0\}$	$\{0\}$
0	$\emptyset$	$\emptyset$

The following is a diagram for this NFA:

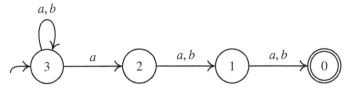

This NFA begins in state 3, its unique initial state. From this state, the NFA may consume any number of a's and b's and remain in this state; the only way to exit this state is to consume an a and move to state 2. From state 2, either symbol permits a unique transition, which is to state 1; from state 1, either symbol permits a unique transition, which is to state 0. While state 0 is accepting, it permits no transitions. Hence, a computation that terminates in state 0 must be timed properly, so that when reading a string, the moment of departure from state 3 allows the coincidence of reaching state 0 and of having scanned the whole string. This coincidence occurs when the a symbol used to transition from state 3 to state 2 is followed by exactly two symbols. We can thus see that a string is accepted by this NFA if and only if it contains three or more symbols, and its third symbol from the right is an a.

The following diagram shows the reachable configurations when this NFA is invoked on the input string *aba*:

$$
\begin{array}{ccccc}
& & & & [3, \epsilon] \\
& & [3, ba] \;\vdash\; [3, a] & \diagup & \\
& & & \diagdown & [2, \epsilon] \\
[3, aba] & \diagup & & & \\
& \diagdown & [2, ba] \;\vdash\; [1, a] \;\vdash\; [0, \epsilon] & &
\end{array}
$$

◇

Remark 1.3.7. For each of the last two example NFA, the reader is invited to ponder how to construct a DFA sharing the NFA's language, and how many states are needed to construct such a DFA. ◇

We next formalize the notions needed to precisely discuss the behavior of an NFA.

Definition 1.3.8. Let $M = (Q, \Sigma, S, T, \Delta)$ be an NFA.

- A **configuration** of M is a pair $[q, y]$ consisting of a state $q \in Q$ and a string $y \in \Sigma^*$.
- An **initial configuration** of M on a string $y \in \Sigma^*$ is a configuration of the form $[s, y]$, where $s \in S$.
- A configuration $[r, x]$ of M is a **successor configuration** of a configuration $[q, y]$ of M if there exists $a \in \Sigma$ such that $y = ax$ and $r \in \Delta(q, a)$.

To discuss configurations of M, we use the relations presented in Definition 1.1.8. ◇

When dealing with an NFA, observe that in order for a configuration $[q, x]$ to have a successor configuration, it must hold that $|x| \geq 1$. On the other hand, even when $|x| \geq 1$, it is not necessary for a configuration $[q, x]$ to have a successor configuration: the set $\Delta(q, a)$ may be empty, where a denotes the leftmost symbol of x.

In general, when dealing with a computational machine such as a DFA or an NFA, we use the term **computation** to refer to a sequence of configurations that begins with an initial configuration, and where each configuration γ in the sequence is followed by a successor configuration of γ, so long as such a successor configuration exists. When invoked on a string, it is possible for an NFA to carry out multiple computations, as the next example will discuss. Say that a computation is *accepting* if it ends with a configuration whose state is an accept state; under this terminology, an NFA M accepts a string x when there *exists* an accepting computation beginning with the initial configuration of M on x.

Example 1.3.9. Let us revisit Example 1.3.3, and consider its NFA M and its first diagram of configurations. The configuration $[0, aa]$ has two successor configurations, $[0, a]$ and $[1, a]$; we can notate this by writing

$$[0, aa] \vdash_M [0, a] \quad \text{and} \quad [0, aa] \vdash_M [1, a].$$

As $[0, aa]$ is a successor configuration of $[0, baa]$, we can write $[0, baa] \vdash_M [0, aa]$; it then follows that

$$[0, baa] \vdash_M^2 [0, a] \quad \text{and} \quad [0, baa] \vdash_M^2 [1, a].$$

As $[0, a] \vdash_M [0, \epsilon]$, $[0, a] \vdash_M [1, \epsilon]$, and $[1, a] \vdash_M [2, \epsilon]$, we may write

$$[0, baa] \vdash_M^3 [0, \epsilon], \quad [0, baa] \vdash_M^3 [1, \epsilon], \quad \text{and} \quad [0, baa] \vdash_M^3 [2, \epsilon].$$

To unpack and expand the last three relationships shown, we have the following three computations of M that begin with the initial configuration $[0, baa]$:

$$[0, baa] \vdash_M [0, aa] \vdash_M [0, a] \vdash_M [0, \epsilon],$$

$$[0, baa] \vdash_M [0, aa] \vdash_M [0, a] \vdash_M [1, \epsilon],$$

$$[0, baa] \vdash_M [0, aa] \vdash_M [1, a] \vdash_M [2, \epsilon].$$

By glancing back at the first diagram in Example 1.3.3, we can see that there are no further computations of M beginning with the configuration $[0, baa]$. ◇

For an NFA $M = (Q, \Sigma, S, T, \Delta)$, we officially define acceptance and rejection of strings as follows.

Definition 1.3.10. Let $y \in \Sigma^*$ be a string. If there exist states $s \in S$ and $t \in T$ such that $[s, y] \vdash_M^* [t, \epsilon]$, then we say that M **accepts** y; otherwise, we say that M **rejects** y. ◇

Definition 1.3.11. We define the **language** of an NFA M, denoted by $L(M)$, to be the set $\{y \in \Sigma^* \mid M \text{ accepts } y\}$. ◇

Example 1.3.12. Let us continue the discussion in Example 1.3.9. For the NFA M under examination, we had $[0, baa] \vdash_M^3 [2, \epsilon]$; since $0 \in S$ and $2 \in T$, we obtain that the NFA M accepts the string *baa*, via Definition 1.3.10. ◇

We have arrived at a critical juncture in our study. We have, in our hands, *two* computational models, the DFA and the NFA. A natural question that one can pose at this point is how we can compare these two models. Above all, we are interested in what our computational models can *do*, that is, in the languages that they can compute. We thus adopt a functional viewpoint and compare our computational models *externally*, by grading each model according to the span of languages that it defines. Indeed, in general it is not altogether clear how one would compare models *internally*: the mechanisms by which one model computes may be quite qualitatively different from those of another model.

We provide our first such model comparison result by arguing the quite plausible result that each language definable by a DFA is also definable by an NFA. This result reveals that, from the external viewpoint that we adopt, the NFA model is at least as powerful as the DFA model. Before providing the argument, let us emphasize that—strictly speaking—a DFA is not an NFA (nor is an NFA a DFA): as noted in Remark 1.3.2, the definitions of NFA and DFA differ in two parts.

Proposition 1.3.13. *For each DFA M, there exists an NFA M' such that $L(M') = L(M)$.*

This proposition can be argued as follows. Let $M = (Q, \Sigma, s, T, \delta)$ be a DFA. Based on this DFA M, we define the NFA $M' = (Q, \Sigma, S', T, \Delta)$ to have initial state set $S' = \{s\}$ and transition function defined by $\Delta(q, a) = \{\delta(q, a)\}$, for each pair $(q, a) \in Q \times \Sigma$. Since M and M' have the same state set, they have the same configurations. We have that the only start state of the NFA M' is the start state of the DFA M, and that when given any state q and symbol a, the NFA M' has exactly one state to which it can transition—namely, the state to which the DFA M transitions. Indeed, if we were to draw both M and M' as diagrams, the results would be identical. Consequently, the notions of successor configuration coincide for M and M', that is, for all configurations α and β of these automata, β is the successor configuration of α according to M (under Definition 1.1.6) if and only if β is a successor configuration of α according to M' (under Definition 1.3.8). To state this symbolically: for all configurations α and β, it holds that $\alpha \vdash_M \beta$ if and only if $\alpha \vdash_{M'} \beta$. It follows that a string is accepted by M if and only if it is accepted by M'; so, the proposition is established.

We will later prove results that imply that one can convert in the other direction, namely, that for each NFA, there exists a DFA having the same language as the NFA (Theorem 1.3.24). Together, the two conversions imply that the classes of languages induced by each of these two models are equal. As a consequence, to show that there exists a DFA for a given language (that is, that a language is regular), it suffices to show that there exists an NFA for the language. This consequence implies a form of programming convenience: for a given language, it may be easier to present an NFA for the language than to present a DFA for the language.

1.3.2 ϵ-NFA

We next present an extension of the NFA model, called the ϵ-*NFA*. We will prove that each ϵ-NFA has a language that is regular, and hence, the ϵ-NFA model provides yet more convenience for establishing the regularity of a language. It will also be useful for showing further closure properties of the regular languages.

The definition of this extended model is built on the definition of NFA, but has the supplementary feature that, from any state of an ϵ-NFA, additional transitions are permitted. These additional transitions are referred to as ϵ-**transitions**; the transition function Δ of an ϵ-NFA specifies the ϵ-transitions by providing, for each state q, a set of states $\Delta(q, \epsilon)$. Operationally, an ϵ-NFA may, at any point in time, freely make a transition from a state q to a state in the set $\Delta(q, \epsilon)$, without consuming any input symbols.

Definition 1.3.14. An ϵ-**NFA** is a 5-tuple $M = (Q, \Sigma, S, T, \Delta)$ where each of the parts is defined as in the definition of NFA (Definition 1.3.1), except the *transition function* is a mapping

$$\Delta \colon Q \times (\Sigma \cup \{\epsilon\}) \to \wp(Q). \qquad \qquad \diamond$$

Recall that $\epsilon \notin \Sigma$ is always assumed.

Example 1.3.15. We present an example ϵ-NFA. In contrast to many of the automata examples given so far, the state set consists of letters, and the input alphabet consists of numbers. The example $N = (Q, \Sigma, S, T, \Delta)$ has state set $Q = \{a, b, c, d\}$, input alphabet $\Sigma = \{1, 2, 3, 4\}$, initial state set $S = \{a\}$, accept state set $T = \{d\}$, and the following transition function:

Δ	1	2	3	4	ϵ
a	$\{a\}$	$\emptyset$	$\emptyset$	$\emptyset$	$\{b\}$
b	$\emptyset$	$\{b\}$	$\emptyset$	$\emptyset$	$\{c\}$
c	$\emptyset$	$\emptyset$	$\{c\}$	$\emptyset$	$\{d\}$
d	$\emptyset$	$\emptyset$	$\emptyset$	$\{d\}$	$\emptyset$

We form the diagram for an ϵ-NFA much in the same way that we formed the diagram for an NFA. The only difference is that we include the ϵ-transitions, so whenever $q \in \Delta(p, i)$, we include an arrow from state p to state q with label i; here, we perform this over each element $i \in \Sigma \cup \{\epsilon\}$, that is, including the case that $i = \epsilon$. The following is a diagram for our example ϵ-NFA N:

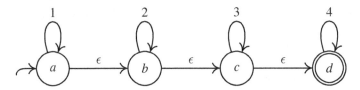

As with DFA and NFA, a *configuration* of an ϵ-NFA consists of a state paired with a string. We fully formalize the behavior of an ϵ-NFA below; as an example, let us examine the configurations reachable when this automaton is invoked on the string 13:

$$
\begin{array}{llllll}
 & & & & & [c,\epsilon] \;\; \vdash \;\; [d,\epsilon] \\
 & [a,3] \;\; \vdash \;\; [b,3] \;\; \vdash \;\; [c,3] \;\; \diagup \\
 & \diagup & & & \diagdown & [d,3] \\
[a,13] & & & & \\
 & \diagdown & & & \\
 & [b,13] \;\; \vdash \;\; [c,13] \;\; \vdash \;\; [d,13]
\end{array}
$$

Let us see cases of how this example ϵ-NFA makes use of ϵ-transitions. Due to the inclusion $b \in \Delta(a,\epsilon)$, from state a the automaton may freely transition to state b without consuming any symbol. This is evidenced in the diagram, where we see the relationships $[a,13] \vdash [b,13]$, and $[a,3] \vdash [b,3]$. Indeed, most of the transitions shown in the diagram can be recognized to be ϵ-transitions.

It can be seen from the diagram of this automaton that, from the initial state a, the accept state d can only be reached by traversing the states a, b, c, and d in order. In the state a, the automaton may consume the symbol 1 and remain in this state, or it may freely progress to the next state in the order. The states b and c behave similarly, but with respect to the symbols 2 and 3. In state d, the automaton may consume the symbol 4 and remain in this state. From this description, it can be seen that a string is accepted by the automaton if and only if it is *sorted* in the sense that, whenever $i,j \in \Sigma$ are such that $i < j$, each occurrence of i appears before each occurrence of j. ◇

We next formalize the behavior of an ϵ-NFA; the difference with the formalization of NFA is that we extend the definition of *successor configuration* to account for ϵ-transitions.

Definition 1.3.16. Let $M = (Q, \Sigma, S, T, \Delta)$ be an ϵ-NFA.

- A **configuration** of M is a pair $[q,y]$ consisting of a state $q \in Q$ and a string $y \in \Sigma^*$.
- An **initial configuration** of M on a string $y \in \Sigma^*$ is a configuration of the form $[s,y]$, where $s \in S$.
- A configuration $[r,x]$ of M is a **successor configuration** of a configuration $[q,y]$ of M if there exists $a \in \Sigma \cup \{\epsilon\}$ such that $y = ax$ and $r \in \Delta(q,a)$.

To discuss configurations of M, we use the relations presented in Definition 1.1.8. To define the notions of acceptance and rejection for M, we put into effect Definition 1.3.10. ◇

So, as was the case for an NFA, an ϵ-NFA M accepts a string x when there *exists* a computation that begins with an initial configuration of M on x, and that is *accepting* in the sense of ending with a configuration having an accept state.

Definition 1.3.17. We define the **language** of an ϵ-NFA M, denoted by $L(M)$, to be the set $\{y \in \Sigma^* \mid M \text{ accepts } y\}$. ◇

We next show how to convert from an NFA to an ϵ-NFA having the same language. This shows that, in the sense made precise, the ϵ-NFA model is at least as powerful as the NFA model. Recall that we previously showed that the NFA model is at least as powerful as the DFA model (Proposition 1.3.13); the present result is in the spirit of that previous result in that it also compares two computational models.

Proposition 1.3.18. *For each NFA M, there exists an ϵ-NFA M' such that $L(M') = L(M)$.*

We can argue this proposition by designing the ϵ-NFA M' to have no ϵ-transitions, and to be otherwise based on the NFA M. To be precise, from an NFA $M = (Q, \Sigma, S, T, \Delta)$, define M' as the ϵ-NFA $(Q, \Sigma, S, T, \Delta')$ where, for each $q \in Q$, we define $\Delta'(q, a)$ as $\Delta(q, a)$ if $a \in \Sigma$, and as the empty set $\emptyset$ if $a = \epsilon$. It is straightforward to verify that M and M' share the same configurations as well as the same notion of successor configuration. The definition of acceptance is the same for both automata and depends only on the set of start states, the set of accept states, and the notion of successor configuration, all three of which are shared in common by M and M'; consequently, a string is accepted by M if and only if it is accepted by M', and we have confirmed the proposition.

At this point, let us identify some facts about the automata models defined so far. Suppose that M is a DFA, NFA, or ϵ-NFA on alphabet Σ, and let $w \in \Sigma^*$ be any string. If one configuration is the successor of another, then adding the string w to the end of each of the configurations does not change the successor relationship; also, if one configuration is the successor of another, then removing the string w from the end of each of the configurations, when it is possible to do so, does not change the successor relationship. We formally state these two facts as follows. First, if it holds that $[r, x]$ is a successor configuration of a configuration $[q, y]$, that is, $[q, y] \vdash_M [r, x]$, then $[q, yw] \vdash_M [r, xw]$. And the converse holds: if, for configurations $[q, y]$ and $[r, x]$, it holds that $[q, yw] \vdash_M [r, xw]$, then $[q, y] \vdash_M [r, x]$. These facts are verified immediately from the definitions of successor configuration. The following proposition is a consequence of these two facts.

Proposition 1.3.19. *Suppose that M is a DFA, NFA, or ϵ-NFA on alphabet Σ, that $w \in \Sigma^*$ is a string, and that $[p, z]$ and $[p', z']$ are configurations of M. Then,*

$$[p, z] \vdash_M^* [p', z'] \quad \text{if and only if} \quad [p, zw] \vdash_M^* [p', z'w].$$

1.3.3   From ϵ-NFA to DFA

So far, we have seen three computational models and we have established that they increase successively in power: each language definable by a DFA is definable by an NFA, and each language definable by an NFA is definable by an ϵ-NFA. We now close the loop by showing that each language definable by an ϵ-NFA is definable by a DFA, and hence that these three computational models have the same power in that they each define the same class of languages.

Theorem 1.3.20. *For each ϵ-NFA M, there exists a DFA M' such that $L(M') = L(M)$.*

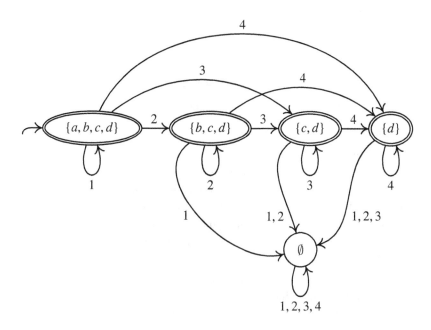

Figure 1.3.1. Part of the DFA $M' = (Q', \Sigma, s', T', \delta)$ obtained by applying the subset construction of Theorem 1.3.20 to the ϵ-NFA $N = (Q, \Sigma, S, T, \Delta)$ of Example 1.3.15. The start state s' contains each state from Q reachable via ϵ-transitions from the start state $a \in S$ of N; each state in Q is reachable in this way, so we have $s' = Q = \{a, b, c, d\}$. The state set Q' of the DFA M' is defined as the power set of Q, but not all states of M' are shown in the diagram; only those reachable from the start state s' via transitions are shown. The ϵ-NFA N has one accept state, d; a state of Q' is an accept state when it contains d. The transition function of the DFA M', given a state U and a symbol a, yields the set of states reachable in N by consuming a along with taking ϵ-transitions, from a state in U. For example, from the state $\{c, d\}$, a transition on 1 yields the empty set: starting from c or d, it is not possible to consume 1 in N, even after making ϵ-transitions. From the state $\{c, d\}$, a transition on 4 yields the set $\{d\}$: in N, from the state d, the symbol 4 can be consumed, but after this no further states can be reached by ϵ-transitions; from the state c, the symbol 4 can be consumed only after making an ϵ-transition to d.

Let $M = (Q, \Sigma, S, T, \Delta)$ be an ϵ-NFA. Our goal is to define a DFA M', based on the ϵ-NFA M, that has the same language as M. One strategy for determining if a string is accepted by an ϵ-NFA is to read in the symbols of the string one-by-one, and to keep in memory *all* of the states that the ϵ-NFA could possibly be in, at each point in time. We show how to construct a DFA M' that, in essence, implements this strategy. The construction of this DFA M' from the ϵ-NFA M is known as the **subset construction**: each state of M' is a subset of the state set of M. An example of this construction is given in Figure 1.3.1.

Define the DFA $M' = (Q', \Sigma, s', T', \delta)$ as follows:

$$Q' = \wp(Q),$$
$$s' = \{u \in Q \mid \exists s \in S \text{ such that } [s, \epsilon] \vdash_M^* [u, \epsilon]\},$$
$$T' = \{V \subseteq Q \mid V \cap T \neq \emptyset\},$$
$$\delta(U, a) = \{v \in Q \mid \exists u \in U \text{ such that } [u, a] \vdash_M^* [v, \epsilon]\}.$$

Let us explain how each of these components is formed.

- This DFA's state set is the power set of Q, since at any point in time, it maintains the set of states from Q that the ϵ-NFA could be in.
- The DFA's start state s' is the set that contains all states reachable from S via ϵ-transitions, in the ϵ-NFA; this set contains S itself, and is the set of all states that the ϵ-NFA could be in prior to reading any symbols. See Figure 1.3.2 for a diagram.
- A state V of the DFA should be regarded as an accept state as long as it contains an accept state of the ϵ-NFA.
- Finally, when U is a state of the DFA and a is a symbol, the state given by the transition function is the set that includes a state v if it is reachable from *some* state in U by consuming a, and possibly allowing ϵ-transitions as well. See Figure 1.3.3 for a diagram.

The following definition is useful for reasoning about our automata.

Definition 1.3.21. Relative to an ϵ-NFA $M = (Q, \Sigma, S, T, \Delta)$, a set $U \subseteq Q$ of states is called ϵ-**closed** when, for each $u \in U$ and each $w \in Q$, if $[u, \epsilon] \vdash_M^* [w, \epsilon]$, then $w \in U$. ◇

So, relative to an ϵ-NFA, a set U of states is ϵ-closed when U contains any state w that is reachable, purely via ϵ-transitions, from a state in U. In reasoning about subsets of Q (that is, sets of states of M), our focus will be on those that are ϵ-closed. The next lemma shows that the set s' has this property.

Lemma 1.3.22. *The set $s' \subseteq Q$ of states is ϵ-closed.*

Proof. Suppose that $u \in s'$ and $w \in Q$ is such that $[u, \epsilon] \vdash_M^* [w, \epsilon]$. By the definition of s', there exists $s \in S$ such that $[s, \epsilon] \vdash_M^* [u, \epsilon]$. It follows that $[s, \epsilon] \vdash_M^* [w, \epsilon]$, and thus by the definition of s', we obtain that $w \in s'$.   □

The following lemma relates the transitions of the DFA M' to the transitions of the ϵ-NFA M; in particular, it characterizes the state W that the DFA will be in when it starts in an ϵ-closed state U and reads a string y.

Lemma 1.3.23. *Let $y \in \Sigma^*$ be a string of length n; suppose that $U \subseteq Q$ is ϵ-closed; and let $W \subseteq Q$ be the unique set such that $[U, y] \vdash_{M'}^n [W, \epsilon]$. Then, it holds that $w \in W$ if and only if there exists $u \in U$ such that $[u, y] \vdash_M^* [w, \epsilon]$.*

Proof. We prove this by induction on n.

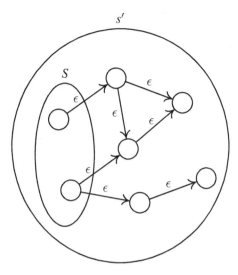

Figure 1.3.2. The start state of the DFA in the subset construction. In the conversion of an ϵ-NFA to a DFA, the start state s' of the DFA is defined as the set of all states reachable from any start state of the ϵ-NFA, by making 0 or more ϵ-transitions. In particular, this start state s' contains the set S of start states of the ϵ-NFA, that is, it holds that $S \subseteq s'$.

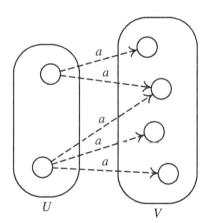

Figure 1.3.3. The transition function of the DFA in the subset construction. In the conversion of an ϵ-NFA to a DFA M', each state of the DFA is a subset of the state set Q of the ϵ-NFA. The transition function of the DFA is defined so that, when given a set $U \subseteq Q$ of ϵ-NFA states along with a symbol a, the function returns the set $V \subseteq Q$ of ϵ-NFA states that can be reached from a state in U after consuming the symbol a. Here, a dotted arrow with label a from a first state to a second state indicates that the second state can be reached from the first by traversing a sequence of states, such that only the symbol a is consumed: thus, in such a traversal, one transition is on the symbol a, and all others are ϵ-transitions.

Suppose that $n = 0$; we then have $y = \epsilon$ and $W = U$. For the forward direction, suppose that $w \in W$; we have $w \in U$ and $[w, y] \vdash_M^* [w, \epsilon]$. For the backward direction, suppose that there exists $u \in U$ such that $[u, y] \vdash_M^* [w, \epsilon]$; then, by the assumption that U is ϵ-closed, it holds that $w \in U = W$.

Suppose that $n > 0$, and write $y = ax$ where $a \in \Sigma$ and $x \in \Sigma^*$. Let $V \subseteq Q$ be the unique set such that $[U, ax] \vdash_{M'} [V, x] \vdash_{M'}^{n-1} [W, \epsilon]$. We have that $V = \delta(U, a)$, implying by the definition of δ that

$$v \in V \quad \Leftrightarrow \quad \text{there exists } u \in U \text{ such that } [u, a] \vdash_M^* [v, \epsilon].$$

The set V is ϵ-closed: suppose that $v \in V$, $w \in Q$, and $[v, \epsilon] \vdash_M^* [w, \epsilon]$; by the above description of V, we have that there exists $u \in U$ such that $[u, a] \vdash_M^* [v, \epsilon]$, implying that $[u, a] \vdash_M^* [w, \epsilon]$, from which it follows that $w \in V$ by the above description of V. By induction, we obtain that

$$w \in W \quad \Leftrightarrow \quad \text{there exists } v \in V \text{ such that } [v, x] \vdash_M^* [w, \epsilon].$$

We now verify each of the two directions of the claim of the lemma.

- For the forward direction, assume that $w \in W$. Then, by the above description of W, there exists $v \in V$ such that $[v, x] \vdash_M^* [w, \epsilon]$. In turn, by the above description of V, there exists $u \in U$ such that $[u, a] \vdash_M^* [v, \epsilon]$, from which it follows that $[u, ax] \vdash_M^* [v, x]$, by Proposition 1.3.19. From the facts that $[u, ax] \vdash_M^* [v, x]$ and $[v, x] \vdash_M^* [w, \epsilon]$, we obtain that $[u, ax] \vdash_M^* [w, \epsilon]$, as desired.

- For the backward direction, assume that there exists $u \in U$ such that $[u, y] \vdash_M^* [w, \epsilon]$; we want to show that $w \in W$. Consider the sequence of configurations that witnesses the relationship $[u, y] \vdash_M^* [w, \epsilon]$: there exist states $q_1, ..., q_k, r \in Q$ (with $k \geq 0$) such that

$$[u, ax] \vdash_M [q_1, ax] \vdash_M \cdots \vdash_M [q_k, ax] \vdash_M [r, x] \vdash_M^* [w, \epsilon].$$

From this, we obtain $[u, a] \vdash_M^* [r, \epsilon]$ (via Proposition 1.3.19) and $[r, x] \vdash_M^* [w, \epsilon]$. By the above description of V and the fact that $[u, a] \vdash_M^* [r, \epsilon]$, we obtain that $r \in V$; then, by the above description of W and the fact that $[r, x] \vdash_M^* [w, \epsilon]$, we conclude that $w \in W$. □

By making use of this lemma, we can now establish the theorem.

Proof of Theorem 1.3.20. Let $y \in \Sigma^*$ be a string of length n, and let $W \subseteq Q$ be the unique state of Q' such that $[s', y] \vdash_{M'}^n [W, \epsilon]$. By Lemma 1.3.22, the set $s' \subseteq Q$ is ϵ-closed. By Lemma 1.3.23, we obtain that

$$w \in W \quad \Leftrightarrow \quad \text{there exists } u \in s' \text{ such that } [u, y] \vdash_M^* [w, \epsilon].$$

We argue that the ϵ-NFA M accepts y if and only if the DFA M' accepts y.

Suppose that the ϵ-NFA M accepts y. Then there exist states $s \in S$ and $t \in T$ giving the relationship $[s, y] \vdash_M^* [t, \epsilon]$. Since $s \in s'$, by the above characterization of W, we have the inclusion $t \in W$. This implies that $W \cap T \neq \emptyset$, so $W \in T'$ and the DFA M' accepts y.

Suppose that the DFA M' accepts y. Then $W \in T'$, implying that $W \cap T \neq \emptyset$. Let t be a state (of Q) that is in $W \cap T$. By the above characterization of W, there exists $u \in s'$ such that $[u, y] \vdash_M^* [t, \epsilon]$. By definition of s', there exists $s \in S$ such that $[s, \epsilon] \vdash_M^* [u, \epsilon]$, implying that $[s, y] \vdash_M^* [u, y]$. From the results $[s, y] \vdash_M^* [u, y]$ and $[u, y] \vdash_M^* [t, \epsilon]$, it follows that $[s, y] \vdash_M^* [t, \epsilon]$. Since $s \in S$ and $t \in T$, we obtain that M accepts y. $\qquad\square$

1.3.4 Summary

The following theorem results from collecting together our comparisons between automata models.

Theorem 1.3.24. *Let B be a language. The following are equivalent:*

- *There exists a DFA M such that $L(M) = B$; that is, B is regular.*
- *There exists an NFA M such that $L(M) = B$.*
- *There exists an ϵ-NFA M such that $L(M) = B$.*

Proof. If there exists a DFA whose language is B, then by Proposition 1.3.13, there exists an NFA whose language is B. If there exists an NFA whose language is B, then by Proposition 1.3.18, there exists an ϵ-NFA whose language is B. And if there exists an ϵ-NFA whose language is B, then by Theorem 1.3.20, there exists a DFA whose language is B. $\qquad\square$

1.4 More closure properties

In this section, we show that the regular languages enjoy two further closure properties. These results help us understand further the extent of the regular languages, and provide insight into what types of languages can be shown to be regular. These results will also have starring roles in the next section, where we will see that the regular languages can in fact be *characterized* using natural closure properties. In the present section, to establish each of the two closure properties under scrutiny, we build an ϵ-NFA whose language is the language claimed to be regular; hence, we rely crucially on the just-established fact that ϵ-NFA define regular languages (this fact follows from Theorem 1.3.24). Let us remark that this fact also allows for an alternative proof that the regular languages are closed under union: given two ϵ-NFA M_B, M_C, one can build an ϵ-NFA whose language is the union $L(M_B) \cup L(M_C)$ essentially by drawing the diagrams of M_B and M_C side by side, and interpreting the overall result as the diagram of an ϵ-NFA.

1.4.1 Concatenation

Let B and C be languages. The **concatenation** of B and C, denoted by $B \cdot C$ or by BC, is defined as $\{xy \mid x \in B \text{ and } y \in C\}$, that is, as the set containing each string that can be obtained by concatenating a string in B with a string in C.

Theorem 1.4.1. *If B and C are both regular languages over the same alphabet Σ, then their concatenation $B \cdot C$ is also a regular language.*

Let $M_B = (Q_B, \Sigma, S_B, T_B, \Delta_B)$ and $M_C = (Q_C, \Sigma, S_C, T_C, \Delta_C)$ be ϵ-NFA with $L(M_B) = B$ and $L(M_C) = C$. We assume that the state sets Q_B and Q_C are disjoint. (If they are not disjoint, the states in one of the sets may be renamed in order to achieve disjointness, without affecting the language of its automaton; Remark 1.1.4 discussed state renaming in DFA, and applies equally well to NFA and ϵ-NFA.) From these two ϵ-NFA, we build a third ϵ-NFA M, whose language is the concatenation $B \cdot C$. On a high level, this is done by including all of the states and transitions in both M_B and M_C, designating the states in S_B as the initial states and the states in T_C as the accept states, and adding ϵ-transitions from each state in T_B to each state in S_C. Figure 1.4.1 gives a diagram indicating this construction.

Essentially, a string will be accepted by M if and only if it can be split into two parts, where the first part allows for M to move from a state in S_B to a state in T_B (that is, the first part is accepted by M_B), and the second part allows for M to move from a state in S_C to a state in T_C (that is, the second part is accepted by M_C). The added ϵ-transitions allow for free passage from T_B to S_C, and are M's only transitions linking the two original ϵ-NFA.

Formally, we define the ϵ-NFA M as $(Q_B \cup Q_C, \Sigma, S_B, T_C, \Delta)$ where the transition function Δ is defined as follows:

- For all $q \in Q_B$ and $a \in \Sigma \cup \{\epsilon\}$, define $\Delta(q, a)$ as $\Delta_B(q, a) \cup S_C$ if $q \in T_B$ and $a = \epsilon$, and as $\Delta_B(q, a)$ otherwise.
- For all $q \in Q_C$ and $a \in \Sigma \cup \{\epsilon\}$, define $\Delta(q, a)$ as $\Delta_C(q, a)$.

So, the definition of Δ naturally imitates those of Δ_B and Δ_C, but in the particular case of a state $q \in T_B$ and the symbol $a = \epsilon$, transitions to the states in S_C are allowed in addition to the transitions given by Δ_B.

Proof of Theorem 1.4.1. We prove that the ϵ-NFA M just defined has $L(M) = B \cdot C$; this suffices by Theorem 1.3.24. We first establish the containment $L(M) \supseteq B \cdot C$, which is readily done. We then establish the containment $L(M) \subseteq B \cdot C$, which involves analyzing the transitions made by an accepting computation of M, and showing that the string accepted can be split into two parts, where the first is accepted by M_B, and the second is accepted by M_C. This latter part of the proof is a bit tedious, but relatively straightforward.

Suppose that $z \in B \cdot C$. Then there exist strings $x \in B$, $y \in C$ such that $z = xy$. Due to the inclusions $x \in L(M_B)$ and $y \in L(M_C)$, there exist states $s_B \in S_B$ and $t_B \in T_B$ such that $[s_B, x] \vdash^*_{M_B} [t_B, \epsilon]$; and there exist $s_C \in S_C$ and $t_C \in T_C$ such that $[s_C, y] \vdash^*_{M_C} [t_C, \epsilon]$.

- From the definition of Δ, we have that $[s_B, x] \vdash^*_M [t_B, \epsilon]$ and $[s_C, y] \vdash^*_M [t_C, \epsilon]$.
- It then follows from Proposition 1.3.19 that $[s_B, xy] \vdash^*_M [t_B, y]$.
- By definition of Δ, we have $s_C \in \Delta(t_B, \epsilon)$, implying that $[t_B, y] \vdash_M [s_C, y]$.

Combining $[s_B, xy] \vdash^*_M [t_B, y]$, $[t_B, y] \vdash_M [s_C, y]$, and $[s_C, y] \vdash^*_M [t_C, \epsilon]$, we obtain immediately that $[s_B, xy] \vdash^*_M [t_C, \epsilon]$, implying that $xy \in L(M)$.

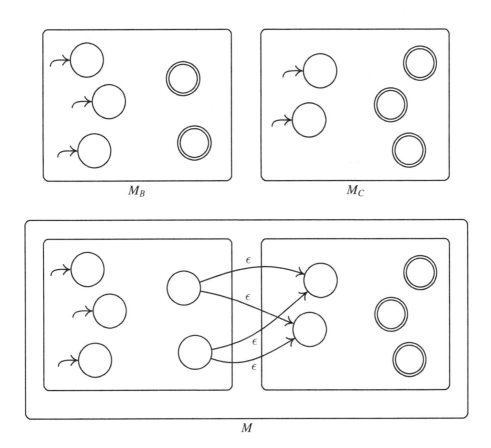

Figure 1.4.1. The construction of Theorem 1.4.1. Given two ϵ-NFA M_B and M_C, a third ϵ-NFA M is formed whose language is equal to the concatenation of the languages $L(M_B)$ and $L(M_C)$. In this diagram, only the start and accept states of M_B and M_C are depicted; the other states and the transitions of these automata are not shown. The ϵ-NFA M is formed by adding ϵ-transitions from the accept states of M_B to the initial states of M_C, by designating the start state set of M to be the start state set of M_B, and by designating the accept state set of M to be the accept state set of M_C.

Suppose that $z \in L(M)$. Then there exist $s_B \in S_B$ and $t_C \in T_C$ such that $[s_B, z] \vdash_M^* [t_C, \epsilon]$. It follows that there exist configurations $\gamma_0, \ldots, \gamma_k$ of M such that $\gamma_0 = [s_B, z]$, $\gamma_k = [t_C, \epsilon]$, and $\gamma_0 \vdash_M \gamma_1 \vdash_M \cdots \vdash_M \gamma_k$. Set q_j to be the state of the configuration γ_j, for each index j.

- Let i be the index such that, in the list $q_0, \ldots, q_k$, it holds that q_i is the first state in Q_C. We have that i is well-defined since $q_k = t_C \in Q_C$; also, as $q_0 = s_B \notin Q_C$, we have the inequality $i > 0$.

- By the definition of Δ, whenever $q \in Q_C$ (and $a \in \Sigma \cup \{\epsilon\}$), the set $\Delta(q, a)$ only contains states in Q_C; it follows that $q_i, q_{i+1}, ..., q_k$ are all elements of Q_C, and $q_0, ..., q_{i-1}$ are all elements of Q_B.

- The transition $\gamma_{i-1} \vdash_M \gamma_i$ must be witnessed by a symbol a such that $q_i \in \Delta(q_{i-1}, a)$; given that $q_{i-1} \in Q_B$ and $q_i \in Q_C$, the definition of Δ implies that $q_{i-1} \in T_B$, $q_i \in S_C$, and $a = \epsilon$. Hence, there exists a string y such that $\gamma_{i-1} = [q_{i-1}, y]$ and $\gamma_i = [q_i, y]$. So, we have $[s_B, z] \vdash_M^* [q_{i-1}, y] \vdash_M [q_i, y] \vdash_M^* [t_C, \epsilon]$.

- Let x be the string such that $z = xy$. From Proposition 1.3.19, $[s_B, z] \vdash_M^* [q_{i-1}, y]$ implies $[s_B, x] \vdash_M^* [q_{i-1}, \epsilon]$, which in turn implies $[s_B, x] \vdash_{M_B}^* [q_{i-1}, \epsilon]$ (by the definition of Δ); we obtain that $x \in L(M_B)$.

- From $[q_i, y] \vdash_M^* [t_C, \epsilon]$, it follows that $[q_i, y] \vdash_{M_C}^* [t_C, \epsilon]$ (by the definition of Δ); we obtain that $y \in L(M_C)$.

We conclude that $z = xy$, where $x \in B$ and $y \in C$. $\square$

1.4.2   Star

When B is a language, we define B^* as the language

$$\{x_1 \cdots x_k \mid k \geq 0 \text{ and } x_1, ..., x_k \in B\};$$

that is, B^* is the language containing each string that is the concatenation of 0 or more strings from B. We sometimes refer to B^* as the **star** of B. In the case that $k = 0$, we understand $x_1...x_k$ to denote the empty string ϵ; so, for any language B, it holds that $\epsilon \in B^*$. In using Σ^* to denote the set of all strings over an alphabet Σ, we have already made use of this notation; observe that this usage is consistent with and generalized by the given definition of B^* for *any* language B.

Theorem 1.4.2. *If B is a regular language, then B^* is also a regular language.*

Let $M = (Q, \Sigma, S, T, \Delta)$ be an ϵ-NFA with $L(M) = B$. From this ϵ-NFA, we build another ϵ-NFA M' whose language is B^*. On a high level, this is done by starting with the states and transitions of M, and adding a new state p, which has ϵ-transitions *to* the initial states of M, and *from* the accept states of M; this state p is defined to be the sole initial state and the sole accept state of M'. A diagram indicating this construction of M' is given in Figure 1.4.2. Formally, define $M' = (Q \cup \{p\}, \Sigma, \{p\}, \{p\}, \Delta')$ where p is assumed to be a new state not in Q, and Δ' is defined as follows. Set $\Delta'(p, \epsilon) = S$ and, for each $a \in \Sigma$, set $\Delta'(p, a) = \emptyset$. For each $q \in Q$ and $a \in \Sigma \cup \{\epsilon\}$, set $\Delta'(q, a)$ to be $\Delta(q, a) \cup \{p\}$ if $q \in T$ and $a = \epsilon$, and to be $\Delta(q, a)$ otherwise.

Proof. We prove that, for the ϵ-NFA M' just defined, it holds that $L(M') = B^*$; this suffices by Theorem 1.3.24. Paralleling the previous proof, the containment $L(M') \supseteq B^*$ is relatively straightforward to show, whereas showing the containment $L(M') \subseteq B^*$ involves analyzing an arbitrary accepting computation of M', and requires more reasoning.

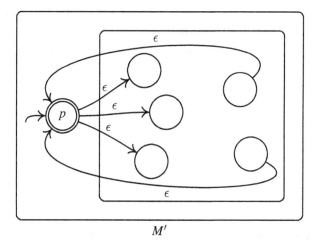

M'

Figure 1.4.2. The construction of Theorem 1.4.2 applied to the ϵ-NFA M_B from Figure 1.4.1. Given an ϵ-NFA M, a second ϵ-NFA M' is formed whose language is equal to the star of M's language. The ϵ-NFA M' is formed by adding a new state p which is both its unique start state and its unique accept state; the state p has ϵ-transitions to each of the initial states of M, and ϵ-transitions from each of the accept states of M.

Suppose that $z \in B^*$. Then there exist strings $x_1, ..., x_k \in B$ such that $z = x_1 \cdots x_k$. For each $i = 1, ..., k$, there thus exist $s_i \in S$ and $t_i \in T$ such that $[s_i, x_i] \vdash_M^* [t_i, \epsilon]$; it follows from the definition of M' that $[s_i, x_i] \vdash_{M'}^* [t_i, \epsilon]$. From Proposition 1.3.19, we obtain that

$$[s_1, x_1 \cdots x_k] \vdash_{M'}^* [t_1, x_2 \cdots x_k], \ [s_2, x_2 \cdots x_k] \vdash_{M'}^* [t_2, x_3 \cdots x_k], \ ..., \ [s_k, x_k] \vdash_{M'}^* [t_k, \epsilon].$$

Using these relationships along with the definition of Δ', we have the following computation of M':

$$[p, x_1 \cdots x_k] \vdash_{M'} [s_1, x_1 \cdots x_k]$$
$$\vdash_{M'}^* [t_1, x_2 \cdots x_k] \vdash_{M'} [p, x_2 \cdots x_k] \vdash_{M'} [s_2, x_2 \cdots x_k]$$
$$\vdash_{M'}^* [t_2, x_3 \cdots x_k] \vdash_{M'} [p, x_3 \cdots x_k] \vdash_{M'} [s_3, x_3 \cdots x_k]$$
$$\vdots$$
$$\vdash_{M'}^* [t_k, \epsilon] \vdash_{M'} [p, \epsilon].$$

As $[p, x_1 \cdots x_k] \vdash_{M'}^* [p, \epsilon]$, we obtain $z \in L(M')$.

Suppose that $z \in L(M')$. If $z = \epsilon$, then clearly $z \in B^*$, so assume that $z \neq \epsilon$. Then, there exist configurations $\gamma_0, ..., \gamma_n$ such that

$$\gamma_0 = [p, z], \quad \gamma_n = [p, \epsilon], \quad \text{and} \quad \gamma_0 \vdash_{M'} \gamma_1 \vdash_{M'} \cdots \vdash_{M'} \gamma_n.$$

Define the strings $z_1, ..., z_\ell$ so that $[p, z_1], ..., [p, z_\ell]$ is a list of the configurations from the list $\gamma_0, ..., \gamma_n$ that have state p, in order; note that $z_1 = z$, $z_\ell = \epsilon$, and $\ell \geq 2$ (as $z \neq \epsilon$). For each index $i = 1, ..., \ell - 1$, it holds that $[p, z_i] \vdash_{M'}^* [p, z_{i+1}]$. Since, according to Δ', the only transitions from p are to states in S, and the only transitions to p are from states in T, there exist states $s_i \in S$, $t_i \in T$ such that

$$[p, z_i] \vdash_{M'} [s_i, z_i] \vdash_{M'}^* [t_i, z_{i+1}] \vdash_{M'} [p, z_{i+1}].$$

By the definition of Δ', it follows that, in the ϵ-NFA M,

$$[s_i, z_i] \vdash_M^* [t_i, z_{i+1}].$$

For each index $i = 1, ..., \ell - 1$, let x_i be the string such that $z_i = x_i z_{i+1}$; by Proposition 1.3.19, we have the relationship

$$[s_i, x_i] \vdash_M^* [t_i, \epsilon],$$

implying that $x_i \in L(M)$. We have that the string z can be expanded as

$$z = z_1 = x_1 z_2 = x_1 x_2 z_3 = \cdots = x_1 \cdots x_{\ell-1} z_\ell = x_1 \cdots x_{\ell-1}.$$

Since each of the strings $x_1, ..., x_{\ell-1}$ is in $L(M)$, we conclude that $z \in B^*$.   □

1.5   Regular expressions

We have studied three computational models, the DFA, the NFA, and the ϵ-NFA. An automaton of any of these three types, as seen, specifies a regular language. In this section, we encounter and study another way, a textual way, of specifying a regular language: giving a *regular expression*, which is a particular type of string. Presenting a regular expression may offer the benefit that there can be a close conceptual correspondence between a regular expression and the language it specifies. Indeed, text searching programs often expect regular expressions as input, although the particular syntax expected may vary.

1.5.1   Definition and evaluation

Definition 1.5.1. Let Σ be an alphabet. We define a **regular expression** over Σ to be a string that can be derived by applying the following rules a finite number of times.

- $\emptyset$ is a regular expression.
- a is a regular expression, for each $a \in \Sigma \cup \{\epsilon\}$.
- $\alpha + \beta$ is a regular expression, when α and β are regular expressions.
- $\alpha\beta$ is a regular expression, when α and β are regular expressions.
- α^* is a regular expression, when α is a regular expression.
- (α) is a regular expression, when α is a regular expression.

Observe that each regular expression over Σ is a string over the alphabet obtained by starting from Σ and adding the symbol $\emptyset$, the symbol ϵ, the symbol +, the symbol *, the left parenthesis, and the right parenthesis. Throughout, we assume that none of these additional symbols is contained in any alphabet Σ over which we form regular expressions.   ◇

Example 1.5.2. Let Σ be the alphabet $\{a, b\}$. The following are examples of regular expressions over Σ:

$$ab + b^*, \quad ab^*, \quad (ab)^* + b, \quad b^*b + aa(a + \epsilon).$$ ◇

Let us emphasize that each regular expression is just a string. We will give semantic meaning to the regular expressions by explaining how each regular expression α *evaluates* to a language, denoted by $L(\alpha)$. While we define this evaluation more precisely in the sequel, let us give a preview of how the evaluation is performed. The expression $\emptyset$ evaluates to the language $\emptyset$; each expression $a \in \Sigma \cup \{\epsilon\}$ evaluates to the language $\{a\}$; and the sum of two expressions evaluates to the union of their languages. The next two cases are evaluated in a natural way: the concatenation of two expressions evaluates to the concatenation of the two corresponding languages, and the star of an expression evaluates to the star of its language. Parentheses are used to control the order of evaluation.

Example 1.5.3. We here present some examples of how regular expressions evaluate to languages. Let Σ be the alphabet $\{a, b\}$.

We have $L(a) = \{a\}$ and $L(b) = \{b\}$. Next, consider the regular expression ab; since it is the concatenation of the regular expressions a and b, its language $L(ab)$ is the concatenation of $L(a)$ and $L(b)$, which is the language $\{a\} \cdot \{b\} = \{ab\}$. More generally, if we take any string $x \in \Sigma^*$, it holds that $L(x) = \{x\}$, that is, x as a regular expression evaluates to the language that contains x as its sole element.

Consider now the regular expression $(ab)^*$. As it arises from applying the star to the expression (ab), its language is the star of $L(ab) = \{ab\}$, that is, $L((ab)^*) = \{ab\}^*$. From the definition of the star operator, we know that $\{ab\}^* = \{\epsilon, ab, abab, ababab, \dots\}$.

Next, consider the regular expression $b + (ab)^*$. This regular expression is the sum of the expressions b and $(ab)^*$, and the language it evaluates to is thus the union of the languages $L(b)$ and $L((ab)^*)$. So,

$$L(b + (ab^*)) = L(b) \cup L((ab)^*) = \{b\} \cup \{\epsilon, ab, abab, ababab, \dots\}.$$ ◇

In order to formally define how the evaluation of regular expressions is performed, we first need to discuss the *precedence* of the operations, that is, the order in which the operations are evaluated. The notion of precedence is likely already familiar to the reader: in arithmetic, by a usual convention, division has *higher precedence* than subtraction, so in evaluating an arithmetic expression such as $9 - 6/3$, it is the convention to evaluate the division before the subtraction, and this expression evaluates to $9 - (6/3) = 9 - 2 = 7$. (Note that if the subtraction was evaluated first, the result would be $3/3 = 1$ and hence different.) In evaluating regular expressions, we adhere to the following convention: the star (*) has the highest precedence, followed by concatenation, followed by sum (+). Let us understand what this implies via an example.

Example 1.5.4. In order to determine the language $L(ab + c^*)$ of the expression $ab + c^*$ in accordance with the precedence just given, we first determine $L(c^*)$, next determine $L(ab)$, and then compute $L(ab + c^*)$ as the union of $L(ab)$ and $L(c^*)$. That is, in evaluating the expression $ab + c^*$, we evaluate the + operator last. So, to determine $L(ab + c^*)$, we view $ab + c^*$ as having the form $\alpha + \beta$ where $\alpha = ab$ and $\beta = c^*$; then, $L(\alpha)$ and $L(\beta)$ are evaluated individually, and $L(\alpha + \beta)$ is evaluated as $L(\alpha) \cup L(\beta)$. We have $L(\alpha) = \{ab\}$ and $L(\beta) = \{\epsilon, c, cc, ccc, \ldots\}$, so we obtain

$$L(ab + c^*) = \{ab\} \cup \{\epsilon, c, cc, ccc, \ldots\}. \qquad \Diamond$$

The use of parentheses allows one to control the order of evaluation, in the usual fashion: in any regular expression α, parenthesized expressions occurring within α are evaluated prior to evaluating operators not contained within parentheses. We illustrate this usage via an example.

Example 1.5.5. Consider the expression $(ab + c)^*$, which differs from the expression in the previous example only in that a pair of parentheses has been added. To evaluate this expression, the parenthesized portion would be completely evaluated prior to evaluating the star. The expression $(ab + c)$ evaluates to $L((ab + c)) = \{ab, c\}$. From this, to determine the language $L((ab + c)^*)$, we apply the star to $L((ab + c))$, so

$$L((ab + c)^*) = L((ab + c))^* = \{ab, c\}^*.$$

Let us underscore that this language is different from the language $L(ab + c^*)$; for instance, it holds that $abab \in L((ab + c)^*)$, but $abab \notin L(ab + c^*)$. $\qquad \Diamond$

The *associativity* of operators is another consideration that ought to be discussed, but turns out to be less important in our present context. In dealing with an expression such as $\epsilon + a + b$, it should technically be specified which of the two + operators should be evaluated first. While the result is independent of the order (as a result of the union $\cup$ being an *associative* operation), we formally adhere to the convention that when dealing with multiple occurrences of +, evaluation proceeds from left to right, so in the example expression, the first instance of + is evaluated prior to the second. The same issue arises in dealing with concatenation (and note that concatenation of languages is also an associative operation); we similarly evaluate multiple occurrences of concatenation from left to right.

We can now officially define the language associated to a regular expression. Let α, β, and γ be regular expressions. We say that γ **has the form** $\alpha + \beta$ if it is syntactically equal to $\alpha + \beta$ and α and β are evaluated prior to the sum indicated by the +, that is, the + is the last operator to be evaluated, according to the presented precedence and associativity. In a similar fashion, we say that γ **has the form** $\alpha\beta$ if it is syntactically equal to $\alpha\beta$ and α and β are evaluated prior to the concatenation; and we say that γ **has the form** α^* if it is syntactically equal to α^* and α is evaluated prior to the star. Lastly, we say that γ **has the form** (α) simply if it is syntactically equal to (α).

Definition 1.5.6. For each regular expression γ over an alphabet Σ, the language $L(\gamma)$ is defined inductively, as follows.

- $L(\emptyset) = \emptyset$.
- $L(a) = \{a\}$, for each $a \in \Sigma \cup \{\epsilon\}$.
- $L(\gamma) = L(\alpha) \cup L(\beta)$, when γ has the form $\alpha + \beta$.
- $L(\gamma) = L(\alpha) \cdot L(\beta)$, when γ has the form $\alpha\beta$.
- $L(\gamma) = L(\alpha)^*$, when γ has the form α^*.
- $L(\gamma) = L(\alpha)$, when γ has the form (α). ◇

Example 1.5.7. As an example, let us consider how to give a regular expression for the language D defined to contain all *alternating strings* over $\Sigma = \{a, b\}$. We here define an **alternating string** to be a string where each occurrence of a, if followed at all, is followed by a b; and where each occurrence of b, if followed at all, is followed by an a. Alternatively, we could say that an alternating string is a string that does not contain two consecutive occurrences of the same symbol.

Consider the regular expressions $(ab)^*$ and $(ba)^*$. Certainly, all of the strings in the languages $L((ab)^*) = \{\epsilon, ab, abab, \ldots\}$ and $L((ba)^*) = \{\epsilon, ba, baba, \ldots\}$ are alternating. However, these languages do not cover all alternating strings, since they do not include any alternating strings of odd length. We may obtain the alternating strings of odd length by considering the regular expressions $a(ba)^*$ and $b(ab)^*$, whose languages are $L(a(ba)^*) = \{a, aba, ababa, \ldots\}$ and $L(b(ab)^*) = \{b, bab, babab, \ldots\}$. Putting things together, we have the following expression δ_1 where $L(\delta_1) = D$:

$$\delta_1 = (ab)^* + (ba)^* + a(ba)^* + b(ab)^*.$$

Observe that the regular expressions $(ab)^*a$ and $(ba)^*b$ yield the same languages as $a(ba)^*$ and $b(ab)^*$, respectively: $L((ab)^*a) = L(a(ba)^*)$ and $L((ba)^*b) = L(b(ab)^*)$. Consequently, we arrive at a second expression δ_2 with $L(\delta_2) = D$:

$$\delta_2 = (ab)^* + (ba)^* + (ab)^*a + (ba)^*b.$$

We may develop another regular expression for D that only uses one instance of the star, as follows. Begin with the expressions $(ab)^*$ and $b(ab)^*$. We want to include all of the strings in the union $L((ab)^*) \cup L(b(ab)^*)$; this union contains all alternating strings that terminate with b. As this union can be obtained by taking each string y in $L((ab)^*)$ and including both y itself and by, it can be seen that this union is equal to $L((\epsilon + b)(ab)^*)$. In effect, placing $(\epsilon + b)$ before $(ab)^*$ allows the strings in $L((ab)^*)$ to optionally be prefixed with b. In an analogous fashion, we can extend the expression $(\epsilon + b)(ab)^*$ so as to allow its strings to optionally end with a, by concatenating $(\epsilon + a)$ to this expression. The resulting expression δ_3 has $L(\delta_3) = D$:

$$\delta_3 = (\epsilon + b)(ab)^*(\epsilon + a).$$

We can actually derive the expression δ_3 from the expression δ_2 above, as follows. First, observe that the language $L(b(ab)^*a)$ contains all non-empty alternating strings that begin with b and end with a, so the empty string is the only string in $L((ba)^*)$ that is not in $L(b(ab)^*a)$. From this observation, it follows that

$$L((ab)^* + (ba)^*) = L((ab)^* + b(ab)^*a),$$

since the empty string is in $L((ab)^*)$. We then have that

$$L(\delta_2) = L((ab)^* + b(ab)^*a + (ab)^*a + (ba)^*b).$$

From this last expression, if we replace $(ba)^*b$ with $b(ab)^*$, and reorder, we obtain

$$(ab)^* + b(ab)^* + (ab)^*a + b(ab)^*a,$$

yet another expression whose language is D. We then have the chain of equalities

$$L((ab)^* + b(ab)^* + (ab)^*a + b(ab)^*a) = L(\epsilon(ab)^*\epsilon + b(ab)^*\epsilon + \epsilon(ab)^*a + b(ab)^*a)$$

$$= L((\epsilon + b)(ab)^*\epsilon + (\epsilon + b)(ab)^*a)$$

$$= L((\epsilon + b)(ab)^*(\epsilon + a)).$$

This gives the claimed derivation, as the last expression appearing is exactly δ_3. In this chain, the latter two equalities can be justified algebraically by distributive laws stating that $L(\gamma(\alpha + \beta)) = L(\gamma\alpha + \gamma\beta)$ and $L((\alpha + \beta)\gamma) = L(\alpha\gamma + \beta\gamma)$, where α, β, and γ denote regular expressions.   ◇

1.5.2 Regular expressions characterize the regular languages

We next establish that regular expressions give another characterization of the regular languages, in the following precise sense.

Theorem 1.5.8. *A language B is regular if and only if there exists a regular expression α such that $L(\alpha) = B$.*

That is, the languages that are representable by regular expressions are exactly the regular languages. This theorem's statement is reminiscent of the automaton-based characterizations of regularity (in Theorem 1.3.24), which each say that a language B is regular if and only if there *exists* an automaton, of some type, whose language is B. Here, instead of positing the existence of an automaton, we posit the existence of a regular expression.

This theorem can be viewed as a characterization of the regular languages *in terms of* closure properties. In essence, the theorem says that if one starts with the language $\emptyset$ and the languages $\{a\}$ for each $a \in \Sigma \cup \{\epsilon\}$, and then closes these languages under union, concatenation, and the star operator, the resulting class of languages is precisely the class of regular languages.

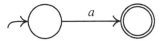

Figure 1.5.1. An ϵ-NFA whose language is $\{a\}$, for any symbol a in an alphabet or for $a = \epsilon$.

Remark 1.5.9. Recall that we proved closure of the regular languages under complementation and intersection (Theorems 1.2.1 and 1.2.2). However, these two operations are not among the operations just mentioned; they are not among the operations permitted in the evaluation of regular expressions! This observation reveals a subtlety lurking under the new characterization of regularity provided by this theorem; consider the following interesting consequences of this characterization. For each regular expression α, there exists a second regular expression α' whose language $L(\alpha')$ is the complement of the language $L(\alpha)$ of the first expression. However, in many cases, it may not be immediately obvious how to explicitly generate the expression α' from the expression α! (Indeed, the reader is invited to ponder how to do this for the example regular expressions seen so far.) Analogously, it is a consequence of the given characterization that, for any two regular expressions α and β, there exists a regular expression γ whose language $L(\gamma)$ is the intersection of $L(\alpha)$ and $L(\beta)$; but in concrete cases it may not be obvious how to generate γ from α and β.[2]

Having multiple characterizations of regularity in hand offers us the general advantage of having multiple characterizations of any property: to establish a result about regularity, we can choose which characterization to work with; a particular result may be easier to establish with one characterization than with another, and different characterizations offer different sources of illumination. See Exercise 1.9.35 for an example of a result on regular languages that can be cleanly established using Theorem 1.5.8.   ◇

We prove Theorem 1.5.8 in the next two theorems, which establish the backward direction and the forward direction, respectively.

Theorem 1.5.10. *For each regular expression γ, it holds that the language $L(\gamma)$ is regular.*

Proof. We prove this result by induction on the structure of the expression γ (Alternatively, the proof may be conceived of as by induction on the length of γ.) We consider cases, depending on the form of the expression γ.

- Suppose $\gamma = \emptyset$. The language $L(\gamma) = \emptyset$ is regular, for example, via a DFA that has no accept states.

---

2. The observant reader might have noticed a similar phenomenon after seeing the characterization of regularity by the NFA model. To wit: for each NFA M, there exists a second NFA M' whose language $L(M')$ is the complement of the language $L(M)$; yet, in many cases, it may not be obvious how to generate such an NFA M' from the NFA M. In general, whenever we have a language class characterized by a model, we can ask how a closure property of the class translates to an operation on realizations of the model.

- Suppose $\gamma = a$, where $a \in \Sigma \cup \{\epsilon\}$. It is straightforward to verify that the language $L(\gamma) = \{a\}$ is regular; see Figure 1.5.1 for an ϵ-NFA whose language is $\{a\}$.
- Suppose γ has the form $\alpha + \beta$. By induction, each of the languages $L(\alpha)$ and $L(\beta)$ is regular. It follows from Theorem 1.2.4 that the language $L(\gamma) = L(\alpha) \cup L(\beta)$ is regular.
- Suppose γ has the form $\alpha\beta$. By induction, each of the languages $L(\alpha)$ and $L(\beta)$ is regular. It follows from Theorem 1.4.1 that the language $L(\gamma) = L(\alpha) \cdot L(\beta)$ is regular.
- Suppose γ has the form α^*. By induction, the language $L(\alpha)$ is regular. It follows from Theorem 1.4.2 that the language $L(\gamma) = L(\alpha)^*$ is regular.
- Suppose γ has the form (α). By induction, the language $L(\alpha)$ is regular, and so the language $L(\gamma) = L(\alpha)$ is regular.   □

Theorem 1.5.11. *For each regular language B, there exists a regular expression α such that $L(\alpha) = B$.*

When B is a regular language, there is an ϵ-NFA $M = (Q, \Sigma, S, T, \Delta)$ such that $L(M) = B$, by Theorem 1.3.24. To establish the theorem, we show how to pass from the automaton M to a regular expression whose language is $L(M)$.[3] We know that a string x is accepted by M if there exists a start state $s \in S$ and an accept state $t \in T$ such that $[s, x] \vdash_M^* [t, \epsilon]$. Thus, to obtain a regular expression for $L(M)$, it would be sufficient to have, for each pair (u, v) of states, a regular expression for the set of strings x such that $[u, x] \vdash_M^* [v, \epsilon]$; one could then take the sum (+) of these expressions over each pair $(s, t) \in S \times T$.

The following key definition presents a restriction of the $\vdash_M^*$ relation, and will facilitate our building the desired regular expressions by induction. Let $P \subseteq Q$, and let $u, v \in Q$ be states. When $x \in \Sigma^*$ is a string, we write

$$[u, x] \vdash_M^{P,*} [v, \epsilon]$$

when there exist configurations $[q_1, y_1], \ldots, [q_k, y_k]$ such that $[q_1, y_1] \vdash_M \cdots \vdash_M [q_k, y_k]$, $[u, x] = [q_1, y_1]$, $[q_k, y_k] = [v, \epsilon]$, $k \geq 1$, and each index j with $1 < j < k$ has $q_j \in P$. That is, the relationship $[u, x] \vdash_M^{P,*} [v, \epsilon]$ holds when the configuration $[v, \epsilon]$ can be reached from the configuration $[u, x]$ by taking successor configurations zero or more times, with the restriction that any strictly intermediate configuration must have a state from P. Note that, in this definition, the configurations $[u, x]$ and $[v, \epsilon]$ themselves need not have states from P. We can make the following observations, which hold for all configurations $[u, x]$ and $[v, \epsilon]$:

- If $[u, x] \vdash_M^0 [v, \epsilon]$ or $[u, x] \vdash_M^1 [v, \epsilon]$, then $[u, x] \vdash_M^{P,*} [v, \epsilon]$, for any subset $P \subseteq Q$.
  (That is, the relations $\vdash_M^0$ and $\vdash_M^1$ are subsets of $\vdash_M^{P,*}$, for any subset $P \subseteq Q$.)
- It holds that $[u, x] \vdash_M^* [v, \epsilon]$ if and only if $[u, x] \vdash_M^{Q,*} [v, \epsilon]$.
  (That is, the relations $\vdash_M^*$ and $\vdash_M^{Q,*}$ are equal.)

---

3. To establish the theorem, it would suffice to show how to pass from a DFA to a regular expression. However, as our proof technique applies quite directly to ϵ-NFA, we carry it out for this model.

The key result concerning this definition is the following.

Lemma 1.5.12. *For all $P \subseteq Q$ and $u, v \in Q$, there exists a regular expression α_{uv}^P where*

$$L(\alpha_{uv}^P) = \{x \mid [u, x] \vdash_M^{P,*} [v, \epsilon]\}.$$

Proof. We prove the result by induction on the size $|P|$ of P.

In the case that $|P| = 0$, we have that $P = \emptyset$ and thus $[u, x] \vdash_M^{P,*} [v, \epsilon]$ if and only if either $[u, x] \vdash_M^0 [v, \epsilon]$ or $[u, x] \vdash_M^1 [v, \epsilon]$. The only strings x that can satisfy this condition must have $|x| \leq 1$. So define the set of strings

$$S = \{x \in \Sigma \cup \{\epsilon\} \mid [u, x] \vdash_M^0 [v, \epsilon] \text{ or } [u, x] \vdash_M^1 [v, \epsilon]\}.$$

If S is empty, then we may take α_{uv}^P to be the regular expression $\emptyset$. If S is non-empty, let $a_1, ..., a_\ell$ be a list of its elements; then, we may take α_{uv}^P to be the sum $a_1 + \cdots + a_\ell$.

In the case that $|P| > 0$, fix an element $p \in P$; we claim that the regular expression

$$\alpha_{uv}^P = \alpha_{uv}^{P\setminus\{p\}} + \alpha_{up}^{P\setminus\{p\}}(\alpha_{pp}^{P\setminus\{p\}})^*\alpha_{pv}^{P\setminus\{p\}}$$

has the desired property, namely, that $L(\alpha_{uv}^P) = \{x \mid [u, x] \vdash_M^{P,*} [v, \epsilon]\}$. Informally, this is because when x is a string such that $[u, x] \vdash_M^{P,*} [v, \epsilon]$, there is a sequence of configurations witnessing this. If this sequence makes no intermediate use of the state p, then x is in the language of $\alpha_{uv}^{P\setminus\{p\}}$; otherwise, based on when the sequence visits the state p, the string x can be broken up into segments $x_0, ..., x_\ell$ where

- x_0 takes the ϵ-NFA from state u to state p,
- each of $x_1, ..., x_{\ell-1}$ takes the ϵ-NFA from state p to state p, and
- x_ℓ takes the ϵ-NFA from state p to state v,

and no visits to the state p are made other than those just mentioned explicitly; so, via the given segments, the string x is in the language of $\alpha_{up}^{P\setminus\{p\}}(\alpha_{pp}^{P\setminus\{p\}})^*\alpha_{pv}^{P\setminus\{p\}}$. Moreover, the reasoning reverses: when x is a string in the language of $\alpha_{uv}^{P\setminus\{p\}}$ or of $\alpha_{up}^{P\setminus\{p\}}(\alpha_{pp}^{P\setminus\{p\}})^*\alpha_{pv}^{P\setminus\{p\}}$, we have the relationship $[u, x] \vdash_M^{P,*} [v, \epsilon]$.

We verify the claim formally as follows; let x be a string.

- Suppose that $x \in L(\alpha_{uv}^P)$; then $x \in L(\alpha_{uv}^{P\setminus\{p\}})$ or $x \in L(\alpha_{up}^{P\setminus\{p\}}(\alpha_{pp}^{P\setminus\{p\}})^*\alpha_{pv}^{P\setminus\{p\}})$.

  In the former case, $[u, x] \vdash_M^{P\setminus\{p\},*} [v, \epsilon]$, implying that $[u, x] \vdash_M^{P,*} [v, \epsilon]$.

  In the latter case, there exist strings $x_0, ..., x_\ell$ (with $\ell \geq 1$) such that $x = x_0...x_\ell$, $x_0 \in L(\alpha_{up}^{P\setminus\{p\}})$, $x_1, ..., x_{\ell-1} \in L((\alpha_{pp}^{P\setminus\{p\}})^*)$, $x_\ell \in L(\alpha_{pv}^{P\setminus\{p\}})$. We thus have that

  - $[u, x_0] \vdash_M^{P\setminus\{p\},*} [p, \epsilon]$,
  - $[p, x_i] \vdash_M^{P\setminus\{p\},*} [p, \epsilon]$ for each i with $1 \leq i < \ell$, and
  - $[p, x_\ell] \vdash_M^{P\setminus\{p\},*} [v, \epsilon]$.

It follows, by the same reasoning that justified Proposition 1.3.19, that

$$[u, x_0...x_\ell] \vdash_M^{P\setminus\{p\},*} [p, x_1...x_\ell] \vdash_M^{P\setminus\{p\},*} \cdots \vdash_M^{P\setminus\{p\},*} [p, x_\ell] \vdash_M^{P\setminus\{p\},*} [v, \epsilon],$$

and we thus obtain that $[u, x] = [u, x_0 \ldots x_\ell] \vdash_M^{P,*} [v, \epsilon]$.

- Suppose that $[u, x] \vdash_M^{P,*} [v, \epsilon]$ holds. If $[u, x] \vdash_M^{P\backslash\{p\},*} [v, \epsilon]$ holds, then $x \in L(\alpha_{uv}^{P\backslash\{p\}})$ holds by induction, and hence $x \in L(\alpha_{uv}^{P})$. Otherwise, there exist configurations $[p_1, y_1], \ldots, [p_k, y_k]$ of M, with $k \geq 1$, such that $p_1, \ldots, p_k \in P$ and

$$[u, x] \vdash_M [p_1, y_1] \vdash_M [p_2, y_2] \vdash_M \cdots \vdash_M [p_k, y_k] \vdash_M [v, \epsilon],$$

where the state p appears among the states $p_1, \ldots, p_k$. Let $[p, z_1], [p, z_2], \ldots, [p, z_\ell]$ be a list, in order, of the configurations among $[p_1, y_1], \ldots, [p_k, y_k]$ whose state is equal to p. We have that

- $[u, x] \vdash_M^{P\backslash\{p\},*} [p, z_1]$,
- $[p, z_i] \vdash_M^{P\backslash\{p\},*} [p, z_{i+1}]$ for each i with $1 \leq i < \ell$, and
- $[p, z_\ell] \vdash_M^{P\backslash\{p\},*} [v, \epsilon]$.

From these relationships, it can be seen that the string z_1 is obtainable from x by removing zero or more symbols from the front of x; likewise, the string z_{i+1} is obtainable from z_i by removing zero or more symbols from the front of z_i (for each i with $1 \leq i < \ell$). Consequently, there exist strings $x_0, \ldots, x_\ell$ such that $x = x_0 z_1$; $z_i = x_i z_{i+1}$ (for each i with $1 \leq i < \ell$); and, $z_\ell = x_\ell$. Observe that $x = x_0 \ldots x_\ell$. By the same reasoning that justified Proposition 1.3.19, we obtain that

- $[u, x_0] \vdash_M^{P\backslash\{p\},*} [p, \epsilon]$,
- $[p, x_i] \vdash_M^{P\backslash\{p\},*} [p, \epsilon]$ for each i with $1 \leq i < \ell$, and
- $[p, x_\ell] \vdash_M^{P\backslash\{p\},*} [v, \epsilon]$.

It follows by induction that $x_0 \in L(\alpha_{up}^{P\backslash\{p\}})$; $x_1, \ldots, x_{\ell-1} \in L(\alpha_{pp}^{P\backslash\{p\}})$; and, $x_\ell \in L(\alpha_{pv}^{P\backslash\{p\}})$. We derive that $x = x_0 \ldots x_\ell \in L(\alpha_{up}^{P\backslash\{p\}} (\alpha_{pp}^{P\backslash\{p\}})^* \alpha_{pv}^{P\backslash\{p\}})$ and hence that $x \in L(\alpha_{uv}^{P})$, as desired.   □

Proof of Theorem 1.5.11. From Lemma 1.5.12, we obtain that, for any string $x \in \Sigma^*$, it holds that $x \in L(\alpha_{uv}^{Q})$ if and only if $[u, x] \vdash_M^{Q,*} [v, \epsilon]$. To conclude the proof, we need to give a regular expression α where $L(\alpha) = L(M)$. We have that $x \in L(M)$ if and only if there exist states $s \in S$ and $t \in T$ such that $[s, x] \vdash_M^* [t, \epsilon]$, or equivalently, such that $[s, x] \vdash_M^{Q,*} [t, \epsilon]$. Hence, we may define α as the sum $(+)$ of α_{st}^{Q} over all $s \in S$ and $t \in T$.   □

1.6 Proving non-regularity

The characterizations of the regular languages seen so far naturally lend themselves to establishing regularity: we can establish that a language B is regular by presenting a DFA, NFA, ϵ-NFA, or regular expression whose language is equal to B. Correspondingly, we have seen numerous positive examples of languages that are regular. This section presents tools for proving that languages are *not* regular.

A motivating example

Before presenting the general theory, we consider the particular language

$$E = \{a^n b^n \mid n \geq 0\},$$

which is perhaps the most classic example of a non-regular language. This language will serve as a running example throughout the section.

Example 1.6.1. Let us try to first gain a heuristic understanding of why the language E ought to be non-regular. As our current situation requests us to show *limits* on the scope of regular languages, it behooves us to revert to working with the simplest, most unadulterated automaton model that characterizes regularity: the DFA. So, let us try to understand why there cannot be a DFA whose language is E. A DFA can only scan a string from left to right, in one shot. Thus, intuitively speaking, a DFA for E would need to count the number n of a's that it sees prior to seeing any b, in a first phase; and then, in a second phase, make sure that the number of b's that follow is exactly equal to n. However, since a DFA by definition can only have a finite number of states, it cannot truly keep count of the number of a's seen so far, in the first phase. Roughly speaking, if one keeps on feeding a's to the DFA and monitors the states that the DFA goes through, the DFA will eventually be seen to confuse two different quantities of a's, lumping them together onto the same state.

Let us be more formal, and also set back our sights by trying to establish that there is no DFA M with 10 or fewer states whose language is E—a goal that is seemingly more modest than proving that there is no DFA whatsoever for E. Consider the 11 strings

$$a^1 = a, \; a^2 = aa, \; ..., \; a^{11} = aaaaaaaaaaa.$$

Assume that M is a DFA with 10 or fewer states. Then, there must exist two distinct strings, among the 11 presented, that cause the DFA to reach the same state. Precisely, there exist distinct values $i, j \in \{1, ..., 11\}$ and there exists a state q such that $[s, a^i] \vdash_M^* [q, \epsilon]$ and $[s, a^j] \vdash_M^* [q, \epsilon]$. Once this shared state q is reached, the DFA cannot and does not distinguish between the two strings a^i and a^j. Let us take the string b^i, which ought to cause the DFA to accept when it follows a^i. Look at the state q' that the DFA reaches after processing b^i from state q, that is, the state q' such that $[q, b^i] \vdash_M^* [q', \epsilon]$. If this state q' is not an accept state, then the DFA does not accept $a^i b^i$, which is in E; hence, the DFA's language is not E. On the other hand, if this state q' is an accept state, then the DFA does accept $a^j b^i$, which is not in E; hence, the DFA's language is not E. Either way, we can conclude that the language of the DFA M is not E.

In fact, the argument just presented generalizes perfectly; it is readily seen that, for *any* number $k \geq 1$, an analogous argument establishes that there is no DFA with k states whose language is E. From this, one may conclude that E is not regular. ◇

We next proceed to give a general framework for establishing non-regularity of languages. However, one can view this general theory as being obtained by simply abstracting out elements that are present in the argument of Example 1.6.1!

Theory

We here present notions and results which culminate in a general theorem allowing one to show non-regularity of languages.

Definition 1.6.2. With respect to a language B over an alphabet Σ, a string $w \in \Sigma^*$ is a **separator** for a pair of strings $x, y \in \Sigma^*$ if exactly one of the two strings xw, yw is in B. ◇

Let us highlight that, in this definition, there is no requirement that the strings x, y be included in—or excluded from—the language B.

Example 1.6.3. Let i and j be distinct natural numbers; consider the pair of strings a^i, a^j. With respect to the language E:

- The string b^i is a separator for the pair a^i, a^j: $a^i b^i$ is in E, but $a^j b^i$ is not in E.
- The string b^j is also a separator for the pair a^i, a^j: $a^i b^j$ is not in E, but $a^j b^j$ is in E.
- When k is a natural number with $k \neq i$ and $k \neq j$, the string b^k is not a separator for the pair a^i, a^j: each of the strings $a^i b^k$, $a^j b^k$ is not in E. ◇

We next argue that two strings having a separator, with respect to the language of a DFA, must be sent to different states by the DFA. (In Example 1.6.1, we used essentially this result in contrapositive form: we derived that the DFA did not decide the desired language by showing that two strings having a separator were sent to the same state.)

Proposition 1.6.4. *Let $M = (Q, \Sigma, s, T, \delta)$ be a DFA, and let $y, y' \in \Sigma^*$ be any strings. Denote by $p, p' \in Q$ the unique states such that $[s, y] \vdash_M^* [p, \epsilon]$ and $[s, y'] \vdash_M^* [p', \epsilon]$ hold. If there exists a separator for y and y' with respect to $L(M)$, then $p \neq p'$.*

Figure 1.6.1 depicts the setup of this proposition's statement.

Proof. We show the contrapositive: we assume that $p = p'$, and prove that there exists no separator for y and y'. Let $w \in \Sigma^*$ be any string. By assumption, we have $[s, y] \vdash_M^* [p, \epsilon]$ and $[s, y'] \vdash_M^* [p, \epsilon]$. We obtain $[s, yw] \vdash_M^* [p, w]$ and that $[s, y'w] \vdash_M^* [p, w]$, via Proposition 1.3.19. Let $q \in Q$ be the unique state such that $[p, w] \vdash_M^* [q, \epsilon]$. Then $[s, yw] \vdash_M^* [q, \epsilon]$ and $[s, y'w] \vdash_M^* [q, \epsilon]$. If $q \in T$, then yw and $y'w$ are both in $L(M)$; if $q \notin T$, then yw and $y'w$ are both not in $L(M)$. Hence, w is not a separator for y and y'. □

Definition 1.6.5. Let us say that a set S of strings is **pairwise separable** with respect to a language B if each pair of distinct strings $x, y \in S$ have a separator with respect to B. ◇

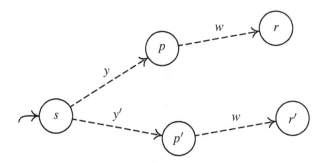

Figure 1.6.1. The setup of Proposition 1.6.4. States from a DFA M are shown. The states p and p' are the states reached by the DFA after reading the strings y and y' from the start state s, respectively. A separator for y and y', with respect to $L(M)$, is a string w such that exactly one of the two strings $yw, y'w$ is in $L(M)$; this is equivalent to the condition that exactly one of the two states r, r' is accepting, where r and r' are the states that the DFA reaches from p and p', respectively, after reading the string w. When such a separator exists, the proposition holds that the states p and p' must be distinct from each other. Note that, in this diagram, we do not indicate which of the states are accepting. Indeed, the proposition's statement and proof are agnostic about whether or not each of the states s, p, and p' is accepting.

Example 1.6.6. We consider separability with respect to the language E. The set of strings $\{a^1, a^2, ..., a^{11}\}$, considered in Example 1.6.1, is pairwise separable; any two distinct strings in this set have a separator, by the discussion of Example 1.6.3. Indeed, by this discussion, the infinite set of strings $\{a^i \mid i \geq 1\}$ is pairwise separable.   ◇

Given a language, the following theorem allows us to establish a lower bound on the number of states of any DFA deciding the language.

Theorem 1.6.7. *Let B be a language over alphabet Σ, and let $k \geq 2$. Suppose that there exists a finite set $Y \subseteq \Sigma^*$ of size k that is pairwise separable with respect to B. Then any DFA M for which $L(M) = B$ has k or more states.*

Proof. Assume that $M = (Q, \Sigma, s, T, \delta)$ is a DFA with $L(M) = B$. Let $y_1, ..., y_k$ denote the strings in Y. Let $q_1, ..., q_k \in Q$ be the states such that $[s, y_i] \vdash_M^* [q_i, \epsilon]$, for each $i = 1, ..., k$. Suppose that $i, j \in \{1, ..., k\}$ are distinct indices; then the strings y_i and y_j have a separator w by assumption, and so by Proposition 1.6.4, it follows that $q_i \neq q_j$. Consequently, the states $q_1, ..., q_k$ are pairwise distinct, and $|Q| \geq k$.   □

From the previous theorem, we derive a sufficient condition for showing non-regularity of a language.

Theorem 1.6.8. *Let B be a language. Suppose that there exists an infinite set Z of strings that is pairwise separable with respect to B. Then the language B is not regular.*

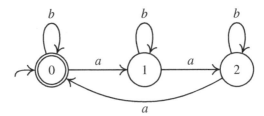

Figure 1.6.2. A DFA deciding the language A of Example 1.6.11. The language A contains a string if and only if the number of a's in the string is a multiple of 3. By swapping the roles of the symbols a and b, one obtains a DFA deciding the language B of Example 1.6.11; the language B contains a string if and only if the number of b's in the string is a multiple of 3.

Proof. We prove this by contradiction. Suppose that there exists a DFA M with $L(M) = B$. Let n denote the number of states that M has. Since the set Z is infinite, it has a subset Y of size $n + 1$. By Theorem 1.6.7, any DFA whose language is B must have $n + 1$ or more states, and we have a contradiction to $L(M) = B$.   □

Applications

We next give two examples that illustrate how Theorem 1.6.8 can be used to prove the non-regularity of languages.

Example 1.6.9. Although we already argued that the language E is not regular (in Example 1.6.1), let us explain how to derive this from Theorem 1.6.8. As discussed in Example 1.6.6, the infinite set of strings $\{a^i \mid i \geq 1\}$ is pairwise separable with respect to E. Hence, by Theorem 1.6.8, we obtain that the language E is not regular.   ◇

Example 1.6.10. Let $\mathrm{rev}(x)$ denote the reversal of a string x. We can define $\mathrm{rev}(x)$ inductively: $\mathrm{rev}(\epsilon) = \epsilon$ and $\mathrm{rev}(ya) = a \cdot \mathrm{rev}(y)$, for all $y \in \Sigma^*$ and $a \in \Sigma$. A **palindrome** is a string x such that $x = \mathrm{rev}(x)$, that is, a string that reads identically forwards and backwards.

Consider the language P containing all palindromes over $\{a, b\}$. We prove that this language is not regular. Set $x_i = a^i b$ for all $i \geq 1$. We show that the set of strings $\{x_1, x_2, \dots\}$ is pairwise separable, with respect to P; this suffices by Theorem 1.6.8.

We argue this as follows. Let $i, j \geq 1$ be distinct indices. We want to show that the pair of strings $x_i = a^i b$ and $x_j = a^j b$ has a separator w. Pick $w = a^i$. We have $x_i w = a^i b a^i \in P$. And, we have $x_j w = a^j b a^i \notin P$: due to i and j being distinct, the two strings $a^j b a^i$ and $\mathrm{rev}(a^j b a^i) = a^i b a^j$ are not equal.   ◇

We next turn to deploy our development in a different way. In the following example (Example 1.6.11), we show that any DFA for a particular *regular* language must have a certain minimum number of states. We exhibit further results of this form in the subsequent example (Example 1.6.12).

Example 1.6.11. Set $\Sigma = \{a, b\}$, and let

$$C = \{y \in \Sigma^* \mid \#_a(y) \text{ and } \#_b(y) \text{ are both multiples of } 3\}.$$

Recall that when d is a symbol and y is a string, $\#_d(y)$ denotes the number of occurrences of d in y. We can view C as the intersection of the following two languages:

$$A = \{y \in \Sigma^* \mid \#_a(y) \text{ is a multiple of } 3\}, \quad B = \{y \in \Sigma^* \mid \#_b(y) \text{ is a multiple of } 3\}.$$

Each of the languages A and B is regular, and has a DFA with 3 states; see Figure 1.6.2. The proof of Theorem 1.2.2 implies that the language C has a DFA with $3 \cdot 3 = 9$ states.

We prove that *any* DFA whose language is C must have 9 or more states, by using Theorem 1.6.7. Consider the set of strings $\{a^i b^j \mid i, j \in \{1, 2, 3\}\}$. We claim that this set is pairwise separable, which suffices, as it contains 9 strings. Let $x = a^i b^j$ and $x' = a^{i'} b^{j'}$ be distinct strings from this set; then either $i \neq i'$ or $j \neq j'$.

- First, consider the case that $i \neq i'$. It can be seen that $|i' - i|$ is equal to 1 or 2, so $i' - i$ is not a multiple of 3. We claim that the string $w = a^{3-i} b^{3-j}$ is a separator for x and x'. We have $xw = a^i b^j a^{3-i} b^{3-j}$, so $\#_a(xw) = \#_b(xw) = 3$ and $xw \in C$. On the other hand, we have $x'w = a^{i'} b^{j'} a^{3-i} b^{3-j}$, so $\#_a(x'w) = i' + 3 - i$. Since $i' - i$ is not a multiple of 3, neither is $i' + 3 - i$, so $x'w \notin C$.

- Next, consider the case that $j \neq j'$. The handling of this case is similar to that of the previous case. We argue that the same string $w = a^{3-i} b^{3-j}$ is a separator for x and x'. We have $xw = a^i b^j a^{3-i} b^{3-j} \in C$, as before. But we now have $\#_b(x'w) = j' + 3 - j$; since $j \neq j'$, we have that $j' - j$ is not a multiple of 3 and hence that $j' + 3 - j$ is not a multiple of 3, implying that $x'w \notin C$. ◇

Recall that, from two given DFA, the *product construction* (of Theorem 1.2.2) allowed us to define a DFA whose language was the intersection of the two given DFA's languages. According to this construction, the new DFA's state set is the product of the state sets of the original two DFA; hence, the new state set's size is the product of the sizes of the given state sets. Example 1.6.11 offers a perspective on the product construction; this example reveals that, in one particular case, the increase in the number of states suggested by this construction is in fact inherent. (Exercise 1.9.32 asks for a general proof that the product construction is optimal in this sense.)

The *subset construction* of a DFA from an ϵ-NFA (given by Theorem 1.3.20) involved an *exponential* increase in the number of states: the state set of the constructed DFA was the *power set* of the state set of the given ϵ-NFA. This observation naturally poses a question: is this exponential increase inherent, or is it merely an artifact of the particular proof method used? In the next example, we show that the exponentiality of the increase is inherent and necessary. That is, in the context of automata theory, nondeterministic computation is exponentially more economical than deterministic computation—when economy is measured according to how many states an automaton has. This result foreshadows a conundrum that will play primary protagonist in our study of complexity theory: there, the

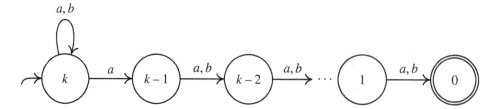

Figure 1.6.3. An NFA with $k + 1$ states whose language is B_k. The language B_k is defined to contain each string x over the alphabet $\Sigma = \{a, b\}$ such that the kth symbol from the right in x exists and is equal to a. The diagram can also be viewed as that of an ϵ-NFA having B_k as its language.

central *P versus NP* question amounts to asking whether or not nondeterministic computation is exponentially more economical than deterministic computation, when economy is measured according to how much *time* a computation takes. In particular, this question asks whether a natural exponential increase, which arises from simulating nondeterministic computation with deterministic computation, is inherent.

Example 1.6.12. Let $\Sigma = \{a, b\}$, and for each $k \geq 1$, let B_k be the language that contains each string x such that $|x| \geq k$ and a is the kth symbol from the right in x. Example 1.3.6 gave a 4-state NFA whose language is B_3. By generalizing the idea in that example, it can be seen that for each $k \geq 1$, there exists a $(k + 1)$-state NFA whose language is B_k. (By Proposition 1.3.18, there also exists a $(k + 1)$-state ϵ-NFA whose language is B_k.) Figure 1.6.3 shows such an NFA.

We prove that, for each $k \geq 1$, *any* DFA whose language is B_k must have at least 2^k states. Let Y_k be the set containing each string over Σ having length k. By appeal to Theorem 1.6.7, it suffices to argue that Y_k is pairwise separable with respect to B_k. Let $y = y_1 \ldots y_k$ and $z = z_1 \ldots z_k$ be distinct strings in Y_k. There exists an index $i \in \{1, \ldots, k\}$ such that $y_i \neq z_i$; it then holds that for the strings $y b^{i-1}$, $z b^{i-1}$, the kth symbols from the right are y_i and z_i, respectively, so exactly one of these two strings is in B_k. We have thus shown that y and z are separable, with respect to B_k.   ◇

1.7 Myhill-Nerode theory

The previous section presented a *sufficient* condition for non-regularity of a language—namely, the existence of an infinite set of pairwise separable strings—and applied this condition to show the non-regularity of some particular languages. A natural question that one can ask about this condition is whether or not it is also *necessary* for non-regularity; this amounts to asking whether or not the presented proof method is *complete*, that is, whether or not it can always succeed when confronted with a non-regular language. In this section, we exhibit yet another characterization of regularity, in terms of an equivalence relation, that permits us to answer this question in the affirmative. Another fruit of our development is to give, for each regular language, a form of canonical minimal DFA, which will be used to prove the correctness of a DFA minimization algorithm in the next section. The development here originates from late 1950s work of John Myhill and Anil Nerode.

We will use the notion of *equivalence relation* and various associated concepts; we briefly review and present these now. An **equivalence relation** $\approx$ on a set U is a binary relation satisfying the following three properties.

- **Reflexivity:** for all $u \in U$, it holds that $u \approx u$.
- **Symmetry:** for all $u, v \in U$, it holds that $u \approx v$ implies $v \approx u$.
- **Transitivity:** for all $u, v, w \in U$, if $u \approx v$ and $v \approx w$, then $u \approx w$.

For each $u \in U$, define $[u]$ as $\{v \in U \mid u \approx v\}$. An **equivalence class of** $\approx$ is a set of the form $[u]$. It is known that two equivalence classes are either equal or disjoint; that is, for all $u, v \in U$, either $[u] = [v]$ or $[u] \cap [v] = \emptyset$. We say that an equivalence relation has **infinite index** if it has infinitely many equivalence classes; and **finite index** if it has finitely many equivalence classes. When an equivalence relation has finite index, its **index** is defined to be its number of equivalence classes. An equivalence relation $\approx$ on a set U **refines** a subset V of U if, for all $u, u' \in U$, it holds that $u \approx u'$ implies $u \in V \Leftrightarrow u' \in V$; equivalently, $\approx$ refines V when, for each $u \in U$, either $[u] \subseteq V$ or $[u] \cap V = \emptyset$.

Characterizing regularity via an equivalence relation

Let $B \subseteq \Sigma^*$ be a language. Define the binary relation $\sim^B$ on Σ^* as follows:

$$x \sim^B y \quad \text{if and only if} \quad \text{for all } w \in \Sigma^*, \text{ it holds that } xw \in B \Leftrightarrow yw \in B.$$

Note that the latter condition is equivalent to saying that there is *no* separator for x and y with respect to B. The relation $\sim^B$ can thus be thought of as the binary relation of *non-separability*, with respect to B. It is straightforwardly verified that $\sim^B$ is an equivalence relation (we leave this to the reader). For each $x \in \Sigma^*$, we use $[x]^B$ to denote the equivalence class of $\sim^B$ containing x, namely, the set $\{y \in \Sigma^* \mid x \sim^B y\}$. Observe that the equivalence relation $\sim^B$ refines the set B: when $x \sim^B y$, it holds that $x \in B \Leftrightarrow y \in B$, by taking $w = \epsilon$ in the definition of $x \sim^B y$.

We may observe the following proposition, which connects the index of $\sim^B$ to the notion of pairwise separability.

Proposition 1.7.1. *Let B be a language. The equivalence relation $\sim^B$ has infinite index if and only if there exists an infinite set of strings that is pairwise separable with respect to B.*

Proof. Suppose that $\sim^B$ has infinite index. Define U to be a set that contains one string from each equivalence class of $\sim^B$. Then for any two distinct strings $x, y \in U$, it does not hold that $x \sim^B y$, and thus there exists a separator for x and y with respect to B.

For the other direction, suppose that U is an infinite set of strings that is pairwise separable. Then, for any two distinct strings $x, y \in U$, it does not hold that $x \sim^B y$, and so $[x]^B \neq [y]^B$. Therefore, no two distinct strings in U fall in the same equivalence class of $\sim^B$, and thus $\sim^B$ has infinitely many equivalence classes. $\square$

We next show that if the condition of Proposition 1.7.1 does not hold, then the language B is regular. This will allow us to characterize the notion of regularity in terms of the equivalence relation $\sim^B$.

Theorem 1.7.2. *Let B be a language. If the equivalence relation $\sim^B$ has finite index, then B is regular; in particular, there exists a DFA M^- such that $L(M^-) = B$ and whose number of states is equal to the index of $\sim^B$.*

Let B be a language over alphabet Σ such that $\sim^B$ has finite index; from B, we define a DFA $M^- = (Q^-, \Sigma, s^-, T^-, \delta^-)$ whose parts are given as follows:

$$Q^- = \left\{ [x]^B \mid x \in \Sigma^* \right\},$$
$$s^- = [\epsilon]^B,$$
$$T^- = \left\{ [x]^B \mid x \in B \right\},$$
$$\delta^-([x]^B, a) = [xa]^B.$$

We have to show that δ^- is well-defined, that is, that its definition depends only on the set $[x]^B$, and not the particular representative chosen.[4] To this end, assume that $[x]^B = [x']^B$, and let $a \in \Sigma$ be arbitrary; then, for each $w \in \Sigma^*$, it holds that $xw \in B \Leftrightarrow x'w \in B$. In particular, for each $v \in \Sigma^*$, it holds that $xav \in B \Leftrightarrow x'av \in B$. It follows that $xa \sim^B x'a$ and that $[xa]^B = [x'a]^B$, as desired.

Example 1.7.3. Let B be the language $\{x \mid \#_b(x) \geq 2\}$ over $\Sigma = \{a, b\}$. (This language was previously seen, in Example 1.1.2.) Relative to this language, let us analyze the structure of the DFA M^- just given.

First, we consider the equivalence class $[\epsilon]^B$. Set $B_0 = \{x \mid \#_b(x) = 0\}$; we observe that

$$B_0 \subseteq [\epsilon]^B,$$

as when x is any string in B_0, it holds that $x \sim^B \epsilon$: for all $w \in \Sigma^*$,

$$xw \in B \quad \Leftrightarrow \quad \#_b(w) \geq 2 \quad \Leftrightarrow \quad \epsilon w \in B.$$

Set $B_1 = \{x \mid \#_b(x) = 1\}$; we observe that

$$B_1 \subseteq [b]^B,$$

---

4. Let us elaborate. The function δ^- needs to be defined on each pair $(q, a) \in Q^- \times \Sigma$; each element $q \in Q^-$ is an equivalence class of $\sim^B$. However, the given definition of δ^- on such a pair (q, a) is in terms of a representative element x of the equivalence class q. To ensure that this definition is proper, we thus need to verify that when x and x' are both elements of the same equivalence class q, that is, when $[x]^B = [x']^B$, the function definition yields the same result on them, that is, $[xa]^B = [x'a]^B$ holds.

as when x is any string in B_1, it holds that $x \sim^B b$: for all $w \in \Sigma^*$,

$$xw \in B \quad \Leftrightarrow \quad \#_b(w) \geq 1 \quad \Leftrightarrow \quad bw \in B.$$

Observe also that

$$B \subseteq [bb]^B,$$

as when x is any string in B, it holds that $x \sim^B bb$: for all $w \in \Sigma^*$, we have the inclusions $xw \in B$ and that $bbw \in B$.

It is straightforwardly verified that the set $\{\epsilon, b, bb\}$ of strings is pairwise separable with respect to B, implying that the equivalence classes $[\epsilon]^B$, $[b]^B$, and $[bb]^B$ are pairwise not equal. As each string in Σ^* falls into either B_0, B_1, or B, we may conclude that

$$B_0 = [\epsilon]^B, \quad B_1 = [b]^B, \quad \text{and} \quad B = [bb]^B.$$

The DFA M^- can be seen to be the bottom DFA shown in Figure 1.7.1 (on page 53). ◇

Proof of Theorem 1.7.2. Since the states in Q^- are precisely the equivalence classes of $\sim^B$, the number of states in Q^- is the index of $\sim^B$. Hence, to conclude the proof of the theorem, we need only verify that $L(M^-) = B$. Let $x = x_1...x_k \in \Sigma^*$ be an arbitrary string of length k. Then, it holds that

$$[[\epsilon]^B, x_1...x_k] \vdash_{M^-} [[x_1]^B, x_2...x_k] \vdash_{M^-} [[x_1 x_2]^B, x_3...x_k] \vdash_{M^-} \cdots \vdash_{M^-} [[x_1...x_k]^B, \epsilon].$$

If $x \in B$, then $[x]^B \in T^-$, and M^- accepts x. On the other hand, if $x \notin B$, then, as $\sim^B$ refines B, we have $[x]^B \cap B = \emptyset$ and hence $[x]^B \notin T^-$; so, M^- rejects x. □

Collecting together the above results, we obtain yet another characterization of the regular languages.

Theorem 1.7.4. *A language B is regular if and only if the equivalence relation $\sim^B$ has finite index.*

Proof. If the equivalence relation $\sim^B$ has infinite index, then it follows from Proposition 1.7.1 and Theorem 1.6.8 that B is not regular. If the equivalence relation $\sim^B$ has finite index, then it follows from Theorem 1.7.2 that B is regular. □

At this point, we can conclude that the sufficient condition for non-regularity presented in the previous section is also necessary, that is, we can establish the converse of Theorem 1.6.8. This result follows directly from Theorem 1.7.4 and Proposition 1.7.1.

Corollary 1.7.5. *Suppose that B is a non-regular language; then, there exists an infinite set of strings that is pairwise separable with respect to B.*

Minimality and canonicity of automata

In the rest of this section, we perform a more detailed study of the DFA M^-, and show that it is a canonical minimal DFA, in a sense made precise. We require the following notions. Let us say that a state q of a DFA M is **reachable** if there exists a string x such that $[s, x] \vdash_M^* [q, \epsilon]$, where s denotes the start state of M. Clearly, states of a DFA that are not reachable can be eliminated without affecting the DFA's behavior.

We next define the notion of a *homomorphism* from a DFA to another DFA. This notion allows us to structurally relate two DFA; in substance, when there exists a homomorphism from a first DFA to a second DFA, the structure of the first DFA is embodied in the structure of the second DFA.

Definition 1.7.6. When $M = (Q, \Sigma, s, T, \delta)$ and $M' = (Q', \Sigma, s', T', \delta')$ are DFA over the same alphabet, a **homomorphism** from M to M' is a map $h \colon Q \to Q'$ such that

- $h(s) = s'$;
- $q \in T \Leftrightarrow h(q) \in T'$, for all $q \in Q$; and,
- $h(\delta(q, a)) = \delta'(h(q), a)$, for all $q \in Q$ and $a \in \Sigma$. $\diamond$

Figure 1.7.1 discusses an example of a homomorphism.

We next establish a theorem essentially showing that, for a regular language B, the structure of any DFA M for B is manifest in the structure of the DFA M^-: precisely, we show that there is a homomorphism from M to M^-.

Theorem 1.7.7. *Let B be a regular language, and let M^- be defined from B as described above; M^- is a DFA via Theorem 1.7.4. If $M = (Q, \Sigma, s, T, \delta)$ is a DFA with $L(M) = B$ and whose states are all reachable, then there exists a unique homomorphism $h \colon Q \to Q^-$ from M to M^-, and moreover, this homomorphism is surjective.*

Both here and in the sequel, we will make use of an equivalence relation $\sim_M$ on Σ^* derived from a DFA $M = (Q, \Sigma, s, T, \delta)$, defined as follows: $x \sim_M y$ if and only if there exists a state $q \in Q$ such that $[s, x] \vdash_M^* [q, \epsilon]$ and $[s, y] \vdash_M^* [q, \epsilon]$. It is straightforward (and left to the reader) to verify that this binary relation is an equivalence relation.

Proof of Theorem 1.7.7. Let $M = (Q, \Sigma, s, T, \delta)$ be a DFA satisfying the hypotheses.

We show that $\sim_M$ is a subset of $\sim^B$, as follows. Suppose that $x \sim_M y$. Then, via Proposition 1.3.19, there exists a state q such that, for each $w \in \Sigma^*$, it holds that $[s, xw] \vdash_M^* [q, w]$ and $[s, yw] \vdash_M^* [q, w]$; hence, for each $w \in \Sigma^*$, it holds that $xw \in L(M) \Leftrightarrow yw \in L(M)$. Thus $x \sim^B y$. (Consequently, each equivalence class of $\sim_M$ is contained in an equivalence class of $\sim^B$, and the index of $\sim^B$ is less than or equal to the index of $\sim_M$, which in turn is the number of states of M; recall our assumption that each state of M is reachable.)

Suppose that g is a homomorphism from M to M^-, and let $q \in Q$ be a state of M. Assume $x = x_1 \ldots x_n$ to be a string such that $[s, x] \vdash_M^* [q, \epsilon]$. We claim that $g(q) = [x]^B$. Let $q_0 = s$, and let $q_1, \ldots, q_n \in Q$ be the states such that

$$[q_0, x_1 \ldots x_n] \vdash_M [q_1, x_2 \ldots x_n] \vdash_M [q_2, x_3 \ldots x_n] \vdash_M \cdots \vdash_M [q_n, \epsilon].$$

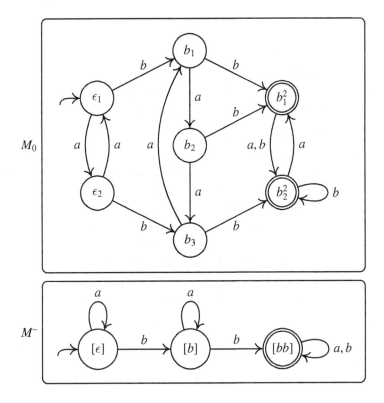

Figure 1.7.1. A pair of DFA related by homomorphism; the bottom DFA M^- is from Example 1.7.3. There is a homomorphism from the top DFA M_0 to the bottom DFA M^-, namely, the mapping h from the top DFA's state set to the bottom DFA's state set defined by $h(\epsilon_1) = h(\epsilon_2) = [\epsilon]$, $h(b_1) = h(b_2) = h(b_3) = [b]$, and $h(b_1^2) = h(b_2^2) = [bb]$. In the definition of homomorphism, the first condition holds that the start state of the first DFA is mapped to the start state of the second; here, we indeed have $h(\epsilon_1) = [\epsilon]$. The second condition holds that a state of the first DFA accepts if and only if it is mapped to an accept state; here, we have that $[bb]$ is the unique accept state of the bottom DFA, and that the states mapped to it, namely b_1^2 and b_2^2, are indeed the only accept states of the top DFA. The third condition holds that, for any state of the first DFA, transitioning on a symbol and passing through the homomorphism yields the same state as first passing through the homomorphism and then transitioning on the same symbol. As one example, consider the state ϵ_2 of the top DFA; transitioning on b leads to the state b_3, and passing through the homomorphism yields the state $[b]$; passing the state ϵ_2 through the homomorphism to obtain $[\epsilon]$ and then transitioning on b also yields the state $[b]$.

Observe that, for each i with $0 \leq i < n$, it holds that

$$g(q_{i+1}) = g(\delta(q_i, x_{i+1})) = \delta^-(g(q_i), x_{i+1}),$$

where the second equality holds by the definition of homomorphism. By the definition of homomorphism, we have $g(q_0) = [\epsilon]^B$. By repeatedly applying our observation about the value of $g(q_{i+1})$ and using the definition of δ^-, we obtain

$$g(q_1) = [x_1]^B, \ g(q_2) = [x_1 x_2]^B, \ \ldots, \ g(q_n) = [x_1 \ldots x_n]^B.$$

Since $q_n = q$, we obtain $g(q) = [x]^B$, as desired.

For each $q \in Q$, define $h(q) = [x]^B$ where x is a string such that $[s, x] \vdash_M^* [q, \epsilon]$. We have that h is well-defined: for any two strings x, x' such that $[s, x] \vdash_M^* [q, \epsilon]$ and $[s, x'] \vdash_M^* [q, \epsilon]$, it holds that $x \sim_M x'$; this implies that $x \sim^B x'$ (as just shown) and that $[x]^B = [x']^B$. We have argued that any homomorphism g must be equal to h. Therefore, if h is indeed a homomorphism from M to M^-, it is the unique such homomorphism.

We verify that h is a homomorphism from M to M^- as follows.

- As $[s, x] \vdash_M^* [q, \epsilon]$ when $q = s$ and $x = c$, we have $h(s) = [\epsilon]^B$, so we obtain $h(s) = s^-$.
- Let $q \in Q$; there exists a string x such that $[s, x] \vdash_M^* [q, \epsilon]$, and $h(q) = [x]^B$.

  - When $q \in T$, the DFA M accepts x, and $x \in B$; then, $[x]^B \in T^-$.
  - When $q \notin T$, the DFA M rejects x, and $x \notin B$; since $\sim^B$ refines B, we have $[x]^B \notin T^-$.

- Let $q \in Q$ and $a \in \Sigma$. Set $x \in \Sigma^*$ so that $[s, x] \vdash_M^* [q, \epsilon]$; then $h(q) = [x]^B$ holds. We have $[s, xa] \vdash_M^* [q, a] \vdash_M [\delta(q, a), \epsilon]$, so $h(\delta(q, a)) = [xa]^B = \delta^-([x]^B, a) = \delta^-(h(q), a)$.

It holds that $h: Q \to Q^-$ is a surjective mapping: for any string y, let p be the state such that $[s, y] \vdash_M^* [p, \epsilon]$; then, $h(p) = [y]^B$. $\square$

Define a DFA M to be **minimal** if there does not exist a DFA M' that has strictly fewer states than M and has $L(M') = L(M)$. That is, a DFA M is minimal if there is no strictly smaller DFA that has the same language, where we measure the size of a DFA according to the number of states.

Let B be a language, and consider a DFA M with $L(M) = B$. Suppose that the DFA M is minimal; since it is minimal, it clearly has only reachable states. Theorem 1.7.7 implies that the DFA M admits a surjective homomorphism to the DFA M^- defined from B; by the surjectivity, M has at least as many states as M^-. It follows that the DFA M^- is minimal, and so we have established the following corollary.

Corollary 1.7.8. *Let B be a regular language, and let M^- be the DFA described above. The DFA M^- is minimal.*

Remark 1.7.9. When M and M' are DFA over the same alphabet, define an **isomorphism** from M to M' to be a homomorphism from M to M' that is bijective. It is straightforwardly verified that if i is an isomorphism from M to M', then its inverse i^{-1} is an isomorphism from M' to M. Say that a DFA is **isomorphic** to another DFA when there exists an isomorphism from one to the other. Diagramatically, two DFA that are isomorphic are the same, up to relabeling the names of their states. It can be verified that relating together each pair of isomorphic DFA yields an equivalence relation (on the class of all DFA).

From Theorem 1.7.7, we learn that any minimal DFA M for a language B is isomorphic to the DFA M^-: when M is minimal, the DFA M and M^- must have the same number of states, implying that the homomorphism provided by the theorem is a bijection and hence an isomorphism. Thus, we can conceive of M^- as a canonical minimal DFA for B. ◇

1.8 DFA minimization

In this section, we present and study an algorithm that, given as input a DFA M, outputs a minimal DFA whose language is that of M.

We employ the following notation in this section. Relative to a DFA $M = (Q, \Sigma, s, T, \delta)$, when $q \in Q$ is a state and $x \in \Sigma^*$ is a string, we use $\widehat{\delta}(q, x)$ to denote the unique state such that $[q, x] \vdash_M^* [\widehat{\delta}(q, x), \epsilon]$. In words, $\widehat{\delta}(q, x)$ denotes the state that the DFA ends up in if it begins in state q and processes the string x. We will invoke the property that, for each state $q \in Q$, each symbol $a \in \Sigma$, and each string $w \in \Sigma^*$, it holds that $\widehat{\delta}(\delta(q, a), w) = \widehat{\delta}(q, aw)$. This property is straightforwardly verified, and in fact could be used to alternatively define the function $\widehat{\delta}$ by induction.

The input to the algorithm is a DFA $M = (Q, \Sigma, s, T, \delta)$. The algorithm performs three phases, in order:

- the *preliminary phase*,
- the *marking phase*, and
- the *collapsing phase*, which outputs the minimized DFA.

In the preliminary phase, the algorithm removes from M each state that is not reachable. This can be done by flagging the start state, and then iteratively flagging each state admitting a transition from a flagged state; when no more states can be flagged, the reachable states will be precisely those that are flagged, and the non-flagged states can be removed. The marking phase and collapsing phase are described and studied in what follows.

1.8.1 Marking phase

The marking phase iteratively marks elements of $Q \times Q$, that is, pairs of states. It is assumed that all pairs are unmarked prior to the commencement of this phase. The marking phase performs the following:

- Initialization: mark all pairs in $T \times (Q \setminus T)$ and in $(Q \setminus T) \times T$.
- Loop, doing the following until no more changes can be made:
  - For each unmarked pair (p, q), if there exists an element $a \in \Sigma$ such that $(\delta(p, a), \delta(q, a))$ is marked, then mark (p, q).

Intuitively, this phase marks each state pair whose states are behaviorally different, and cannot be collapsed together. The initialization marks each state pair where exactly one state is an accept state; the states of such a pair behave differently. The loop marks a state pair (p, q) as different when making a transition from these states, based on a common symbol, would lead to a pair of states already marked as being different.

Let us introduce some symmetric binary relations, each of which is a subset of $Q \times Q$, for the sake of reasoning about this algorithm. First, define

$$R_0 = (T \times (Q \setminus T)) \cup ((Q \setminus T) \times T).$$

The relation R_0 contains the pairs that are marked after the initialization step. Next, for each value $i \geq 0$, define the relation

$$R_{i+1} = R_i \cup \{(p, q) \in Q \times Q \mid \exists a \in \Sigma \text{ such that } (\delta(p, a), \delta(q, a)) \in R_i\}.$$

Clearly, we have the inclusions

$$R_0 \subseteq R_1 \subseteq R_2 \subseteq \cdots.$$

What is the meaning of the relations R_{i+1}? The relation R_{i+1} contains those pairs that are marked after the $(i + 1)$th iteration of the loop body, so long as this iteration is performed. The loop terminates as soon as no changes can be made; letting k be the lowest value such that $R_k = R_{k+1}$, the loop terminates after $k + 1$ executions of the loop body. Observe that, for this value k, it holds that $R_k = R_{k+1} = R_{k+2} = \cdots$. We nonetheless define R_{i+1} for all values $i \geq 0$, for the purpose of analyzing the algorithm.

Figure 1.8.1 discusses an example of the marking phase's behavior.

Define $R = \bigcup_{j \geq 0} R_j$. Observe that R contains a pair if and only if the pair is marked by the algorithm. We will use $\overline{R}$ to denote the complement of R with respect to $Q \times Q$; that is, we use $\overline{R}$ to denote the set $(Q \times Q) \setminus R$. We thus have that the pairs in $\overline{R}$ are precisely the pairs that are not marked by the algorithm. The following lemma provides a characterization of the set $\overline{R}$, and thus implicitly, a characterization of the set R, as well.

Lemma 1.8.1. *A pair (p, q) of states is in $\overline{R}$ if and only if for all $w \in \Sigma^*$, it holds that $\widehat{\delta}(p, w) \in T \Leftrightarrow \widehat{\delta}(q, w) \in T$. Consequently, the binary relation $\overline{R} \subseteq Q \times Q$ is an equivalence relation.*

Proof. The second statement about $\overline{R}$ being an equivalence relation is readily verified from the first statement. We prove the first statement. Let (p, q) be an arbitrary pair of states of M.

We prove the forward direction by establishing its contrapositive. Suppose that there exists $w \in \Sigma^*$ such that exactly one of $\widehat{\delta}(p, w)$, $\widehat{\delta}(q, w)$ is in T; we prove that (p, q) is not in $\overline{R}$. Let $w = w_1 \ldots w_n$. Set $p_0 = p$ and $q_0 = q$. For each index $i = 1, \ldots, n$ in sequence, define the two states $p_i = \delta(p_{i-1}, w_i)$ and $q_i = \delta(q_{i-1}, w_i)$. We have

$$[p, w_1 \ldots w_n] \vdash_M [p_1, w_2 \ldots w_n] \vdash_M [p_2, w_3 \ldots w_n] \vdash_M \cdots \vdash_M [p_n, \epsilon],$$

$$[q, w_1 \ldots w_n] \vdash_M [q_1, w_2 \ldots w_n] \vdash_M [q_2, w_3 \ldots w_n] \vdash_M \cdots \vdash_M [q_n, \epsilon].$$

	ϵ_1	ϵ_2	b_1	b_2	b_3	b_1^2	b_2^2
ϵ_1			1	1	1	0	0
ϵ_2			1	1	1	0	0
b_1	1	1				0	0
b_2	1	1				0	0
b_3	1	1				0	0
b_1^2	0	0	0	0	0		
b_2^2	0	0	0	0	0		

Figure 1.8.1. The marking phase's behavior on the DFA M_0 of Figure 1.7.1. This DFA has state set $Q = \{\epsilon_1, \epsilon_2, b_1, b_2, b_3, b_1^2, b_2^2\}$ and accept state set $T = \{b_1^2, b_2^2\}$. The relation R_0 is defined to contain all pairs that are initially marked, which are the pairs containing one accept state and one non-accept state; these pairs are indicated with a 0 in the table. The relation R_1 contains all pairs marked by the 1st iteration of the loop, as well as the pairs in R_0; in this case, R_1 newly includes each pair of the form (ϵ_i, b_j) and its transposition, as for such a pair we have $(\delta(\epsilon_i, b), \delta(b_j, b)) \in R_0$. The pairs in R_1 but not in R_0 are indicated with a 1 in the table. After the first iteration of the loop, no further pairs are marked by the marking phase, and we have $R_1 = R_2 = \cdots$. When the marking phase is concluded, the unmarked pairs always form an equivalence relation on the state set; this is established by Lemma 1.8.1. Here, this equivalence relation has the equivalence classes $\{\epsilon_1, \epsilon_2\}$, $\{b_1, b_2, b_3\}$, and $T = \{b_1^2, b_2^2\}$.

By hypothesis, exactly one of the states p_n, q_n is in T. Hence, we have $(p_n, q_n) \in R_0$. Since $(p_n, q_n) = (\delta(p_{n-1}, w_n), \delta(q_{n-1}, w_n))$, it follows from the definition of R_1 that the inclusion $(p_{n-1}, q_{n-1}) \in R_1$ holds. Repeating this reasoning, we obtain that $(p_{n-i}, q_{n-i}) \in R_i$ for each index $i = 0, \ldots, n$, and so $(p, q) = (p_0, q_0) \in R_n \subseteq R$. We have shown that (p, q) is not in $\overline{R}$.

We prove the backward direction also by establishing its contrapositive. Suppose the inclusion $(p, q) \in R$; we show that there exists $w \in \Sigma^*$ such that exactly one of the two states $\widehat{\delta}(p, w)$, $\widehat{\delta}(q, w)$ is in T. We prove by induction that for each $i \geq 0$, if $(p, q) \in R_i$, then there exists a string w with the stated property. In the case of $i = 0$, it is clear that the string $w = \epsilon$ has the stated property. For the induction, assume that the statement holds for i; we show that it holds for $i + 1$. Let $(p, q) \in R_{i+1}$. If $(p, q) \in R_i$, we are finished, by the induction hypothesis. Otherwise, by the definition of R_{i+1}, there exists $a \in \Sigma$ such that $(\delta(p, a), \delta(q, a)) \in R_i$. By the induction hypothesis, there exists a string w' such that the set T contains exactly one of the two states $\widehat{\delta}(\delta(p, a), w')$, $\widehat{\delta}(\delta(q, a), w')$. As we have the equalities $\widehat{\delta}(\delta(p, a), w') = \widehat{\delta}(p, aw')$ and $\widehat{\delta}(\delta(q, a), w') = \widehat{\delta}(q, aw')$, we can take $w = aw'$. $\quad\square$

1.8.2 Collapsing phase

The collapsing phase of the algorithm computes and outputs a minimized DFA N, described as follows. Let us use $[q]$ to denote the equivalence class of a state $q \in Q$ with respect to the equivalence relation $\overline{R}$, the set of unmarked pairs. Essentially, the DFA N is obtained from the DFA $M = (Q, \Sigma, s, T, \delta)$ by taking each equivalence class $[q]$, and collapsing all of its states into one state. Intuitively, this is justified due to all states in an equivalence class $[q]$ being behaviorally equivalent. To be formal, let us define the DFA $N = (Q_N, \Sigma, s_N, T_N, \delta_N)$ as follows:

$$Q_N = \{[q] \mid q \in Q\},$$

$$s_N = [s],$$

$$T_N = \{[t] \mid t \in T\},$$

$$\delta_N([q], a) = [\delta(q, a)].$$

We need to argue that the transition function δ_N is well-defined; in particular, we need to argue that, assuming $a \in \Sigma$, if $(p, q) \in \overline{R}$, then $(\delta(p, a), \delta(q, a)) \in \overline{R}$. We prove the contrapositive. Suppose that $(\delta(p, a), \delta(q, a)) \in R$. Then there exists an index $j \geq 0$ such that $(\delta(p, a), \delta(q, a)) \in R_j$. But then it follows by the definition of the relations R_i that $(p, q) \in R_{j+1}$, and hence $(p, q) \in R$.

In the next two theorems, the correctness of the algorithm is established. We assume, for these two theorems, that M is a DFA whose states are all reachable, and that N is the DFA defined from M as just described. These theorems show that the new DFA N has the same language as the original DFA M, and that the new DFA N is minimal.

Theorem 1.8.2. $L(M) = L(N)$.

Proof. Let $x = x_1 \ldots x_k$ be an arbitrary string. Let $q_1, \ldots, q_k \in Q$ be the states such that

$$[s, x_1 \ldots x_k] \vdash_M [q_1, x_2 \ldots x_k] \vdash_M [q_2, x_3 \ldots x_k] \vdash_M \cdots \vdash_M [q_k, \epsilon].$$

From the definition of δ_N, it follows that

$$[[s], x_1 \ldots x_k] \vdash_N [[q_1], x_2 \ldots x_k] \vdash_N [[q_2], x_3 \ldots x_k] \vdash_N \cdots \vdash_N [[q_k], \epsilon].$$

We show that $x \in L(M)$ if and only if $x \in L(N)$. In order to do this, we argue that for any state $q_k \in Q$, it holds that $q_k \in T$ if and only if $[q_k] \in T_N$. The forward direction follows immediately from the definition of T_N. For the backward direction, suppose that $[q_k] \in T_N$; then, there exists $t \in T$ such that $[t] = [q_k]$, that is, such that $(t, q_k) \in \overline{R}$. But by Lemma 1.8.1, we have

$$t = \widehat{\delta}(t, \epsilon) \in T \quad \Leftrightarrow \quad q_k = \widehat{\delta}(q_k, \epsilon) \in T,$$

so it follows that $q_k \in T$.   □

Theorem 1.8.3. *The DFA N is minimal.*

Proof. By our assumption that all states of M are reachable, it follows that all states of N are reachable. Let $B = L(N)$; by Theorem 1.8.2, we have that $B = L(M)$. We will prove the claim that $\sim^B$ is a subset of $\sim_N$. This implies that each equivalence class of $\sim^B$ is contained in an equivalence class of $\sim_N$, which in turn implies that the index of $\sim^B$ is greater than or equal to the index of $\sim_N$. The index of $\sim^B$ is equal to $|Q^-|$, the number of states of M^-

(defined from B in the previous section). The index of $\sim_N$ is equal to $|Q_N|$, the number of states of N; this holds since all states of N are reachable. Since M^- is known to be minimal (by Corollary 1.7.8), it follows that N is minimal. (We remark that the proof of Theorem 1.7.7 yields that $\sim_N$ is a subset of $\sim^B$, here implying that $\sim_N$ and $\sim^B$ are equal.)

To establish the claim, assume that $x \sim^B y$; then, by definition we have that for each string $w \in \Sigma^*$, it holds that

$$xw \in B \quad \Leftrightarrow \quad yw \in B.$$

Since $B = L(M)$, we obtain that, for each string $w \in \Sigma^*$, it holds that

$$\widehat{\delta}_M(s, xw) \in T \quad \Leftrightarrow \quad \widehat{\delta}_M(s, yw) \in T,$$

and consequently that

$$\widehat{\delta}_M(\widehat{\delta}_M(s, x), w) \in T \quad \Leftrightarrow \quad \widehat{\delta}_M(\widehat{\delta}_M(s, y), w) \in T.$$

By Lemma 1.8.1, we obtain that $[\widehat{\delta}_M(s, x)] = [\widehat{\delta}_M(s, y)]$. It follows from the first paragraph of the proof of the previous theorem (Theorem 1.8.2) that

$$\delta_N([s], x) = [\widehat{\delta}_M(s, x)] \quad \text{and} \quad \delta_N([s], y) = [\widehat{\delta}_M(s, y)].$$

Therefore, we have that $\delta_N([s], x) = \delta_N([s], y)$ which, by definition of $\sim_N$, yields that the relationship $x \sim_N y$ holds. $\qquad \Box$

1.9 Exercises and notes

Exercise 1.9.1. List each string of length 3 or less that is accepted by the following DFA:

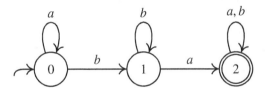

$\Diamond$

Note 1.9.2: Automata as finite descriptions of languages. Observe that an automaton (of one of the defined brands) is an inherently finite object: from the supposition that each automaton has a finite state set, each part of an automaton may be presented by expending a finite amount of ink on paper. Likewise, a regular expression is by definition a string having finite length, and is also a finite object in this sense.

On the other hand, each automaton and regular expression describes a language, which is potentially an infinite object, in that there are infinitely many strings that may belong to a language, and presenting a particular language involves specifying (explicitly or implicitly) which of those strings are members. So, automata and regular expressions may be viewed as *finite* descriptions of generally *infinite* objects. $\Diamond$

Note 1.9.3. To continue the discussion of Note 1.9.2, fix an alphabet Σ. A corollary of the observation that each DFA admits a finite representation is that the number of possible DFA over Σ is countably infinite. This can be seen, in fact, by observing that each DFA (over Σ) can itself be represented as a string over an alphabet, and that the number of strings over any particular alphabet is countably infinite.

As a consequence, one obtains from size considerations that there exists a language not decided by any DFA (that is, a language that is not regular), for the number of languages over Σ is uncountably infinite. Indeed, the vast majority of languages are inaccessible in that they lack representation via DFA. The same phenomenon will persist throughout our study; for each of the studied computational models, the number of particular realizations of the model will be countably infinite, implying immediately that there are languages without representation in the model.   ◇

Note 1.9.4. While the argument of Note 1.9.3 imparts that there *exist* languages that are not regular, it does not at all render uninteresting the techniques we developed for proving non-regularity of languages. The developed techniques allow us to explicitly present natural specimens of non-regular languages; more generally, they offer the possibility of analyzing whether a given language of relevance is regular or not.

As our study progresses, we will identify further classes of languages; one broad goal of the theory of computation is to understand, when confronted with a relevant language (possibly arising from the real world!), to which classes it belongs and to which classes it does not, thereby clarifying the computational resources demanded by language.   ◇

Note 1.9.5: On the trivial languages and DFA. Relative to an alphabet Σ, the trivial languages $\emptyset$ and Σ^* are indeed among the most innocuous languages with which we will deal. They are the only two languages that are decidable by 1-state DFA, a fact which assures us that monikering them as *trivial* was reasonable. They fall into the families of *finite* and *cofinite* languages (respectively), which are the principals of Exercise 1.9.7.   ◇

Note 1.9.6. As has already been suggested, the regular languages are the smallest class of languages and the least difficult languages that we will study computationally. That the trivial languages are clearly regular suggests that the subset and superset relations will, in general, not be of high utility for comparing the difficulty of languages. For the trivial languages bookend all other languages: over an alphabet Σ, each language is a subset of Σ^*, and a superset of the empty set $\emptyset$.   ◇

Exercise 1.9.7: Regularity of finite languages. Prove that each finite language is regular.

This implies, via Theorem 1.2.1, that each *cofinite* language is also regular; a cofinite language is a language whose complement is finite.   ◇

Exercise 1.9.8: On infinite state sets. It is certainly a legitimate move to define a mathematical object more general than the DFA, by lifting off the assumption that the state set be finite. Define a **deterministic automaton (DA)** in exactly the same way that a DFA is defined, but without the restriction that the state set be finite. For a DA $M = (Q, \Sigma, s, T, \delta)$, we can define the notions of *configuration*, *successor configuration*, *acceptance*, and *rejection* just as we did for DFA.

Prove that for *every* language B, there exists a DA M with $L(M) = B$.   ◇

Note 1.9.9. The result of Exercise 1.9.8 highlights the cruciality of the assumption that each DFA has a *finite* state set. In the absence of this assumption, the computational model becomes trivialized in that its power becomes overwhelming: every language becomes describable. Correspondingly, the theory goes flat, not permitting any interest in or technique for showing the non-describability of languages; also, the describable languages trivially possess any closure property.   ◇

Exercise 1.9.10: Symmetric differences of regular languages. The **symmetric difference** of two languages B and C is defined as the set $(B \setminus C) \cup (C \setminus B)$; it is the language containing each string that is in exactly one of B and C.

Prove that when B and C are regular languages over the same alphabet Σ, their symmetric difference is also a regular language.   ◇

Note 1.9.11. When one has a language B of interest in hand, each string over the language's alphabet poses a question to a potential DFA for deciding the language B: is the string inside B? Whether or not there is a DFA deciding B is not affected by modifying the answer to this decision question for a finite number of strings: by Exercises 1.9.7 and 1.9.10, regularity of a language is preserved under taking a symmetric difference with a finite language. And, this statement holds not just for the DFA model, but for each of the principal computational models that we will consider in this book.

What we are building, then, is not so much a theory of individual decision questions, but rather, a theory of how decision questions behave in an aggregate fashion and in relation to each other.   ◇

Note 1.9.12. In some of the following exercises, you are asked to present an automaton or a regular expression whose language is a given one. Also, strive for comprehensibility: to the extent possible, design and present automata and regular expressions so that their functionality is transparent and readily graspable. And, with comprehensibility in mind, strive for brevity: when presenting automata, attempt to use as few states as is feasible, and when presenting regular expressions, try to minimize the length of expressions.   ◇

Exercise 1.9.13: Building DFA. Let $\Sigma = \{a, b\}$. For each of the languages over Σ that is given below, present a DFA with input alphabet Σ whose language is the given one.

1. The language containing each string with exactly 4 occurrences of b.
2. The language containing each string that ends with either aa or ab.
3. The language containing each string x such that $|x|$ is a multiple of 4.

4.   The language containing each string x such that $|x|$ is a multiple of 2 or 3.

5.   The language containing each string x such that $\#_a(x)$ is odd.

6.   The language containing each string x such that $\#_a(x)$ is odd, equal to 2, or equal to 6.

7.   The language containing each string that does not have *abb* as a substring.

8.   The language containing each string x such that each occurrence of *baab* as a substring is either followed by *aa*, or is at the end of x.

9.   The language containing each string x such that *ab* is a substring of x if and only if *ba* is a substring of x.

10. The language containing each string x where, for each prefix w of x, it holds that $|\#_a(w) - \#_b(w)| \leq 3$.

11. The language containing each string x where, for each prefix w of x, it holds that $|2\#_a(w) - \#_b(w)| \leq 3$.

12. The language containing each string that contains *ab* as a substring an odd number of times.

13. The language containing each string that ends with either *aaa*, *aab*, or *aba*.

14. The language containing each string that contains exactly two *b*'s or contains an odd number of *a*'s.

15. The language containing each string that contains exactly two *b*'s and contains an odd number of *a*'s.   ◇

Exercise 1.9.14: Building more DFA. Let $\Sigma = \{0, 1, 2, 3, 4, 5, 6, 7, 8, 9\}$. For each of the languages over Σ that is given below, present a DFA with input alphabet Σ whose language is the given one.

1.   The language B containing each string that is a number between 1 and 420, inclusive, written without any leading 0's. As examples, $0 \notin B$, $04 \notin B$, $1 \in B$, $4 \in B$, $44 \in B$, $50 \in B$, $050 \notin B$, $404 \in B$, $420 \in B$, $444 \notin B$, and $500 \notin B$.

2.   The language C containing each string that is a number between 1 and 2046, inclusive, written without any leading 0's. As examples, $0 \notin C$, $042 \notin C$, $42 \in C$, $142 \in C$, $0142 \notin C$, $1024 \in C$, and $2401 \notin C$.

3.   The language D containing each string that is a number between 1984 and 2001, inclusive, written without any leading 0's.   ◇

Exercise 1.9.15: Building NFA. Let $\Sigma = \{a, b, c\}$. For each of the languages over Σ that is given below, present an NFA with input alphabet Σ whose language is the given one.

1.   The language containing each string that contains both *ca* and *bb* as substrings.

2.   The language containing each string that contains at least one of *aab* or *aac* as a substring.

3.   The language containing each string x such that the second symbol from the right in x exists, and is equal to the second symbol from the left in x.

4. The language containing each string x such that if the 5th symbol from the right exists in x, it is equal to c.
5. The language containing each string having 3 consecutive symbols that are equal.
6. The language containing each string x such that there exist natural numbers $k, \ell \geq 0$ where $|x| = 5k + 7\ell$.
7. The language containing each string where each occurrence of a is followed immediately by an occurrence of b. ◇

Exercise 1.9.16: Building more NFA. Let $\Sigma = \{a, b\}$. For each of the languages over Σ that is given below, present an NFA with input alphabet Σ whose language is the given one.

1. The language containing each string x such that $|x| \geq 1$ and the first symbol of x is equal to the last symbol of x.
2. The language B containing each string x such that $|x| \geq 4$ and the first two symbols of x are equal to the last two symbols of x. As examples, $aaa \notin B$, $abab \in B$, and $abba \notin B$.
3. The language C containing each string x such that $|x| \geq 2$ and the first two symbols of x are equal to the last two symbols of x. As examples, $aaa \in C$, $aba \notin C$, $abab \in C$, and $abba \notin C$. ◇

Exercise 1.9.17. List all strings of length 3 and of length 4 that do not belong to the language $L(a^* b^* a^*)$. ◇

Exercise 1.9.18: Describing languages of regular expressions. For each of the following regular expressions, give a natural language description of the language represented, and list all of the strings of length 6 or less that belong to the language represented. If there are more than 15 such strings, then you may list the first 15 strings in a length-ascending order.

1. $(ab)^* + (ba)^*$
2. $(ab)^* c + (bc)^*$
3. $(aab)^* + (bba)^*$
4. $(a + bb)^* + (b + aa)^*$
5. $(ab + ba)(aa + bb)^*$
6. $(ab + ba)^*$
7. $(ab + c + b)^*$
8. $(abb + c)^*$
9. $(a + ab)^*(\epsilon + b)$
10. $(abb + b)^*$
11. $((b^*) + (aa)^*)^*$ ◇

Exercise 1.9.19: Building regular expressions. Let $\Sigma = \{a, b\}$. For each of the languages over Σ given below, present a regular expression whose language is the given one.

1. The language containing each string that contains 3 or more a's.
2. The language containing each string that contains 3 or fewer a's.
3. The language containing each string that contains *abba* as a substring.
4. The language containing each string x such that $|x| \geq 4$ and the 4th symbol from the right is b.
5. The language containing each string that contains *baa* as a substring 2 or fewer times.
6. The language containing each string that does not contain two consecutive a's.
7. The language containing each string that begins or ends with *abba*.
8. The language containing each string having even length.
9. $L(b^*a^*) \cap L(a^*b^*)$.
10. $L(b^*a^*b^*) \cap L(a^*b^*a^*)$.
11. $L(b^*ab^*) \cap L(a^*ba^*)$.   ◇

Exercise 1.9.20. The DFA of Example 1.1.3 can be viewed as the DFA that results by applying the product construction, given at the beginning of Section 1.2.2, to two DFA. Which two DFA?   ◇

Exercise 1.9.21: Unary alphabets and ultimate periodicity. This exercise characterizes the structure of regular languages over a unary alphabet. Define a subset $S \subseteq \mathbb{N}$ of the natural numbers to be **ultimately periodic** if there exist numbers $n \geq 0$ and $p > 0$ such that for all $m \geq n$, it holds that $m \in S$ if and only if $m + p \in S$.

Let Σ be the unary alphabet $\{a\}$. Prove that a language B over Σ is regular if and only if the set $\{n \in \mathbb{N} \mid a^n \in B\}$ is ultimately periodic.   ◇

Exercise 1.9.22. Prove that if B is a regular language over Σ, then for any $a \in \Sigma$, the language $B' = \{x \mid xa \in B\}$ is also regular. Prove this by first assuming that M is a DFA with $L(M) = B$, and then showing how to construct a DFA M' with $L(M') = B'$ and whose set of states is equal to that of M.   ◇

Exercise 1.9.23. Prove that if B is a regular language over Σ, then the language

$$P = \big\{ x \in \Sigma^* \mid \exists v \in \Sigma^* \text{ such that } xv \in B \big\}$$

is also regular. The language P contains each prefix of each string in B.   ◇

Exercise 1.9.24. Prove that if B is a regular language over Σ, then the language

$$B' = \big\{ x \in \Sigma^* \mid xx \in B \big\}$$

is also regular. Hint: let $M = (Q, \Sigma, s, T, \delta)$ be a DFA with $L(M) = B$; it may be useful to consider the functions $h_a \colon Q \to Q$, defined for each $a \in \Sigma$, by $h_a(q) = \delta(q, a)$.   ◇

Exercise 1.9.25. For each language B over Σ, define

$$\text{FirstHalf}(B) = \left\{ x \in \Sigma^* \mid \exists y \in \Sigma^* \text{ such that } xy \in B \text{ and } |x| = |y| \right\}.$$

That is, FirstHalf(B) contains the first half of every even-length string in B. Prove that if B is a regular language, then FirstHalf(B) is also regular. ◇

Exercise 1.9.26. Let D denote the language $\{a^m b^n \mid 0 \le n < m\}$. Answer each of the following questions, and justify your answer.

1. Does the pair of strings (a, aa) have a separator, with respect to D?
2. Does the pair of strings (ab, abb) have a separator, with respect to D? ◇

Exercise 1.9.27: Proving non-regularity. For each of the given languages over the alphabet $\Sigma = \{a, b\}$, prove that the language is not regular.

1. The language $\{a^i b^j \mid i, j \ge 0, i \ne j\}$.
2. The language $\{a^i b^j \mid i \ge 0, i^2 = j\}$.
3. The language containing each string x such that $\#_a(x) \le \#_b(x)$.
4. The language containing each string x such that $2 \cdot \#_a(x) = 3 \cdot \#_b(x)$.
5. The language containing each string x such that $\#_a(x) \ge 2^{\#_b(x)}$.
6. The language containing each string over Σ whose length is a square, that is, whose length has the form n^2 for a natural number $n \ge 0$.
7. The language containing each string over Σ whose length is a power of 2, that is, whose length has the form 2^n for a natural number $n \ge 0$.
8. The language $\{xx \mid x \in \Sigma^*\}$. (It may be didactic to compare this language with that of Exercise 1.9.24.) ◇

Exercise 1.9.28: Deciding regularity. For each of the following languages over the alphabet $\Sigma = \{a, b\}$, state whether or not the language is regular, and prove your assertion.

1. The language $\{a^i b^j \mid i, j \ge 0 \text{ and } (i + j) \text{ is even}\}$.
2. The language B that contains each string x such that the number of occurrences of ab as a substring in x is one more than the number of occurrences of ba as a substring in x. As examples, $ab \in B$ and $abba \notin B$.
3. The language C that contains each string x such that the number of occurrences of abb as a substring in x is one more than the number of occurrences of baa as a substring in x. As examples, $ab \notin C$ and $abba \in C$. ◇

Exercise 1.9.29. Let B be the language containing each string over $\{a, b\}$ that has *babbab* as a substring. Show that any DFA whose language is B must have 7 or more states. ◇

Exercise 1.9.30: Multiples of 7. Let B_7 be the language containing each string over the alphabet $\Sigma = \{0, 1, \ldots, 9\}$ that represents a number (base 10) that is a multiple of 7. Leading zeroes should be ignored, in the sense that a string x is in B_7 if and only if $0x$ is in B_7. Hence, we have $0, 007, 14, 014, 42, 217, 1729 \in B_7$, and we have $6, 06, 10, 237 \notin B_7$.

Give a DFA whose language is B_7. (A diagram is not necessary; the DFA may be specified in any way.)   ◇

Exercise 1.9.31: Multiples of 99. Let B_{99} be the language containing each string over the alphabet $\Sigma = \{0, 1, \ldots, 9\}$ that represents a number (base 10) that is a multiple of 99. (As in Exercise 1.9.30, leading zeroes should be ignored.) Prove that any DFA whose language is B_{99} must contain 99 or more states.   ◇

Exercise 1.9.32: Optimality of the product construction. For each pair of natural numbers $k, \ell \geq 1$, give a DFA M having k states, a DFA M' having ℓ states, and a proof that any DFA whose language is $L(M) \cap L(M')$ must have at least $k \cdot \ell$ states. In a sense, this exercise witnesses the optimality of the product construction of Theorem 1.2.2; this theorem established closure under intersection, for the regular languages.   ◇

Exercise 1.9.33: A product construction for NFA. Show how to directly construct, from two NFA $M_1 = (Q_1, \Sigma, \Delta_1, S_1, T_1)$ and $M_2 = (Q_2, \Sigma, \Delta_2, S_2, T_2)$, a third NFA M with state set $Q_1 \times Q_2$ such that $L(M) = L(M_1) \cap L(M_2)$, and prove that your construction works.   ◇

Exercise 1.9.34. Consider the ϵ-NFA with state set $Q = \{1, 2\}$, input alphabet $\Sigma = \{a, b\}$, initial state set $S = \{1\}$, accept state set $T = \{1\}$, and the following transition function:

Δ	a	b	ϵ
1	$\{1, 2\}$	$\{2\}$	$\emptyset$
2	$\emptyset$	$\{1\}$	$\emptyset$

Use the subset construction of Theorem 1.3.20 to convert the given ϵ-NFA to a DFA. The resulting DFA will have the same language as the given ϵ-NFA.   ◇

Exercise 1.9.35: Reversing regular languages. Prove that if B is a regular language, then the language

$$B' = \{\text{rev}(x) \mid x \in B\}$$

is also regular. Here, $\text{rev}(x)$ denotes the reversal of the string x, as in Example 1.6.10. That is, prove that if one starts from a regular language and reverses every single one of its strings, the resulting language is also regular. Hint: try using Theorem 1.5.8.   ◇

Exercise 1.9.36: String homomorphisms. Let Σ and Γ be alphabets. For each mapping of the form $h \colon \Sigma \to \Gamma^*$, define the mapping $\overline{h} \colon \Sigma^* \to \Gamma^*$ by $\overline{h}(x_1 \ldots x_n) = h(x_1) \cdots h(x_n)$. Each mapping $\overline{h} \colon \Sigma^* \to \Gamma^*$ that arises from a mapping $h \colon \Sigma \to \Gamma^*$ in this way is called a **string homomorphism**. Prove the following statements.

1. If $h \colon \Sigma \to \Gamma^*$ is any mapping, and B is a regular language over Σ, then the language $\{\overline{h}(x) \mid x \in B\}$ is also regular. This result is typically referred to as *closure under homomorphism*.

2. If $h: \Sigma \to \Gamma^*$ is any mapping, and C is a regular language over Γ, then the language $\{x \in \Sigma^* \mid \overline{h}(x) \in C\}$ is also regular. This result is typically referred to as *closure under inverse homomorphism*. ◇

Exercise 1.9.37: Rotating regular languages. When B is a language over alphabet Σ, define the *language of rotations of B* as

$$\text{Rotations}(B) = \{yx \mid x, y \in \Sigma^* \text{ and } xy \in B\}.$$

Prove that if B is regular, then $\text{Rotations}(B)$ is also regular. ◇

Exercise 1.9.38: Myhill-Nerode relations. Let B be a language over alphabet Σ. Define a **Myhill-Nerode relation** for B to be an equivalence relation $\approx$ on Σ^* that has finite index, refines B, and is a **right congruence** in that, for all strings $x, y \in \Sigma^*$ and for each $a \in \Sigma$, it holds that $x \approx y$ implies $xa \approx ya$. Prove that a language B is regular if and only if there exists a Myhill-Nerode relation for B. ◇

Note 1.9.39. One way to prove the forward direction of Exercise 1.9.38 is by invoking Theorem 1.7.4 and by confirming that $\sim^B$ is a Myhill-Nerode relation. This exercise can thus be interpreted as showing that the notion of *Myhill-Nerode relation* abstracts out the vital properties of $\sim^B$ that ensure regularity of B. ◇

Exercise 1.9.40: The pumping lemma. Prove the *pumping lemma*, which is the following statement. Suppose that B is a regular language over Σ; then, there exists a natural number $K \geq 1$ such that for any string $w \in B$ with $|w| \geq K$, there exist $x, y, z \in \Sigma^*$ such that the following hold:

* $w = xyz$,
* $|xy| \leq K$,
* $y \neq \epsilon$, and
*   for all $n \geq 0$, it holds that $xy^n z \in B$.

The pumping lemma gives a necessary condition for regularity. Its contrapositive form thus gives a sufficient condition for non-regularity, and indeed a typical use of this lemma is to show non-regularity of a language via the contrapositive form.

As a hint sketch, this lemma can be proved along the following lines. Let $M = (Q, \Sigma, s, T, \delta)$ be a DFA whose language is B, and set $K = |Q|$. Let $w = w_1 \ldots w_m$ be a string of length $m \geq K$, set $q_0 = s$, and let $q_1, \ldots, q_m$ be the states that the DFA passes through upon processing w, that is, the states such that

$$[q_0, w_1 \ldots w_m] \vdash_M [q_1, w_2 \ldots w_m] \vdash_M [q_2, w_3 \ldots w_m] \vdash_M \cdots \vdash_M [q_m, \epsilon].$$

Then, exploit the fact that two of the $K + 1$ states in the list $q_0, q_1, \ldots, q_K$ must be equal. ◇

Exercise 1.9.41: Non-regularity of the primes. Let B be the language $\{1^n \mid n$ is a prime$\}$ containing the primes in unary representation. Prove, using the pumping lemma (of Exercise 1.9.40), that the language B is not regular.   ◇

Exercise 1.9.42: Between one string and infinitely many. Let M be a DFA with state set Q. Prove that the language $L(M)$ is infinite if and only if there exists a string $x \in L(M)$ such that the inequalities $|Q| \leq |x| \leq 2|Q| - 1$ hold.   ◇

Exercise 1.9.43: The tip of the pyramid. Let Σ be the alphabet $\{r, g, b\}$, whose symbols represent the colors *red*, *green*, and *blue*. Define $d \colon \Sigma^* \setminus (\{\epsilon\} \cup \Sigma) \to \Sigma^*$ as the function that, on a non-empty string $x_1 \ldots x_m$ of length $m \geq 2$, returns the string $y_1 \ldots y_{m-1}$ where, for each $i = 1, \ldots, m - 1$, the symbol y_i is defined as x_i if $x_i = x_{i+1}$, and as the unique element of $\Sigma \setminus \{x_i, x_{i+1}\}$ if $x_i \neq x_{i+1}$. That is, the color y_i is derived from the colors x_i and x_{i+1} as follows: if the colors x_i and x_{i+1} are the same, then the color y_i is set equal to them; if the colors x_i and x_{i+1} are different, then the color y_i is set to the unique color that is different from each of them. Define $d^+ \colon \Sigma^* \setminus \{\epsilon\} \to \Sigma$ as the function that, on a non-empty string x, returns the symbol obtained by applying the function d to x repeatedly, a total of $|x| - 1$ many times. In other words, when x is a non-empty string, $d^+(x)$ is defined as the symbol that results from applying d repeatedly to x until a single symbol remains.

Prove or disprove: the language $B = \{x \in \Sigma^* \setminus \{\epsilon\} \mid d^+(x) = b\}$ is regular.   ◇

Exercise 1.9.44: Bisimulations. Let $M = (Q, \Sigma, s, T, \delta)$, $M' = (Q', \Sigma, s', T', \delta')$ be DFA sharing the same input alphabet Σ. Define a **bisimulation** between M and M' as a relation $R \subseteq Q \times Q'$ where, for each pair $(q, q') \in R$, the following hold: $q \in T \Leftrightarrow q' \in T'$, and for each $a \in \Sigma$, the pair $(\delta(q, a), \delta'(q', a))$ is in R. Note that this definition does not depend on the start states of the DFA.

Say that two states $q \in Q$, $q' \in Q'$ are **bisimilar** if there exists a bisimulation between M and M' of which the pair (q, q') is an element. Let us presuppose that what one can observe about a state is whether or not it is accepting, and that one can also subject a state to a transition, based on a given symbol. Then, bisimilar states can be described as being *observationally indistinguishable*: they produce the same observations, and subjecting them to transitions based on a common symbol leads to states that are again indistinguishable.

1. Prove that there exists a bisimulation R between M and M' such that $(s, s') \in R$ if and only if $L(M) = L(M')$.

2. Let $g \colon Q \to Q'$ be a map, and let $R_g = \{(q, g(q)) \mid q \in Q\}$ be its graph. Prove that g is a homomorphism from M to M' if and only if R_g is a bisimulation between M and M' such that $(s, s') \in R_g$.

3. Prove that when R_1, R_2 are bisimulations between M and M', their union $R_1 \cup R_2$ is also a bisimulation between M and M'. This result implies that, when looking at the

bisimulations between two DFA, there is a *greatest bisimulation*—namely, the union of all such bisimulations.

4. Let $\approx_M$ be the **bisimilarity relation** on M, defined as the set containing each pair of states $(p, q) \in Q \times Q$ such that there exists a bisimulation between M and itself of which the pair (p, q) is an element. This relation is clearly the greatest bisimulation between M and itself, in the just-introduced sense. Prove that the relation $\approx_M$ is equal to the relation $\overline{R}$ treated by Lemma 1.8.1.

5. By modifying the *marking phase* in Section 1.8, give an algorithm for computing the complement of the greatest bisimulation between M and M'; here, the complement is with respect to the set $Q \times Q'$. The resulting algorithm allows us to determine whether or not M and M' are equivalent in the sense of having the same language: by part 1 of this exercise, we have that $L(M) = L(M')$ if and only if the pair (s, s') is not in this complement. Hint: first mark the states in $T \times (Q' \setminus T')$ and in $(Q \setminus T) \times T'$.   ◇

1.10   Bibliographic discussion

General references on the theory of computation include the books by Hopcroft, Motwani, and Ullman (2007); Kozen (1997, 2006); Moore and Mertens (2011); Papadimitriou (1994); and Sipser (2013).

An early study of finite-state systems was conducted in an article of McCulloch and Pitts (1943). In the 1950s, versions of the DFA model were presented and studied (Huffman 1954; Mealy 1955; Moore 1956; Kleene 1956). The NFA model is due to an article of Rabin and Scott (1959), who established the equivalence to the DFA model, in the sense of Theorem 1.3.24. Closure properties of the regular languages were studied by many authors, including Kleene (1956); Ginsburg and Rose (1963); and, Rabin and Scott (1959). The characterization of regular languages via regular expressions given in Theorem 1.5.8 is due to Kleene (1956); our presentation of this result is based on that of Kozen (1997). The Myhill-Nerode theory in and around Section 1.7, and in Exercise 1.9.38, is due to Myhill (1957) and Nerode (1958). DFA minimization procedures were studied by numerous authors, including Huffman (1954), Moore (1956), Nerode (1958), and Hopcroft (1971).

Our discussion in Example 1.5.7 of the language of *alternating strings* stems from a textbook discussion of this language (Hopcroft, Motwani, and Ullman 2007, Chapter 3). The pumping lemma of Exercise 1.9.40 is due to Bar-Hillel, Perles, and Shamir (1961). Exercise 1.9.44 is based on an article of Rutten (1998).

2 Computability Theory

> I wonder why. I wonder why.
> I wonder why I wonder.
> I wonder why I wonder why
> I wonder why I wonder!
> — Richard Feynman

> The problem with introspection is that it has no end.
> — Philip K. Dick, *The Transmigration of Timothy Archer*

The finite-state automata of the previous chapter were relatively limited computational models: an automaton could only make one pass through an input string, and had no working space, apart from its bounded memory. This chapter turns to study *Turing machines*, computational models which are considerably more general and more powerful than automata, and which indeed are the most powerful models that we will study. A particular type of Turing machine, the *halting deterministic Turing machine*, will be presented as a formalization of the intuitive notion of *algorithm*; the corresponding class of languages that these machines define are called the *computable languages*. Just as the previous chapter explored both the scope and the boundaries of the regular languages, this chapter engages in a kindred exploration of the computable languages.

2.1 Deterministic Turing machines

2.1.1 Introduction

The notion of *algorithm* is an informal and intuitive one; an early known example of an algorithm, from ancient Greece, is *Euclid's algorithm* for computing the greatest common divisor of two positive natural numbers. By an **algorithm**, we here refer to a procedure with the following properties. An algorithm is specified via a finite list of instructions; each instruction is finite and unambiguously describes an action performable mechanically, without recourse to judgement or creativity. An algorithm operates deterministically, and in discrete time steps. When executed on an input, an algorithm terminates after a finite number of steps, producing the desired output.

This section presents the *deterministic Turing machine (DTM)*, a general-purpose, full-fledged computational model that is recognized as providing a formalization of the intuitive notion of *algorithm*, and thus as capturing the concept of computation in a broad sense. The DTM is a mathematical object, a construct for performing analysis—as was the case for the DFA and the other automata models previously seen. The definition of DTM will naturally lead us to define the notion of a *computable* language, which amounts to a language for which there exists an algorithm determining membership. In this chapter, the quantity of time and space consumed during a computation is not in any way restricted, for the focus is on the power of computation *in principle*.

The DTM was introduced in a 1937 publication by Alan Turing. Around this time, there were in fact numerous proposals of computational models, in addition to the DTM, that aimed to formalize the notion of algorithm. These proposals stemmed from mathematical questions of the era about whether certain problems were solvable by algorithms; in order to rigorously address these questions, a precise definition of algorithm was needed. At the time, the proposed computational models seemed quite qualitatively different from each other; for example, one was based on functions defined on the natural numbers, and another, the λ-*calculus*, was based on a simple, abstract view of function formation and application. Remarkably, these differences were revealed to be superficial: all of these computational models turned out to be provably equivalent, in that membership in a language could be computed by one model if and only if it could be computed by another. Typical programming languages used in practice, when formalized, also yield computational models that are equivalent to the original ones. This rich system of equivalences signals the robustness and the stability of the notion of *computable* language. These equivalences back the non-mathematical claim that each of these models provides a suitable formalization of the intuitive notion of algorithm—a claim known as the *Church-Turing thesis*, and credited to the 1937 article of Turing and a 1936 article of Alonzo Church.

The situation of having a single mathematical notion with an abundance of seemingly disparate characterizations strongly suggests that this notion is natural and primal. But, if there are numerous computational models that formalize the notion of algorithm, why do we focus on the DTM in our study? A prime reason is the *simplicity* of the DTM model. It can be presented with relative ease (particularly when the DFA model has been understood), and its stripped-down nature facilitates proving the types of results that are of interest to us. Furthermore, the DTM model makes it easy and natural to impose time or space bounds on computation; such bounds are central to the study of complexity theory. What is lost and traded off by considering such a simple model is that it can be cumbersome to precisely present sophisticated algorithms. However, the precise presentation of algorithms by DTMs is not our focus, and we typically specify algorithms informally, appealing to the reader's sense that they could be implemented by DTMs—if laboriously.

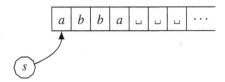

Figure 2.1.1. The initial configuration of a DTM on the input string *abba*. The *control* is depicted by a polygon enclosing the current state, which in this case is the DTM's start state *s*. The *head* is depicted by the tip of an arrow that emanates out of the control. The *worktape* here contains the string *abba* in its initial 4 cells, and the *blank symbol* in all other cells.

2.1.2 Model

We begin with an overview of the model. A deterministic Turing machine (DTM) has a one-dimensional working space, its *worktape*. The input string of a DTM is presented on this tape, with each symbol in a memory unit; beyond the input string, this tape has further memory units, each capable of holding one symbol, with which the DTM can compute. While a DTM accesses its tape via a *head* that is located at and can operate on one memory unit at a time, this head can move in both directions, and can write symbols in addition to reading them. A more comprehensive, informal description of the DTM model follows.

Architecture-wise, a DTM consists of a **control**, a **head**, and a **worktape**. The worktape constitutes the working space of a DTM; it is a one-dimensional array, which we conceive of as horizontally positioned. The worktape is infinite to the right, but has a left end; it consists of discrete memory units called **cells**, each of which can store one symbol. At any point in time, the control is in a state, and the head is located at a single worktape cell. A DTM can move its head both to the left and right during a computation, and can both read from and write to the worktape via its head; this is in contrast to a DFA, which scans its input just once, from left to right, in a read-only fashion.

Given an input, a DTM begins in the configuration where the control is in the DTM's *start state*; the head is at the leftmost cell of the worktape; and the worktape contains the input in its initial cells but otherwise contains a special symbol, the **blank symbol** ⊔. Figure 2.1.1 illustrates an initial configuration of a DTM.

A DTM operates in discrete time steps, as with a DFA. In each time step, a DTM makes a transition based on its current state and the symbol in the cell where its head is located. To make a transition, a DTM performs three changes:

- It changes state.
- It writes a tape symbol at the location of its head.
- It moves its head left or right.

Correspondingly, a DTM's *transition function* needs to specify, for each state and symbol, three pieces of information: a state, a symbol, and a direction—left or right, to be represented by −1 and +1, respectively. Recall that a DFA made a transition simply by changing state; correspondingly, its transition function specified, for each state and symbol, just one piece of information, a state.

When run on an input, a DTM makes transitions until it enters its *accept state* or its *reject state*, at which point it comes to rest and ceases to make transitions; so, formally, the transition function is not defined on these two states. It is certainly possible that, when invoked on an input, a DTM will never enter its accept state or its reject state, but rather, runs infinitely without *halting*—in this case, we will say that the DTM *loops* on the input.

We next turn to present the formal definition of a DTM.

Definition 2.1.1. A **deterministic Turing machine (DTM)** is a 7-tuple $(Q, \Sigma, \Gamma, s, t, r, \delta)$ where:

- Q is a finite set called the **state set**,
- Σ is an alphabet called the **input alphabet**,
- Γ is an alphabet called the **tape alphabet** and is such that $\Gamma \supseteq \Sigma$,
- $s \in Q$ is a state called the **start state** or **initial state**,
- $t \in Q$ is a state called the **accept state**,
- $r \in Q$ is a state called the **reject state** and is such that $r \neq t$, and
- $\delta \colon (Q \setminus \{t, r\}) \times \Gamma \to Q \times \Gamma \times \{-1, +1\}$ is a function called the **transition function**.

It is required that the *blank symbol* $\sqcup$ is an element of $\Gamma \setminus \Sigma$. $\diamond$

Let us remark that there are multiple ways to define the DTM; here, we elected a definition of minimalist design.

As mentioned, when a DTM is invoked on a particular input string, its tape is initialized to contain the string at the left end, followed by an infinite sequence of blank symbols; and the DTM's head is located at the leftmost position of the tape. Each input string is required to be over the input alphabet Σ; the assumption that the blank symbol is not in Σ permits the DTM to detect where the input string ends. In carrying out a computation, a DTM may write elements from the tape alphabet Γ onto the tape, and its transition function must be fully defined on all pairs consisting of a state (that is not t nor r) and a symbol from Γ.

We next formalize the notion of a *configuration* of a DTM. Recall that a configuration ought to contain all of the information that one needs to know, at a particular point in time, about how a computation will proceed. For a DTM, then, a configuration will provide the state of its control, the entire contents of its tape, and the location of its head. We assume that the worktape cells are numbered with indices, starting from the left end, by $1, 2, 3, \ldots$; this is depicted in Figure 2.1.2. So, a head location can be specified as an element of $\mathbb{N}^+$; and, the tape contents can be given by a function that maps a cell's number to the symbol that it contains, that is, by a function from the set $\mathbb{N}^+$ to the tape alphabet Γ.

1	2	3	4	5	6	7	
a	b	b	a	$\sqcup$	$\sqcup$	$\sqcup$	$\cdots$

Figure 2.1.2. A DTM's worktape cells are numbered with indices, starting from 1 on the left. The example tape contents given here are represented by a function $\tau\colon \mathbb{N}^+ \to \Gamma$ where $\tau(1) = a$, $\tau(2) = b$, $\tau(3) = b$, $\tau(4) = a$, and $\tau(i)$ is the blank symbol for all $i \geq 5$.

We also next give the definition of *successor configuration* of a configuration. To define this notion comprehensively, it is necessary to specify what occurs if a DTM tries to move its head left when it is at the leftmost cell; the convention we use is that, in this case, the DTM's head remains at the leftmost cell. Hence, if the DTM's head is at location $\ell \in \mathbb{N}^+$ and a transition calls for the head to move in the direction $d \in \{-1, +1\}$, the next location will be $\ell + d$ unless this sum is 0, in which case the next location should be 1; this value is expressed below as $\max(\ell + d, 1)$.

Definition 2.1.2. Let $M = (Q, \Sigma, \Gamma, s, t, r, \delta)$ be a DTM.

- A **configuration** of M is a triple $[q, \tau, \ell]$ where $q \in Q$ is a state, τ is a function from $\mathbb{N}^+$ to Γ representing tape contents, and $\ell \in \mathbb{N}^+$ is a head location.
- The **successor configuration** of a configuration $[q, \tau, \ell]$ is defined when $q \in Q \setminus \{t, r\}$. In this case, set $(p, a, d) = \delta(q, \tau(\ell))$; then, the successor configuration of $[q, \tau, \ell]$ is defined as the configuration $[p, \tau[\ell \mapsto a], \max(\ell + d, 1)]$; here, $\tau[\ell \mapsto a]$ denotes the function that maps ℓ to a, and is otherwise equal to τ.

To discuss configurations of a DTM M, we use the previously given definitions of the relations $\vdash_M$, $\vdash_M^n$, and $\vdash_M^*$ presented in Definition 1.1.8. ⬦

In order to smoothly present configurations of DTMs, we need a convenient way to specify a function $\tau\colon \mathbb{N}^+ \to \Gamma$ giving the tape contents; such a function is an infinite object. To this end, we view such a function as an infinite string, that is, as the infinite sequence of symbols $\tau(1)\tau(2)\tau(3)\ldots$; and we use the notation $\sqcup\ldots$ to indicate the infinite string consisting solely of blanks. So, for example, we will use the notation $bab\sqcup\ldots$ to denote the function $\tau\colon \mathbb{N}^+ \to \Gamma$ that maps 1 to b, 2 to a, 3 to b, and each other element of $\mathbb{N}^+$ to $\sqcup$; as another example, we will use the notation $abba\sqcup\ldots$ to denote the tape contents and the function given in Figure 2.1.2. (Note that the tape contents, when viewed as an infinite string, will always terminate with an infinite sequence of blanks.)

DTM examples

We next examine two examples of DTMs.

Example 2.1.3. Consider the DTM $M = (Q, \Sigma, \Gamma, s, t, r, \delta)$, presented in Figure 2.1.3, where $Q = \{s, t, r, h, e, g\}$, $\Sigma = \{a, b\}$, and $\Gamma = \{a, b, \sqcup\}$.

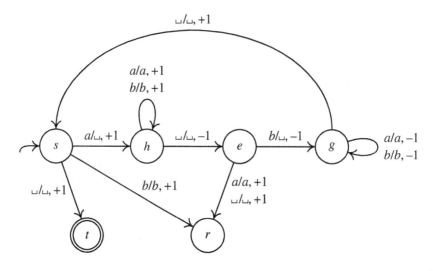

Figure 2.1.3. The DTM given in Example 2.1.3. In general, we form the diagram for a DTM as follows. Each state is placed in a circle; the initial state is indicated by an unlabeled arrow that points to it; the accept state has a double circle placed around it. Each transition $\delta(q, c) = (p, a, d)$ is indicated by an arrow with label $c/a, d$ from the state q to the state p; multiple transitions having the same source and target states are indicated using multiple labels on a shared arrow. Thus, to determine the behavior of the transition function δ given a state q and a read symbol c, one looks for an arrow coming out of state q having a label whose first component is c; the label's remaining components specify the symbol to be written and the direction of movement, and the arrow's target is the state to be entered. The accept and reject states are the only states with no outgoing arrows.

This DTM's transition function δ is given by the following table:

δ	a	b	$\sqcup$
s	$(h, \sqcup, +1)$	$(r, b, +1)$	$(t, \sqcup, +1)$
h	$(h, a, +1)$	$(h, b, +1)$	$(e, \sqcup, -1)$
e	$(r, a, +1)$	$(g, \sqcup, -1)$	$(r, \sqcup, +1)$
g	$(g, a, -1)$	$(g, b, -1)$	$(s, \sqcup, +1)$

On the input string a, this DTM begins in the initial configuration $[s, a\sqcup\dots, 1]$. We have

$$[s, a\sqcup\dots, 1] \vdash_M [h, \sqcup\sqcup\dots, 2]$$

$$\vdash_M [e, \sqcup\sqcup\dots, 1]$$

$$\vdash_M [r, \sqcup\sqcup\dots, 2].$$

Once in the configuration $[r, \sqcup\sqcup\dots, 2]$, the machine halts in its reject state r. The string a is considered *rejected*.   ◇

Remark 2.1.4. Before proceeding further, let us add a detail to the fashion in which we present configurations. To enhance readability, when displaying concrete configurations, we will typically underline the symbol in the tape string where the head is located. This convention should facilitate determining successor configurations of DTMs. ◇

As in the previous chapter, we use the term **computation** to refer to a sequence of all configurations that a machine passes through when invoked on an input string.

Example 2.1.5. Having put the convention of Remark 2.1.4 in effect, we exhibit further computations of the DTM M from Example 2.1.3.

On the input string ab, this DTM begins in the initial configuration $[s, \underline{a}b\sqcup\sqcup\ldots, 1]$. We have the computation

$$[s, \underline{a}b\sqcup\sqcup\ldots, 1] \vdash_M [h, \sqcup\underline{b}\sqcup\sqcup\ldots, 2]$$
$$\vdash_M [h, \sqcup b\underline{\sqcup}\sqcup\ldots, 3]$$
$$\vdash_M [e, \sqcup\underline{b}\sqcup\sqcup\ldots, 2]$$
$$\vdash_M [g, \underline{\sqcup}\sqcup\sqcup\sqcup\ldots, 1]$$
$$\vdash_M [s, \sqcup\underline{\sqcup}\sqcup\sqcup\ldots, 2]$$
$$\vdash_M [t, \sqcup\sqcup\underline{\sqcup}\sqcup\ldots, 3].$$

Once in the configuration $[t, \sqcup\sqcup\underline{\sqcup}\sqcup\ldots, 3]$, the machine halts, in its accept state t; the string ab is considered *accepted*.

On the input string abb, this DTM M begins in the initial configuration $[s, \underline{a}bb\sqcup\sqcup\ldots, 1]$. We have the computation

$$[s, \underline{a}bb\sqcup\sqcup\ldots, 1] \vdash_M [h, \sqcup\underline{b}b\sqcup\sqcup\ldots, 2]$$
$$\vdash_M [h, \sqcup b\underline{b}\sqcup\sqcup\ldots, 3]$$
$$\vdash_M [h, \sqcup bb\underline{\sqcup}\sqcup\ldots, 4]$$
$$\vdash_M [e, \sqcup b\underline{b}\sqcup\sqcup\ldots, 3]$$
$$\vdash_M [g, \sqcup\underline{b}\sqcup\sqcup\sqcup\ldots, 2]$$
$$\vdash_M [g, \underline{\sqcup}b\sqcup\sqcup\sqcup\ldots, 1]$$
$$\vdash_M [s, \sqcup\underline{b}\sqcup\sqcup\sqcup\ldots, 2]$$
$$\vdash_M [r, \sqcup b\underline{\sqcup}\sqcup\sqcup\ldots, 3].$$

Here, the DTM halts in its reject state, so the string abb is *rejected* by this DTM. ◇

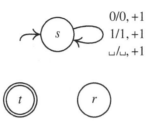

Figure 2.1.4. The DTM N given in Example 2.1.6. The diagram is formed from the specification of N in the manner described by Figure 2.1.3. Neither the accept state nor the reject state is ever entered by this DTM, and so this DTM does not halt on any input.

Example 2.1.6 (A runaway DTM). Let us give, as another example, a tiny DTM. Consider the DTM $N = (Q, \Sigma, \Gamma, s, t, r, \delta)$, presented in Figure 2.1.4, where $Q = \{s, t, r\}$, $\Sigma = \{0, 1\}$, $\Gamma = \{0, 1, \sqcup\}$, and δ is given by the following table:

δ	0	1	$\sqcup$
s	$(s, 0, +1)$	$(s, 1, +1)$	$(s, \sqcup, +1)$

At each time step, this DTM simply moves to the right, mindlessly! For example, on the input string 10, we have the computation

$$[s, \underline{1}0\sqcup\sqcup\ldots, 1] \vdash_N [s, 1\underline{0}\sqcup\sqcup\ldots, 2] \vdash_N [s, 10\underline{\sqcup}\sqcup\ldots, 3] \vdash_N [s, 10\sqcup\underline{\sqcup}\ldots, 4] \vdash_N \cdots$$

In particular, this DTM never enters its accept state or its reject state, and thus does not accept or reject any string. To make use of terminology formalized below, on every input string $x \in \Sigma^*$, this DTM does not *halt*, but *loops*.   ◇

Outcomes

Let us define precisely the outcomes possible when a DTM is run on an input string. Let $M = (Q, \Sigma, \Gamma, s, t, r, \delta)$ be a DTM.

Definition 2.1.7. Define the **initial configuration** of M on a string $x \in \Sigma^*$ as the configuration $[s, x\sqcup\ldots, 1]$.   ◇

Definition 2.1.8. We say that a configuration $[q, \tau, \ell]$ of M is

- an **accepting configuration** if $q = t$;
- a **rejecting configuration** if $q = r$; and,
- a **halting configuration** if $q \in \{t, r\}$, that is, if it is either accepting or rejecting.   ◇

Definition 2.1.9. Let $x \in \Sigma^*$ be a string; let α_x be the initial configuration of M on x.

- We say that M **accepts** x if there exists an accepting configuration β such that $\alpha_x \vdash_M^* \beta$.
- We say that M **rejects** x if there exists a rejecting configuration β such that $\alpha_x \vdash_M^* \beta$.

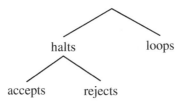

Figure 2.1.5. Tree showing the possible outcomes when a DTM is run on an input string.

- In the case that M accepts or rejects x, we say that M **halts** on x; otherwise, we say that M **loops** on x.   ◇

Definition 2.1.10. We define the **language** of a DTM M, denoted by $L(M)$, to be the set $\{x \in \Sigma^* \mid M \text{ accepts } x\}$.   ◇

Let us offer some remarks on the introduced definitions. During a computation, once a DTM enters a halting configuration, it ceases to make transitions; a configuration that is halting is (by definition) either accepting or rejecting, but cannot be both, by the proviso that $r \neq t$ (in Definition 2.1.1). So, on an input, a DTM either halts or loops, but not both; if it halts, it either accepts or rejects, but not both. Consequently, we can observe that, when a DTM is run on an input, exactly one of three outcomes occurs: the DTM accepts, rejects, or loops. (This is a point of contrast with the DFA model; recall that when a DFA is run on an input, exactly one of two outcomes occurs: the DFA either accepts or rejects.) These three DTM outcomes are depicted in Figure 2.1.5. Thus, when a string y is in the language $L(M)$ of a DTM M, it holds that M accepts y; and when a string y is not in the language $L(M)$ of a DTM M, what can be generally inferred is that M either rejects y or loops on y.

Let us emphasize that we here use the word *loops* in a specific terminological fashion: a DTM is said to *loop* on a string when it does not halt on the string. When a DTM loops on a string in this sense, it is not necessarily the case that the DTM's computation on the string has a configuration that appears more than once. (For example, when invoked on any input string, the DTM of Example 2.1.6 never repeats configuration.)

Example 2.1.11 (Continuation of Example 2.1.3). The DTM M of Example 2.1.3 halts on each input, and its language $L(M)$ is in fact equal to a key language previously seen (in Section 1.6): the language $E = \{a^n b^n \mid n \geq 0\}$. Let us explain why.

On a high level, when invoked in the state s, this DTM attempts to remove an instance of the symbol a from the left boundary of the string that starts from the head location; to then remove an instance of the symbol b from the right boundary of this string; and then to move back to the new left boundary and to iterate this process.

More concretely, let us assume that the DTM is invoked in state s and at a location such that, beginning from the location and continuing to the right, the tape consists of a string in $\{a,b\}^*$ followed by blank symbols. The DTM rejects if the symbol scanned is b, and accepts if the symbol scanned is the blank symbol. (This act of acceptance is consistent with the desire to accept the strings in the language E: we have that the empty string ϵ is included in E.) If the symbol scanned is a, this symbol is overwritten with the blank symbol, and the DTM changes to state h. In state h, one can then think of the DTM as holding an instance of the symbol a.

Once in state h, the DTM iteratively moves to the right and stays in h so long as it sees the symbol a or the symbol b. When it encounters a blank, it transitions to state e, wherein it is ready to **e**at an instance of the symbol b. After first transitioning into state e, the DTM's head is located at the last non-blank symbol—if this exists. If the symbol at the head is not b, then the DTM rejects; if it is, then the DTM transitions into the state g, overwrites the b with a blank symbol (in effect, eating the b), and steps to the left.

In the state g, the DTM tries to **g**o to the leftmost boundary of the string; it does this by staying in the state g until it encounters a blank symbol. Note that in the configuration where the state g is first entered, there is either a blank at the head's location or to the left of the head, since a blank was written when the DTM most recently came out of the s state. When a blank is encountered in state g, the DTM transitions to state s and moves to the right, and hence iterates the just-described process on a shorter string in $\{a,b\}^*$.   ◇

Further DTM examples

We next give two more examples of DTMs.

Example 2.1.12. Consider the DTM $M = (Q, \Sigma, \Gamma, s, t, r, \delta)$, presented in Figure 2.1.6, where $Q = \{s, u, t, r\}$, $\Sigma = \{a, b, c\}$, $\Gamma = \{a, b, c, \sqcup\}$, and δ is given by the following table:

δ	a	b	c	$\sqcup$
s	$(t,a,+1)$	$(r,b,+1)$	$(u,c,+1)$	$(u,\sqcup,+1)$
u	$(u,a,+1)$	$(u,b,+1)$	$(u,c,+1)$	$(u,\sqcup,+1)$

This DTM accepts immediately if its input begins with the symbol a; it rejects immediately if its input begins with the symbol b; and otherwise, it enters state u and walks indefinitely to the right. Thus, its language $L(M)$ is the set of all strings over Σ that begin with the symbol a; and this DTM halts on precisely the strings that begin with either the symbol a or the symbol b.

Let us consider some example computations. When invoked on the input string *abba*, this DTM accepts after making one transition:

$$[s, \underline{a}bba\sqcup..., 1] \vdash_M [t, a\underline{b}ba\sqcup..., 2].$$

And, when invoked on the input string *ca*, this DTM makes a head move to the right at each step, and thus loops:

$$[s, \underline{c}a\sqcup\sqcup..., 1] \vdash_M [u, c\underline{a}\sqcup\sqcup..., 2] \vdash_M [u, ca\underline{\sqcup}\sqcup..., 3] \vdash_M \cdots.   ◇$$

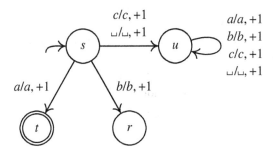

Figure 2.1.6. The DTM given in Example 2.1.12. The diagram is formed using the conventions described in Figure 2.1.3.

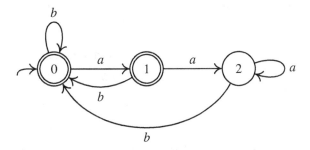

Figure 2.1.7. The DFA discussed in Example 2.1.13.

Example 2.1.13 (A DTM based on a DFA). We revisit the DFA $M = (Q, \Sigma, s, T, \delta)$ of Example 1.1.5. This DFA M, shown in Figure 2.1.7, has $Q = \{0, 1, 2\}$, $\Sigma = \{a, b\}$, $s = 0$, $T = \{0, 1\}$, and transition function δ defined by:

δ	a	b
0	1	0
1	2	0
2	2	0

We here give a DTM M' based on the DFA M. In particular, each input string is accepted or rejected by M' according to whether it is accepted or rejected by M. We define the DTM M', which is displayed in Figure 2.1.8, as $(Q', \Sigma, \Gamma, 0, t, r, \delta')$ where 0 is the start state, $Q' = \{0, 1, 2, t, r\}$, $\Gamma = \{a, b, \sqcup\}$, and δ' is given by the following table:

δ'	a	b	$\sqcup$
0	$(1, a, +1)$	$(0, b, +1)$	$(t, \sqcup, +1)$
1	$(2, a, +1)$	$(0, b, +1)$	$(t, \sqcup, +1)$
2	$(2, a, +1)$	$(0, b, +1)$	$(r, \sqcup, +1)$

It can be seen that the state component of $\delta'(q, d)$, for each $q \in Q$ and $d \in \Sigma$, is equal to the value $\delta(q, d)$ provided by the transition function δ of the DFA M. Indeed, this DTM imitates the behavior of the DFA M: as long as it reads symbols from $\Sigma = \{a, b\}$, it takes steps to the right and makes precisely the state transitions that the DFA M would make.

As an example, let us consider the input string *aaba*. When invoked on this string, the DFA M produces the following computation:

$$[0, aaba] \vdash_M [1, aba]$$

$$\vdash_M [2, ba]$$

$$\vdash_M [0, a]$$

$$\vdash_M [1, \epsilon].$$

When invoked on this string, the DTM M' produces the following computation:

$$[0, \underline{a}aba_{\sqcup\sqcup\sqcup}\ldots, 1] \vdash_{M'} [1, a\underline{a}ba_{\sqcup\sqcup\sqcup}\ldots, 2]$$

$$\vdash_{M'} [2, aa\underline{b}a_{\sqcup\sqcup\sqcup}\ldots, 3]$$

$$\vdash_{M'} [0, aab\underline{a}_{\sqcup\sqcup\sqcup}\ldots, 4]$$

$$\vdash_{M'} [1, aaba_{\underline{\sqcup}\sqcup\sqcup}\ldots, 5]$$

$$\vdash_{M'} [t, aaba_{\sqcup\underline{\sqcup}\sqcup}\ldots, 6].$$

Recall that, by definition, a DTM has a unique accept state, while a DFA may have multiple accept states, as is the case for the DFA M considered here. Despite this difference in definition, we have succesfully presented a DTM whose behavior is faithful to that of the DFA M; as soon as the DTM reads a blank symbol, it knows that it has reached the end of the input string and then enters its accept state t or its reject state r depending on whether or not its state (0, 1, or 2) was an accept or reject state of the DFA M, respectively.

In this example, we showed how to imitate a particular DFA by a DTM; the ideas we used to do so can be generalized to show that any DFA can be imitated by a DTM. We formulate this claim below as Proposition 2.1.18; see also the discussion that follows.   ◇

2.1.3   Classes of languages

We next define two classes of languages using the DTM model. First and foremost, we define what it means for a language to be *computable*; this definition is intended to formalize what it means for membership in the language to be decidable by an algorithm. Recall that an *algorithm* is presupposed to terminate after a finite number of steps, on any input. Correspondingly, to define the notion of *computable* language, we want to only permit a DTM if it halts after a finite number of steps, on each input; such a DTM is formalized

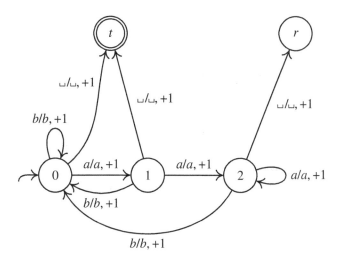

Figure 2.1.8. The DTM given in Example 2.1.13; this DTM is constructed based on the DFA given in Figure 2.1.7. The diagram is formed using the conventions described in Figure 2.1.3.

here as a *halting DTM*. Indeed, imagine that one initiates a DTM computation on an input; the utility of doing this is not at all clear if the computation is not guaranteed to halt.[5]

Definition 2.1.14. A DTM M with input alphabet Σ is called **halting** if M halts on every string $x \in \Sigma^*$. When M is a halting DTM, we say that M **decides** its language $L(M)$. ◇

Definition 2.1.15. A language B is **computable** if there exists a halting DTM M such that $B = L(M)$. ◇

Note that computable languages were historically referred to as *recursive* languages, and are also referred to as *decidable* languages.

Example 2.1.16. Let us examine the four example DTMs in the previous section to see which are halting:

- The DTM of Example 2.1.3 is halting, as discussed in Example 2.1.11.
- The DTM of Example 2.1.6 is not halting; indeed, it does not halt on any input.
- The DTM of Example 2.1.12 does not halt on all inputs; in particular, it does not halt on inputs beginning with the symbol c; thus, this DTM is not halting.
- The DTM of Example 2.1.13 is halting: on any input, it moves to the right until it scans the blank symbol, at which point it halts.

---

5. Even if there is such a guarantee, the amount of time that the computation will take should also be considered; but that is the concern of the next chapter.

Note that even if a DTM M is not halting, its *language $L(M)$* may be computable; there may still exist a halting DTM sharing the same language. For example, the DTM N of Example 2.1.6 is not halting, but its language $L(N)$, the empty set $\emptyset$, is computable, via (for example) a DTM that immediately rejects each input string.   ◇

This is an opportune moment to define what it means for a *function* to be computable. Essentially, a function $f\colon \Sigma^* \to \Sigma^*$ is defined to be *computable* if there exists a DTM M such that, when M is run on any string $x \in \Sigma^*$, it terminates in an accepting configuration where the tape contains $f(x)$ followed by blank symbols, and the head is at the leftmost location (namely, the location numbered 1).

Definition 2.1.17. A DTM $M = (Q, \Sigma, \Gamma, s, t, r, \delta)$ **computes** a function $f\colon \Sigma^* \to \Sigma^*$ if, for each string $x \in \Sigma^*$, it holds that

$$[s, x\sqcup..., 1] \vdash_M^* [t, f(x)\sqcup..., 1].$$

A function $f\colon \Sigma^* \to \Sigma^*$ is **computable** if there exists a DTM that computes it.   ◇

We can observe that any DTM computing a function is a halting DTM.

Let us next compare the notions of regular language and computable language. On the one hand, we have the following.

Proposition 2.1.18. *Each language that is regular is also computable.*

This proposition can be proved by showing how to pass from a DFA to a DTM that imitates the behavior of the DFA; this can be done by generalizing the idea of Example 2.1.13, where a concrete DFA was converted to a DTM. We leave the arguing of this proposition as an exercise (Exercise 2.10.13).

The converse of Proposition 2.1.18 does not hold; the following proposition implies that the class of computable languages strictly contains the class of regular languages.

Proposition 2.1.19. *The language $\{a^n b^n \mid n \geq 0\}$ is computable but is not regular.*

Proof. By the discussion in Example 2.1.11, the DTM given in Example 2.1.3 is halting, and its language is the specified one. Hence, this language is computable. Example 1.6.9 established that this language is not regular.   □

We now present the second class of languages defined in terms of the DTM model. The definition of *computable* language, as discussed, is a formalization of what it means for a language to be computable by an algorithm. In contrast, the class of languages that we next define are presented for the purpose of analysis.

Definition 2.1.20. A language B is **computably enumerable** (for short, **CE**) if there exists a DTM M such that $B = L(M)$.   ◇

Computably enumerable languages were historically referred to as *recursively enumerable* languages, and are also referred to as *semi-decidable* languages.

According to the definitions, the requirement for a language to be computably enumerable is clearly a relaxation of the requirement for a language to be computable; the stipulation that the DTM be *halting* is lifted. We record this fact, to be used tacitly in the sequel, as follows.

Proposition 2.1.21. *Each language that is computable is also computably enumerable.*

To recapitulate, a language B is computable if there exists a DTM that accepts each string in B, and rejects each string outside B; a language B is computably enumerable if there exists a DTM that accepts each string in B, and does not accept any string outside B—so, the DTM either rejects or loops on each string outside B. One might succinctly say that the definition of *computable* is based on the distinction between acceptance and rejection, whereas the definition of *computably enumerable* is based on the distinction between acceptance and nonacceptance.

Remark 2.1.22 (On the presentation of DTMs). When we claim the existence of a DTM with a particular behavior, in the sequel we typically do *not* present a DTM formally by giving all parts of the 7-tuple in the definition of DTM, as we did in Examples 2.1.3, 2.1.6, 2.1.12, and 2.1.13. Rather, we give a high-level description of what the DTM should do; we appeal to the reader's sense, intuition, and judgment that the description could be implemented by a DTM (if arduously). Recall that the original impetus behind introducing the DTM was, in any case, to formalize the *intuitive* notion of algorithm.   ◇

2.1.4 Summary of models and language classes

The following table shows the computational models that have been studied so far, along with the language classes that they define:

Computational model	Defined class of languages	Justification
DFA	regular languages	Definition 1.1.1
NFA	regular languages	Theorem 1.3.24
ϵ-NFA	regular languages	Theorem 1.3.24
halting DTM	computable languages	Definition 2.1.15
DTM	CE languages	Definition 2.1.20

As discussed in Section 2.1.3, each language that is regular is also computable, but not vice versa; and each language that is computable is also CE. The relationship between the computable languages and the CE languages will be clarified later in this chapter (specifically, in Section 2.5.1).

2.2 Encoding objects as strings

Throughout our subsequent studies, we will want to be able to present various mathematical objects to Turing machines as input. For example, we will want to discuss situations where a Turing machine is presented a *graph* as input. As defined, however, the Turing machine model always takes a string as input. Hence, in order to present a graph as input to a Turing machine, we will fix a way of encoding graphs as strings. More generally, for each type of object that we want to present as input to a Turing machine, we need to fix a way of encoding instances as strings. It turns out that for the issues that we want to study, the particular encoding methods that we use are typically immaterial; natural, reasonable encoding methods tend to behave equivalently for these issues. Due to this, we usually will not devote much energy to precisely specifying encoding methods; our attitude is that this involves low-level details that could ultimately be formalized if necessary, resembling our attitude toward the specification of DTMs, in Remark 2.1.22. Nonetheless, in this section we give a discussion of how certain types of objects can be encoded. We assume that the particular encodings given in this section are, by default, used throughout the book.

We typically use the braces notation $\ulcorner \cdot \urcorner$ to denote a string encoding of an object; for example, when G is a graph, we will use $\ulcorner G \urcorner$ to denote its string encoding. We focus on giving encodings over the alphabet $\{0, 1\}$. The encoding methods we give can readily be adapted to other alphabets having two or more symbols, by using two distinct symbols to play the roles of 0 and 1.

Encoding digraphs and graphs

We define a **digraph** (short for *directed graph*) to be a pair (V, E) where V is a finite set and $E \subseteq V \times V$. The elements of V are called **vertices**, and the elements of E are called **edges**. For example, define

$$V_0 = \{v_1, v_2, v_3, v_4\}$$

and

$$E_0 = \{(v_1, v_2), (v_1, v_3), (v_2, v_3), (v_3, v_4), (v_4, v_2)\}.$$

Define H_0 to be the pair (V_0, E_0); then, H_0 is an example of a digraph. Following a usual convention, we depict a digraph by representing each vertex with a circle containing the name of the vertex, and each edge (u, v) with an arrow from the vertex u to the vertex v; as an example, the following is a diagram for the digraph H_0:

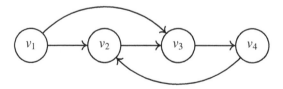

We define a **graph** to be a pair (V, E) where V is a finite set and it holds that E is a subset of $\big\{\{v, v'\} \mid v, v' \in V \text{ and } v \neq v'\big\}$, that is, E is a set whose elements are size 2 subsets of V. As for a digraph, the elements of V are called **vertices**, and the elements of E are called

edges. For example, define

$$V_1 = \{v_1, v_2, v_3, v_4\}$$

and

$$E_1 = \{\{v_1, v_2\}, \{v_1, v_3\}, \{v_1, v_4\}, \{v_2, v_3\}, \{v_3, v_4\}\}.$$

Define G_1 to be the pair (V_1, E_1); then, G_1 is an example of a graph. It is the norm to depict a graph by representing each vertex with a circle, and each edge with a line between its vertices; the following is a diagram for the graph G_1:

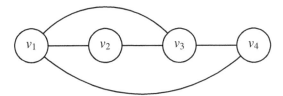

Consider a digraph whose vertices have the names $v_1, v_2, ..., v_n$. Define the **adjacency matrix** of such a digraph to be the $n \times n$ matrix where the entry at the ith row and jth column is 1 or 0, depending on whether or not the pair (v_i, v_j) is in E, respectively. For example, the adjacency matrix of the example digraph H_0 is:

0110

0010

0001

0100

With this notion in hand, a digraph may be encoded as a string over the alphabet $\Sigma = \{0, 1\}$ that gives the rows of the adjacency matrix, in order. For example, the encoding of the digraph H_0, denoted by $\ulcorner H_0 \urcorner$, would be the string 0110 0010 0001 0100 of length 16, where the extra spacing has been added for the sake of readability.

Similarly, for a graph whose vertices have the names $v_1, ..., v_n$, we define the **adjacency matrix** to be the $n \times n$ matrix where the entry at the ith row and jth column is 1 or 0, depending on whether or not the pair $\{v_i, v_j\}$ is in E, respectively. For example, the adjacency matrix of the example graph G_1 is

0111

1010

1101

1010

As in the case of digraphs, a graph's adjacency matrix can be encoded as the string giving the rows of the matrix, in order. For example, the encoding of the graph G_1, denoted by $\ulcorner G_1 \urcorner$, would be the string 0111 1010 1101 1010. Observe that a graph's adjacency matrix is always *symmetric* with respect to the diagonal: the entry at row i and column j is always equal to the entry at row j and column i. Observe also that a graph's adjacency matrix has a *zero diagonal*: for each index i, the entry at row i and column i is equal to 0.

Given an arbitrary digraph or graph with n vertices, we may rename its vertices so that they have the names $v_1, v_2, ..., v_n$, and then apply the respective encoding just described. While in general there will be multiple ways to perform this renaming, our focus will be on properties that do not depend on the renaming chosen.

A key fact about these encodings is that it can be checked computably whether or not a given string is the encoding of a digraph or graph. For a digraph, checking this amounts to deciding whether a given string has length n^2, for some natural number n; for a graph, it needs to be further checked that the resulting matrix is symmetric and has a zero diagonal.

Proposition 2.2.1. *The languages* $\{\ulcorner H \urcorner \mid H$ is a digraph$\}$ *and* $\{\ulcorner G \urcorner \mid G$ is a graph$\}$ *are computable.*

An analogous property will hold for all encoding methods that we present: the language containing all valid encodings will be computable. We tacitly assume that this property holds, as well, for all encoding methods that are not explicitly presented.

Encoding DTMs

We will also want to present DTMs themselves as input strings. So, let us describe one method for encoding DTMs. In particular, we show how to encode DTMs whose input alphabet is $\Sigma = \{0, 1\}$; the encodings themselves will also be strings over this alphabet.

Let $M = (Q, \Sigma, \Gamma, s, t, r, \delta)$ be such a DTM. We assume that the state set Q has the form $\{1, 11, ..., 1^n\}$ where $n = |Q|$; if Q does not have this form, the states therein may be renamed so that it does. The encoding $\ulcorner M \urcorner$ of M begins with the initial string

$$1^{|Q|} \, 0 \, 1^{|\Gamma|} \, 0 \, s \, 0 \, t \, 0 \, r \, 0.$$

This string provides the size of Q in unary representation, the size of Γ in unary representation, the initial state, the accept state, and the reject state; each of these five objects is a string over $\{1\}$, and each is followed by a 0 for the sake of delimitation.

Example 2.2.2. Let us use as a running example the DTM N of Example 2.1.6. To begin to encode this DTM, we need to rename the states so that the state set has the above form. Let us label s as 1, t as 11, and r as 111. This particular DTM has $|Q| = 3$ and $|\Gamma| = 3$, so the above initial string would be

$$1^3 \, 0 \, 1^3 \, 0 \, s \, 0 \, t \, 0 \, r \, 0 = 11101110101101110.$$ ◇

It remains to encode the transition function δ. To this end, we give a unary representation for each element of Γ, and each of the directions $+1$ and -1. By our assumption that the input alphabet Σ is $\{0, 1\}$, we have that Γ contains at least three symbols, 0, 1, and $\sqcup$. To represent the elements of Γ, let us use the convention that 1 is represented by 1, 0 is represented by 11, $\sqcup$ is represented by 111, and any other symbols in Γ are represented by longer strings of 1's, namely, by the strings 1^4, 1^5, ..., $1^{|\Gamma|}$. For each $a \in \Gamma$, let $\mathrm{rep}_\Gamma(a)$ denote the representation of a. Let us represent the directions $+1$ and -1 by the strings 1 and 11, respectively; set $\mathrm{dir}(+1) = 1$ and $\mathrm{dir}(-1) = 11$. Then, a transition $\delta(q, b) = (p, a, d)$ can be encoded by the string

$$q\, 0\, \mathrm{rep}_\Gamma(b)\, 0\, p\, 0\, \mathrm{rep}_\Gamma(a)\, 0\, \mathrm{dir}(d)\, 0.$$

The encoding $\ulcorner M \urcorner$ of the DTM M is the string obtained by beginning with the initial string, and concatenating to this the encodings of all transitions.

Example 2.2.3. For the DTM N of Example 2.1.6, the transition $\delta(s, 0) = (s, 0, +1)$ would be encoded by

$$s\, 0\, \mathrm{rep}_\Gamma(0)\, 0\, s\, 0\, \mathrm{rep}_\Gamma(0)\, 0\, \mathrm{dir}(+1)\, 0 = 101101011010.$$

The transition $\delta(s, 1) = (s, 1, +1)$ would be encoded by the string

$$s\, 0\, \mathrm{rep}_\Gamma(1)\, 0\, s\, 0\, \mathrm{rep}_\Gamma(1)\, 0\, \mathrm{dir}(+1)\, 0 = 1010101010,$$

and the transition $\delta(s, \sqcup) = (s, \sqcup, +1)$ would be encoded by the string

$$s\, 0\, \mathrm{rep}_\Gamma(\sqcup)\, 0\, s\, 0\, \mathrm{rep}_\Gamma(\sqcup)\, 0\, \mathrm{dir}(+1)\, 0 = 10111010111010.$$

The full encoding $\ulcorner N \urcorner$ of the DTM N consists of the initial string followed by the encodings of the three transitions, namely, the string

$$11101110101101110\ 101101011010\ 1010101010\ 10111010111010,$$

where the extra spacing has been included for readability. ◇

We have the following fact, which is analogous to Proposition 2.2.1.

Proposition 2.2.4. *The language* $\{\ulcorner M \urcorner \mid M \text{ is a DTM}\}$ *is computable.*

Encoding pairs

We will also want to allow Turing machines to be presented inputs that consist of a pair of objects. So, we will assume that, for any alphabet Σ, there is an encoding method for representing pairs of strings; in particular, we assume that each pair $(x, y) \in \Sigma^* \times \Sigma^*$ of strings has an encoding, denoted by $\langle x, y \rangle \in \Sigma^*$.

Let us provide a concrete description of how encoding of pairs can be performed in the case that $\Sigma = \{0, 1\}$; we will later make use of this particular encoding. Let $x = x_1 \ldots x_m$ and $y = y_1 \ldots y_n$ be strings of length m and n, respectively. Define the encoding $\langle x, y \rangle$ of the pair (x, y) to be the string

$$x_1 x_1 x_2 x_2 \ldots x_m x_m 01 y_1 y_2 \ldots y_n.$$

That is, the encoding $\langle x, y \rangle$ is the string of length $2m + 2 + n$ which is formed by duplicating each symbol in x, concatenating 01, and then concatenating y. As examples, we have $\langle 101, 00 \rangle = 1100110100$, $\langle 01, 01 \rangle = 00110101$, $\langle 1, \epsilon \rangle = 1101$, and $\langle \epsilon, 100 \rangle = 01100$.

Given such a string $\langle x, y \rangle$, one can determine x by continually reading in pairs of symbols until 01 is encountered, and then determine y by taking the remainder of the string. Note that, for this encoding method, not every string over $\Sigma = \{0, 1\}$ encodes a pair; for example, no string beginning with 10 encodes a pair. Nonetheless, it is possible to determine computably whether or not a string encodes a pair, and in the case that it does, the original pair of strings can be computably determined. We record these facts here.

Proposition 2.2.5. *The encoding of pairs satisfies the following properties.*

- *The language $\left\{ \langle x, y \rangle \mid x, y \in \Sigma^* \right\}$ is computable.*
- *There exist computable functions p_1, p_2 such that, for all $x, y \in \Sigma^*$, it holds that $p_1(\langle x, y \rangle) = x$ and $p_2(\langle x, y \rangle) = y$.*

We remark that for any alphabet Σ containing at least two distinct symbols a_0, a_1, a similar approach can be used to provide an encoding of each pair (x, y) of strings over Σ: denoting $x = x_1 \ldots x_m$ and $y = y_1 \ldots y_n$, define $\langle x, y \rangle$ as the string

$$x_1 x_1 x_2 x_2 \ldots x_m x_m a_0 a_1 y_1 y_2 \ldots y_n.$$

An encoding method for pairs can be extended to an encoding method for tuples of longer length, in a natural inductive fashion. Namely, for each $k \geq 3$, inductively define

$$\langle x_1, \ldots, x_k \rangle = \langle x_1, \langle x_2, \ldots, x_k \rangle \rangle,$$

for all strings $x_1, \ldots, x_k \in \Sigma^*$.

Encoding natural numbers

By default, we assume that each positive natural number is represented according to its binary representation that begins with 1, and that the number 0 is represented by the string 0. So, as examples, we have $\ulcorner 0 \urcorner = 0$, $\ulcorner 1 \urcorner = 1$, $\ulcorner 2 \urcorner = 10$, $\ulcorner 3 \urcorner = 11$, and $\ulcorner 4 \urcorner = 100$.

2.3 Universal Turing machines

If we want to use an algorithm in the form of a concrete DTM to perform computations in the physical world, we need a physical realization thereof. A priori, each time we design a DTM that we want to use, we need to produce a physical realization—a seemingly cumbersome cycle! This consideration naturally leads to the question of whether there exists a *single* DTM that can simulate the behavior of any other. An affirmative answer to this question would obviate the need to physically realize each DTM of interest on an individual basis.

Let us formalize what we are asking for. Fix an alphabet Σ, and let us restrict attention to DTMs whose input alphabet is Σ. We would like a DTM M_u that, when given as input a pair $\langle \ulcorner M \urcorner, x \rangle$ consisting of the encoding $\ulcorner M \urcorner$ of a DTM and a string $x \in \Sigma^*$, behaves exactly as M does when given x as input. That is, we would like that, on the respective inputs, M_u accepts if M accepts, M_u rejects if M rejects, and M_u loops if M loops. Such a DTM M_u is called a **universal Turing machine**. It is a fundamental fact about DTMs and hence about algorithms that such DTMs exist. The notion of *universal Turing machine*, indeed, provides a theoretical basis for the modern general-purpose programmable computer.[6]

The notion of a DTM that receives another DTM's encoding as part of its input may seem exotic, at first blush. However, this notion should not be mysterious at all to the reader with computer programming experience: it is analogous to that of a computer program that takes other computer programs as input, such as a compiler, an interpreter, or a code analyzer.

The existence of universal Turing machines

Let us explain briefly why universal Turing machines exist, by describing a universal Turing machine M_u on a high level. We assume that $\Sigma = \{0, 1\}$ and that DTMs are encoded as described in Section 2.2. Given an input $\langle \ulcorner M \urcorner, x \rangle$, the DTM M_u simulates the computation of $M = (Q, \Sigma, \Gamma, s, t, r, \delta)$ on x, by first determining the initial configuration $[s, x \sqcup \ldots, 1]$ of M and then repeatedly determining the successor configuration; the DTM M_u accepts if an accepting configuration of M is ever encountered, and rejects if a rejecting configuration of M is ever encountered.

A configuration $[q, \tau, \ell]$ of M can be represented by M_u as follows. In line with the described encoding of DTMs, a state $q \in Q$ is already a string over $\{1\}$. The tape contents τ will always be equal to a string $y = y_1 \ldots y_k$ followed by an infinite sequence of blanks; it can be represented by the string $\text{rep}_\Gamma(y_1)0\text{rep}_\Gamma(y_2)0 \ldots \text{rep}_\Gamma(y_k)0$, where, $\text{rep}_\Gamma(a)$ is a representation of the symbol $a \in \Gamma$, as described in Section 2.2. The location ℓ can be represented by the string $\ulcorner \ell \urcorner$. These three parts of the configuration need to be delimited from each other. From the encoding $\ulcorner M \urcorner$ of M and from the string x, the representation of the initial configuration $[s, x \sqcup \ldots, 1]$ can be readily determined.

The DTM M_u always maintains two pieces of information on its tape: the given encoding $\ulcorner M \urcorner$ and the current configuration γ of the simulation. From these two pieces of information, the successor configuration of γ can be determined: when $\gamma = [q, \tau, \ell]$ is the current configuration and is non-halting, the DTM M_u can determine which symbol a is at the head location ℓ with respect to the tape contents τ, and then, by making use of $\ulcorner M \urcorner$, determine the transition $\delta(q, a)$ to be taken, and then determine the successor configuration

---

6. Indeed, thanks to the form of universality discussed here, a modern-day user of physical computation devices likely has a small number of such devices, each having many application programs—as opposed to one such device for each application program!

of $[q, \tau, \ell]$. The DTM M_u then checks if this successor configuration is halting; if it is, the DTM M_u accepts or rejects accordingly, and if not, the DTM M_u updates the current configuration to be this successor configuration, and repeats the process of this paragraph.

Define the **acceptance problem** as the language

$$\mathsf{AP} = \big\{ \langle \ulcorner M \urcorner, x \rangle \mid M \text{ is a DTM}, x \in \Sigma^*, \text{ and } M \text{ accepts } x \big\}.$$

It is clear that this language AP is the language $L(M_u)$ of any universal Turing machine M_u, and the following theorem is hence a consequence of our discussion.

Theorem 2.3.1. *There exists a DTM M_u where $L(M_u) =$ AP. Thus, the language AP is CE.*

2.4   A non-CE language

The definitions of *computable language* and *CE language* naturally lend themselves to proving positive results. For example, to show that a language B is computable, it suffices by definition to present a DTM, and argue that it is halting and has B as its language. These definitions leave less clear how one should go about negatively proving that a language is *not* computable, or *not* CE. (We previously encountered this phenomenon; the definition of *regular language* exhibits a similar asymmetry.)

In this section, we explicitly construct a first example of a language that is not CE, and hence not computable (recall that each computable language is CE; this was Proposition 2.1.21). Later, we will see further techniques for establishing that languages are not computable, or not CE. Throughout this section, we assume that all strings under discussion are over a fixed alphabet Σ. Following the discussion in Section 2.2, each Turing machine M has an encoding $\ulcorner M \urcorner$ which is a string over Σ^*.

Our aim is to construct a language B that is *not* CE. Thus, we need to ensure that for *no* DTM M does it hold that $L(M) = B$. By definition, it is the case that $L(M) = B$ when, for each string x, the following property holds:

$$x \in B \quad \text{if and only if} \quad M \text{ accepts } x.$$

To construct the desired language B, we should try to ensure that, for each DTM M, there is at least one string x where this property does *not* hold. That is, for each DTM M we would like to ensure that there exists a string x such that

$$x \in B \quad \text{if and only if} \quad M \text{ does not accept } x.$$

We already have, in our hands, a natural way to allocate a string to each DTM! Namely, to each DTM M we can allocate its encoding $\ulcorner M \urcorner$. So, we can try to define a language B satisfying the criterion that, for each DTM M, it holds that

$$\ulcorner M \urcorner \in B \quad \text{if and only if} \quad M \text{ does not accept } \ulcorner M \urcorner.$$

Following these ideas, we introduce a language, which we call the **self-acceptance problem** and denote by SAP. We define

$$\text{SAP} = \{\ulcorner M \urcorner \mid M \text{ is a DTM that accepts } \ulcorner M \urcorner\}.$$

Informally, we can say that a DTM is included in this language precisely when it accepts itself, or when it is in its own language. It can be seen that $\overline{\text{SAP}}$, the complement of this language, satisfies the criterion just identified: the encoding $\ulcorner M \urcorner$ of a DTM is in SAP if and only if M accepts $\ulcorner M \urcorner$; so, the encoding $\ulcorner M \urcorner$ of a DTM is in $\overline{\text{SAP}}$ if and only if M does not accept $\ulcorner M \urcorner$. We thus have that the language $\overline{\text{SAP}}$ is not CE.

Theorem 2.4.1. *The language* $\overline{\text{SAP}}$ *is not CE, and is hence not computable.*

We can describe the salient features of the languages in play, as follows: when $\ulcorner M \urcorner$ is the encoding of a DTM, we have that

$$\ulcorner M \urcorner \in \text{SAP} \quad \text{if and only if} \quad \ulcorner M \urcorner \in L(M),$$

and thus we have that

$$\ulcorner M \urcorner \in \overline{\text{SAP}} \quad \text{if and only if} \quad \ulcorner M \urcorner \notin L(M).$$

Our construction of the language $\overline{\text{SAP}}$ invokes a general technique called *diagonalization*.[7] See Figure 2.4.1 for a diagrammatic explanation.

Although Theorem 2.4.1 follows from the above discussion, we believe it didactic to provide a proof[8] that proceeds directly from the definition of SAP.

Proof of Theorem 2.4.1. Each language that is computable is also CE, by Proposition 2.1.21. It thus suffices to prove that $\overline{\text{SAP}}$ is not CE. We prove this by contradiction; suppose that M is a DTM with $L(M) = \overline{\text{SAP}}$. We consider two cases.

- If M accepts $\ulcorner M \urcorner$, then $\ulcorner M \urcorner \in L(M)$; thus $\ulcorner M \urcorner \in \overline{\text{SAP}}$ and $\ulcorner M \urcorner \notin \text{SAP}$.
  From the definition of SAP, it follows that M does not accept $\ulcorner M \urcorner$, a contradiction.
- If M does not accept $\ulcorner M \urcorner$, then $\ulcorner M \urcorner \notin L(M)$; thus $\ulcorner M \urcorner \notin \overline{\text{SAP}}$ and $\ulcorner M \urcorner \in \text{SAP}$.
  From the definition of SAP, it follows that M accepts $\ulcorner M \urcorner$, a contradiction. □

Let us underscore the import of Theorem 2.4.1. This theorem shows an absolute limit on computation, as formalized by Turing machines: no DTM whatsoever has $\overline{\text{SAP}}$ as its language. Whereas the automata models studied in the previous chapter were strongly limited by the amount of memory and storage that they could use, the DTM model has no

---

7. This construction channels Groucho Marx's quip, "I don't care to belong to any club that will have me as a member," which he stated upon resigning from a club.

8. The proof that we give recalls self-referential paradoxes, such as the paradox of the barber, resident in a village, who claims to shave exactly the persons in the village who do not shave themselves. If one asks whether or not the barber shaves themself, either of the answers *yes* or *no* leads to a contradiction.

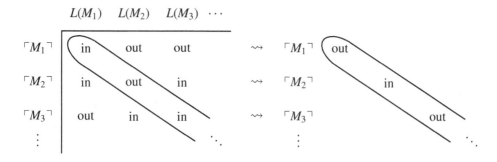

Figure 2.4.1. The definitions of the languages SAP and $\overline{\text{SAP}}$. We assume $M_1, M_2, \ldots$ to be an enumeration of all DTMs. Our motivation is to construct a non-CE language, that is, a language different from each of the languages $L(M_1), L(M_2), \ldots$ On the left, a table is given that shows, for each DTM encoding and each language $L(M_i)$, whether the encoding is in the language. (The particular values in the table were invented, for the purposes of illustration.) We defined the language SAP according to the diagonal of the diagram on the left: a DTM encoding is included in SAP when the encoding is accepted by the DTM, or equivalently, is in the DTM's language. It follows that the language $\overline{\text{SAP}}$, shown on the right, contains a DTM encoding when the encoding is *not* in the DTM's language. The language $\overline{\text{SAP}}$ is thus different from each of the languages $L(M_1), L(M_2), \ldots$ by construction. This construction of the set $\overline{\text{SAP}}$ from the presented table is an instance of a general technique known as *diagonalization*.

such limitation, and is considered to formalize the notions of computation and of algorithm in a fully-fledged fashion!

2.5 Closure properties

We here investigate basic closure properties of the introduced language classes: the computable languages and the CE languages. Our motivations are similar to those that we had when considering closure properties of the regular languages: knowing when these properties hold helps us to understand the scope and structure of a language class, and can aid us in reasoning about whether or not a particular language is inside a class or not. Indeed, as we saw in our study of regular languages, establishing that closure properties held amounted to showing that automata could be modified and composed together in various natural ways; examining closure properties thus gave insight into the power of computational models, and it will here as well.

2.5.1 Complementation

We first observe that the computable languages are closed under complementation.

Proposition 2.5.1. *If B is a computable language, then its complement $\overline{B}$ is also a computable language.*

Proof. Let $M = (Q, \Sigma, \Gamma, s, t, r, \delta)$ be a halting DTM with $L(M) = B$. Then, let $M' = (Q, \Sigma, \Gamma, s, r, t, \delta)$ be the DTM derived from M by interchanging the accept and reject states. The DTM M' is halting, and has $L(M') = \overline{L(M)} = \overline{B}$. □

In contrast, the CE languages are not closed under complementation, as witnessed by the language SAP.

Theorem 2.5.2. *The language* SAP *is CE, but the language* $\overline{\text{SAP}}$ *is not CE. Hence, the CE languages are not closed under complementation.*

Proof. Theorem 2.4.1 showed that $\overline{\text{SAP}}$ is not CE. We thus argue that SAP is CE. Let M_u be the DTM from Theorem 2.3.1; recall that $L(M_u) = $ AP. Define M_0 to be a DTM that, on an input string y, runs M_u on $\langle y, y \rangle$, and accepts if this computation accepts. We have that $y \in L(M_0)$ if and only if $\langle y, y \rangle \in L(M_u) = $ AP. By definition of AP, the latter condition holds if and only if there exists a DTM M such that $y = \ulcorner M \urcorner$ and M accepts $\ulcorner M \urcorner$, which in turn holds exactly when $y \in$ SAP. We conclude that $L(M_0) = $ SAP. □

Since the CE languages are not closed under complementation, if we take the complements of all languages that are CE, we obtain a different class of languages. It will be wieldy to assign a name to this class, as we will want to investigate and understand it.

Definition 2.5.3. A language B is **co-computably enumerable** (for short, **coCE**) if its complement $\overline{B}$ is CE. ◇

An initial observation that we can make about this class is the following, which we shall use tacitly in the sequel.

Proposition 2.5.4. *Each language that is computable is also coCE.*

Proof. Immediate from Propositions 2.5.1 and 2.1.21. □

We next give a corollary summarizing our knowledge of the languages SAP and $\overline{\text{SAP}}$. This corollary holds that the class of computable languages is *strictly* contained in the class of CE languages: there is a language that is CE but not computable, namely, the language SAP. Likewise, this corollary also holds that the class of computable languages is strictly contained in the class of coCE languages, via the language $\overline{\text{SAP}}$.

Corollary 2.5.5. *The language* SAP *is CE but not coCE, and hence not computable; the language* $\overline{\text{SAP}}$ *is coCE but not CE, and hence not computable.*

Proof. That each computable language is both CE and coCE follows from Propositions 2.1.21 and 2.5.4. Given this, the first statement is immediate from Theorem 2.5.2, and the second statement follows from the first, along with the definition of coCE. □

Knowing that each computable language is both CE and coCE, it is instinctive to inquire about the exact relationship between the computable languages and the languages that are both CE and coCE; a natural question is whether or not these two classes of languages are equal. The following theorem beautifully answers this question in the affirmative.

Theorem 2.5.6. *A language is computable if and only if it is CE and coCE.*

To prove this theorem's backward direction, we suppose that a language B is both CE and coCE, which implies that there are DTMs M and M' with $L(M) = B$ and $L(M') = \overline{B}$. It thus holds that, on any string x, exactly one of these two DTMs accepts, and our goal is to present a halting DTM that, on an input string x, determines *which one* of the two DTMs accepts x. A first reaction to this goal might be to design a DTM that performs a sequenced execution, and first runs one of the DTMs—say, the DTM M—on the input string, with the idea that the second DTM will be run if the first one does not accept. This strategy, however, does not work as is: the first DTM might never halt, which would disallow detecting that the second DTM accepts. To overcome this issue, we present a DTM that alternately runs each of the two DTMs M, M' for longer and longer amounts of time—in essence, performing a parallel execution of the two DTMs. This permits detecting which of the two DTMs accepts, even if the other does not halt.

Proof of Theorem 2.5.6. The truth of the forward direction was established by Propositions 2.1.21 and 2.5.4, so we prove the backward direction. Suppose that B is a language that is both CE and coCE; we want to show that B is computable. Let M be a DTM such that $L(M) = B$, and let M' be a DTM such that $L(M') = \overline{B}$.

Let M_0 be a DTM that, on input x, performs the following.

- Assign $i := 1$.
- Iterate:

  ○ Run M on x for i time steps; if this computation accepts, then accept.
  ○ Run M' on x for i time steps; if this computation accepts, then reject.
  ○ Assign $i := i + 1$.

We show that the DTM M_0 is halting and has $L(M_0) = B$.

Let x be an arbitrary string; since either $x \in B$ or $x \in \overline{B}$, we have that either $x \in L(M)$ or $x \in L(M')$, that is, that either M accepts x or M' accepts x. Thus, after a sufficiently large number of iterations, the DTM M_0, when run on input x, either accepts (due to M accepting x) or rejects (due to M' accepting x); we conclude that M_0 is halting.

Observe that if M_0 accepts a string x, it does so only because running M on x resulted in acceptance, so $L(M_0) \subseteq L(M)$. Let us establish the opposite containment $L(M) \subseteq L(M_0)$. Suppose that x is a string that is accepted by M; then, $x \in L(M) = B$ and $x \notin L(M') = \overline{B}$. Thus, running M' on x will never result in acceptance, but running M on x for a sufficiently large number of time steps will result in acceptance; it follows that x is accepted by M_0, and we obtain that $L(M) \subseteq L(M_0)$. We thus have established the equality $L(M_0) = L(M)$, which implies that $L(M_0) = B$. □

2.5.2 Intersection and union

We next consider closure under intersection and union.

Theorem 2.5.7. *If B and C are computable languages, then both $B \cap C$ and $B \cup C$ are also computable languages.*

Proof. Let M_B and M_C be halting DTMs such that $L(M_B) = B$ and $L(M_C) = C$. Define $M_\cap$ to be a DTM that, on an input string x, performs the following.

- Run M_B on x until the computation halts; then run M_C on x until the computation halts.
- If both computations accepted, then accept; otherwise, reject.

It is clear that the DTM $M_\cap$ is halting and that $L(M_\cap) = B \cap C$.

The proof for union is similar; the difference is that one defines a DTM that, on an input string x, accepts if at least one of M_B, M_C accepts x. □

Theorem 2.5.8. *If B and C are CE languages, then $B \cap C$ is also a CE language.*

Proof. Let M_B and M_C be DTMs such that $L(M_B) = B$ and $L(M_C) = C$. On a high level, we define a DTM M whose language is $B \cap C$ by sequencing M_B and M_C: the DTM M first runs M_B, and, if it accepts, passes control to M_C. Precisely, let M be a DTM that, on an input x, performs the following two-stage process.

- Stage 1: Run M_B on x. If this computation rejects, reject; if this computation accepts, proceed to stage 2.
- Stage 2: Run M_C on x. If this computation rejects, reject; if this computation accepts, accept.

We claim that $L(M) = B \cap C$. If M accepts a string x, then this can only be because it accepted in stage 2; in this case, both M_B and M_C accepted x, so $x \in L(M_B) \cap L(M_C)$. On the other hand, suppose $x \in L(M_B) \cap L(M_C)$; when M is run on x, in stage 1, the computation will eventually accept, so M will proceed to stage 2, where the computation will eventually accept; thus, M accepts x. We obtain $L(M) = L(M_B) \cap L(M_C)$, implying $L(M) = B \cap C$. □

Theorem 2.5.9. *If B and C are CE languages, then $B \cup C$ is also a CE language.*

In the proof of this theorem, we present a DTM that is conceptually similar to that presented in the proof of Theorem 2.5.6. The DTM's design makes use of the same parallel execution idea discussed prior to that theorem's proof, and contrasts with the sequenced execution found in the proof of Theorem 2.5.8.

Proof. Let M_B and M_C be DTMs such that $L(M_B) = B$ and $L(M_C) = C$.

Let M be a DTM that performs the following.

- Assign $i := 1$.
- Iterate:
  - Run M_B on x for i time steps; if this computation accepts, then accept.
  - Run M_C on x for i time steps; if this computation accepts, then accept.
  - Assign $i := i + 1$.

We claim that $L(M) = B \cup C$. First, observe that if M accepts a string x, then it holds that either M_B or M_C accepts x. On the other hand, if either M_B or M_C accepts x, then after a sufficiently large number of iterations, M will accept x. We have thus established the equality $L(M) = L(M_B) \cup L(M_C)$, which implies that $L(M) = B \cup C$. $\quad\square$

Corollary 2.5.10. *If B and C are coCE languages, then both $B \cap C$ and $B \cup C$ are also coCE languages.*

Proof. These facts are immediate from Theorems 2.5.8 and 2.5.9, in combination with De Morgan's laws (Proposition 1.2.5). $\quad\square$

2.6 Nondeterministic Turing machines

As previously discussed (in Section 1.3), the *nondeterministic* mode of computation is a theoretical apparatus which, in multiple contexts, offers great insight in the analysis of computation; our first contact with nondeterministic computation was in the presentation of the NFA and ϵ-NFA computational models. In this section, we present the *nondeterministic Turing machine (NTM)*, whose computations have the ability to *branch*, as those of the NFA model did: a configuration may have multiple successor configurations. The NTM model can be conceived of as a generalization of the DTM model;[9] recall that each configuration of a DTM could have at most one successor configuration. Formally, the definition of NTM is a simple variant of the definition of DTM: all parts are defined in the same way, except the transition function of an NTM, when given a state and symbol, describes a *set* of transitions, instead of just a single transition, as the transition function of a DTM did.

In general, a question that one can ask about a computational model is whether augmenting it with an additional feature makes it more powerful, in any sense. In automata theory, we saw that allowing nondeterminism allowed for extra succinctness: we exhibited NFA for which the smallest DFA having equivalence—in terms of language decided—had an exponentially larger state size (Example 1.6.12). On the other hand, from our language-theoretic point of view, NFA are equivalent in power to DFA in the sense that the language classes that they define are the same. In this language-theoretic sense, the situation is

---

9. Proposition 2.6.11 below is a formalization of this claim.

similar for NTMs and DTMs: in addition to defining the NTM, we will define the *halting NTM* and show that these two models define the same language classes as the DTM and halting DTM models, respectively. However, the distinction between determinism and nondeterminism will definitively take center stage in a drama to be unraveled in our study of complexity theory: when we bound the behavior of halting Turing machines even further to give abstractions of *efficient* computation, whether or not deterministic computation is as powerful as nondeterministic computation will be seen to be a paramount, pivotal question.

2.6.1 Model

We give the definition of nondeterministic Turing machine.

Definition 2.6.1. A **nondeterministic Turing machine (NTM)** is defined as a 7-tuple $(Q, \Sigma, \Gamma, s, t, r, \Delta)$ where each of the parts is described as in the definition of DTM (Definition 2.1.1), except the *transition function* Δ is a mapping

$$\Delta\colon (Q \setminus \{t, r\}) \times \Gamma \to \wp(Q \times \Gamma \times \{-1, +1\}).$$ ◇

The notion of *configuration* is defined for NTMs just as it is defined for DTMs. The notion of *successor configuration* is defined based on the transition function Δ.

Definition 2.6.2. Let $M = (Q, \Sigma, \Gamma, s, t, r, \Delta)$ be an NTM.

- A **configuration** of M is a triple $[p, \tau, \ell]$ where $p \in Q$ is a state, τ is a function from $\mathbb{N}^+$ to Γ representing tape contents, and $\ell \in \mathbb{N}^+$ is a head location.
- A configuration $[p', \tau', \ell']$ of M is a **successor configuration** of a configuration $[p, \tau, \ell]$ of M if $p \notin \{t, r\}$ and there exists $(q, a, d) \in \Delta(p, \tau(\ell))$ such that $p' = q$, $\tau' = \tau[\ell \mapsto a]$, and $\ell' = \max(\ell + d, 1)$.

To discuss configurations of the NTM M, we use the previously given definitions of the relations $\vdash_M$, $\vdash_M^n$, and $\vdash_M^*$ presented in Definition 1.1.8.

We define the **initial configuration** of the NTM M on a string $x \in \Sigma^*$ as the configuration $[s, x\sqcup\ldots, 1]$ (following Definition 2.1.7). For the NTM M, we put into effect Definition 2.1.8, that is, we define the notions of **accepting configuration**, **rejecting configuration**, and **halting configuration** just as they were defined for DTMs. ◇

Remark 2.6.3. Observe that a halting configuration of an NTM has no successor configurations; the same holds for a halting configuration of a DTM.

On the other hand, observe that a non-halting configuration of an NTM may have multiple successor configurations; also, a non-halting configuration may have zero successor configurations. In this sense, the definition of NTM bears resemblance to the definition of NFA; an NFA configuration whose string is nonempty may have multiple successor configurations, or zero successor configurations. ◇

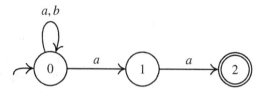

Figure 2.6.1. The NFA used in Example 2.6.4.

Example 2.6.4. We give an example NTM that is based on and imitates the behavior of the NFA $M = (Q, \Sigma, S, T, \Delta)$ presented in Example 1.3.3 and shown in Figure 2.6.1; this NFA has $Q = \{0, 1, 2\}$, $\Sigma = \{a, b\}$, $S = \{0\}$, $T = \{2\}$, and the following transition function Δ:

Δ	a	b
0	$\{0, 1\}$	$\{0\}$
1	$\{2\}$	$\emptyset$
2	$\emptyset$	$\emptyset$

Define M' to be the NTM $(Q', \Sigma, \Gamma, 0, t, r, \Delta')$, shown in Figure 2.6.2, that has $Q' = \{0, 1, 2, t, r\}$, $\Gamma = \{a, b, \sqcup\}$, and the following transition function Δ':

Δ	a	b	$\sqcup$
0	$\{(0, a, +1), (1, a, +1)\}$	$\{(0, b, +1)\}$	$\{(r, \sqcup, +1)\}$
1	$\{(2, a, +1)\}$	$\emptyset$	$\{(r, \sqcup, +1)\}$
2	$\emptyset$	$\emptyset$	$\{(t, \sqcup, +1)\}$

This NTM imitates the behavior of the given NFA in the following manner. As long as this NTM reads symbols from $\Sigma = \{a, b\}$, it moves to the right and is able to enter the states that the NFA M is able to enter. Once the NTM reads a blank symbol, it knows that it has reached the end of the input string, and then enters its accept state t or its reject state r depending on whether its state (0, 1, or 2) was an accept or reject state of the NFA M.

The following diagram provides a look at the configurations that can be reached when this NTM is run on the input string *baa*. This NTM never changes a symbol on its tape; here, we use w to denote $baa\sqcup...$, which is the tape contents of this NTM's initial configuration on this input string.

$$[0, w, 4] \vdash [r, w, 5]$$
$$[0, w, 3]$$
$$[1, w, 4] \vdash [r, w, 5]$$
$$[0, w, 1] \vdash [0, w, 2]$$
$$[1, w, 3] \vdash [2, w, 4] \vdash [t, w, 5]$$

It can be remarked that the derivation of the NTM M' from the NFA M is analogous to the derivation of the DTM in Example 2.1.13 from the DFA in Example 1.1.5.   ◇

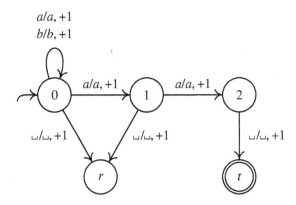

Figure 2.6.2. The NTM presented in Example 2.6.4. This diagram is formed similarly to the way in which the diagrams for DTMs were formed; see Figure 2.1.3. Here, each transition $(p, a, d) \in \Delta'(q, c)$ is indicated by an arrow from the state q to the state p, with label $c/a, d$.

We next define, for an NTM, the outcomes of *accepting* and *halting*. In the following, we assume that the input alphabet of each Turing machine is denoted by Σ.

Definition 2.6.5. Let M be an NTM, let $x \in \Sigma^*$ be a string, and let α_x be the initial configuration of M on x.

- We say that M **accepts** x if there exists an accepting configuration β such that $\alpha_x \vdash_M^* \beta$.
- We say that M **halts on** x if there exists $C \in \mathbb{N}$ such that for each configuration γ of M and each $k \in \mathbb{N}$, the relationship $\alpha_x \vdash_M^k \gamma$ implies $k \leq C$. $\diamond$

Acceptance is defined in terms of possibility (as it was for NFA): an NTM accepts a string if there *exists* a computation ending with an accepting configuration. And, halting may be thought of in terms of a time limit, as illustrated in Figure 2.6.3: an NTM halts on a string if there is a number C (depending on the string) such that it is not possible, from the initial configuration, to take a successor configuration more than C times—that is, no computation on the string lasts for more than C steps. The existence of such a number is equivalent to saying that all computations starting from the initial configuration must eventually terminate: it is not possible to take a successor configuration indefinitely.

Note that here, we do not explicitly define any notion of an NTM *rejecting* a string.

The following two key definitions conclude our formalization of NTMs.

Definition 2.6.6. We define the **language** of an NTM M, denoted by $L(M)$, to be the set $\{x \in \Sigma^* \mid M \text{ accepts } x\}$. $\diamond$

Definition 2.6.7. We say that an NTM M is **halting** if it halts on each string $x \in \Sigma^*$. $\diamond$

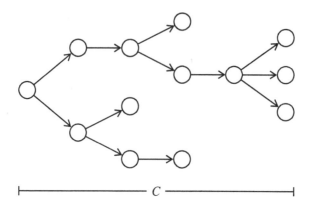

Figure 2.6.3. An illustration of what it means for an NTM M to *halt* on a string x. Each circle represents a configuration of the NTM M, where the leftmost configuration is the initial configuration of M on x. An arrow from a first configuration to a second indicates that the second configuration is a successor configuration of the first. While different computations may have different lengths, the NTM M is considered to halt on a string x when there exists a constant C, depending on the string x, that bounds the length of all computations on x.

Example 2.6.8. The NTM given in Example 2.6.4 is halting: so long as it makes transitions, it only moves to the right, and as soon as it encounters a blank symbol, it enters either its reject or its accept state.   ◇

Our definition of what it means for an NTM to halt on a string may, on its face, appear to have a different character from the definition of what it means for a DTM to halt on a string. However, we can observe that the definition of halting on a string for NTMs (Definition 2.6.5), when applied to a DTM, coincides with the official definition of halting on a string for DTMs (Definition 2.1.9).

Proposition 2.6.9. *Let M be a DTM; let $x \in \Sigma^*$ be a string; let α_x be the initial configuration of M on x. The DTM M halts on x if and only if there exists a value $C \in \mathbb{N}$ where, for each configuration γ of M and each $k \in \mathbb{N}$, the relationship $\alpha_x \vdash_M^k \gamma$ implies $k \leq C$.*

This proposition can be argued in the following way. First, suppose that M halts on x. Then, there exists a halting configuration β such that $\alpha_x \vdash_M^* \beta$; it follows that there exists a value C such that $\alpha_x \vdash_M^C \beta$. Since each non-halting configuration of the DTM M has exactly one successor configuration, the constant C has the claimed property. Next, suppose that x is a string such that the constant C has the stated property. Then, from the initial configuration α_x, the DTM M must reach a halting configuration within taking the successor configuration up to C times.

2.6.2 Relationship to the DTM model

We next study the relationship between the NTM and DTM models. Recall that we defined two types of languages directly from the DTM model: the computable languages were defined via halting DTMs, and the CE languages were defined via DTMs. Here, we show that the computable languages can also be characterized using halting NTMs, and that the CE languages can also be characterized using NTMs. We hence show that, with respect to the genres of DTMs and NTMs presented so far, the two models are in a sense equivalent.

To prove this equivalence of models, we will use the following notion, which formalizes what it means for one machine to produce the same outcomes as a second machine. In this section, we apply this definition to DTMs and NTMs.

Definition 2.6.10. Let M, M' be machines sharing the same input alphabet Σ. We say that M' **outcome-simulates** M when, for each input string $x \in \Sigma^*$, the following hold:

- M halts on x implies that M' halts on x.
- M accepts x if and only if M' accepts x. ◇

In Definition 2.6.10, the first condition guarantees that when M is halting, M' is halting as well; note that this condition's converse is not needed for our purposes. The second condition guarantees that the languages of M and of M' are the same.

We begin by arguing that each DTM can be converted to an NTM.

Proposition 2.6.11. *For each DTM M, there exists an NTM M' that outcome-simulates M.*

Essentially, this proposition holds because deterministic computation, as carried out by a DTM, can be viewed as a degenerate form of nondeterministic computation, as carried out by an NTM. In particular, given a DTM M, an NTM M' can be constructed whose behavior imitates that M in all relevant senses.

We argue this proposition precisely as follows. Let $M = (Q, \Sigma, \Gamma, s, t, r, \delta)$ be a DTM. We define the transition function $\Delta \colon (Q \setminus \{t, r\}) \times \Gamma \to \wp(Q \times \Gamma \times \{-1, +1\})$ of the NTM M' according to the rule $\Delta(q, a) = \{\delta(q, a)\}$; the NTM M' is defined as $(Q, \Sigma, \Gamma, s, t, r, \Delta)$. That is, we define the NTM M' to imitate the DTM M; their definitions are equal, except the transition function Δ of M' simply permits, in each case, the sole transition given by the transition function δ of M. These two machines have the same initial configurations on any string in Σ^*, and have the same non-halting configurations. In addition, it is readily seen that for each non-halting configuration γ, each of the two machines provides one successor configuration of γ, and the two provided successor configurations are equal. Hence, the DTM M accepts a string x if and only if the NTM M' accepts x; and, the DTM M halts on a string x if and only if the NTM M' halts on x (recall Proposition 2.6.9).

We next show how to convert in the other direction, from an NTM to a DTM.

Theorem 2.6.12. *For each NTM M, there exists a DTM M' that outcome-simulates M.*

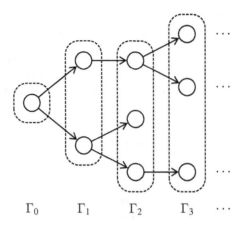

$$\Gamma_0 \qquad \Gamma_1 \qquad \Gamma_2 \qquad \Gamma_3 \quad \cdots$$

Figure 2.6.4. Sets computed by the DTM given in the proof of Theorem 2.6.12; this DTM is constructed based on an NTM. As in Figure 2.6.3, each circle represents a configuration of the NTM, and an arrow from a first configuration to a second indicates that the second configuration is a successor configuration of the first. Given an input string x, the DTM computes, for increasing values of i, the set Γ_i of all configurations that the NTM could be in after i transitions, when run on x. The set Γ_0 contains just the initial configuration of the NTM on the input string.

To establish this theorem, from an NTM M, we show how to construct a DTM M' having the desired properties. The construction of the DTM M' from the NTM M is more involved than the construction of the previous result. On a high level, the DTM M' performs the following. On an input x, it iteratively computes, for larger and larger i, the set Γ_i containing *all* of the configurations that M could reach after i transitions; see Figure 2.6.4. If it ever encounters an accepting configuration, then it accepts; if it never encounters an accepting configuration but discovers that, after some number of transitions, there are no configurations that M could reach, then it knows that M halts on the input without accepting, and it rejects. In computer science terminology, on each input string x, the DTM M' performs a *breadth-first* search on the tree of configurations yielded by invoking the NTM M on string x: all configurations at the same distance from the tree's root are considered prior to any configurations at a longer distance from the root. This breadth-first strategy copes properly with the possibility that, on an input string, the NTM M may have both a computation that continues indefinitely, and a computation that terminates by accepting.

Proof of Theorem 2.6.12. For each string $x \in \Sigma^*$, let α_x denote the initial configuration of M on x. Let M' be a DTM that, on an input string $x \in \Sigma^*$, performs the following:

- Assign $\Gamma_0 := \{\alpha_x\}$.

- Assign $i := 0$.
- Iterate:
  - If Γ_i contains an accepting configuration, accept.
  - If Γ_i is empty, reject.
  - Assign $\Gamma_{i+1} := \bigcup_{\gamma \in \Gamma_i} \{\gamma' \mid \gamma \vdash_M \gamma'\}$.
  - Assign $i := i + 1$.

From the way that the algorithm determines Γ_0 and the way that the algorithm computes Γ_{i+1} from Γ_i, we can observe that whenever a set Γ_j is computed by the algorithm, it is the set of all configurations reachable from the initial configuration after j transitions, that is, it is equal to $\left\{\gamma \mid \alpha_x \vdash_M^j \gamma\right\}$.

Suppose that M halts on a string x. Let C be a constant satisfying the property given in Definition 2.6.5; if M' does not halt prior to computing Γ_{C+1}, it will reject after computing Γ_{C+1}, since this set will be empty. Thus, M' halts on x.

We argue that M accepts a string x if and only if M' accepts x.

- Suppose that M accepts a string x. Then, there exists $D \in \mathbb{N}$ such that $\alpha_x \vdash_M^D \beta$, where β is an accepting configuration. Let $D \in \mathbb{N}$ be the minimum value such that this holds. On the input string x, the DTM M' computes the sets $\Gamma_0, \Gamma_1, \ldots, \Gamma_D$: due to the choice of D, each of the sets is nonempty, but none of these sets, other than Γ_D, contains an accepting configuration. It follows that M' accepts x.
- Suppose that M' accepts a string x; this must be because one of the sets Γ_i contained an accepting configuration β, which implies that $\alpha_x \vdash_M^* \beta$ and hence that M accepts x. □

Remark 2.6.13 (Simulating NTMs with DTMs). While this chapter is not concerned with the amount of time that Turing machines consume, this issue will be of prime concern in the next chapter.

The just-presented theorem (Theorem 2.6.12) showed that each NTM could be simulated by a DTM in the precise sense that, on any input string, the outcome of the DTM was the same as the outcome of the NTM. However, the way in which the DTM simulates computations of the NTM requires the DTM to expend a significant amount of time effort. Since each configuration of an NTM may have 2 or more successor configurations, with the passing of each time step during an NTM computation, the number of configurations that the NTM could possibly be in may be multiplied by 2 (or more). The simulation of the theorem has the DTM maintain *all* of the configurations that the NTM could be in after i transitions, for increasing values of i; the number of such configurations could be 2^i or more, and thus could be *exponential* in the amount of elapsed time.[10] This simulation thus incurs a severe time penalty, and is not at all an efficient one. Whether or not such a severe

---

10. This phenomenon is reminiscent of the exponential blowup in state size that can occur when converting from an NFA to a DFA. This blowup was discussed in and right before Example 1.6.12.

penalty is inevitable is a deep issue that is the essence of the *P versus NP question*, and that is at the heart of the next chapter.   ◇

We can now observe, as formalized in the following two theorems, that the notions of *computable* and *computably enumerable* language can be characterized by halting NTMs and NTMs, respectively. These two theorems follow quite directly from the simulation results established by Proposition 2.6.11 and Theorem 2.6.12.

Theorem 2.6.14. *A language B is computable if and only if there exists a halting NTM M such that B = L(M).*

Proof. If B is computable, then by definition there exists a halting DTM M' such that $L(M') = B$; by Proposition 2.6.11, there exists an NTM M that outcome-simulates M'. The definition of *outcome-simulates* yields that the NTM M is halting and has $L(M) = B$.

If there exists a halting NTM M such that $L(M) = B$, then by Theorem 2.6.12, there exists a DTM M' that outcome-simulates M. The definition of *outcome-simulates* yields that the DTM M' is halting and has $L(M') = B$, implying that B is computable.   □

Theorem 2.6.15. *A language B is computably enumerable if and only if there exists an NTM M such that B = L(M).*

Proof. If B is CE, then by definition there exists a DTM M' such that $L(M') = B$; by Proposition 2.6.11, there exists an NTM M that outcome-simulates the DTM M', and thus has $L(M) = B$. On the other hand, if there exists an NTM M such that $L(M) = B$, then by Theorem 2.6.12, there exists a DTM M' that outcome-simulates the NTM M, and thus has $L(M') = B$; this implies that B is CE.   □

Let us emphasize the parallelism between the two theorem statements just given and the definitions of *computable language* and of *CE language* (Definitions 2.1.15 and 2.1.20).

2.6.3   Summary of models and language classes

The following is an expansion of a table previously seen in this chapter (in Section 2.1.4); it gives the computational models seen so far, along with their accompanying language classes.

Computational model	Defined class of languages	Justification
DFA	regular languages	Definition 1.1.1
NFA	regular languages	Theorem 1.3.24
ϵ-NFA	regular languages	Theorem 1.3.24
halting DTM	computable languages	Definition 2.1.15
halting NTM	computable languages	Theorem 2.6.14
DTM	CE languages	Definition 2.1.20
NTM	CE languages	Theorem 2.6.15

The following Venn diagram relates the language classes seen so far. In particular, we see here that the computable languages are the languages that are both CE and coCE, and that they properly contain the regular languages.

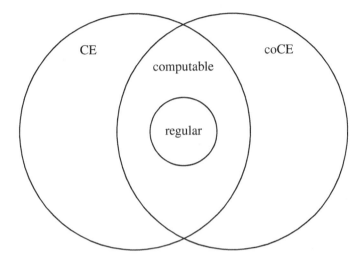

The following diagram shows the inclusion structure of the language classes seen so far:

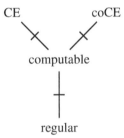

Here, a line from a language class to a language class above it indicates inclusion of the first class in the second, and the hash mark on such a line indicates that the inclusion is proper. For example, the line with a hash mark from the regular languages to the computable languages indicates that each regular language is computable, but that there exists a computable language that is not regular.

2.7 The robustness of computability

As discussed in the first section of this chapter, numerous computational models are known to define the notion of *computable language*. This notion is indeed remarkably robust and is certainly quite impervious to changes to the basic DTM model. For example, as we saw in the previous section, the nondeterministic variant of the halting DTM, the *halting NTM*, also defines the class of computable languages. Varying other features of the basic DTM model also leaves unchanged the class of defined languages: for example, changing the geometry of the tape so that it is infinite in both directions, or even multidimensional (as opposed to one-dimensional); allowing the head to move left or right multiple cells instead of just one cell, in a time step; or allowing multiple heads on the tape.

In this optional section, we present and study two further computational models that both are instructive to study in their own right, and are of utility in the theory of computation. The first model is the *multitape DTM*, an extension of the DTM where a machine may have multiple tapes, each with its own head. This model is useful for formalizing computation where the amount of *space* permitted is bounded to be smaller than the input string.[11] The second model is the *random access machine (RAM)*. Under this model, so-called *random access* to an infinite memory is allowed: to read or write the contents at a memory location, the machine can execute single instructions which specify the location. In terms of time consumption, the RAM model is viewed as more faithful to modern computers than the DTM model, where many head movements are necessary to move between and manipulate tape cells that are far apart. Consequently, versions of the RAM are often employed to analyze the running time of algorithms. Nonetheless, as is the norm, in this book the DTM is chosen over the RAM as the main model for studying computability and complexity. This choice is due to the DTM having a relatively simple formulation; also, the specific requirement that a DTM head must move locally, step by step, often renders DTMs easier to reason about.

While it is most possible to do so, we do not explicitly study nondeterministic versions of the models presented here. We mention here that, for each of the presented models, the natural generalizations allowing nondeterminism do not add any expressive power in that the defined language classes remain the same.

2.7.1 Multitape DTMs

We here introduce *multitape DTMs*, generalizations of the DTM model where the control has the ability to read from and write to multiple tapes, as opposed to just one single tape.

A multitape DTM consists of a control, a finite sequence of worktapes, and a head for each worktape. Each worktape is identical in form to the worktape of a DTM; namely, each worktape consists of discrete cells, and is infinite to the right. As with a DTM, a multitape DTM operates in discrete time steps. In each time step, a multitape DTM makes a transition based on its current state and the symbols in the cells where its heads are located. In making a transition, a multitape DTM changes state; it writes a symbol at the location of each of its heads; and it moves each head left or right. When a multitape DTM is invoked on an input

11. Typically, this is done by only allowing reading from the tape with the input string, and restricting the space usage of a second tape, which serves as a workspace; see Section 4.6.2.

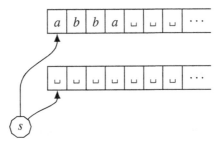

Figure 2.7.1. A configuration of a 2-tape DTM. Such a DTM has 2 tapes and one head for each tape. The heads may be moved independently of each other. The displayed configuration is the initial configuration of a 2-tape DTM on the string *abba*; here, *s* denotes the DTM's start state.

string x, its first tape is initialized to contain the string at the left end, followed by blank symbols; all other tapes are initialized to purely contain blank symbols; and, each head is located at the leftmost cell of its tape (namely, the cell numbered 1). Figure 2.7.1 shows an example initial configuration.

Multitape DTMs are formally defined as follows.

Definition 2.7.1. For each $k \geq 1$, a k-**tape DTM** is a 7-tuple $(Q, \Sigma, \Gamma, s, t, r, \delta)$ where each of the parts is described as in the definition of DTM (Definition 2.1.1), except the *transition function* is a mapping

$$\delta \colon (Q \setminus \{t, r\}) \times \Gamma^k \to Q \times \Gamma^k \times \{-1, +1\}^k. \qquad \Diamond$$

Based on the discussion so far, the reader may be able to anticipate how to formalize the behavior of a multitape DTM, and how to make precise notions such as *configuration* and *acceptance*. We briefly present a formalization thereof. Let $M = (Q, \Sigma, \Gamma, s, t, r, \delta)$ be a k-tape DTM.

- A **configuration** of M is a tuple $[q, \tau_1, \ldots, \tau_k, \ell_1, \ldots, \ell_k]$ where $q \in Q$ is a state; $\tau_1, \ldots, \tau_k$ are functions from $\mathbb{N}^+$ to Γ giving the tape contents of the k tapes, respectively; and, $\ell_1, \ldots, \ell_k \in \mathbb{N}^+$ are values giving the head locations.

- The **successor configuration** of a configuration $[q, \tau_1, \ldots, \tau_k, \ell_1, \ldots, \ell_k]$ is defined when $q \in Q \setminus \{t, r\}$; when this holds, set $(p, a_1, \ldots, a_k, d_1, \ldots, d_k) = \delta(q, \tau_1(\ell_1), \ldots, \tau_k(\ell_k))$; then, the successor configuration of the presented configuration is defined as

$$[p, \tau_1[\ell_1 \mapsto a_1], \ldots, \tau_k[\ell_k \mapsto a_k], \max(\ell_1 + d_1, 1), \ldots, \max(\ell_k + d_k, 1)].$$

  Here, following the previously introduced convention, if on any tape M tries to move its head left when it is already at the leftmost cell, the head remains at that cell.

- To discuss configurations of the k-tape DTM M, we use the relations $\vdash_M$, $\vdash_M^n$, and $\vdash_M^*$ presented in Definition 1.1.8.

- A configuration $[q, \tau_1, ..., \tau_k, \ell_1, ..., \ell_k]$ is **accepting** if $q = t$, **rejecting** if $q = r$, and **halting** if $q \in \{t, r\}$. These definitions follow Definition 2.1.8.
- Let $x \in \Sigma^*$ be a string. Set τ_1 to be $x\sqcup...$, and set each of $\tau_2, ..., \tau_k$ to be $\sqcup...$. Set α_x to be the configuration $[s, \tau_1, ..., \tau_k, 1, ..., 1]$, which is the **initial configuration** when M is invoked on x: the first tape contains the string x, starting from its left end, and otherwise all cells contain the blank symbol.

  By analogy to Definition 2.1.9, we say that

  - M **accepts** x if there exists an accepting configuration β such that $\alpha_x \vdash_M^* \beta$;
  - M **rejects** x if there exists a rejecting configuration β such that $\alpha_x \vdash_M^* \beta$; and
  - M **halts** on x if it accepts or rejects x.

- We define the language of M, denoted by $L(M)$, as $\{x \in \Sigma^* \mid M \text{ accepts } x\}$.
- We say that M is **halting** if for each string $x \in \Sigma^*$, it holds that M halts on x.

Example 2.7.2. We present a halting 2-tape DTM $M = (Q, \Sigma, \Gamma, s, t, r, \delta)$ whose language is the set of all palindromes over the alphabet $\Sigma = \{a, b\}$. Define $Q = \{s, t, r, y, f, g, e\}$ and define $\Gamma = \{a, b, \sqcup\}$. To define the transition function

$$\delta: (Q \setminus \{t, r\}) \times \Gamma \times \Gamma \to Q \times \Gamma \times \Gamma \times \{-1, +1\} \times \{-1, +1\},$$

consider the following table:

δ	(a, a)	(b, b)	$(a, \sqcup)$	$(b, \sqcup)$	$(\sqcup, \sqcup)$
s			$(y, a, \sqcup, -1, +1)$	$(y, b, \sqcup, -1, +1)$	$(t, \sqcup, \sqcup, -1, -1)$
y			$(y, a, a, +1, +1)$	$(y, b, b, +1, +1)$	$(f, \sqcup, \sqcup, -1, -1)$
f	$(f, a, a, -1, -1)$	$(f, b, b, -1, -1)$	$(g, a, \sqcup, -1, -1)$	$(g, b, \sqcup, -1, -1)$	
g			$(g, a, \sqcup, +1, -1)$	$(g, b, \sqcup, +1, -1)$	$(e, \sqcup, \sqcup, -1, +1)$
e	$(e, a, a, -1, +1)$	$(e, b, b, -1, +1)$	$(t, a, \sqcup, -1, -1)$	$(t, b, \sqcup, -1, -1)$	

For each triple $(q, c_1, c_2) \in Q \times \Gamma \times \Gamma$, define $\delta(q, c_1, c_2)$ according to the given table whenever there is an entry present at the row with label q and the column with label (c_1, c_2); define $\delta(q, c_1, c_2)$ as any 5-tuple whose first entry is the state r, otherwise. In fact, when reasoning about the resulting 2-tape DTM, the only assumption made about δ on entries omitted by the table is that each of the tuples $\delta(e, a, b)$ and $\delta(e, b, a)$ has r as its first entry.

Let us argue that the machine M is halting and that it accepts exactly the palindromes.

- The machine begins in state s with each of its two heads at location 1 of their tapes. When the input string is empty, the heads see the symbols $(\sqcup, \sqcup)$, and the machine enters its accept state t. When the input string is not empty, the heads see the symbols $(a, \sqcup)$ or $(b, \sqcup)$, and the machine enters the state y and moves the second head to the right.

  As a running example, we consider the action of the machine on the input string $abba$; the first transition is

  $$[s, \underline{a}bba\sqcup..., \underline{\sqcup}\sqcup\sqcup..., 1, 1] \vdash_M [y, \underline{a}bba\sqcup..., \sqcup\underline{\sqcup}\sqcup..., 1, 2].$$

- In state y, the machine makes a copy of each symbol on the first tape onto the second tape, and moves each head to the right. This is performed until the blank symbol is seen on the first tape, at which point the state f is entered, and the entirety of the input string has been copied to the second tape: letting x denote the input string, the first tape's contents is x⊔... (it has not been changed), and the second tape's contents is ⊔x⊔.... The tapes' contents will not be further changed.

  In our running example, we have

  $$[y, \underline{a}bba⊔..., ⊔\underline{⊔}⊔..., 1, 2] \vdash_M [y, a\underline{b}ba⊔⊔..., ⊔a\underline{⊔}⊔⊔⊔⊔..., 2, 3]$$

  $$\vdash_M^3 [y, abba\underline{⊔}⊔..., ⊔abba\underline{⊔}⊔..., 5, 6]$$

  $$\vdash_M [f, abb\underline{a}⊔⊔..., ⊔abb\underline{a}⊔⊔..., 4, 5].$$

- In state f, each of the heads is moved to the left until the second head sees the blank symbol, at which point each of the heads will be at location 1; the machine then enters the state g.

  Continuing our running example, we have

  $$[f, abb\underline{a}⊔⊔..., ⊔abb\underline{a}⊔⊔..., 4, 5] \vdash_M^3 [f, \underline{a}bba⊔⊔..., ⊔\underline{a}bba⊔⊔..., 1, 2]$$

  $$\vdash_M [f, \underline{a}bba⊔⊔..., \underline{⊔}abba⊔⊔..., 1, 1]$$

  $$\vdash_M [g, \underline{a}bba⊔⊔..., \underline{⊔}abba⊔⊔..., 1, 1].$$

- In state g, the first head is moved to the right until it sees a blank symbol. When it does, the first head is at the first blank symbol after the input string; and, the second head is at location 1 and sees a blank symbol that directly precedes the copy of the input string. Then, the state e is entered, the first head is moved left to see the last symbol of the input string, and the second head is moved right to see the first symbol of the input string.

  In our running example, we have

  $$[g, \underline{a}bba⊔⊔..., \underline{⊔}abba⊔⊔..., 1, 1] \vdash_M^4 [g, abba\underline{⊔}⊔..., \underline{⊔}abba⊔⊔..., 5, 1]$$

  $$\vdash_M [e, abb\underline{a}⊔⊔..., ⊔\underline{a}bba⊔⊔..., 4, 2].$$

  The last configuration just given is depicted in Figure 2.7.2.

- In state e, the machine checks for equality of the symbols seen by the heads.

  Suppose these seen symbols are both in the input alphabet $\{a, b\}$; when they are not equal, the machine rejects (here we utilize the assumption on how δ behaves outside of the given table), and when they are equal, the machine stays in the state e, moves the first head to the left, and moves the second head to the right.

  Otherwise, on the second tape, the second head has reached the blank symbol directly following the input string, and the input string has been fully traversed on each tape. Since all equality checks were successful, the machine accepts.

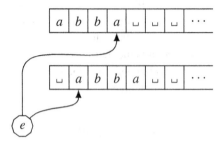

Figure 2.7.2. The first configuration where the state e is entered, in the computation discussed in Example 2.7.2. This example discusses the execution of a particular 2-tape DTM on the input string *abba*.

In our running example, we have

$$[e, ab\underline{b}a\text{⊔⊔}..., \text{⊔}\underline{a}bba\text{⊔⊔}..., 4, 2] \vdash_M [e, ab\underline{b}a\text{⊔⊔}..., \text{⊔}a\underline{b}ba\text{⊔⊔}..., 3, 3]$$
$$\vdash_M [e, a\underline{b}ba\text{⊔⊔}..., \text{⊔}ab\underline{b}a\text{⊔⊔}..., 2, 4]$$
$$\vdash_M [e, \underline{a}bba\text{⊔⊔}..., \text{⊔}abb\underline{a}\text{⊔⊔}..., 1, 5]$$
$$\vdash_M [e, \underline{a}bba\text{⊔⊔}..., \text{⊔}abba\text{⊔}_\text{⊔}..., 1, 6]$$
$$\vdash_M [t, \underline{a}bba\text{⊔⊔}..., \text{⊔}abb\underline{a}\text{⊔⊔}..., 1, 5].$$

It can be verified that, in the computation of this machine on an input string x, the number of configurations with state y is at most $|x| + 1$, the number of configurations with state f is at most $|x| + 1$, the number of configurations with state g is at most $|x|$, and the number of configurations with state c is at most $|x| + 1$. The final configuration will have state r or t, and thus, including the initial configuration, the total number of configurations is less than or equal to $4|x| + 5$.   ◇

We show that (for each $k \geq 1$) the DTM and k-tape DTM models are equivalent in power. We use the definition of *outcome-simulates* (Definition 2.6.10) to relate DTMs and k-tape DTMs. We first show that each DTM is simulable by a k-tape DTM.

Proposition 2.7.3. *Let $k \geq 1$. For each DTM M, there exists a k-tape DTM M' that outcome-simulates M.*

This proposition can be proved as follows. Given a DTM M, we construct a k-tape DTM M' that imitates the behavior of the DTM M on its first tape, but does not make real use of any other of its tapes, on which each head always requests a left movement (so that it stays in the leftmost location). Formally, let $M = (Q, \Sigma, \Gamma, s, t, r, \delta)$ be a DTM. We define M' to be the k-tape DTM having the same components but with the transition function δ' defined as follows. For each $q \in Q \setminus \{t, r\}$ and for each $(c_1, ..., c_k) \in \Gamma^k$, we

$(a,\sqcup)$	$(b,\hat{a})$	(b,b)	$(\hat{a},b)$	$(\sqcup,a)$	$(\sqcup,\sqcup)$	$(\sqcup,\sqcup)$	$\cdots$

Figure 2.7.3. A DTM simulates a 2-tape DTM M by representing the tape contents and head locations of M using pairs. The pair in the ith cell contains the symbols in the ith cells of M's tapes; a symbol has a carat over it if the respective head of M is located at the symbol. The presented tape contents represent the respective parts of the configuration depicted in Figure 2.7.2.

define $\delta'(q, c_1, ..., c_k)$ as $(p, a, \sqcup, ..., \sqcup, d, -1, ..., -1)$, where $p \in Q$, $a \in \Gamma$, and $d \in \{-1, +1\}$ are the values such that $(p, a, d) = \delta(q, c_1)$. Thus, the transition function δ' of M' imitates the transition function δ of M on the first tape, but on each other tape, always writes a blank symbol and requests to move left.

We next show that each k-tape DTM is simulable by a DTM.

Theorem 2.7.4. *Let $k \geq 1$. For each k-tape DTM M, there exists a DTM M' that outcome-simulates M.*

Let us explain how Theorem 2.7.4 can be proved. Let $M = (Q, \Sigma, \Gamma, s, t, r, \delta)$ be a k-tape DTM. We design a DTM M' that simulates the action of M.[12] During the simulation, the tape contents of M' will represent the tape contents of M, along with the locations of the heads of M. (Recall that in general, during a computation, the heads of M may be at different locations.) Specifically, the ith cell of the tape of M' will store a tuple $(c_1, ..., c_k)$ where each c_j is the symbol in the ith cell of the jth simulated tape; the symbol c_j will be marked with a carat if the simulated head of the jth tape is located at the ith cell. See Figure 2.7.3 for an example. We define the tape alphabet Γ' of M' as $\Sigma \cup \{\sqcup\} \cup (\Gamma \cup \hat{\Gamma})^k$, where $\hat{\Gamma}$ is defined as the set that contains each symbol in Γ with a carat over it, that is, $\hat{\Gamma}$ is defined as $\{\hat{c} \mid c \in \Gamma\}$.[13] The DTM M' acts as follows:

Step 1. In an initialization phase, M' first replaces the symbol $b \in \Sigma \cup \{\sqcup\}$ in the 1st cell with the tuple

$$(\hat{b}, \hat{\sqcup}, ..., \hat{\sqcup})$$

of carated symbols that contains $\hat{b}$ in the first entry and $\hat{\sqcup}$ in each other entry, and then moves right. The DTM M' then iteratively checks if the symbol at its head is an element $c \in \Sigma$; if so, M' replaces this symbol c with the tuple

$$(c, \sqcup, ..., \sqcup)$$

that contains c in the first entry and $\sqcup$ in each other entry, and then moves right. This phase terminates when the first blank symbol on the tape is encountered. From this

---

12. There are certainly multiple ways to perform this simulation; we attempt to present a simulation that lends itself to a relatively clean exposition.

13. It is assumed that Γ and $\hat{\Gamma}$ are disjoint.

$(\hat{a},\hat{\sqcup},\hat{\sqcup})$	$(b,\sqcup,\sqcup)$	$(b,\sqcup,\sqcup)$	$(a,\sqcup,\sqcup)$	$(\sqcup,\sqcup,\sqcup)$	$(\sqcup,\sqcup,\sqcup)$	$(\sqcup,\sqcup,\sqcup)$	$\cdots$

Figure 2.7.4. For a DTM to simulate a k-tape DTM M, it first performs an initialization phase which transforms each symbol of its input string into a k-tuple, so that its tape contents represent the initial tape contents and initial head locations of M. The displayed tape contents show the result of this initialization phase on the input string *abba*, in the simulation of a 3-tape DTM. The blank symbols following the DTM's input string need not be changed; they are treated and shown here as k-tuples of blank symbols.

point on, we associate together the blank symbol $\sqcup \in \Gamma'$ and the k-tuple of blanks $(\sqcup, ..., \sqcup) \in \Gamma'$, that is, we treat them equally and as if they were the same symbol. Thus, after all replacements have been performed, the tape contents of M' represents the initial tape contents of M, in the described fashion; see Figure 2.7.4 for an example. The DTM M', as part of its own state, tracks the state of M as s. Then, the DTM proceeds to the next step.

Step 2. In a reading phase, M' moves left until it has determined the symbols seen by each of the simulated heads; it stores these symbols as part of its state. It then moves right until its location is to the right of each head location of M', and then proceeds to the next step.

Step 3. Based on the tracked state q of M and the symbols $(c_1, ..., c_k)$ determined in the reading phase, M' simulates a transition of M, as follows. Moving left, it looks for each simulated head of each simulated tape (that is, it looks for elements of $\hat{\Gamma}$ in the tuple in each cell), and when found, it updates both the symbol at the simulated head and the location of the simulated head, based on $\delta(q, c_1, ..., c_k)$. Once it has done this for each simulated tape, it moves right until it has passed all of the simulated heads, and it updates the tracked state of M according to the state given by $\delta(q, c_1, ..., c_k)$. If the new tracked state is t or r, then M' itself accepts or rejects, respectively; otherwise, it goes to step 2 in order to simulate one more transition.

It can be verified that this behavior can be implemented by a DTM. In particular, to implement this behavior, only a finite amount of information needs to be maintained at any time point. For example, step 2 just needs to track the state of M and, for each tape of M, whether or not it has determined the symbol at the tape's head, and if so, what the symbol is.

As consequences of the simulations just given, we have the following results.

Theorem 2.7.5. *Let $k \geq 1$. A language B is computable if and only if there exists a halting k-tape DTM such that $B = L(M)$.*

Theorem 2.7.6. *Let $k \geq 1$. A language B is computably enumerable if and only if there exists a k-tape DTM such that $B = L(M)$.*

	-1	0	1	2	3	4	5	6	
$\cdots$	0	0	1	2	2	1	0	0	$\cdots$

Figure 2.7.5. The memory of a RAM consists of a one-dimensional array of cells which is infinite in both directions. Each cell is indexed with an integer, and can contain an integer.

These results follow directly from the given simulations, in the same way that Theorems 2.6.14 and 2.6.15 followed from Proposition 2.6.11 and Theorem 2.6.12. We omit giving explicit proofs of these results.

2.7.2 Random access machines

We next describe the random access machine (RAM) model. In contrast to the previously introduced models, the primitive memory units—the *cells*—of a RAM hold integers, as opposed to symbols of an alphabet. We here use $\mathbb{Z}$ to denote the set $\{\ldots, -2, -1, 0, 1, 2, \ldots\}$ of integers. As with the other computational models, there are many possible definitions of the RAM; we present one of minimalist design. Architecturally, a RAM consists of a *program counter*, a *memory*, and a *register*.

- Each particular RAM has an associated **program**, which is an indexed sequence of **instructions**. During a computation, the **program counter** holds the index of an instruction, namely, the instruction to be executed next.

- The **memory** is a one-dimensional array of **cells** and is infinite in both directions; each cell can hold an integer, and so the memory is formalized as a mapping $\mu \colon \mathbb{Z} \to \mathbb{Z}$. See Figure 2.7.5 for a visualization. We refer to a value $i \in \mathbb{Z}$ as a *location* when we are interested in discussing the value $\mu(i)$ stored in the ith cell.

- The **register** is a special cell apart from the memory array. The register can hold one integer value, which is typically denoted by ρ. It is used for working with the memory and controlling the flow of execution.

In order to give the formal definition of a RAM, we first formally define the notion of the *program* of a RAM.

Definition 2.7.7. A **RAM program** is a finite sequence Π of **instructions** $\pi_1, \ldots, \pi_\ell$ (with $\ell \geq 1$), where each instruction is drawn from the table in Figure 2.7.6 and obeys the respective condition. It is required that the last instruction π_ℓ of each RAM program is either *accept* or *reject*; this convention ensures that the program counter is never incremented past the value ℓ. $\diamond$

A RAM operates in discrete time steps; in each time step, the instruction referenced by the program counter is atomically executed. Other than for each of the last three instruction types, after each instruction is executed, the program counter is incremented by 1.

Instruction	Condition	Informal description
read i	$i \in \mathbb{Z}$	sets the register's value ρ to $\mu(i)$
read ↑ i	$i \in \mathbb{Z}$	sets the register's value ρ to $\mu(\mu(i))$
write i	$i \in \mathbb{Z}$	updates μ to map i to the register's value ρ
write ↑ i	$i \in \mathbb{Z}$	updates μ to map $\mu(i)$ to the register's value ρ
assign c	$c \in \mathbb{Z}$	sets the register's value ρ to c
add c	$c \in \mathbb{Z}$	adds c to the register's value ρ
jump-if-pos j	$j \in \{1, ..., \ell\}$	if $\rho \in \mathbb{N}^+$, changes the program counter to j
accept		causes the machine to accept
reject		causes the machine to reject

Figure 2.7.6. Table giving the instructions allowed in RAM programs; this table forms part of Definition 2.7.7.

We remark that many formalizations of the RAM permit, as primitive instructions, basic arithmetic operations on stored values, such as addition or multiplication.

We proceed to give the formal definition of a RAM.

Definition 2.7.8. A **random access machine (RAM)** is a triple (Π, Σ, e) where

- Π is a RAM program,
- Σ is an alphabet called the **input alphabet**, and
- $e \colon \Sigma \to \mathbb{N}^+$ is an injective function called the **encoding**.   ◇

For a RAM $M = (\Pi, \Sigma, e)$, an input string over Σ is provided to the RAM via the encoding e: on an input string $x_1 \ldots x_n \in \Sigma^*$, the RAM's memory μ is initially set so that the values $\mu(1), \ldots, \mu(n)$ are set to $e(x_1), \ldots, e(x_n)$, respectively. That is, the input string is placed in the n consecutive memory cells starting at location 1. All other memory cells and the register are initially set to 0; this value is something of an analog of the blank symbol used by Turing machines, and in particular delimits the end of the input string.

Example 2.7.9. Consider a RAM having the input alphabet $\Sigma = \{a, b\}$ and the encoding $e \colon \Sigma \to \mathbb{N}^+$ where $e(a) = 1$ and $e(b) = 2$. The initial setting of the RAM's memory under the input string *abba* would be that depicted in Figure 2.7.5: the symbols of the string, mapped under the encoding, are placed in the memory starting from the cell with index 1, and all other cells are initialized with the value 0.   ◇

Relative to a RAM, we next define the notions of *configuration* and *successor configuration*, and also identify a few types of configurations. The following definitions are analogs of Definitions 2.1.2 and 2.1.8, which concerned configurations of DTMs.

Definition 2.7.10. Let $M = (\Pi, \Sigma, e)$ be a RAM whose program Π is $\pi_1, \ldots, \pi_\ell$.

Instruction given by π_κ	Successor configuration of $[\kappa, \mu, \rho]$
read i	$[\kappa+1, \mu, \mu(i)]$
read $\uparrow$ i	$[\kappa+1, \mu, \mu(\mu(i))]$
write i	$[\kappa+1, \mu[i \mapsto \rho], \rho]$
write $\uparrow$ i	$[\kappa+1, \mu[\mu(i) \mapsto \rho], \rho]$
assign c	$[\kappa+1, \mu, c]$
add c	$[\kappa+1, \mu, \rho+c]$
jump-if-pos j	$[j, \mu, \rho]$ when $\rho \in \mathbb{N}^+$; $[\kappa+1, \mu, \rho]$ otherwise

Figure 2.7.7. Table describing the successor configuration of a configuration $[\kappa, \mu, \rho]$; this table forms part of Definition 2.7.10.

- A **configuration** of M is a triple $[\kappa, \mu, \rho]$ where $\kappa \in \{1, ..., \ell\}$ provides the value of the program counter; μ is a function from $\mathbb{Z}$ to $\mathbb{Z}$ giving the memory contents; and $\rho \in \mathbb{Z}$ specifies the value of the register.
- The **successor configuration** of a configuration $[\kappa, \mu, \rho]$ is defined whenever the instruction π_κ is not in $\{accept, reject\}$, and is defined according to the table in Figure 2.7.7. ◇

Definition 2.7.11. Let M be a RAM whose program Π is $\pi_1, ..., \pi_\ell$. We say that a configuration $[\kappa, \mu, \rho]$ of M is an **accepting configuration** if $\pi_\kappa = accept$; a **rejecting configuration** if $\pi_\kappa = reject$; and, a **halting configuration** if it is an accepting or a rejecting configuration. ◇

We next conclude our formalization of RAM behavior; let $M = (\Pi, \Sigma, e)$ be a RAM.

- To discuss configurations of the RAM M, we use the relations $\vdash_M$, $\vdash_M^n$, and $\vdash_M^*$ presented in Definition 1.1.8.
- Let $x = x_1...x_n \in \Sigma^*$ be a string of length n. Define $\mu_x: \mathbb{Z} \to \mathbb{Z}$ to be the function that maps the values $1, 2, ..., n$ to $e(x_1), e(x_2), ..., e(x_n)$, respectively, and every other integer value to 0. Set $\alpha_x = [1, \mu_x, 0]$; this is the **initial configuration** of M on x.
  - We say that M **accepts** x if there exists an accepting configuration β where $\alpha_x \vdash_M^* \beta$.
  - We say that M **rejects** x if there exists a rejecting configuration β where $\alpha_x \vdash_M^* \beta$.
  - We say that M **halts** on x if M accepts or rejects x.
- We define the language of M, denoted by $L(M)$, as $\{x \in \Sigma^* \mid M \text{ accepts } x\}$.
- We say that M is **halting** if for each string $x \in \Sigma^*$, it holds that M halts on x.

Example 2.7.12. We present a RAM $M = (\Pi, \Sigma, e)$ whose language is the set of palindromes over $\Sigma = \{a, b\}$. Let $e: \Sigma \to \mathbb{N}^+$ be the encoding where $e(a) = 1$ and $e(b) = 2$. The program Π is defined as the sequence $\pi_1, ..., \pi_{25}$ of instructions presented in Figure 2.7.8. Let us explain why the language of this RAM is the set of palindromes.

$$\pi_1 = read\ -1 \qquad\qquad \pi_{14} = read \uparrow -2$$
$$\pi_2 = add\ 1 \qquad\qquad \pi_{15} = add\ -1$$
$$\pi_3 = write\ -1 \qquad\qquad \pi_{16} = jump\text{-}if\text{-}pos\ 22$$
$$\pi_4 = read \uparrow -1$$
$$\pi_5 = jump\text{-}if\text{-}pos\ 1 \qquad\qquad \pi_{17} = read \uparrow -1$$
$$\pi_{18} = add\ -1$$
$$\pi_6 = read\ -1 \qquad\qquad \pi_{19} = jump\text{-}if\text{-}pos\ 25$$
$$\pi_7 = add\ -1 \qquad\qquad \pi_{20} = assign\ 1$$
$$\pi_8 = write\ -1 \qquad\qquad \pi_{21} = jump\text{-}if\text{-}pos\ 6$$
$$\pi_9 = jump\text{-}if\text{-}pos\ 11$$
$$\pi_{10} = accept \qquad\qquad \pi_{22} = read \uparrow -1$$
$$\pi_{11} = read\ -2 \qquad\qquad \pi_{23} = add\ -1$$
$$\pi_{12} = add\ 1 \qquad\qquad \pi_{24} = jump\text{-}if\text{-}pos\ 6$$
$$\pi_{13} = write\ -2 \qquad\qquad \pi_{25} = reject$$

Figure 2.7.8. An example RAM program, discussed in Example 2.7.12.

On a high level, the behavior of the program Π resembles that of the 2-tape DTM of Example 2.7.2. As with that DTM, the program Π compares the input's first symbol with its last symbol, then its second symbol with its second-to-last symbol, and so on, rejecting if a mismatch is ever found, and accepting when the entire string has been traversed. While the DTM makes a copy of its input, the program Π works directly on the given input.

The instructions $\pi_1, \ldots, \pi_5$ constitute a preliminary phase that configure the value $\mu(-1)$ to point to the first memory cell that follows the input. These instructions increment $\mu(-1)$ by 1, examine the value of $\mu(\mu(-1))$, and repeat, so long as this value is positive. As $\mu(-1)$ begins at the value 0, these instructions in effect examine the values of $\mu(1)$, $\mu(2)$, ... in sequence; when these instructions finish, $\mu(-1)$ is equal to the lowest value $k \geq 1$ such that $\mu(k) = 0$, which is the index of the first memory cell right after the input.

To aid in the understanding of this RAM, we consider its behavior on the input string ab. As above, we use μ_{ab} to denote the initial memory contents on the string ab, namely, the function mapping 1 to 1, 2 to 2, and each other integer to 0. On this input string, the instructions $\pi_1, \ldots, \pi_5$ perform the following:

$$[1, \mu_{ab}, 0] \vdash [2, \mu_{ab}, 0]$$
$$\vdash [3, \mu_{ab}, 1]$$
$$\vdash [4, \mu_{ab}[-1 \mapsto 1], 1]$$

$$\vdash [5, \mu_{ab}[-1 \mapsto 1], 1]$$

$$\vdash [1, \mu_{ab}[-1 \mapsto 1], 1]$$

$$\vdash^4 [5, \mu_{ab}[-1 \mapsto 2], 2]$$

$$\vdash^5 [5, \mu_{ab}[-1 \mapsto 3], 0]$$

$$\vdash [6, \mu_{ab}[-1 \mapsto 3], 0].$$

When execution reaches instruction π_6, the value of $\mu(-1)$ and the value of $\mu(-2)$ are viewed as pointers to the input to be moved left and right, respectively, such that after each move, it is checked whether $\mu(\mu(-1))$ and $\mu(\mu(-2))$ are equal. The first time that instruction π_6 is reached, the value of $\mu(-1)$ is the location number immediately to the right of the input, and the value of $\mu(-2)$ is the location number immediately to the left of the input, namely, 0.

On a high level, the instructions $\pi_6, \ldots, \pi_{13}$ decrement $\mu(-1)$ by 1 and increment $\mu(-2)$ by 1. The instructions π_6, π_7, π_8 decrement the value $\mu(-1)$. If after this decrementing, the value $\mu(-1)$ is detected by instruction π_9 to be no longer positive, this indicates that this left-moving pointer has moved past the left end of the input and thus that each of the pointers has traversed the whole input; in this case, the program accepts in instruction π_{10}. (In particular, if the input string was empty, the program accepts here the first time this block of instructions is executed.) Continuing our running example, where π_6 has been reached for the first time, this segment of instructions decrements $\mu(-1)$ to 2, and increments $\mu(-2)$ to 1:

$$[6, \mu_{ab}[-1 \to 3], 0] \vdash [7, \mu_{ab}[-1 \mapsto 3], 3]$$

$$\vdash [8, \mu_{ab}[-1 \mapsto 3], 2]$$

$$\vdash [9, \mu_{ab}[-1 \mapsto 2], 2]$$

$$\vdash [11, \mu_{ab}[-1 \mapsto 2], 2]$$

$$\vdash [12, \mu_{ab}[-1 \mapsto 2], 0]$$

$$\vdash [13, \mu_{ab}[-1 \mapsto 2], 1]$$

$$\vdash [14, \mu_{ab}[-2 \mapsto 1, -1 \mapsto 2], 1].$$

The remaining instructions $\pi_{14}, \ldots$ carry out the task of checking equality of the values $\mu(\mu(-1))$ and $\mu(\mu(-2))$, which at this point in the program must necessarily hold encodings of input symbols. Instructions $\pi_{14}, \pi_{15}, \pi_{16}$ examine $\mu(\mu(-2))$; if its value is 1 (representing a), execution resumes at instruction π_{17}, and if its value is 2 (representing b), execution resumes at instruction π_{22}. In our running example, this segment of instructions discovers that $\mu(\mu(-2))$ is 1, and so execution resumes at instruction π_{17}:

$$[14, \mu_{ab}[-2 \mapsto 1, -1 \mapsto 2], 1] \vdash [15, \mu_{ab}[-2 \mapsto 1, -1 \mapsto 2], 1]$$

$$\vdash [16, \mu_{ab}[-2 \mapsto 1, -1 \mapsto 2], 0]$$

$$\vdash [17, \mu_{ab}[-2 \mapsto 1, -1 \mapsto 2], 0].$$

Instructions $\pi_{17}, \ldots, \pi_{21}$ examine $\mu(\mu(-1))$; if its value is 2, a mismatch is detected, and the program rejects by jumping to instruction π_{25}, and if its value is 1, the program jumps back to instruction π_6. Analogously, instructions $\pi_{22}, \ldots, \pi_{25}$ examine $\mu(\mu(-1))$, jumping back to instruction π_6 if its value is 2, and rejecting if its value is 1. In our running example, a mismatch is detected:

$$[17, \mu_{ab}[-2 \mapsto 1, -1 \mapsto 2], 0] \vdash [18, \mu_{ab}[-2 \mapsto 1, -1 \mapsto 2], 2]$$

$$\vdash [19, \mu_{ab}[-2 \mapsto 1, -1 \mapsto 2], 1]$$

$$\vdash [25, \mu_{ab}[-2 \mapsto 1, -1 \mapsto 2], 1]. \qquad \diamond$$

Via simulation arguments, we next show that DTMs and RAMs are equivalent in power. We use the definition of *outcome-simulates* (Definition 2.6.10) to relate DTMs and RAMs.

Theorem 2.7.13. *For each DTM M, there exists a RAM M' that outcome-simulates M.*

We briefly explain how this theorem can be proved. Let $(Q, \Sigma, \Gamma, s, t, r, \delta)$ denote the DTM M. We describe a RAM M' that performs a step-by-step simulation of the DTM M. Fix $f: \Gamma \to \mathbb{Z}$ to be an injective mapping such that $f(a) \in \mathbb{N}^+$ for each $a \in \Sigma$, and $f(\sqcup) = 0$. The encoding e of the RAM M' is defined as the restriction of f to Σ, that is, as the mapping $e: \Sigma \to \mathbb{N}^+$ where $e(a) = f(a)$ for each $a \in \Sigma$. Let $\tau: \mathbb{N}^+ \to \Gamma$ denote the tape contents of M at some point in time during the simulation; these contents will be represented in the memory μ of M', via the mapping f, at positive-indexed locations: the memory will satisfy the condition that $\mu(i) = f(\tau(i))$ for each $i \in \mathbb{N}^+$. Observe that, for any string $x \in \Sigma^*$, the initial memory contents of M' on x already satisfy this condition relative to the initial tape contents of M on x. The position of the DTM's head will be maintained as $\mu(-1)$, which the RAM initializes to 1.

The RAM has a segment of instructions for each state of the DTM, and the segment for the start state s comes before all others in Π, effecting that the RAM begins with the DTM in state s. In such a segment for a state q that is neither the accept state nor the reject state, the tape symbol at the DTM's head is obtained by an instruction *read* $\uparrow -1$, and then, depending on the value b of this symbol, a transition $\delta(q, b) = (q', c, d)$ is simulated:

- the simulated tape is written to via instructions of the form *assign c, write* $\uparrow -1$;
- the simulated tape head is moved via instructions of the form *read* -1, *add d, write* -1, where $d \in \{-1, +1\}$ is the direction of movement; and,
- a jump is performed to the segment of the next state q'.

The segment of the accept state consists simply of the instruction *accept*, and the segment of the reject state consists simply of the instruction *reject*; these two segments are placed after all of the other segments.

Theorem 2.7.14. *For each RAM M, there exists a DTM M' that outcome-simulates M.*

Let us briefly indicate how this theorem can be proved. The DTM M' simulates the behavior of the RAM M in a step-by-step fashion. The DTM maintains, on its tape, a configuration of the RAM: the program counter, the memory contents, and the register contents of the RAM. Throughout a computation, the memory contents can be represented using a finite amount of space: at any point in time, the number of memory cells that are not mapped to 0 is finite, and thus it suffices to represent the finite set of pairs (i, c) such that $i \in \mathbb{Z}$ is a memory location, $c = \mu(i)$ is the integer stored at the location, and $c \neq 0$. By looking at the program counter, the DTM can determine whether or not the represented configuration has a successor configuration; if so, based on the program counter, the DTM can enter a state that implements the determination of the successor configuration. The DTM performs this iteratively; if and when the represented configuration becomes a halting configuration, the DTM accepts or rejects depending on whether the represented configuration is accepting or rejecting.

The following theorems are consequences of the just-presented simulations.

Theorem 2.7.15. *A language B is computable if and only if there exists a halting RAM M such that B = L(M).*

Theorem 2.7.16. *A language B is computably enumerable if and only if there exists a RAM M such that B = L(M).*

These theorems follow directly from the simulations, in the same way that Theorems 2.6.14 and 2.6.15 followed directly from Proposition 2.6.11 and Theorem 2.6.12. We omit explicit proofs of these theorems.

2.8 Reductions

The diagonalization argument in Section 2.4 allowed us to derive that the languages SAP and $\overline{\text{SAP}}$ are not computable (Corollary 2.5.5). In this section, we introduce a tool that will allow us to demonstrate the non-computability of further languages, by piggybacking on established non-computability results. In particular, we introduce a notion of *reduction*, which will allow us to speak of one language *reducing* to another. A reduction can be thought of as a means for translating a membership question about one language to a membership question about another language. A key property of the reduction notion to be presented is that if a non-computable language reduces to a second language, then this establishes the non-computability of the second language. As we already have a couple of non-computable languages in our hands, presenting reductions will allow us to demonstrate the non-computability of further languages.

We begin the discussion with a motivating example. Recall the language definitions

$$AP = \{\langle \ulcorner M \urcorner, x \rangle \mid M \text{ is a DTM}, x \in \Sigma^*, \text{ and } M \text{ accepts } x\},$$

$$SAP = \{\ulcorner M \urcorner \mid M \text{ is a DTM that accepts } \ulcorner M \urcorner\}.$$

Example 2.8.1. We prove that the language AP is *not* computable, by building atop the fact that SAP is not computable.

Suppose, for a contradiction, that AP is computable, and let M_A be a halting DTM whose language is AP. We can then show that SAP is computable, as follows. Define a DTM M_S that performs the following: on an input $\ulcorner M \urcorner$, compute the pair $\langle \ulcorner M \urcorner, \ulcorner M \urcorner \rangle$, and then run the DTM M_A on this pair; if the computation accepts, then accept, and if the computation rejects, then reject. (If the input to M_S is not the encoding of a DTM, then M_S simply rejects.) The DTM M_S is clearly halting; moreover, its language is SAP, since we have

$$\ulcorner M \urcorner \in SAP \quad \Leftrightarrow \quad M \text{ accepts } \ulcorner M \urcorner$$
$$\Leftrightarrow \quad \langle \ulcorner M \urcorner, \ulcorner M \urcorner \rangle \in AP$$
$$\Leftrightarrow \quad M_S \text{ accepts } \ulcorner M \urcorner.$$

This establishes that SAP is computable; as this is a contradiction, we conclude that the language AP is not computable.

Intuitively speaking, we have shown that the language SAP can be viewed as a special case of the language AP. Indeed, a key component of this argument was to convert a string $x = \ulcorner M \urcorner$, for which we wanted to answer the question of whether $x \in SAP$, into a second string $y = \langle \ulcorner M \urcorner, \ulcorner M \urcorner \rangle$, for which knowing whether $y \in AP$ would answer the original question. We next introduce a concept of *reduction* that formalizes this process of converting membership questions about one language (in our case, SAP) to membership questions about another language (in our case, AP). ◇

The following definition of reduction builds on the notion of computable function (presented in Definition 2.1.17).

Definition 2.8.2. Let B and C be languages over the same alphabet Σ. A **many-one reduction from B to C** is a computable function $\rho: \Sigma^* \to \Sigma^*$ satisfying the condition that, for each string $x \in \Sigma^*$, the equivalence $x \in B \Leftrightarrow \rho(x) \in C$ holds. We refer to this condition as the **correctness** of the function ρ. To indicate that there exists a many-one reduction from B to C, we use the notation $B \leq_m C$ and say that B **many-one reduces** to C. ◇

The correctness condition is illustrated in Figure 2.8.1.

Remark 2.8.3. A many-one reduction ρ from B to C maps each string x to another string $\rho(x)$ so that when x is in B, the result $\rho(x)$ is in C, and when x is not in B, the result $\rho(x)$ is not in C. We can think of a reduction as a translation. Suppose we want to answer the question of whether a string x is in B, and we have such a reduction ρ in hand; then, computing $\rho(x)$ gives us a string such that, if we could answer whether $\rho(x)$ is in C,

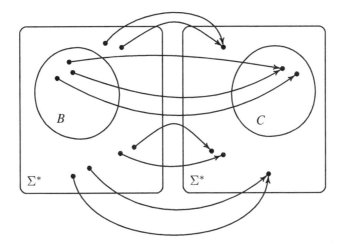

Figure 2.8.1. The correctness of a many-one reduction from a language B to a language C. Each point represents a string. Correctness holds that strings in B are mapped to strings in C, and that strings outside of B are mapped to strings outside of C. It is permitted that two distinct strings are mapped by a reduction to the same string.

this would answer the original question of whether x is in B. Indeed, as we will formalize below, assuming we have a reduction as described, the computability of C implies the computability of B.

Let us emphasize that when a many-one reduction ρ is applied to a string x, knowledge of the result $\rho(x)$ does *not*, in general, allow one to immediately resolve the *yes-or-no* question of whether x is in B; rather, the result $\rho(x)$ is a new string such that the question of whether $\rho(x)$ is in C has *the same answer* to the stated question of whether x is in B. Indeed, while a many-one reduction f is computable by definition, it could very well be that the language C is not computable, and thus that deciding whether $\rho(x) \in C$ is, on its face, much harder than deriving $\rho(x)$ from x.   ◇

Example 2.8.4 (A many-one reduction from SAP **to** AP**).** The discussion in Example 2.8.1 suggests a way of giving a reduction from SAP to AP, namely, try to define a map $\rho \colon \Sigma^* \to \Sigma^*$ by $\rho(\ulcorner M \urcorner) = \langle \ulcorner M \urcorner, \ulcorner M \urcorner \rangle$. Note, however, that this definition is formally incomplete, as it defines ρ only on DTM encodings, whereas ρ needs to be defined on all strings; this definition can be remedied and made complete as follows. Fix a string y_0 that is not in AP. Define $\rho(x)$ to be $\langle \ulcorner M \urcorner, \ulcorner M \urcorner \rangle$ if x has the form $\ulcorner M \urcorner$, and as y_0 if x is not the encoding of any DTM. This remedy parallels our having needed, in Example 2.8.1, to specify that the DTM M_S rejects each string that is not the encoding of any DTM.

Let us show that ρ is a reduction from SAP to AP. We have that ρ is computable (recall Proposition 2.2.4). We verify the correctness of ρ, namely, that $x \in$ SAP $\Leftrightarrow \rho(x) \in$ AP holds for all strings x.

- If x is not the encoding of any DTM, then $x \notin$ SAP and $\rho(x) = y_0 \notin$ AP.
- If x is the encoding $\ulcorner M \urcorner$ of a DTM M, then we have

$$x = \ulcorner M \urcorner \in \text{SAP} \quad \Leftrightarrow \quad M \text{ accepts } \ulcorner M \urcorner$$

$$\Leftrightarrow \quad \rho(x) = \langle \ulcorner M \urcorner, \ulcorner M \urcorner \rangle \in \text{AP}. \qquad \diamond$$

Remark 2.8.5. When presenting reductions, we will often neglect to define a reduction on strings that are obviously outside the initial language, that is, the language that we reduce *from*. For example, if each string in the initial language is an encoding $\ulcorner M \urcorner$ of a DTM M, we will typically only define the reduction on the strings that are DTM encodings. As discussed in Example 2.8.4, this is formally incomplete, but in all cases where we will do it, such a definition can be made complete by precisely the maneuver employed in this example: the strings on which the reduction is not defined can all be mapped to a fixed string that is outside the language reduced *to*. $\diamond$

2.8.1 Properties

We present here some basic properties of many-one reducibility. First, we show that the existence of a reduction between two languages is preserved under taking the complements of the two languages.

Proposition 2.8.6. *Let B and C be languages where $B \leq_m C$ holds; then $\overline{B} \leq_m \overline{C}$ holds.*

Proof. A many-one reduction ρ from B to C is also a many-one reduction from $\overline{B}$ to $\overline{C}$: the condition $x \in B \Leftrightarrow \rho(x) \in C$ implies the condition $x \in \overline{B} \Leftrightarrow \rho(x) \in \overline{C}$. (Indeed, these two conditions are equivalent.) $\square$

Our next theorem shows that when we have a reduction from a first language to a second language, and the second language is in one of the language classes introduced in this chapter, then the first language is as well. For example, the next theorem shows that when a language B reduces to a language C that is computable, the language B must also be computable. Placing a language in one of these classes is sometimes referred to as an *upper bound*; following the use of this terminology, one can say that when a first language reduces to a second, any upper bound on the second applies to the first. (This lingo indeed jives with our symbolic notation $\leq_m$ for indicating the existence of reductions.)

Figure 2.8.2. The behavior of a DTM M_B defined in the proof of Theorem 2.8.7's first part. This part holds that, assuming that there exists a many-one reduction ρ from a language B to a computable language C, it follows that the language B is computable. To argue this, let M_ρ be a DTM computing ρ, let M_C be a halting DTM whose language is C, and construct a DTM M_B behaving as shown in the diagram: on an input x, it invokes the DTM M_ρ to compute the string $\rho(x)$, and then invokes the DTM M_C on this latter string. This DTM M_B is halting and has B as its language. A similar construction shows that when C is assumed just to be CE, the language B is also CE.

Theorem 2.8.7. *Suppose that B and C are languages such that $B \leq_m C$. The following implications hold:*

- *If C is computable, then B is computable.*
- *If C is CE, then B is CE.*
- *If C is coCE, then B is coCE.*

Let us make two remarks about this theorem. First, let us underscore that we will often use this theorem's claims in their contrapositive form. For example, the first claim implies that if $B \leq_m C$ and B is *not* computable, then C is also *not* computable. Second, observe that this theorem's claims can be viewed as asserting that the various classes of languages enjoy a certain closure property. For example, the first claim says that if C is computable, then any language that many-one reduces to C is also computable.

Proof of Theorem 2.8.7. Assume that ρ is a many-one reduction from B to C, and let M_ρ be a DTM that computes ρ. We prove the claims in order.

Suppose that C is computable. Let M_C be a halting DTM such that $L(M_C) = C$. Define M_B to be the DTM that, on an input x, first invokes the DTM M_ρ on x, and then invokes the DTM M_C on the result $\rho(x)$; the DTM M_B accepts if M_C accepts, and rejects if M_C rejects. For each string x, we have

$$
\begin{aligned}
x \in L(M_B) \quad &\Leftrightarrow \quad \rho(x) \in L(M_C) \\
&\Leftrightarrow \quad \rho(x) \in C \\
&\Leftrightarrow \quad x \in B.
\end{aligned}
$$

The first equivalence holds by the definition of M_B, the second equivalence holds by the choice of M_C, and the third equivalence holds by the assumption that ρ is a many-one reduction from B to C. We obtain that $L(M_B) = B$. Moreover, since M_C is a halting DTM, the DTM M_B is halting as well. Thus, M_B is a halting DTM with $L(M_B) = B$, and we conclude that B is computable. Figure 2.8.2 shows the behavior of the DTM M_B.

Suppose that C is CE. Let M_C be a DTM such that $L(M_C) = C$. Let M_B be the DTM defined just as in the previous argument. We obtain that $L(M_B) = B$ by the same reasoning as in the previous argument, allowing us to conclude that B is CE.

Suppose that C is coCE. Then $\overline{C}$ is CE. By Proposition 2.8.6, we have that $\overline{B} \leq_m \overline{C}$. By applying the previous result, we obtain that $\overline{B}$ is CE, and hence that B is coCE.   □

Remark 2.8.8. Example 2.8.4 showed that SAP $\leq_m$ AP. The language SAP was previously shown to be not coCE and hence not computable (recall Corollary 2.5.5). Via Theorem 2.8.7, we obtain that AP is not coCE and hence not computable.   ◇

Remark 2.8.9. The result that SAP is CE, previously shown in Theorem 2.5.2, can be derived from Theorem 2.8.7 in conjunction with the facts that SAP $\leq_m$ AP (Example 2.8.4) and that AP is CE (Theorem 2.3.1). Indeed, the proof of Theorem 2.5.2 showing that SAP is CE can be interpreted as giving a reduction from SAP to AP.   ◇

We exhibit further properties of the relation $\leq_m$ arising from many-one reducibility. First, let us record that it is reflexive, as a consequence of the identity mapping being computable.

Proposition 2.8.10. *For each language B, it holds that $B \leq_m B$.*

We next show the transitivity of the relation $\leq_m$; this is proved essentially by showing that reductions can be composed.

Theorem 2.8.11. *Let A, B, and C be languages such that $A \leq_m B$ and $B \leq_m C$. Then it holds that $A \leq_m C$.*

Proof. Let f be a many-one reduction from A to B, and let g be a many-one reduction from B to C. Set $\rho \colon \Sigma^* \to \Sigma^*$ to be the function defined by $\rho(x) = g(f(x))$, that is, ρ is the composition of f and g. We claim that ρ is a many-one reduction from A to C.

Let M_f be a DTM that computes f, and let M_g be a DTM that computes g. Consider the DTM M that, on an input x, first invokes the DTM M_f, and when the computation accepts, then invokes the DTM M_g, accepting when this second computation accepts. The DTM M clearly computes the function ρ. We have thus established that ρ is computable.

For each string $x \in \Sigma^*$, we have

$$
\begin{aligned}
x \in A \quad &\Leftrightarrow \quad f(x) \in B \\
&\Leftrightarrow \quad g(f(x)) \in C \\
&\Leftrightarrow \quad \rho(x) \in C.
\end{aligned}
$$

The first two equivalences follow from the correctness of f and g as many-one reductions, and the third equivalence is immediate from the definition of ρ. We conclude that ρ is a many-one reduction from A to C.   □

2.8.2 Further examples

We next present three further examples of reductions. In doing so, we use the convention presented in Remark 2.8.5: we may neglect to define a reduction on strings that are obviously outside the initial language. Also, we will in each example assert that the function claimed to be a reduction is computable, without explicitly verifying this; for verification, we appeal to the reader's judgement. In the first two examples, we reduce *from* the language AP; since we established that this language is not computable (Remark 2.8.8), it follows that the languages that we reduce *to* are not computable (via Theorem 2.8.7).

Define the **halting problem**, denoted by HP, to be the language

$$\{\langle \ulcorner M \urcorner, x \rangle \mid M \text{ is a DTM}, x \in \Sigma^*, \text{ and } M \text{ halts on } x\}.$$

Theorem 2.8.12. AP *many-one reduces to* HP.

Proof. Let ρ be the computable function that, on a string of the form $\langle \ulcorner M \urcorner, x \rangle$ with M a DTM, returns $\langle \ulcorner M' \urcorner, x \rangle$ where $\ulcorner M' \urcorner$ is the encoding of a DTM M' described as follows. On an input x, the DTM M' performs the following: it runs M on x; if this computation accepts, M' accepts, and if this computation rejects, M' loops. Thus,

- if M accepts x, then M' accepts x;
- if M rejects x, then M' loops on x; and,
- if M loops on x, then M' loops on x.

It follows that M accepts x if and only if M' halts on x; so,

$$\langle \ulcorner M \urcorner, x \rangle \in \text{AP} \quad \Leftrightarrow \quad \langle \ulcorner M' \urcorner, x \rangle \in \text{HP}$$

and we have verified that ρ is a many-one reduction from AP to HP. $\quad\square$

Define ACCEPT-ALL to be the language $\{\ulcorner M \urcorner \mid L(M) = \Sigma^*\}$. That is, ACCEPT-ALL is the language that contains the encoding of each DTM that accepts all possible input strings.

Theorem 2.8.13. AP *many-one reduces to* ACCEPT-ALL.

Proof. Let ρ be the computable function that, on a DTM encoding $\langle \ulcorner M \urcorner, x \rangle$, returns the encoding $\ulcorner M' \urcorner$ of a DTM M' described as follows. The DTM M' invokes M with input string x, accepting if M accepts, and rejecting if M rejects. Note that M' ignores its input; independent of what its input is, it runs M on x.

We verify that ρ is a many-one reduction from AP to ACCEPT-ALL, as follows.

- Suppose $\langle \ulcorner M \urcorner, x \rangle \in \text{AP}$; then the DTM M accepts x, from which it follows that the DTM M' accepts every string and that $\ulcorner M' \urcorner \in \text{ACCEPT-ALL}$.
- Suppose $\langle \ulcorner M \urcorner, x \rangle \notin \text{AP}$; then the DTM M does not accept x, from which it follows that the DTM M' does not accept any string, and that $\ulcorner M' \urcorner \notin \text{ACCEPT-ALL}$. $\quad\square$

Define ACCEPT-SAME to be the language $\{\langle \ulcorner M_1 \urcorner, \ulcorner M_2 \urcorner \rangle \mid L(M_1) = L(M_2)\}$. So, the language ACCEPT-SAME contains a pair of two DTM encodings when the two DTMs share the same language.

Theorem 2.8.14. ACCEPT-ALL *many-one reduces to* ACCEPT-SAME.

Proof. Fix M_{Σ^*} to be a DTM such that $L(M_{\Sigma^*}) = \Sigma^*$; for instance, we can take M_{Σ^*} to be the DTM that always accepts immediately. Let ρ be the computable function that, on a string of the form $\ulcorner M \urcorner$, outputs the pair $\langle \ulcorner M \urcorner, \ulcorner M_{\Sigma^*} \urcorner \rangle$. We have the equivalences

$$\ulcorner M \urcorner \in \text{ACCEPT-ALL} \quad \Leftrightarrow \quad L(M) = L(M_{\Sigma^*}) \quad \Leftrightarrow \quad \langle \ulcorner M \urcorner, \ulcorner M_{\Sigma^*} \urcorner \rangle \in \text{ACCEPT-SAME}.$$

Hence, ρ is a many-one reduction from ACCEPT-ALL to ACCEPT-SAME. □

Via the three reductions just presented, we may infer information about the non-inclusion of the discussed languages in the language classes presented. We summarize the results in the following theorem.

Theorem 2.8.15. *Each of the following languages is not coCE, and hence not computable:* AP, HP, ACCEPT-ALL, ACCEPT-SAME.

Proof. Remark 2.8.8 established that the language AP is not coCE. Theorems 2.8.13, 2.8.13, and 2.8.14 establish that AP $\leq_m$ HP, AP $\leq_m$ ACCEPT-ALL, and ACCEPT-ALL $\leq_m$ ACCEPT-SAME, respectively. By applying the second claim of Theorem 2.8.7 three times, we obtain that the languages HP, ACCEPT-ALL, and ACCEPT-SAME are not coCE. □

2.9 Rice's theorem

This section presents a generic theorem allowing one to deduce the non-computability of many languages, in one blow. In essence, this theorem shows the non-computability of deciding, given a DTM, anything interesting about the DTM's language. This theorem is named after Henry Gordon Rice, a mathematician who published it in the early 1950s.

Fix an alphabet Σ over which strings and languages will be formed. We define a **property** of the CE languages to be a mapping $\mathcal{P}$ that assigns each CE language either the value 0 or 1; notationally, for each CE language B, we have $\mathcal{P}(B) = 0$ or $\mathcal{P}(B) = 1$. When $\mathcal{P}(B) = 1$, we say that the property $\mathcal{P}$ **holds** on B. A property $\mathcal{P}$ of the CE languages is called **nontrivial** if there exist CE languages D_0, D_1 such that $\mathcal{P}(D_0) = 0$ and $\mathcal{P}(D_1) = 1$; that is, a property $\mathcal{P}$ is nontrivial if it does not map all CE languages to the same value.

Example 2.9.1. Let $\mathcal{F}$ be the property of *finiteness*; that is, $\mathcal{F}$ holds on a CE language B if and only if B is finite. Observe that $\mathcal{F}$ is nontrivial, for $\emptyset$ and Σ^* are CE languages such that $\mathcal{F}(\emptyset) = 1$ and $\mathcal{F}(\Sigma^*) = 0$. ◇

Example 2.9.2. Let $\mathcal{C}$ be the property of being computable, so that $\mathcal{C}$ holds on a CE language B if and only if B is computable. The property $\mathcal{C}$ is nontrivial: in this chapter, we saw both examples of computable languages (in Section 2.1) and examples of non-computable languages (starting from Section 2.4).   ◇

Theorem 2.9.3 (Rice's theorem). *Let $\mathcal{P}$ be a nontrivial property of the CE languages. The following language is not computable:*

$$L_{\mathcal{P}} = \{\ulcorner M \urcorner \mid M \text{ is a DTM such that the property } \mathcal{P} \text{ holds on } L(M)\}.$$

In this theorem statement, the necessity of assuming that the property $\mathcal{P}$ is nontrivial should be apparent: in the case that $\mathcal{P}$ is always equal to 0, the language $L_{\mathcal{P}}$ is the empty set, which is computable; in the case that $\mathcal{P}$ is always equal to 1, the language $L_{\mathcal{P}}$ is the set containing all DTM encodings, which is computable (recall Proposition 2.2.4).

We underscore that this theorem only applies directly to languages of the form $L_{\mathcal{P}}$; such a language contains only DTM encodings as elements. Whether or not a DTM encoding $\ulcorner M \urcorner$ is included in a language $L_{\mathcal{P}}$ depends only on the *language $L(M)$* of M: for any property $\mathcal{P}$, two DTMs sharing the same language will either both be included in $L_{\mathcal{P}}$ or both be excluded from $L_{\mathcal{P}}$.

Proof of Theorem 2.9.3. We first prove the theorem under the assumption that $\mathcal{P}(\emptyset) = 0$. We present a many-one reduction from SAP to $L_{\mathcal{P}}$. Since $\mathcal{P}$ is assumed to be nontrivial, there exists a CE language B such that $\mathcal{P}(B) = 1$. Fix M_B to be a DTM such that $L(M_B) = B$.

Define σ to be the computable function that, given a string $\ulcorner M \urcorner$ where M is a DTM, outputs the encoding $\ulcorner M' \urcorner$ of a DTM M' that behaves as follows. On an input string x, the DTM M' performs the following two-stage process:

Stage 1. Run M on $\ulcorner M \urcorner$. If this computation rejects, then M' rejects; if this computation accepts, then proceed to stage 2.

Stage 2. Run M_B on x. If this computation rejects, then M' rejects; if this computation accepts, then M' accepts.

In accordance with Remark 2.8.5, we neglect to define σ on strings that are not DTM encodings.

We now make two observations, accompanied with justifications, which will allow us to argue that this function σ is a many-one reduction from SAP to $L_{\mathcal{P}}$.

- If $\ulcorner M \urcorner \notin$ SAP, then $L(M') = \emptyset$.
  Justification: suppose $\ulcorner M \urcorner \notin$ SAP; then M, when run on input $\ulcorner M \urcorner$, either loops or rejects. By the description of M', it follows that on any input, M' will loop or reject (respectively), never entering stage 2. So, it holds that $L(M') = \emptyset$.

- If $\ulcorner M \urcorner \in$ SAP, then $L(M') = B$.
  Justification: suppose $\ulcorner M \urcorner \in$ SAP; then M accepts input $\ulcorner M \urcorner$. So, the DTM M' will enter stage 2, and will accept an input x if and only if M_B accepts x. It follows that $L(M') = L(M_B) = B$.

From these observations, we obtain the following.

- If $\ulcorner M \urcorner \notin$ SAP, then $L(M') = \emptyset$, and so $\ulcorner M' \urcorner \notin L_{\mathcal{P}}$.
- If $\ulcorner M \urcorner \in$ SAP, then $L(M') = B$, and so $\ulcorner M' \urcorner \in L_{\mathcal{P}}$.

Hence, we have that σ is a many-one reduction from SAP to $L_{\mathcal{P}}$. Since SAP is not computable (by Corollary 2.5.5), we obtain by Theorem 2.8.7 that $L_{\mathcal{P}}$ is not computable.

We have established the theorem under the assumption that $\mathcal{P}(\emptyset) = 0$. We next consider the case that $\mathcal{P}(\emptyset) = 1$. In this case, since $\mathcal{P}$ is nontrivial, there exists a CE language B such that $\mathcal{P}(B) = 0$. Fix M_B to be a DTM such that $L(M_B) = B$. We claim that the computable function σ defined above is a many-one reduction from $\overline{\text{SAP}}$ to $L_{\mathcal{P}}$. Indeed, by the observations above, we obtain the following.

- If $\ulcorner M \urcorner \in \overline{\text{SAP}}$, then $L(M') = \emptyset$, and so $\ulcorner M' \urcorner \in L_{\mathcal{P}}$.
- If $\ulcorner M \urcorner \notin \overline{\text{SAP}}$, then $L(M') = B$, and so $\ulcorner M' \urcorner \notin L_{\mathcal{P}}$.

Thus, the claim holds. Since $\overline{\text{SAP}}$ is not computable (by Theorem 2.4.1), we obtain by Theorem 2.8.7 that $L_{\mathcal{P}}$ is not computable. $\square$

Remark 2.9.4. We previously established that the language ACCEPT-ALL is not computable, in Theorem 2.8.15. We can also derive directly from Theorem 2.9.3 that the language ACCEPT-ALL is not computable; this can be done by invoking this theorem on the property that holds only on Σ^*, the set of all strings. $\diamond$

Remark 2.9.5. The proof of Theorem 2.9.3 transparently reveals that, whenever $\mathcal{P}$ is a nontrivial property of the CE languages,

$$\mathcal{P}(\emptyset) = 0 \text{ implies SAP} \leq_m L_{\mathcal{P}} \quad \text{and} \quad \mathcal{P}(\emptyset) = 1 \text{ implies } \overline{\text{SAP}} \leq_m L_{\mathcal{P}}.$$

Thus, via Corollary 2.5.5 and Theorem 2.8.7, when $\mathcal{P}(\emptyset) = 0$, the language $L_{\mathcal{P}}$ is not coCE; and, when $\mathcal{P}(\emptyset) = 1$, the language $L_{\mathcal{P}}$ is not CE. $\diamond$

2.10 Exercises and notes

Exercise 2.10.1. For the DTM of Example 2.1.3, give traces of the computations of this DTM on the string *aaa* and on the string *aab*. That is, give an ordered list showing all of the configurations that this DTM passes through when *aaa* is the input string, and likewise for the string *aab*. $\diamond$

Note 2.10.2: On the finiteness of DTM state sets. One might approximately conceive of a DTM as a DFA having read/write access to an infinite-size storage space, namely, an infinite one-dimensional tape. In moving from the DFA model to the DTM model, the requirement that the state set be finite is retained, and it is crucial not to confuse this with the infinity of the DTM's storage. Recall the effect of modifying even the DFA model to permit an infinite state set (explored in Exercise 1.9.8): every language becomes definable. Making the analogous change to the DTM model also causes every language to be definable—in fact, by a DTM that only reads each input symbol once, and never makes any change to its tape. ◇

Note 2.10.3. In computer programming terms, the requirement that a DTM's state set be *finite* corresponds to the requirement that a computer program consist of a *finite* list of instructions! This is fairly visible from the simulations given to justify Theorems 2.7.13 and 2.7.14: a DTM with an infinite state set would translate to a RAM with an infinite sequence of instructions, and vice versa. ◇

Note 2.10.4: Building DTMs. In the following exercises, when it is requested that you *give* a DTM, you should fully specify all parts of the DTM. ◇

Exercise 2.10.5. Give a halting DTM, with $\Sigma = \{a, b\}$, that decides the language

$$\{x \in \{a, b\}^* \mid x \text{ is a palindrome}\}.$$

◇

Exercise 2.10.6. Give a halting DTM, with input alphabet $\Sigma = \{a, b\}$, that decides the language $\{a^i b^j \mid i \geq j\}$. ◇

Exercise 2.10.7. For each of the following languages over $\Sigma = \{a, b\}$, give a halting DTM that decides it.

1. $\{a^{2n} b^n \mid n \geq 0\}$.
2. $\{a^{n^2} b^n \mid n \geq 0\}$.
3. $\{a^{2^n} b^n \mid n \geq 0\}$. ◇

Exercise 2.10.8. For each of the following languages over $\Sigma = \{a, b\}$, give a halting DTM that decides it.

1. $\{x \in \{a, b\}^* \mid \#_a(x) = \#_b(x)\}$.
2. $\{x \in \{a, b\}^* \mid \#_a(x) > \#_b(x)\}$.
3. $\{x \in \{a, b\}^* \mid \#_a(x) = 2\#_b(x)\}$.
4. $\{x \in \{a, b\}^* \mid \#_a(x) > 2\#_b(x)\}$.
5. $\{x \in \{a, b\}^* \mid \#_a(x) = \#_b(x)^2\}$.
6. $\{x \in \{a, b\}^* \mid \#_a(x) = 2^{\#_b(x)}\}$. ◇

Exercise 2.10.9. Let $\Sigma = \{1\}$. For each of the following functions, give a DTM that computes it.

1. The function $f: \Sigma^* \to \Sigma^*$ defined by $f(1^n) = 1^{2n}$.
2. The function $f: \Sigma^* \to \Sigma^*$ defined by $f(1^n) = 1^{n^2}$.
3. The function $f: \Sigma^* \to \Sigma^*$ defined by $f(1^n) = 1^{2^n}$. ◇

Exercise 2.10.10: Delimiting a DTM's input. In designing DTMs, it is sometimes convenient to delimit where the input string *begins*, by inserting, before the input string, a symbol that is not in the input alphabet. Let Σ be an alphabet. Give a DTM M with input alphabet Σ such that, for each $x \in \Sigma^*$, it holds that $[s, x \sqcup ..., 1] \vdash_M^* [t, \sqcup x \sqcup ..., 1]$. That is, on any input string, the DTM in effect inserts a blank symbol before the input string, and halts at the leftmost cell.   ◇

Exercise 2.10.11. This exercise asks you to present a DTM M with input alphabet Σ that undoes what the DTM of Exercise 2.10.10 did. Present a DTM that, when initiated on a tape that begins with a blank symbol, in effect deletes this blank symbol. Precisely, let Σ be an alphabet; give a DTM M with input alphabet Σ such that, for each $x \in \Sigma^*$, it holds that $[s, \sqcup x \sqcup ..., 1] \vdash_M^* [t, x \sqcup ..., 1]$.   ◇

Exercise 2.10.12: Duplicating strings. Let Σ be an alphabet, and let $f \colon \Sigma^* \to \Sigma^*$ be the function defined by $f(x) = xx$; give a DTM that computes this function.   ◇

Exercise 2.10.13: Converting a DFA to a DTM. Argue Proposition 2.1.18; show how to construct, from any DFA $M = (Q, \Sigma, s, T, \delta)$, a halting DTM M' such that $L(M') = L(M)$. In particular, precisely give all 7 components of such a DTM M', and provide an explanation as to why its language is equal to that of the DFA M. Hint: this can be carried out by generalizing the construction in Example 2.1.13.   ◇

Exercise 2.10.14: Right-moving Turing machines. Let us say that a DTM $M = (Q, \Sigma, \Gamma, s, t, r, \delta)$ is *right-moving* if, for each $q \in Q \setminus \{t, r\}$ and $a \in \Gamma$, it holds that the third entry of $\delta(q, a)$ is equal to $+1$; that is, the transition function only specifies $+1$ as the direction of movement. Likewise, let us say that an NTM $M = (Q, \Sigma, \Gamma, s, t, r, \Delta)$ is *right-moving* if, for each $q \in Q \setminus \{t, r\}$ and $a \in \Gamma$, it holds that the third entry of each element in the set $\Delta(q, a)$ is equal to $+1$. Prove the following statements:

1. For any DTM M that is right-moving, the language $L(M)$ is regular.
2. For any NTM M that is right-moving, the language $L(M)$ is regular.   ◇

Exercise 2.10.15: Characteristic functions. Assume that Σ is an alphabet containing the symbols 0 and 1. The *characteristic function* $\chi_B \colon \Sigma^* \to \{0, 1\}$ of a language B is the function defined by the rule $\chi_B(x) = 1 \Leftrightarrow x \in B$. Argue that a language B over Σ is computable if and only if its *characteristic function* $\chi_B \colon \Sigma^* \to \{0, 1\}$ is computable.   ◇

Exercise 2.10.16: Halting versus non-halting. It was explained that the definition of *computably enumerable* is based on the distinction between acceptance and non-acceptance. This exercise shows that the computably enumerable languages could alternatively be defined based on the distinction between halting and non-halting. Prove the following statement: a language B (over alphabet Σ) is CE if and only if there exists a DTM M such that, for each string $x \in \Sigma^*$, it holds that $x \in B \Leftrightarrow M$ halts on x.   ◇

Exercise 2.10.17: A bijective encoding of the natural numbers. Let $\Sigma = \{0, 1\}$. For each string $y \in \Sigma^*$, let $\text{nat}(y)$ denote the natural number having y as a base 2 representation.

As examples, $\mathrm{nat}(1) = 1$, $\mathrm{nat}(10) = 2$, and $\mathrm{nat}(11) = 3$. Prove that the mapping $h\colon \Sigma^* \to \mathbb{N}$ defined by $h(x) = \mathrm{nat}(1x) - 1$ is a bijection between Σ^* and $\mathbb{N}$. $\diamond$

Exercise 2.10.18: Closure under concatenation. In this exercise, you are asked to prove the closure under concatenation of this chapter's introduced language classes.

1. Prove that, when B and C are computable languages, the language $B \cdot C$ is also computable.
2. Prove that, when B and C are CE languages, the language $B \cdot C$ is also CE.
3. Prove that, when B and C are coCE languages, the language $B \cdot C$ is also coCE. $\diamond$

Exercise 2.10.19: Closure under star. This exercise asks you to prove the closure under star of this chapter's introduced language classes.

1. Prove that, when B is a computable language, the language B^* is also computable.
2. Prove that, when B is a CE language, the language B^* is also CE.
3. Prove that, when B is a coCE language, the language B^* is also coCE. $\diamond$

Exercise 2.10.20: Differences of languages. For each of the following assertions, state if it is true or false, and prove your answer.

1. For any CE language A and any computable language B, it holds that $A \setminus B$ is CE.
2. For any computable language A and any CE language B, it holds that $A \setminus B$ is CE. $\diamond$

Exercise 2.10.21: CE languages as projections. Here, we give an alternative characterization of the CE languages; we show that each CE language can be obtained as the projection of a computable language. Prove that a language B is CE if and only if there exists a computable language R such that $B = \{x \mid \exists y \in \Sigma^* \text{ such that } \langle x, y \rangle \in R\}$. $\diamond$

Exercise 2.10.22: Computable partial functions. In this exercise, we see further characterizations of the CE languages. A *partial function* $f\colon \Sigma^* \to \Sigma^*$ may be defined on some strings in Σ^*, but undefined on other strings. Let us say that a partial function $f\colon \Sigma^* \to \Sigma^*$ is **computable** when there exists a DTM M such that, for all $x \in \Sigma^*$:

- If f is defined on x, then $[s, x \sqcup \ldots, 1] \vdash_M^* [t, f(x) \sqcup \ldots, 1]$.
- If f is not defined on x, then M loops on x.

Prove the following statements.

1. A language B over Σ is CE if and only if there exists a computable partial function $f\colon \Sigma^* \to \Sigma^*$ such that $B = \{x \mid x \in \Sigma^* \text{ and } f \text{ is defined on } x\}$.
2. A language B over Σ is CE if and only if there exists a computable partial function $f\colon \Sigma^* \to \Sigma^*$ such that $B = \{f(x) \mid x \in \Sigma^* \text{ and } f \text{ is defined on } x\}$. $\diamond$

Exercise 2.10.23. Prove that a partial function $f\colon \Sigma^* \to \Sigma^*$ is computable if and only if the language $\{\langle x, f(x) \rangle \mid x \in \Sigma^* \text{ and } f \text{ is defined on } x\}$ is CE. $\diamond$

Exercise 2.10.24: Enumerating CE languages. This exercise presents yet another characterization of the CE languages. Prove that a nonempty language B is CE if and only if there exists a computable function f such that $B = \{f(x) \mid x \in \Sigma^*\}$. Note that, when this condition holds, a machine that computes f can be thought of as enumerating the elements of B; this exercise thus provides something of a justification for the nomenclature *computably enumerable*.   ◇

Exercise 2.10.25. Let us say that a function $f: \Sigma^* \to \Sigma^*$ is **length-monotone** if for all strings $x, y \in \Sigma^*$, it holds that $|x| \leq |y|$ implies $|f(x)| \leq |f(y)|$. Prove that a nonempty language B is computable if and only if there exists a length-monotone computable function f such that $B = \{f(x) \mid x \in \Sigma^*\}$. (This exercise is a variation of Exercise 2.10.24.)   ◇

Exercise 2.10.26: Contrarian subsets. Prove the following statements.

1. Each infinite computable language has a subset that is not computable.
2. Each infinite CE language has an infinite subset that is computable.   ◇

Exercise 2.10.27: CE languages forming a partition. Let Σ be an alphabet, let $k \geq 2$, and suppose that $B_1, ..., B_k \subseteq \Sigma^*$ are languages that *partition* Σ^*, by which it is meant that the union $B_1 \cup \cdots \cup B_k$ is equal to Σ^*, and each pair of sets B_i, B_j (with $i \neq j$) has an empty intersection. Prove that if each of the languages B_i is CE, then each of the languages B_i is computable. (This exercise can be viewed as a generalization of Theorem 2.5.6.)   ◇

Note 2.10.28: Completeness. Fix an alphabet Σ over which strings and languages are formed, for the purposes of this note. Example 2.8.4 gave a reduction from a particular CE language to the language AP. It turns out that *every* CE language (over Σ) reduces to the language AP, and hence that AP is in a sense universal among the CE languages. Here is why. Let B be an arbitrary CE language. Then, there exists a DTM M_B such that $L(M_B) = B$. The function f defined by $f(x) = \langle \ulcorner M_B \urcorner, x \rangle$ is a many-one reduction from B to AP: for any string x, it holds that

$$x \in B \quad \Leftrightarrow \quad M_B \text{ accepts } x \quad \Leftrightarrow \quad \langle \ulcorner M_B \urcorner, x \rangle \in \mathsf{AP}.$$

This universality allows us to *characterize* the CE languages in terms of the language AP and the notion of many-one reduction: a language B is CE if and only if B many-one reduces to AP. The forward direction was just argued; the backward direction follows from the fact that AP is CE and Theorem 2.8.7.

In the next chapter, we will re-encounter and study this phenomenon of characterizing a class of languages in terms of a single member language to which each language in the class reduces. Indeed, this phenomenon, known as *completeness*, will take center stage in our study of complexity theory.   ◇

Example 2.10.29. Fix an alphabet Σ. Prove that a language B over Σ is CE if and only if B many-one reduces to SAP. Here, we assume that each DTM encoding is over the alphabet Σ, so that SAP is also over the alphabet Σ. (Note 2.10.28 showed that an analogous result held, for AP in place of SAP.) ◇

Note 2.10.30: On reducing to trivial languages. We previously suggested (in Note 1.9.5) that, relative to a language Σ, the trivial languages $\emptyset$ and Σ^* can be regarded as the simplest languages, from our point of view. These languages are very restrictive in terms of permitting reductions from other languages: it is readily verified that the only language that many-one reduces to $\emptyset$ is $\emptyset$ itself, and likewise the only language that many-one reduces to Σ^* is Σ^* itself. Indeed, these languages often need to be left behind when proving general statements about many-one reducibility; this phenomenon is witnessed in Exercises 2.10.31 and 2.10.32, which follow. ◇

Exercise 2.10.31. As a complement to Note 2.10.30, this exercise asks one to show that— other than the two languages discussed in that note—*any* language admits a reduction from a computable language. Prove that, for any computable language B and any language C that is nontrivial, it holds that $B \leq_m C$. ◇

Exercise 2.10.32: Equivalence from reducibility. Fix an alphabet Σ; define $\equiv_m$ as the binary relation, on languages over Σ, where $B \equiv_m C$ if and only if $B \leq_m C$ and $C \leq_m B$.

1. Prove that $\equiv_m$ is an equivalence relation.
2. Let B be any nontrivial computable language. Prove that $B \equiv_m C$ if and only if C is a nontrivial computable language.

The second part establishes that the class of all nontrivial computable languages forms an equivalence class of the equivalence relation $\equiv_m$. We can observe that each nontrivial language that is finite or cofinite belongs to this equivalence class. (Each such language is regular by Exercise 1.9.7, and is hence computable.) ◇

Exercise 2.10.33. Prove that the relation $\leq_m$ is not symmetric on nontrivial languages, that is, that there exist nontrivial languages B and C such that $B \leq_m C$ holds, but $C \leq_m B$ does not hold. ◇

Exercise 2.10.34: Marked unions. When B and C are languages over $\Sigma = \{0, 1\}$, define their **marked union**, denoted by $B \dot\cup C$, to be the language $\{0x \mid x \in B\} \cup \{1y \mid y \in C\}$. Prove that, for any languages B, C, and D, the relationship $B \dot\cup C \leq_m D$ holds if and only if both of the relationships $B \leq_m D$ and $C \leq_m D$ hold. ◇

Exercise 2.10.35: Reachable states. Let us say that a state q of a DTM M is **reachable** if there exists an input string x such that, during the computation of M on x, the state q is entered. Define E as the language

$$\{\langle \ulcorner M \urcorner, \ulcorner q \urcorner \rangle \mid M \text{ is a DTM, and } q \text{ is a reachable state of } M\}.$$

Prove that the language E is not computable. (Hint: one way to proceed is to give a reduction that always outputs pairs of the form $\langle \ulcorner M \urcorner, \ulcorner t \urcorner \rangle$, where M is a DTM and t is its accept state.)   ◇

Note 2.10.36: Reachable code. The computer programming analog of a reachable DTM state is *reachable code*—that is, code for which there exists an input under which the code is executed. Relative to any common programming language, Exercise 2.10.35 implies the non-computability of deciding, given a computer program and a line of code, whether the line of code is reachable. This is because each DTM can be computably converted to a computer program where there is a group of instructions for each state of the DTM, and the first instruction in such a group is reached under an input if and only if the corresponding DTM state is reached under the input. (Indeed, the justification of Theorem 2.7.13 can be viewed as providing such a conversion.)

This non-computability result is often read as indicating the impossibility of performing perfect code optimization: non-reachable code can clearly be removed without affecting functionality, but detecting it is not computable in general!   ◇

Exercise 2.10.37: Evenly-CE languages. Say that a language B is *evenly-CE* if there exists a computable language R of pairs such that the following holds:

- For each string x, the set R_x, defined as $\{y \mid \langle x, y \rangle \in R\}$, is finite.
- For each string x, it holds that $x \in B$ if and only if the size $|R_x|$ is an even number.

Show the following results.

1. Prove that each CE language is an evenly-CE language.
2. Prove that the evenly-CE languages are closed under complementation; that is, if B is evenly-CE, then $\overline{B}$ is also evenly-CE.
3. Prove that the evenly-CE languages are closed under intersection; that is, if B and C are evenly-CE, then $B \cap C$ is also evenly-CE.   ◇

Exercise 2.10.38: Categorizing languages. Consider the following languages.

1. Define the *rejection problem*, denoted by RP, to be the language
$$\{\langle \ulcorner M \urcorner, x \rangle \mid M \text{ is a DTM that rejects } x\}.$$

2. Define the *self-rejection problem*, denoted by SRP, to be the language
$$\{\ulcorner M \urcorner \mid M \text{ is a DTM that rejects } \ulcorner M \urcorner\}.$$

3. Say that a DTM M *left-halts* on a string x if, when run on that string, it halts at the leftmost location; precisely, if there exists a halting configuration $[q, \tau, \ell]$ such that $\alpha_x \vdash_M^* [q, \tau, \ell]$ and $\ell = 1$. Here, α_x denotes the initial configuration of M on x. Define the *left-halting problem*, denoted by LHP, to be the language
$$\{\langle \ulcorner M \urcorner, x \rangle \mid M \text{ is a DTM that left-halts on } x\}.$$

4. Define HALT-ALL to be the language

$$\{\ulcorner M \urcorner \mid M \text{ is a halting DTM}\}.$$

That is, the encoding $\ulcorner M \urcorner$ of a DTM M is included in HALT-ALL if and only if M halts on all strings.

5. Define ACCEPTS-DOZEN to be the language

$$\{\ulcorner M \urcorner \mid L(M) \text{ contains exactly 12 strings}\}.$$

6. Define ACCEPTS-DOZEN-PLUS to be the language

$$\{\ulcorner M \urcorner \mid L(M) \text{ contains 12 or more strings}\}.$$

7. Define ACCEPTS-ACCEPTS-DOZEN-PLUS to be the language

$$\{\ulcorner M \urcorner \mid L(M) = \text{ACCEPTS-DOZEN-PLUS}\}.$$

For each of these languages, do the following.

- Prove that the language is not computable.
- State if the language is CE, and prove your answer.
- State if the language is coCE, and prove your answer. ◇

Exercise 2.10.39: Busy beavers. This exercise is based on a sequence of numbers called the *busy beaver* numbers. For $n \geq 1$, the nth busy beaver number is defined as the maximum number of steps taken by an n-state deterministic Turing machine whose tape alphabet contains the blank symbol and one other symbol, when invoked on a tape having only blank symbols. The classical definition of these numbers uses a tape that is infinite in both directions, and does not include the accept state or the reject state in the count n; however, we can formalize a function that is based on the busy beaver numbers using DTMs as we have defined them, and which retains the interesting properties of the busy beaver numbers.

Set $\Sigma = \{1\}$ and $\Gamma = \{1, \sqcup\}$. Let $b \colon \Sigma^* \to \Sigma^*$ be the function where $b(\epsilon) = b(1) = \epsilon$, and where for each $n \geq 2$, the value $b(1^n)$ is defined to be 1^m, where m is the maximum number of transitions made by an n-state DTM on the empty string. Here, the maximum is taken over all n-state DTMs that halt on the empty string, and that have input alphabet Σ and tape alphabet Γ.

Prove that there is no computable function g greater than b; that is, prove that there is no computable function $g \colon \Sigma^* \to \Sigma^*$ where for each $n \geq 0$, it holds that $|b(1^n)| \leq |g(1^n)|$. This in particular implies that the function $b \colon \Sigma^* \to \Sigma^*$ is itself not computable. ◇

Note 2.10.40: Gödel incompleteness via computability theory. Using our development in this chapter, we can prove a version of *Gödel's first incompleteness theorem*. This meta-mathematical theorem concerns the notion of a *formal system*, which provides a way of proving mathematical statements. We say that a formal system is *consistent* if it does not prove both a statement and its negation, and *complete* if, for any statement, it proves either the statement or its negation. In brief, Gödel's first incompleteness theorem (in its usual presentation) holds that any formal system that is consistent cannot be complete—so long as it is sufficiently rich to make enough *arithmetic* statements. In our version here, we use a stand-in for this clause about arithmetic statements: we assume that each formal system is expressive enough to make statements about DTM acceptance, and in this way, exploit our knowledge of computability theory. A precise development follows.

Let Σ be an alphabet that includes the $\neg$ symbol. Define a **formal system** to be a computable language S where each element thereof is a pair $\langle x, \pi \rangle$ where x and π are strings over Σ. We assume that each formal system has, associated to it, a language $W \subseteq \Sigma^*$ of **statements**, and that when y is a statement, $\neg y$ is as well; the statement $\neg y$ is intended to have a truth value equal to the negation of that of the statement y. We write $\vdash_S x$ when x is a statement such that there exists $\pi \in \Sigma^*$ having $\langle x, \pi \rangle \in S$; when this holds, π is conceived of as a proof that x is true. We write $\nvdash_S x$ to indicate that $\vdash_S x$ does not hold.

Let S be a formal system.

- We say that S is **expressive** when there exists a computable function $h \colon \Sigma^* \to \Sigma^*$ where, for each DTM M, the string $h(\ulcorner M \urcorner)$ is a statement such that

$$\vdash_S h(\ulcorner M \urcorner) \quad \Leftrightarrow \quad \ulcorner M \urcorner \in \mathsf{SAP}.$$

Intuitively, this condition says that S is rich enough to be able to provide accurate statements about the acceptance of DTMs.

- We say that S is **consistent** when, for each statement x, at least one of $\vdash_S x$ and $\vdash_S \neg x$ fails to hold, that is, it is not the case that both hold.

- We say that S is **complete** when, for each statement x, either $\vdash_S x$ or $\vdash_S \neg x$ holds.

Note that the conditions of *consistency* and *completeness* are readily achieved in isolation: a formal system S where $\vdash_S y$ does not hold for any statement y—that is, which does not prove anything—is consistent; on the other extreme, a formal system S where $\vdash_S y$ holds for every statement y—that is, which proves everything—is complete.

We establish the following claim: *If S is an expressive and consistent formal system, then it is not complete; in particular, there exists a DTM M such that both $\nvdash_S h(\ulcorner M \urcorner)$ and $\nvdash_S \neg h(\ulcorner M \urcorner)$ hold.*

We argue this claim as follows. Define $A_\neg$ as the language

$$\{ \ulcorner M \urcorner \mid M \text{ is a DTM such that } \vdash_S \neg h(\ulcorner M \urcorner) \}.$$

We have $A_\neg \subseteq \overline{\mathsf{SAP}}$: when $\ulcorner M \urcorner \in A_\neg$, it holds that M is a DTM with $\vdash_S \neg h(\ulcorner M \urcorner)$; by the consistency of S, it follows that $\nvdash_S h(\ulcorner M \urcorner)$, and thus by the expressiveness of S, we obtain that $\ulcorner M \urcorner \notin \mathsf{SAP}$. It is readily verified, from the computability of h and S, that the language

$$R = \left\{ \langle \ulcorner M \urcorner, \pi \rangle \mid M \text{ is a DTM such that } \langle \neg h(\ulcorner M \urcorner), \pi \rangle \in S \right\}$$

is computable; by Exercise 2.10.21, the language $A_\neg$ is CE, as it is the projection of R. Since the language $\overline{\mathrm{SAP}}$ is not CE (recall Corollary 2.5.5), we obtain that $A_\neg$ is a proper subset of $\overline{\mathrm{SAP}}$. Thus, there exists a DTM M_0 such that $\ulcorner M_0 \urcorner \in \overline{\mathrm{SAP}} \setminus A_\neg$. From $\ulcorner M_0 \urcorner \notin A_\neg$, we obtain directly that $\nvdash_S \neg h(\ulcorner M_0 \urcorner)$, and from $\ulcorner M_0 \urcorner \in \overline{\mathrm{SAP}}$ and the expressiveness of S, we obtain that $\nvdash_S h(\ulcorner M_0 \urcorner)$. Thus, the DTM M_0 has the claimed properties. ◇

2.11 Bibliographic discussion

The Turing machine was introduced by Turing in a now-classic 1936 article (Turing 1936). Initial studies of the λ-calculus and its relevance to computation were given, starting in the 1930s, by Church (1932, 1936b, 1936a, 1941), Kleene (1935), and Turing (1936). The Church-Turing thesis is credited to articles of Church (1936b) and Turing (1936). Turing's article (1936) introduced the notion of *universal Turing machine*, as well as the use of diagonalization to exhibit non-computability results. Post (1944) performed an initial study of reductions in computability theory. Rice's theorem is due to Rice (1953). Gödel's incompleteness theorems, the first of which is considered in Note 2.10.40, are due to Gödel (1931). An anthology of Davis (2004) collects together a number of early articles on computability theory and on logical undecidability. General references on computability theory include the books by Rogers (1987) and Soare (2016).

3   Complexity Theory

When confronted with a language of interest, a first question is whether or not there exists an algorithm for deciding membership in the language; developing the ability to answer this question was the previous chapter's concern. Once the existence of an algorithm has been achieved, however, another consideration rears its head: whether or not there exists an efficient algorithm for the language, an algorithm that will provide answers to inputs within a reasonable amount of time. To be blunt about the matter, the value of invoking a computation is not clear if there is no guarantee that the computation will halt; but this value is also not clear if the computation will only halt after a time duration exceeding the lifespan of the persons interested in the computation's outcome!

In each of the previous two chapters, a class of languages was defined from a computational model and then explored: recall that the first chapter studied DFA and their corresponding languages, the regular languages; and that the second chapter studied halting DTMs and their corresponding languages, the computable languages. Continuing with this theme, this chapter formalizes a notion of efficient algorithm, and then studies the class of languages that admit efficient algorithms. The study of this class, however, is infused with a tantalizing enigma: there is a wide range of natural, relevant languages for which it is unknown whether or not they belong to this class.

In this chapter, starting from Section 3.5, it is assumed by default that each language is over the alphabet $\Sigma = \{0, 1\}$.

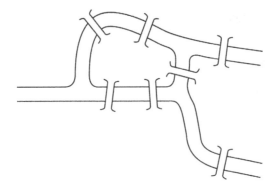

Figure 3.1.1. The seven bridges of the 18th-century town of Königsberg.

3.1 Two tales

In order to develop some first intuitions about how one should go about defining a notion of efficient algorithm, we present two tales. In each, a pair of languages is presented and discussed. Before narrating the tales, let us review and introduce the graph-theoretic notions that we will make use of in this chapter.

Graph-theoretic notions

We will use the term *graph* to refer to an undirected graph, and will use the term *digraph* to refer to a directed graph. When V is a set, we use $\binom{V}{2}$ to denote the set containing each size 2 subset of V; that is, $\binom{V}{2}$ is defined as the set $\{\{v, v'\} \mid v, v' \in V \text{ and } v \neq v'\}$. Recall that we define a **graph** as a pair (V, E) where V is a finite set and $E \subseteq \binom{V}{2}$, and that we define a **digraph** as a pair (V, E) where V is a finite set and $E \subseteq V \times V$. When (V, E) is a graph or digraph, the elements of V are called **vertices**, and the elements of E are called **edges**; when (V, E) is a digraph and v is a vertex in V, an edge of the form (v, w) is called an **outgoing edge** of v, and an edge of the form (u, v) is called an **incoming edge** of v. A vertex of a graph or digraph is **isolated** if it does not occur in any edge.

A **walk** in a graph $G = (V, E)$ is a sequence $v_1, \ldots, v_m \in V$ of vertices (with $m \geq 1$) such that for each $i \in \{1, \ldots, m-1\}$, it holds that $\{v_i, v_{i+1}\} \in E$; we define a **walk** in a digraph $G = (V, E)$ in the same way, but the condition that $\{v_i, v_{i+1}\} \in E$ is replaced by the condition that $(v_i, v_{i+1}) \in E$. In a graph or digraph, a walk $v_1, \ldots, v_m$ is **closed** if $v_m = v_1$, that is, if the walk concludes at its starting point; and a vertex v is **reachable** from a vertex u if there exists a walk beginning with u and ending with v. A graph or digraph is **connected** if every vertex is reachable from every other vertex.

Relative to a graph $G = (V, E)$, the **degree** of a vertex $v \in V$ is the number of edges that contain it, that is, $|\{e \in E \mid v \in e\}|$; and we use the term **triangle** to refer to three vertices where each pair forms an edge.

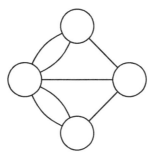

Figure 3.1.2. A graph-theoretic view of the land masses and bridges of Königsberg, which are shown in Figure 3.1.1. Each land mass is represented by a vertex, depicted by a circle, and each bridge is represented by an edge between the two vertices of the land masses that it connects. The presented object is technically a *multigraph*, wherein two vertices may have multiple edges between them.

3.1.1 Cycles in graphs

Our first tale begins in the 18th century, when the town of Königsberg in Prussia—which is now the city of Kaliningrad in Russia—was divided by a river and contained two islands. Seven bridges linked the land masses together, as depicted in Figure 3.1.1. It was popularly asked whether or not one could take a stroll that crossed each bridge exactly once. As was recognized by the mathematician Euler, the situation could be modeled graph-theoretically, by representing each land mass by a vertex and each bridge by an edge, as in Figure 3.1.2.

We here study a closely related notion, named after Euler. Whereas in Königsberg it was asked if there was a walk that traversed each edge once, we here ask about the existence of a *closed* walk that traverses each edge once, known as an *Eulerian cycle*. Formally, an **Eulerian cycle** in a graph $G = (V, E)$ is a closed walk $v_1, ..., v_m$ in G such that each edge in E appears exactly once in the list

$$\{v_1, v_2\}, \{v_2, v_3\}, ..., \{v_{m-1}, v_m\}.$$

Two example graphs are shown in Figure 3.1.3; in the left graph, we have that the walk $u_1, u_2, u_3, u_4, u_5, u_3, u_1$ is an Eulerian cycle (and there are others); in the right graph, as we will explain, there is no Eulerian cycle.

How can one tell if a given graph has an Eulerian cycle? Let us discuss the general question using the computational notions that we have been developing, by formalizing it as a language. Recalling that $\ulcorner G \urcorner$ denotes the string encoding of a graph, define

$$\text{EUL-CYCLE} = \{\ulcorner G \urcorner \mid G \text{ is a graph that has an Eulerian cycle}\}.$$

A first observation that we can make is that this language is most certainly computable; it is possible to design a halting DTM that, given a graph, examines all orderings of the edges, and accepts if and only if one of the orderings corresponds to an Eulerian cycle. This naive, exhaustive examination of all orderings is costly in terms of time: the number

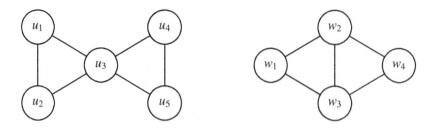

Figure 3.1.3. Two example graphs. The left graph consists of two triangles, $\{u_1, u_2, u_3\}$ and $\{u_3, u_4, u_5\}$, which share a vertex; the right graph consists of two triangles, $\{w_1, w_2, w_3\}$ and $\{w_2, w_3, w_4\}$ which share two vertices and thus an edge.

of orderings of an edge set E is $|E|$ factorial, denoted by $|E|!$; this quantity grows mercilessly and unmanageably as the number of edges $|E|$ increases. (Throughout this chapter, we use the ! notation to denote the factorial operation.)

Let us focus on connected graphs for the moment. Is there a faster method to determine if a given connected graph has an Eulerian cycle? Can we overcome the crude, brute-force examination of all edge orderings? Actually, we can—by exploiting the following characterization of the connected graphs having Eulerian cycles, a characterization that is considered one of the inaugural results of the field of graph theory!

Proposition 3.1.1. *A connected graph has an Eulerian cycle if and only if each vertex of the graph has even degree.*

The proposition's forward direction can be verified as follows: when $v_1, ..., v_m$ is an Eulerian cycle of a graph $G = (V, E)$, each occurrence of a vertex v in the vertex sequence $v_1, ..., v_{m-1}$ witnesses it being included in two edges in the edge sequence $\{v_1, v_2\}, \{v_2, v_3\}, ..., \{v_{m-2}, v_{m-1}\}, \{v_{m-1}, v_m\}$; since this latter list contains each edge in E exactly once, each vertex is included in an even number of edges. This direction implies that the graph on the right in Figure 3.1.3 has no Eulerian cycle: this graph has vertices of odd degree, namely, v_2 and v_3. This proposition's backward direction can be established by showing that, in the graph, if one takes a maximal-length walk that uses no edge more than once, such a walk must be an Eulerian cycle; we omit a full argument.

The proposition's characterization suggests a simple and faster algorithm for checking if a given connected graph has an Eulerian cycle: examine each vertex one by one; if a vertex with odd degree is encountered, reject the graph, and if no such vertex is encountered, accept the graph. In essence, this algorithm needs only consider and check each vertex once, *locally*; its behavior contrasts with that of the exhaustive algorithm, which examines all edge orderings, *globally*.

Let us now turn to consider a different type of cycle in a graph. Whereas an Eulerian cycle is a closed walk that traverses each *edge* exactly once, a *Hamiltonian cycle* is a closed walk that traverses each *vertex* exactly once. Formally, a **Hamiltonian cycle** in a graph or digraph $G = (V, E)$ is a closed walk $v_1, ..., v_m$ in G such that each vertex in V appears exactly once in the list $v_1, ..., v_{m-1}$. Looking again at Figure 3.1.3, in the right graph, the walk w_1, w_2, w_4, w_3, w_1 is a Hamiltonian cycle, whereas in the left graph, it can be verified that there is no Hamiltonian cycle.

In order to investigate this notion computationally, let us define the language

$$\text{HAM-CYCLE} = \{\ulcorner G \urcorner \mid G \text{ is a graph that has a Hamiltonian cycle}\}.$$

As for the language EUL-CYCLE, it is straightforward to argue that the language HAM-CYCLE is computable; to check if a graph $G = (V, E)$ has a Hamiltonian cycle, one can exhaustively consider all orderings of the vertices, of which there are $|V|!$—again, a quantity that grows prohibitively out of control as the number of vertices $|V|$ increases. The notions of Eulerian cycle and Hamiltonian cycle seem to be of the same spirit, to be innocuous variations on the same theme. But to check if a given graph has a Hamiltonian cycle, is it possible to circumvent brute-force search, as was achieved for the notion of Eulerian cycle? For the moment, we ask the reader to ponder this.

3.1.2 Graph coloring

To begin our second tale, suppose that we have a set of persons, and want to split them up into k teams, subject to a condition: certain pairs of persons are not compatible, and should not be placed on the same team; these incompatible pairs are given as the edge set of a graph G, whose vertex set contains all persons under consideration.

Denote the teams using the numbers $1, ..., k$; what we are seeking, then, is a way of assigning each vertex of the graph to a team in a way that any two vertices v, v' forming an edge are not assigned to the same team. A successful assignment can be formalized as follows. Let $k \geq 1$; a k-**coloring** of a graph $G = (V, E)$ is a mapping $c: V \to \{1, ..., k\}$ such that each edge $\{v, v'\} \in E$ is **respected** in that $c(v) \neq c(v')$. Often, the elements of the set $\{1, ..., k\}$ are referred to as *colors*, or, in place of this set, a size k set of actual colors is used to define a k-*coloring*. Under this view, a k-coloring assigns each vertex to one of k colors, such that each edge's vertices are assigned to distinct colors. Let us say that a graph G is k-**colorable** if there exists a k-coloring of G. Observe that a k-coloring of a graph G can be viewed as an ℓ-coloring of G for each $\ell > k$, and hence if G is k-colorable, it is also ℓ-colorable for each value $\ell > k$. See Figure 3.1.4 for examples of graph colorings.

For each value $k \geq 1$, we inquire how difficult it is to decide if a given graph is k-colorable. Defining the following languages will allow us to address this issue; for each value $k \geq 1$, let

$$k\text{-COL} = \{\ulcorner G \urcorner \mid G \text{ is a } k\text{-colorable graph}\}.$$

Deciding if a graph is 1-colorable can be performed readily. There is only one potential 1-coloring of a graph—namely, the mapping that sends each vertex to the value 1. It is immediate from the definition of k-*coloring* that this mapping is a 1-coloring of a graph G

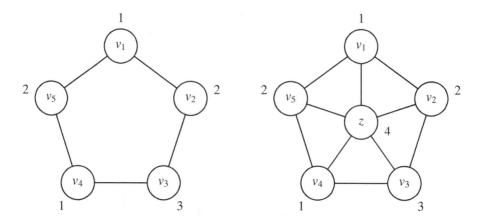

Figure 3.1.4. Two example graphs with colorings. The left graph is known as a 5-*cycle*, and the right graph is obtained from the left graph by adding a vertex z, along with edges between z and each other vertex. A 3-coloring of the left graph is indicated: next to each vertex is the color that the vertex is mapped to. A 4-coloring of the right graph is similarly indicated; this 4-coloring extends the coloring of the left graph. It is possible to verify that the left graph is not 2-colorable, and that the right graph is not 3-colorable.

if and only if G has no edges; hence, a graph is 1-colorable if and only if it has no edges—or put equivalently, if and only if every vertex in the graph is isolated.

Next, consider a value $k \geq 2$. One algorithm for deciding if an input graph $G = (V, E)$ has a k-coloring is to exhaustively examine each mapping $c \colon V \to \{1, \ldots, k\}$ as a candidate k-coloring. The number of such mappings, however, is equal to $k^{|V|}$; this quantity grows exponentially and prohibitively rapidly as $|V|$ increases, naturally prompting again the question of whether or not an exhaustive examination can be evaded.

There is, in fact, a relatively efficient algorithm for deciding if a graph is 2-colorable. Consider the following routine, which is applied to a graph:

- Arbitrarily pick an *initial vertex* u and a color $b \in \{1, 2\}$, and assign u to have the color b.
- Then, repeat the following until no further vertices can be assigned values:

  ◦ For any edge where exactly one vertex has been assigned a color, assign the other vertex to have the other color.

See Figure 3.1.5 for example executions of this routine.

After this routine has been performed, if there exists a **bad edge** where both vertices have been assigned the same color, we can conclude that the graph is not 2-colorable. This is because each time the routine assigned a color to a vertex other than the initial vertex, the choice was unique in that assigning the other color could not have possibly yielded a

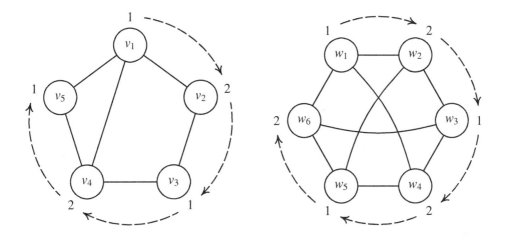

Figure 3.1.5. Example executions of a routine that helps to decide whether or not a graph is 2-colorable. In the left graph, the vertex v_1 is first assigned the color 1, after which the edges $\{v_1, v_2\}$, $\{v_2, v_3\}$, $\{v_3, v_4\}$, and $\{v_4, v_5\}$ are considered in sequence. Each time an edge is considered, one vertex therein has been assigned a color, and so the other vertex therein is assigned the other color. After the color of the vertex v_5 has been set, the edge $\{v_1, v_5\}$ is a bad edge in that both vertices have been assigned the same color; based on this bad edge, it can be concluded that the left graph has no 2-coloring. In the right graph, the vertex w_1 is first assigned the color 1, and then the edges $\{w_1, w_2\}$, $\{w_2, w_3\}$, $\{w_3, w_4\}$, $\{w_4, w_5\}$, and $\{w_5, w_6\}$ are considered in sequence. No bad edge is ever encountered, and so the assigned colors constitute a 2-coloring of the right graph.

2-coloring; and changing the particular choice of the initial vertex's color would only have the effect of swapping the symmetric roles of the two colors throughout the routine.

If there is no such *bad edge* after the routine has been performed, then it can be seen that the vertices that are reachable from the initial vertex u are those that have been assigned colors, and that each edge between these vertices consists of two vertices that have been assigned different colors. In this case, we hence can remove all such reachable vertices, and the edges between them, to obtain a smaller graph that is 2-colorable if and only if the original graph was; we can then iteratively apply the routine to the smaller graph. We thus obtain the following algorithm for deciding 2-colorability of a graph.

- Repeatedly perform the following, accepting if it results in an empty graph with no vertices:
  - Apply the routine given above.
  - If the routine results in a bad edge, then reject. Otherwise, remove each vertex that has been assigned a color, and each edge that contains any such vertex.

A salient point here is that, when a vertex is assigned a color by the algorithm, this assignment is irrevocable and binding in that the algorithm never recolors the vertex. That is, the algorithm builds up a 2-coloring by assigning one vertex at a time, but is committal in that it never modifies already made assignments. This algorithm's committal nature contrasts starkly with the brute-force character of exhaustively examining *all* candidate 2-colorings.

The reader is invited to ponder whether or not exhaustive examination can be overcome in deciding the property of *k*-colorability, when $k \geq 3$.

3.1.3   Outlook

We saw various languages, whose elements were graphs, that were readily classifiable as being computable—due to their having *exhaustive* algorithms that perform a brute-force, comprehensive consideration of all possibilities in a large, but finite, search space. For the properties of having an Eulerian cycle and of 2-colorability, we saw algorithms that circumvent a brute-force examination, and exploit structural features of the graphs under scrutiny. As will be discussed, these algorithms are, in a crucial and critical sense, faster than the exhaustive algorithms; they outpace and surpass the exhaustive algorithms along the important dimension of time. In the next sections, we present and develop a framework that, in effect, allows one to distinguish between languages that have time-efficient algorithms, and those that do not.

3.2   Polynomial-time computation

In this section, we formalize what it means for a Turing machine to be time-bounded; we then consider and begin to justify *polynomial* time bounds.

3.2.1   Time-bounded computation

Our first order of business is to define the amount of time that a halting Turing machine M uses on an input string x, a quantity that we denote by $\text{time}_M(x)$. Figures 3.2.1 and 3.2.2 illustrate the definition.

Definition 3.2.1. Let M be a halting DTM or a halting NTM with input alphabet Σ. We define the function $\text{time}_M \colon \Sigma^* \to \mathbb{N}$ as follows. Let $x \in \Sigma^*$ be a string, and let α_x denote the initial configuration of M on x.

- When M is a halting DTM, the value $\text{time}_M(x)$ is defined as the number of time steps used by the computation of M on the input string x.

  We consider the number of time steps used by a computation to be the number of configurations in the computation.[14] So formally, we define $\text{time}_M(x)$ as 1 plus the unique value k such that there exists a halting configuration γ with $\alpha_x \vdash_M^k \gamma$.

---

14. Measuring the time of a computation according to its number of configurations (as opposed to, say, its number of transitions) is a technical convention which will later be handy. This convention comes into play when we need to closely analyze Turing machine computations; this need arises, for example, in this chapter's Section 3.6, where we prove our first *NP-completeness* result.

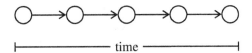

Figure 3.2.1. For a halting DTM, the time used on an input string x is the number of time steps before halting. Here, each circle represents a configuration; the leftmost circle is the initial configuration of the Turing machine on x, and an arrow from a configuration leads to a successor configuration thereof. A configuration with no outgoing arrows is understood to be a halting configuration.

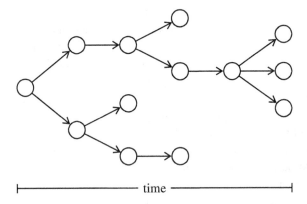

Figure 3.2.2. For a halting NTM, the time used on an input string is the maximum number of time steps used before halting, over all computations. This diagram is formed using the conventions given in Figure 3.2.1.

- When M is a halting NTM, the value $\text{time}_M(x)$ is defined as the maximum number of time steps used, over *all* computations of M on the input string x.

    Formally, we define $\text{time}_M(x)$ as $1 + k$, where k is the maximum value such that there exists a halting configuration γ with $\alpha_x \vdash_M^k \gamma$. ◇

Having defined the running time of a Turing machine on a single string, we want next to be able to upper bound the time that a Turing machine takes, over all input strings, in aggregate. To anticipate how we will do this, consider Turing machines that deal with graphs as inputs; one can often naturally describe the running time in terms of the number of vertices. As a concrete example of this, we above discussed a naive algorithm for the language HAM-CYCLE, and stated that it needs to examine $|V|!$ orderings, where $|V|$ is the size of the input graph's vertex set V; so, the time needed grows as a function of the graph size. One would indeed expect in general that larger input objects would require more computation time. The suggestion here is to measure running time in terms of the size of an input object—with more running time permitted on larger input objects. We follow this suggestion, which will lead to a theory that is both useable and useful.

Inputs to Turing machines are always ultimately strings. Typically, the larger an object is, the longer its encoding as a string will be. Hence, it is natural to upper bound the running time of a machine via a function of the input string length, as we formalize next.

Definition 3.2.2. Let M be a DTM or an NTM, and let $T\colon \mathbb{N} \to \mathbb{N}$ be a function. We say that M **runs within time** T if M is halting and it holds that $\text{time}_M(x) \le T(|x|)$, for each string $x \in \Sigma^*$.   ◇

Now that we can speak of a Turing machine running within time T, where T is a function on the natural numbers, let us ponder what class of such functions should be permitted in a reasonable, robust formulation of *efficient* computation. Certainly, an efficient computation should be allowed to read its entire input, and thus the class should contain the function $T(n) = n$. With the aim of arriving at a robust formulation, let us examine various ways of combining computations. We should consider as efficient the sequencing of one efficient computation on an input followed by another on the same input, and so the class should be closed under addition. We should also consider as efficient an efficient computation that, at each step, invokes another efficient computation as a subroutine, and so the class should be closed under multiplication. Finally, we should consider as efficient the invocation of an efficient computation on the result of another efficient computation, and so the class should be closed under composition. We are naturally led to the class of *polynomials*, which can be verified to be the smallest class of functions that contains all constants and that satisfies the stated properties.

For our purposes here, a **polynomial** is a function $P\colon \mathbb{N} \to \mathbb{N}$ such that $P(n)$ can be expressed as the finite sum of *terms*, where a **term** has the form cn^d with $c, d \in \mathbb{N}$. Three examples of polynomials are the functions $P_1, P_2, P_3\colon \mathbb{N} \to \mathbb{N}$ defined by $P_1(n) = n^2 + 3$; $P_2(n) = 5n^{17}$; and $P_3(n) = 14n^{10} + 7n^5 + 42$. Here, we define the **degree** of a term cn^d as 0 if $c = 0$, and as d otherwise; we extend this to define the **degree** of a polynomial as the maximum degree of its terms. As examples, the degrees of P_1, P_2, and P_3 are 2, 17, and 10, respectively. We use the term **linear polynomial** to refer to a degree 1 polynomial, and the term **quadratic polynomial** to refer to a degree 2 polynomial. We will sometimes tacitly use the fact that polynomials, as we have defined them, are *monotonic*: when P is a polynomial and $i, j \in \mathbb{N}$ are values such that $i \le j$, it holds that $P(i) \le P(j)$.

Definition 3.2.3. Let M be a DTM or an NTM; we say that M **runs within polynomial time** if there exists a polynomial $P\colon \mathbb{N} \to \mathbb{N}$ such that M runs within time P. We define a **polynomial-time DTM** to be a DTM that runs within polynomial time; likewise, we define a **polynomial-time NTM** to be an NTM that runs within polynomial time.   ◇

Remark 3.2.4. Let us consider so-called *exponential* functions; these include $f(n) = n!$, $f(n) = 2^n$, $f(n) = (1.01)^n$, and indeed any function $f(n) = c^n$ where c is a real number strictly greater than 1. It is known that such exponential functions, as well as their scalings by positive multiplicative factors, such as $f(n) = (0.0001) \cdot (1.01)^n$, always dominate polynomials in the limit. Precisely, for each such function $f(n)$ and any polynomial $P(n)$, there exists a value $C \in \mathbb{N}$ such that, for each value $i \geq C$, it holds that $f(i) > P(i)$; that is, this last inequality holds for all but finitely many values in $\mathbb{N}$.

Some such exponential functions appear frequently in the analysis of brute-force algorithms: as examples, $n!$ is number of ways to order n distinct items, whereas 2^n is the number of ways to assign one of two values to each of n items.

Consider again the presented algorithms for determining the existence of an Eulerian cycle and for deciding 2-colorability. These algorithms overcame exhaustive searching, and natural implementations of them will run within polynomial time. The notion of polynomial time hence provides us with a quantitative, formal instrument for differentiating between efficient algorithms and and exhaustive, brute-force algorithms.   ◇

Let us point out that the definition of *running within polynomial time* (Definition 3.2.3) is *asymptotic* in nature: if one knows just that a Turing machine runs within polynomial time, this does not permit making predictions about how much time the machine takes on input strings of any particular length. Rather, knowing this makes a statement about how the time used by the machine *scales*, in the limit, as input strings get larger and larger.

Let us also point out that the definition of *running within time T* (Definition 3.2.2) is *worst case* in nature, in that a Turing machine M runs within time T if, for *every* input x, the running time of M on x does not exceed $T(|x|)$. A natural question that may arise is whether or not these definitions can be relaxed so that one can speak of, for example, a Turing machine that runs within polynomial time on *typical* inputs, or *on average*. While such notions have been developed and studied in the research literature, they are often more complicated to cope with; indeed, their formalization suggests the need to define, relative to languages of interest, probability distributions over input strings—a weighty issue itself.

3.2.2   PTIME languages

Definitions and discussion

Whereas the halting DTM is widely taken to be a reasonable formalization of the notion of *algorithm*, the polynomial-time DTM is widely taken to be a reasonable formalization of the notion of *efficient algorithm*. The idea of formulating efficient computation via DTMs that run within polynomial time has its origins in and is credited to 1960s articles of Alan Cobham and Jack Edmonds. The following definitions give names to the languages and functions that the polynomial-time DTM model is able to decide and compute, respectively.

Definition 3.2.5. A language B is **PTIME** if there exists a polynomial-time DTM M such that $B = L(M)$.   ◇

Definition 3.2.6. A function $f: \Sigma^* \to \Sigma^*$ is **polynomial-time computable** if there exists a polynomial-time DTM that computes it.   ◇

We argued above that polynomials were a natural class of functions to permit for a formulation of efficiency; we here offer further defense that polynomial-time deterministic computation is a reasonable formulation of *efficient* computation.

An objection that one may raise to the given formulation is that the notion of *polynomial-time DTM* seems overpermissive: surely, one might say, a polynomial-time DTM that does not run within time P, for (say) any polynomial P of degree 1000, implements an algorithm that is not feasibly useable in practice, and consequently such DTMs should be excluded by the definition.

As a first response to this suggestion, which is in its own right a justification of the definition of polynomial time, we highlight the mathematical robustness of this definition. In addition to the pointed-out fact that the class of polynomials enjoys natural and relevant closure properties, the notion of polynomial time is known to be robust across changes in computational model: the languages that are PTIME would not change even if, in Definition 3.2.5, the DTM was replaced with another conventional computational model, such as the 8-tape DTM or the RAM (these two models were presented in Section 2.7). This *model independence* gives us confidence that the property of being PTIME is a basic, intrinsic property of languages—just as the robustness of the computable languages gave us confidence that the property of being computable was a timeless, fundamental property. Indeed, a language that has polynomial running time on one model may require a strictly larger polynomial on another model;[15] this suggests that truncating the class of all polynomials, to only permit some of them, would be an artificial, model-specific move.

Allowing the class of all polynomials also offers us other forms of independence. One is that the notion of *running within polynomial time* enjoys a certain imperviousness to changes in technology: for example, it remains the same under a new machine realization that runs two times faster—or any constant rate faster—than a previous one. In a similar fashion, this notion is not tied to any particular unit of time, in that it is not affected by multiplicatively scaling the unit of time used to measure computations: for example, if we define a *kilostep* to be a thousand steps, running within a polynomial number of kilosteps is the same as running within a polynomial number of steps. Additionally, this notion frees us from expending excessive attention on encoding methods of objects: as long as two encoding methods permit polynomial-time translations between each other, a set of encoded objects will be PTIME, or not, independently of the encoding method used. We

---

15. As a case in point, from the simulation given by Theorem 2.7.4, it can be verified that for any multitape DTM M running within time $T: \mathbb{N} \to \mathbb{N}$, there exists a quadratic (degree 2) polynomial Q and a single-tape DTM M' that runs within time $Q \circ T$ and outcome-simulates M. (Here, $Q \circ T$ denotes the composition of the two functions, defined as the mapping sending each $n \in \mathbb{N}$ to $Q(T(n))$.) That is, this simulation can be done with at most a quadratic slowdown. Interestingly enough, it can be proved that this quadratic slowdown is necessary and inherent: for the language of palindromes, we gave a 2-tape DTM that runs within linear time (that is, within time U for a linear polynomial U) in Example 2.7.2—but, it can be proved that *any* 1-tape DTM requires quadratic time!

do coarsen our perspective by blurring the distinction among different polynomials, stirring them all into the same soup, but in doing so, we arrive at deeper, more eternal questions.

Let us present another justification of polynomial-time deterministic computation as a formulation of efficient computation. This justification has a different character; it is of a post-hoc, empirical nature, and it is this: by and large, real-world evidence shows that natural languages that are classified to be in PTIME can be efficiently solved in practice, and conversely, natural languages that defy placement in PTIME tend to be difficult to cope with in practice. Indeed, natural languages that are shown to be in PTIME are, for the most part, shown to have algorithms whose running times can be upper bounded by reasonable, low-degree polynomials. In the analysis of algorithms, fast-growing polynomials, such as polynomials of degree 100 or more, tend not to arise; on the flip side, nor do slow-growing exponential functions, such as $(1.01)^n$.

We offered *prescriptive* justifications of our formulation, arguing that it is mathematically robust and mathematically useable, as well as *descriptive* justifications, defending it based on empirical experience. To be sure, the notion of *polynomial-time DTM* is ultimately a mathematical abstraction, and, in this capacity, serves as an idealized version of a real-world phenomenon—namely, efficient computation. As has been suggested, numerous criticisms can be leveled at this notion's ability to capture the phenomenon under focus; the research literature has certainly responded to some such criticisms by investigating refinements and variations of this notion. Nonetheless, this notion both allows for the development of a clean, resilient theory (as the reader will hopefully be convinced of by this chapter!) and has been evidenced to proficiently inform practical, real-world situations.

Remark 3.2.7. Throughout, we will tacitly use the fact that polynomials are themselves polynomial-time computable. By this, we mean that, for each polynomial $P \colon \mathbb{N} \to \mathbb{N}$ and for each alphabet Σ (assumed to contain 1 as a symbol), one has polynomial-time computability of the mapping sending each string $x \in \Sigma^*$ to the unary representation $1^{P(|x|)}$ of $P(|x|)$. This fact can be verified fairly straightforwardly, by using the result that pairs of numbers in unary representation can be added and multiplied in polynomial time. ◇

Examples and relationships

Let us now position the PTIME languages by providing examples thereof, and by comparing them with the classes of languages we have already seen. The following proposition furnishes numerous examples of PTIME languages, via the examples of regular languages that we have given.

Proposition 3.2.8. *Each language that is regular is also PTIME.*

We briefly argue Proposition 3.2.8 as follows. Each regular language can be decided by a DTM that moves right in each time step, simulating the transitions of a DFA for the language, until encountering a blank symbol, at which point the DTM transitions to its accept or reject state; this is shown in one particular case in Example 2.1.13. Such a DTM runs within time $T(n) = n + 2$, and hence is a polynomial-time DTM.

Let us point out that the converse to the just-given proposition does not hold.

Proposition 3.2.9. *There exists a language that is PTIME but not regular.*

Proposition 3.2.9 is witnessed by the language $\{a^n b^n \mid n \geq 0\}$. This language was proved to be not regular in Example 1.6.9. But this language is PTIME: a DTM M deciding this language is presented and discussed in Examples 2.1.3 and 2.1.11; it can be verified that this DTM M runs within *quadratic time*, that is, within time P for a quadratic (degree 2) polynomial P. (Exercise 3.10.5 calls for such a verification.)

Each PTIME language is the language of a DTM that runs within polynomial time, which by definition is a halting DTM; this yields the following fact.

Proposition 3.2.10. *Each language that is PTIME is also computable.*

Having established these basic relationships, our next objective is to give further examples of PTIME languages; before doing so, we briefly discuss encodings.

Remark 3.2.11. As suggested by the discussion in Section 2.2, the particular way in which mathematical objects are encoded as strings is typically immaterial for the issues that we want to study; natural encoding methods tend to behave equivalently for these issues. The reader may find it helpful to and is welcome to keep in mind some of the concrete encodings that have been presented. However, as our study progresses, we will appeal to the reader's judgment, and will even neglect to present concrete encoding methods for some of the objects to be encountered.

One assumption that we will make throughout is that, for each type of object discussed, the language consisting of all encodings is PTIME. This is verifiable for all of the encoding methods presented so far. Indeed, all of the languages and functions claimed to be computable in Section 2.2 are PTIME and polynomial-time computable, respectively.   ◇

We next present further examples of PTIME languages, along with justifications that they are indeed PTIME. We emphasize that each of our arguments that there exists a polynomial-time DTM (or NTM) will generally be high level, and will not delve into low-level implementation details—which in each case *could* be spelled out (if laboriously). Accordingly, in estimating running times, focus will be placed on quantifying the number of high-level operations.

Example 3.2.12. The language EUL-CYCLE is PTIME; this language was introduced in Section 3.1.1. We give a justification by describing, on a high level, a polynomial-time DTM whose language is EUL-CYCLE. We first observe that when a graph has an Eulerian cycle, every non-isolated vertex must appear in the cycle, and thus the non-isolated vertices must be mutually reachable, that is, each must be reachable from any other.

Consider a DTM that behaves as follows. On an input string x, the machine first checks to see if x is the encoding $\ulcorner G \urcorner$ of a graph having vertices; if it is not, the machine rejects. (This can be done within polynomial time, as mentioned in Remark 3.2.11.) Let $G = (V, E)$ denote the graph. The machine then checks if all vertices in V are isolated; if so, G trivially contains an Eulerian cycle, and the DTM accepts.

The machine then checks if the non-isolated vertices of the graph $G = (V, E)$ are mutually reachable. This can be performed by placing one non-isolated vertex v_0 into a set, and continually adding, to this set, any vertex that is adjacent to one in the set, until no more vertices can be added. The resulting set contains all vertices reachable from v_0. The machine rejects in the case that there is a non-isolated vertex that is not in the resulting set.

At this point, if the machine has not yet halted, removing the isolated vertices (which have degree 0) from the vertex set of G would result in a connected graph, so by Proposition 3.1.1, the graph G has an Eulerian cycle if and only if each vertex has even degree. Thus, the machine next considers each row r_i of the adjacency matrix; it scans each row once by looking at each symbol one time, and while doing so it keeps track of whether or not the number of 1s seen so far (in the row) is even or odd. If it encounters a row with an odd number of 1s, then the vertex corresponding to the row has odd degree, and the machine rejects; if no such row is encountered, the machine accepts.

The described DTM has EUL-CYCLE as its language. Let us consider the time that it takes. Consider a graph G, and set $\ell = |\ulcorner G \urcorner|$, that is, set ℓ to be the length of G's encoding, which we suppose to be the adjacency matrix encoding. The search for a non-isolated vertex takes time proportional to ℓ. The mutual reachability check updates the set no more than $|V|$ times, since vertices are only added to the set; we have $|V| \leq \ell$. The row-by-row examination of the adjacency matrix takes time proportional to ℓ, since each symbol of each row is looked at just once. Thus, the number of high-level operations performed by the machine can be bounded by a polynomial in ℓ. Here, we assume—for example—that there is an efficient routine for isolating each of the rows for examination. We do not explicitly argue that there is such a routine; in general, when presenting Turing machine descriptions, we assume the existence of primitive routines of this sort. $\diamond$

Example 3.2.13. The language 2-COL is PTIME; this language was introduced and discussed in Section 3.1.2. Following the previous example, we justify this claim by giving a high-level description of a polynomial-time DTM whose language is 2-COL.

Let us first estimate the running time of the routine described in Section 3.1.2, on a graph $G' = (V', E')$. After the initial vertex is picked and assigned a color, a loop is performed. In the body of the loop, an examination of the edges is performed; each time, this examination takes at most $|V'|^2$ time steps, due to the adjacency matrix representation of Section 2.2 (which we assume is used). The loop terminates when no further vertices can be assigned values; thus, the number of times the body is invoked is at most $|V'|$. We can thus estimate the routine's running time as being bounded above by $|V'| \cdot |V'|^2 = |V'|^3$.

We next analyze a DTM implementing the overall algorithm. Input strings that are not encodings of graphs can be discarded as in the previous example, so assume that the input string is the encoding $\ulcorner G \urcorner$ of a graph G. The DTM repeatedly applies the routine and removes vertices given colors by the routine. Let $G_1 = G, G_2, \ldots, G_k$ be the graphs on which the routine is invoked before the DTM halts; denote each G_i by (V_i, E_i). The amount of time used is at most

$$|V_1|^3 + \cdots + |V_k|^3.$$

For each of the graphs G_i, we have $V_i \subseteq V$, so we have $|V_i| \leq |V|$. Since at least one vertex is removed each time the routine is invoked, it holds that $k \leq |V|$. Thus we can upper bound the amount of time used by the DTM by $k|V|^3$, which in turn can be upper bounded by the quantity $|V| \cdot |V|^3 = |V|^4$. Set $n = |\ulcorner G \urcorner|$; under our encoding of graphs, we have $|V|^2 = n$ and $|V|^4 = n^2$, establishing a polynomial bound on the time used.

Again, our argument neglects low-level detail; for example, in the routine, bookkeeping is needed to record a color assignment to vertices. ◇

Example 3.2.14. Let us define PROPER-DIVISOR to be the language

$$\left\{ \langle \ulcorner n \urcorner, \ulcorner d \urcorner \rangle \mid n, d \in \mathbb{N}^+ \text{ and } d \text{ is a proper divisor of } n \right\}.$$

The language PROPER-DIVISOR is known to be in PTIME. This is due to the existence of division algorithms, implementable by polynomial-time DTMs, that can divide a natural number n by another natural number $d > 0$, and report the remainder; this remainder is 0 if and only if d is a divisor of n. ◇

There are many further examples of natural languages in PTIME. One example is the language containing each solvable system of linear equations over $\{0, 1\}$, where multiplication is the *and* operation ($\wedge$) and addition is the *exclusive-or* operation ($\oplus$). A second example is the language containing each *linear program* (over the rational numbers) having a *feasible solution*, which is an assignment to the program's variables satisfying each of the program's inequalities. A typical textbook on algorithms contains numerous polynomial-time algorithms!

3.2.3 NP languages

Definitions and discussion

For many languages of interest, deciding membership of an input string amounts to deciding whether there *exists* an object of a desired form. As examples, a graph belongs to the language HAM-CYCLE if and only if there *exists* a Hamiltonian cycle of the graph; and a graph belongs to the language 3-COL if and only if there *exists* a 3-coloring of the graph.

For many languages of the described type, including the two languages HAM-CYCLE and 3-COL, it is not known whether or not they are PTIME. However, by adjusting and expanding the definition of the PTIME languages to allow for *nondeterministic* machines, we obtain an umbrella class of languages—the NP languages—which covers not just the languages HAM-CYCLE and 3-COL, but literally thousands of further relevant languages.

It should not be wholly surprising that a nondeterministic flavor of polynomial-time computation characterizes languages where membership is concerned with the existence of a desired object. Rather, this should be suggested by the parallelism between the membership condition of such languages, and the acceptance condition of nondeterministic machines: membership holds, for a string, when there *exists* a desired object, and a nondeterministic machine accepts a string when there *exists* an accepting computation. Indeed, this parallelism—this close alignment—suggests that for such languages, one might design nondeterministic machines where, on a string, the different computations correspond to the different possible objects under consideration, and a computation accepts when its object is one of the desired type. We will follow this general design strategy.

We formalize the definition of the NP languages as follows; as indicated, this definition is just the modification of the definition of PTIME language (Definition 3.2.5) where the DTM model is replaced with the NTM model.

Definition 3.2.15. A language B is *NP* if there exists a polynomial-time NTM M such that $B = L(M)$. $\diamond$

The just-discussed parallelism between the search for a desired object and nondeterministic computation goes beyond the fact that the class of NP languages *includes* languages such as HAM-CYCLE and 3-COL. As we will see later in this chapter, the connection between this class and certain of its members is much tighter: in an apparent inversion, it is possible to take single NP languages, such as the language HAM-CYCLE or the language 3-COL, and show that each of these in turn *characterizes* the entire class of NP languages, in a sense to be made precise. Such privileged NP languages will be referred to as *NP-complete* languages.

Relationships

We next relate the NP languages to previously identified language classes. Here and in the sequel, we use $\mathcal{P}$ to denote the class of all PTIME languages, and $\mathcal{NP}$ to denote the class of all NP languages. So under this notation, a language B is PTIME if and only if $B \in \mathcal{P}$, and is NP if and only if $B \in \mathcal{NP}$.

Proposition 3.2.16. *Each language that is PTIME is also NP. (That is, $\mathcal{P} \subseteq \mathcal{NP}$.)*

Essentially, Proposition 3.2.16 holds because an NTM M' can be constructed whose behavior imitates that of a given DTM M, and in particular that has both the same language and the same time consumption as M.

Let us give a more precise justification. Suppose that B is a PTIME language, and let M be a polynomial-time DTM where $L(M) = B$. We make use of a previously given construction—the construction given in the argument of Proposition 2.6.11. This argument shows how to construct, from a DTM M, an NTM M' having the same language as M and having the property that for any non-halting configuration of M, each of M and M' has one successor configuration, and these successor configurations are equal. It thus holds that M' is halting and that, for each input string x, the two machines M and M' use the same amount of time; formally, for each input string x, it holds that $\text{time}_M(x) = \text{time}_{M'}(x)$. Since M is a polynomial-time DTM, it follows that M' is a polynomial-time NTM, and thus that the language B is NP.

Proposition 3.2.17. *Each language that is NP is also computable.*

Proposition 3.2.17 is a direct consequence of Theorem 2.6.12: this theorem shows that, for each halting NTM M, there exists a halting DTM M' whose language $L(M')$ is equal to the language $L(M)$ of M.

We record here that the converse of Proposition 3.2.17 is known not to hold; an explanation is given in Note 3.10.11.

Proposition 3.2.18. *There exists a computable language that is not NP.*

The *P versus NP* question

Whether or not the converse of Proposition 3.2.16 holds—that is, whether or not each NP language is also a PTIME language—is an open question. Using the class notation, this question asks whether or not the containment $\mathcal{NP} \subseteq \mathcal{P}$ holds; in light of Proposition 3.2.16, this containment is tantamount to the equivalence $\mathcal{P} = \mathcal{NP}$. This question, which is often referred to as the *P versus NP question*, is considered critical due to the many relevant languages that are NP, but not known to be PTIME. For these languages, the existence of deterministic polynomial-time algorithms could have monumental consequences: if these languages were to have such algorithms permitting efficient implementations, then many languages of practical interest, from a wide variety of domains, would be solvable in a manner dramatically faster than known possible at the time of writing.

This question of whether or not $\mathcal{P}$ equals $\mathcal{NP}$ has a neat conceptual interpretation: it asks whether, in the context of polynomial-time computation, nondeterminism offers any advantage over determinism. We can recall that there was provably no such advantage in some previous comparisons: the DFA and NFA models were shown to define the same languages in Theorem 1.3.24; and the DTM and NTM models were shown to define the same languages in Theorems 2.6.14 and 2.6.15. On the other hand, Example 1.6.12 exposed an exponential gap between the *number* of states needed by the DFA and NFA models, for a particular family of languages.

To wax philosophical, many areas of human endeavor deal with tasks that seem to embody the spirit of the NP languages, in that these tasks involve trying to produce an object, from a large space of possibilities, that satisfies some readily checkable criteria. Consider the following examples of workers and tasks. A scientist strives to generate a theory that is consistent with and explains a body of empirical data; an engineer tries to create a design that meets a set of given constraints; an artist aims to construct a work that summons aesthetic pleasure; a mathematician attempts to generate a proof of a mathematical statement having interest. Throughout human experience, the act of *creating* has been felt to be distinctly more challenging than the act of *evaluating* a creation;[16] whether or not this perceived discrepancy is genuine, in the milieu of polynomial-time computation, can be seen as the heart of the P versus NP question!

Examples

We next look at examples of NP languages; for each, we give an explanation of why they are NP. In each case, the explanation has a similar form: we give a polynomial-time NTM that, on an input string *x*, nondeterministically *guesses* a string, and then checks whether the guessed string witnesses that *x* is in the language; if it does, the NTM accepts, and otherwise, the NTM rejects. By *guessing a string*, we mean that the NTM repeatedly guesses bits in the following way: it repeatedly enters a configuration having two successor configurations, one in which the NTM records 0 on the tape and moves right, and one in which the NTM records 1 on the tape and moves right; it does this until the number of recorded bits reaches a length limit.

In the following presentation of examples, we argue on a high level, as we did when giving examples of PTIME languages; in particular, we do not engage in low-level discussion of how NTMs operate, but rather, assume the existence of basic primitive routines.

Example 3.2.19. Let us argue that the language HAM-CYCLE is NP; this language was introduced and discussed in Section 3.1.1.

We describe a polynomial-time NTM whose language is HAM-CYCLE. Overall, given a graph, the NTM will guess a string, and then check to see if the string represents a Hamiltonian cycle in the graph. How long should the guessed string be? Consider a graph with r vertices. A Hamiltonian cycle can be specified by giving an ordering $u_1, ..., u_r$ of the vertices. Each vertex can be specified by giving an index $i \in \{1, ..., r\}$. Such an index can be encoded using $\lceil \log_2 r \rceil$ bits, and so an ordering of the vertices can be encoded using a total of $r \cdot \lceil \log_2 r \rceil$ bits.

The NTM, when given as input the encoding $\ulcorner G \urcorner$ of a graph $G = (V, E)$, behaves as follows. Set $r = |V|$. The NTM guesses a bit string y of length $r \cdot \lceil \log_2 r \rceil$; since $r \leq |\ulcorner G \urcorner|$, this process takes polynomial time. It then checks to see if the string y represents a Hamiltonian cycle in G; to do this, it checks to see if y represents an ordering $u_1, ..., u_r$ of the vertices in V, and then checks that each pair of consecutive vertices—as well as the first and last—form an edge in E. This check can be carried out in polynomial time. The NTM accepts if the check discovered y to represent a Hamiltonian cycle in G; it rejects otherwise.

16. As the time-tested adage goes, *everyone's a critic*.

It is readily seen that, for any graph G, its encoding $\ulcorner G \urcorner$ is in the language of this NTM M if and only if G has a Hamiltonian cycle. For the forward direction, we observe that if $\ulcorner G \urcorner \in L(M)$, then there exists a string y under which the NTM accepted; but this occurs only when y represents a Hamiltonian cycle. For the backward direction, when G has a Hamiltonian cycle, there exists a string y (of the described length) that represents the cycle, and under which the NTM accepts, implying that $\ulcorner G \urcorner \in L(M)$.   ◇

Example 3.2.20. Let us argue that the language 3-COL is NP; this language was introduced and discussed in Section 3.1.2.

We design a polynomial-time NTM whose language is 3-COL by following the schema of the previous example. Upon being presented an input graph $G = (V, E)$, the NTM guesses a string, and checks whether or not the string represents a 3-coloring of the graph; it accepts if so, and rejects otherwise. How long need the guessed string be in this case? Here, a color—an element of $\{1, 2, 3\}$—can be represented by 2 bits; an assignment $f: V \to \{1, 2, 3\}$ can thus be represented by a string of length $2|V|$.

Thus, the NTM, when given as input the encoding $\ulcorner G \urcorner$ of a graph $G = (V, E)$, behaves as follows. The NTM guesses a bit string y of length $2|V|$; since $|V| \leq |\ulcorner G \urcorner|$, this process takes polynomial time. It then checks to see if y represents an assignment $f: V \to \{1, 2, 3\}$; if so, it checks whether or not this assignment f is a 3-coloring of G, by examining each edge in E. In particular, if it finds an edge $\{v, v'\}$ such that f maps both v and v' to the same value, it rejects; if it finds no such edge, it accepts.

It can be seen that the encoding $\ulcorner G \urcorner$ of a graph G is in the language of this NTM if and only if G has a 3-coloring. Thus, this NTM's language is 3-COL.   ◇

We have already argued that the languages EUL-CYCLE and 2-COL are PTIME, which entails (by Proposition 3.2.16) that they are NP. We remark in passing that, via reasoning similar to that of the previous two examples, one could argue directly that these two languages are NP.

Example 3.2.21. What can we say about the prime numbers, with respect to the language classes defined in this chapter so far? That is, we ask what can be said about the language

$$\text{PRIMES} = \{\ulcorner t \urcorner \mid t \in \mathbb{N}^+ \text{ and } t \text{ is prime}\}.$$

Here and below, we use $\ulcorner t \urcorner$ to denote the binary encoding of a natural number t (as presented in Section 2.2).

In fact, probably the most obvious thing we can say about this language is that this language's *complement*, the language of composite numbers, is an NP language. Define

$$\text{COMPOSITES} = \{\ulcorner t \urcorner \mid t \in \mathbb{N}^+ \text{ and } t \text{ has a proper divisor}\}.$$

Note that, technically, the two languages PRIMES and COMPOSITES are complements with respect to the base set $\{\ulcorner t \urcorner \mid t \in \mathbb{N} \setminus \{0, 1\}\}$; these two languages only contain strings that are encodings of natural numbers that are greater than or equal to 2, and we concern ourselves only with such strings for the moment.

Why is the language COMPOSITES an NP language? On a high level, one can design a polynomial-time NTM for this language as follows. The NTM, when given as input the encoding $\ulcorner t \urcorner$ of a positive natural number t, guesses the encoding $\ulcorner d \urcorner$ of a natural number where $d \leq t$; it then checks whether d is a proper divisor of t, accepting if this is so, and rejecting otherwise. The guessing process can be carried out in polynomial time; when $d \leq t$, we have $|\ulcorner d \urcorner| \leq |\ulcorner t \urcorner|$. The checking can also be carried out in polynomial time, as discussed in Example 3.2.14.

The language PRIMES was actually shown to be PTIME in the year 2002; this result implies that the language COMPOSITES is PTIME as well. Unfortunately, presenting a proof of this result is beyond our present scope. ◇

Remark 3.2.22. Unless mentioned otherwise, in complexity theory, we assume all natural numbers to be represented by the binary encoding (presented in Section 2.2). The binary encoding can behave quite differently from the unary encoding of numbers, whereby a number n is represented with the string a^n, for some symbol a. For example, the language of prime numbers under the unary encoding is very readily verified to be PTIME, via an exhaustive algorithm that, when given a string a^n, checks whether each number $i < n$ is a divisor of n. Intuitively speaking, the unary encoding is exponentially longer than the binary encoding, and so under the unary encoding, DTMs operating relatively slowly can still qualify as running within polynomial time. ◇

One can identify a pattern, in these examples, of designing polynomial-time NTMs that guess a string and then check whether or not it represents some desired object. In each case, the checking can be carried out deterministically; it is the guessing that uses and exploits nondeterminism. This pattern is actually not a coincidence: we next see a characterization of the NP languages that in effect isolates and separates these two phases, and formalizes this so-called "guess-and-check" or "guess-and-verify" paradigm.

Characterization by verifiers

We conclude this section by giving an alternative characterization of the NP languages. As discussed, to show that a language is NP, it is often natural to design a two-phase NTM that, on an input x, first guesses a string y, and then verifies whether or not y represents some desired object, relative to x. In such a design, it is crucial that the guessed string y has length bounded by a polynomial in x—that is, that the guessing can be carried out in polynomial time—and it is typical that the verification phase can be carried out deterministically. We give a characterization of the NP languages that formalizes this two-phase design.

The characterization states that a language is NP if and only if it has a verifier. Intuitively speaking, a verifier carries out the verification phase; it is presented a pair $\langle x, y \rangle$, and needs to efficiently decide whether or not y verifies that x is in the language under consideration; it accepts if so, and rejects otherwise. Formally, a verifier will be a polynomial-time DTM whose language consists of pairs $\langle x, y \rangle$ of strings and satisfies a further property, which ensures that a verifier only considers pairs $\langle x, y \rangle$ where y has length bounded by a polynomial in the length of x. The precise definitions are as follows.

Definition 3.2.23. Define a **polynomially balanced relation** over an alphabet Σ to be a language R such that

- R is a subset of $\left\{ \langle x, y \rangle \mid x, y \in \Sigma^* \right\}$, that is, R is a language of pair encodings; and
- there exists a polynomial $P_R \colon \mathbb{N} \to \mathbb{N}$ where (for all $x, y \in \Sigma^*$) if $\langle x, y \rangle \in R$, then the inequality $|y| \leq P_R(|x|)$ holds.   ◇

Definition 3.2.24. A **verifier** is a polynomial-time DTM M whose language $L(M)$ is a polynomially balanced relation. When B is a language and M is a verifier, we say that M is a **verifier for** B if

$$B = \left\{ x \mid \exists y \in \Sigma^* \text{ such that } \langle x, y \rangle \in L(M) \right\}.$$ ◇

To break down this last definition, a verifier M is *for* a language B if for each $x \in B$, there exists a string y such that M accepts $\langle x, y \rangle$; and, conversely, if there exists a string y such that M accepts $\langle x, y \rangle$, then $x \in B$. When x is a string, and y is a string such that M accepts $\langle x, y \rangle$, we may conceive of y as a **certificate** for x that witnesses the membership of x in B. Under this view, a verifier is *for* a language B when we have both that *each* string in B has a certificate, and that *only* the strings in B have certificates.

Example 3.2.25. Consider the language PROPER-DIVISOR, introduced in Section 3.2.2. This language is a polynomially balanced relation, because each of its elements is a pair, and for each pair $\langle \ulcorner n \urcorner, \ulcorner d \urcorner \rangle \in$ PROPER-DIVISOR, it holds that $d \leq n$, which implies $|\ulcorner d \urcorner| \leq |\ulcorner n \urcorner|$. This language thus satisfies the conditions of Definition 3.2.23 via the polynomial defined as $P_R(n) = n$.

As discussed in Example 3.2.14, there exists a polynomial-time DTM M whose language is PROPER-DIVISOR. It follows that this DTM is a verifier; moreover, it is a verifier for the language COMPOSITES, as is evident from the definitions of these two languages.   ◇

We next give the promised characterization of the NP languages.

Theorem 3.2.26. *Let Σ be an alphabet such that $|\Sigma| \geq 2$. A language B over Σ is NP if and only if there exists a verifier for B.*

Observe that this theorem provides a characterization of NP in terms of verifiers, whose languages are PTIME. Hence, this theorem can be taken as a characterization of NP in terms of PTIME. So computationally speaking, this is a characterization of NP that does not make explicit reference to NTMs, but rather is based on DTMs.

Proof. We begin with the backward direction. Suppose that M is a verifier for B, and let P_M be a polynomial such that M runs within time P_M. The language $L(M)$ is polynomially balanced; let P_R be a polynomial satisfying the second condition in the definition of *polynomially balanced*.

Define M' to be an NTM that, on input x, first guesses a string y such that $|y| \leq P_R(|x|)$, and then invokes the DTM M on $\langle x, y \rangle$, accepting if M accepts, and rejecting if M rejects. This NTM has $L(M') = B$, since $x \in B$ if and only if there exists a string y with $|y| \leq P_R(|x|)$ such that M accepts $\langle x, y \rangle$. The value $P_R(|x|)$ can be computed in polynomial time (recall Remark 3.2.7); it takes at most $P_R(|x|)$ time steps to guess the string y, and at most $P_M(\langle x, y \rangle)$ time steps to run M on $\langle x, y \rangle$. Hence, the NTM M' is a polynomial-time NTM.

We next prove the forward direction. Let $M = (Q, \Sigma, \Gamma, s, t, r, \Delta)$ be a polynomial-time NTM such that $L(M) = B$; let P be a polynomial such that M runs within time P. The proof idea of this direction is to give a polynomial-time DTM that accepts a string $\langle x, y \rangle$ when y specifies a sequence of nondeterministic choices under which the NTM M accepts x.

Set $b = P(|x|) - 1$, and let c be a length b sequence $(q_1, a_1, d_1), \ldots, (q_b, a_b, d_b)$ of elements from $Q \times \Gamma \times \{-1, +1\}$. Set $p_1 = s$, $\tau_1 = x_\sqcup \ldots$, $\ell_1 = 1$, and $\gamma_1 = [p_1, \tau_1, \ell_1]$; we have that γ_1 is the initial configuration of M on x. Let us say that the NTM M *accepts x under choices c* if there exists $k \in \mathbb{N}^+$, with $k \leq P(|x|)$, and there exist configurations $\gamma_2 = [p_2, \tau_2, \ell_2], \ldots, \gamma_k = [p_k, \tau_k, \ell_k]$ of M where

- γ_k is an accepting configuration; and
- for each index $i \in \{2, \ldots, k\}$,

  - $(q_{i-1}, a_{i-1}, d_{i-1}) \in \Delta(p_{i-1}, \tau_{i-1}(\ell_{i-1}))$, and
  - $p_i = q_{i-1}$, $\tau_i = \tau_{i-1}[\ell_{i-1} \mapsto a_{i-1}]$, $\ell_i = \max(\ell_{i-1} + d_{i-1}, 1)$.

That is, for each such index i, the transition (q_i, a_i, d_i) is allowed from configuration γ_{i-1}, and γ_i is the successor configuration of γ_{i-1} resulting from taking this transition.

Observe that M accepts x if and only if there exists a sequence c (of the described form) such that M accepts x under choices c.

Let $D \in \mathbb{N}$ be a sufficiently large constant so that there exists a surjective function $f \colon \Sigma^D \to Q \times \Gamma \times \{-1, +1\}$; such a constant exists by our assumption on the alphabet that $|\Sigma| \geq 2$. Define R as the set of string pairs that contains a pair $\langle x, y \rangle$ of strings from Σ^* if and only if the following hold: $|y| = b \cdot D$, where $b = P(|x|) - 1$; and when y is viewed as the concatenation $z_1 \cdots z_b$ with each $z_i \in \Sigma^D$, the verifier M accepts x under choices $f(z_1), \ldots, f(z_b)$. By the surjectivity of f and the observation, we have that $B = \{ x \mid \exists y \in \Sigma^* \text{ such that } \langle x, y \rangle \in R \}$. It is straightforward to verify that there exists a polynomial-time DTM M' with $L(M') = R$; essentially, such a DTM need only check, given a pair $\langle x, y \rangle$, whether y represents a sequence of valid transitions for M that leads to acceptance from the initial configuration of M on x. We also have that R is polynomially balanced, since for each string $\langle x, y \rangle$ in R it holds that $|y| = (P(|x|) - 1) \cdot D$. We thus have that M' is a verifier for B.   □

Remark 3.2.27. Let us point out, for future use, that for each NP language B, the proof of Theorem 3.2.26 reveals that there exists a verifier M for B and a polynomial Q such that, for all $x, y \in \Sigma^*$, it holds that $\langle x, y \rangle \in L(M)$ implies $|y| = Q(|x|)$.   ◇

One can adopt something of a metamathematical perspective on the class of NP languages. Let B be a language, and consider the assertions having the form "$x \in B$", over all strings x. Then, one can view a verifier as taking in a string x along with a potential proof y of the assertion that $x \in B$, and accepting when it considers y to be a proof of the assertion. Under this perspective, a verifier is *for B* (in the sense of Definition 3.2.24) when it acts as a proof system that is both *sound*—meaning that each assertion having a proof is true—and *complete*—meaning that each true assertion has a proof.

As another take, the NP languages are sometimes depicted by a game between an omnipotent wizard *Prover*, and a humbler, limited *Verifier* that computes deterministically in polynomial time. Let B be a language; in this game, an input string x is presented to both of them, the Prover can pass a message to the Verifier aiming to convince the Verifier that $x \in B$, and then the Verifier decides whether or not it was convinced. According to this storyline, a language B is NP if one can exhibit a Prover and Verifier such that for each $x \in B$, the Prover's message successfully convinces the Verifier, and for each $x \notin B$, no message convinces the Verifier. Our definition of *verifier* in effect plays the role of the Verifier described here.

With this game story in mind, one might succinctly say that the PTIME languages are those where one can *efficiently compute* whether membership holds, and that the NP languages are those where one can be *efficiently convinced* that membership holds.

3.2.4 Summary of models and language classes

The following is an update of the running table (last seen in Section 2.6.3) giving the computational models studied so far, along with their accompanying language classes.

Computational model	Defined class of languages	Justification
DFA	regular languages	Definition 1.1.1
NFA	regular languages	Theorem 1.3.24
ϵ-NFA	regular languages	Theorem 1.3.24
polynomial-time DTM	PTIME languages	Definition 3.2.5
polynomial-time NTM	NP languages	Definition 3.2.15
halting DTM	computable languages	Definition 2.1.15
halting NTM	computable languages	Theorem 2.6.14
DTM	CE languages	Definition 2.1.20
NTM	CE languages	Theorem 2.6.15

The following diagram summarizes the inclusion structure of the language classes studied so far, along with the *coNP languages*, introduced in the following section.

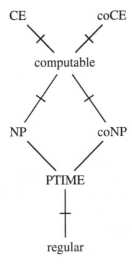

As before, a line from a language class to a language class above it indicates inclusion of the first class in the second, and the hash mark on such a line indicates that the inclusion is known to be proper.

3.3 Closure properties

We here study the closure properties of the PTIME languages and of the NP languages.

3.3.1 Complementation

We first observe that the PTIME languages are closed under complementation. This is because for any polynomial-time DTM M, the DTM M' derived from M by interchanging the accept and reject states is also a polynomial-time DTM, and has $L(M') = \overline{L(M)}$.

Proposition 3.3.1. *If B is a PTIME language, then $\overline{B}$ is also a PTIME language.*

What about the NP languages—are they closed under complementation? Let us first observe that if one takes an NTM M, and derives an NTM M' from M by interchanging its accept and reject states, the resulting NTM M' will not in general have $L(M') = \overline{L(M)}$. To see this, consider a situation where, on an input string x, an NTM M has at least one computation that ends in an accepting configuration, and at least one computation that ends in a rejecting configuration; then, on that input string x, the NTM M' could imitate the latter computation of M, which for M' would end in an accepting configuration. Thus in this situation, it would hold both that $x \in L(M)$ and $x \in L(M')$. (This argument applies to common nondeterministic computational models: interchanging the accept and reject states of a nondeterministic machine does not, in general, have the effect of complementing the machine's language.)

In fact, it is *not known* if the NP languages are closed under complementation. As a concrete example, the language 3-COL is an NP language, but it is not known whether or not its complement $\overline{\text{3-COL}}$ is an NP language. Let us speak on an intuitive level to try to get a feeling for what this means. Recall that the language 3-COL is NP in virtue of it being possible for a powerful prover to readily convince someone, by passing them a short message, that a graph is 3-colorable: simply give them a 3-coloring! The question of whether or not its complement $\overline{\text{3-COL}}$ is NP amounts to asking whether or not it is possible to readily convince someone that a graph is *not* 3-colorable. For a non-3-colorable graph $G = (V, E)$, it is possible to create a message listing each assignment $f: V \to \{1, 2, 3\}$ along with an edge $e \in E$ that is not colored properly (that is, not respected) by the assignment; however, such a message will not be short in general, as there are $3^{|V|}$ such assignments from V to $\{1, 2, 3\}$. While such a message certifies the non-3-colorability of G, the named question might be thought of as asking if there is a very condensed version of this message that properly conveys non-3-colorability. Rephrased, this question asks whether one can always present a succinct certificate that witnesses the lack of a certificate holding a 3-coloring! As with many questions in complexity theory, the question of whether or not the NP languages are closed under complement seems to pose a conundrum of philosophical proportions: *Is non-certifiability certifiable?*

We introduce the following name for the languages whose complements are NP, so as to be able to deftly discuss them.

Definition 3.3.2. A language B is *coNP* if its complement $\overline{B}$ is NP.   ◇

Remark 3.3.3. The naming convention of Definition 3.3.2 follows the precedent of Definition 2.5.3, where the *coCE* languages were defined.   ◇

Following a typical convention, we use $\text{co}\mathcal{NP}$ to denote the class of all coNP languages. Using this class notation, the question of whether or not the NP languages are closed under complement is the question of whether or not the containment $\text{co}\mathcal{NP} \subseteq \mathcal{NP}$ holds. The following proposition holds that this containment is equivalent both to its reverse containment, as well as to the equivalence of the two implicated classes.

Proposition 3.3.4. *The following are equivalent:*

(1)   Each coNP language is NP. (That is, $\text{co}\mathcal{NP} \subseteq \mathcal{NP}$.)

(2)   Each NP language is coNP. (That is, $\mathcal{NP} \subseteq \text{co}\mathcal{NP}$.)

(3)   A language is NP if and only if it is coNP. (That is, $\mathcal{NP} = \text{co}\mathcal{NP}$.)

Proof. Clearly (3) implies (1) and (2); indeed, (3) is equivalent to the conjunction of (1) and (2). We have that (2) implies (1), since if each NP language is coNP, for any coNP language B, it holds that $\overline{B}$ is NP and hence coNP, implying that B is NP; (1) implies (2) by a dual argument. Thus, (1), (2), and (3) are equivalent. □

As we did for the NP languages, we can position the coNP languages as being located in between the PTIME languages and the computable languages, as follows.

Proposition 3.3.5. *Each language that is PTIME is also coNP (that is, $\mathcal{P} \subseteq \text{co}\mathcal{NP}$); and each language that is coNP is also computable.*

Proof. Let B be a language that is PTIME. By Proposition 3.3.1, the language $\overline{B}$ is also PTIME. By Proposition 3.2.16, the language $\overline{B}$ is NP, and so the language B is coNP.

Let C be a language that is coNP; by definition, the language $\overline{C}$ is NP. By Proposition 3.2.17, the language $\overline{C}$ is computable. As the computable languages are closed under complementation (Proposition 2.5.1), we have that the language C is computable. □

It is natural to ask about the converses of the statements of Proposition 3.3.5. Concerning the second statement, as mentioned earlier there exists a computable language C that is not NP (Proposition 3.2.18); its complement $\overline{C}$ is clearly a computable language that is not coNP (recall that the computable languages are closed under complementation—Proposition 2.5.1). We record this separation as follows.

Proposition 3.3.6. *There exists a computable language that is not coNP.*

We next consider the converse of the first statement of Proposition 3.3.5, which is the statement that each coNP language is PTIME; we show that this holds if and only if each NP language is PTIME.

Proposition 3.3.7. *The following statements are equivalent.*

- *Each language that is NP is also PTIME. (That is, $\mathcal{NP} \subseteq \mathcal{P}$.)*
- *Each language that is coNP is also PTIME. (That is, $\text{co}\mathcal{NP} \subseteq \mathcal{P}$.)*

Proof. Assume the first statement. Let B be a language that is coNP. Then the language $\overline{B}$ is NP, and by the assumption, the language $\overline{B}$ is PTIME; it follows by Proposition 3.3.1 that B is PTIME.

Assume the second statement. Let B be a language that is NP. Then the language $\overline{B}$ is coNP, and by the assumption, the language $\overline{B}$ is PTIME; it follows by Proposition 3.3.1 that B is PTIME. □

Remark 3.3.8. From Proposition 3.3.7, we see that if $\mathcal{P} = \mathcal{NP}$, then both of these classes are equal to $\text{co}\mathcal{NP}$ as well. It follows that the research project of showing that $\mathcal{NP} \neq \text{co}\mathcal{NP}$ is at least as ambitious as that of showing that $\mathcal{P} \neq \mathcal{NP}$: demonstrating the first statement would imply the second. Indeed, showing that $\mathcal{NP} \neq \text{co}\mathcal{NP}$ is equivalent to showing that $\mathcal{NP}$ is not closed under complementation (by Proposition 3.3.4), and would imply that $\mathcal{NP}$ is not equal to any language class already known to be closed under complementation. ◇

3.3.2   Intersection and union

We next turn to consider closure under intersection and union. Each of the classes under focus is closed under these operations.

Theorem 3.3.9. *If B and C are PTIME languages, then both $B \cap C$ and $B \cup C$ are also PTIME languages.*

Proof. Let M_B and M_C be polynomial-time DTMs such that $L(M_B) = B$ and $L(M_C) = C$. Define $M_\cap$ to be a DTM that, on an input string x, performs the following algorithm:

- Make a copy of the string x.
- Run M_B on the copy of x until the computation halts; then clear the tape so that just the original string x remains, and run M_C on x until the computation halts.
- If both computations accepted, then accept; otherwise, reject.

It is clear that $L(M_\cap) = B \cap C$. Let P_B be a polynomial such that M_B runs within time P_B, and let P_C be a polynomial such that M_C runs within time P_C. Putting aside the polynomial amount of time needed to copy x and clear the tape, we may estimate $\mathrm{time}_{M_\cap}(x)$ as $\mathrm{time}_{M_B}(x) + \mathrm{time}_{M_C}(x)$, which is bounded above by $P_B(|x|) + P_C(|x|)$. Hence, the DTM $M_\cap$ is a polynomial-time DTM.

The proof for union is similar; the difference is that one defines a DTM that, on an input string x, accepts if at least one of M_B, M_C accepts x. (We can also obtain the result for union via De Morgan's laws, Proposition 1.2.5, at this point.)   □

Theorem 3.3.10. *If B and C are NP languages, then both $B \cap C$ and $B \cup C$ are also NP languages.*

See Figure 3.3.1 for a diagram explaining this theorem's proof.

Proof. The proof is actually similar to that of Theorem 3.3.9. Let M_B and M_C be polynomial-time NTMs such that $L(M_B) = B$ and $L(M_C) = C$. Define $M_\cap$ to be an NTM that, on an input string x, performs the algorithm described in the proof of Theorem 3.3.9. Observe that, for any string x, there exists a computation of $M_\cap$ on x that results in acceptance if and only if there exists a computation of M_B on x that results in acceptance, and a computation of M_C on x that results in acceptance. Hence, $L(M_\cap) = B \cap C$. As in the proof of Theorem 3.3.9, we may estimate $\mathrm{time}_{M_\cap}(x)$ as $\mathrm{time}_{M_B}(x) + \mathrm{time}_{M_C}(x)$, and so by reasoning as in that proof, the NTM $M_\cap$ is a polynomial-time NTM.

The proof for union is similar; the difference is that one defines an NTM that, on an input string x, accepts if at least one of M_B, M_C accepts x.   □

As an immediate consequence of the NP languages being closed under intersection and union, we obtain that the coNP languages are also closed under these operations.

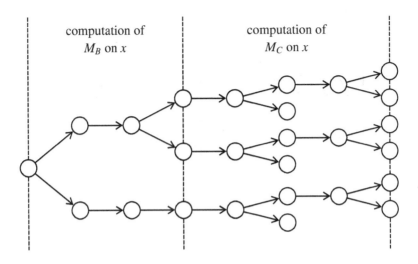

computation of
M_B on x

computation of
M_C on x

Figure 3.3.1. In order to prove that the NP languages are closed under intersection and union, we construct an NTM from two polynomial-time NTMs M_B and M_C. This constructed NTM, on an input string x, runs M_B on x, and when the computation halts, runs M_C on x. The resulting computation tree thus, in general, contains many occurrences of the computation tree of M_C on x. (In this diagram, each computation of M_B on x takes the same amount of time, but this need not hold, in general, for the computations of a halting NTM on a string.)

Corollary 3.3.11. *If B and C are coNP languages, then both $B \cap C$ and $B \cup C$ are also coNP languages.*

Proof. Immediate from Theorem 3.3.10 and De Morgan's laws (Proposition 1.2.5). ☐

3.4 Reductions

In the previous chapter, the notion of *many-one reduction* helped us understand the scope of the computable languages. In particular, once a first non-computable language was identified, this notion of reduction allowed us to prove that further languages were non-computable: exhibiting a reduction from a non-computable language to a second language established that the second language was non-computable. Here, we present a notion of reduction that will analogously help us understand the scope of the PTIME languages; for this notion, a key property is that exhibiting a reduction from a non-PTIME language to a second language establishes that the second language is non-PTIME.

The new reduction notion, called *polynomial-time many-one reduction*, is a refinement of the many-one reduction; a polynomial-time many-one reduction is, in fact, simply a many-one reduction that is polynomial-time computable.

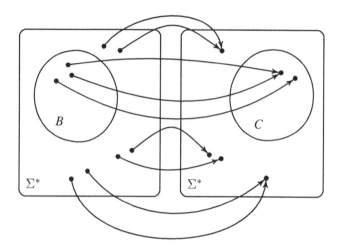

Figure 3.4.1. The correctness of a many-one reduction from a language B to a language C. Each point represents a string. Correctness holds that strings in B are mapped to strings in C, and that strings outside of B are mapped to strings outside of C. It is permitted that two distinct strings are mapped by a reduction to the same string.

Definition 3.4.1. Let B and C be languages over the same alphabet Σ. A **polynomial-time many-one reduction from B to C** is defined as a polynomial-time computable function $\rho\colon \Sigma^* \to \Sigma^*$ satisfying the condition that, for all $x \in \Sigma^*$, the equivalence

$$x \in B \quad \Leftrightarrow \quad \rho(x) \in C$$

holds. We refer to this condition as the **correctness** of the function ρ; see Figure 3.4.1 for an illustration. To indicate the existence of a polynomial-time many-one reduction from B to C, we write $B \leq_m^p C$ and say that B **polynomial-time many-one reduces** to C. $\diamond$

Remark 3.4.2. The relationship of polynomial-time many-one reductions to the PTIME languages enjoys analogies to the relationship of many-one reductions (Definition 2.8.2) to the computable languages. For example, it is very much possible to relate, by a polynomial-time many-one reduction, two languages that are not PTIME or not believed to be PTIME, just as it was possible to present many-one reductions between non-computable languages.

When a polynomial-time many-one reduction ρ from B to C is applied to a string x, the result $\rho(x)$ does not by itself allow one, in general, to immediately resolve the *yes-or-no* question of whether x is in B; rather, it yields a string such that the question of whether $\rho(x)$ is in C has the same answer to the question of whether x is in B. One may conceive of a many-one reduction (polynomial-time or not) as a translation between languages, as opposed to a device that reveals the nature of a single language. (Similar points were made about many-one reductions in Remark 2.8.3). ◇

Remark 3.4.3. When presenting polynomial-time many-one reductions, we will typically follow the convention set in Remark 2.8.5: we will neglect to define a reduction on strings that are obviously outside the language that we reduce from. Such a partial definition can be completed to a full definition by the following maneuver (which is analogous to one described in that remark): on a partial definition of a reduction, the language of strings where the result of the mapping is not described will always be a PTIME language; thus, the definition can be completed by mapping all such strings to a fixed string outside the language reduced *to*. ◇

In the remainder of this chapter, we often use the term *reduction* to refer succinctly to *polynomial-time many-one reduction*.

3.4.1 Examples

To give a first example of a reduction in the setting of complexity theory, we consider two graph-theoretic notions. An *independent set* of a graph is a set S of vertices such that there are no edges between any two vertices in S; or, equivalently, such that each edge contains at most one vertex of S. Formally, an **independent set** of a graph (V, E) is a set $S \subseteq V$ of vertices such that for any two distinct vertices $v, v' \in S$, it holds that $\{v, v'\} \notin E$. A *clique* of a graph is a set of vertices such that there is an edge between any two vertices in S. Formally, a **clique** of a graph (V, E) is a set $S \subseteq V$ of vertices such that for any two distinct vertices $v, v' \in S$, it holds that $\{v, v'\} \in E$. It is immediately verified that, in a graph, any subset of an independent set is also an independent set, and analogously, any subset of a clique is also a clique.

Example 3.4.4. For the Petersen graph shown in Figure 3.4.2, the set $\{u_2, v_3, v_4, u_5\}$ is an independent set of size 4: no two distinct vertices in this set form an edge. Moreover, it can be verified that this independent set has maximal size: this graph has no independent set of size 5. Each edge of this graph is a clique of size 2; it can be verified that this graph has no clique of size 3. ◇

Example 3.4.5. For the 3-by-3 grid graph shown in Figure 3.4.3, it holds that the set $\{(1, 1), (3, 1), (2, 2), (1, 3), (3, 3)\}$ is an independent set of size 5. It can be verified that this independent set has maximal size: this graph has no independent set of size 6. As with the Petersen graph, while each edge of this grid graph is a clique of size 2, it can be verified that this grid graph has no clique of size 3. ◇

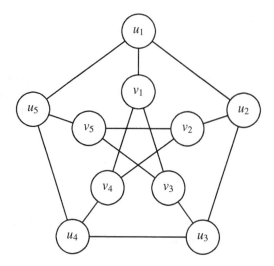

Figure 3.4.2. An example graph, known as the *Petersen graph*.

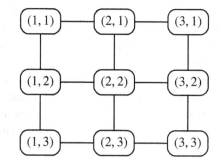

Figure 3.4.3. An example graph, the so-called 3-*by*-3 *grid graph*. For each $k \geq 1$, the k-*by*-k *grid graph* is defined as the graph with vertex set $\{1, ..., k\} \times \{1, ..., k\}$, and where two vertices $(i, j), (i', j')$ form an edge if and only if $|i - i'| + |j - j'| = 1$.

Based on the just-defined notions, we define the languages

$$\text{INDEP-SET} = \left\{ \langle \ulcorner G \urcorner, \ulcorner k \urcorner \rangle \mid G \text{ is a graph, } k \in \mathbb{N}, \text{ and } G \text{ has a size } k \text{ independent set} \right\},$$

$$\text{CLIQUE} = \left\{ \langle \ulcorner G \urcorner, \ulcorner k \urcorner \rangle \mid G \text{ is a graph, } k \in \mathbb{N}, \text{ and } G \text{ has a size } k \text{ clique} \right\}.$$

The **complement** of a graph $G = (V, E)$, denoted by $\overline{G}$, is the graph $(V, \binom{V}{2} \setminus E)$. That is, the complement of a graph is obtained by toggling the edge status of each pair $\{u, v\}$ of vertices: each edge becomes a non-edge, and each non-edge becomes an edge. The following proposition is immediate from the given definitions.

Proposition 3.4.6. *Let* $G = (V, E)$ *be a graph, and let* $S \subseteq V$. *The set* S *is an independent set of* G *if and only if the set* S *is a clique of* $\overline{G}$.

With this proposition in hand, we can give an example of a reduction.

Proposition 3.4.7. INDEP-SET *polynomial-time many-one reduces to* CLIQUE.

Proof. Define $\rho \colon \Sigma^* \to \Sigma^*$ by $\rho(\langle \ulcorner G \urcorner, \ulcorner k \urcorner \rangle) = \langle \ulcorner \overline{G} \urcorner, \ulcorner k \urcorner \rangle$, for each graph G and $k \in \mathbb{N}$. That is, given encodings of a graph and of a natural number, the function ρ replaces the graph with its complement. We argue that ρ is a polynomial-time many-one reduction from INDEP-SET to CLIQUE. The mapping ρ is polynomial-time computable; under the adjacency matrix encoding of graphs (discussed in Section 2.2), the string $\ulcorner \overline{G} \urcorner$ can be computed from the string $\ulcorner G \urcorner$ simply by toggling each bit corresponding to an edge (that is, each bit not on the matrix diagonal).

We verify the correctness of ρ as follows. For each graph G and $k \in \mathbb{N}$:

- When $\langle \ulcorner G \urcorner, \ulcorner k \urcorner \rangle \in$ INDEP-SET, there exists a size k independent set S in G; Proposition 3.4.6 implies that S is a size k clique in $\overline{G}$, and so $\rho(\langle \ulcorner G \urcorner, \ulcorner k \urcorner \rangle) \in$ CLIQUE.
- When $\rho(\langle \ulcorner G \urcorner, \ulcorner k \urcorner \rangle) \in$ CLIQUE, there exists a size k clique S in $\overline{G}$; Proposition 3.4.6 implies that S is a size k independent set in G, and so $\langle \ulcorner G \urcorner, \ulcorner k \urcorner \rangle \in$ INDEP-SET. $\quad\square$

Let us next consider another graph-theoretic notion. A *vertex cover* of a graph is a set S of vertices that covers each edge in the sense that each edge contains a vertex in S. Formally, a **vertex cover** of a graph (V, E) is a set $S \subseteq V$ where for each $e \in E$, it holds that $e \cap S \neq \emptyset$. From this notion, it is natural to define the following language:

VERTEX-COVER = $\{ (G, k) \mid G$ is a graph, $k \in \mathbb{N}$, and G has a size k vertex cover$\}$.

In the same way that Proposition 3.4.6 served as a principle for presenting a reduction from INDEP-SET to CLIQUE, the following proposition will aid us in defining a reduction from INDEP-SET to VERTEX-COVER. It states that, in a graph, the complement of an independent set is a vertex cover, and vice versa. (Here, we take the complement with respect to the graph's vertex set.)

Proposition 3.4.8. *Let* $G = (V, E)$ *be a graph, and let* $S \subseteq V$. *The set* S *is an independent set of* G *if and only if the set* $V \setminus S$ *is a vertex cover of* G.

Proof. First, suppose that S is an independent set; then, each edge in E contains at most one vertex in S, and hence contains at least one vertex in $V \setminus S$; so, $V \setminus S$ is a vertex cover. For the other direction, we reverse the reasoning. Suppose that $V \setminus S$ is a vertex cover; then, each edge in E contains at least one vertex in $V \setminus S$, and thus contains at most one vertex in S; so, S is an independent set. $\quad\square$

Example 3.4.9. In Figure 3.4.2's graph, the set $\{u_2, v_3, v_4, u_5\}$ is an independent set; according to Proposition 3.4.8, its complement with respect to the graph's entire vertex set, namely, the set $\{u_1, u_3, u_4, v_1, v_2, v_5\}$, is a vertex cover of this graph. ◇

Proposition 3.4.10. INDEP-SET *polynomial-time many-one reduces to* VERTEX-COVER.

Proof. Define $\rho \colon \Sigma^* \to \Sigma^*$ so that when G is a graph with n vertices and $k \in \mathbb{N}$, the pair $\langle \ulcorner G \urcorner, \ulcorner k \urcorner \rangle$, is mapped by ρ to the pair $\langle \ulcorner G \urcorner, \ulcorner n - k \urcorner \rangle$. We assume here that $k \leq n$, as if this does not hold, the initial pair is clearly not in INDEP-SET.

We argue that ρ is a polynomial-time many-one reduction from INDEP-SET to VERTEX-COVER. It can be verified that ρ is polynomial-time computable: this is because $\ulcorner n \urcorner$ can be computed from $\ulcorner G \urcorner$, and the difference $\ulcorner n - k \urcorner$ is readily computable from $\ulcorner n \urcorner$ and $\ulcorner k \urcorner$. We verify correctness as follows. For each graph G and each value k:

- When $\langle \ulcorner G \urcorner, \ulcorner k \urcorner \rangle \in$ INDEP-SET, there exists an independent set S of size k in G; Proposition 3.4.8 implies that $V \setminus S$ is a vertex cover of size $n - k$ in G, and hence we obtain that $\rho(\langle \ulcorner G \urcorner, \ulcorner k \urcorner \rangle) \in$ VERTEX-COVER.
- When $\rho(\langle \ulcorner G \urcorner, \ulcorner k \urcorner \rangle) \in$ VERTEX-COVER, there exists a vertex cover S' of size $n - k$ in G; Proposition 3.4.8 implies that $V \setminus S'$ is an independent set of size k in G, and hence we obtain that $\langle \ulcorner G \urcorner, \ulcorner k \urcorner \rangle \in$ INDEP-SET. □

Remark 3.4.11. We mention that the reduction given in the proof of Proposition 3.4.7 is also a polynomial-time many-one reduction in the other direction, from CLIQUE to INDEP-SET. In the same way, the reduction given in the proof of Proposition 3.4.10 is also a polynomial-time many-one reduction from VERTEX-COVER to INDEP-SET. It is not at all common that a reduction from a first language to a second simultaneously serves as a reduction from the second language to the first! ◇

Remark 3.4.12. Note that the graph property of *having an independent set of size k* is the same as that of *having an independent set of size greater than or equal to k*. The first property clearly implies the second, and when the second holds, the first does as well: in a graph, removing vertices from an independent set always yields an independent set. A similar comment applies to the cliques of a graph. The situation is reversed for vertex covers: in a graph, *adding* vertices to a vertex cover always yields a vertex cover. ◇

3.4.2 Properties

We here present some basic properties of polynomial-time many-one reducibility. Our development strongly parallels the corresponding development of many-one reducibility (in Section 2.8.1).

We begin by observing that the relationship of reducibility between two languages is preserved by complementation of the languages.

Proposition 3.4.13. *Suppose that B and C be languages where $B \leq_m^p C$. Then, it holds that $\overline{B} \leq_m^p \overline{C}$.*

Proof. When ρ is a polynomial-time many-one reduction from B to C, it is also a polynomial-time many-one reduction from $\overline{B}$ to $\overline{C}$, since the condition $x \in B \Leftrightarrow \rho(x) \in C$ directly implies the condition $x \in \overline{B} \Leftrightarrow \rho(x) \in \overline{C}$. $\square$

We next show that the language classes introduced in this chapter are closed under reduction: when C is a language in one of these classes and a language B reduces to C, then B is also in the class.

Theorem 3.4.14. *Suppose that B and C are languages such that $B \leq_m^p C$. The following implications hold:*

- *If C is PTIME, then B is PTIME.*
- *If C is NP, then B is NP.*
- *If C is coNP, then B is coNP.*

Let us emphasize that the contrapositive of the first part of this theorem statement provides that, when $B \leq_m^p C$, if the language B is not PTIME, then the language C is not PTIME. In complexity theory, our typical use of reductions will be this: we will start with a language B for which there is evidence (or at least suspicion!) that it is not PTIME, and then exhibit a reduction from B to C; we then obtain evidence that C is not PTIME—for if it were PTIME, then the theorem would yield that B was PTIME as well.

Proof. Assume that ρ is a polynomial-time many-one reduction from B to C, let M_ρ be a polynomial-time DTM that computes ρ, and let P_ρ be a polynomial such that M_ρ runs within time P_ρ.

Suppose that C is PTIME. Let M_C be a polynomial-time DTM such that $L(M_C) = C$, and let P_C be a polynomial such that M_C runs within time P_C. Define M_B to be the DTM that, on an input x, first invokes the DTM M_ρ on x, and then invokes the DTM M_C on the resulting string $\rho(x)$. We have

$$\mathrm{time}_{M_B}(x) = \mathrm{time}_{M_\rho}(x) + \mathrm{time}_{M_C}(\rho(x))$$
$$\leq P_\rho(|x|) + P_C(|\rho(x)|)$$
$$\leq P_\rho(|x|) + P_C(P_\rho(|x|)).$$

Hence, the DTM M_B runs within polynomial time: it runs within time P_B, where P_B is the polynomial defined by $P_B(n) = P_\rho(n) + P_C(P_\rho(n))$. For each string x, we have

$$x \in L(M_B) \quad \Leftrightarrow \quad \rho(x) \in L(M_C)$$
$$\Leftrightarrow \quad \rho(x) \in C$$
$$\Leftrightarrow \quad x \in B.$$

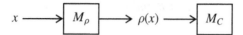

Figure 3.4.4. The behavior of a DTM M_B defined in the proof of Theorem 3.4.14's first part. This part holds that, assuming that there exists a polynomial-time many-one reduction ρ from a language B to a PTIME language C, it follows that the language B is PTIME. To argue this, let M_ρ be a polynomial-time DTM computing ρ, let M_C be a polynomial-time DTM whose language is C, and construct a DTM M_B behaving as shown in the diagram: on an input x, it invokes the DTM M_ρ to compute the string $\rho(x)$, and then invokes the DTM M_C on this latter string. This DTM M_B is polynomial-time and has B as its language. A similar construction shows that when C is assumed to be NP, the language B is also NP.

The first equivalence holds by the definition of M_B, the second equivalence holds by the choice of M_C, and the third equivalence holds by the correctness of ρ as a many-one reduction from B to C. We obtain that $L(M_B) = B$. Since we have established that M_B is a polynomial-time DTM, we conclude that B is PTIME. See Figure 3.4.4 for a diagram showing the behavior of the DTM M_B.

Suppose that C is NP. Let M_C be a polynomial-time NTM such that $L(M_C) = C$, and let P_C be a polynomial such that M_C runs within time P_C. Define M_B to be the NTM that, on an input x, first invokes the DTM M_ρ on x, and then invokes the NTM M_C on the result $\rho(x)$. We obtain that $L(M_B) = B$ and that M_B is a polynomial-time NTM by reasoning as in the previous argument.

Suppose that C is coNP. Then $\overline{C}$ is NP. By Proposition 3.4.13, we have that $\overline{B} \leq_m^p \overline{C}$. By applying the previous argument, we obtain that $\overline{B}$ is NP, and hence that B is coNP.   □

Remark 3.4.15. The two results just presented can be taken as analogs of results on many-one reducibility shown in the previous chapter. In particular, Proposition 3.4.13 is a refinement of Proposition 2.8.6. And Theorem 3.4.14 is highly parallel to Theorem 2.8.7; in fact, the former theorem's proof contains elements of the latter theorem's proof.   ◇

Remark 3.4.16. It is instructive to consider the effect on Theorem 3.4.14 of increasing the power of the reduction notion. In particular, let us consider many-one reducibility from the previous chapter. Assume that $B \leq_m C$, and that C is PTIME. What can we conclude about B? It turns out that we can no longer conclude that B is PTIME, but can only conclude that B is computable. Indeed, any computable language many-one reduces to a PTIME language (see Exercise 3.10.16): this is essentially because a many-one reduction can itself determine membership in a computable language. It no longer follows from the assumptions that B is PTIME due to the reduction notion being overly powerful; intuitively speaking, the language C has limited power, but the difficulty of deciding an arbitrary computable language B has been pushed into the reduction itself.

From this parable, we learn a general moral. Suppose we have a class of languages defined by a computational model. In order to understand the scope of the class using reductions, in particular, to present reductions under which the class is closed (in the sense of Theorem 3.4.14), the notion of reduction should not have computational power exceeding that of the computational model. ◇

Let us note that the relation $\leq^p_m$ is reflexive; this is an immediate consequence of the polynomial-time computability of the identity function.

Proposition 3.4.17. *For each language B, it holds that* $B \leq^p_m B$.

Finally, we show transitivity of the relation $\leq^p_m$, establishing a polynomial-time analog of the transitivity of the relation $\leq_m$ (Theorem 2.8.11).

Theorem 3.4.18. *Let A, B, and C be languages such that* $A \leq^p_m B$ *and* $B \leq^p_m C$. *Then it holds that* $A \leq^p_m C$.

Proof. Let ρ be a polynomial-time many-one reduction from A to B, and let σ be a polynomial-time many-one reduction from B to C. Set $\tau \colon \Sigma^* \to \Sigma^*$ to be the function defined by $\tau(x) = \sigma(\rho(x))$, that is, τ is the composition of ρ and σ.

Let M_ρ be a polynomial-time DTM that computes ρ, and let P_ρ be a polynomial such that M_ρ runs within time P_ρ. Let M_σ be a polynomial-time DTM that computes σ, and let P_σ be a polynomial such that M_σ runs within time P_σ. Define M to be the DTM that, on an input x, first invokes the DTM M_ρ, and when the computation accepts, then invokes the DTM M_σ, accepting when this second computation accepts. The DTM M clearly computes the function τ. We have

$$\text{time}_M(x) = \text{time}_{M_\rho}(x) + \text{time}_{M_\sigma}(\rho(x))$$
$$\leq P_\rho(|x|) + P_\sigma(|\rho(x)|)$$
$$\leq P_\rho(|x|) + P_\sigma(P_\rho(|x|)).$$

Hence, the DTM M runs within polynomial time, and so τ is polynomial-time computable. (This just-seen chain of relationships is analogous to one given in the proof of the first item of Theorem 3.4.14.)

For each string $x \in \Sigma^*$, we have

$$x \in A \quad \Leftrightarrow \quad \rho(x) \in B$$
$$\Leftrightarrow \quad \sigma(\rho(x)) \in C$$
$$\Leftrightarrow \quad \tau(x) \in C.$$

The first two equivalences follow from the correctness of ρ and σ as polynomial-time many-one reductions, and the third equivalence is immediate from the definition of τ.

We conclude that τ is a polynomial-time many-one reduction from A to C. ☐

When B and C are languages such that the relationship $B \leq^p_m C$ holds, we can intuitively conceive of the $\leq^p_m$ relation as expressing that the language C is *at least as hard* as the language B, as far as efficient algorithmic solvability is concerned. From this vantage point, the properties just given in Theorem 3.4.14, Proposition 3.4.17, and Theorem 3.4.18 are properties that one would naturally expect of a relation comparing hardness in this way.

3.5 NP-completeness

In this section, we introduce notions that will allow us to strongly tighten the relationship between the overall class of NP languages and some of its members. Using these notions, we will be able to show that certain members of this class—including the already-seen languages HAM-CYCLE, 3-COL, INDEP-SET, CLIQUE, and VERTEX-COVER—characterize the entire class, in precise senses. In terminology to be presented soon, we will show that they are *NP-complete*. One key property possessed by an NP-complete language is that it is PTIME if and only if *every* NP language is PTIME; thus, its relationship to PTIME reflects the relationship to PTIME of the whole class that it represents. On an intuitive level, this property entails that all of the phenomena covered by the NP languages are captured by and embodied in these single, individual languages. One can read the NP-completeness of HAM-CYCLE (for example) as stating that HAM-CYCLE is an all-encompassing NP language: if it were possible to efficiently resolve the existence questions that it poses—given a graph, decide whether or not there exists a Hamiltonian cycle—then it would be possible to efficiently resolve the existence questions posed by an arbitrary NP language.

Remark 3.5.1. *For the rest of the chapter, we assume that all languages under discussion are over the alphabet* $\Sigma = \{0, 1\}$, *unless otherwise mentioned.* We will sometimes repeat this assumption for emphasis. This assumption permits us to be able to meaningfully speak of a language admitting a reduction from every NP language; without this assumption, we could not do so—at least with our current definition of reduction—which only allows us to relate two languages over the same alphabet.[17]   ◇

We begin by defining the conditions of *NP-hardness* and *NP-completeness*, which are located at the conceptual epicenter of this chapter. A language is NP-hard if it is at least as hard as each NP language, under reductions; it is NP-complete if, in addition, it is NP. Thus, the NP-complete languages can be conceived of as being the hardest NP languages.

Definition 3.5.2. A language B is **NP-hard** if for each NP language A, the relationship $A \leq_m^p B$ holds.   ◇

Definition 3.5.3. A language B is **NP-complete** if it is NP and it is NP-hard.   ◇

A crucial property of the NP-hard languages is the following.

---

17. It is certainly possible to define reductions between languages on different alphabets. The author has elected not to do so, and holds the view that not much extra insight is yielded by that approach, which comes at the expense of adding technicalities to some of the definitions. In any case, for any language B over an alphabet Σ_B, one can define a language B' over the alphabet $\{0, 1\}$ that retains all relevant properties of B (see Exercise 3.10.17).

Theorem 3.5.4. *Suppose that B is an NP-hard language. If B is PTIME, then each NP language is PTIME. (That is, $B \in \mathcal{P}$ implies $\mathcal{NP} \subseteq \mathcal{P}$.)*

Proof. Let A be an arbitrary NP language. Since B is NP-hard, it holds that $A \leq_m^p B$. As B is PTIME by assumption, it follows from Theorem 3.4.14 that A is PTIME. □

We next show the mentioned key property of the NP-complete languages; indeed, that this property holds can be taken both as the motivation for and as a justification of the definition of NP-completeness.

Theorem 3.5.5. *Suppose that B is an NP-complete language. It holds that B is PTIME if and only if each NP language is PTIME. (That is, it holds that $B \in \mathcal{P}$ if and only if $\mathcal{NP} \subseteq \mathcal{P}$.)*

Proof. The backward direction is immediate. Since each NP-complete language is by definition NP-hard, the forward direction follows from Theorem 3.5.4. □

A direct consequence of Theorem 3.5.5 is that either all of the NP-complete languages are PTIME, or that none of them are; as it is sometimes said, the NP-complete languages stand or fall together.

Theorem 3.5.6. *When B and C are NP-complete languages, it holds that B is PTIME if and only if C is PTIME.*

Proof. This theorem is immediate from Theorem 3.5.5: each of the two statements of this theorem is equivalent to the statement that each NP language is PTIME. □

Indeed, it follows immediately from the definition of *NP-complete* that any NP-complete language admits reductions both to and from any other NP-complete language; in this sense, all NP-complete languages are equivalent under reductions.

Discussion

A primary fruit of the theory of NP-completeness is that it yields the ability to equate different hypotheses. For instance, the languages HAM-CYCLE, 3-COL, and INDEP-SET will be shown to be NP-complete; from these results and Theorem 3.5.6, the hypothesis that HAM-CYCLE is a PTIME language is the same as the hypothesis that 3-COL is a PTIME language, which in turn is the same as the hypothesis that INDEP-SET is a PTIME language. On the research level, this implies that trying to establish the truth of one of these hypotheses is the same as trying to establish the truth of any of the other hypotheses; likewise, trying to establish the falsity of one of these hypotheses is the same as trying to establish the falsity of any of the other hypotheses. These equivalences hold despite any sensation that these languages and further NP-complete languages are quite qualitatively different from one another. Indeed, the NP-complete languages interestingly exhibit an awesome diversity, and occur in many fields of human inquiry. The reader will hopefully cultivate a rounded sense of this diversity in Section 3.8, where a variety of NP-complete languages will be presented.

As shown by Theorem 3.5.5, the hypothesis that an NP-complete language is not PTIME is equivalent to the assumption that $\mathcal{NP} \not\subseteq \mathcal{P}$, which is equivalent to the assumption that $\mathcal{P} \neq \mathcal{NP}$. The ubiquity and relevance of the NP-complete languages thus exposes and underscores the criticality of the P versus NP question. The assumption that $\mathcal{P} \neq \mathcal{NP}$ is, at the time of writing, generally accepted as a valid working hypothesis. In accordance with Theorem 3.5.4, a proof that a language is NP-hard is thus commonly construed as evidence that the language is not PTIME. (By that theorem, having an NP-hard language that was also PTIME would imply that $\mathcal{P} = \mathcal{NP}$.) Pragmatically speaking, a proof that a language is NP-hard suggests that the ambition of showing that the language is PTIME should be approached with extreme caution: showing this would imply that $\mathcal{P} = \mathcal{NP}$. Indeed, over the years, many persons have attempted to exhibit efficient algorithms for NP-hard languages, and thus in effect tried to prove that $\mathcal{P} = \mathcal{NP}$—in some cases, perhaps unknowingly!

Further properties

In the next section, we will present a first example of an NP-complete language: the language CIRCUIT-SAT, which consists of the *satisfiable circuits*. After this, we will want to prove the NP-completeness of further languages, such as the languages HAM-CYCLE, 3-COL, and INDEP-SET. Typically, the challenge in establishing the NP-completeness of a language is in showing NP-hardness; to show that languages are NP, straightforward arguments along the lines of those already seen often suffice. The following proposition presents a main tool that will be used to show NP-hardness of languages: one exhibits a reduction from a language already established as NP-hard.

Proposition 3.5.7. *Suppose that B is an NP-hard language, and that C is a language such that $B \leq_m^p C$. Then, the language C is NP-hard.*

Proof. Let A be an arbitrary NP language. By the NP-hardness of the language B, we have that $A \leq_m^p B$. By the hypothesis that $B \leq_m^p C$ and Theorem 3.4.18, we obtain the relationship $A \leq_m^p C$. □

The following theorem presents an offshoot of the existence of NP-complete languages: an alternative characterization of the class of NP languages. In particular, the following theorem shows that this class can be characterized solely in terms of an NP-complete language B and the notion of polynomial-time many-one reduction.

Theorem 3.5.8. *Suppose that B is an NP-complete language. Then, an arbitrary language A is NP if and only if $A \leq_m^p B$.*

Proof. The forward direction follows immediately from the NP-hardness of B. The backward direction follows from Theorem 3.4.14 and the assumption that B is NP. □

Remark 3.5.9. Theorem 3.5.8 reveals that we actually could have equivalently defined the NP languages by taking a language known to be NP-complete, such as CIRCUIT-SAT, and defining a language to be NP if and only if it reduces to CIRCUIT-SAT. Observe that this alternative definition makes no explicit reference to nondeterministic computation; the only computational notion it directly refers to is that underlying a reduction, namely, the notion of a polynomial-time computable function. (This is the second characterization of the NP languages that does not refer expressly to nondeterminism; the first was the characterization via verifiers, given by Theorem 3.2.26.)

This alternative definition would still allow us to exhibit NP-completeness results, which in turn would still allow us to equate the hypotheses stating that each of the various NP-complete languages is PTIME (recall Theorem 3.5.6). If we can carry out all of these results without any notion of nondeterministic computation, why should we use such a notion to define the NP languages in the first place? Relative to the alternative definition, the official definition that we have given in terms of polynomial-time NTMs (Definition 3.2.15) gives us additional perspective; it gives us another way to reason about whether or not languages are NP. In particular, this definition facilitates the act of showing inclusion of a language in the class of NP languages: to do so, we can present a polynomial-time NTM for the language. (In many cases, presenting such an NTM is arguably more intuitive and natural than presenting a reduction to a known NP-complete language.) On a more conceptual level, this machine-based definition renders vivid the computational phenomena encompassed by the class, and therefore also the computational phenomena encompassed by the class's complete problems.   ◇

Remark 3.5.10. The act of defining *complete* languages for a language class is not specific to the NP languages, but in fact can be carried out for many language classes of interest. We explore this act in a general setting in Exercises 3.10.23 and 3.10.25.   ◇

3.6 Circuit satisfiability

In this section, we establish our first NP-completeness result, which is for the language whose elements are the *satisfiable circuits*.[18] We first introduce the requisite terminology and concepts; we then define the language and prove it to be NP-complete.

---

18. The adoption of the term *NP-complete* stems from a 1974 article of D. E. Knuth, in which a number of alternative name proposals are discussed. Among these proposals, one can find *hard-ass*, suggested as shorthand for *hard as satisfiability*.

Definition 3.6.1. A **circuit** consists of

- a sequence $v_1, \ldots, v_n$ of **inputs**, where $n \geq 0$;
- a sequence $g_1, \ldots, g_m$ of **gates**, where $m \geq 1$;
- a map I that sends each gate g to its **instruction** $I(g)$; and
- a distinguished gate g_u called the **output gate**.

We define the following notions.

- We use G_0 to denote the set $\{v_1, \ldots, v_n\} \cup \{\underline{0}, \underline{1}\}$, that is, the set containing all inputs as well as two special values $\underline{0}$ and $\underline{1}$ that represent the propositional values 0 and 1, respectively. We refer to the elements of G_0 as the **sources** of the circuit.
- For each $i \in \{1, \ldots, m\}$, define $G_{<i} = G_0 \cup \{g_j \mid 1 \leq j < i\}$. That is, the set $G_{<i}$ contains all sources, and all gates prior to the ith gate.

For each $i \in \{1, \ldots, m\}$, the instruction $I(g_i)$ of gate g_i must have one of the following forms:

- $\neg h$, where $h \in G_{<i}$;
- $h_1 \wedge \cdots \wedge h_k$, where $k \geq 1$ and $h_1, \ldots, h_k \in G_{<i}$; or
- $h_1 \vee \cdots \vee h_k$, where $k \geq 1$ and $h_1, \ldots, h_k \in G_{<i}$.   ◇

Note that the values $\underline{0}$ and $\underline{1}$ are explicitly allowed in instructions; this will allow us to easily replace variables with constant values.

Example 3.6.2. Let us present an example of a circuit, depicted as a directed graph in Figure 3.6.1. Let C be the circuit with inputs v_1, v_2, v_3, and with gates g_1, g_2, g_3, g_4, where g_4 is the output gate; we define the instructions of the gates as follows:

$$I(g_1) = v_1 \wedge v_2 \wedge v_3,$$

$$I(g_2) = \neg v_3,$$

$$I(g_3) = g_1 \vee g_2,$$

$$I(g_4) = \neg g_3.$$ ◇

When we have a circuit in hand, an assignment to its inputs naturally induces an assignment to each of its gates; see Figure 3.6.2 for examples. We formalize this as follows.

Definition 3.6.3. Let C be a circuit, whose parts are notated as in Definition 3.6.1. An assignment $f\colon \{v_1, \ldots, v_n\} \to \{0, 1\}$ to the inputs can be naturally extended to an assignment $f_C\colon G_0 \cup \{g_1, \ldots, g_m\}$ which, for each gate, gives the value in $\{0, 1\}$ that the gate evaluates to under f. In particular, the definition f_C is built inductively:

- First, define f_C on G_0 as the extension of f such that $f_C(\underline{0}) = 0$ and $f_C(\underline{1}) = 1$.
- For each $i \in \{1, \ldots, m\}$, define f_C on g_i inductively according to the instructions.

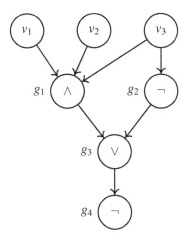

Figure 3.6.1. The circuit from Example 3.6.2. Each circuit can be visualized as a directed graph, in the following way. The sources that are used are presented as labeled vertices. Each gate is represented with a vertex whose label indicates the connective ($\neg$, $\wedge$, or $\vee$) of the gate's instruction, and next to the vertex is the gate's name. Each gate has incoming edges from the vertices appearing in the gate's instruction. Following a custom, the sources are placed at the top, and the output gate is placed at the bottom.

Precisely, define $f_C(g_i)$ as

- $\neg f_C(h)$, when $I(g_i) = \neg h$;
- $f_C(h_1) \wedge \cdots \wedge f_C(h_k)$, when $I(g_i) = h_1 \wedge \cdots \wedge h_k$; and
- $f_C(h_1) \vee \cdots \vee f_C(h_k)$, when $I(g_i) = h_1 \vee \cdots \vee h_k$.   ◇

We remark that in the just-given definition of $f_C(g_i)$, the symbols $\neg$, $\wedge$, and $\vee$ are being used in two senses: when applied to a value $f_C(h)$ or values $f_C(h_j)$, they are viewed as operations over the set $\{0, 1\}$; when appearing in instructions, they are treated as syntax indicating how the instructions should be interpreted.

Example 3.6.4. Consider the circuit C from Example 3.6.2. We indicate how two example assignments to the inputs are extended to all of the gates; see Figure 3.6.2 for diagrams, where the value assigned to each input and each gate is given to the right of the corresponding vertex.

- Define $f\colon \{v_1, v_2, v_3\} \to \{0, 1\}$ as the assignment where $f(v_1) = 1$ and $f(v_2) = f(v_3) = 0$. It is readily verified that $f_C(g_1) = 0, f_C(g_2) = 1, f_C(g_3) = 1$, and $f_C(g_4) = 0$.
- Define $f'\colon \{v_1, v_2, v_3\} \to \{0, 1\}$ as the assignment where $f'(v_1) = f'(v_2) = 0$ and $f'(v_3) = 1$. It is readily verified that $f'_C(g_1) = 0, f'_C(g_2) = 0, f'_C(g_3) = 0$, and $f'_C(g_4) = 1$.   ◇

We use the following notions to discuss the satisfiability of circuits.

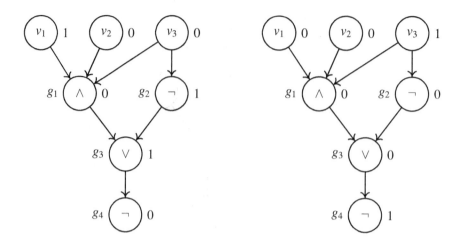

Figure 3.6.2. Two examples of how assignments to the inputs of a circuit are extended to all gates.

Definition 3.6.5. Let C be a circuit with inputs $v_1, \ldots, v_n$ and output gate g_u.

- An assignment $f \colon \{v_1, \ldots, v_n\} \to \{0, 1\}$ **satisfies** the circuit C if, under f, its output gate evaluates to 1; formally, if its described extension f_C has $f_C(g_u) = 1$.
- A circuit is called **satisfiable** if there exists an assignment that satisfies it, and is called **unsatisfiable** otherwise.
- We naturally view a length n string $x_1 \ldots x_n$ over the alphabet $\{0, 1\}$ as **defining** an assignment $f \colon \{v_1, \ldots, v_n\} \to \{0, 1\}$, namely, the assignment where $f(v_i) = x_i$ for each index $i \in \{1, \ldots, n\}$; in this way, we can speak of a string satisfying (or not satisfying) the circuit C.   ◇

Example 3.6.6. Let us illustrate the notions of Definition 3.6.5. We continue the discussion of Example 3.6.4; let C be the circuit from Example 3.6.2.

- The string 100 does not satisfy the circuit C. This string defines the assignment f given in Example 3.6.4; this assignment's extension f_C maps the output gate g_4 to 0.
- On the other hand, the string 001 does satisfy the circuit C. This string defines the assignment f' given in Example 3.6.4; this assignment's extension f'_C maps the output gate g_4 to 1. The circuit C is thus satisfiable.
- In fact, we can observe that for any assignment $e \colon \{v_1, v_2, v_3\} \to \{0, 1\}$ having $e(v_3) = 0$, it holds that e does not satisfy C. This is because such an assignment e will have $e_C(g_2) = 1$, $e_C(g_3) = 1$, and $e_C(g_4) = 0$. See the left diagram of Figure 3.6.3.   ◇

Example 3.6.7. We can create, starting from the circuit C of Example 3.6.2, a second circuit C' by *instantiating* the input v_3 with the value 0. The circuit C' is depicted in the right diagram of Figure 3.6.3. Formally, the circuit C' has inputs v_1, v_2; it excludes the

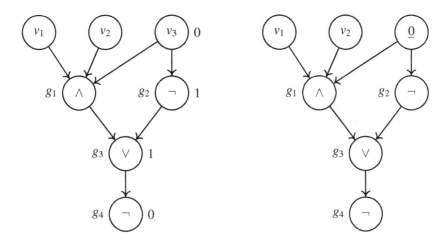

Figure 3.6.3. The left diagram indicates how, for the given circuit, any assignment mapping v_3 to 0 will map the output gate g_4 to 0; this is discussed in Example 3.6.6. The right diagram shows the circuit obtained from the circuit on the left by *instantiating* the input v_3 with the value 0; refer to Example 3.6.7 for a discussion.

input v_3 of C. The gates of C' are those of C, namely, g_1, g_2, g_3, g_4, and the output gate of C' is that of C, namely, g_4. The gate instructions of C' are modified from those of C so that each occurrence of v_3 is replaced with the source $\underline{0}$:

$$I'(g_1) = v_1 \wedge v_2 \wedge \underline{0},$$

$$I'(g_2) = \neg\underline{0},$$

$$I'(g_3) = g_1 \vee g_2,$$

$$I'(g_4) = \neg g_3.$$

It is straightforward to verify that C' is satisfied by an assignment $h' \colon \{v_1, v_2\} \to \{0, 1\}$ if and only if C is satisfied by the extension $h \colon \{v_1, v_2, v_3\} \to \{0, 1\}$ of h' where $h(v_3) = 0$. Thus, by the last point of Example 3.6.6, the circuit C' is unsatisfiable. ◇

We formally define the process of instantiating circuit inputs, which was just exemplified, as follows.

Definition 3.6.8 (Instantiation of circuit inputs). When C is a circuit and $w_1, \ldots, w_k$ are among the inputs of C, the circuit C' obtained by **instantiating** the inputs $w_1, \ldots, w_k$ with the values $b_1, \ldots, b_k \in \{0, 1\}$ is defined as the circuit derived from C where $w_1, \ldots, w_k$ are removed from the sequence of inputs, the gates remain the same, and each occurrence of an input w_i in an instruction is replaced with the source $\underline{b_i}$. ◇

Let us identify a key fact concerning this type of instantiation, to be used tacitly in the sequel. When C' is a circuit obtained by instantiating inputs from a circuit C as notated in Definition 3.6.8, and when f is an assignment to the inputs of C', it holds that f satisfies C' if and only if the extension of f mapping each w_i to b_i satisfies C. (This fact was exemplified in Example 3.6.7.)

A basic fact on circuits, which we state and argue next, is that any propositional formula can be converted to a circuit.

Proposition 3.6.9 (Formulas as circuits). *For any propositional formula ϕ whose variables are drawn from a variable sequence $v_1, \ldots, v_n$, there exists a circuit C_ϕ with inputs $v_1, \ldots, v_n$ that represents ϕ in the following sense:*

an assignment $f: \{v_1, \ldots, v_n\} \to \{0, 1\}$ satisfies ϕ if and only if it satisfies C_ϕ.

We briefly argue Proposition 3.6.9 as follows; see Figure 3.6.5 for an example. To convert from a propositional formula ϕ to a circuit C_ϕ, we view the formula ϕ as a rooted tree where each leaf corresponds to a variable occurrence, and each internal vertex corresponds to a connective occurrence. This rooted tree is converted to a circuit by making each internal vertex into a gate, whose instruction is defined according to the formula; the tree's root becomes the output gate. It is worth mentioning that this conversion from formulas to circuits is efficient in that there exists a polynomial-time DTM that carries it out.

Example 3.6.10. Let us present a second example of a circuit, depicted as a directed graph in Figure 3.6.4. This example circuit has inputs v_1, v_2, v_3 and has gates $g_1, \ldots, g_8$; the gate g_8 is the output gate, and the instructions are given as follows:

$$I(g_1) = v_1 \vee v_2, \qquad\qquad I(g_5) = g_4 \vee v_3,$$

$$I(g_2) = v_1 \wedge v_2, \qquad\qquad I(g_6) = g_4 \wedge v_3,$$

$$I(g_3) = \neg g_2, \qquad\qquad\qquad I(g_7) = \neg g_6,$$

$$I(g_4) = g_1 \wedge g_3, \qquad\qquad I(g_8) = g_5 \wedge g_7.$$

It can be verified that, under any assignment $f: \{v_1, v_2, v_3\} \to \{0, 1\}$, the gate g_8 evaluates to the *parity* of the values $f(v_1), f(v_2)$, and $f(v_3)$; that is, to 1 if the number of 1's among these values is odd, and to 0 if this number is even. An assignment $f: \{v_1, v_2, v_3\} \to \{0, 1\}$ thus satisfies this circuit if and only if it maps either exactly one input or all three inputs to the value 1. To use the string notation, the strings 001, 010, 100, and 111 satisfy this circuit, and the strings 000, 011, 101, and 110 do not.   ◇

Remark 3.6.11. Let us observe some general facts linking a circuit diagram to its circuit's instructions, which are readily verified for the seen example circuits. For a source or a gate, the number of outgoing edges in the diagram is the number of times it appears in the instructions; for a gate, the number of incoming edges in the diagram is the number of sources and gates appearing in its instruction.

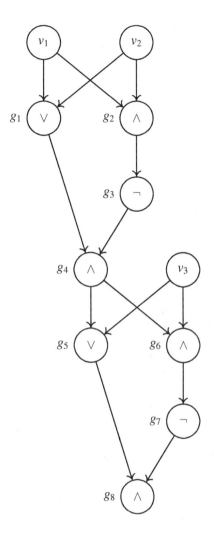

Figure 3.6.4. The circuit from Example 3.6.10, which computes the parity of its three input values.

When a formula is converted to a circuit (as described in conjunction with Proposition 3.6.9) the resulting circuit satisfies a property that does not hold in general on a circuit: no gate appears more than once in an instruction. In terms of the circuit diagrams we have shown, this property holds that no gate has more than one outgoing edge. Indeed, in such a resulting circuit, the output gate will have no outgoing edges, and each other gate will have exactly one outgoing edge. ◇

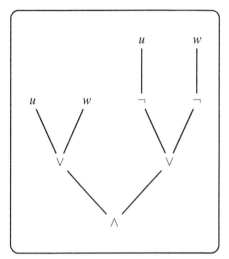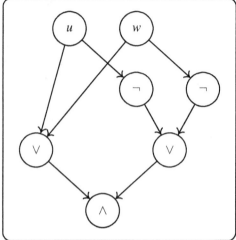

Figure 3.6.5. Example of a conversion from a formula to a circuit. The diagram shows how the formula $(u \lor w) \land (\neg u \lor \neg w)$ can be converted to a circuit. First, the formula is viewed as a rooted tree, as shown on the left; here, the tree's root is drawn at the bottom, and so the leaves, which correspond to variable occurrences, appear at the top. Then, to perform the conversion, each variable of the formula is viewed as a circuit input, and each internal vertex of the formula tree becomes a circuit gate; the resulting circuit is shown on the right.

We can next proceed to this section's main result. Define the language

$$\text{CIRCUIT-SAT} = \{\ulcorner C \urcorner \mid C \text{ is a satisfiable circuit}\}.$$

Theorem 3.6.12. *The language* CIRCUIT-SAT *is NP-complete.*

We will prove this theorem in two steps.

- In the first step, the upcoming Theorem 3.6.15, we show that any PTIME language can be efficiently represented by circuits, in a sense to be made precise.
- In the second step, we make use of the first step's theorem in combination with the previously given characterization of NP languages in terms of verifiers—whose languages are PTIME.

On a high level, we argue this theorem as follows. The crux is to establish that the language CIRCUIT-SAT is NP-hard. To do so, we want to translate, for any NP language B, a question of whether or not a string x is in B to a question of whether or not a circuit is satisfiable. With a particular string x in hand, the question of whether $x \in B$ can be viewed as a question about whether or not there exists a string y that causes a certain polynomial-time computation to accept, via the verifier-based characterization of the NP languages (Theorem 3.2.26). Specifically, this theorem provides a verifier M for the language B; the verifier M is by definition a polynomial-time DTM; and it holds that $x \in B$ if and only if there exists a string y such that $\langle x, y \rangle \in L(M)$. The upcoming theorem (Theorem 3.6.15), which characterizes the PTIME languages in terms of circuits, allows us to translate the question of whether such a string y exists to a question about whether a circuit is satisfiable.

How are we to characterize a language using circuits? Observe that a circuit only renders judgment on strings of a fixed length: a circuit with n inputs is either satisfied or not by each string of length n, but does not render any judgment on strings that are not of length n. In contrast, a language confers a membership judgment on each string (over the language's alphabet), regardless of length: a language either contains or does not contain a given string. So, a natural way to characterize a language using circuits would be to provide one circuit C_n for each possible string length $n \geq 0$; this is what we do. We formalize the needed notions as follows.

Definition 3.6.13. A **circuit family** is an infinite sequence $(C_n)_{n \in \mathbb{N}}$ of circuits such that (for each $n \in \mathbb{N}$) the circuit C_n has n inputs. ◇

Definition 3.6.14. A circuit family $(C_n)_{n \in \mathbb{N}}$ **computes** a language B over $\Sigma = \{0, 1\}$ when, for each string $x \in \Sigma^*$, it holds that x satisfies the circuit $C_{|x|}$ if and only if $x \in B$ holds. A circuit family $(C_n)_{n \in \mathbb{N}}$ is **polynomial-time uniform** if there exists a polynomial-time computable function $f \colon \Sigma^* \to \Sigma^*$ such that, for all $n \in \mathbb{N}$, it holds that $f(1^n) = \ulcorner C_n \urcorner$. ◇

The following is our circuit-based characterization of the PTIME languages.

Theorem 3.6.15. *For each PTIME language B over the alphabet $\{0, 1\}$, there exists a polynomial-time uniform circuit family that computes B.*

Let us give a preview of this theorem's proof. The high-level idea behind the proof is not complicated, although its precise implementation requires a certain attention to detail.[19] Let M be a polynomial-time DTM such that $L(M) = B$, and let P be a polynomial such that M runs within time P. For each $n \geq 0$, we need to construct a circuit C_n that, on a string x of length n, outputs 1 if and only if $x \in B$.

Upon being given an input string x of length n, the machine M begins in its initial configuration on x, denoted here by γ_1, and passes through a sequence of configurations $\gamma_1 \vdash_M \gamma_2 \vdash_M \gamma_3 \vdash_M \cdots$ before halting. For each $i > 1$, the configuration γ_i, if defined, can be determined from γ_{i-1}. The circuit determines the configurations $\gamma_1, \gamma_2, \gamma_3, \ldots$ in order, and outputs 1 if the final such configuration is accepting; the number of configurations encountered up to halting is at most $P(n)$.

A priori, however, each configuration $\gamma_i = [q_i, \tau_i, \ell_i]$ is an infinite object: the mapping τ_i, giving the tape contents, is defined on an infinite set—the positive natural numbers—and ℓ_i

---

19. Of this proof, the author would say that there is no *devil in the details*. Once the proof's overall strategy is established, carrying out the details is relatively straightforward, if somewhat taxing; perhaps, *the message is the tedium.*

	1	2	3	4	5	6	7	8
1	(a, s)	$(b, \bot)$	$(\sqcup, \bot)$	$(\sqcup, \bot)$	$(\sqcup, \bot)$	$(\sqcup, \bot)$	$(\sqcup, \bot)$	$(\sqcup, \bot)$
2	$(\sqcup, \bot)$	(b, h)	$(\sqcup, \bot)$	$(\sqcup, \bot)$	$(\sqcup, \bot)$	$(\sqcup, \bot)$	$(\sqcup, \bot)$	$(\sqcup, \bot)$
3	$(\sqcup, \bot)$	$(b, \bot)$	$(\sqcup, h)$	$(\sqcup, \bot)$	$(\sqcup, \bot)$	$(\sqcup, \bot)$	$(\sqcup, \bot)$	$(\sqcup, \bot)$
4	$(\sqcup, \bot)$	(b, e)	$(\sqcup, \bot)$	$(\sqcup, \bot)$	$(\sqcup, \bot)$	$(\sqcup, \bot)$	$(\sqcup, \bot)$	$(\sqcup, \bot)$
5	$(\sqcup, g)$	$(\sqcup, \bot)$	$(\sqcup, \bot)$	$(\sqcup, \bot)$	$(\sqcup, \bot)$	$(\sqcup, \bot)$	$(\sqcup, \bot)$	$(\sqcup, \bot)$
6	$(\sqcup, \bot)$	$(\sqcup, s)$	$(\sqcup, \bot)$	$(\sqcup, \bot)$	$(\sqcup, \bot)$	$(\sqcup, \bot)$	$(\sqcup, \bot)$	$(\sqcup, \bot)$
7	$(\sqcup, \bot)$	$(\sqcup, \bot)$	$(\sqcup, t)$	$(\sqcup, \bot)$	$(\sqcup, \bot)$	$(\sqcup, \bot)$	$(\sqcup, \bot)$	$(\sqcup, \bot)$
8	$(\sqcup, \bot)$	$(\sqcup, \bot)$	$(\sqcup, t)$	$(\sqcup, \bot)$	$(\sqcup, \bot)$	$(\sqcup, \bot)$	$(\sqcup, \bot)$	$(\sqcup, \bot)$

Figure 3.6.6. An example computation table T, based on the computation of a DTM on the input string ab (namely, the DTM from Example 2.1.3). The rows and columns are numbered, starting from 1. Each row represents a configuration; row 1 represents the initial configuration. Each entry of the table is a pair; the entry at the ith row and jth column is denoted $T_{(i,j)}$. The first part of $T_{(i,j)}$ is the symbol in the jth cell, in the ith configuration. The second part of $T_{(i,j)}$ indicates the head location and state of the ith configuration: it is the DTM's state when the head is located at the jth cell, and is the value $\bot$ otherwise. As examples, the entry $T_{(3,2)}$ is the pair $(b, \bot)$, which indicates that, in the 3rd configuration, the symbol in the 2nd cell is b and the head is not located at this cell; the entry $T_{(4,2)}$ is the pair (b, e), which indicates that, in the 4th configuration, the symbol in the 2nd cell is b, the head is located at this cell, and the DTM state is e. The computation's configurations are represented by rows 1 through 7. In row 7, a halting configuration is reached; its entries are repeated in row 8.

is itself a positive natural number. A key observation is that, once we fix the length n of the input string x, we can represent each configuration γ_i using a *finite* amount of information. On an input string of length n, the head location starts at 1 and increases by at most 1 in each time step, so during the computation, the head location never exceeds $P(n)$. On such an input string, then, each configuration can be described by the status of its tape cells up to the $P(n)$th: it suffices to specify, for each of these tape cells, the symbol that it contains, and in the case that the head is located at it, the configuration's state. The circuit uses a sequence of gates to represent each potential configuration; each configuration can be represented by a number of gates that is proportional to $P(n)$, and the number of potential configurations is $P(n)$. These are the two dimensions along which the circuit is constructed; the total number of gates will be proportional to $P(n)^2$.

Proof of Theorem 3.6.15. Let $M = (Q, \Sigma, \Gamma, s, t, r, \delta)$ be a polynomial-time DTM such that $L(M) = B$, and let P be a polynomial such that M runs within time P; we can assume that $P(n) \geq n$ (for each $n \in \mathbb{N}$).[20] For each $n \geq 0$, we describe a circuit C_n such that a string x of length n satisfies C_n if and only if $x \in B$.

---

20. In the case that this inequality fails to hold, the polynomial P can be replaced with the polynomial P' defined by $P'(n) = P(n) + n$.

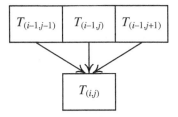

Figure 3.6.7. The property of *locality*. In a non-initial row of a computation table, each entry $T_{(i,j)}$ can be determined from at most three entries in the previous row: the entry $T_{(i-1,j)}$ immediately above it, and the adjacent entries $T_{(i-1,j-1)}$ and $T_{(i-1,j+1)}$. When one of these adjacent entries is not defined, the entry $T_{(i,j)}$ can be determined without it.

The following notion of *computation table*, which serves as a transcript of a computation, will be used to present the circuit C_n; see Figure 3.6.6 for an example. For a value $K \geq 1$ and a string x, the **K-by-K computation table** of M on x is the table T that, for each pair of values $i, j \in \{1, ..., K\}$, has an entry $T_{(i,j)}$ defined as follows.

- For each $i \in \{1, ..., K\}$, the ith row of the table represents a configuration κ_i. The configuration represented by the 1st row, κ_1, is the initial configuration of M on x. For each $i \in \{2, ..., K\}$, the configuration κ_i is defined as the successor configuration of κ_{i-1} when κ_{i-1} is not a halting configuration, and as equal to κ_{i-1} when κ_{i-1} is a halting configuration. So, the 1st row represents the initial configuration, and each following row represents the successor configuration of the previous row's configuration until a halting configuration is reached, at which point each subsequent row is simply a copy of the previous one.

- The ith row of the table represents the defined configuration κ_i in the following precise fashion. For each $j \in \{1, ..., K\}$, the entry $T_{(i,j)}$ is defined as the pair (a, q) from the set $\Gamma \times (Q \cup \{\perp\})$ where a is the symbol in the jth cell (according to κ_i); and where q is $\perp$ when κ_i's head location is not j, and is the state component of the configuration κ_i, otherwise. (We assume $\perp$ to be a value not contained in Q.) Thus, the second value q of the entry $T_{(i,j)}$ indicates information about the head location: it is set to $\perp$ or not depending on whether or not the head is absent at location j (in κ_i). In each row, exactly one entry $T_{(i,j)}$ will have a value q that is set to an element of Q, since in a configuration the head is located at exactly one cell.

We will only form the K-by-K computation table of M on x when $K \geq P(|x|)$, which ensures that the table has enough columns so that each row can fully represent its corresponding configuration, and has enough rows to determine the computation's outcome.

The circuit C_n, when given a string x of length n, determines a computation table of the DTM M on x. As discussed just prior to the proof, during a computation of M on a length n input string, the head location (of M) never exceeds $P(n)$. From this observation and our

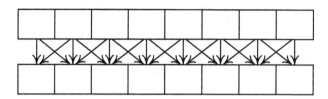

Figure 3.6.8. In a computation table, the entries of each row, apart from the initial row, can be determined via locality from the previous row's entries.

assumption that $P(n) \geq n$, we have that, during such a computation, each tape cell beyond the $P(n)$th remains blank, and is never reached by the head. Thus, so long as $K \geq P(n)$, determining the K-by-K computation table is sufficient for determining the outcome of M on x. In particular, if M accepts x, such a computation table will contain a row representing an accepting configuration, and all subsequent rows will represent the same configuration. So, the final row of such a computation table will contain an occurrence of the accept state if and only if M accepts x.

In order to present the circuit C_n, we observe that the computation table satisfies a property which is called **locality**, and which is depicted in Figures 3.6.7 and 3.6.8: once the 1st row has been fixed, in any later row—say, the ith row—the jth column's entry $T_{(i,j)}$ can be determined from the previous row by inspecting at most three entries: the entry $T_{(i-1,j)}$ above $T_{(i,j)}$, and the two directly adjacent entries $T_{(i-1,j-1)}$ and $T_{(i-1,j+1)}$. (If either of these two adjacent entries is not defined, it is not needed to determine the entry $T_{(i,j)}$.) Why is this?

- The first part $a \in \Gamma$ of the entry $T_{(i,j)}$ can be determined from the entry $T_{(i-1,j)}$: when in row $i-1$'s configuration the head is not located at j, this value a is equal to the first part of $T_{(i-1,j)}$; otherwise, this value a is determined by the transition function's value under the state and symbol of $T_{(i-1,j)}$.

- Assuming $j > 1$, the second part $q \in Q \cup \{\bot\}$ of the entry $T_{(i,j)}$ is $\bot$ unless one of the following holds, on row $i-1$'s configuration: the head location is $j-1$ and the transition function calls for a right movement; the head location is $j+1$ and the transition function calls for a left movement; or, the head location is j and the configuration is halting. Thus, this second part q can be determined from the entry $T_{(i-1,j-1)}$, the entry $T_{(i-1,j)}$, and (if defined) the entry $T_{(i-1,j+1)}$.

  When $j = 1$, this second part $q \in Q \cup \{\bot\}$ can be determined from the entries $T_{(i-1,1)}$ and $T_{(i-1,2)}$, by similar reasoning; one needs to account for our convention that the head remains at location 1 when the head is at this location and the transition function calls for a left movement.

Each circuit C_n determines a K-by-K computation table T, where we take $K = P(n) + 1$. This choice of K will facilitate our presentation, as it ensures that in the rightmost column, the Kth column, each entry will be equal to $(\sqcup, \perp)$. In the circuit C_n, each entry $T_{(i,j)}$ is represented by a sequence of gates. For entries in the initial row, each gate's instruction is given in terms of the circuit's sources. Via locality, each other gate's instruction can be written using a fixed number of gates of the previous row, and thus requires just a constant amount of circuitry. The total number of gates needed to construct each circuit C_n is thus linear in the number of entries in the computation table, so we can upper bound the total number of gates by an expression $R(P(n)^2)$, where R is a linear (degree 1) polynomial. Each circuit C_n will be evidently constructed in a highly uniform manner, and it will be straightforwardly verifiable from the description below that this circuit family is polynomial-time uniform.

As stated, each entry $T_{(i,j)}$ of the computation table T is a pair $(a, q) \in \Gamma \times (Q \cup \{\perp\})$; we refer to a as the **symbol** of $T_{(i,j)}$, and to q as the **state** of $T_{(i,j)}$. Each entry $T_{(i,j)}$ is represented in the circuit by a set of gates

$$\left\{ \mathsf{sym}^a_{(i,j)} \mid a \in \Gamma \right\} \cup \left\{ \mathsf{state}^q_{(i,j)} \mid q \in Q \cup \{\perp\} \right\},$$

which will be defined so that, under an input string x, a gate $\mathsf{sym}^a_{(i,j)}$ evaluates to 1 if and only if the symbol of $T_{(i,j)}$ is a, and a gate $\mathsf{state}^q_{(i,j)}$ evaluates to 1 if and only if the state of $T_{(i,j)}$ is q. So, the entry $T_{(i,j)}$ is represented by having exactly one of the gates in $\left\{ \mathsf{sym}^a_{(i,j)} \mid a \in \Gamma \right\}$ evaluate to 1, and exactly one of the gates in $\left\{ \mathsf{state}^q_{(i,j)} \mid q \in Q \cup \{\perp\} \right\}$ evaluate to 1.

We explain in detail how to construct the circuit C_n, row-by-row. We begin by showing how to define the instructions for the 1st row's gates.

- Define $I(\mathsf{state}^s_{(1,1)}) = \underline{1}$, and for each $q \in (Q \cup \{\perp\}) \setminus \{s\}$, define $I(\mathsf{state}^q_{(1,1)}) = \underline{0}$.
- For each j with $1 < j \leq K$, define $I(\mathsf{state}^{\perp}_{(1,j)}) = \underline{1}$, and for each $q \in Q$, define $I(\mathsf{state}^q_{(1,j)}) = \underline{0}$.
- For each j with $1 \leq j \leq n$, define $I(\mathsf{sym}^a_{(1,j)})$ as $\neg v_j$ if $a = 0$, as v_j if $a = 1$, and as $\underline{0}$ otherwise.
- For each j with $n < j \leq K$, define $I(\mathsf{sym}^{\sqcup}_{(1,j)}) = \underline{1}$, and, for each $a \in \Gamma \setminus \{\sqcup\}$, define $I(\mathsf{sym}^a_{(1,j)}) = \underline{0}$.

These instructions specify that the state of $T_{(1,1)}$ is s, and the state of each other entry $T_{(1,j)}$ in the 1th row is $\perp$. And they specify that the symbol of each entry $T_{(1,j)}$ with $1 \leq j \leq n$ is equal to the value of the input v_j, and that the symbol of each other entry $T_{(1,j)}$ is the blank symbol $\sqcup$.

For the later rows, we define the instruction of most of the corresponding gates by providing a propositional formula, whose variables are gates from the previous row. This formula can be converted into circuitry via the translation given for Proposition 3.6.9.[21] Let i be the index of a non-initial row, so that it satisfies $1 < i \leq K$.

We show how to define the instruction of each symbol gate. For each symbol $a \in \Gamma$ and each value $j \in \{1, \ldots, K\}$, the formula for $I(\text{sym}_{(i,j)}^a)$ is the disjunction

$$(\text{sym}_{(i-1,j)}^a \wedge (\text{state}_{(i-1,j)}^\perp \vee \text{state}_{(i-1,j)}^t \vee \text{state}_{(i-1,j)}^r)) \vee (\bigwedge_{q',a'} (\text{sym}_{(i-1,j)}^{a'} \wedge \text{state}_{(i-1,j)}^{q'}))$$

where the big conjunction is over all pairs $(q', a') \in (Q \setminus \{t, r\}) \times \Gamma$ such that $\delta(q', a')$ has the form $(\cdot, a, \cdot)$. So, this big conjunction is true when the previous configuration is non-halting and has the head at j, and the transition calls for the symbol a to be written. This big conjunction is thus true whenever the symbol of $T_{(i,j)}$ should be a, in all cases where the state of $T_{(i-1,j)}$ is a non-halting state in Q. When the state of $T_{(i-1,j)}$ is equal to $\perp$ or one of the halting states $t, r \in Q$, the symbol of $T_{(i,j)}$ should be a copy of the symbol of $T_{(i-1,j)}$, so, the symbol of $T_{(i,j)}$ should be a whenever the symbol of $T_{(i-1,j)}$ is a; this is specified by the first disjunct of the overall formula given.

We next turn to define the instruction of each state gate. By our choice of the value K, the state of each entry in the rightmost column is $\perp$. We thus define $I(\text{state}_{(i,K)}^\perp) = \underline{1}$, and $I(\text{state}_{(i,K)}^q) = \underline{0}$, for each $q \in Q$. In order to present the instructions for the state gates of the remaining entries, we present auxiliary formulas. For all $i', j' \in \{1, \ldots, K\}$, and for all $q' \in Q, d' \in \{-1, +1\}$, define the formula

$$\theta_{(i',j')}^{q',d'} = \bigvee_{(p',a')} (\text{sym}_{(i',j')}^{a'} \wedge \text{state}_{(i',j')}^{p'}),$$

where the disjunction is over each pair $(p', a') \in (Q \setminus \{t, r\}) \times \Gamma$ such that $\delta(p', a')$ has the form $(q', \cdot, d')$. So, the given formula holds when in the i'th row, the head is at location j', and the transition calls for the state to be changed to q', and movement in the direction d'.

Let j be a value with $1 < j < K$, representing a column that is neither the leftmost nor rightmost column. When $q \in Q \setminus \{t, r\}$, define $I(\text{state}_{(i,j)}^q)$ by the formula $\sigma_{(i,j)}^q$ defined by

$$\sigma_{(i,j)}^q = \theta_{(i-1,j-1)}^{q,+1} \vee \theta_{(i-1,j+1)}^{q,-1}.$$

This formula evaluates to true when in row $(i-1)$'s configuration, the head is positioned at location $j - 1$, and the transition calls for the state to be changed to q and for a right movement; or, the head is positioned at location $j + 1$, and the transition calls for the state to be changed to q and for a left movement. When $q \in \{t, r\}$, define $I(\text{state}_{(i,j)}^q)$ by the same formula but with $\text{state}_{(i-1,j)}^q$ added as a disjunct, that is, by the formula $\sigma_{(i,j)}^q$ defined by

$$\sigma_{(i,j)}^q = \theta_{(i-1,j-1)}^{q,+1} \vee \theta_{(i-1,j+1)}^{q,-1} \vee \text{state}_{(i-1,j)}^q.$$

---

21. Note that when this proposition is applied literally to a formula, the formula's variables become circuit inputs. Here, the setup is slightly different in that the formula's variables are gates, but the described conversion can be applied equally well.

This extra disjunct accounts for the behavior that an entry should copy the state of the entry above it, when that state is one of the halting states $t, r \in Q$.

When $j = 1$ and $q \in Q$, we define the instruction $I(\text{state}^q_{(i,j)})$ by the formula $\sigma^q_{(i,j)}$ defined as above, but where $\theta^{q,+1}_{(i-1,j-1)}$ is replaced with $\theta^{q,-1}_{(i-1,1)}$. This replacement adapts the instruction to accommodate the behavior that the DTM should remain in location 1 when, from location 1, a transition calls for a left movement.

Finally, let j be a column number with $1 \leq j < K$, so that j denotes a column other than the rightmost column. We define the instruction $I(\text{state}^{\perp}_{(i,j)})$ according to the formula $\bigwedge_{q \in Q} \neg \sigma^q_{(i,j)}$. This formula holds that the state of the entry $T_{(i,j)}$ should be $\perp$ precisely when it is not defined as a state $q \in Q$ according to the formulas above.

The output gate of the circuit C_n is an additional gate whose instruction is

$$\text{state}^t_{(K,1)} \vee \text{state}^t_{(K,2)} \vee \cdots \vee \text{state}^t_{(K,K)},$$

so that the circuit outputs 1 if and only if the final row of the computation table contains an occurrence of the DTM M's accept state. $\quad\square$

Remark 3.6.16. The just-presented theorem offers a first whiff of an area of study known as *circuit complexity*. In this area, circuit families of various forms are considered as computational models, and the resulting computational models are compared both to each other and to other computational models.

We mention that the existence of a polynomial-time uniform circuit family that computes a language B *exactly* characterizes the condition of the language B being PTIME. (Exercise 3.10.19 requests a proof of this fact.) $\quad\diamond$

We next prove Theorem 3.6.12; the crux is to prove that CIRCUIT-SAT is NP-hard. Our approach is as follows. Let B be an NP language; we need to present a reduction that, given a string x, outputs a circuit C^x that is satisfiable if and only if $x \in B$. We describe how the circuit C^x is constructed. Fix M to be a verifier for B; and let x be an arbitrary string.

- We have that $x \in B$ if and only if there exists a string y of a certain length ℓ (depending on the length of x) such that $\langle x, y \rangle$ in $L(M)$.
- The just-given theorem (Theorem 3.6.15) shows how to construct a circuit C that is satisfied by a pair $\langle x, y \rangle$ if and only if y has length ℓ and the pair is in $L(M)$.

Chaining these observations together, we have that $x \in B$ if and only if there exists a string y such that $\langle x, y \rangle$ satisfies C. By hard-coding the value of x in the circuit C, we obtain a circuit C^x that is satisfied by a string y if and only if C is satisfied by the pair $\langle x, y \rangle$. It follows that $x \in B$ if and only if C^x is satisfiable.

Proof of Theorem 3.6.12. It is straightforward to verify that the language CIRCUIT-SAT is NP, so we prove that this language is NP-hard. Let B be an arbitrary NP language. We show that there exists a polynomial-time many-one reduction from B to CIRCUIT-SAT. By Theorem 3.2.26 and Remark 3.2.27, there exists a verifier R for B and a polynomial P

such that, for any pair $\langle x, y \rangle$ in R, it holds that $|y| = P(|x|)$. Let $x = x_1 \ldots x_n$ be any string of length $n \in \mathbb{N}$ over $\Sigma = \{0, 1\}$.

We have that $x \in B$ if and only if

there exists a string $y_1 \ldots y_{P(n)} \in \{0, 1\}^{P(n)}$ such that $\langle x, y_1 \ldots y_{P(n)} \rangle \in R$.

Let $(C_i)_{i \in \mathbb{N}}$ be a polynomial-time uniform circuit family that computes R. Under the pair encoding presented in Section 2.2, we have that $\langle x, y_1 \ldots y_{P(n)} \rangle = x_1 x_1 \ldots x_n x_n 01 y_1 \ldots y_{P(n)}$ and that this string has length $2n + 2 + P(n)$. We obtain that $x \in B$ if and only if

there exists a string $y_1 \ldots y_{P(n)} \in \{0, 1\}^{P(n)}$ where $x_1 x_1 \ldots x_n x_n 01 y_1 \ldots y_{P(n)}$ satisfies $C_{2n+2+P(n)}$.

Let $v_1, \ldots, v_{2n+2}, w_1, \ldots, w_{P(n)}$ denote the inputs of the circuit $C_{2n+2+P(n)}$. Let C^x be the circuit obtained from $C_{2n+2+P(n)}$ by instantiating the inputs $v_1, \ldots, v_{2n+2}$ respectively with the values $x_1, x_1, \ldots, x_n, x_n, 0, 1$; this circuit C^x is considered to have $w_1, \ldots, w_{P(n)}$ as its inputs. By *instantiation* of an input v_j with a value $z \in \{0, 1\}$, we mean that every occurrence of v_j in an instruction is replaced with the source $\underline{z}$; this type of instantiation was presented in Definition 3.6.8.

We then have

$$x \in B \quad \Leftrightarrow \quad \text{there exists a string } y_1 \ldots y_{P(n)} \in \{0, 1\}^{P(n)} \text{ satisfying } C^x$$

$$\Leftrightarrow \quad \text{the circuit } C^x \text{ is satisfiable}$$

$$\Leftrightarrow \quad \ulcorner C^x \urcorner \in \mathsf{CIRCUIT\text{-}SAT}.$$

We claim that the mapping $\rho \colon \Sigma^* \to \Sigma^*$ defined by $\rho(x) = \ulcorner C^x \urcorner$ is a polynomial-time many-one reduction from B to CIRCUIT-SAT. We just established the correctness of ρ, namely, that $x \in B \Leftrightarrow \rho(x) \in$ CIRCUIT-SAT. The mapping ρ is polynomial-time computable, for given a string x, the string $\rho(x)$ can be computed as follows: set n to be the length of x; compute $m = 2n + 2 + P(n)$; compute $\ulcorner C_m \urcorner$, which is doable within polynomial time from the string 1^m due to the polynomial-time uniformity of the circuit family $(C_i)_{i \in \mathbb{N}}$; then, determine $\ulcorner C^x \urcorner$ from $\ulcorner C_m \urcorner$ by performing the described instantiation of inputs. $\square$

We have just established our first NP-hardness result, on the language CIRCUIT-SAT, by proving explicitly that each NP language reduces to CIRCUIT-SAT. We give many further NP-hardness results in Section 3.8; in each case, we establish NP-hardness by presenting a reduction from a language already established as NP-hard; thus, each such further result is ultimately based on the NP-hardness of CIRCUIT-SAT. While we could in principle prove the NP-hardness of another language D by again proving that each NP language reduces to D, doing so typically involves low-level reasoning about every polynomial-time NTM.[22] Our NP-hardness proof for CIRCUIT-SAT in a sense encapsulates this low-level reasoning for once and for all, and indeed many of the NP-hardness proofs given in the sequel are

---

22. Here, to reason about a polynomial-time NTM, we passed through the verifier characterization of Theorem 3.2.26.

notably shorter than that for CIRCUIT-SAT. The situation here is not dissimilar to the way in which non-computability results were obtained in the previous chapter: we established a first non-computable language (namely, $\overline{SAP}$) via a diagonalization argument that reasoned about all DTMs, and then established each further non-computability result by giving a reduction from a language already established as non-computable—without ever using diagonalization a second time!

Remark 3.6.17 (An alternative presentation of a first NP-complete language). An NP-complete language is universal in that it holds information about whether or not each string is accepted by each polynomial-time NTM. We actually could have presented, as our first example of an NP-complete language, a language that contains this information in a rather direct fashion; in this optional remark, we explain how.

Define a language, denoted by NTIME-BAP and called the *nondeterministic-time bounded acceptance problem*, as follows. This language contains each triple $\langle \ulcorner M \urcorner, x, 1^t \rangle$ such that

- $\ulcorner M \urcorner$ is the encoding of an NTM M,
- x is a string over the alphabet $\Sigma = \{0, 1\}$,
- $t \in \mathbb{N}^+$,

and M *accepts x within t steps*; formally, by this it is meant that there exists an accepting configuration γ of M and a value $t' < t$ such that $\alpha_x \vdash_M^{t'} \gamma$, where α_x denotes the initial configuration of M on x. This language can be viewed as a variant of the *acceptance problem*—the language AP—studied in the previous chapter. It is described as *bounded* due to one only having to consider, when given a candidate string for the language, the behavior of a Turing machine as long as the machine obeys a certain resource bound—in our case, a time bound. (Here, we omit a description of how NTMs can be encoded; this can be done via simple, natural extensions of the encoding of DTMs previously given in Section 2.2.)

Let us briefly explain why this language is NP-complete.

We first explain why this language is NP-hard. Let B be an arbitrary NP language, and let M be an NTM with $L(M) = B$ and such that M runs within time P, where P is a polynomial. Consider the function that maps a string x to the triple $\langle \ulcorner M \urcorner, x, 1^{P(|x|)} \rangle$. This is a reduction from B to NTIME-BAP: when $x \in B$, it holds that the NTM M has a computation accepting x within $P(|x|)$ steps, and so the given triple is in NTIME-BAP; when $x \notin B$, the NTM M has no computation accepting x at all, and so the given triple is outside of NTIME-BAP. Also, this function is readily seen to be polynomial-time computable: given a string x, a DTM computing this function needs to produce the presented triple; the string $\ulcorner M \urcorner$ is fixed, so the main work is to compute the value $P(|x|)$ in the form of the string $1^{P(|x|)}$.

Let us explain why this language is NP. It is possible to design a polynomial-time NTM N that, given a triple $\langle \ulcorner M \urcorner, x, 1^t \rangle$, simulates the computation of M on x for up to t time steps, accepting if an accepting configuration is encountered, and rejecting if a rejecting configuration is encountered. The way in which N simulates various NTMs is similar to the way in which a universal Turing machine M_u simulates a given DTM on a given string. The difference is that the NTM N needs to simulate nondeterminism; this can be done (for example) as follows. When the NTM N is simulating an NTM $M = (Q, \Sigma, \Gamma, s, t, r, \Delta)$ in configuration $[p, \tau, \ell]$, to proceed to the next time step, it nondeterministically guesses a value (q, a, d) in $\wp(Q \times \Gamma \times \{-1, +1\})$; if $(q, a, d) \in \Delta(p, \tau(\ell))$, it makes the corresponding transition, and it rejects otherwise.

The idea here of exhibiting a complete language by defining a bounded version of the acceptance problem is a general one that can be applied in further contexts: in many cases, such bounded versions serve as complete languages for other language classes. With the perspective of this discussion, the language CIRCUIT-SAT can be conceived of as a natural rendering of the language NTIME-BAP—a rendering which deals with circuits instead of dealing directly with machines and their computations. Indeed, a benefit of establishing the language CIRCUIT-SAT as our first official NP-complete language is that the question of whether a circuit is satisfiable is a straightforwardly grasped combinatorial question concerning a relatively simple object, the circuit. Thanks to this, we will be able to readily establish the NP-completeness of further languages by using this language as a basis.   ◇

3.7   coNP languages

In this section, we study a number of aspects of the coNP languages, including notions of hardness and completeness. However, the strenuous work has arguably been done, and the results that we present are largely consequences of the theory of NP languages that has been developed. This, of course, reflects the close relationship between the coNP languages and the NP languages.

Definition 3.7.1. We define hardness and completeness for the coNP languages as follows.

- A language B is **coNP-hard** if for each each coNP language A, it holds that $A \leq_m^p B$.
- A language B is **coNP-complete** if it is coNP and it is coNP-hard.   ◇

The following theorem holds that, via complementation, each NP-hard language yields a coNP-hard language, and vice versa; and likewise, each NP-complete language yields a coNP-complete language, and vice versa.

Theorem 3.7.2. *For any language B, the following hold:*

- *B is NP-hard if and only if $\overline{B}$ is coNP-hard.*
- *B is NP-complete if and only if $\overline{B}$ is coNP-complete.*

Proof. The second statement is immediate from the first statement via the definition of coNP, so we prove the first statement. For the forward direction, suppose that B is NP-hard; then, for any coNP language A, we have that $\overline{A} \leq_m^p B$, from which we obtain that $A \leq_m^p \overline{B}$, via Proposition 3.4.13. The backward direction is analogous: suppose that $\overline{B}$ is coNP-hard;

then, for any NP language A, we have that $\overline{A} \leq_m^p \overline{B}$, from which we obtain that $A \leq_m^p B$, via Proposition 3.4.13. $\qquad\square$

The following proposition will facilitate giving examples of coNP-hard languages; it is an analog of Proposition 3.5.7, which concerned NP-hard languages.

Proposition 3.7.3. *Suppose that B is a coNP-hard language, and that C is a language such that $B \leq_m^p C$. Then, the language C is coNP-hard.*

Proof. Let A be an arbitrary coNP language. By the coNP-hardness of B, we have that $A \leq_m^p B$. By the hypothesis that $B \leq_m^p C$ and Theorem 3.4.18, which established the transitivity of the $\leq_m^p$ relation, we obtain that $A \leq_m^p C$. $\qquad\square$

Let us present a natural example of a coNP-complete language. Define

$$\text{CIRCUIT-UNSAT} = \{ \ulcorner C \urcorner \mid C \text{ is an unsatisfiable circuit}\}.$$

Theorem 3.7.4. CIRCUIT-UNSAT *is coNP-complete.*

Via Theorems 3.6.12 and 3.7.2, we have that the language $\overline{\text{CIRCUIT-SAT}}$ is coNP-complete, and so by the just-given Proposition 3.7.3, to prove the theorem, it suffices to exhibit a reduction from this language. For each circuit C, it is readily apparent that $\ulcorner C \urcorner \in \overline{\text{CIRCUIT-SAT}}$ if and only if $\ulcorner C \urcorner \in \text{CIRCUIT-UNSAT}$. The difference between these two languages is rather superficial: each string that is not a circuit encoding is in $\overline{\text{CIRCUIT-SAT}}$, but outside of CIRCUIT-UNSAT. We need to deal properly with such non-encodings to formally give this theorem's proof, which is something of a technicality and could be safely skipped by the reader.

Proof. We first argue that the language CIRCUIT-UNSAT is a coNP language. Let M be a polynomial-time NTM that, on an input x, does the following:

- First, M simulates a polynomial-time DTM that decides whether x is the encoding $\ulcorner C \urcorner$ of a circuit C, and accepts if it is not.
- Then, M guesses an assignment y for the circuit C, accepting if y satisfies C, and rejecting otherwise.

We have $L(M) = \overline{\text{CIRCUIT-UNSAT}}$: M accepts each non-encoding of a circuit, and accepts a circuit encoding if and only if the circuit has a satisfying assignment (so, if and only if the encoding is not in CIRCUIT-UNSAT). This shows that the language $\overline{\text{CIRCUIT-UNSAT}}$ is NP, and thus that the language CIRCUIT-UNSAT is coNP.

We next argue that CIRCUIT-UNSAT is coNP-hard. By Theorems 3.6.12 and 3.7.2, we have that the language $\overline{\text{CIRCUIT-SAT}}$ is coNP-complete. Thus, by Proposition 3.7.3, it suffices to give a reduction from $\overline{\text{CIRCUIT-SAT}}$ to CIRCUIT-UNSAT, which we now do. Fix z_0 to be an element of CIRCUIT-UNSAT; that is, fix z_0 to be an unsatisfiable circuit's encoding. Consider the mapping ρ that maps a string x to z_0 if x is not the encoding of a circuit, and

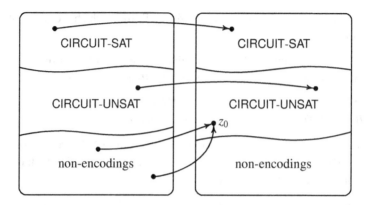

Figure 3.7.1. The reduction from $\overline{\text{CIRCUIT-SAT}}$ to CIRCUIT-UNSAT given by Theorem 3.7.4. Strings outside CIRCUIT-SAT are mapped to strings inside CIRCUIT-UNSAT, and strings inside CIRCUIT-SAT are mapped to strings outside CIRCUIT-UNSAT. In particular, since non-encodings of circuits are outside CIRCUIT-SAT, they are mapped to a fixed string z_0 in CIRCUIT-UNSAT.

to x otherwise; see Figure 3.7.1 for a diagram. This mapping is seen to be polynomial-time computable. To conclude that it gives the desired reduction, we verify correctness:

- When x is not the encoding of a circuit, it holds that $x \in \overline{\text{CIRCUIT-SAT}}$ and that

$$\rho(x) = z_0 \in \text{CIRCUIT-UNSAT}.$$

- When x is the encoding of a circuit, it holds that $\rho(x) = x$ and that

$$x \in \overline{\text{CIRCUIT-SAT}} \quad \Leftrightarrow \quad \rho(x) \in \text{CIRCUIT-UNSAT}. \qquad \square$$

We next give another example of a coNP-complete language, which can be taken as a simple variant of the language CIRCUIT-UNSAT. A circuit with inputs $v_1, \ldots, v_n$ is a **tautology** if it is satisfied by every assignment $f: \{v_1, \ldots, v_n\} \to \{0, 1\}$; define

$$\text{CIRCUIT-TAUT} = \{\ulcorner C \urcorner \mid C \text{ is a circuit that is a tautology}\}.$$

Theorem 3.7.5. CIRCUIT-TAUT *is coNP-complete.*

The idea of the proof is to reduce from CIRCUIT-UNSAT; given the encoding $\ulcorner C \urcorner$ of a circuit, the reduction simply outputs the encoding $\ulcorner C' \urcorner$ of a circuit C' whose output gate evaluates to the negation of the output gate of C. It is readily verified that this function maps an unsatisfiable circuit to a tautology, and a satisfiable circuit to a non-tautology.

Proof. We first argue that the language CIRCUIT-TAUT is a coNP language. Define M' to be the polynomial-time NTM that behaves as the NTM M in the proof of Theorem 3.7.4, but where after guessing an assignment y, the NTM M' accepts if y does not satisfy C, and rejects otherwise. We have $L(M') = \overline{\text{CIRCUIT-TAUT}}$: M' accepts each non-encoding of a circuit, and accepts a circuit encoding if and only if the circuit has a non-satisfying assignment—so, if and only if the circuit is not a tautology.

We next prove that CIRCUIT-TAUT is coNP-hard. By Proposition 3.7.3, it suffices to exhibit a reduction ρ from CIRCUIT-UNSAT to CIRCUIT-TAUT. When x is the encoding $\ulcorner C \urcorner$ of a circuit C, the string $\rho(x)$ is defined as the encoding $\ulcorner C' \urcorner$ of a circuit C' derived from C as follows: let g_u denote the output gate of C; add an additional gate g'_u where $I(g'_u) = \neg g_u$; set g'_u as the output gate of C'. We have that C is unsatisfiable if and only if C' is tautological: there does not exist an assignment satisfying C if and only if every assignment satisfies C'. Thus, when x is the encoding of a circuit, we have the equivalence $x \in$ CIRCUIT-UNSAT $\Leftrightarrow \rho(x) \in$ CIRCUIT-TAUT. $\qquad\square$

Remark 3.7.6. The properties of satisfiability and being a tautology are said to be *dual* to each other, for the negation of an unsatisfiable circuit is a tautology, and the negation of a non-tautological circuit is satisfiable. $\qquad\diamond$

We conclude this section with a result that again exhibits the phenomenon whereby the behavior of complete languages reflects the behavior of the classes for which they are complete. The following proposition can be viewed as an expansion of Proposition 3.3.4; each of the two propositions shows that three statements are equivalent, and they share their third statement. This proposition entails, for example, that if there is a coNP-complete language that is NP, then *every* coNP language is NP (this is the implication (1') $\Rightarrow$ (1), which is proved below).

Proposition 3.7.7. *The following are equivalent:*

(1') *There exists a coNP-complete language that is NP.*

(2') *There exists an NP-complete language that is coNP.*

(3) *A language is NP if and only if it is coNP. (That is,* $\mathbb{NP} = \mathrm{co}\mathbb{NP}$.)

Proof. Clearly (3) implies (2'), as we have the existence of an NP-complete language by Theorem 3.6.12. Similarly, (3) implies (1'), as we have the existence of a coNP-complete language by Theorems 3.6.12 and 3.7.2.

We establish that (1') implies (3) by showing that (1') implies (1) of Proposition 3.3.4. Suppose that C is a coNP-complete language that is NP, and let B be an arbitrary coNP language; we have that B polynomial-time many-one reduces to C, and thus by Theorem 3.4.14 that B is NP. By a dual argument, it can be established that (2') implies (3) by showing that (2') implies (2) of Proposition 3.3.4. $\qquad\square$

Remark 3.7.8. It can be argued directly that statements (1') and (2') of Proposition 3.7.7 are equivalent: a language is NP-complete and coNP if and only if its complement is coNP-complete and NP, by Theorem 3.7.2 and Definition 3.3.2. $\qquad\diamond$

3.8 Further hardness results

In this section, we present a variety of reductions that establish hardness results for a diversity of languages. For the most part, these results are NP-hardness results, although we do include a couple of coNP-hardness results. Our starting point is CIRCUIT-SAT, the main language established as NP-hard thus far. We obtain the NP-hardness of further languages by successively giving reductions from languages established as NP-hard.

Throughout this section, we will employ the following conventions.

- When claiming that a language is NP-complete, we typically omit an argument that the language is NP. Along these lines, we customarily omit arguing that a presented reduction is polynomial-time computable. We omit these arguments due to their being relatively straightforward. In general, each presented reduction is accompanied by a *correctness proof* verifying the reduction's correctness.

- We make tacit use of the result that a reduction from an NP-hard language to a second language establishes NP-hardness of the second language (Proposition 3.5.7).

- Eschewing precision for readability, we often reduce symbolic clutter by omitting the $\ulcorner \cdot \urcorner$ notation for specifying the encoding of an object, and likewise, we use the conventional pair notation $(\cdot, \cdot)$ in place of the pair encoding notation $\langle \cdot, \cdot \rangle$. Hence, for example, we use (G, k) in place of $\langle \ulcorner G \urcorner, \ulcorner k \urcorner \rangle$. We practice this notational simplification both here and in the rest of this book. In general, we freely neglect to distinguish between the encoding of an object and the object itself.

- When $k \geq 1$ is a positive natural number, we use the notation $[k]$ to denote the set $\{1, ..., k\}$ containing the first k positive natural numbers.

- Following Remark 3.4.3, we will neglect to define reductions on strings that are obviously outside of the language being reduced *from*. In particular, when defining a reduction, we usually assume that the input is *well-formed* in that it consists of objects each having the expected type (formula, graph, number, etc.).

  Relative to a language, we generally use the term **instance** to refer to a string that is well-formed in this sense; for instance, a string is an instance of the language CLIQUE when it has the form (G, k) where G is a graph and $k \in \mathbb{N}$. We emphasize that, under our terminology, an instance of a language may or may not be an element of the language; what is certain is that each non-instance of a language is not an element of the language.

Remark 3.8.1. In the theory of computation at large, it is standard to alternatively view a language as a **decision problem**, which is defined as a mapping from the set Σ^* of all strings (over an alphabet Σ) to the set $\{0, 1\}$, where 0 signifies *no*, and 1 signifies *yes*. In this view, relative to a decision problem, each string poses a yes/no question. A language can be naturally translated to the decision problem where the strings inside the language are mapped to 1, and all other strings are mapped to 0; in the other direction, a decision problem naturally defines the language containing each string mapped to 1. A decision

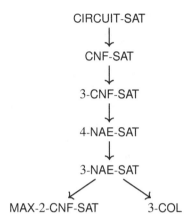

Figure 3.8.1. The web of reductions given for satisfiability problems. Here, an arrow from a first language to a second language indicates that we present a reduction from the first language to the second.

problem is often specified by defining its *instances*, which typically are the strings that are well-formed in the sense described above (and omit only strings whose answer is *no*); and by presenting a yes/no *question* concerning an instance. For example, the language CIRCUIT-SAT could be presented by defining an instance as an encoding of a circuit, and the question as: *is the circuit satisfiable?* While this book has thus far adhered mostly to the *language* view, in the sequel we will speak interchangeably of *problems* and *languages*. ◇

Remark 3.8.2 (A reading suggestion). This section contains numerous reductions. Let us offer a suggestion to the reader wishing to acquire an initial taste of how reductions are constructed and proved correct. Such a reader might consider first studying Reductions 3.8.5 and 3.8.8, which are located in Section 3.8.1 and establish the hardness of two languages, CNF-SAT and 3-CNF-SAT, which deal with propositional satisfiability; and also Reduction 3.8.34 and Theorem 3.8.38, which are located in Section 3.8.2 and establish the hardness of two languages: INDEP-SET and a restricted version of the language VERTEX-COVER, denoted by REST-VERTEX-COVER.

Then, a selection could be made from the remaining reductions; one proposal would be to start by choosing among Reductions 3.8.42, 3.8.46, and 3.8.56. ◇

3.8.1 Satisfiability problems

We begin by studying *satisfiability problems*, by which we refer broadly to problems where the question is to decide if given variables can be assigned values in a fixed set so as to satisfy a conjunction of requirements. See Figure 3.8.1 for a summary of the presented reductions; as this figure shows, our point of departure is the hardness of CIRCUIT-SAT.

Hardness of CNF-satisfiability problems

We start with the problem of deciding the satisfiability of so-called *CNF-formulas*; the abbreviation *CNF* is short for *conjunctive normal form*. Let us briefly review the relevant notions from propositional logic. Recall that a **propositional formula** is built from variables, negation ($\neg$), disjunction ($\vee$), and conjunction ($\wedge$). Suppose that ϕ is a propositional formula, and that $f\colon V \to \{0, 1\}$ is an assignment defined on each variable of ϕ. Under the assignment f, the formula ϕ evaluates to 0 or 1. When ϕ evaluates to 1 under f, we call f a **satisfying assignment** of ϕ; in this case, f is also said to **satisfy** ϕ. A propositional formula ϕ is **satisfiable** if there exists an assignment that satisfies it, and is **unsatisfiable** otherwise.

In order to define the particular type of formulas that we are interested in, some further terminology is needed. A **literal** is a variable v or the negation $\neg v$ of a variable v. A literal that is a variable v is a **positive literal**; a literal that is the negation $\neg v$ of a variable is a **negative literal**. We say that two literals are **complementary** if one is a positive literal v and the other is the negative literal $\neg v$ on the same variable; for two such literals, we say that each is the **complement** of the other. When λ is a literal, we use $\overline{\lambda}$ to denote the complement of λ; so, $\overline{\lambda}$ is defined as the literal $\neg v$ when $\lambda = v$ for a variable v, and as the literal v when $\lambda = \neg v$ for a variable v. A **clause** is a disjunction of literals; the **size** of a clause is defined to be the number of its disjuncts, that is, the number of literal occurrences in the clause. A **CNF-formula** is a conjunction of clauses.

Example 3.8.3. Consider the CNF-formula $\psi = (u \vee w) \wedge (\neg u \vee \neg w)$; it contains 2 clauses, each having size 2. Let us consider example assignments:

- Let $f\colon \{u, w\} \to \{0, 1\}$ be the assignment where $f(u) = 1$ and $f(w) = 1$. This assignment is not a satisfying assignment of ψ; under this assignment, ψ evaluates to the value $(1 \vee 1) \wedge (\neg 1 \vee \neg 1) = 1 \wedge 0 = 0$.
- Let $g\colon \{u, w\} \to \{0, 1\}$ be the assignment where $g(u) = 0$ and $g(w) = 1$. This assignment is a satisfying assignment of ψ; under this assignment, ψ evaluates to the value $(0 \vee 1) \wedge (\neg 0 \vee \neg 1) = 1 \wedge 1 = 1$. Hence, the formula ψ is satisfiable.

It can be verified that an assignment $h\colon \{u, w\} \to \{0, 1\}$ satisfies the CNF-formula ψ if and only if $h(u) \neq h(w)$, that is, if and only if u and w are assigned to different values. $\diamond$

Remark 3.8.4. In some contexts, it is natural to permit a clause to be an empty disjunction, or to permit a CNF-formula to be an empty conjunction. However, throughout this section, we always assume a clause to be a disjunction of one or more literals, and a CNF-formula to be a conjunction of one or more clauses. $\diamond$

We show that the problem of deciding satisfiability of a CNF-formula is NP-hard. Define

$$\text{CNF-SAT} = \{\ulcorner \phi \urcorner \mid \phi \text{ is a satisfiable CNF-formula}\}.$$

Reduction 3.8.5: from CIRCUIT-SAT **to** CNF-SAT. Let C be a circuit, whose parts are notated as in Definition 3.6.1; the reduction maps C to a CNF-formula ϕ defined as follows.

Each variable occurring in ϕ will be a source or a gate of C. The clauses of ϕ are defined as follows. There are clauses $\neg\underline{0}$, $\underline{1}$, and g_u, which enforce that any satisfying assignment of ϕ must map $\underline{0}$, $\underline{1}$, and g_u to the values 0, 1, and 1, respectively. For each gate g of the circuit, there is a set of clauses $S(g)$ defined depending on the form of the instruction $I(g)$, as follows:

- When $I(g) = \neg h$, the set $S(g)$ contains the 2 clauses $h \vee g$ and $\neg h \vee \neg g$.
- When $I(g) = h_1 \wedge \cdots \wedge h_k$, the set $S(g)$ contains the clause $\neg h_1 \vee \cdots \vee \neg h_k \vee g$ along with the k clauses $h_1 \vee \neg g, \ldots, h_k \vee \neg g$.
- When $I(g) = h_1 \vee \cdots \vee h_k$, the set $S(g)$ contains the clause $h_1 \vee \cdots \vee h_k \vee \neg g$ along with the k clauses $\neg h_1 \vee g, \ldots, \neg h_k \vee g$.

In summary, the formula ϕ is defined as the conjunction of the clauses in the set $\{\neg\underline{0}, \underline{1}, g_u\} \cup \bigcup_{g \in G} S(g)$, which set we denote by $S(C)$. ◇

Example 3.8.6. When applied to the circuit C of Example 3.6.2, which has inputs v_1, v_2, v_3 and gates g_1, g_2, g_3, g_4, the just-given reduction (Reduction 3.8.5) produces the formula ϕ whose clauses are $\neg\underline{0}, \underline{1}, g_4$, and all clauses in the sets $S(g_1)$, $S(g_2)$, $S(g_3)$, and $S(g_4)$. The set of variables occurring in ϕ is

$$\{v_1, v_2, v_3, \underline{0}, \underline{1}, g_1, g_2, g_3, g_4\}.$$

Let us look concretely at a couple of the sets $S(g_i)$.

- We have $I(g_1) = v_1 \wedge v_2 \wedge v_3$; the set $S(g_1)$ contains 4 clauses, and is equal to

$$S(g_1) = \{\neg v_1 \vee \neg v_2 \vee \neg v_3 \vee g_1, \ v_1 \vee \neg g_1, \ v_2 \vee \neg g_1, \ v_3 \vee \neg g_1\}.$$

- We have $I(g_2) = \neg v_3$; the set $S(g_2)$ contains 2 clauses, and is equal to

$$S(g_2) = \{v_3 \vee g_2, \ \neg v_3 \vee \neg g_2\}. \quad ◇$$

A key aspect of the construction (of Reduction 3.8.5), captured in the next lemma, is that each set $S(g)$ of clauses enforces the behavior of the circuit. For example, when g is a gate with $I(g) = h_1 \wedge \cdots \wedge h_k$, an assignment b satisfies the clauses in $S(g)$ if and only if it holds that $b(g) = b(h_1) \wedge \cdots \wedge b(h_k)$. In essence, an assignment that satisfies the clauses in $S(g)$ necessarily imitates the circuit's behavior on the gate g. Knowing that an assignment satisfies all clauses in $S(C)$ then implies that the assignment is completely determined by where it maps the inputs.

Lemma 3.8.7. *Let C be a circuit, whose parts are notated as in Definition 3.6.1, and let G denote the set $G_0 \cup \{g_1, \ldots, g_m\}$ of all sources and gates of C. Let $f \colon \{v_1, \ldots, v_n\} \to \{0, 1\}$ be an assignment to the inputs of C, and let f_C be the assignment given by Definition 3.6.3. The assignment f_C is the unique mapping from G to $\{0, 1\}$ that extends f and satisfies all clauses in $S(C) \setminus \{g_u\}$.*

This somewhat technical lemma holds that, for any assignment f to the inputs of C, the extension f_C of f satisfies all clauses in $S(C)$, leaving out the clause g_u for the output gate; and moreover, that it is the *only* extension of f, with domain G, that satisfies all of these clauses.

Proof. Let $f\colon \{v_1, \ldots, v_n\} \to \{0,1\}$ be any assignment; let $b\colon G \to \{0,1\}$ be an extension of f that satisfies all clauses in $S(C) \setminus \{g_u\}$. We show both that f_C satisfies all clauses in $S(C) \setminus \{g_u\}$ and that $b = f_C$. First, observe that since $f_C(\underline{0}) = 0$ and $f_C(\underline{1}) = 1$ by definition of f_C, the mapping f_C satisfies the clauses $\neg \underline{0}$ and $\underline{1}$; since b satisfies these clauses and extends f, it agrees with f_C on the set G_0.

To establish the lemma from here, it suffices to consider each of the gates $g_1, \ldots, g_m$ in order and show, for each gate g_i:

- the assignment f_C satisfies all clauses in $S(g_i)$; and
- b and f_C agree on g_i, that is, $b(g_i) = f_C(g_i)$.

Consider a gate g_i of the circuit C. When $I(g_i)$ has the form $h_1 \wedge \cdots \wedge h_k$, since each of the gates $h_1, \ldots, h_k$ lies in $G_{<i}$, by appeal to induction we may assume that f_C and b agree on each element of this sequence. Letting g denote the gate g_i, we branch into two cases.

- Suppose that $b(h_1) = \cdots = b(h_k) = 1$. We have $f_C(h_1) = \cdots = f_C(h_k) = 1$, by induction. By hypothesis, b satisfies the clause $\neg h_1 \vee \cdots \vee \neg h_k \vee g$ in $S(g)$; since each of the literals $\neg h_1, \ldots, \neg h_k$ evaluates to 0 under b, it must hold that $b(g) = 1$. From the definition of f_C, we have $f_C(g) = f_C(h_1) \wedge \cdots \wedge f_C(h_k) = 1$; f_C is then seen to satisfy each clause in $S(g)$, as each such clause contains one of $g, h_1, \ldots, h_k$ as a positive literal.
- Suppose that there exists an index j such that $b(h_j) = 0$. We have $f_C(h_j) = 0$, by induction. By hypothesis, b satisfies the clause $h_j \vee \neg g$ in $S(g)$, implying that $b(g) = 0$. From the definition of f_C, we have $f_C(g) = f_C(h_1) \wedge \cdots \wedge f_C(h_k) = 0$. The assignment f_C is then seen to satisfy all clauses in $S(g)$: it satisfies the clause $\neg h_1 \vee \cdots \vee \neg h_k \vee g$, as $f_C(h_j) = 0$; each other clause in $S(g)$ contains $\neg g$ as a literal, and is satisfied since $f_C(g) = 0$.

When $I(g_i)$ has the form $h_1 \vee \cdots \vee h_k$, the reasoning is dual to that just given; we omit presenting it explicitly. When $I(g_i)$ has the form $\neg h$, the argumentation is relatively straightforward, and is also omitted; we remark that, in this situation, the clauses in $S(g_i)$ are those occurring in the formula of Example 3.8.3, up to renaming of variables.   □

Correctness proof of Reduction 3.8.5. We show that the circuit C is satisfiable if and only if the CNF-formula ϕ is.

For the forward direction, suppose that the circuit C is satisfiable; then, there exists an assignment $f\colon \{v_1, \ldots, v_n\} \to \{0,1\}$ satisfying C. By Lemma 3.8.7, the assignment f_C is defined on all variables of ϕ and satisfies all clauses in $S(C) \setminus \{g_u\}$. However, since f satisfies C, we have $f_C(g_u) = 1$, and so f_C satisfies the clause g_u, and thus each clause of ϕ.

For the backward direction, suppose that the formula ϕ is satisfiable; then, there exists a mapping $b\colon G_0 \cup \{g_1, ..., g_m\} \to \{0, 1\}$ that satisfies ϕ and hence all clauses in $S(C)$. Define $f\colon \{v_1, ..., v_n\} \to \{0, 1\}$ as the restriction of b to the inputs, that is, as the mapping where $f(v_i) = b(v_i)$ for each $i = 1, ..., n$. By Lemma 3.8.7, it holds that b and f_C are equal. Since $b(g_u) = 1$, we have $f_C(g_u) = 1$, implying that f satisfies C. □

Even when a language is NP-complete, typical instances of interest may have surface-level features that are not captured by the original language definition. In such a situation, it may be possible to define a restricted version of the original language, and then investigate the complexity of this new version, in hopes of discovering a positive PTIME result. For example, a readily visible feature of a CNF-formula is the length of the clauses appearing. If for some particular application the CNF-formulas that require solution tend to have short clauses, one might very well ask: to what extent is the hardness of CNF-SAT due to allowing clauses of arbitrarily long length? We next show a result suggesting that long clauses are not the crux of this hardness: even when we impose the *syntactic* restriction that clauses may have size at most 3, a hardness result on satisfiability can be established.

For each $k \geq 1$, define a k-**CNF-formula** to be a CNF-formula where each clause has size k or less. Define the language

$$k\text{-CNF-SAT} = \{\ulcorner \phi \urcorner \mid \phi \text{ is a satisfiable } k\text{-CNF-formula}\}.$$

We give a reduction from CNF-SAT to 3-CNF-SAT which, when given a CNF-formula ϕ with clauses $C^1 \wedge \cdots \wedge C^m$, maps it to a 3-CNF-formula ϕ' in the following way:

- For each clause C^i that is already of size 3 or less, the clause C^i is itself included in the formula ϕ'.
- For each clause C^i that is of size 4 or greater, let k_i denote its size (that is, its number of literals). In the formula ϕ', the clause C^i is represented by k_i clauses, denoted by $C^{i,1}, ..., C^{i,k_i}$, that contain the literals in C^i as well as literals over new variables. This clause sequence is designed so that any assignment satisfying the clause C^i can be extended to an assignment satisfying the clauses $C^{i,1}, ..., C^{i,k_i}$, and conversely, any assignment that satisfies the clauses $C^{i,1}, ..., C^{i,k_i}$ also satisfies the clause C^i.

The precise reduction follows.

Reduction 3.8.8: from CNF-SAT **to** 3-CNF-SAT**.** Let ϕ be a CNF-formula, whose clauses are denoted $C^1 \wedge \cdots \wedge C^m$. For each index $i \in [m]$, let k_i denote the number of literals in the clause C^i, and let $\lambda_1^i \vee \cdots \vee \lambda_{k_i}^i$ denote the clause C^i, where each λ_j^i is a literal.

The reduction produces a 3-CNF-formula ϕ' as follows. For each index $i \in [m]$:

- If $k_i \leq 3$, it includes, in the formula ϕ', the clause C^i.

- If $k_i > 3$, it includes, in the formula ϕ', the k_i clauses

$$C^{i,1} = \lambda_1^i \vee x_1^i,$$

$$C^{i,j} = \neg x_{j-1}^i \vee \lambda_j^i \vee x_j^i, \quad \text{for } j = 2, \ldots, k_i - 1,$$

$$C^{i,k_i} = \neg x_{k_i-1}^i \vee \lambda_{k_i}^i.$$

Here, the variables $x_1^i, \ldots, x_{k_i-1}^i$ are new variables assumed not to occur in ϕ.   ◇

Example 3.8.9. Let us consider Reduction 3.8.8's behavior on the formula ϕ of Example 3.8.6. We saw that this formula includes the 4 clauses

$$\neg\underline{0}, \quad \underline{1}, \quad g_4, \quad \text{and} \quad \neg v_1 \vee \neg v_2 \vee \neg v_3 \vee g_1,$$

which we denote by C^1, C^2, C^3, and C^4, respectively. The clauses $C^1 = \neg\underline{0}$, $C^2 = \underline{1}$, and $C^3 = g_4$ are included in the formula ϕ' as-is, since they each already have size at most 3. The clause $C^4 = \neg v_1 \vee \neg v_2 \vee \neg v_3 \vee g_1$ is translated to 4 clauses:

$$C^{4,1} = \neg v_1 \vee x_1^4,$$

$$C^{4,2} = \neg x_1^4 \vee \neg v_2 \vee x_2^4,$$

$$C^{4,3} = \neg x_2^4 \vee \neg v_3 \vee x_3^4,$$

$$C^{4,4} = \neg x_3^4 \vee g_1.$$ ◇

Correctness proof of Reduction 3.8.8. We prove that ϕ is satisfiable if and only if ϕ' is satisfiable. The verification, although slightly lengthy, is relatively routine. Let V be the set of variables appearing in the CNF-formula ϕ, and let X be the set of all variables x_j^i that are introduced in the 3-CNF-formula ϕ'.

For the backward direction, let $f' : V \cup X \to \{0, 1\}$ be a satisfying assignment for ϕ'. We show that the assignment f' satisfies ϕ, by arguing that the assignment f' satisfies each clause C^i of ϕ. Consider any clause C^i of ϕ (that is, consider an index $i \in [m]$). When $k_i \leq 3$, the clause C^i is included in ϕ', and is thus satisfied by f'. When $k_i > 3$, we reason in cases as follows.

- If $f'(x_1^i) = 0$, then since f' satisfies the clause $C^{i,1}$, we have that f' satisfies the literal λ_1^i, and hence satisfies the clause C^i.
- If for each $j \in [k_i]$ it holds that $f'(x_j^i) = 1$, then since f' satisfies the clause C^{i,k_i}, we have that f' satisfies the literal $\lambda_{k_i}^i$, and hence satisfies the clause C^i.
- Otherwise, we have that $f'(x_1^i) = 1$ and that there exists $j \in [k_i]$ such that $f'(x_j^i) = 0$. Let $\ell \in [k_i]$ be the minimum value such that $f'(x_\ell^i) = 0$; we have $\ell > 1$. We have that $f'(x_{\ell-1}^i) = 1$ and $f'(x_\ell^i) = 0$; since f' satisfies the clause $C^{i,\ell}$, it follows that f' satisfies the literal λ_ℓ^i, and hence satisfies the clause C^i.

For the forward direction, let $f : V \to \{0, 1\}$ be a satisfying assignment for ϕ; we define an extension $f' : V \cup X \to \{0, 1\}$ of f as follows. Let $i \in [m]$ be an index such that $k_i > 3$.

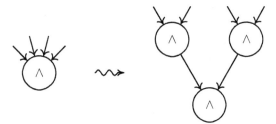

Figure 3.8.2. Each gate of a circuit can be locally transformed so that each gate has a *fan-in* of 2 or less. In terms of circuit diagrams, the **fan-in** of a gate is the number of incoming arrows. This diagram shows how this transformation can be performed in the case of a gate with fan-in 4.

In order to define f' on the variables $x_1^i, \ldots, x_{k_i-1}^i$ and to argue that f' satisfies the clauses $C^{i,1}, \ldots, C^{i,k_i}$, we consider cases; the reasoning in essence reverses that of the previous direction. Let $j \in [k_i]$ be the minimum value such that λ_j^i is satisfied by f.

- If $j = 1$, set $f'(x_1^i) = \cdots = f'(x_{k_i-1}^i) = 0$. The clause $C^{i,1}$ is satisfied by f' since the literal λ_1^i is satisfied by f'; each clause $C^{i,2}, \ldots, C^{i,k_i}$ is satisfied by f' since these clauses contain the literals $\neg x_1^i, \ldots, \neg x_{k_i-1}^i$, respectively.
- If $j = k_i$, set $f'(x_1^i) = \cdots = f'(x_{k_i-1}^i) = 1$. The clause C^{i,k_i} is satisfied by f' since the literal $\lambda_{k_i}^i$ is satisfied by f'; each clause $C^{i,1}, \ldots, C^{i,k_i-1}$ is satisfied by f' since these clauses contain the literals $x_1^i, \ldots, x_{k_i-1}^i$, respectively.
- Otherwise, set $f'(x_1^i) = \cdots = f(x_{j-1}^i) = 1$, and $f'(x_j^i) = \cdots = f(x_{k_i-1}^i) = 0$. The clause $C^{i,j}$ is satisfied by f' since the literal λ_j^i is satisfied by f'; each clause $C^{i,1}, \ldots, C^{i,j-1}$ is satisfied by f' since these clauses contain the literals $x_1^i, \ldots, x_{j-1}^i$, respectively; and each clause $C^{i,j+1}, \ldots, C^{i,k_i}$ is satisfied by f' since these clauses contain the literals $\neg x_j^i, \ldots, \neg x_{k_i-1}^i$, respectively. $\qquad\square$

Remark 3.8.10. The reduction just given from CNF-SAT to 3-CNF-SAT is a quintessential example of a reduction employing *local replacement*, whereby each instance of the first language is viewed as consisting of certain basic units, and each unit is replaced with a component forming part of the created instance. In the reduction at hand, the given CNF-formula was viewed as having clauses as its basic units; each clause was independently replaced with 1 or more clauses, according to a uniform rule. This reduction supplies a very pure example of the local replacement technique.

The reduction from CIRCUIT-SAT to CNF-SAT (Reduction 3.8.5) can also be construed as employing this technique: each gate g is translated to a set $S(g)$ of clauses. However, this latter reduction also exhibits a global behavior: there are 3 clauses of size 1 that are always included in the output CNF-formula. Most of our reductions between satisfiability problems can be viewed as utilizing the local replacement technique, at least in part. $\qquad\Diamond$

Remark 3.8.11. We here elected to prove the hardness of 3-CNF-SAT by exhibiting a reduction from CNF-SAT, as we believe that the reduction is instructive. Let us remark that it is also possible to present a direct reduction from CIRCUIT-SAT to 3-CNF-SAT, as follows. Given a circuit, first transform it so that each instruction of the form $h_1 \wedge \cdots \wedge h_k$ or $h_1 \vee \cdots \vee h_k$ has $k \leq 2$; that is, so that the *fan-in* of each gate, the number of previous sources/gates operated on, is at most 2. This can be done by replacing each gate with fan-in 3 or greater with multiple gates; an example of such a replacement is illustrated in Figure 3.8.2. Then, one can apply the presented reduction from CIRCUIT-SAT to CNF-SAT (Reduction 3.8.5); it is readily seen that all clauses in the resulting CNF-formula will have 3 or fewer literals.   ◇

Remark 3.8.12. If we push further the idea of restricting clause length of CNF-formulas, we do arrive at a positive complexity result. The language 2-CNF-SAT is PTIME; this is the content of Exercise 3.10.33. This result suggests that any reduction establishing the NP-hardness of 3-CNF-SAT, such as Reduction 3.8.8, must utilize size 3 clauses!   ◇

Based on the given reductions to CNF-SAT and to 3-CNF-SAT, we obtain the following complexity results.

Theorem 3.8.13. CNF-SAT *and* 3-CNF-SAT *are NP-complete.*

Proof. It is straightforwardly verified that these languages are NP. They are NP-hard by Theorem 3.6.12 in conjunction with Reductions 3.8.5 and 3.8.8.   □

Remark 3.8.14. The fact that the langugaes CNF-SAT and 3-CNF-SAT are NP, along with the result that the language CIRCUIT-SAT is NP-complete (Theorem 3.6.12), imply that there *exist* reductions to CIRCUIT-SAT both from CNF-SAT and from 3-CNF-SAT. It is worth observing that, from these two languages, such reductions can be presented explicitly and relatively simply: the conversion of CNF-formulas into circuits (as described by Proposition 3.6.9) acts as such a reduction, in both cases.   ◇

coNP-hardness results

We present a couple of consequences of the NP-hardness results just obtained in Theorem 3.8.13. First, we show the coNP-completeness of deciding *unsatisfiability* of a given 3-CNF-formula. Define the language

$$3\text{-CNF-UNSAT} = \{\ulcorner \phi \urcorner \mid \phi \text{ is an unsatisfiable 3-CNF-formula}\}.$$

Corollary 3.8.15. 3-CNF-UNSAT *is coNP-complete.*

Let us explain how to prove Corollary 3.8.15. By Theorem 3.7.2 and the result that 3-CNF-SAT is NP-complete, we obtain that $\overline{\text{3-CNF-SAT}}$ is coNP-complete. Observe that, for a 3-CNF-formula ϕ, we have the equivalence

$$\ulcorner \phi \urcorner \in \overline{\text{3-CNF-SAT}} \quad \text{if and only if} \quad \ulcorner \phi \urcorner \in \text{3-CNF-UNSAT}.$$

The difference between the languages $\overline{\text{3-CNF-SAT}}$ and 3-CNF-UNSAT is that each string that is not the encoding of a 3-CNF-formula is in $\overline{\text{3-CNF-SAT}}$, but not in 3-CNF-UNSAT. The situation is analogous to that of the proof of Theorem 3.7.4, and arguing in an analogous fashion yields the present corollary.

Having established the coNP-completeness of the property of *unsatisfiability* for 3-CNF-formulas, we can next establish the coNP-completeness of the property of being a *tautology* for so-called 3-*DNF-formulas*; these formulas are dual to 3-CNF-formulas, that is, they are obtained by negating 3-CNF-formulas. A propositional formula is a **tautology** if it is satisfied by every assignment defined on its variables. Define a **dual clause** to be a conjunction of literals. Define a **DNF-formula** to be a disjunction of dual clauses, and for $k \geq 1$, define a k-**DNF-formula** to be a DNF formula where each dual clause has k or fewer literals. The abbreviation *DNF* is short for *disjunctive normal form*.

In the following, we write $\psi \equiv \psi'$ to indicate that two propositional formulas are **logically equivalent**, by which is meant that any assignment defined on their variables satisfies one if and only if it satisfies the other. Recall that, when λ is a literal, $\overline{\lambda}$ denotes its complement; observe that $\neg\lambda \equiv \overline{\lambda}$ holds. Define the **dual** of a clause $C = \lambda_1 \vee \cdots \vee \lambda_k$ to be the dual clause $D = \overline{\lambda_1} \wedge \cdots \wedge \overline{\lambda_k}$; by De Morgan's laws, we have

$$\neg C \equiv (\neg\lambda_1) \wedge \cdots \wedge (\neg\lambda_k) \equiv \overline{\lambda_1} \wedge \cdots \wedge \overline{\lambda_k} = D.$$

The following reduction yields the coNP-hardness of the language defined as

$$\text{3-DNF-TAUT} = \{\ulcorner \phi \urcorner \mid \phi \text{ is a 3-DNF-formula that is a tautology}\}.$$

Reduction 3.8.16: from 3-CNF-UNSAT **to** 3-DNF-TAUT. Let $\phi = C^1 \wedge \cdots \wedge C^m$ be an instance of 3-CNF-UNSAT. For each clause C^i, let D^i denote the dual of C^i. The reduction maps the formula ϕ to the 3-DNF-formula $\phi' = D^1 \vee \cdots \vee D^m$. ◇

Correctness proof of Reduction 3.8.16. It holds that

$$\neg\phi = \neg(C^1 \wedge \cdots \wedge C^m)$$
$$\equiv \neg C^1 \vee \cdots \vee \neg C^m$$
$$\equiv D^1 \vee \cdots \vee D^m$$
$$= \phi'.$$

Here, the second equivalence holds by De Morgan's laws. We have that ϕ is unsatisfiable if and only if $\neg\phi$ is a tautology; this latter condition holds, by the just-given equivalences, if and only if ϕ' is a tautology. □

Corollary 3.8.15 and Reduction 3.8.16 together entail the coNP-hardness of 3-DNF-TAUT. The language 3-DNF-TAUT can be verified to be coNP; one way to do this is to argue that 3-DNF-TAUT reduces to 3-CNF-UNSAT, by essentially inverting Reduction 3.8.16. We obtain the following result.

Corollary 3.8.17. 3-DNF-TAUT *is coNP-complete.*

We remark that the language of satisfiable DNF-formulas and the language of tautological CNF-formulas are both PTIME; proofs of these facts are left as exercises.

NAE-satisfiability problems

We next consider *not-all-equal (NAE) satisfiability problems*; as with CNF-SAT and 3-CNF-SAT, an instance consists of a sequence of requirements on variables, and the question is to determine if there exists a 0/1 assignment to the variables satisfying all of them. However, the requirements here are not clauses: now, each requirement is specified by a variable tuple, and is satisfied when not all variables in the tuple are mapped to be equal.

For each $k \geq 2$, define a k-**NAE-system** to be a sequence $t^1, \ldots, t^m$ where each t^i is a k-tuple of variables. Let $f \colon V \to \{0, 1\}$ be an assignment defined on the variables of a k-NAE-system T denoted by $t^1, \ldots, t^m$, and (for each $i \in [m]$) denote t^i by $(v_1^i, \ldots, v_k^i)$; we say that f is a **satisfying assignment** of T, or that f **satisfies** T, when for each index $i \in [m]$, it holds that $\{0, 1\} \subseteq \{f(v_1^i), \ldots, f(v_k^i)\}$. That is, f is a satisfying assignment of an instance if, for each tuple, the tuple's variables are mapped to values that are *not all equal*. A k-NAE-system T is **satisfiable** if there exists an assignment that satisfies T. We define

$$k\text{-NAE-SAT} = \{\ulcorner T \urcorner \mid T \text{ is a satisfiable } k\text{-NAE-system}\}.$$

Example 3.8.18. Consider the 2-NAE-system T defined as $(a, b), (a, c), (b, c)$. By definition, an assignment $f \colon \{a, b, c\} \to \{0, 1\}$ satisfies T when

$$\{0, 1\} \subseteq \{f(a), f(b)\}, \quad \{0, 1\} \subseteq \{f(a), f(c)\}, \quad \text{and} \quad \{0, 1\} \subseteq \{f(b), f(c)\}.$$

It follows that f satisfies T when $f(a) \neq f(b)$, $f(a) \neq f(c)$, and $f(b) \neq f(c)$. It is readily seen that there is no such assignment f satisfying these conditions, and so T is not satisfiable.

In contrast, consider the 2-NAE-system T' defined as $(a, b), (a, c)$, and obtained from T by eliminating its last tuple. It can be readily confirmed that T' is satisfied by the assignment $f' \colon \{a, b, c\} \to \{0, 1\}$ defined by $f'(a) = 0$ and $f'(b) = f'(c) = 1$. Thus, we have that T' is satisfiable. ◇

The following proposition, which is straightforward to verify, states that, for any k-NAE-system, satisfying assignments come in pairs: flipping every bit of a satisfying assignment yields another satisfying assignment.[23]

Proposition 3.8.19. *For any $k \geq 2$, if $f \colon V \to \{0, 1\}$ is a satisfying assignment of a k-NAE-system T, then the assignment $g \colon V \to \{0, 1\}$ defined (for all $v \in V$) by $g(v) = \neg f(v)$ is also a satisfying assignment of T.*

We exhibit a reduction from 3-CNF-SAT to 4-NAE-SAT. Given a 3-CNF-formula ϕ using variables $U = \{u_1, \ldots, u_n\}$, the reduction creates a 4-NAE-system which uses the expanded

---

23. This proposition yields that, for any k-NAE-system, the number of satisfying assignments is even!

set of variables $U \cup \{u'_1, \ldots, u'_n\} \cup \{z\}$. The system enforces that any satisfying assignment map u_i and its primed version u'_i to different values, via a tuple (u_i, u_i, u'_i, u'_i); this gives a way to simulate negation. (Note that the tuples in a k-NAE-system can only contain variables, and cannot contain negations of variables.) In addition, the system contains, for each clause C^i of the formula ϕ, a tuple (v^i_1, v^i_2, v^i_3, z) which simulates the clause's effect. By Proposition 3.8.19, the system is satisfiable if and only if it has a satisfying assignment mapping z to 0, and so in reasoning about the system's satisfiability, we may restrict attention to assignments mapping z to 0. An assignment f sending z to 0 fulfills the requirement $\{0, 1\} \subseteq \{f(v^i_1), f(v^i_2), f(v^i_3), f(z)\}$ imposed by the tuple (v^i_1, v^i_2, v^i_3, z) if and only if *at least* one of the values $f(v^i_1), f(v^i_2), f(v^i_3)$ is equal to 1; in this way, the tuple enforces the disjunctive character of a clause.

Reduction 3.8.20: from 3-CNF-SAT **to** 4-NAE-SAT. Let ϕ be a 3-CNF-formula with clauses $C^1 \wedge \cdots \wedge C^m$, and let $U = \{u_1, \ldots, u_n\}$ denote the variables occurring in ϕ. We assume that each clause C^i contains exactly 3 literals; this can be obtained by duplicating literals in a clause, if necessary. For each $i \in [m]$, denote the clause C^i by $\lambda^i_1 \vee \lambda^i_2 \vee \lambda^i_3$.

The reduction produces a 4-NAE-system T as follows. Define $U' = \{u'_1, \ldots, u'_n\}$ to be the set that contains a primed copy of each variable in U, and let z be a new variable.

- For each $i \in [n]$, define s^i to be the tuple (u_i, u_i, u'_i, u'_i).
- For each $i \in [m]$ and $j \in [3]$, define v^i_j as u if λ^i_j is equal to a variable $u \in U$, and as u' if λ^i_j is equal to the negation $\neg u$ of a variable $u \in U$.
- For each $i \in [m]$, define t^i to be the tuple (v^i_1, v^i_2, v^i_3, z).

The 4-NAE-system T is defined as the sequence $s^1, \ldots, s^n, t^1, \ldots, t^m$ of length $n + m$.   ◇

Example 3.8.21. Let us consider the 4-NAE-system produced by Reduction 3.8.20 when given the 3-CNF-formula $\psi = C^1 \wedge C^2 \wedge C^3$, where we have

$$C^1 = a \vee b \vee c, \quad C^2 = \neg b \vee \neg b \vee c, \quad C^3 = \neg a \vee b \vee \neg c.$$

We have that $U = \{a, b, c\}$ are the variables occurring in ψ. Thus, we have $U' = \{a', b', c'\}$. For each variable in U, there is a tuple s^i; in our case, we have

$$s^1 = (a, a, a', a'), \quad s^2 = (b, b, b', b'), \quad s^3 = (c, c, c', c').$$

For each clause of ψ, there is a tuple t^i; we have

$$t^1 = (a, b, c, z), \quad t^2 = (b', b', c, z), \quad t^3 = (a', b, c', z).$$

Each tuple t^i is obtained from the clause C^i by including the literals of the clause, with priming in place of negation, and adding on the variable z. The produced system is the sequence $s^1, s^2, s^3, t^1, t^2, t^3$.   ◇

Correctness proof of Reduction 3.8.20. We show that a 3-CNF-formula ϕ is satisfiable if and only if the defined instance T of 4-NAE-SAT is satisfiable.

For the forward direction, suppose that $f\colon U \to \{0,1\}$ is a satisfying assignment of ϕ. Define $g\colon U \cup U' \cup \{z\} \to \{0,1\}$ as the extension of f where $g(z) = 0$ and, for each variable $u_i' \in U'$, it holds that $g(u_i') = \neg g(u_i)$. We argue that g is a satisfying assignment of T. For each $i \in [n]$, consider the tuple s^i; we have $\{0,1\} \subseteq \{g(u_i), g(u_i), g(u_i'), g(u_i')\}$. Next, for each $i \in [m]$, consider the tuple t^i. Observe that g satisfies v_j^i if and only if f satisfies λ_j^i. Thus, it holds that at least one of the three values $g(v_1^i), g(v_2^i), g(v_3^i)$ is equal to 1. Since $g(z) = 0$, we obtain that $\{0,1\} \subseteq \{g(v_1^i), g(v_2^i), g(v_3^i), g(z)\}$.

For the backward direction, suppose that T is satisfiable. By Proposition 3.8.19, there exists a satisfying assignment $g\colon U \cup U' \cup \{z\} \to \{0,1\}$ of T where $g(z) = 0$. For each index $i \in [n]$, due to the presence of the tuple $s^i \in T$, it holds that $g(u_i) = \neg g(u_i')$. From this, we may observe that g satisfies v_j^i if and only if it satisfies λ_j^i. For any index $i \in [m]$, consider the clause C^i. Due to the presence of the tuple t^i in T, we have the containment $\{0,1\} \subseteq \{g(v_1^i), g(v_2^i), g(v_3^i), g(z)\}$. Since $g(z) = 0$, we have that at least one of the three values $g(v_1^i), g(v_2^i), g(v_3^i)$ is equal to 1; by the observation, it follows that g satisfies at least one of the three literals $\lambda_1^i, \lambda_2^i, \lambda_3^i$, and hence satisfies the clause C^i. $\square$

We next present a reduction from 4-NAE-SAT to 3-NAE-SAT. The reduction bears a conceptual resemblance to the already presented reduction from CNF-SAT to 3-CNF-SAT (Reduction 3.8.8); there, each sufficiently long clause was replaced with multiple clauses containing new variables. Here, each tuple r^i of the given 4-NAE-system will be replaced with three tuples, which are denoted $r^{i,1}, r^{i,2}, r^{i,3}$ and which contain two new variables denoted x^i, y^i. Chaining together the behavior of these three tuples will achieve the effect of the tuple t^i.

Reduction 3.8.22: from 4-NAE-SAT to 3-NAE-SAT. Let T be a 4-NAE-system denoted as $r^1, \ldots, r^m$, and let V be the set of variables occurring in the tuples r^i. For each $i \in [m]$, denote $r^i = (v_1^i, v_2^i, v_3^i, v_4^i)$. We define a 3-NAE-system T' as follows:

- Let $x^1, \ldots, x^m, y^1, \ldots, y^m$ be new variables not in V, and define V' as the set
$$V \cup \{x^1, \ldots, x^m\} \cup \{y^1, \ldots, y^m\}.$$

  The variables appearing in T' will be drawn from V'.

- For each $i \in [m]$, the instance T' contains 3 tuples, denoted $r^{i,1}, r^{i,2}, r^{i,3}$, which simulate the effect of the tuple r^i in T. In particular, for each $i \in [m]$, define

  - $r^{i,1} = (v_1^i, v_2^i, x^i)$,
  - $r^{i,2} = (x^i, x^i, y^i)$,
  - $r^{i,3} = (y^i, v_3^i, v_4^i)$.

The instance T' is defined as the sequence $r^{1,1}, r^{1,2}, r^{1,3}, \ldots, r^{m,1}, r^{m,2}, r^{m,3}$ of length $3m$. $\diamond$

Example 3.8.23. Consider the 4-NAE-system T generated in Example 3.8.21. When Reduction 3.8.22 is applied to this system, each tuple of T contributes 3 tuples to the produced 3-NAE-system T'. As an example, consider the first tuple $s^1 = (a, a, a', a')$ of T, and denote it by r^1; it contributes the tuples

$$r^{1,1} = (a, a, x^1), \quad r^{1,2} = (x^1, x^1, y^1), \quad r^{1,3} = (y^1, a', a').$$

As another example, consider the last tuple $t^3 = (a', b, c', z)$ of T, and denote it by r^6; it contributes the tuples

$$r^{6,1} = (a', b, x^6), \quad r^{6,2} = (x^6, x^6, y^6), \quad r^{6,3} = (y^6, c', z).$$

As the system T has 6 tuples and each one of these tuples contributes 3 tuples to the produced system T', the system T' has a total of $3 \cdot 6 = 18$ tuples. $\diamond$

Correctness proof of Reduction 3.8.22. We show that the 4-NAE-system T is satisfiable if and only if the 3-NAE-system T' is satisfiable.

For the backward direction, suppose that $g \colon V' \to \{0, 1\}$ satisfies T'. We show that g satisfies T. Consider an index $i \in [m]$.

- Due to the presence of the tuple $r^{i,2}$ in T', it holds that $g(x^i) \neq g(y^i)$, and thus $\{0, 1\} = \{g(x^i), g(y^i)\}$.
- Due to the presence of the tuple $r^{i,1}$ in T', it holds that $\{0, 1\} \subseteq \{g(v_1^i), g(v_2^i), g(x^i)\}$, which implies that $g(y^i) \in \{g(v_1^i), g(v_2^i)\}$.
- And due to the presence of the tuple $r^{i,3}$ in T', it holds that $\{0, 1\} \subseteq \{g(y^i), g(v_3^i), g(v_4^i)\}$, which implies that $g(x^i) \in \{g(v_3^i), g(v_4^i)\}$.

It follows that $\{0, 1\} = \{g(x^i), g(y^i)\} \subseteq \{g(v_1^i), g(v_2^i), g(v_3^i), g(v_4^i)\}$.

For the forward direction, suppose that $f \colon V \to \{0, 1\}$ satisfies T. We define an extension $f' \colon V' \to \{0, 1\}$ of f and show that it satisfies T'. For each $i \in [m]$:

- If $f(v_1^i) = f(v_2^i)$, set $f'(x^i) = \neg f(v_1^i)$ and $f'(y^i) = f(v_1^i)$. Due to the presence of the tuple r^i in T, we have $\{0, 1\} \subseteq \{f(v_1^i), f(v_2^i), f(v_3^i), f(v_4^i)\}$, implying that $\neg f(v_1^i) \in \{f(v_3^i), f(v_4^i)\}$. We verify that the conditions on the tuples $r^{i,1}, r^{i,2}, r^{i,3}$ hold:

$$\{0, 1\} = \{f'(v_1^i)\} \cup \{\neg f'(v_1^i)\} \subseteq \{f'(v_1^i), f'(v_2^i)\} \cup \{f'(x^i)\},$$

$$\{0, 1\} = \{\neg f'(v_1^i), f'(v_1^i)\} \subseteq \{f'(x^i), f'(y^i)\},$$

$$\{0, 1\} = \{f'(v_1^i)\} \cup \{\neg f'(v_1^i)\} \subseteq \{f'(y^i)\} \cup \{f'(v_3^i), f'(v_4^i)\}.$$

- If $f(v_1^i) \neq f(v_2^i)$, set $f'(x^i) = f(v_3^i)$ and $f'(y^i) = \neg f(v_3^i)$. We verify that the conditions on the tuples $r^{i,1}, r^{i,2}, r^{i,3}$ hold:

$$\{0, 1\} = \{f'(v_1^i), f'(v_2^i)\} \subseteq \{f'(v_1^i), f'(v_2^i), f'(x^i)\},$$

$$\{0, 1\} = \{f'(v_3^i), \neg f'(v_3^i)\} \subseteq \{f'(x^i), f'(y^i)\},$$

$$\{0, 1\} = \{\neg f'(v_3^i)\} \cup \{f'(v_3^i)\} \subseteq \{f'(y^i)\} \cup \{f'(v_3^i), f'(v_4^i)\}. \qquad \square$$

From the given reductions to the languages 4-NAE-SAT and 3-NAE-SAT, we obtain the following.

Theorem 3.8.24. 4-NAE-SAT *and* 3-NAE-SAT *are NP-complete.*

Proof. The NP-hardness of these languages follows from Theorem 3.8.13 along with Reductions 3.8.20 and 3.8.22.   □

In fact, 3-NAE-SAT can be viewed as a special case of 4-NAE-SAT: a 3-NAE-system can be readily expanded into a 4-NAE-system having the same satisfying assignments simply by duplicating one variable in each tuple. This idea can also be used to obtain that, for each $k \geq 5$, the language k-NAE-SAT is NP-hard. We remark that the language 2-NAE-SAT is PTIME: it is readily shown to be a formulation of and reducible to the language 2-COL, which was previously argued to be PTIME (in Example 3.2.13).

Hardness from NAE-satisfiability

Having established that 3-NAE-SAT is NP-complete, we can derive further NP-completeness results in a relatively smooth fashion.

Our first such result concerns an optimization variant of the 2-CNF-SAT language. The question associated with the original language is to decide whether a given 2-CNF-formula is satisfiable, that is, whether or not there is an assignment satisfying all of the formula's clauses. The following language is a generalization; its question is to decide, given a 2-CNF-formula and a number $\ell \geq 0$, whether or not there is an assignment satisfying ℓ or more of the formula's clauses. Interestingly, this optimization variant is NP-hard, in sharp contrast to the original language being PTIME (Exercise 3.10.33).

Define MAX-2-CNF-SAT to be the language containing each pair (ϕ, ℓ) where ϕ is a 2-CNF-formula, $\ell \in \mathbb{N}$, and there exists an assignment $f: V \to \{0,1\}$ defined on the variables of ϕ that satisfies ℓ or more of the clauses in ϕ. We show that 3-NAE-SAT reduces to this language. In doing so, we will make use of the following lemma, whose proof is left as an exercise (Exercise 3.10.28).

Lemma 3.8.25. *Let* (u, w, x) *be a 3-tuple of variables, and let* $f : V \to \{0,1\}$ *be an assignment defined on these variables. Consider the following 6 clauses:*

$$u \vee w, \ u \vee x, \ w \vee x, \ \neg u \vee \neg w, \ \neg u \vee \neg x, \ \neg w \vee \neg x.$$

If it holds that $\{f(u), f(w), f(x)\} = \{0,1\}$, *then exactly 5 of these 6 clauses are satisfied by* f; *otherwise, exactly 3 of these 6 clauses are satisfied by* f.

Reduction 3.8.26: from 3-NAE-SAT **to** MAX-2-CNF-SAT. Let T be a 3-NAE-system with tuples $t^1, ..., t^m$. For each $i \in [m]$, define $C^{i,1}, ..., C^{i,6}$ to be the 6 clauses derived from the tuple t^i, as described in the statement of Lemma 3.8.25. The produced instance of MAX-2-CNF-SAT is $(\phi, 5m)$ where ϕ is the conjunction of the $6m$ derived clauses, that is, we have

$$\phi = (C^{1,1} \wedge \cdots \wedge C^{1,6}) \wedge \cdots \wedge (C^{m,1} \wedge \cdots \wedge C^{m,6}). \qquad \diamond$$

Correctness proof. We verify that T is satisfiable if and only if there exists an assignment satisfying $5m$ or more clauses of ϕ. This follows quite directly from Lemma 3.8.25.

Suppose that the 3-NAE-system T is satisfiable; let $f\colon V \to \{0,1\}$ be a satisfying assignment of T. By Lemma 3.8.25, for each $i \in [m]$, the assignment f satisfies 5 of the clauses $C^{i,1}, \ldots, C^{i,6}$. Thus, the assignment f satisfies $5m$ of the clauses in ϕ.

Suppose that there exists an assignment g that satisfies $5m$ or more clauses of ϕ. By Lemma 3.8.25, for each $i \in [m]$, any assignment satisfies either 3 or 5 of the clauses in $C^{i,1}, \ldots, C^{i,6}$. Thus, for each $i \in [m]$, the assignment g satisfies 5 of the clauses in $C^{i,1}, \ldots, C^{i,6}$. Denoting t^i by (v_1^i, v_2^i, v_3^i), from Lemma 3.8.25 we obtain $\{g(v_1^i), g(v_2^i), g(v_3^i)\} = \{0,1\}$. Thus, the assignment g satisfies the instance T. $\quad\square$

From Theorem 3.8.24 and Reduction 3.8.26, we obtain the following result.

Theorem 3.8.27. MAX-2-CNF-SAT *is NP-complete.*

We next return to graph colorings, and prove that the language 3-COL admits a reduction from the language 3-NAE-SAT. In order to relate graph colorings to propositional assignments and 3-NAE-systems in the proof, it will be convenient to slightly generalize the definition of k-coloring given in Section 3.1.2, and say that a k-**coloring** of a graph $G = (V, E)$ is a mapping $c\colon V \to D$ such that D is *any* k-element set and, for each edge $\{v, v'\} \in E$, the edge is **respected** in that $c(v) \neq c(v')$. Clearly, it holds that a graph is k-*colorable*, under the definition given in Section 3.1.2, if and only if the graph has a k-coloring, under the just-given definition: renaming the elements of D does not affect whether or not any edge is respected. A particular case of this principle is encapsulated by the following proposition, which maintains that if one starts with a coloring and applies a permutation to the colors, the result is another coloring.[24]

Proposition 3.8.28. *Let $k \geq 1$, and suppose that $c\colon V \to D$ is a k-coloring of a graph G. Let $\pi\colon D \to D$ be a bijection, and define $c'\colon V \to D$ as the mapping where $c'(v) = \pi(c(v))$, for each $v \in V$. Then, c' is also a k-coloring of G.*

The following is the reduction to the language 3-COL. An example of its application is given in Figure 3.8.3. From a 3-NAE-system with variables U, the reduction generates a graph where each variable u in U is included as a vertex, and forms an edge $\{u, z\}$ with a vertex z. To create a 3-coloring of the graph, the vertex z must receive one color, and for each variable in U, there are then two colors to choose from; any 3-coloring of the graph thus induces a two-valued (propositional) assignment on the variables in U.

---

24. Proposition 3.8.28 can be conceived of as an analog of Proposition 3.8.19 for graph colorings, and implies that the number of k-colorings of any graph is a multiple of $k!$.

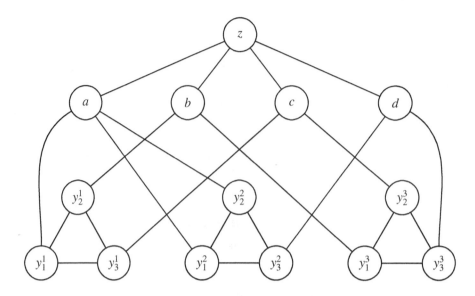

Figure 3.8.3. The reduction from 3-NAE-SAT to 3-COL (Reduction 3.8.29) applied to the 3-NAE-system T having the 3 tuples $t^1 = (a, b, c), t^2 = (a, a, d)$, and $t^3 = (b, c, d)$. The produced graph's vertex set contains a new vertex z, a vertex for each variable appearing in T, and for each tuple index $i = 1, 2, 3$, three vertices y_1^i, y_2^i, y_3^i forming a triangle. The vertex z forms an edge with each variable. Each tuple t^i is encoded via edges between the triangle y_1^i, y_2^i, y_3^i and the respective entries of the tuple. For example, the tuple $t^1 = (a, b, c)$ is encoded via the edges $\{a, y_1^1\}, \{b, y_2^1\}, \{c, y_3^1\}$.

Reduction 3.8.29: from 3-NAE-SAT to 3-COL. Let T be a 3-NAE-system whose tuples are $t^1, \dots, t^m$. Let U be the set of variables appearing in T; denote each tuple t^i by (u_1^i, u_2^i, u_3^i). Based on the system T, the reduction produces a graph $G = (V, E)$ as follows.

- Define the vertex set V as $U \cup \{z\} \cup \{y_j^i \mid i \in [m], j \in [3]\}$, where z and the y_j^i are new variables not in U. We have $|V| = |U| + 1 + 3m$.
- Define the edge set E as the union $E_1 \cup E_2 \cup E_3$, where the sets E_1, E_2, and E_3 are defined in the following way:

  - The set E_1 contains, for each $u \in U$, the pair $\{u, z\}$. Thus $|E_1| = |U|$.
  - The set E_2 contains, for each $i \in [m]$, each of the pairs $\{u_1^i, y_1^i\}, \{u_2^i, y_2^i\}$, and $\{u_3^i, y_3^i\}$. Thus $|E_2| = 3m$.
  - The set E_3 contains, for each $i \in [m]$, each of the pairs $\{y_1^i, y_2^i\}, \{y_1^i, y_3^i\}$, and $\{y_2^i, y_3^i\}$. Thus $|E_3| = 3m$. The set E_3 enforces, for each $i \in [m]$, that y_1^i, y_2^i, and y_3^i form a triangle. ◇

To confirm that this is a reduction, we need to verify that there exists a 3-coloring of the graph G if and only if the 3-NAE-system T has a satisfying assignment. The idea of our proof is as follows. For the forward direction, by appeal to Proposition 3.8.28, there exists a 3-coloring $h\colon V \to \{0,1,2\}$ such that $h(z) = 2$. It can then be verified that the restriction of the coloring h to the variables U is a satisfying assignment of T: the edges in E_1 enforce that for each $u \in U$, it holds that $h(u) \in \{0,1\}$, and the edges in E_2 and E_3 enforce that each 3-tuple of T is mapped to values that are not all equal. For the backward direction, the reasoning is, in some sense, reversed. Given a satisfying assignment $f\colon U \to \{0,1\}$ of the system T, we show that f can be extended to a 3-coloring $h\colon V \to \{0,1,2\}$ of G where $h(z) = 2$. The assumption that f satisfies T permits us to define h on the vertices y_j^i in a way that respects the edges in E_2 and E_3.

Correctness proof of Reduction 3.8.29. Suppose that G is 3-colorable. Then there exists a 3-coloring $h^-\colon V \to \{0,1,2\}$ of G. In light of Proposition 3.8.28, by applying an appropriately chosen permutation to h^-, we may obtain a 3-coloring $h\colon V \to \{0,1,2\}$ of G such that $h(z) = 2$. We claim that the restriction of h to U yields a satisfying assignment of T. For each $u \in U$, we obtain from the equality $h(z) = 2$ and from the presence of the edge $\{u,z\}$ that $h(u) \in \{0,1\}$. It thus suffices to argue that, for each $i \in [m]$, that $\{0,1\} \subseteq \{h(u_1^i), h(u_2^i), h(u_3^i)\}$. We argue this by contradiction; if it does not hold, there exists an index $i \in [m]$ such that

$$\{h(u_1^i), h(u_2^i), h(u_3^i)\} = \{0\} \quad \text{or} \quad \{h(u_1^i), h(u_2^i), h(u_3^i)\} = \{1\}.$$

Since the vertices y_1^i, y_2^i, y_3^i form a triangle, it holds that

$$\{h(y_1^i), h(y_2^i), h(y_3^i)\} = \{0,1,2\}.$$

It follows that there exists an index $j \in [3]$ such that $h(u_j^i) = h(y_j^i)$; this contradicts that h is a 3-coloring of G, since the pair $\{u_j^i, y_j^i\}$ is an edge in E.

Suppose that $f\colon U \to \{0,1\}$ is a satisfying assignment of T. Based on f, we define a map $h\colon V \to \{0,1,2\}$ as follows.

- Set $h(u) = f(u)$, for each $u \in U$.
- Set $h(z) = 2$.
- For each $i \in [m]$, the sequence of values $f(u_1^i), f(u_2^i), f(u_3^i)$ are used as a basis to set the sequence of values $h(y_1^i), h(y_2^i)$, and $h(y_3^i)$, as follows. In the former sequence, there is one value $p \in \{0,1\}$ that occurs exactly once. In order to respect the edges in E_2, we set the corresponding entry of the latter sequence to the *other* value in $\{0,1\}$, and then set the other entries of the latter sequence so that each color in $\{0,1,2\}$ occurs once. Concretely, we can use the table in Figure 3.8.4 to set the values $h(y_j^i)$.

We argue that h is a 3-coloring of G. First, consider the edges in E_1. For each $u \in U$, we have $h(u) = f(u) \in \{0,1\}$, so $h(u) \neq 2 = h(z)$. Next, consider the edges in E_2; it is straightforward to verify that they are respected, given the above definition of the values $h(y_j^i)$ from the values $f(u_j^i)$. The edges in E_3 are respected, since in every case above, the three values $h(y_1^i), h(y_2^i)$, and $h(y_3^i)$ are assigned pairwise distinct values. $\qquad\square$

Values of $(f(u_1^i), f(u_2^i), f(u_3^i))$	Setting for $(h(y_1^i), h(y_2^i), h(y_3^i))$
$(0,0,1)$	$(1,2,0)$
$(0,1,0)$	$(2,0,1)$
$(1,0,0)$	$(0,1,2)$
$(1,1,0)$	$(0,2,1)$
$(1,0,1)$	$(2,1,0)$
$(0,1,1)$	$(1,0,2)$

Figure 3.8.4. Table which aids in passing from a satisfying assignment f to a 3-coloring h in the correctness proof of Reduction 3.8.29.

In the just-given proof, we can conceive of the colors 0 and 1 as representing the respective propositional values, and the color 2 as a *flexible* color. Under a 3-coloring of the produced graph, each triangle $\{y_1^i, y_2^i, y_3^i\}$ must receive each color once: a vertex y_j^i receiving the color 0 or 1 ensures that the variable u_j^i receives the color 1 or 0, respectively, and a vertex y_j^i receiving the color 2 allows the variable u_j^i to receive either 0 or 1 as a color (regarding the edge $\{u_j^i, y_j^i\}$). In this way, each triangle enforces that its corresponding vertices in U receive each of the colors 0 and 1 at least once—equivalently, that these vertices' colors are *not all equal*.

The reduction to 3-COL that we just gave establishes this language's hardness. With this hardness result as a basis, we can quite readily prove the hardness of k-COL for all $k \geq 3$, by bootstrapping: we exhibit a reduction from k-COL to $(k+1)$-COL. The reduction we present transforms a given graph G by expanding it into a new graph that contains a new vertex z having an edge to each vertex in the original graph G.

Reduction 3.8.30: from k-COL to $(k+1)$-COL, when $k \geq 3$. Given a graph $G = (V, E)$, the reduction produces the graph $G' = (V', E')$ having vertex set $V' = V \cup \{z\}$, where z is a new vertex assumed to be outside of V, and edge set $E' = E \cup \{\{v,z\} \mid v \in V\}$. ◇

Example 3.8.31. Looking back at Figure 3.1.4 (on page 146), when the just-given reduction is applied to the left graph, the right graph is produced. ◇

Correctness proof of Reduction 3.8.30. We verify that G is k-colorable if and only if G' is $(k+1)$-colorable.

Suppose that $h: V \to \{1, \ldots, k\}$ is a k-coloring of G. Define $h': V' \to \{1, \ldots, k+1\}$ as the extension of h where $h'(z) = k+1$. The mapping h' is a $(k+1)$-coloring of G': each edge $\{v,z\}$ is respected since z is the only vertex mapped by h' to $k+1$, and each edge in E is respected since h' extends h.

Suppose that $h^-: V' \to \{1, \ldots, k+1\}$ is a $(k+1)$-coloring of G. Due to Proposition 3.8.28, an appropriately chosen permutation can be applied to the map h^- to obtain a $(k+1)$-coloring $h': V' \to \{1, \ldots, k+1\}$ such that $h'(z) = k+1$. Due to the edges of the

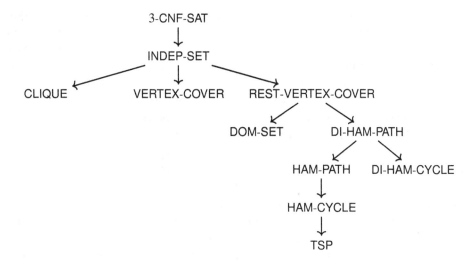

Figure 3.8.5. The web of reductions given for graph-theoretic problems in Section 3.8.2.

form $\{v, z\}$, each vertex $v \in V$ has $h'(v) \in \{1, \dots, k\}$. Since h' respects all edges in E, it thus holds that the restriction of h' to V is a k-coloring of G. $\square$

Theorem 3.8.32. *For each $k \geq 3$, it holds that k-COL is NP-complete.*

Proof. The language 3-COL is NP-hard by Theorem 3.8.24 and Reduction 3.8.29. For each $k \geq 4$, the language k-COL is NP-hard via applying Reduction 3.8.30 inductively. $\square$

Remark 3.8.33. The *unsatisfiability* versions of the languages 4-NAE-SAT and 3-NAE-SAT can be shown to be coNP-complete, by using Theorem 3.8.24 along with an argument analogous to that given to establish Corollary 3.8.15. Similarly, for each $k \geq 3$, the language consisting of *k-uncolorable* graphs, that is, of the graphs that are *not* k-colorable, can be shown to be coNP-complete, by using Theorem 3.8.32 and such an argument. $\diamond$

3.8.2 Graph-theoretic problems

We next consider a number of further graph-theoretic problems; a summary of the reductions to be shown is given in Figure 3.8.5. We begin by revisiting the languages that were used to give initial examples of reductions (in Section 3.4.1).

   Our first reduction, which is from 3-CNF-SAT to INDEP-SET, serves as a bridge between satisfiability problems and the graph-theoretic problems treated here. These two languages may at first appear to be quite qualitatively different from each other: one deals with logical formulas, and the other, with graphs. The reduction needs to translate a 3-CNF-formula to a graph and a value k such that the formula is satisfiable if and only if the graph has an independent set of size k. So, the reduction needs to relate the existence of a satisfying assignment—which chooses a value of 0 or 1 for each variable of the formula—to the existence of an independent set—which chooses k vertices from the vertex set of a graph.

In order to present the reduction, we adopt a particular perspective on the satisfiability of a 3-CNF-formula. Rather than conceiving of an assignment as choosing a 0/1 value for each variable, we conceive of an assignment as choosing one literal from each clause, in such a way that all chosen literals are consistent with each other. (Recall that an assignment satisfies a clause when it satisfies *at least* one literal in the clause.) Following this line of thought, let us contemplate how to guarantee that an independent set chooses one literal from each clause. We can assume each clause to have 3 literals; since we view satisfiability as a choice of literals, it is natural to introduce, for each clause, 3 vertices representing the clause's literals. As an independent set can include at most one vertex from each edge, if we turn the 3 vertices representing a clause into a triangle, we enforce that each independent set of the constructed graph can include *at most one* of these 3 vertices. To ensure that each independent set of the constructed graph includes *at least one* of the 3 vertices in each such triangle, we request an independent set whose size is the number of clauses in the formula.

To secure that, from an independent set, we will be able to assemble a satisfying assignment—and vice versa—we need to require that the chosen literals are consistent with each other. A satisfying assignment certainly never chooses two literals that are complementary, since it can only satisfy one out of two complementary literals. To impose this requirement, we place an edge between each pair of complementary literals. It turns out that these edges are sufficient for ensuring the desired correspondence between satisfying assignments and independent sets; in particular, from any set of literals not containing complementary literals, one can assemble an assignment satisfying all literals in the set.

We next present the precise reduction; Figure 3.8.6 gives an example application thereof.

Reduction 3.8.34: from 3-CNF-SAT **to** INDEP-SET. Let ϕ be a 3-CNF-formula, and let $C^1, \ldots, C^m$ denote the clauses of ϕ. We assume that each clause contains exactly 3 literals; this can be achieved by just duplicating literals within a clause, if necessary.[25] For each index $i \in [m]$, we denote the clause C^i by $\lambda_1^i \vee \lambda_2^i \vee \lambda_3^i$.

Given the formula ϕ, the reduction produces the pair (G, m), where $G = (V, E)$ is the graph defined in the following way:

- The vertex set V is defined as

$$\{v_j^i \mid i \in [m], j \in [3]\}.$$

That is, there is a vertex v_j^i for each literal occurrence λ_j^i in ϕ. We have $|V| = 3m$.

---

25. This assumption is mainly for ease of presentation; in fact, the idea of the reduction that we present can be readily adapted to yield a direct reduction from CNF-SAT to INDEP-SET.

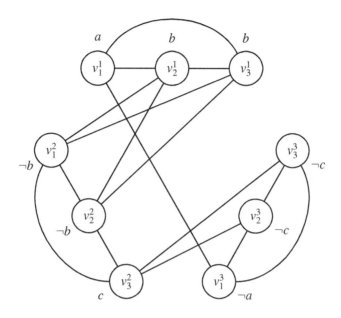

Figure 3.8.6. The graph produced by the reduction from 3-CNF-SAT to INDEP-SET, when applied to the example 3-CNF-formula with the clauses $C^1 = a \vee b \vee b$, $C^2 = \neg b \vee \neg b \vee c$, and $C^3 = \neg a \vee \neg c \vee \neg c$. The literal occurrences $\lambda_1^i, \lambda_2^i, \lambda_3^i$ of each clause C^i are represented by a triangle of vertices v_1^i, v_2^i, v_3^i, respectively. In the figure, the literal occurrence represented by a vertex is placed next to the vertex; technically, each such literal occurrence is not part of the graph. Two vertices $v_j^i, v_{j'}^{i'}$ from different clauses (that is, with $i \neq i'$) form an edge when their represented literals are complementary.

- The edge set E is defined by the following rule. Let $v_j^i, v_{j'}^{i'}$ be distinct elements of V; then, place $\{v_j^i, v_{j'}^{i'}\}$ in E if and only if at least one of the following two conditions holds:
  (1) $i = i'$; (2) the literals λ_j^i and $\lambda_{j'}^{i'}$ are complementary. Condition (1) places edges between vertices whose literals are in the same clause; condition (2) places edges between vertices representing complementary literals, which are precisely the pairs of literals that cannot be simultaneously satisfied by an assignment. ◇

Correctness proof. We prove that the 3-CNF-formula ϕ is satisfiable if and only if the graph G has a size m independent set.

Let f be a satisfying assignment of the 3-CNF-formula. Let S be a size m subset of V that contains, for each $i \in [m]$, a vertex v_j^i whose corresponding literal λ_j^i is satisfied by f. Let us argue that S is an independent set of G. Let v_j^i and $v_{j'}^{i'}$ be distinct vertices in S. It does not hold that $i = i'$, since for each i, the set S contains exactly one of the vertices v_1^i, v_2^i, v_3^i. Also, by the specification of S, the assignment f satisfies both of the literals λ_j^i and $\lambda_{j'}^{i'}$, and hence they cannot be complementary literals. We thus have $\{v_j^i, v_{j'}^{i'}\} \notin E$.

Suppose S is a size m independent set of the graph G. For each $i \in [m]$, the set S contains at most one of the vertices v_1^i, v_2^i, v_3^i, since each pair of these vertices forms an edge. But since $|S| = m$, we observe that S must contain, for each $i \in [m]$, exactly one of the vertices v_1^i, v_2^i, v_3^i. Define $S' = \{\lambda_j^i \mid v_j^i \in S\}$. By the observation just made, S' must contain at least one literal of each clause. But S' does not contain complementary literals by the definition of E. Hence, there exists an assignment f to the variables of ϕ under which all literals of S' are true, and this assignment f satisfies ϕ.   □

Remark 3.8.35. In the graphs produced by Reduction 3.8.34, the triangles representing clauses are examples of what are known as *gadgets* in the setting of complexity-theoretic reductions. Although there is no formal definition of the term *gadget*, it typically refers to a device that appears in an instance produced by a reduction and simulates a component or behavior of the original instance. In Reduction 3.8.34, each triangle v_1^i, v_2^i, v_3^i in effect simulates the need to choose one literal from the clause that it represents (namely, the clause C^i). Each inter-clause edge between a pair of complementary literals' vertices can also be conceived of as a gadget, which simulates the behavior that no assignment can satisfy both literals in such a pair.   ◇

From Theorem 3.8.13 and Reduction 3.8.34, we obtain the following hardness result.

Theorem 3.8.36. INDEP-SET *is NP-complete.*

We can now revisit the languages CLIQUE and VERTEX-COVER; each of these languages was earlier shown to admit a reduction from the language INDEP-SET (in Section 3.4.1). As the language INDEP-SET was just established to be hard, we may conclude the hardness of these two languages.

Theorem 3.8.37. CLIQUE *and* VERTEX-COVER *are NP-complete.*

Proof. By Theorem 3.8.36, the language INDEP-SET is NP-hard. By Proposition 3.4.7, we obtain that the language CLIQUE is NP-hard, and by Proposition 3.4.10, we obtain that the language VERTEX-COVER is NP-hard.   □

We next identify a slightly restricted version of the language VERTEX-COVER that remains NP-hard, which will facilitate the presentation of some of the reductions to come. Define REST-VERTEX-COVER to be the language containing each pair (G, k) in VERTEX-COVER satisfying the additional restrictions that each vertex of the graph G has degree 2 or greater, and $k \geq 1$.

Theorem 3.8.38. REST-VERTEX-COVER *is NP-complete.*

Proof. The reduction from 3-CNF-SAT to INDEP-SET given by Reduction 3.8.34 maps a 3-CNF-formula ϕ with m clauses to a pair (G, m), where G is a graph with $|V| = 3m$; recall that we have $m \geq 1$ (by Remark 3.8.4). Observe that each vertex of G is part of a triangle, and thus has degree 2 or greater. The reduction from INDEP-SET to VERTEX-COVER given by Proposition 3.4.10 maps such a pair (G, m) to the pair $(G, |V| - m) = (G, 2m)$. The pair $(G, 2m)$ is thus a pair satisfying the additional restrictions given in the definition of REST-VERTEX-COVER, and so the composition of these two reductions gives a reduction from 3-CNF-SAT to REST-VERTEX-COVER. (The composition of two reductions is always a reduction; this follows from the proof of Theorem 3.4.18.) □

Remark 3.8.39. It is possible to alternatively prove Theorem 3.8.38 by presenting a direct reduction from VERTEX-COVER to the restricted version thereof. ◇

A vertex cover of a graph was a set of vertices that, in a particular sense, covered all *edges*. We next consider the notion of a **dominating set** of a graph, which is a set of vertices that, in a sense to be defined, covers all *vertices*.

Let $G = (V, E)$ be a graph. We say that a vertex u **dominates** a vertex v if either $u = v$ or $\{u, v\}$ is an edge in E. Let $U \subseteq V$ be a set of vertices; we say that U **dominates** a vertex v if there exists a vertex $u \in U$ that dominates v. To deal with these concepts, the following notation will be handy. Define the **neighborhood** of a vertex $u \in V$, denoted by $N_G[u]$, as the set $\{u\} \cup \{v \mid \{u, v\} \in E\}$; and define the **neighborhood** of a set $U \subseteq V$ of vertices, denoted by $N_G[U]$, as the set $\bigcup_{u \in U} N_G[u]$. It is readily seen that a vertex u dominates a vertex v if and only if $v \in N_G[u]$, and that a set U of vertices dominates a vertex v if and only if $v \in N_G[U]$. Define a **dominating set** of a graph $G = (V, E)$ to be a set U of vertices such that $V = N_G[U]$, that is, such that each vertex of G is dominated by U.

Example 3.8.40. In the Petersen graph of Figure 3.4.2 (on page 172), the set $\{u_1, v_3, v_4\}$ is a dominating set of size 3; by symmetry, there are numerous other dominating sets of size 3. This graph has no dominating set of size 2: each vertex has degree 3 and thus has a neighborhood of size 4; so, any 2 vertices dominate at most $2 \cdot 4 = 8$ vertices. ◇

Example 3.8.41. In the 3-by-3 grid graph presented by Figure 3.4.3 (on page 172), the set $\{(1, 2), (3, 1), (3, 3)\}$ is a dominating set of size 3. It is verifiable that this graph has no dominating set of size 2. ◇

The notion of dominating set is related to the notion of vertex cover. It is straightforwardly verified that, in a graph with no isolated vertices, each vertex cover is a dominating set. The converse, however, fails dramatically. Consider, for $n \geq 3$, the *complete graph* on n vertices, denoted K_n, which is defined to have edges between each pair of distinct vertices. In such a complete graph K_n, any single vertex dominates all of the vertices, so there exist dominating sets of size 1. On the other hand, there is no vertex cover of size $n - 2$ (or less), since omitting two vertices from a purported vertex cover would leave uncovered the edge between the two omitted vertices. In the graph K_n, each size $n - 1$ subset of the vertex set is seen to be a vertex cover.

We next establish the hardness of the language

DOM-SET $= \{(G, k) \mid G$ is a graph, $k \in \mathbb{N}$, and G has a size k dominating set$\}$

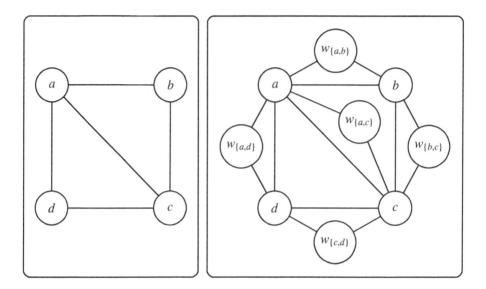

Figure 3.8.7. The reduction establishing the hardness of DOM-SET transforms a graph into a second graph by expanding each edge of the original graph into a triangle.

by presenting a reduction from REST-VERTEX-COVER. When given a pair (G, k), the reduction's essential behavior is to produce a pair (G', k), where G' is a graph obtained from G by adding vertices and edges. More specifically, for each edge $e = \{x, y\}$ of G, a new vertex w_e is added, and the edges $\{x, w_e\}$, $\{y, w_e\}$ are added, so that $\{x, y, w_e\}$ forms a triangle in G'. See Figure 3.8.7 for an example of the transformation from G to G'.

A vertex cover of G is readily seen to be a dominating set of G'; this observation yields one direction of the correctness proof. For the other direction, one needs to show that the existence of a dominating set U' of G' implies the existence of a vertex cover of G having the same size as U'. In general, a dominating set U' of G' may contain the added vertices of the form w_e, and may not necessarily itself be a vertex cover of G. However, by adjusting such a dominating set U', we will obtain a dominating set U of G' that does not contain any of the added vertices (that is, which contains only vertices of G), and which will yield a vertex cover of G as desired.

Reduction 3.8.42: from REST-VERTEX-COVER **to** DOM-SET. Given a pair (G, k) where $k \geq 1$ and $G = (V, E)$ is a graph where each vertex has degree at least 2, the reduction behaves as follows. When $k > |V|$, clearly G has no vertex cover of size k, and the reduction produces a fixed string outside of DOM-SET. When $k \leq |V|$, the reduction produces the pair (G', k), where $G' = (V', E')$ is the graph defined as follows:

$$V' = V \cup \left\{ w_{\{x,y\}} \mid \{x, y\} \in E \right\},$$

$$E' = E \cup \left\{ \{x, w_{\{x,y\}}\}, \{y, w_{\{x,y\}}\} \mid \{x, y\} \in E \right\}.$$

That is, the vertex set V' is the set obtained from V by adding a new vertex w_e for each edge e in E. The edge set E' is defined so that, for each edge $e \in E$, the 3 vertices in the set $e \cup \{w_e\}$ form a triangle. Observe that $|V'| = |V| + |E|$, and $|E'| = 3|E|$. ◇

Correctness proof. Assuming that $k \leq |V|$, we verify that there exists a size k vertex cover of G if and only if there exists a size k dominating set of G'.

Suppose that there exists a size k vertex cover U of G. We claim that U is a size k dominating set of G'. To establish this, we confirm that, in the graph G', each vertex in V' is dominated by a vertex in U:

- Let v be an arbitrary vertex in V; since there are no isolated vertices in G, there exists a vertex $v' \in V$ such that $\{v, v'\} \in E \subseteq E'$. Because U is a vertex cover of G, one of the vertices in $\{v, v'\}$ is in U; let u denote such a vertex. It holds that $v \in N_{G'}[u]$.
- Consider an arbitrary vertex in V' having the form $w_{\{x,y\}}$. Since $\{x, y\} \in E$ and U is a vertex cover of G, one of the vertices in $\{x, y\}$ is in U; let u denote such a vertex. We have $\{u, w_{\{x,y\}}\} \in E'$, and so $w_{\{x,y\}} \in N_{G'}[u]$.

Suppose that there exists a size k dominating set U' of G'. Based on U', we define a set U according to the following procedure. Initialize U to be the empty set; then, consider each element $u' \in U'$, and perform the following:

- If $u' \in V$, add u' to U.
- If u' has the form $w_{\{x,y\}}$, arbitrarily pick one of the vertices x, y and add it to U.

Clearly, it holds that $U \subseteq V$ and that $|U| \leq |U'|$. We establish that there exists a size k vertex cover of G in a few steps.

1. We claim that U is a dominating set of G'. This holds because, for each $u' \in U$, a vertex was added to U that dominates all vertices dominated by u': this is vacuously true when $u' \in V$, and when u' has the form $w_{\{x,y\}}$, it holds that $N_{G'}[w_{\{x,y\}}] = \{w_{\{x,y\}}, x, y\}$, which is a subset of both $N_{G'}[x]$ and $N_{G'}[y]$.

2. We next claim that U is a vertex cover of G. Consider any edge $\{x, y\} \in E$. Since U is a dominating set of G', there exists a vertex $u \in U$ that dominates the vertex $w_{\{x,y\}} \in E'$; since $u \in V$, it must then hold that u is equal to x or y, because x and y are the only vertices in V that dominate $w_{\{x,y\}}$ in G'.

3. We have that U is a vertex cover of G with $|U| \leq |U'| = k$. Let U^+ be any superset of U that consists of vertices from V and has size k; such a superset exists by our assumption that $k \leq |V|$. We then have that U^+ is a size k vertex cover of G, as desired. □

From Theorem 3.8.38 and Reduction 3.8.42, we obtain the following result.

Theorem 3.8.43. DOM-SET *is NP-complete.*

Hamiltonian paths and cycles

We next study a handful of languages related to Hamiltonian cycles, including the language HAM-CYCLE itself. Let $G = (V, E)$ be a graph or digraph. Define a **Hamiltonian path** in G to be a walk $v_1, \ldots, v_m$ in G where each vertex in V appears exactly once; when $s, t \in V$ are vertices, define an (s, t)-**Hamiltonian path** in G to be a Hamiltonian path starting at s and ending at t, that is, a Hamiltonian path $v_1, \ldots, v_m$ where $s = v_1$ and $t = v_m$.

Example 3.8.44. The Petersen graph of Figure 3.4.2 (on page 172) has Hamiltonian paths; for example,

$$v_1, v_4, v_2, v_5, v_3, u_3, u_4, u_5, u_1, u_2$$

is a (v_1, u_2)-Hamiltonian path. It can be proved that this graph has no Hamiltonian cycle; however, deleting any vertex from this graph (and the edges containing it) can be verified to yield a graph having a Hamiltonian cycle.   ◇

Example 3.8.45. The 3-by-3 grid graph presented in Figure 3.4.3 (on page 172) has a $((1, 1), (3, 3))$-Hamiltonian path; one example is

$$(1, 1), (2, 1), (3, 1), (3, 2), (2, 2), (1, 2), (1, 3), (2, 3), (3, 3).$$

This graph has no Hamiltonian cycle (see Exercise 3.10.49).   ◇

Define HAM-PATH to be the language containing each triple (G, s, t) such that G is a graph obeying the following conditions:

- s and t are vertices of G, and
- G has an (s, t)-Hamiltonian path.

Define DI-HAM-PATH to be the digraph version of HAM-PATH, namely, the language containing each triple (G, s, t) such that G is a digraph satisfying the stated conditions. We show the hardness of both of these languages, beginning with DI-HAM-PATH.

To prove the hardness of DI-HAM-PATH, we present a reduction from the language REST-VERTEX-COVER. In Figure 3.8.8, we provide an illustration of the reduction's behavior, which the reader is encouraged to peruse before studying the reduction.

Reduction 3.8.46: from REST-VERTEX-COVER **to** DI-HAM-PATH. Let (G, k) be a pair where G is a graph without isolated vertices and $k \geq 1$; denote G by (U, E). The reduction produces the triple (H, x_1, x_{k+1}), where the digraph $H = (V, F)$ is defined as follows.

The vertex set V is defined as

$$\{x_1, \ldots, x_{k+1}\} \cup \{(u, e, \text{in}), (u, e, \text{out}) \mid u \in e, e \in E\}.$$

We refer to the vertices x_i as **anchors**; there are $k + 1$ of them. For each edge $e \in E$, there are 4 vertices in V having the form $(\cdot, e, \cdot)$, so we have $|V| = (k + 1) + 4|E|$.

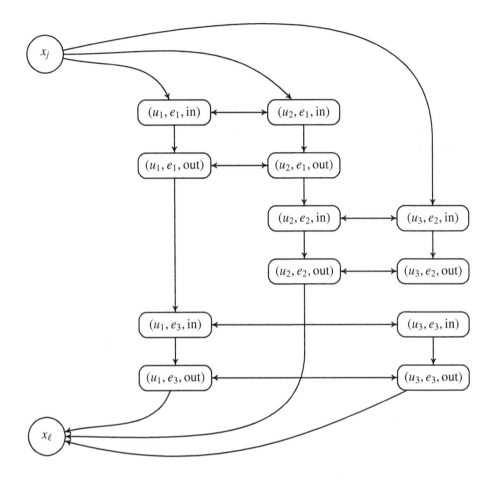

Figure 3.8.8. Part of the digraph H produced by Reduction 3.8.46 when applied to the triangle graph $G = (U, E)$ having vertex set $U = \{u_1, u_2, u_3\}$ and edge set $\{e_1, e_2, e_3\}$, where $e_1 = \{u_1, u_2\}$, $e_2 = \{u_2, u_3\}$, and $e_3 = \{u_1, u_3\}$. For each vertex u in U, a so-called *u-walk* is created, which has two vertices (with labels in and out) for each edge containing u. The u_1-walk is the sequence $(u_1, e_1, \text{in}), (u_1, e_1, \text{out}), (u_1, e_3, \text{in}), (u_1, e_3, \text{out})$; the u_2-walk is the sequence $(u_2, e_1, \text{in}), (u_2, e_1, \text{out}), (u_2, e_2, \text{in}), (u_2, e_2, \text{out})$; and the u_3-walk is the sequence $(u_3, e_2, \text{in}), (u_3, e_2, \text{out}), (u_3, e_3, \text{in}), (u_3, e_3, \text{out})$. Directed edges between these walks are placed between vertices whose second and third entries are equal; these edges run horizontally in the diagram. There are also vertices $x_1, \ldots, x_{k+1}$ called *anchors*; x_j is presumed to be among the first k anchors $x_1, \ldots, x_k$, which each have an outgoing edge to each vertex starting a u-walk; x_ℓ is presumed to be among the last k anchors $x_2, \ldots, x_{k+1}$, which each have an incoming edge from each vertex ending a u-walk.

The edge set F contains three types of edges. Precisely, we define F as the union of sets $F_1 \cup F_2 \cup F_3$, where F_1, F_2, and F_3 are defined as follows:

- For each vertex $u \in U$ (in G), let $d(u)$ denote the degree of u, and let $e_1^u, \ldots, e_{d(u)}^u$ be a listing of the edges in E that contain u. We place—into F_1—the edges needed to ensure that, for each $u \in U$, the sequence

$$(u, e_1^u, \text{in}), (u, e_1^u, \text{out}), \ (u, e_2^u, \text{in}), (u, e_2^u, \text{out}), \ \ldots, \ (u, e_{d(u)}^u, \text{in}), (u, e_{d(u)}^u, \text{out}),$$

is a walk; let us refer to this sequence as the u-**walk**. Each such u-walk is nonempty, by our assumption that the original graph G does not contain any isolated vertices.

Formally, we define F_1 as the union of the two sets

$$\bigcup_{u \in U} \left\{ ((u, e_i^u, \text{in}), (u, e_i^u, \text{out})) \mid i \in [d(u)] \right\},$$

$$\bigcup_{u \in U} \left\{ ((u, e_i^u, \text{out}), (u, e_{i+1}^u, \text{in})) \mid i \in [d(u) - 1] \right\}.$$

- For each anchor among $x_1, \ldots, x_k$, we allow an outgoing edge to each vertex (u, e_1^u, in); and, for each anchor among $x_2, \ldots, x_{k+1}$, we permit an incoming edge from each vertex $(u, e_{d(u)}^u, \text{out})$. Formally, we define

$$F_2 = \bigcup_{u \in U} \left\{ (x_j, (u, e_1^u, \text{in})), \ ((u, e_{d(u)}^u, \text{out}), x_{j+1}) \mid j \in [k] \right\}.$$

- For each edge $e = \{u, u'\}$ in E, we place edges between (u, e, in) and (u', e, in) in both directions; and we place edges between (u, e, out) and (u', e, out) in both directions. Formally, we define

$$F_3 = \left\{ ((u, e, \text{in}), (u', e, \text{in})), \ ((u, e, \text{out}), (u', e, \text{out})) \mid e = \{u, u'\}, e \in E \right\}. \qquad \diamond$$

Let us take stock of the construction. The digraph H should be designed in such a way that it has a Hamiltonian path from x_1 to x_{k+1} if and only if the original graph G has a vertex cover. When G has a vertex cover $C = \{u_1, \ldots, u_k\}$ of size k, the construction will provide that H has a Hamiltonian path that begins at x_1, traverses a vertex sequence corresponding to u_1, goes to x_2, traverses a vertex sequence corresponding to u_2, and so on. It is instructive to see which vertices in H can be traversed, using the first two types of edges (that is, using the edges in $F_1 \cup F_2$), if we attempt to construct a Hamiltonian path. A walk can start from x_1, take the u_1-walk, go to x_2, take the u_2-walk, and continue in this fashion, ending at x_{k+1}. However, in doing this, this walk traverses just the anchors and the vertices of the form $(u_i, e, \cdot)$, where u_i is in the vertex cover C; it does not traverse any vertex of the form $(u, e, \cdot)$ where u is not in the vertex cover C. But, for any such vertex $(u, e, \cdot)$ of this latter type, it must be the case that the *other* vertex in e *is* in the vertex cover C—by the definition of vertex cover! So as to allow a Hamiltonian path in H to traverse these vertices $(u, e, \cdot)$, the third type of edge (the edges in F_3) allow that, in traversing the vertices in a u_i-walk, a walk in H may make detours to also traverse vertices

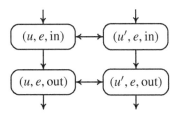

Figure 3.8.9. A view showing, for an edge $e = \{u, u'\}$ in E, the digraph H localized to the four vertices (u, e, in), (u', e, in), (u, e, out), (u', e, out). We refer to these vertices along with the edges between them as the *edge gadget* for the edge e. The horizontal edges are supplied by the set F_3.

of the form $(u, \{u, u_i\}, \cdot)$. This is done by placing edges *between* different u-walks; see Figure 3.8.9 for an illustration.

We next establish a result concerning the behavior of Hamiltonian paths in H, and then establish correctness of the reduction.

Lemma 3.8.47. *Consider an edge gadget in the digraph H as shown in Figure 3.8.9. Suppose that W is a Hamiltonian path in H where the vertex (u, e, in) is preceded by a vertex not in the gadget. Then, in W, the vertex (u, e, in) is either followed by the vertex (u, e, out) and a vertex not in the gadget; or, by the vertices (u', e, in), (u', e, out), and (u, e, out).*

Proof. The vertex (u, e, in) must be followed by (u, e, out) or (u', e, in), as those are the only two vertices receiving incoming edges from (u, e, in).

First, suppose that (u, e, in) is followed by (u, e, out). The vertex (u, e, out) cannot be followed by (u', e, out), as then there would be no vertex to follow (u', e, in), which must appear somewhere in the Hamiltonian path W. It follows that (u, e, out) must be followed by a vertex not in the gadget.

Next, suppose that (u, e, in) is followed by (u', e, in). The vertex (u', e, in) must be followed by (u', e, out), since the vertex (u', e, in) only has outgoing edges to (u, e, in) and (u', e, out). The vertex (u', e, out) must be followed by (u, e, out); if not, there would be no vertex to precede (u, e, out) in the Hamiltonian path W. $\square$

Relative to a graph, suppose that W' is a walk $v'_1, \ldots, v'_m$, and that W'' is a walk $v''_1, \ldots, v''_n$. When the last vertex of W' is equal to the first vertex of W'', that is, when $v'_m = v''_1$, we define the **concatenation** of W' and W'' as the walk whose vertices are those of W' followed by those of W'' but without repeating the vertex $v'_m = v''_1$, that is, as the walk $v'_1, \ldots, v'_m, v''_2, \ldots, v''_n$. This operation is naturally extended to any sequence of walks.

Correctness proof of Reduction 3.8.46. We prove that, under the given reduction, the graph G has a vertex cover of size k if and only if the digraph H has an (x_1, x_{k+1})-Hamiltonian path.

232 Chapter 3

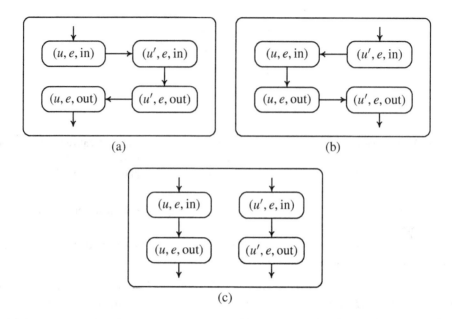

(a) (b)

(c)

Figure 3.8.10. Three possible traversals of an edge gadget, as shown in Figure 3.8.9. These traversals correspond to the cases where (a) u is in the vertex cover, but u' is not; (b) u' is in the vertex cover, but u is not; and (c) both u and u' are in the vertex cover.

Suppose that $C = \{u_1, \ldots, u_k\}$ is a vertex cover of G having size k. We construct an (x_1, x_{k+1})-Hamiltonian path in H as follows. For each $j \in [k]$, define W_j as the walk constructed in the following way. The walk W_j starts at x_j. For each $i = 1, \ldots, d(u_j)$ in sequence, the walk then includes vertices as follows: letting $\{u_j, u'\}$ denote $e_i^{u_j}$, in the case that $u' \in C$, the walk includes

$$(u_j, \{u_j, u'\}, \text{in}), \ (u_j, \{u_j, u'\}, \text{out});$$

otherwise, the walk includes

$$(u_j, \{u_j, u'\}, \text{in}), \ (u', \{u_j, u'\}, \text{in}), \ (u', \{u_j, u'\}, \text{out}), \ (u_j, \{u_j, u'\}, \text{out}).$$

The walk then ends at x_{j+1}. That is, the walk W_j starts from x_j and ends at x_{j+1}; in between, it traverses the vertices in the u_j-walk and, for each edge gadget, it either traverses just the two vertices corresponding to u_j or it takes a detour to traverse all four vertices, depending on whether or not both vertices in the corresponding edge (of G) are in C; see Figure 3.8.10. Let us make an observation: in the walk W_j, other than the anchors, each vertex is of the form $(\cdot, e, \cdot)$ where $u_j \in e$.

Let W be the concatenation of the walks $W_1, \ldots, W_k$; we claim that the walk W is an (x_1, x_{k+1})-Hamiltonian path in H. The walk W clearly begins at x_1 and ends at x_{k+1}, so we verify that W is a Hamiltonian path. By construction, each anchor vertex x_i appears exactly once in W. Now consider an arbitrary non-anchor vertex v in V; it has the form (u, e, in) or (u, e, out) where $u \in e$. Set $e = \{u, u'\}$. We argue that the vertex v appears exactly once in W; we split into two cases depending on whether or not $u \in C$.

- When $u \in C$, set $u_i = u$. We have that v appears once in the walk W_i. By the observation, v could only appear in another walk W_j if u' was equal to u_j; but if that occurred, the walk W_j, by construction, would omit v when traversing the edge gadget for e.
- When $u \notin C$, then $u' \in C$ since C is a vertex cover; set $u_j = u'$. In this case, by the observation, W_j is the only one of the walks $W_1, \ldots, W_k$ that could include v; it does include v once, as by construction, when traversing the edge gadget for e, the walk W_j takes a detour to traverse v.

Suppose next that there exists an (x_1, x_{k+1})-Hamiltonian path W of H. Since W begins at the anchor x_1 and ends at the anchor x_{k+1}, we may view W as the concatenation of walks where each begins at an anchor $x_i \in \{x_1, \ldots, x_k\}$ and ends as soon as another anchor is encountered; let us call such a walk the **segment starting at** x_i.

Let x_i be an anchor in $\{x_1, \ldots, x_k\}$; then, x_i only has outgoing edges to vertices of the form (u, e_1^u, in). We let u_i denote the vertex of G such that $(u_i, e_1^{u_i}, \text{in})$ follows x_i (in W). By Lemma 3.8.47, $(u_i, e_1^{u_i}, \text{in})$ is either followed in W by $(u_i, e_1^{u_i}, \text{out})$, or by $(u', e_1^{u_1}, \text{in})$, $(u', e_1^{u_1}, \text{out})$, $(u_i, e_1^{u_i}, \text{out})$, where u' is the vertex such that $e_1^{u_1} = \{u_1, u'\}$. That is, after traversing $(u_i, e_1^{u_i}, \text{in})$, the walk either proceeds directly to $(u_i, e_1^{u_i}, \text{out})$, or takes a detour to traverse $(u', e_1^{u_1}, \text{in})$ and $(u', e_1^{u_1}, \text{out})$ before proceeding to $(u_i, e_1^{u_i}, \text{out})$. After $(u_i, e_1^{u_i}, \text{out})$, the walk proceeds to $(u_i, e_2^{u_i}, \text{in})$, as long as it exists, that is, as long as $d(u_i) \geq 2$. Then, by similar reasoning, the walk either proceeds directly to $(u_i, e_2^{u_i}, \text{out})$, or takes a detour to traverse the other two vertices in the edge gadget for $e_2^{u_i}$ before proceeding to $(u_i, e_2^{u_i}, \text{out})$. Repeating this reasoning, the walk traverses all vertices in the u_i-walk, possibly taking detours, and then after traversing the last vertex in the u_i-walk, goes to an anchor. The key observation here is this: in the segment starting at x_i, each vertex of the form $(\cdot, e, \cdot)$ that is traversed has the property that $u_i \in e$.

We claim that the set $C = \{u_1, \ldots, u_k\}$ is a vertex cover of G. Let e be an arbitrary edge of G. Let v be a vertex of the form $(\cdot, e, \cdot)$ in H. Since W is a Hamiltonian path in H, the vertex v is traversed by W. Thus, there exists $i \in [k]$ such that v is traversed by the segment starting at x_i; it follows, by the observation, that $u_i \in e$. We have shown that an arbitrary edge of G must contain an element of C, so may conclude that C is a vertex cover of G. □

We next show the hardness of the language HAM-PATH, which is the graph version of the language DI-HAM-PATH of digraphs. We in fact establish hardness by reducing from the language DI-HAM-PATH. In order to present the reduction, we present two transformations; an example of their behavior is shown in Figure 3.8.11. The first transforms a digraph G to a second digraph G' that in a sense holds the structure of G; the second transforms the digraph G' into a graph G'' that captures the relevant features of G'.

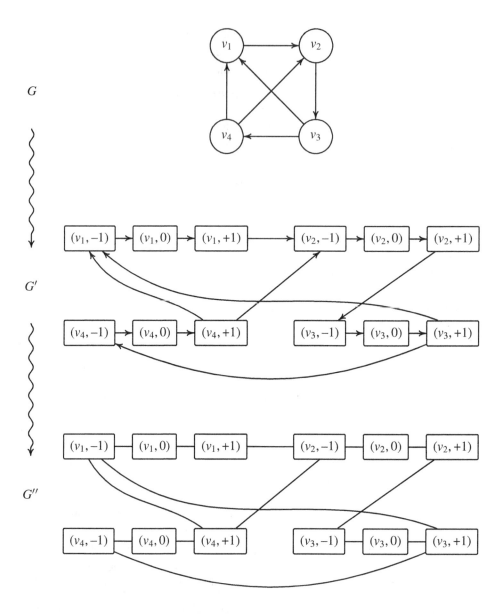

Figure 3.8.11. Examples of the graph transformations used to prove the hardness of HAM-PATH. The first transformation transforms a digraph G to another digraph G': each vertex v of G is expanded into 3 vertices $(v, -1)$, $(v, 0)$, $(v, 1)$ forming a walk, where $(v, -1)$ receives the incoming edges of v, and $(v, +1)$ emits the outgoing edges of v. The second transformation transforms the digraph G' to a graph G'' by disregarding the directions of the edges of G'. In this example, the original digraph G has 4 vertices and has exactly one edge between each pair of distinct vertices.

More specifically, the first transformation expands each vertex v of a digraph G into a walk of three vertices—$(v, -1)$, $(v, 0)$, and $(v, +1)$—where $(v, -1)$ receives the incoming edges of v, and $(v, +1)$ emits the outgoing edges of v. Precisely, when $G = (V, E)$ is a digraph, we define the digraph $G' = (V', E')$ by

$$V' = \{(v, a) \mid v \in V, a \in \{-1, 0, +1\}\},$$

$$E' = \{((v, -1), (v, 0)), ((v, 0), (v, +1)) \mid v \in V\} \cup \{((v, +1), (w, -1)) \mid (v, w) \in E\}.$$

Observe that $|V'| = 3|V|$, and $|E'| = 2|V| + |E|$. The following lemma presents a key property of this transformation: the (s, t)-Hamiltonian paths of G are reflected in G'.

Lemma 3.8.48. *Let $s, t \in V$, and set $s' = (s, -1)$, $t' = (t, +1)$. The digraph G has an (s, t)-Hamiltonian path if and only if the digraph G' has an (s', t')-Hamiltonian path.*

Proof. For the forward direction, assume that $v_1, \ldots, v_n$ is an (s, t)-Hamiltonian path in G. By replacing each vertex v_i in this path with the walk $(v_i, -1), (v_i, 0), (v_i, +1)$, we obtain

$$(v_1, -1), (v_1, 0), (v_1, +1), \ (v_2, -1), (v_2, 0), (v_2, +1), \ \ldots, \ (v_n, -1), (v_n, 0), (v_n, +1),$$

a sequence that is an (s', t')-Hamiltonian path in G', as can be verified using the definitions of E', s', and t'.

For the backward direction, assume that there is an (s', t')-Hamiltonian path W' of G'. Observe that, in G', a vertex of the form $(v, -1)$ has a single outgoing edge to $(v, 0)$; a vertex of the form $(v, 0)$ has a single outgoing edge to $(v, +1)$; and a vertex of the form $(v, +1)$ only has outgoing edges to vertices of the form $(w, -1)$. Since the walk W' begins at a vertex of the form $(v, -1)$, it must be of the form

$$(v_1, -1), (v_1, 0), (v_1, +1), \ (v_2, -1), (v_2, 0), (v_2, +1), \ \ldots, \ (v_n, -1), (v_n, 0), (v_n, +1)$$

where $v_1, \ldots, v_n$ are vertices in V with $v_1 = s$ and $v_n = t$. By the definition of the edge set E', we obtain that the sequence W defined as $v_1, \ldots, v_n$ is a walk in G; since the walk W' is a Hamiltonian path, the walk W is a Hamiltonian path as well. $\square$

The second transformation defines a graph $G'' = (V'', E'')$ from the digraph G', where

$$V'' = V',$$

$$E'' = \{\{x, y\} \mid (x, y) \in E'\}.$$

That is, the graph G'' is derived from the digraph G' simply by turning each edge of G' into an edge in G'' by forgetting about the edge's directionality. This transformation retains information about certain Hamiltonian paths of the digraph to which it is applied, in the following fashion.

Lemma 3.8.49. *Let $s' \in V'$ be a vertex of the form $(s, -1)$, and let $t' \in V'$ be a vertex of the form $(t, +1)$. The digraph G' has an (s', t')-Hamiltonian path if and only if the graph G'' has an (s', t')-Hamiltonian path.*

Proof. For the forward direction, assume that W' is an (s', t')-Hamiltonian path in G'; it is immediately verified from the definition of E'' that W' is an (s', t')-Hamiltonian path in G''.

For the backward direction, assume that W'' is an (s', t')-Hamiltonian path in G''. We make an observation: in W'', if a vertex of the form $(v, -1)$ is not preceeded by $(v, 0)$, then $(v, -1)$ is followed by $(v, 0)$ and $(v, +1)$. This observation holds due to the following: each vertex of the form $(v, 0)$ forms an edge with exactly two vertices in G'', namely, $(v, -1)$ and $(v, +1)$; since the walk W'' does not begin or end with $(v, 0)$, the walk W'' contains, as consecutive vertices, either $(v, -1), (v, 0), (v, +1)$ or $(v, +1), (v, 0), (v, -1)$.

Now consider the walk W''. It begins at a vertex of the form $(v_1, -1)$; by the observation, this vertex is followed by $(v_1, 0)$ and $(v_1, +1)$. Suppose that the vertex $(v_1, +1)$ is followed by a vertex; then, $(v_1, +1)$ must be followed by a vertex of the form $(\cdot, -1)$, since such vertices are the only ones forming an edge with $(v_1, +1)$ in G'', other than the vertex $(v, 0)$. Let $(v_2, -1)$ denote the vertex following $(v_1, +1)$. Applying the observation and this reasoning again, in W'', the vertex $(v_2, -1)$ must be followed by $(v_2, 0)$ and $(v_2, +1)$, and then a vertex of the form $(\cdot, -1)$. By repeating this argumentation, the walk W'' has the form

$$(v_1, -1), (v_1, 0), (v_1, +1), \quad (v_2, -1), (v_2, 0), (v_2, +1), \quad \ldots, \quad (v_n, -1), (v_n, 0), (v_n, +1).$$

It is readily verified, from the definitions of E' and E'', that W'' is a walk in G'. Since W'' is an (s', t')-Hamiltonian path in G'' and the graphs G'', G' share the same vertex set $V'' = V'$, we obtain that W'' is an (s', t')-Hamiltonian path in G'.   □

Reduction 3.8.50: from DI-HAM-PATH **to** HAM-PATH. Given a triple (G, s, t) where G is a digraph having s and t as vertices, the reduction produces the instance (G'', s', t') where G'' is the graph derived from G as described above, $s' = (s, -1)$, and $t' = (t, +1)$.   ◇

Correctness proof. It follows immediately from Lemmas 3.8.48 and 3.8.49 that G has an (s, t)-Hamiltonian path if and only if G'' has an (s', t')-Hamiltonian path.   □

From the NP-hardness of REST-VERTEX-COVER (Theorem 3.8.38) and the previous two reductions (Reductions 3.8.46 and 3.8.50), we obtain the following.

Theorem 3.8.51. DI-HAM-PATH *and* HAM-PATH *are NP-complete.*

Having established the hardness of the languages concerning the existence of Hamiltonian paths, we are poised to readily establish the hardness of languages concerning the existence of Hamiltonian cycles. We first consider the directed case; define the language

DI-HAM-CYCLE $= \{ G \mid G$ is a digraph that has a Hamiltonian cycle $\}$.

We establish hardness by reducing from the language DI-HAM-PATH; the behavior of the reduction is depicted in Figure 3.8.12.

Reduction 3.8.52: from DI-HAM-PATH **to** DI-HAM-CYCLE. Let (G, s, t) be a triple where $G = (V, E)$ is a digraph and $s, t \in V$. Let z be a new vertex not in V. Based on the given triple, the reduction produces the digraph $G' = (V', E')$ defined from G by adding

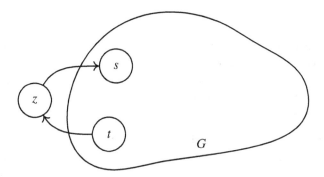

Figure 3.8.12. An illustration of the behavior of Reduction 3.8.52, a reduction from DI-HAM-PATH to DI-HAM-CYCLE. Given a graph G with two distinguished vertices s and t, the reduction produces the graph G' obtained from G by adding a new vertex z which has edges to s and from t. When G has an (s, t)-Hamiltonian path, augmenting this path with the vertex z yields a Hamiltonian cycle of G'. Conversely, from a Hamiltonian cycle of G', removing the vertex z yields an (s, t)-Hamiltonian path of G.

the new vertex z, giving it an outgoing edge to s, and giving it an incoming edge from t. Formally, we define $V' = V \cup \{z\}$, and $E' = E \cup \{(z, s), (t, z)\}$. $\Diamond$

Correctness proof. We verify that G has an (s, t)-Hamiltonian path if and only if G' has a Hamiltonian cycle.

Suppose that $v_1, \ldots, v_n$ is an (s, t)-Hamiltonian path in G. Then, $z, v_1, \ldots, v_n, z$ is readily verified to be a Hamiltonian cycle in G'.

Suppose that there is a Hamiltonian cycle in G'. By reordering the vertices if necessary, we may obtain a Hamiltonian cycle in G' of the form $z, v_1, \ldots, v_n, z$. Since z only has one outgoing edge which is to s, we have $v_1 = s$; since z only has one incoming edge which is from t, we have $v_n = t$. Hence, $v_1, \ldots, v_n$ is an (s, t)-Hamiltonian path in G. $\square$

We next consider Hamiltonian cycles in graphs. The reduction and proof of correctness are highly similar to those just given, but here, we reduce from the language HAM-PATH. Recall the language definition

$$\text{HAM-CYCLE} = \{\ulcorner G \urcorner \mid G \text{ is a graph that has a Hamiltonian cycle}\}.$$

Reduction 3.8.53: from HAM-PATH to HAM-CYCLE. Let (G, s, t) be a triple where $G = (V, E)$ is a graph and $s, t \in V$. Let z be a new vertex not in V. The production produces the graph $G' = (V', E')$ where $V' = V \cup \{z\}$, and $E' = E \cup \{\{z, s\}, \{t, z\}\}$. $\Diamond$

Correctness proof. We verify that G has an (s, t)-Hamiltonian path if and only if G' has a Hamiltonian cycle.

Suppose that $v_1, \ldots, v_n$ is an (s, t)-Hamiltonian path in G. Then, $z, v_1, \ldots, v_n, z$ is readily verified to be a Hamiltonian cycle in G'.

Suppose that there is a Hamiltonian cycle in G'. By reordering the vertices, we may obtain a Hamiltonian cycle W' in G' of the form $z, v_1, \ldots, v_n, z$. Since z only occurs in edges with the vertices s and t, either $v_1 = s$ and $v_n = t$; or, $v_1 = t$ and $v_n = s$. In the former case, $v_1, \ldots, v_n$ is seen to be an (s, t)-Hamiltonian path in G; in the latter case, $v_n, \ldots, v_1$ is seen to be an (s, t)-Hamiltonian path in G. □

The term *sequencing problem* is used broadly to refer to a problem where the question is to decide if there is a way to sequence the elements of a set such that some condition is satisfied. The problems HAM-CYCLE and DI-HAM-CYCLE are problems of this form: these problems involve deciding if the vertex set of a given graph can be sequenced so that consecutive vertex pairs form edges. We next show hardness of another sequencing problem, a famous and well-known problem known as the *traveling salesperson problem (TSP)*. In an instance of this problem, there is a set of cities, a cost associated with traveling between each pair of cities, and a budget. The question is to decide whether or not a traveling salesperson could start at a city, visit all of the cities in some sequence, and then return to the starting city—without exceeding the budget. Formally, define a **TSP instance** to be a triple (V, c, B) where

- V is a finite set of cities, assumed to be of size 2 or greater;
- $c\colon \binom{V}{2} \to \mathbb{N}$ is called the **cost function**, and specifies the cost of traveling between two cities in V; and
- $B \in \mathbb{N}$ is a value called the **budget**.

Relative to such an instance, a **tour** T is an ordering $v_1, \ldots, v_n$ of the elements in V, whose **cost**, denoted by c_T, is defined as $c_T = (\sum_{i \in [n-1]} c(\{v_i, v_{i+1}\})) + c(\{v_n, v_1\})$. That is, the value c_T is the total cost of traveling from each city in the tour to the following city, where the last city v_n is considered to be followed by the starting city v_1. Define TSP to be the language containing each TSP instance (V, c, B) such that there exists a tour T whose cost satisfies $c_T \leq B$.

We present a simple reduction from the last language proven hard: the language HAM-CYCLE. Given a graph, the reduction takes the graph's vertex set to be the set of cities, and assigns each pair of vertices a cost of 1 or 2 depending on whether or not it forms an edge; the budget is simply the number of cities.

Reduction 3.8.54: from HAM-CYCLE to TSP. Let $G = (V, E)$ be a graph, and set $n = |V|$; we assume $n \geq 2$.

- Define $c\colon \binom{V}{2} \to \mathbb{N}$ as follows: for each $f \in \binom{V}{2}$, set $c(f)$ as 1 if $f \in E$, and as 2 if $f \notin E$.
- Define $B = n$.

From the graph G, the reduction produces the TSP instance (V, c, B).   ◇

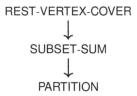

Figure 3.8.13. The web of reductions given for numeric problems.

Correctness proof. We prove that G has a Hamiltonian cycle if and only if the produced TSP instance has a tour T with $c_T \leq B$.

Suppose that (V, E) has a Hamiltonian cycle $v_1, v_2, ..., v_{n-1}, v_n, v_1$. Then the sequence $v_1, v_2, ..., v_{n-1}, v_n$ can be seen to be a tour of cost n, and is hence a tour T with $c_T \leq B$.

Suppose that the TSP instance has a tour T, denoted $v_1, ..., v_n$, with $c_T \leq n$. Since c_T is the sum of n values, each of which is greater than or equal to 1, it follows that each of those values must be equal to 1. That is, each of the values $c(\{v_1, v_2\})$, $c(\{v_2, v_3\})$, ..., $c(\{v_{n-1}, v_n\})$, $c(\{v_n, v_1\})$ is equal to 1. It follows that each of the underlying pairs is in E, and thus that $v_1, v_2, ..., v_{n-1}, v_n, v_1$ is a Hamiltonian cycle of (V, E). □

From Theorem 3.8.51 and Reductions 3.8.52, 3.8.53, and 3.8.54, we conclude the following.

Theorem 3.8.55. DI-HAM-CYCLE, HAM-CYCLE, *and* TSP *are NP-complete.*

3.8.3 Numeric problems

We close this section by considering a pair of problems that crucially involve numeric quantities. The reductions to be given are shown in Figure 3.8.13.

When $S \subseteq \mathbb{N}$ is a finite set of natural numbers, define the **sum** of S as the sum of its elements, namely, as $\sum_{u \in S} u$. We consider the problem of deciding whether there exists a selection of numbers from a given set $Z \subseteq \mathbb{N}$ whose sum is a specified target value t. Precisely, define SUBSET-SUM to be the language containing each pair (Z, t) such that Z is a finite subset of $\mathbb{N}$, $t \in \mathbb{N}$, and there exists a subset $S \subseteq Z$ whose sum is t. We establish the hardness of this language by exhibiting a reduction from REST-VERTEX-COVER. In presenting and discussing this reduction, we use the base 10 representation of each natural number; we index the digits starting from 0 and from the right, so we refer to the rightmost digit as the 0th digit, the second-to-rightmost digit as the 1st digit, and so on. See Figure 3.8.14 for an example of this reduction's behavior.

Viewing the numbers as rows (as in Figure 3.8.14), the idea of the reduction is as follows. Let m denote the number of edges in the given graph G, and let k be the size of the sought vertex cover. Each of the rightmost m columns represents an edge. In the produced set D of numbers, there is a number a_v for each vertex v of the graph G, as well as a number b_i

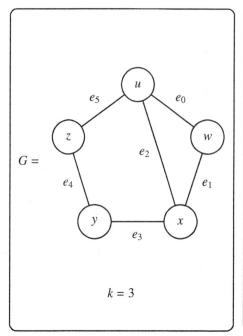

		digit index						
		6	5	4	3	2	1	0
a_u	=	1	1	0	0	1	0	1
a_w	=	1	0	0	0	0	1	1
a_x	=	1	0	0	1	1	1	0
a_y	=	1	0	1	1	0	0	0
a_z	=	1	1	1	0	0	0	0
b_0	=	0	0	0	0	0	0	1
b_1	=	0	0	0	0	0	1	0
b_2	=	0	0	0	0	1	0	0
b_3	=	0	0	0	1	0	0	0
b_4	=	0	0	1	0	0	0	0
b_5	=	0	1	0	0	0	0	0
t	=	3	2	2	2	2	2	2

D labels the set of a and b numbers. $G =$ on the left, with $k = 3$.

Figure 3.8.14. An example of the behavior of Reduction 3.8.56. On the left is a pair (G, k) consisting of a graph and a value; the graph G has 5 vertices, and we have $k = 3$. From this pair, the reduction produces a set D of natural numbers and a target value t, shown on the right. The set D includes a number a_v for each vertex v of G; this number begins with the digit 1, and then indicates the edges that contain the vertex. Let m denote the number of edges in the graph; the rightmost m digits, which in the table are the rightmost m columns, represent the graph's edges. The set D also includes, for each edge e_i, a number b_i which simply indicates the respective edge. The target value t consists of the number k followed by m occurrences of the digit 2.

for each edge e_i of the graph G. When there exists a size k vertex cover C of G, taking the numbers a_v whose vertex v is in the cover and adding them up yields a sum that begins with k, and in the remaining columns has either the value 1 or 2 depending on whether or not the corresponding edge is covered by 1 or 2 vertices in C. In each such column where the sum is 1, the sum can be brought up to 2 by including the corresponding number b_i. In this way, one can attain the target value t, defined as the number k followed by m occurrences of the digit 2. The reasoning reverses; whenever the target value t is attained by a subset of D, the subset must contain exactly k numbers of the form a_v, and the respective vertices form a size k vertex cover.

Reduction 3.8.56: from REST-VERTEX-COVER to SUBSET-SUM. Let (G, k) be a pair where G is a graph where each vertex has degree 2 or greater, and $k \geq 1$. Denote the graph G by (V, E), set $m = |E|$, and set $e_0, \ldots, e_{m-1}$ to be a list of the edges in E. We define a set D of natural numbers, each of which has $m + 1$ or fewer digits, as follows.

- For each vertex $v \in V$, define the natural number a_v as follows: the mth digit of a_v is 1; for each $i \in \{0, \ldots, m-1\}$, the ith digit of a_v is 1 if the ith edge e_i includes v, and is 0 otherwise. In notation, we define $a_v = 10^m + \sum_{i:e_i \ni v} 10^i$.
- For each $i \in \{0, \ldots, m-1\}$, define the natural number b_i so that its ith digit is 1, and each other digit is 0. That is, define $b_i = 10^i$.

We define D as the set containing each of the numbers just defined, that is, we define

$$D = \{a_v \mid v \in V\} \cup \{b_i \mid i \in \{0, \ldots, m-1\}\}.$$

Define t as the number $k \cdot 10^m + \sum_{i=0}^{m-1} (2 \cdot 10^i)$, which, in base 10, consists of the number k followed by m occurrences of the number 2. The reduction outputs the pair (D, t). ◇

In this reduction, it is evident that for each index $i \in \{0, \ldots, m-1\}$, there are exactly 3 numbers in D that have 1 as the ith digit, namely, the number b_i and the numbers a_v such that $v \in e_i$; each other number has 0 as the ith digit. Thus, for such an index i, when taking the sum of any subset of D, the ith digit does not provoke a carry—that is, the sum of the ith digits will never be 10 or greater, and thus will not contribute to any other digit of the sum.[26] We will use this fact in our analysis.

Correctness proof. We begin by making an initial observation about the numbers defined in Reduction 3.8.56: when $u, v \in V$ are distinct vertices, the numbers a_u and a_v are not equal. This is because, in looking at the edges where the vertices u and v appear, these vertices can have at most 1 edge in common (namely, the set $\{u, v\}$); yet each of these vertices appears in 2 or more edges, so there is an edge index $i \in \{0, \ldots, m-1\}$ such that $u \in e_i$ and the ith digit of a_u is 1, but $v \notin e_i$ and the ith digit of a_v is 0.

We turn to verify the correctness of the reduction, that is, that G has a size k vertex cover if and only if D has a subset whose sum is t.

Suppose that C is a size k vertex cover of G. Based on the vertices in the set C, define the following subsets of D:

$A = \{a_v \mid v \in C\}$,

$B = \{b_i \mid i \in \{0, \ldots, m-1\}$ and the ith digit of the sum of A is equal to 1$\}$,

$S = A \cup B$.

Let us analyze the sum of S.

- Let $i \in \{0, \ldots, m-1\}$; we examine the ith digit of the numbers in S. There are exactly two numbers of the form a_v whose ith digit is equal to 1: the two numbers corresponding

---

26. We note that even if the numbers here were viewed as being in base 4, no such carries would be provoked and the presented reduction would still work.

to the two vertices in the edge e_i. Each other such number a_v has its ith digit equal to 0. Since C is a vertex cover, A contains at least one number whose ith digit is equal to 1. Thus, the ith digit of A's sum is equal to 1 or 2. The value $b_i = 10^i$ is defined to be in B exactly when the former case occurs; so, the ith digit of the sum of S is 2.

- If we examine the mth digit of the numbers in S, the values a_v have mth digit equal to 1, and the values b_v have mth digit equal to 0; so, the mth digits of the elements in S contribute $|A| \cdot 10^m$ to the sum of S. By the initial observation, we have $|A| = |C| = k$.

The sum of S is thus $k \cdot 10^m + \sum_{i=0}^{m-1} (2 \cdot 10^i)$ and is equal to t, as desired.

Suppose that S is a subset of D having sum t. We can view t as the sum of $k \cdot 10^m$ and a number which is 2 in the ith digit for each $i \in \{0, \dots, m-1\}$. Define $C = \{v \in V \mid a_v \in S\}$; that is, define C to contain each vertex v of G whose corresponding number a_v is in S. Each element $a_v \in S$ has 1 in the mth digit, and each element $b_i \in S$ has 0 in the mth digit. These mth digits sum up to k; there is no carrying over to the mth digit in taking the sum of S; and no two vertices share the same number a_v. So, we must have that $|C| = k$.

We claim that C is a vertex cover of G; this suffices, since then G has a vertex cover of size k. Let $e_i = \{u, u'\}$ be an arbitrary edge of G. As observed, the only numbers in X that have 1 as the ith digit are b_i, a_u, and $a_{u'}$; each other number in X has 0 as the ith digit. We have that the ith digit of t is equal to 2. So, the set S must contain a value a_v having 1 in the ith digit; it follows that C must contain a vertex v such that a_v has 1 in the ith digit, implying that either u or u' is in C. Thus C is a vertex cover of G. □

The language SUBSET-SUM involves deciding, given a set of numbers, if there is a subset whose sum is a specified target value. We next look at a language where the question is to decide if a set of numbers can be split into two parts, each having the same sum. Let us say that a pair of sets (U, U') is a **partition** of a set Y if $U \cup U' = Y$ and $U \cap U' = \emptyset$, that is, if Y is the disjoint union of U and U'. When Y is a finite set of natural numbers, we say that a partition (U, U') of Y is **balanced** if the sum of U is equal to the sum of U', that is, $\sum_{u \in U} u = \sum_{u' \in U'} u'$. Define the language

PARTITION $= \{Y \subseteq \mathbb{N} \mid Y$ is a finite set having a balanced partition$\}$.

We establish the hardness of this language by reducing from the language SUBSET-SUM. From an instance (D, t) of this latter language, we define a set Y by starting with D and including 3 extra numbers, each of which exceeds the sum of D. These extra numbers are configured so that the highest of them combined with a subset of D summing to t gives one set in a balanced partition of Y; conversely, any balanced partition of Y must contain, as one of its sets, this highest extra number along with a subset of D summing to t.

Reduction 3.8.57: from SUBSET-SUM to PARTITION. Let (D, t) be a pair where $D \subseteq \mathbb{N}$ is a finite set and $t \in \mathbb{N}$. Set p to be the sum of D; that is, set $p = \sum_{d \in D} d$. We may assume that $t \leq p$ (if not, $p < t$, and we have $(D, t) \notin$ SUBSET-SUM). From the given pair, the reduction produces the set

$$Y = D \cup \{1 + p, \ 2 + p + t, \ 3 + 3p - t\}. \qquad \qquad \diamond$$

Correctness proof. We first make some observations about the reduction. It is straightforward to verify that

$$p < 1 + p < 2 + p + t < 3 + 3p - t,$$

so the numbers $1 + p$, $2 + p + t$, and $3 + 3p - t$ are different from each other, and also not contained in D. Observe that the sum of Y is

$$\sum_{y \in Y} y = p + (1 + p) + (2 + p + t) + (3 + 3p - t) = 6 + 6p,$$

so a partition (U, U') of Y is balanced if and only if each of the sets U, U' has sum $3 + 3p$.

With these observations in place, we verify that the set D has a subset with sum t if and only if the set Y has a balanced partition.

Suppose that D has a subset S whose sum is t. Define the sets $U = S \cup \{3 + 3p - t\}$ and $U' = Y \setminus U$. The sum of U is equal to $3 + 3p$. Hence, (U, U') is a balanced partition of Y.

Suppose that Y has a balanced partition (U, U'). One of the sets U, U' must contain the value $3 + 3p - t$; let us assume for the sake of notation that U contains this element. Define the set $S = U \setminus \{3 + 3p - t\}$. Since the sum of U is $3 + 3p$, the sum of S must be t. In particular, it must be that each element of S is less than or equal to t, and hence less than or equal to p; so, $S \subseteq D$. Thus S is a subset of D whose sum is t. $\qquad \qquad \square$

From the NP-hardness of REST-VERTEX-COVER (Theorem 3.8.38) and the last two reductions (Reductions 3.8.56 and 3.8.57), we obtain the following.

Theorem 3.8.58. SUBSET-SUM *and* PARTITION *are NP-complete.*

Remark 3.8.59. While here we formulated the languages SUBSET-SUM and PARTITION using *sets* of numbers, some treatments formulate them using *sequences* of numbers, where repetitions are allowed. $\qquad \qquad \diamond$

3.9   Connecting decision and search

Our development thus far has focused on *languages* as the objects subject to computation; for each language of interest, we have been striving to understand what type of machine can, upon being given a string, *decide* whether or not the string is in the language. When dealing with an NP language, however, relative to a string, the *search* for a certificate witnessing the string's membership in the language—should one exist—is arguably just as natural. For example, a traveling salesperson, when confronted with an instance of the TSP, might want to know of an under budget tour when one exists—as opposed to merely being assured of the *existence* of an under budget tour! Similarly, with a circuit or propositional formula in hand, one might very well want to obtain a satisfying assignment when one exists, and not solely an indication of the existence.

In this section, we link the notions of decision and search for NP languages, and show that efficient search is possible if and only if efficient decision is possible; in both contexts, our notion of efficiency is that of polynomial-time computation. This result endorses our focus on *decision* and languages: their fate is inevitably entangled with the fate of *search*.

We begin by defining the notion of a *search function*, which intuitively speaking is a function that, when given a string x, outputs a certificate witnessing that x belongs to a language. What constitutes certificates for the strings in an NP language is made definitive via the notion of a *verifier* (introduced in Section 3.2.3).

Definition 3.9.1. A **search function** for a verifier M is a function $f : \Sigma^* \to \Sigma^*$ such that, for each $x \in \Sigma^*$, the following holds:

- if there does not exist a string y such that $\langle x, y \rangle \in L(M)$, then $f(x) = 0$;
- otherwise, $f(x)$ has the form $1y$ where y is a string such that $\langle x, y \rangle \in L(M)$.   ◇

Recall that, relative to a verifier M, we say that y is a **certificate** of x if $\langle x, y \rangle \in L(M)$. To rephrase Definition 3.9.1, a *search function* is a function f where, for each string x, if there is no certificate of x, then $f(x) = 0$; and otherwise, $f(x) = 1y$ where y is a certificate of x. Note that, in general, a verifier may have multiple search functions since—relative to a verifier—a string may have multiple certificates.

This section's main theorem holds that each verifier has a search function that is polynomial-time computable if and only if all NP languages are.

Theorem 3.9.2. *Each verifier has a polynomial-time computable search function if and only if each NP language is PTIME (that is, if and only if $\mathbb{NP} \subseteq \mathbb{P}$).*

While proving this theorem's forward direction is relatively straightforward, to prove the backward direction, we will need to give a polynomial-time computable search function for each verifier. With this aim, the next lemma defines a helpful auxiliary language which is NP—and hence, is PTIME under the hypothesis that each NP language is PTIME.

Lemma 3.9.3. *Let M be a verifier, and define R_M as the language*

$$\left\{ \langle x, u \rangle \mid \text{there exists } v \in \Sigma^* \text{ such that } \langle x, uv \rangle \in L(M) \right\}.$$

The language R_M is a polynomially balanced relation that is NP.

We may view the language R_M as containing each pair $\langle x, u \rangle$ such that u can be extended to a certificate of x, relative to the verifier M. Recall that a relation consisting of pairs is *polynomially balanced* when there exists a polynomial P such that for each pair $\langle x, y \rangle$ in the relation, it holds that $|y| \leq P(|x|)$.

Proof. Let P be a polynomial witnessing that $L(M)$ is polynomially balanced. Then, for each string $\langle x, u \rangle \in R_M$, there exists $v \in \Sigma^*$ such that $\langle x, uv \rangle \in L(M)$; so, the inequalities $|u| \leq |uv| \leq P(|x|)$ hold and thus P witnesses that R_M is polynomially balanced.

To prove that R_M is NP, we give a verifier M' for R_M, which suffices by Theorem 3.2.26. We define M' to be a polynomial-time DTM such that

$$L(M') = \big\{ \langle \langle x, u \rangle, v \rangle \mid \langle x, uv \rangle \in L(M) \big\}.$$

Such a polynomial-time DTM exists: it checks whether or not its input has the form $\langle \langle x, u \rangle, v \rangle$; if it does not, it rejects, and if it does, it invokes M on the pair $\langle x, uv \rangle$, accepting if M accepts, and rejecting otherwise. For each string $\langle \langle x, u \rangle, v \rangle \in L(M')$, it holds that $\langle x, uv \rangle \in L(M)$, from which we may derive that $|v| \leq |uv| \leq P(|x|) \leq P(|\langle x, u \rangle|)$. Hence, P witnesses that $L(M')$ is polynomially balanced, and we have that M' is a verifier. We have that $\langle x, u \rangle \in R_M$ if and only if there exists $v \in \Sigma^*$ such that $\langle \langle x, u \rangle, v \rangle \in L(M')$; thus, M' is a verifier for R_M. $\square$

Proof of Theorem 3.9.2. We first prove the forward direction. Let B be an arbitrary NP language. By Theorem 3.2.26, there exists a verifier M_B for B. By hypothesis, the verifier M_B has a polynomial-time computable search function f; let M_f be a polynomial-time DTM that computes f. Define M to be the DTM that does the following: given an input string x, compute $f(x)$ using M_f; reject if the result is 0, and accept otherwise. The DTM M runs within polynomial time, since M_f does. As f is a search function for the verifier M_B, for each string x it holds that $f(x) = 0$ if and only if $x \notin B$; thus, $L(M) = B$.

We next prove the backward direction. Let M be an arbitrary verifier, let R_M be the language given by Lemma 3.9.3, and let P be a polynomial witnessing that R_M is polynomially balanced. By this lemma, the language R_M is NP; by hypothesis, this language R_M is PTIME.

Consider the following procedure:

- Given an input string x, check if $\langle x, \epsilon \rangle \in R_M$; if not, halt with output 0.

  Otherwise, set w to be ϵ; note that $\langle x, w \rangle \in R_M$ at this point.

- Iterate the following loop:

  - Check if $\langle x, w \rangle \in L(M)$.

    If so, halt with output $1w$.

  - Check if $\langle x, w0 \rangle \in R_M$.

    If so, replace w with $w0$; otherwise, replace w with $w1$.

When this procedure halts, it evidently outputs a string having the form required by Definition 3.9.1: in particular, when $\langle x, \epsilon \rangle \notin R_M$, there does not exist a string y such that $\langle x, y \rangle \in L(M)$. We thus need to argue that the procedure always halts; it suffices to argue that the procedure always halts whenever it enters the loop. Let us observe that the invariant $\langle x, w \rangle \in R_M$ holds prior to each iteration of the loop: it was already noted that this holds prior to the first iteration; assuming that it holds prior to any iteration, it also holds after an iteration (that does not invoke a halt) since a string w' for which $\langle x, w' \rangle \notin L(M)$ and $\langle x, w' \rangle \in R_M$ must have either $\langle x, w'0 \rangle \in R_M$ or $\langle x, w'1 \rangle \in R_M$. The length of the string w increases by 1 after each iteration; due to the invariant and the polynomial balancedness of R_M, throughout the procedure's execution, it holds that $|w| \leq P(|x|)$; thus, the number of loop iterations is bounded above by $P(|x|)$. To sum up, this procedure can be implemented by a polynomial-time DTM; the checks of the procedure can be carried out by invoking the polynomial-time DTM M and a polynomial-time DTM with language R_M.   □

Remark 3.9.4. Let M be a verifier. Observe that the proof of the backward direction of Theorem 3.9.2 provides a polynomial-time computable search function for M directly from the assumption that the language R_M is PTIME. That is, this direction's use of the hypothesis that *each NP language is PTIME* is limited to using the assumption that the single language R_M is PTIME.   ◇

Remark 3.9.5. Let us concretely consider what the observation of Remark 3.9.4 implies for the language CIRCUIT-SAT. Let N be the verifier for CIRCUIT-SAT whose language $L(N)$ naturally contains each pair $\langle \ulcorner C \urcorner, x \rangle$ where C is a circuit, and $x \in \{0,1\}^*$ is a satisfying assignment of C. (Recall our view of strings as assignments, from Definition 3.6.5.)

Consider the procedure in the proof of Theorem 3.9.2 for this verifier's search problem. Each membership query $\langle \ulcorner C \urcorner, y \rangle \in R_N$ can in fact be reformulated as a membership query to CIRCUIT-SAT: the condition $\langle \ulcorner C \urcorner, y \rangle \in R_N$ holds when y has an extension satisfying C; instantiating the first $|y|$ inputs of C as y yields a circuit C_y that is satisfiable if and only if this condition holds. (The notion of instantiation used here was described in Definition 3.6.8.) Via this reformulation, the given procedure yields polynomial-time computability of a search problem (for N) directly from the assumption that CIRCUIT-SAT *is PTIME*. Here, we underscore the directness; as seen earlier in this chapter, this assumption is implied by and is indeed equivalent to the hypothesis that $\mathbb{NP} \subseteq \mathbb{P}$.

In essence, we have argued that when taking a natural verifier for the language CIRCUIT-SAT, its search problem reduces directly to this language. Using a similar argument, an analogously direct reduction can also be given for the languages CNF-SAT and 3-CNF-SAT; see also Exercise 3.10.66.   ◇

Let us close by pointing out that, in dealing with NP languages and verifiers, there are further natural computational tasks that can be considered. For example, relative to a verifier, one may investigate the problem of *enumerating* all certificates of an input string, or of *counting* the certificates of an input string.[27] Certain NP languages also lend themselves to the study of optimization problems: for example, given a CNF-formula, one may desire

---

27. These two tasks are examined in Sections 3.10.4 and 3.10.6, respectively.

an assignment that maximizes the number of satisfied clauses; or, given a graph, one may desire a minimum size vertex cover.

3.10 Exercises and notes

Following general exercises and notes, in Section 3.10.1, this section is organized according to themes: *satisfiability*, in Section 3.10.2; *graphs and hypergraphs*, in Section 3.10.3; *search and enumeration*, in Section 3.10.4; *subproblems*, in Section 3.10.5; and *counting*, in Section 3.10.6.

Throughout this section, for notational simplicity, we often will omit the encoding notation $\ulcorner \cdot \urcorner$, as well as the pairing notation $\langle \cdot, \cdot \rangle$, as we did in Section 3.8. That is, we neglect to distinguish between objects and their encodings.

3.10.1 General

Note 3.10.1: Coping with hardness. Given the prevalence of hard problems, how should their instances be confronted and dealt with? One practical approach is to adopt an engineering stance: try to develop heuristics, techniques, tactics, and so forth, that are experimentally effective for solving instances that arise.

Theoretical computer science has also developed a set of approaches for proving theoretical results that help to mitigate and understand computational hardness. Classical approaches in this vein include studying restricted versions of problems; presenting algorithms with running time bounds that improve over exhaustive search; and, for optimization problems, presenting approximation algorithms with provable performance guarantees (see Exercise 3.10.54 for an example). Another approach, which we take up in the next chapter, is the study of so-called *parameterized algorithms*, wherein it is required that a *parameter* be associated to each instance of a language, and the notion of polynomial time is relaxed by allowing a non-polynomial dependence on the parameter of an instance. ◇

Note 3.10.2. We point out that in Definition 3.2.1, the definition of $\text{time}_M(x)$ for a halting NTM M could also be used to define $\text{time}_M(x)$ for a halting DTM, and thus a single uniform definition is possible. That is, for either a halting DTM or a halting NTM, the value $\text{time}_M(x)$ is equal to 1 plus the maximum value k such that there exists a halting configuration γ with $\alpha_x \vdash_M^k \gamma$; this value $\text{time}_M(x)$ can also be characterized as 1 plus the maximum value k such that there exists a configuration γ with $\alpha_x \vdash_M^k \gamma$. ◇

Note 3.10.3. The PTIME languages are commonly referred to as being *polynomial-time decidable*, *polynomial-time tractable*, or simply *tractable*. ◇

Note 3.10.4. One way to perceive the contrast between polynomial and exponential running times is to consider how an increase in computing power affects the size of the largest instances that are solvable in a fixed amount of time. To wit, let n denote the size of an instance. Consider an algorithm that runs in time proportional to n; doubling the algorithm's execution speed has the effect of doubling the size of the largest solvable instances. Next, consider an algorithm that runs in time proportional to 2^n; doubling the algorithm's speed has the effect of increasing the size of the largest solvable instances by one!   ◇

Exercise 3.10.5. Argue that the DTM presented and discussed in Example 2.1.11 runs within *quadratic time*, that is, within time P for a polynomial P having degree 2. (This helps to establish Proposition 3.2.9.)   ◇

Exercise 3.10.6: Pseudo-verifiers. This exercise studies the role that being polynomially balanced plays in the definition of *verifier*; in particular, it studies the class of languages that results when this condition is dropped. Define a **pseudo-verifier** to be a polynomial-time DTM whose language is a subset of $\{\langle x, y \rangle \mid x, y \in \Sigma^*\}$. When B is a language, say that a **pseudo-verifier for** B is a pseudo-verifier M such that $B = \{x \mid \exists y \in \Sigma^* \text{ such that } \langle x, y \rangle \in R\}$.

Characterize the class of languages for which there are pseudo-verifiers, by identifying one of the classes of languages presented thus far, and proving that a language is in the identified class if and only if there exists a pseudo-verifier for the language.   ◇

Note 3.10.7: An analogy between computability theory and complexity theory. The PTIME languages and the NP languages can be taken as complexity-theoretic analogs of the computable languages and the CE languages, respectively. One needs be cautious in pushing the analogy too far, however: the basic result that there exists a CE language that is not computable translates into the wide open question of whether or not there exists an NP language that is not PTIME! Another fundamental result, that any language assumed to be both CE and coCE is computable, also translates into an open question, namely, whether or not each language that is both NP and coNP is PTIME. (More information on this latter question is given in Note 3.10.65.)

The analogy between the NP languages and the CE languages is accentuated by considering the characterizations thereof given by Theorem 3.2.26 and Exercise 2.10.21.   ◇

Note 3.10.8: Deciding NP languages in deterministic time. It is natural to ask how quickly NP languages can be decided by DTMs. Not much can be generally said beyond that which is relatively obvious. Let B be an NP language, and consider a verifier M for B. A naive method for deciding membership in B of a string x is this: for all strings y up to the length bound given by the polynomial balancedness of $L(M)$, check if M accepts $\langle x, y \rangle$; accept if at least one such check passes, and reject otherwise. This method can be implemented by a DTM running within time $T(n) = 2^{Q(n)}$, where Q is a polynomial.   ◇

Note 3.10.9: Graph encodings. The encoding of graphs via adjacency matrix was presented in Section 2.2. Another natural encoding of graphs is to provide, for each graph (V, E), a list of the elements in V, followed by a list of the elements in E. That these representations behave equivalently for the complexity issues concerning us can be formalized by arguing that conversion from one of these encodings to the other can be performed in polynomial time. In this way, it can be seen that each language of graphs (for example, 3-COL or INDEP-SET) under one encoding has polynomial-time many-one reductions both to and from the same language under the other encoding. Thus, from the perspective of complexity theory as presented in this chapter, two such paired languages are, for all intents and purposes, one and the same. ◇

Note 3.10.10. In Section 3.2.2, we argued that the notion of *polynomial time* frees us from having to tie a step of a Turing machine to any particular unit of time. In some situations, this notion also gives us the freedom to adjust what polynomial time is measured as a function of. The default norm, as set forth by Definitions 3.2.2 and 3.2.3, is to bound the allowed time by a polynomial in the input string size. If we examine the case of graphs as inputs, however, we can see that the number of vertices is polynomially related to the graph encoding size, at least, for the encodings considered in Note 3.10.9: the number of vertices is bounded above by the graph encoding size, and the graph encoding size is bounded above by a polynomial in the number of vertices (as the number of potential edges is not more than the square of the number of vertices). So, being bounded above by a polynomial in a graph's encoding size is equivalent to being bounded above by a polynomial in the graph's number of vertices. ◇

Note 3.10.11: Computable languages outside of complexity classes. In this note, we show how to construct languages that are computable but outside of common complexity classes, such as $\mathcal{P}$ and $\mathcal{NP}$. Fix $\Sigma = \{0, 1\}$ as the alphabet over which strings and languages are formed. Define a **computable presentation** of a class $\mathcal{C}$ of languages as a computable function $r\colon \Sigma^* \to \Sigma^*$ such that the following hold:

- For every string $w \in \Sigma^*$, it holds that the string $r(w)$ is the encoding $\ulcorner M \urcorner$ of a halting DTM or a halting NTM.
- A language B is in $\mathcal{C}$ if and only if there exists a string $w \in \Sigma^*$ such that the string $r(w)$ is the encoding $\ulcorner M \urcorner$ of a machine M where $B = L(M)$.

As an example, we explain why the class $\mathcal{P}$ has a computable presentation. Fix M_- to be a DTM that always rejects immediately. We define r as a computable function that, on each pair $\langle \ulcorner M \urcorner, \ulcorner c \urcorner \rangle$ encoding a DTM M and a number $c \in \mathbb{N}$, outputs the encoding $\ulcorner M_c \urcorner$ of a *clocked version* M_c of M that we explain momentarily, and on each other string, outputs $\ulcorner M_- \urcorner$. For a DTM M and a number $c \in \mathbb{N}$, the **clocked version** M_c of M is a DTM performing the following: on each input string x, it runs M on x, but also counts, at each step, the total number of time steps that the computation of M has consumed; if $cn^c + c$ time steps have elapsed in this computation without M halting, then the DTM M_c halts (by either accepting or rejecting); if M halts before this time limit is reached, then M_c accepts if M accepts, and rejects if M rejects. We have the following:

- The natural design of clocked DTMs M_c is such that they are all polynomial-time DTMs. Thus, we can achieve that each string $r(w)$, over all $w \in \Sigma^*$, is the encoding of a polynomial-time DTM.
- For any language $B \in \mathcal{P}$, there is a clocked DTM whose language is B: take a polynomial-time DTM N such that $L(N) = B$, and let $c \in \mathbb{N}$ be a sufficiently high value such that N runs within time $T(n) = cn^c + c$, which is possible since each polynomial is bounded by this function for a sufficiently high value of c; then, the clocked DTM N_c has $L(N_c) = L(N) = B$.

In a similar way, it can be argued that the class $\mathcal{NP}$ has a computable presentation; the main difference is that one uses NTMs in place of DTMs.

We prove the following statement: *Suppose that $\mathcal{C}$ is a class of languages that has a computable presentation. Then, there exists a computable language that is not in $\mathcal{C}$.*

Toward proving this, define D as the language defined by the following rule: for each string $w \in \Sigma^*$,

$$w \in D \quad \Leftrightarrow \quad \text{the machine } M \text{ such that } r(w) = \ulcorner M \urcorner \text{ does } not \text{ accept } w.$$

We show that the language D has the claimed properties. First, let us see why the language D is not in $\mathcal{C}$. Let B be any language in $\mathcal{C}$; we show that B is not equal to D. By the definition of *computable presentation*, there exists a string $w \in \Sigma^*$ such that $r(w)$ is the encoding $\ulcorner M \urcorner$ of a halting DTM or NTM with $B = L(M)$.

- If $w \in B$, then M accepts w, and so $w \notin D$.
- If $w \notin B$, then M does not accept w, and so $w \in D$.

Thus, the languages B and D are not equal. If this argument seems reminiscent of the diagonalization argument given in Section 2.4, it is because the two arguments are quite similar: there, we used a DTM encoding $\ulcorner M \urcorner$ itself to ensure that the constructed language was different from the language $L(M)$, over *all* DTMs; here, we use the string w to ensure that the constructed language is different from the language of the machine $r(w)$, over all machines in the image of r.

The language D is computable, via a halting DTM M_D behaving as follows: given a string w, it computes $r(w)$, and then invokes a universal Turing machine on the pair $\langle r(w), w \rangle$ to determine whether or not w is accepted by the machine M encoded by $r(w)$; if M accepts w, then M_D rejects, and otherwise, M_D accepts. (Although we did not explicitly discuss universal Turing machines in conjunction with NTMs, by combining Theorems 2.3.1 and 2.6.12, we can obtain a DTM N_u that, when given a pair $\langle \ulcorner M \urcorner, x \rangle$ consisting of an NTM encoding and a string, faithfully simulates the computation of M on x, accepting if and only if M accepts x, and halting if and only if M halts on x.) We have thus established the statement.

In this argument, we only used the forward direction of the equivalence in the definition of *computable presentation*. Indeed, the statement holds so long as the class $\mathcal{C}$ is *contained* in a class of languages having a computable presentation.   ◇

Exercise 3.10.12. Define the language

$$Y = \{\ulcorner M \urcorner \mid M \text{ is a polynomial-time DTM}\}.$$

Show that the language Y is not computable. (This result contrasts with the computable presentation of the complexity class $\mathcal{P}$ given in Note 3.10.11.)   ◇

Exercise 3.10.13: Proof systems. Let Σ be the alphabet $\{0, 1\}$. In complexity theory, a **proof system** for a language B is a polynomial-time computable function $S \colon \Sigma^* \to \Sigma^*$ such that $B = \{S(\pi) \mid \pi \in \Sigma^*\}$. A proof system S for a language B is **polynomially bounded** if there exists a polynomial P such that, for each $x \in B$, there exists $\pi \in \Sigma^*$ where $S(\pi) = x$ and $|\pi| \leq P(|x|)$. When S is a proof system for a language B, one can think of π as a proof that the string $S(\pi)$ is contained in B; the condition of being *polynomially bounded* essentially means that each string x in B has a proof that is not much larger than x.

1. Prove that a nonempty language B is NP if and only if there exists a polynomially bounded proof system for B. (It may be didactic to compare this exercise with Exercise 2.10.24.)

2. When S and S' are proof systems for the same language B, say that S' **simulates** S if there exists a polynomial P' such that for all $\pi \in \Sigma^*$, there exists $\pi' \in \Sigma^*$ where $|\pi'| \leq P(|\pi|)$ and $S'(\pi') = S(\pi)$. Prove that if S is polynomially bounded and S' simulates S, then S' is polynomially bounded.   ◇

Exercise 3.10.14: Operations on verifiers. This exercise investigates whether or not the closure of NP under intersection and union can be obtained by applying the respective operation to verifiers' languages. Assume that B and C are NP languages, that M_B is a verifier for B, and that M_C is a verifier for C. Let $M_\cap$ be a polynomial-time DTM whose language is $L(M_B) \cap L(M_C)$, and let $M_\cup$ be a polynomial-time DTM whose language is $L(M_B) \cup L(M_C)$; such DTMs exist by Theorem 3.3.10. Answer the following questions, and defend each answer with a proof.

1. Under the assumptions, is $M_\cap$ always a verifier for the language $B \cap C$?
2. Under the assumptions, is $M_\cup$ always a verifier for the language $B \cup C$?   ◇

Exercise 3.10.15: Closure under concatenation. In this exercise, you are asked to prove the closure under concatenation of this chapter's introduced language classes.

1. Prove that, when B and C are PTIME languages, the language $B \cdot C$ is also PTIME.
2. Prove that, when B and C are NP languages, the language $B \cdot C$ is also NP.
3. Prove that, when B and C are coNP languages, the language $B \cdot C$ is also coNP.   ◇

Exercise 3.10.16. Prove that a language B is computable if and only if there exists a PTIME language C such that $B \leq_m C$. ◊

Exercise 3.10.17: Representing languages over the binary alphabet. Let B and C be arbitrary languages over an alphabet Σ, and let $e \colon \Sigma \to \{0, 1\}^k$ be an injective mapping from the alphabet Σ to the set of length k strings over $\{0, 1\}$. For any string $x = x_1 \ldots x_n \in \Sigma$, let $e^+(x)$ denote the string $e(x_1) \ldots e(x_n)$ of length $k \cdot n$, that is, the string where each symbol of x is mapped under e, in order. Set $B' = \{e^+(x) \mid x \in B\}$, and set $C' = \{e^+(x) \mid x \in C\}$. Prove the following statements:

1. The language B is PTIME if and only if the language B' is PTIME.
2. The language B is NP if and only if the language B' is NP.
3. The language B is coNP if and only if the language B' is coNP.
4. $B \leq_m^p C$ if and only if $B' \leq_m^p C'$. ◊

Exercise 3.10.18: Characterizing completeness via completeness. This exercise calls for characterizations of NP-completeness and coNP-completeness.

1. Suppose that B is an NP-complete language. Prove that an arbitrary language C is NP-complete if and only if $B \leq_m C$ and $C \leq_m B$.
2. Suppose that B is an coNP-complete language. Prove that an arbitrary language C is coNP-complete if and only if $B \leq_m C$ and $C \leq_m B$. ◊

Exercise 3.10.19. Suppose that there exists a polynomial-time uniform circuit family computing a language B. Prove that B is a PTIME language. (This result is the converse of Theorem 3.6.15.) ◊

Exercise 3.10.20: Non-symmetry of polynomial-time reducibility. Prove that the relation $\leq_m^p$ is not symmetric on nontrivial languages, that is, that there exist nontrivial languages B and C such that $B \leq_m^p C$ holds, but $C \leq_m^p B$ does not hold. (This result is a variation of Exercise 2.10.33.) ◊

Exercise 3.10.21. Fix $\Sigma = \{0, 1\}$ as the alphabet over which strings and languages are formed. Define $\equiv_m^p$ as the binary relation, on languages over Σ, where $B \equiv_m^p C$ holds if and only if $B \leq_m^p C$ and $C \leq_m^p B$.

1. Prove that $\equiv_m^p$ is an equivalence relation.
2. Prove that the set of all nontrivial PTIME languages is an equivalence class of $\equiv_m^p$.
3. Prove that the set of all NP-complete languages is an equivalence class of $\equiv_m^p$.
4. Prove that the two equivalence classes in parts 2 and 3 are equal if and only if each NP language is a PTIME language (that is, if and only if $\mathcal{NP} \subseteq \mathcal{P}$).

This exercise can be taken as a complexity-theoretic version of Exercise 2.10.32. ◊

Note 3.10.22: Complements as twins. A language B and its complement $\overline{B}$ are in many senses mirror twins of each other. The operation of complementation toggles between them, and what can be said about one of the twins is often reflected by the other. The trait of being PTIME is shared among twins: a language is PTIME if and only if its complement is (Proposition 3.3.1). The trait of being computable is also thusly shared (Proposition 2.5.1). With respect to other language classes, twins do not obviously stick together: when a language is known to be NP, what can be said is that its twin is coNP, and vice versa; and when a language is known to be CE, what can be said is that its twin is coCE, and vice versa. (Here, it is also worth recalling that when a language is NP-hard, its twin is coNP-hard, and vice versa—as shown by Theorem 3.7.2.) Along these lines, the class of NP languages and the class of coNP languages can themselves be conceived of as twins to each other. As twin classes, they also share some crucial properties; for example, that of being equal to the class of PTIME languages (Proposition 3.3.7)!

Complementation also preserves the important relationship of reducibility: a first language B reduces to a second language C (under either of the notions of reduction studied so far—recall Definitions 2.8.2 and 3.4.1) if and only if the first language's twin $\overline{B}$ reduces to the second language's twin $\overline{C}$, as shown by Propositions 2.8.6 and 3.4.13. ◇

Exercise 3.10.23: Reduction relations. In this exercise and its sequel, Exercise 3.10.25, we establish some of this chapter's results on hardness and completeness in a general setting. Fix $\Sigma = \{0, 1\}$ as the alphabet over which strings and languages are formed. When $\leq$ is a binary relation on languages (over Σ), say that $\leq$ is a **reduction relation** when it is reflexive and transitive.

Let $\mathcal{C}$ be a set of languages (over Σ). Say that $\mathcal{C}$ is **closed** under a reduction relation $\leq$ when (for all languages B, C) it holds that $B \leq C$ and $C \in \mathcal{C}$ implies $B \in \mathcal{C}$. With respect to a reduction relation $\leq$, say that a language D is $\mathcal{C}$-**hard** when, for each language $B \in \mathcal{C}$, it holds that $B \leq D$; say that D is $\mathcal{C}$-**complete** when, in addition, it holds that $D \in \mathcal{C}$.

Let $\mathcal{C}$, $\mathcal{C}'$ be sets of languages, each of which is closed under a reduction relation $\leq$. Prove the following:

1. If B is $\mathcal{C}$-hard and $B \leq B^+$, then B^+ is $\mathcal{C}$-hard.
2. If B is $\mathcal{C}$-hard and $B \in \mathcal{C}'$, then $\mathcal{C} \subseteq \mathcal{C}'$.
3. Suppose that B is $\mathcal{C}$-complete; then, $B \in \mathcal{C}'$ if and only if $\mathcal{C} \subseteq \mathcal{C}'$.
4. Suppose that B is $\mathcal{C}$-complete; then, $A \in \mathcal{C}$ if and only if $A \leq B$ (for each language A).
5. Suppose that B is a language where $A \in \mathcal{C}$ if and only if $A \leq B$ (for each language A); then, B is $\mathcal{C}$-complete. ◇

Note 3.10.24: The co- operator. When $\mathcal{C}$ is a set of languages over an alphabet Σ, define co-$\mathcal{C}$ as the set $\{\overline{C} \mid C \in \mathcal{C}\}$, that is, as the set containing the complement of each language in $\mathcal{C}$. This unary operation on sets of languages behaves radically differently from the complementation of sets of languages. It *preserves* containment, that is, when $\mathcal{C}$ and $\mathcal{D}$ are sets of languages (over the same alphabet Σ) such that $\mathcal{C} \subseteq \mathcal{D}$, it holds that co-$\mathcal{C} \subseteq$ co-$\mathcal{D}$. This is in sharp contrast to complementation, which *reverses* containment: when $\mathcal{C} \subseteq \mathcal{D}$, it holds that $\overline{\mathcal{D}} \subseteq \overline{\mathcal{C}}$. Here, the complement $\overline{\mathcal{B}}$ of a set $\mathcal{B}$ of languages is the set of all languages (over Σ) that are not in $\mathcal{B}$.

For any set $\mathcal{C}$ of languages, it holds that co-(co-$\mathcal{C}$) $= \mathcal{C}$. So, the containments $\mathcal{C} \subseteq$ co-$\mathcal{C}$ and co-$\mathcal{C} \subseteq \mathcal{C}$ are seen to be generically equivalent to each other, and are also equivalent to the equality $\mathcal{C} =$ co-$\mathcal{C}$.   ◇

Exercise 3.10.25. This exercise is a sequel to Exercise 3.10.23; we make use of the setup and terminology introduced there, as well as the definition of co-$\mathcal{C}$ from Note 3.10.24.

Assume that $\leq$ is a reduction relation where (for all languages A, B) the relationship $A \leq B$ implies the relationship $\overline{A} \leq \overline{B}$, and assume $\mathcal{C}$ to be a set of languages that is closed under $\leq$. Prove the following:

1. A language B is $\mathcal{C}$-hard if and only if $\overline{B}$ is co-$\mathcal{C}$-hard.
2. A language B is $\mathcal{C}$-complete if and only if $\overline{B}$ is co-$\mathcal{C}$-complete.
3. Suppose that B is $\mathcal{C}$-complete; then, $B \leq \overline{B}$ if and only if $\mathcal{C} \subseteq$ co-$\mathcal{C}$.   ◇

Note 3.10.26: Ladner's theorem. In looking at naturally occurring NP languages, the overwhelming majority of them can be catalogued as being either PTIME or NP-complete. This ostensibly dichotomic behavior instinctively raises the question of whether or not it is possible that all NP languages are indeed either PTIME or NP-complete. This is absolutely and arguably uninterestingly the case if $\mathcal{P} = \mathcal{NP}$: in this case, all NP languages are PTIME *and* all nontrivial NP languages are NP-complete (by Exercise 3.10.21). It is thus most reasonable to ask this question under the assumption that $\mathcal{P} \neq \mathcal{NP}$; in this case, it has been proved that there exist NP languages that are neither PTIME nor NP-complete, and which are thus intermediate between these two typical extremes. This result, known as Ladner's theorem, was proved by Richard Ladner in 1975.   ◇

3.10.2 Satisfiability

Exercise 3.10.27: Non-tautologies. On propositional formulas, we studied the properties of satisfiability, of unsatisfiability, and of being a tautology. It is thus only fair that we consider the property of *not* being a tautology. Define the following languages:

CNF-NONTAUT $= \{\phi \mid \phi$ is a CNF-formula that is not a tautology$\}$,

DNF-NONTAUT $= \{\phi \mid \phi$ is a DNF-formula that is not a tautology$\}$.

Each of these two languages can be proved to be PTIME, NP-complete, or coNP-complete. Do it.   ◇

Exercise 3.10.28. Prove Lemma 3.8.25, which concerned the 6 clauses created for each tuple in the reduction from 3-NAE-SAT to MAX-2-CNF-SAT.   ◇

Note 3.10.29: Propositional resolution. There are many proof systems for certifying the unsatisfiability of propositional formulas. Here, we take a look at one of the most basic ones, *resolution*. Starting from a CNF-formula, clauses can be derived under this system; when the *empty clause* with no literals is derivable, this implies that the original CNF-formula is unsatisfiable.

In order to introduce resolution, we put into effect a couple of conventions. First, we allow an empty disjunction of literals to serve as a clause; we refer to this empty disjunction as the **empty clause**, denote it by $\perp$, and consider it as not satisfied by any assignment, since it has no literals that can be satisfied. Next, when C is a clause, we use litset(C) to denote the set of literals appearing in the clause C; as examples, litset($u \vee \neg x$) = $\{u, \neg x\}$, litset($\neg w \vee \neg u \vee \neg w$) = $\{\neg w, \neg u\}$, and litset($\perp$) = $\emptyset$.

With these conventions in place, we can present the resolution proof system. Let ϕ be a CNF-formula. A **resolution proof** Π for ϕ is a sequence $D_1, ..., D_\ell$ of clauses, where each clause D_i is derived according to one of the following rules.

- **Download:** the clause D_i appears as a clause in ϕ.
- **Structural:** the clause D_i satisfies litset(D_i) = litset(D_j) for a clause D_j appearing before D_i (that is, with $j < i$).
- **Cut:** the clause D_i is equal to $C \vee C'$, where C and C' are clauses such that there exists a variable x and clauses D_j, D_k appearing before D_i (that is, with $j < i$ and $k < i$) where

$$D_j = C \vee x \quad \text{and} \quad D_k = \neg x \vee C'.$$

The *structural* rule implies in particular that from any clause D in a proof, we can derive any clause obtained from D by reordering literals, and by removing duplicate literals. Note that in the *cut* rule, one or both of the clauses C, C' may be the empty clause. Figure 3.10.1 presents an example of a resolution proof.

For convenience, we say that a clause D is **derivable** from a CNF-formula ϕ when there exists a resolution proof for ϕ in which the clause D appears. When ϕ is a CNF-formula with variables from a set V, we say that a clause with variables from V is **entailed** by ϕ when each assignment $f: V \rightarrow \{0, 1\}$ satisfying ϕ also satisfies D. A key property of this proof system is that any clause derivable from a CNF-formula is entailed by the formula. We formalize this property, known as **soundness**, as follows:

> When ϕ is a CNF-formula, and D is any clause derivable from ϕ,
> it holds that ϕ entails D.

We establish that soundness holds by fixing a CNF-formula ϕ and a resolution proof for ϕ, and by considering the clauses of the proof in sequence. Suppose $f: V \rightarrow \{0, 1\}$ to be an assignment satisfying ϕ; we show that it satisfies each clause D_i of the proof by considering which derivation rule was used.

- *Download:* Suppose that D_i appears as a clause in ϕ. Then, it is evident that f satisfies D_i.

$$D_1 = u \lor x \qquad\qquad\qquad \text{(download)}$$

$$D_2 = u \lor \neg x \qquad\qquad\qquad \text{(download)}$$

$$D_3 = \neg x \lor u \qquad\qquad\qquad \text{(structural: } D_2\text{)}$$

$$D_4 = u \lor u \qquad\qquad\qquad \text{(cut: } D_1, D_3\text{)}$$

$$D_5 = u \qquad\qquad\qquad \text{(structural: } D_4\text{)}$$

$$D_6 = \neg u \lor y \qquad\qquad\qquad \text{(download)}$$

$$D_7 = y \qquad\qquad\qquad \text{(cut: } D_5, D_6\text{)}$$

$$D_8 = \neg y \lor \neg z \qquad\qquad\qquad \text{(download)}$$

$$D_9 = \neg z \qquad\qquad\qquad \text{(cut: } D_7, D_8\text{)}$$

$$D_{10} = \neg u \lor \neg y \lor z \qquad\qquad\qquad \text{(download)}$$

$$D_{11} = \neg u \lor \neg y \qquad\qquad\qquad \text{(cut: } D_{10}, D_9\text{)}$$

$$D_{12} = \neg y \qquad\qquad\qquad \text{(cut: } D_5, D_{11}\text{)}$$

$$D_{13} = \bot \qquad\qquad\qquad \text{(cut: } D_7, D_{12}\text{)}$$

Figure 3.10.1. The presented sequence of clauses is an example resolution proof for the CNF-formula $\phi = (u \lor x) \land (u \lor \neg x) \land (\neg u \lor y) \land (\neg y \lor \neg z) \land (\neg u \lor \neg y \lor z)$. Each clause is annotated with the respective rule used.

- *Structural:* Suppose that D_i is a clause such that $\text{litset}(D_i) = \text{litset}(D_j)$ for a clause D_j appearing before D_i. We may assume by induction that f satisfies D_j, which implies that f satisfies a literal λ in D_j. Since λ also appears in D_i, we obtain that f satisfies D_i.
- *Cut:* Suppose that D_i is a clause that, as in the rule description, is equal to $C \lor C'$, where there is a variable x and clauses D_j, D_k appearing before D_i with $D_j = C \lor x$ and $D_k = \neg x \lor C'$. We may assume by induction that f satisfies both D_j and D_k. Consider the value $f(x)$. If $f(x) = 0$, then the literal x evaluates to 0 under f; since f satisfies D_j, it must then satisfy C, and hence also D_i. If $f(x) = 1$, then the literal $\neg x$ evaluates to 0 under f; since f satisfies D_k, it must then satisfy C', and hence also D_i.

A consequence of the soundness property is that whenever the empty clause $\bot$ is derivable from a CNF-formula ϕ, the formula ϕ must be unsatisfiable. This is because no assignment satisfies the empty clause, so when it is derivable, soundness implies that there is no assignment satisfying ϕ. Indeed, a primary use of resolution is to certify the unsatisfiability of CNF-formulas by showing derivability of the empty clause.   ◇

Exercise 3.10.30: Completeness of resolution. This exercise requests proofs of versions of *completeness* for resolution.

1. Prove that for any unsatisfiable CNF-formula ϕ, the empty clause $\bot$ is derivable from ϕ, using resolution. This property is known as **refutation-completeness**; along with soundness, it implies that a CNF-formula ϕ is unsatisfiable *if and only if* the empty clause $\bot$ is derivable from ϕ.

   One possible strategy for establishing this property is as follows. Let ϕ be a CNF-formula with variables V. By the structural rule, from each derivable clause, one can derive an equivalent clause without repeated literals. Focus on the set $\mathcal{D}$ of derivable clauses without repeated literals; there are finitely many such clauses (since each has variables drawn from V). Show by induction on $|U|$ that for any subset $U \subseteq V$, an assignment $g: V \setminus U \to \{0, 1\}$ satisfies all clauses in the set $\mathcal{D}$ having variables from $V \setminus U$ if and only if g can be extended to a satisfying assignment $g': V \to \{0, 1\}$ of ϕ.

2. Here, you are asked to generalize the previous result, and show a version of a property known as **completeness**. Prove that for any clause C not containing complementary literals (that is, for any clause C that is not tautological) and any CNF-formula ϕ, if the formula ϕ entails the clause C, then there exists a clause D that is derivable from ϕ with $\mathrm{litset}(D) \subseteq \mathrm{litset}(C)$.

   Essentially, what is being requested is a proof that for each clause C entailed by a CNF-formula, there is a clause derivable from the formula that is at least as strong as C. As a hint, consider that when ϕ entails a clause $\lambda_1 \vee \cdots \lambda_m$, the CNF-formula $\phi \wedge (\neg \lambda_1) \wedge \cdots \wedge (\neg \lambda_m)$ is unsatisfiable. ◇

Note 3.10.31: Resolution as a proof system. Propositional resolution, as presented in Note 3.10.29, gives a proof system for the language of unsatisfiable CNF-formulas, in the sense of Exercise 3.10.13. Here is why. Fix ψ_0 to be an unsatisfiable CNF-formula. Consider the function $S: \Sigma^* \to \Sigma^*$ defined as follows. When the string z is a pair $\langle \phi, \Pi \rangle$ consisting of a CNF-formula ϕ and a resolution proof of Π containing $\bot$, the string $S(z)$ is defined as ϕ; otherwise, the string $S(z)$ is defined as ψ_0.

The image of S is the language of all unsatisfiable CNF-formulas, since $\bot$ is derivable from a CNF-formula ϕ if and only if ϕ is unsatisfiable (by Exercise 3.10.30, part 1). The function S is polynomial-time computable; given a candidate resolution proof for a CNF-formula, it can be checked in polynomial time that each line is justified according to one of the presented rules.

It has been proved unconditionally that, as a proof system, propositional resolution is not polynomially bounded! ◇

Note 3.10.32. In the presented reduction from CNF-SAT to 3-CNF-SAT (Reduction 3.8.8), each clause $\lambda_1 \vee \cdots \vee \lambda_k$ of size $k > 3$ was translated to k clauses, each having size at most 3. The clause $\lambda_1 \vee \cdots \vee \lambda_k$ is readily seen to be derivable, by resolution, from the introduced k clauses. Along with this observation, the soundness of resolution (presented in Note 3.10.29) implies the backward direction of this reduction's correctness.   ◇

Exercise 3.10.33. Prove that the language 2-CNF-SAT is PTIME.   ◇

Exercise 3.10.34: Bounded-occurrence CNF-formulas. For each $k \geq 1$, define the language k-OCC-CNF-SAT to contain each satisfiable CNF-formula ϕ such that each variable occurs k or fewer times, that is, such that if one looks through the literals of ϕ one by one, each variable is seen k or fewer times.

1. Prove that the language 2-OCC-CNF-SAT is PTIME.
2. Prove that the language 3-OCC-CNF-SAT is NP-complete.   ◇

Exercise 3.10.35: Horn satisfiability. Define a **Horn clause** to be a clause containing at most one positive literal; define a **Horn-CNF-formula** to be a CNF-formula where each clause is a Horn clause. Prove that, for any Horn-CNF-formula ϕ, the following procedure correctly decides satisfiability:

*   Assign P to be the empty set $\emptyset$.
*   Iteratively do the following, until no positive literal literals can be added to P:
    For each clause C (of ϕ) that contains a positive literal v, add v to P if P contains the complement of each negative literal in C. (In particular, add a positive literal v to P if v itself appears as a clause of ϕ.)
*   If there exists a clause C (of ϕ) where each literal is negative and has its complement contained in P, report *unsatisfiable*; otherwise, report *satisfiable*.

This procedure admits a polynomial-time implementation.

   Unit resolution is the case of resolution where, for each application of the cut rule, one of the two parent clauses must be a **unit clause**—a 1-literal clause. The above procedure's correctness indicates that unit resolution is refutation-complete for Horn-CNF-formulas. (The terms used here are explained in Note 3.10.29 and Exercise 3.10.30.)   ◇

Exercise 3.10.36: Guaranteed satisfiability. Let $k \geq 1$. Suppose that ϕ is a CNF-formula having strictly fewer than 2^k clauses, and where each clause of ϕ has k or more literals and has no repeated literals. Prove that the formula ϕ is satisfiable. (Here, we do not assume any upper bound on the number of variables occurring in the formula ϕ.) So, this exercise shows that when dealing with clauses each having k or more pairwise distinct literals, at least 2^k clauses are needed to enforce unsatisfiability.   ◇

Exercise 3.10.37: Barely 3-CNF-formulas. Define a **barely-3-CNF-formula** as a 3-CNF-formula having at most 99 clauses of size 3; that is, all but at most 99 of the clauses must have size 2 or less. Define BARELY-3-CNF-SAT as the language containing each satisfiable barely-3-CNF-formula. Prove either that this language is PTIME, or that it is NP-complete.   ◇

Exercise 3.10.38: Exact 3-CNF-formulas. Define a 3-CNF-formula to be **exact** if each clause of ϕ contains three pairwise distinct variables, that is, each clause of ϕ has 3 literals, no two of which are over the same variable. Prove NP-completeness of the language EXACT-3-CNF-SAT, defined as containing each satisfiable exact 3-CNF-formula. ◇

Exercise 3.10.39. For an exact 3-CNF-formula (defined in Exercise 3.10.38), consider a random assignment to its variables, where each variable is set to 0 or 1 independently depending on the outcome of a coin flip. In expectation, such a random assignment satisfies $\frac{7}{8}$ of the clauses: each clause contains 3 variables, there are $2^3 = 8$ assignments to these variables, and exactly 1 of these 8 assignments fails to satisfy the clause. That is, when we take the average of the fraction of clauses satisfied, over all assignments, we obtain $\frac{7}{8}$; this implies that there *exists* an assignment satisfying at least $\frac{7}{8}$ of the clauses.

Show that there is a polynomial-time computable function that, when given an exact 3-CNF-formula ϕ with m clauses, outputs an assignment to the variables of ϕ that satisfies $\frac{7m}{8}$ or more clauses of ϕ. In essence, this exercise asks that you show a probabilistic *existence* argument to be polynomial-time *constructive*. ◇

Exercise 3.10.40: Positive formulas. A propositional formula is called **positive** when it makes no use of negation. So, a CNF-formula is positive if every literal is positive. Clearly, each positive formula is satisfied by the assignment that maps each variable to 1 (assuming that no disjunction in the formula is empty). As a consequence, the satisfiability problem for such formulas is not interesting. However, the satisfiability problem can be made interesting again if we only consider satisfiability by assignments having a limited number of variables that can be set to 1. Precisely, when $k \in \mathbb{N}$, let us say that a formula ϕ on variables V is ($\leq k$)-*satisfiable* if there exists an assignment $f: V \to \{0, 1\}$ with $\left|\{v \mid f(v) = 1\}\right| \leq k$ that satisfies ϕ; that is, if ϕ is satisfied by an assignment that sets k or fewer variables to the value 1.

Define LIMITED-POS-CNF-SAT as the language containing each pair (ϕ, k) such that $k \in \mathbb{N}$ and ϕ is a positive CNF-formula that is ($\leq k$)-satisfiable. Prove that this language is NP-complete. ◇

Exercise 3.10.41: 1-in-3 satisfiability. This exercise considers a satisfiability problem known as 1-**in**-3-**SAT**. An *instance* here is a sequence of 3-tuples of variables (and is thus identical in form to a 3-*NAE-system*, as presented in Section 3.8.1). An instance is *satisfiable* if there exists a mapping $f: V \to \{0, 1\}$ that is defined on all variables appearing in the instance, and such that for each 3-tuple (u, v, w) in the instance, exactly one of the three values $f(u), f(v), f(w)$ is equal to 1. Prove that the language 1-in-3-SAT, defined as the set containing each satisfiable instance, is NP-complete. ◇

Exercise 3.10.42: Inequalities. Define an *inequality system* as a sequence of *constraints*, each having the form $u \leq v$ or $u \neq v$, where u and v are variables. Say that such an inequality system S is *satisfiable* if there exists a mapping $f: V \to \mathbb{N}$ defined on all variables appearing in S such that for each constraint of the form $u \leq v$ in S, it holds that $f(u) \leq f(v)$, and for each constraint of the form $u \neq v$ in S, it holds that $f(u) \neq f(v)$. Define INEQUALITIES as the language containing each satisfiable inequality system. Prove either that this language is PTIME or that it is NP-complete.   ◇

Exercise 3.10.43: Half-satisfiability of monotone circuits. A circuit is **monotone** if it contains no instances of negation; that is, if each instruction is an AND ($\wedge$) or an OR ($\vee$). For a monotone circuit, satisfiability is readily checked: if there is any satisfying assignment at all, the assignment setting each input to 1 is a satisfying assignment. Let us say that a circuit with an even number of inputs is $\frac{1}{2}$-*satisfiable* if it has a satisfying assignment that assigns exactly half of its inputs to the value 1. Define MONO-CIRCUIT-$\frac{1}{2}$-SAT as the language containing each monotone circuit that has an even number of inputs and that is $\frac{1}{2}$-satisfiable. Prove that this language is NP-complete.   ◇

Exercise 3.10.44: Equivalence problems. We say that two propositional formulas ϕ, ϕ' are **logically equivalent** when, for any assignment $f: V \rightarrow \{0, 1\}$ defined on all variables appearing in the formulas, it holds that f satisfies ϕ if and only if f satisfies ϕ'. Let us say that two circuits C, C' are **logically equivalent** when they are defined on the same inputs $v_1, \ldots, v_n$ and for any assignment $f: \{v_1, \ldots, v_n\} \rightarrow \{0, 1\}$, it holds that f satisfies C if and only if f satisfies C'.

1. Define 2-CNF-EQUIV as the language containing each pair (ϕ, ϕ') of 2-CNF-formulas that are logically equivalent.

2. Define BARELY-3-CNF-EQUIV as the language containing each pair (ϕ, ϕ') of barely-3-CNF-formulas that are logically equivalent. (See Exercise 3.10.37 for the definition of *barely-3-CNF-formula*.)

3. Define MONO-CIRCUIT-EQUIV as the language containing each pair (C, C') of *monotone circuits* that are logically equivalent. (The notion of *monotone circuit* was defined in Exercise 3.10.43.)

For each of these languages, prove either that it is PTIME, or that it is coNP-complete.   ◇

Exercise 3.10.45: Expressiveness by widening clauses. Prove that there exists a 3-CNF-formula that is not logically equivalent to any 2-CNF-formula.   ◇

Exercise 3.10.46: Computing parity via CNF-formulas. Let $V = \{v_1, \ldots, v_k\}$ be a finite set of variables, with $k \geq 1$. Say that a CNF-formula ϕ *computes the parity of V* when ϕ is logically equivalent to the propositional formula $v_1 \oplus \cdots \oplus v_k$, that is, when an assignment $f: V \rightarrow \{0, 1\}$ satisfies ϕ if and only if the number $|\{v \in V \mid f(v) = 1\}|$ of variables set to 1 by f is odd. Prove that, for each $k \geq 1$, any CNF-formula that computes the parity of $V = \{v_1, \ldots, v_k\}$ has 2^{k-1} or more clauses.   ◇

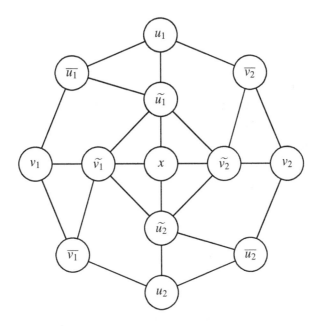

Figure 3.10.2. A planar graph studied in Exercise 3.10.48.

Exercise 3.10.47: Precoloring. The language 9-COL consisting of the 9-colorable graphs was demonstrated to be hard, by Theorem 3.8.32. This exercises asks you to show, essentially, that this language remains hard even when each graph is presented along with a 10-coloring. Define PRECOLORED-9-COL as the language containing each pair (G,f) where G is a 9-colorable graph and f is a 10-coloring of G. Prove that this language is NP-complete. ◇

Exercise 3.10.48: 3-colorability of planar graphs. A graph is **planar** if there is a way to draw it in the plane so that no two edges cross. It is known that the restriction of the language 3-COL to planar graphs is NP-complete. One way to prove this result is to give a reduction from the language 3-COL itself, along the following lines. The reduction first draws its given graph in the plane in a way that each edge touches no vertices other than its own endpoints, and at any point does not touch more than one other edge. The planar graph given in Figure 3.10.2 can then be used to help cope with points where two edges cross. Let V denote this graph's vertex set; prove that this graph has the following key properties.

1. For any two values $a, b \in \{1, 2, 3\}$, there exists a 3-coloring $f\colon V \to \{1, 2, 3\}$ of the graph such that $f(u_1) = f(u_2) = a$ and $f(v_1) = f(v_2) = b$.
2. Any 3-coloring $f\colon V \to \{1, 2, 3\}$ of the graph satisfies $f(u_1) = f(u_2)$ and $f(v_1) = f(v_2)$.

Together, these properties imply that, when one takes the 3-colorings of the given graph and restricts attention to the vertices u_1, u_2, u_3, and u_4, one obtains precisely the mappings sending u_1 and u_2 to the same color, and sending v_1 and v_2 to the same color.   ◇

3.10.3   Graphs and hypergraphs

Exercise 3.10.49: Hamiltonicity of grid graphs. In this exercise, we classify the grid graphs having Hamiltonian cycles. Grid graphs were defined in Figure 3.4.3 on page 172.

1. Prove that the 3-by-3 grid graph has no Hamiltonian cycle.
2. Describe the values $k \geq 4$ such that the k-by-k grid graph has a Hamiltonian cycle. Prove that your description is correct.   ◇

Exercise 3.10.50: Finding any Hamiltonian path. We defined the language HAM-PATH so that an instance consists of a triple (G, s, t) where s and t are vertices of G prescribing where the sought Hamiltonian path must begin and end. In this exercise, you are to show that this language remains hard even when there is no such prescription. Define ANY-HAM-PATH as the language containing each graph G having a Hamiltonian path. Prove that this language is NP-complete.   ◇

Exercise 3.10.51: Finding any Eulerian path. An **Eulerian path** in a graph $G = (V, E)$ is a walk $v_1, \ldots, v_m$ in G such that each edge in E appears exactly once in the list

$$\{v_1, v_2\}, \{v_2, v_3\}, \ldots, \{v_{m-1}, v_m\}.$$

That is, an Eulerian path in a graph is a walk that traverses each edge exactly once. Define ANY-EUL-PATH as the language containing each graph G having an Eulerian path. Prove that this language is PTIME.   ◇

Exercise 3.10.52: Complexity under bounded degree. In this exercise, we consider the effect of bounding the degree of the permitted graphs, for some of the considered languages involving graphs. When $G = (V, E)$ is a graph, let $\deg_G(v)$ denote the degree of the vertex v in G, and define the **degree** of the graph G, denoted by $\deg(G)$, as $\max_{v \in V} \deg_G(v)$. So, the degree of a graph G is defined as the maximum degree over all of its vertices; and, for a number d, the condition $\deg(G) \leq d$ holds that every vertex of G occurs in at most d edges.

For each $d \geq 1$, define the following languages:

$$d\text{-DEG-HAM-CYCLE} = \{G \in \text{HAM-CYCLE} \mid \deg(G) \leq d\},$$
$$d\text{-DEG-CLIQUE} = \{(G, k) \in \text{CLIQUE} \mid \deg(G) \leq d\},$$
$$d\text{-DEG-INDEP-SET} = \{(G, k) \in \text{INDEP-SET} \mid \deg(G) \leq d\},$$
$$d\text{-DEG-3-COL} = \{G \in \text{3-COL} \mid \deg(G) \leq d\}.$$

Prove the following results:

1. The language 2-DEG-HAM-CYCLE is PTIME.
2. The language 6-DEG-CLIQUE is PTIME.

3. The language 6-DEG-INDEP-SET is NP-complete.
4. The language 6-DEG-3-COL is NP-complete. ◇

Exercise 3.10.53: Fractional-sized vertex covers. For the language VERTEX-COVER, an instance consisted of a graph G along with a number k, and the question was whether or not the graph contained a vertex cover of size k. In this exercise, we show that this language remains hard even when the size of the sought vertex cover is fixed as a constant fraction of the number of vertices.

Define $\frac{1}{4}$-VERTEX-COVER as the language containing each graph G whose number n of vertices is a multiple of 4 and that contains a vertex cover of size $\frac{n}{4}$; define $\frac{3}{4}$-VERTEX-COVER similarly, but with the difference that each graph must contain a vertex cover of size $\frac{3n}{4}$.

1. Prove that the language $\frac{1}{4}$-VERTEX-COVER is NP-complete.
2. Prove that the language $\frac{3}{4}$-VERTEX-COVER is NP-complete. ◇

Exercise 3.10.54: Approximation algorithm for vertex cover. Consider the following algorithm for computing a vertex cover of a given graph $G = (V, E)$:

- Initialize C to be $\emptyset$.
- While E is nonempty:
  - Pick any edge $\{u, v\} \in E$.
  - Place the vertices u and v in C.
  - Remove the vertices u and v from G.
- Output C.

Here, by removal of a vertex from a graph, we mean that it is removed from the graph's vertex set, and that any edge containing the vertex is removed from the graph's edge set.

Prove that the set C output by the algorithm is a vertex cover of the original graph, and that for *any* vertex cover D of the original graph, it holds that $|C| \leq 2|D|$. This in particular implies that the size of the algorithm's output vertex cover is is at most 2 times the size of the graph's smallest vertex cover.

It is not known how to polynomial-time compute a graph's smallest vertex cover, or even the size of such a vertex cover (see Exercise 3.10.67). Yet, the algorithm here *approximates* this quantity within a factor of 2, and can be seen to do so within polynomial time. ◇

Note 3.10.55. Exercise 3.10.54 discusses the predicament of being able to efficiently find a vertex cover of any given graph that is at most 2 times the size of a smallest vertex cover, without being able to efficiently find a smallest vertex cover. This pickle recalls a quip attributed to the American retailer John Wanamaker: "Half the money I spend on advertising is wasted; the trouble is I don't know which half." ◇

Exercise 3.10.56: Set covers. In a graph, we saw that a *vertex cover* is a set of vertices that covers all *edges*, in a certain precise sense; and that a *dominating set* is a set of vertices that covers all *vertices*, in a certain precise sense. In this exercise, we show how these notions can be viewed as special cases of a more general notion, by showing that the associated languages reduce to a more general language.

Define a **hypergraph** as a pair (U, F) where U is a finite set, and $F \subseteq \wp(U)$, that is, F is a set whose elements are subsets of U. The elements of F are called **edges** or **hyperedges**. Relative to a hypergraph (U, F), a **cover** is a subset $C \subseteq F$ where $U = \bigcup_{f \in C} f$, that is, where for each element $u \in U$, there is an edge $f \in C$ in which u appears. Define SET-COVER as the language containing each triple (U, F, k) such that (U, F) is a hypergraph having a cover of size k. In effect, given such a triple, the question is to determine if it is possible to select k sets from F that cover the entire set U.

1. Prove that there is a reduction from VERTEX-COVER to SET-COVER behaving as follows: for any graph $G = (V, E)$, the reduction maps a pair (G, k) to a triple of the form $(E, \cdot, k)$. That is, define a reduction mapping each such pair (G, k) to a triple (E, F, k) where you specify the definition of the set F, and prove the reduction's correctness.

2. Prove that there is a reduction from DOM-SET to SET-COVER behaving as follows: for any graph $G = (V, E)$, a pair (G, k) is mapped to a triple of the form $(V, \cdot, k)$.

Each of these reductions establishes the NP-hardness of SET-COVER: Theorems 3.8.37 and 3.8.43 gave the NP-hardness of VERTEX-COVER and DOM-SET. ◇

Note 3.10.57: Proof by restriction. The form of hardness proof requested in Exercise 3.10.56 has been referred to as *proof by restriction*: the proof's reduction reveals that the instances of a first language can be viewed quite directly as instances of a second language, and thus that the first language is in effect a restricted version of the second. The next exercise, Exercise 3.10.58, also requests proofs of this form. ◇

Exercise 3.10.58: Graph homomorphisms. When $H = (V_H, E_H)$ and $H' = (V'_H, E'_H)$ are graphs, define a **homomorphism** from H to H' as a mapping $f: V_H \to V'_H$ such that for each edge $\{u, v\} \in E_H$, it holds that $\{f(u), f(v)\} \in E'_H$. That is, a homomorphism from a first graph to a second graph is a mapping f from the first vertex set to the second vertex set that *preserves edge containment*, meaning that taking any edge of the first graph and sending its endpoints through f yields an edge of the second graph.

Define INJ-GRAPH-HOM as the language containing each pair (H, H') of graphs such that there exists an *injective* homomorphism from $H = (V_H, E_H)$ to $H' = (V'_H, E'_H)$, that is, a homomorphism f that is injective as a mapping from V_H to V'_H. This problem is also known as the **subgraph isomorphism problem**, for there is an injective homomorphism from H to H' if and only if H is isomorphic to a subgraph of H'.

1. Prove that CLIQUE reduces to INJ-GRAPH-HOM via a polynomial-time many-one reduction that sends each pair (G, k) to a pair of the form $(\cdot, G)$, that is, to a pair where G is the second entry.

2. Prove that HAM-CYCLE reduces to INJ-GRAPH-HOM via a polynomial-time many-one reduction that sends each graph G to a pair of the form $(\cdot, G)$.

3. Prove that ANY-HAM-PATH reduces to INJ-GRAPH-HOM via a polynomial-time many-one reduction that sends each graph G to a pair of the form $(\cdot, G)$. (The language ANY-HAM-PATH was presented in Exercise 3.10.50.) ◇

Exercise 3.10.59: Homomorphisms to cycles. For each $k \geq 2$, the k-**cycle** is the graph with vertex set $\{0, ..., k-1\}$ and edge set $\{\{i, i+1\} \mid i \in \{0, ..., k-2\}\} \cup \{\{k-1, 0\}\}$. That is, two vertices form an edge if and only if they differ by 1, modulo k. Define k-CYCLE-COL as the language containing each graph having a homomorphism *to* the k-cycle. (The notion of homomorphism between graphs was defined in Exercise 3.10.58.)

For each of the languages 4-CYCLE-COL and 5-CYCLE-COL, prove either that it is PTIME or that it is NP-complete. (Hint: it may be didactic to understand which graphs have a homomorphism to the 2-cycle, and likewise for the 3-cycle.) ◇

Exercise 3.10.60: Homomorphisms between cycles. Describe the set containing each pair $(i, j) \in \mathbb{N} \times \mathbb{N}$ where $i, j \geq 2$ and there exists a homomorphism from the i-cycle to the j-cycle. Prove that your description is correct. (Homomorphisms between graphs were defined in Exercise 3.10.58, and cycle graphs were defined in Exercise 3.10.59.) ◇

Exercise 3.10.61: Hardness of maximum cut. When $G = (V, E)$ is a graph, a **cut** of G is a partition (U, U') of the vertex set V, that is, a pair of sets U, U' such that V is the disjoint union of U and U'; the **weight** of the cut (U, U') is $\left| \{e \in E \mid e \cap U \neq \emptyset, e \cap U' \neq \emptyset\} \right|$. That is, the weight of a cut is the number of edges that cross the cut, where an edge is said to cross the cut if it has one vertex in one set of the cut, and one vertex in the other set of the cut. Define MAX-CUT as the language containing each pair (G, k) such that G is a graph, $k \in \mathbb{N}$, and G has a cut of weight k or more.

Show that the following mapping is a polynomial-time many-one reduction from the language 3-NAE-SAT to the language MAX-CUT, by proving its correctness. Given a 3-NAE-system T with m tuples, the mapping outputs the pair $(G^-, 5m)$, where $G^- = (V^-, E^-)$ is the graph defined from T in Reduction 3.8.29, but excluding the vertex z and all edges containing z. In the notation of Reduction 3.8.29, we have $V^- = U \cup \{y_j^i \mid i \in [m], j \in [3]\}$ as the vertex set, and $E^- = E_2 \cup E_3$ as the edge set. ◇

Exercise 3.10.62: Hypergraph splits. Let $H = (U, F)$ be a hypergraph (defined in Exercise 3.10.56). Define a **pure split** of H to be a partition (W, W') of the vertex set U such that both W and W' are nonempty, and for each edge $f \in F$, either $f \subseteq W$ or $f \subseteq W'$ holds; that is, each of the two parts is nonempty, and each edge is purely in one of the two parts. Define an **impure split** of H to be a partition (W, W') of the vertex set U where, for each edge $f \in F$, neither $f \subseteq W$ nor $f \subseteq W'$ holds; that is, no edge is purely in one of the two parts.

Define PURE-SPLIT as the language containing each hypergraph having a pure split; define IMPURE-SPLIT as the language containing each hypergraph having an impure split. For each of these two languages, prove either that it is PTIME or that it is NP-complete.   ◇

Exercise 3.10.63: The complexity of avoiding rainbows. The notion of a *hypergraph* was defined in Exercise 3.10.56; when $d \geq 1$, let us say that a hypergraph (U, F) is *d-uniform* if each edge $f \in F$ has size d. When $H = (U, F)$ is a 4-uniform hypergraph, let us say that a mapping $h: U \to \{1, 2, 3, 4\}$ is a *no-rainbow-4-coloring* of H when, for each edge $\{u_1, u_2, u_3, u_4\} \in F$, it holds that $\big|\{h(u_1), h(u_2), h(u_3), h(u_4)\}\big| \leq 3$. That is, no edge in F takes on all possible colors, under h. Let NO-RAINBOW-4-COL be the language containing each 4-uniform hypergraph H such that there exists a *surjective* no-rainbow-4-coloring of H. Prove either that this language is PTIME, or that it is NP-complete.   ◇

3.10.4   Search and enumeration

Exercise 3.10.64: Decision and search for factoring. It is known that each positive natural number can be written as a product $p_1 \cdots \cdots p_k$ of prime numbers $p_1, \ldots, p_k$; this product form is known as a **prime decomposition** of the number, and is known to be unique up to reordering the primes appearing in it. **Prime factoring** is the problem of computing, given a number, a prime decomposition of the number. While this problem is not a decision problem and is perhaps not obviously formulable as a language, in this exercise, we show that there exists a language that is PTIME if and only if this factoring problem is. To wit, define PRIME-FACTOR as the language containing each triple $\langle \ulcorner m \urcorner, \ulcorner a \urcorner, \ulcorner b \urcorner \rangle$ such that $m, a, b \in \mathbb{N}$ and there exists a prime divisor p of m satisfying $a \leq p \leq b$. To carry out this exercise, you may use the known fact that the language PRIMES is PTIME.

1. Prove that the language PRIME-FACTOR is both NP and coNP. (Hint: consider using prime decompositions as certificates.)

2. Prove that the following statements are equivalent:

    i.   PRIME-FACTOR is PTIME.

    ii. There exists a polynomial-time computable function f such that for each natural number $m \geq 2$ having a proper divisor (that is, for each composite number), it holds that $f(\ulcorner m \urcorner)$ is the encoding $\ulcorner d \urcorner$ of a proper divisor d of m.

    iii. There exists a polynomial-time computable function f' such that for each natural number $m \geq 2$, it holds that $f'(\ulcorner m \urcorner)$ is a prime decomposition of m.   ◇

Note 3.10.65: Good characterizations. The languages that are both NP and coNP—that is, the languages in $\mathbb{NP} \cap co\mathbb{NP}$—have long been referred to as those having a *good* *characterization*; for such a language, each string either has a succinct certificate of membership, or a succinct certificate of nonmembership. While it is not known whether or not $\mathcal{NP} \cap \mathrm{co}\mathcal{NP}$ is equal to $\mathcal{P}$, there are very few natural languages known to be in $\mathcal{NP} \cap \mathrm{co}\mathcal{NP}$ that are not also known to be in $\mathcal{P}$; the language PRIME-FACTOR is an example of such a language (a prime example, at that). By Exercise 3.10.64, anyone who believes that $\mathcal{NP} \cap \mathrm{co}\mathcal{NP} = \mathcal{P}$ necessarily also believes that factoring can be performed in polynomial time; contrapositively, anyone who believes that factoring cannot be performed in polynomial time perforce believes that $\mathcal{NP} \cap \mathrm{co}\mathcal{NP} \neq \mathcal{P}$.

It is surely the case that certain languages were first placed in the complexity class $\mathcal{NP} \cap \mathrm{co}\mathcal{NP}$ prior to being placed in $\mathcal{P}$. This phenomenon definitively occurred for the language PRIMES: it is straightforwardly shown to be in $\mathrm{co}\mathcal{NP}$ (see Example 3.2.21), was shown to be in $\mathcal{NP}$ in the year 1975, and was shown to be in $\mathcal{P}$ in the year 2002!   ◇

Exercise 3.10.66: From search to decision for 3-colorability. Let M be a verifier for 3-COL whose language $L(M)$ contains each pair (G, f) such that G is a graph, and f is a 3-coloring of G. Prove directly from the assumption that 3-COL is PTIME that the verifier M has a polynomial-time computable search function. That is, explicitly present a procedure computing a search function for M that makes membership queries to the language 3-COL and, aside from these queries, is implementable in polynomial time.   ◇

Exercise 3.10.67. A **minimum vertex cover** of a graph G is a vertex cover having the smallest size, over all vertex covers of G. Prove that the following are equivalent:

1. The language VERTEX-COVER is PTIME.
2. There exists a polynomial-time computable function that, given a graph G, returns the size of a minimum vertex cover of G.
3. There exists a polynomial-time computable function that, given a graph G, returns a minimum vertex cover of G.   ◇

Exercise 3.10.68. Let ϕ be a CNF-formula, and let V be the set of variables appearing in ϕ. Define a **clause-maximum assignment** of ϕ to be an assignment $f: V \rightarrow \{0, 1\}$ that satisfies the maximum number of clauses from ϕ, over all assignments from V to $\{0, 1\}$. Prove that the following are equivalent:

1. The language CNF-SAT is PTIME.
2. There exists a polynomial-time computable function that, given a CNF-formula ϕ, returns the number of clauses satisfied by a clause-maximum assignment of ϕ.
3. There exists a polynomial-time computable function that, given a CNF-formula ϕ, returns a clause-maximum assignment of ϕ.   ◇

Exercise 3.10.69: Output polynomial time. When computing functions where the output size may far exceed the input size, the notion of polynomial time may be unsuitable. For, if a function's output size cannot be bounded by a polynomial in the input size, then there is no chance for a polynomial-time DTM to even write down the output, and thus a polynomial-time DTM is automatically disqualified from computing such a function. Examples of such functions are provided by enumeration problems, where the goal is to list all objects fulfilling a criterion—for example, all satisfying assignments of a given propositional formula, of which there can be exponentially many, as a function of the formula length. To be able to discuss what it means for such a function to be efficiently computable, it is natural to relax the definition of polynomial time so as to allow an amount of time that grows as the output size does. When M is a DTM computing a function $f : \Sigma^* \to \Sigma^*$, say that M is **output-polynomial-time** if there exists a polynomial P such that, for all $x \in \Sigma^*$, it holds that $\text{time}_M(x) \leq P(|x| + |f(x)|)$.

Prove that the following are equivalent:

- The language CNF-SAT is PTIME.
- There exists an output-polynomial-time DTM computing a function f where, for each CNF-formula ϕ, it holds that $f(\phi)$ is a list of all satisfying assignments of ϕ.   ◇

3.10.5 Subproblems

When one has a language B that is not known to be polynomial-time tractable, it is very natural to seek restricted versions of the language that do exhibit tractable behavior. That is, it is natural to attempt to identify sets of instances on which the language behaves like a polynomial-time tractable language. When such a set X of instances is itself polynomial-time tractable, one can simply study the language $B \cap X$ obtained by intersecting the original language with the instances of interest. We have already done this; for example, the language 2-CNF-SAT can be viewed as the intersection of the language CNF-SAT and the set of all 2-CNF-formulas. However, it may be that the set X of instances is not itself polynomial-time tractable. So, it is useful to clarify what it means for a set X of instances to be tractable, relative to a language B. Here and in the next exercises, we identify and explore a few such notions of tractability.

Define a **subproblem** as a pair (B, X) of languages over the same alphabet Σ; the language B is conceived as the language relative to which one wants to decide membership, and the language X is conceived as containing the instances of interest. We define the following notions of tractability for subproblems.

- A subproblem (B, X) is **strongly tractable** if X is PTIME and there exists a PTIME language B' such that, for each $x \in X$, it holds that $x \in B \Leftrightarrow x \in B'$.
- A subproblem (B, X) is **robustly tractable** if there exists a superset Y of X such that (B, Y) is strongly tractable.
- A subproblem (B, X) is **promise tractable** if there exists a PTIME language B' such that, for each $x \in X$, it holds that $x \in B \Leftrightarrow x \in B'$.

It is readily verified that these notions of tractability successively weaken: any strongly tractable subproblem is robustly tractable, and any robustly tractable subproblem is promise tractable.

Exercise 3.10.70. Prove that a subproblem (B, X) is strongly tractable if and only if both X and $B \cap X$ are PTIME languages. ◇

Exercise 3.10.71. In this exercise, we characterize the introduced tractability notions, via polynomial-time DTMs that can output three values. To be precise, we consider polynomial-time DTMs computing functions $f: \Sigma^* \to \{0, 1, ?\}$, where the value ? is understood to be represented by a string other than 0 or 1. Relative to a subproblem (B, X), the output of such a function f is interpreted as follows: 0 indicates that the input string is not in B; 1 indicates that the input string is in B; and ? indicates that it is not known whether or not the input string is in B. Let us say that a function $f: \Sigma^* \to \{0, 1, ?\}$ is B-**sound** when, for each string $z \in \Sigma^*$, it holds that $f(z) = 1 \Rightarrow z \in B$, and that $f(z) = 0 \Rightarrow z \notin B$.

1. Prove that a subproblem (B, X) is strongly tractable if and only if there exists a polynomial-time computable function $f: \Sigma^* \to \{0, 1, ?\}$ that is B-sound and where, for each $z \in \Sigma^*$, it holds that $f(z) = ? \Leftrightarrow z \notin X$. So, the function f reports ignorance on precisely the strings outside of X.

2. Prove that a subproblem (B, X) is robustly tractable if and only if there exists a polynomial-time computable function $f: \Sigma^* \to \{0, 1, ?\}$ that is B-sound and where, for each $z \in \Sigma^*$, it holds that $f(z) = ? \Rightarrow z \notin X$. So, the function f reports ignorance only on strings outside of X.

    This exercise gives something of a justification for the name *robustly tractable*: a function that behaves as described gives a definitive response (0 or 1) for each string in X, and is robust in that whenever it gives a definitive response, it does so soundly.

3. Prove that a subproblem (B, X) is promise tractable if and only if there exists a polynomial-time computable function $f: \Sigma^* \to \{0, 1, ?\}$ having the property that, for each string $z \in X$, it holds that $f(z) = 1 \Rightarrow z \in B$, and that $f(z) = 0 \Rightarrow z \notin B$. This property can be taken as a notion of B-soundness relativized to the set X.

    This exercise, in turn, gives something of a justification for the name *promise tractable*: a function having the stated property produces the correct response when its input is promised to be in X, but no guarantee applies to its response when its input is outside of X. ◇

Exercise 3.10.72: Separating tractability notions. In this exercise, we separate the introduced tractability notions.

1. Prove that there exists a subproblem (B, X) that is promise tractable, but not robustly tractable.

2. Prove that there exists a subproblem (B, X) that is robustly tractable, but not strongly tractable. ◇

Note 3.10.73: Comparing tractability results. When a subproblem is strongly tractable, it is also robustly tractable. But should a *strongly tractable* result be viewed as preferable to a *robustly tractable* result? On the one hand, when a subproblem (B, X) is strongly tractable, the set X of instances is itself PTIME and thus has a low-complexity characterization; but on the other hand, when (B, X) is robustly tractable, one has strong tractability of a subproblem (B, Y) where Y contains all instances in X, and possibly more!   ◇

3.10.6   Counting

Relative to an NP language, each instance can be viewed as posing the question of whether or not a desired object *exists*. An NP language naturally extends to the counting problem where for each instance, the goal is to count the *number* of desired objects. We here study counting problems, some associated complexity classes, and notions of reduction for comparing such problems.

Fix the alphabet Σ as $\{0, 1\}$. Define a **counting problem** as a mapping from Σ^* to $\mathbb{N}$. We define the following complexity classes of counting problems.

- Define $\mathcal{FP}$ as the set containing each counting problem $h\colon \Sigma^* \to \mathbb{N}$ such that there exists a polynomial-time computable function g where, for each string $x \in \Sigma^*$, it holds that $\ulcorner h(x) \urcorner = g(x)$. (That is, it is required that the map sending each string x to the encoding $\ulcorner h(x) \urcorner$ of the number $h(x)$ is polynomial-time computable.)

- Define #$\mathcal{P}$ as the set containing each counting problem $h\colon \Sigma^* \to \mathbb{N}$ such that there exists a verifier M where, for each string $x \in \Sigma^*$, it holds that $h(x) = \left| \left\{ y \mid \langle x, y \rangle \in L(M) \right\} \right|$. That is, for each string x, the value $h(x)$ is the number of certificates that x has, relative to the verifier M.

  In this definition, when M is a verifier for a language B, computing $h(x)$ is at least as hard as determining whether or not x is in B: it holds that $x \in B$ if and only if $h(x) > 0$, that is, if and only if the number of certificates is positive.

The classes $\mathcal{FP}$ and #$\mathcal{P}$ can be viewed as counting analogs of the classes $\mathcal{P}$ and $\mathcal{NP}$, respectively. We remark that #$\mathcal{P}$ can alternatively be characterized as containing a counting problem h when there exists a polynomial-time NTM N such that, for each string x, the value $h(x)$ is the number of accepting computations of N on input string x; here, by *accepting computation*, we mean a computation that ends with an accepting configuration.

A first example of a counting problem in #$\mathcal{P}$ is #CIRCUIT-SAT, which we define as mapping each circuit C to the number of satisfying assignments $f\colon \{v_1, ..., v_n\} \to \{0, 1\}$ of C; we here use $v_1, ..., v_n$ to denote the inputs of C. Here and in the sequel, we understand a counting problem to be defined as 0 on any string not explicitly discussed. Each of the propositional satisfiability problems studied so far also naturally gives rise to a counting problem in #$\mathcal{P}$: map each formula (or system) under consideration to the number of satisfying assignments $f\colon V \to \{0, 1\}$, where V is the set of all variables occurring in the formula (or system). In this way, we obtain counting problems #3-CNF-SAT, #4-NAE-SAT, and so on.

Exercise 3.10.74: Closure properties of #$\mathcal{P}$. It is relatively straightforward to argue that the complexity class $\mathcal{FP}$ is closed under addition ($+$) and multiplication ($\cdot$); these closure properties follow quite directly from the fact that addition and multiplication of natural numbers can be performed in polynomial time. Here, you are to establish that the complexity class #$\mathcal{P}$ also enjoys these closure properties.

1. Prove that for any two counting problems h, h' in #$\mathcal{P}$, it holds that $h + h'$ is in #$\mathcal{P}$.
2. Prove that for any two counting problems h, h' in #$\mathcal{P}$, it holds that $h \cdot h'$ is in #$\mathcal{P}$.

The sum $h + h'$ of two mappings $h, h' \colon \Sigma^* \to \mathbb{N}$ is defined by $(h + h')(x) = h(x) + h'(x)$, for each string $x \in \Sigma^*$. The product $h \cdot h'$ is defined analogously.   ◊

Note 3.10.75: Parsimonious reductions. The most basic form of reduction that is commonly used to compare counting problems is that of *parsimonious reduction*. Suppose that $g, h \colon \Sigma^* \to \mathbb{N}$ are counting problems; a **parsimonious reduction** from g to h is a polynomial-time computable function $\rho \colon \Sigma^* \to \Sigma^*$ such that, for each string $x \in \Sigma^*$, it holds that $g(x) = h(\rho(x))$.

Let M and N be verifiers for NP languages B and C, respectively. When g and h are counting problems in #$\mathcal{P}$ arising from the verifiers M and N, a parsimonious reduction ρ from g to h is also a polynomial-time many-one reduction from B to C. This is because a parsimonious reduction maps each string x to a string $\rho(x)$ in such a way that the number of certificates x has under M is equal to the number of certificates $\rho(x)$ has under N; in particular, there thus exists a certificate of x under M—that is, $x \in B$—if and only if there exists a certificate of $\rho(x)$ under N—that is, $\rho(x) \in C$. Consequently, in attempting to define a parsimonious reduction between two verifiers' counting problems, it is natural to start from a many-one reduction between the verifiers' NP languages.

It is known that the counting problem #CIRCUIT-SAT is complete for #$\mathcal{P}$ under parsimonious reductions: this problem is in #$\mathcal{P}$, and is hard for #$\mathcal{P}$ in that each problem in #$\mathcal{P}$ admits a parsimonious reduction to it. This hardness of #CIRCUIT-SAT can be derived from an examination of the proof of Theorem 3.6.12. The counting problem #3-CNF-SAT is another problem complete for #$\mathcal{P}$.

In Section 3.4.1, we considered a few problems—INDEP-SET, CLIQUE, and VERTEX-COVER—where an instance consists of a graph G and a number k, and the question is whether or not there is a size k set of vertices satisfying some property—for example, forming an independent set, in the case of INDEP-SET. We obtain the counting problems #INDEP-SET, #CLIQUE, and #VERTEX-COVER by asking for the *number* of size k sets of vertices satisfying the respective property. It is straightforwardly verified that the many-one reductions given in Section 3.4.1 are parsimonious reductions between the corresponding counting problems. For example, the number of size k independent sets in a graph is equal to the number of size k cliques in the graph's complement, so graph complementation (as deployed in Proposition 3.4.7) yields a parsimonious reduction from #INDEP-SET to #CLIQUE. ◇

Exercise 3.10.76: Closure under parsimonious reductions. This exercise asks you to show that the two introduced classes of counting problems are closed under parsimonious reductions (presented in Note 3.10.75).

1. Prove that the complexity class $\mathcal{FP}$ is closed under parsimonious reductions. That is, prove that when $g, h \colon \Sigma^* \to \mathbb{N}$ are counting problems where $h \in \mathcal{FP}$ holds and there exists a parsimonious reduction from g to h, then $g \in \mathcal{FP}$ holds.
2. Prove that the complexity class #$\mathcal{P}$ is closed under parsimonious reductions. ◇

Exercise 3.10.77. In this exercise, we consider parsimonious reductions (defined in Note 3.10.75) between particular concrete languages.

1. Argue that Reduction 3.8.34 is *not* a parsimonious reduction from #3-CNF-SAT to #INDEP-SET.
2. Give a function that is a parsimonious reduction from #3-CNF-SAT to #INDEP-SET, and prove that it is a parsimonious reduction.
3. State whether or not Reduction 3.8.50 is a parsimonious reduction from #DI-HAM-PATH to #HAM-PATH, and prove your assertion. As should be expected, #HAM-PATH and #DI-HAM-PATH are the counting problems where an instance is a triple (G, s, t) consisting of a graph or digraph G (respectively) having s and t as vertices; such an instance is mapped to the number of (s, t)-Hamiltonian paths in G. ◇

Exercise 3.10.78: Turing reductions. Parsimonious reductions (from Note 3.10.75) are not general enough to relate pairs of counting problems in #$\mathcal{P}$ that have the same status as regards containment in $\mathcal{FP}$. This can occur for at least a couple of different reasons. Some counting problems may only have certain types of numbers in their images; for example, since each NAE-system has an even number of satisfying assignments (recall Proposition 3.8.19), there is no way to present (for example) a parsimonious reduction from #3-CNF-SAT to #4-NAE-SAT, since there are most certainly 3-CNF-formulas having an odd number of satisfying assignments. It also occurs—as this exercise shows—that there are problems whose decision version is known to be PTIME, but whose natural counting version is hard; to such a problem, there is not much hope for giving a parsimonious reduction from a problem whose decision version is NP-complete: this would imply a many-one reduction from an NP-complete language to a PTIME language, and thus that $\mathcal{P} = \mathcal{NP}$!

A more general notion of reduction, under which the class $\mathcal{FP}$ is closed, is that of **polynomial-time Turing reduction**, under which a counting problem g reduces to a counting problem h when there exists a polynomial-time algorithm for g that may make black-box queries to h, and receive the answers immediately (in one time step). In the following exercises, you are to show, in a number of situations, that one counting problem g is in $\mathcal{FP}$ assuming that a second counting problem h is in $\mathcal{FP}$. The suggested way to proceed is to give a polynomial-time algorithm for computing g which makes black-box use of a polynomial-time algorithm for computing h—thus, in essence, exhibiting a Turing reduction from g to h.

1. Prove that #DNF-SAT $\in \mathcal{FP}$ if and only if #CNF-SAT $\in \mathcal{FP}$.
2. Prove that #3-CNF-SAT $\in \mathcal{FP}$ if and only if #CNF-SAT $\in \mathcal{FP}$.
3. Prove that #POS-CNF-SAT $\in \mathcal{FP}$ if and only if #CNF-SAT $\in \mathcal{FP}$.
4. Prove that #4-NAE-SAT $\in \mathcal{FP}$ if and only if #3-CNF-SAT $\in \mathcal{FP}$.

Here, #DNF-SAT is defined as the problem of counting the satisfying assignments of a DNF-formula, and #POS-CNF-SAT is defined as the problem of counting the satisfying assignments of a positive CNF-formula (defined in Exercise 3.10.40). ◇

Note 3.10.79: Needles in haystacks. The class of NP languages, as well as each of the NP-complete languages, are often colorfully said to characterize the difficulty of finding a needle in a haystack; a more precise analogy would be to the difficulty of determining if there *exists* a needle in a haystack! The difficulty of so *finding* a needle would be more accurately linked to the search functions studied in Section 3.9.

And if we want to continue with the analogy, we can identify the counting problems in #$\mathcal{P}$ as characterizing the difficulty of *counting* the number of needles in a haystack, a task which is evidently at least as hard as determining if there exists a needle in a haystack. ◇

3.11 Bibliographic discussion

The modern study of resource-bounded computation is viewed as originating with an article of Hartmanis and Stearns (1965), entitled "On the Computational Complexity of Algorithms," whose investigation focused on time-bounded Turing machines. Early systematic discussions on the useability of polynomial time as a formalization of efficient computation were given in the mid 1960s by Cobham (1965) and Edmonds (1965b). An informal discussion of nondeterministic polynomial-time computation was given by Edmonds (1965a); the notion of *good characterization*, as presented in Note 3.10.65, is credited to this discussion. Some of the notions in these early works on computational complexity were studied in the then-Soviet Union starting from the 1950s, as described in a survey by Trakhtenbrot (1984); this literature contains early appearances of the question of whether or not exhaustive search—referred to as *perebor* in the Russian language—can be improved upon, for natural problems. A presentation of the history of computational complexity is given by Fortnow and Homer (2003).

The first NP-completeness results were proved independently in the early 1970s by Cook (1971) and Levin (1973); the NP-completeness of the language CNF-SAT, given in this book by Theorem 3.8.13, is often referred to as the *Cook-Levin theorem*. Subsequently, an article of Karp (1972) used polynomial-time many-one reductions to show the NP-completeness of 21 problems, the majority of which make an appearance in the present chapter. The adoption of the term *NP-complete* is due to an article of Knuth (1974). Ladner's theorem, discussed in Note 3.10.26, is due to Ladner (1975). In the late 1970s, a comprehensive book examination of the theory of NP-completeness at the time was published by Garey and Johnson (1979). Surveys on the P versus NP question include those of Sipser (1992), Wigderson (2007), Allender (2009), and Aaronson (2016). For further reading on philosophical aspects of the P versus NP question, the reader is directed to articles of Wigderson (2009) and Aaronson (2013).

The result that the language PRIMES is PTIME, mentioned in Example 3.2.21, is due to Agrawal, Kayal, and Saxena (2004). Our treatment of satisfiability problems in Section 3.8.1 is based on that of the book by Moore and Mertens (2011). The presentation of Reduction 3.8.46, which shows the NP-hardness of DI-HAM-PATH, is based on the presentation of a similar reduction by Erickson (2019, Chapter 12).

The notion of proof system and its accompanying notions, as presented in Exercise 3.10.13, are due to Cook and Reckhow (1979). Exercise 3.10.63 on no-rainbow-colorings is based on work of Zhuk (2021) and Chen (2020). Our presentation of notions of subproblem tractability in Section 3.10.5 is based on discussions of Chen and Dalmau (2005) and Chen (2017, Section 10). An early discussion of the notion of *output polynomial time* was given by Johnson, Papadimitriou, and Yannakakis (1988). The study of counting complexity, as covered in Section 3.10.6, has origins in an article of Valiant (1979); see also the references therein.

In addition to the general references on the theory of computation given in Section 1.10, we can name the books by Arora and Barak (2009), Goldreich (2008, 2010), and Wigderson (2019) as general references on complexity theory. General references on algorithms include the books by Cormen, Leiserson, Rivest, and Stein (2009); Dasgupta, Papadimitriou, and Vazirani (2008); Erickson (2019); and Kleinberg and Tardos (2006).

4 Further Complexity Theory

> L'amour, c'est l'espace et le temps rendus sensibles au coeur.
> — Marcel Proust, *La Prisonnière*

> How much wood would a woodchuck chuck
> if a woodchuck could chuck wood?
> — English-language tongue-twister

In this chapter, we explore a number of further topics in complexity theory. The previous chapter focused on *time-bounded* computation; in Section 4.1, we offer an initiation to *space-bounded* computation. Next, in Section 4.2, we present *hierarchy theorems*; the first such theorem formalizes the claim that Turing machines having more time can decide languages that are not decidable by Turing machines having less time, and a second hierarchy theorem is analogous, but addresses the resource of *space* in place of *time*. Section 4.3 introduces a relaxation of polynomial-time tractability called *fixed-parameter tractability*, whereby computation time is measured both in terms of input string length as well as a *parameter* associated to each input string. A complexity-theoretic framework complementing this tractability notion is presented in Section 4.4; the framework, known as *parameterized complexity theory*, allows one to present evidence of non-tractability. Finally, Section 4.5 presents a complexity-theoretic framework for studying the *compilability* of problems; many concepts in this framework can be viewed as restrictions of concepts in parameterized complexity theory.

Throughout this chapter, we assume by default that each language is over the alphabet $\Sigma = \{0, 1\}$. Also, when $P, U \colon \mathbb{N} \to \mathbb{N}$ are functions on the natural numbers, we throughout use $P \circ U$ to denote the composed function that maps each number $n \in \mathbb{N}$ to $P(U(n))$.

4.1 Space complexity

While the previous chapter focused on studying computations that were bounded in terms of *time*, this section examines the effects of bounding the amount of *space* with which computations may work. We will see that, as a computational resource, *space* exhibits a behavior quite qualitatively different from that of *time*. Crucially, and in strong contrast to time, it is possible to reuse space: over the course of a computation, the contents of a memory unit can be rewritten numerous times. In addition, when space restrictions are imposed, nondeterministic computation is provably not much more powerful than deterministic computation.

4.1.1 Space-bounded computation

We begin by defining the amount of space that a halting Turing machine M uses on an input string x, a quantity that we denote by $\text{space}_M(x)$. The definition is somewhat analogous to the corresponding definition for time, but instead of measuring the amount of time elapsed prior to halting, here we measure the number of distinct tape cells accessed prior to halting. For a computation, this number is equal to the rightmost tape index accessed, since each Turing machine begins with its head at the leftmost tape index (namely, index 1).

Definition 4.1.1. Let M be a halting DTM or a halting NTM with input alphabet Σ. Define the function $\text{space}_M \colon \Sigma^* \to \mathbb{N}$ as follows. Let $x \in \Sigma^*$ be an input string.

- When M is a halting DTM, the value $\text{space}_M(x)$ is defined as the number of distinct tape cells accessed by the head of M, during the computation of M on x.
- When M is a halting NTM, the value $\text{space}_M(x)$ is defined as the maximum number of distinct tape cells accessed by the head of M, over all computations of M on x.

To give a formal definition of $\text{space}_M(x)$, let α_x denote the initial configuration of M on x. Then, $\text{space}_M(x)$ is the maximum value, over all configurations γ with $\alpha_x \vdash_M^* \gamma$, of the head location of γ. ◇

We next introduce a definition that allows us to discuss bounds on the space that a Turing machine uses, over all input strings. As we did when treating time as a resource, we bound the amount of space used as a function of the input string length.

Definition 4.1.2. Let M be a DTM or an NTM, and let $S \colon \mathbb{N} \to \mathbb{N}$ be a function. We say that M **runs within space** S if M is halting and it holds that $\text{space}_M(x) \le S(|x|)$, for each string $x \in \Sigma^*$. ◇

Definition 4.1.2 is intended for use with functions $S \colon \mathbb{N} \to \mathbb{N}$ where $S(n) \ge n$, that is, where the amount of space allowed is at least the input string length. There are established ways to discuss space bounds where the amount of allowed space is less than the input string length; such bounds are typically formalized using a computational model where there is a workspace apart from the input string, and the input string must be accessed in a read-only fashion.[28]

The next proposition morally says that *space is at least as valuable as time*: whatever can be done within a certain amount of time, can also be done within that amount of space.

Proposition 4.1.3. *Suppose that M is a DTM or an NTM that runs within time T*: $\mathbb{N} \to \mathbb{N}$. *Then, M runs within space T.*

Proposition 4.1.3 follows from the observation that in the kth configuration of a computation, the head location must be k or less: the head begins at location 1, and its location can increase by at most 1 whenever one transition is made.

We just observed a space bound on time-bounded Turing machines. In the other direction, the following proposition provides a time bound on space-bounded Turing machines.

Proposition 4.1.4. *Let S*: $\mathbb{N} \to \mathbb{N}$ *be a function; suppose that M is a DTM or an NTM that runs within space S. Then, there exists a constant c > 1 such that M runs within time c^S.*

Proof. Based on the machine M, we can define an alphabet Δ having the following property: in any computation where the head stays within the initial k tape locations, each configuration can be represented by a string of length k over Δ, that is, by an element of Δ^k. Specifically, the alphabet Δ can be defined so that each symbol can represent the following information about a tape location: the location's tape symbol, an indication of whether or not the head is located at the corresponding location, and the state of the machine when the head is so located.[29]

Suppose that x is an input string, and set $k = \text{space}_M(x)$. Consider a computation of M on the input x. Since the head always stays within the initial k tape locations, we can specify each configuration by a string of length k over the alphabet Δ, where the string's symbols correspond to the tape locations $1, \dots, k$, respectively. Since the machine M is halting, no computation repeats a configuration, and thus, in any computation of M on x, the total number of configurations is at most $|\Delta|^k$, the number of length k strings over Δ. The proposition thus holds with $c = |\Delta|$. □

---

28. For more information, see Section 4.6.2.

29. Precisely, the alphabet Δ can be defined as the set $\Gamma \times (Q \cup \{\bot\})$, which appeared in the proof of Theorem 3.6.15; here, the set Γ is the tape alphabet of M, the set Q is the state set of M, and $\bot$ is an extra symbol outside of Q. A configuration is represented by a string $(a_1, q_1)\dots(a_k, q_k)$ when (for each i) the symbol a_i is the symbol in the configuration's ith tape cell; and the value q_i is equal to the configuration's state if the configuration's head location is i, and is equal to $\bot$ otherwise. We refer the interested reader to the mentioned proof for more details and discussion.

4.1.2 PSPACE languages

We saw in the previous chapter that bounding computation time by polynomials gave rise to a robust and relevant theory. We next focus on analogously bounding computation space by polynomials, and studying the resulting language classes.

Definition 4.1.5. Let M be a DTM or an NTM; we say that M **runs within polynomial space** if there exists a polynomial $P \colon \mathbb{N} \to \mathbb{N}$ such that M runs within space P. We define a **polynomial-space DTM** to be a DTM that runs within polynomial space; likewise, we define a **polynomial-space NTM** to be an NTM that runs within polynomial space. ◇

We next name the languages decidable by DTMs running within polynomial space.

Definition 4.1.6. A language B is **PSPACE** if there exists a polynomial-space DTM M such that $B = L(M)$. We use the notation $\mathcal{PSPACE}$ to denote the class containing each language that is PSPACE. ◇

Our observation that space is at least as valuable as time, Proposition 4.1.3, implies that any polynomial-time DTM is also a polynomial-space DTM, which in turn entails the following fact.

Proposition 4.1.7. *Each language that is PTIME is also PSPACE. (That is, the containment $\mathcal{P} \subseteq \mathcal{PSPACE}$ holds.)*

Closure properties

The PSPACE languages are closed under complementation: for any polynomial-space DTM M, the DTM derived from M by interchanging the accept and reject states is a polynomial-space DTM whose language is the complement of $L(M)$.

Proposition 4.1.8. *If B is a PSPACE language, then its complement $\overline{B}$ is also a PSPACE language.*

The PSPACE languages are also closed under intersection and union.

Proposition 4.1.9. *If B and C are PSPACE languages, then $B \cap C$ and $B \cup C$ are also PSPACE languages.*

Proof. Let M_B and M_C be polynomial-space DTMs whose languages are B and C, respectively. Consider the DTM M that makes a copy of its input string; invokes M_B on the copy; clears its tape so that just the original input string is left; invokes M_C on the original input string; and then accepts if both invocations accepted, and rejects otherwise. This DTM has $L(M) = B \cap C$; we can obtain a DTM with language $B \cup C$ simply by appropriately adjusting the rule for acceptance. On each input string x, the space needed to keep a copy of x is around $|x|$ cells; putting this aside, we can estimate $\mathrm{space}_M(x)$ as $\max(\mathrm{space}_{M_B}(x), \mathrm{space}_{M_C}(x))$. That is, we can estimate the space usage of M as the *maximum* space usage of the two invoked DTMs; let us remark that the time usage of M would be reasonably estimated as the *sum* of the time usage of the two invoked DTMs. For the purposes of arguing that the DTM M is polynomial-space, we observe that $\max(\text{space}_{M_B}(x), \text{space}_{M_C}(x)) \leq \text{space}_{M_B}(x) + \text{space}_{M_C}(x)$ for each string x. Letting P_B and P_C be polynomials such that M_B and M_C run within space P_B and P_C, respectively, we can then estimate that M runs within space $P_B + P_C$. $\qquad \square$

Relationships

We can directly relate the PSPACE languages to the NP languages and the coNP languages.

Proposition 4.1.10. *Each language that is NP is also PSPACE. (That is, the containment* $\mathcal{NP} \subseteq \mathcal{PSPACE}$ *holds.)*

Proposition 4.1.10 is essentially argued by presenting, for each NP language B, a polynomial-space DTM that when run on an input string x, exhaustively searches for a certificate for x, relative to a verifier for B. By ecologically reusing tape cells, this exhaustive search can be performed in a polynomial amount of space.

Proof. Suppose that B is an NP language. By the verifier characterization of the NP languages (Theorem 3.2.26), there exists a verifier for B, implying that there exists a polynomial-time DTM M and a polynomial P such that a string x is in B if and only if there exists a string y where $|y| \leq P(|x|)$ and $\langle x, y \rangle \in L(M)$.

Consider a DTM M^+ behaving as follows: on an input string x, it loops over each string y such that $|y| \leq P(|x|)$, and invokes M on the pair $\langle x, y \rangle$; the DTM accepts if at least one invocation of M accepts, and rejects otherwise. This DTM M^+ clearly has B as its language. Such a DTM M^+ can be implemented to run within polynomial space: at any point in time, the working value of y can be maintained using space at most $P(|x|)$, and the invocations of M can each use the same space. Letting Q be a polynomial such that M runs within time Q, we can estimate $\text{space}_{M^+}(x)$ as the amount of space needed to maintain x and the working value of y, plus the amount of space used by each invocation of M; so, we can estimate

$$\text{space}_{M^+}(x) \leq |x| + P(|x|) + \max_y Q(|\langle x, y \rangle|),$$

where the maximum is taken over all strings y with $|y| \leq P(|x|)$. From this estimate and the closure of polynomials under addition and composition, it is evident that the DTM M^+ is a polynomial-space DTM. Observe that this DTM M^+ heavily reuses space; the working value of y is changed, in general, an exponential number of times, and the DTM M is invoked on each such value. $\qquad \square$

We saw that the complement of any PSPACE language is also PSPACE (Proposition 4.1.8); the following fact thus follows directly from Proposition 4.1.10.

Proposition 4.1.11. *Each language that is coNP is also PSPACE. (That is, the containment* $\mathcal{coNP} \subseteq \mathcal{PSPACE}$ *holds.)*

Each of Propositions 4.1.10 and 4.1.11 strengthens and implies Proposition 4.1.7's containment $\mathcal{P} \subseteq \mathcal{PSPACE}$, in light of the containments $\mathcal{P} \subseteq \mathcal{NP}$ and $\mathcal{P} \subseteq \mathcal{coNP}$.

Each DTM that runs within polynomial space is halting by definition, implying the folowing fact.

Proposition 4.1.12. *Each language that is PSPACE is also computable.*

Remark 4.1.13. At the time of writing, the question of whether $\mathcal{P} = \mathcal{PSPACE}$ is open. Due to the containments $\mathcal{P} \subseteq \mathcal{NP} \subseteq \mathcal{PSPACE}$, a proof that $\mathcal{P} \neq \mathcal{NP}$ would imply that $\mathcal{P} \neq \mathcal{PSPACE}$.   ◇

4.1.3 PSPACE-completeness

We next turn to develop a completeness theory for PSPACE.

Definition 4.1.14. We define hardness and completeness for the PSPACE languages as follows.

- A language B is **PSPACE-hard** if for each PSPACE language A, it holds that $A \leq_m^p B$.
- A language B is **PSPACE-complete** if it is PSPACE and it is PSPACE-hard.   ◇

Defining hardness and completeness for the PSPACE languages with respect to polynomial-time many-one reductions allows us to meaningfully relate these conditions to the conditions of being PTIME, NP, or coNP: for example, it is straightforwardly verified that when B is a PSPACE-complete language, it holds that B is PTIME if and only if every PSPACE language is PTIME. (The issue of how the computational power of a reduction notion relates to its use was previously discussed in Remark 3.4.16.)

The closure of the PSPACE languages under reduction is a basic fact.

Theorem 4.1.15. *Suppose that B and C are languages such that $B \leq_m^p C$. If C is PSPACE, then B is PSPACE.*

We omit the proof of this theorem; it can be established using argumentation similar to that in the proof of the closure of the PTIME languages under polynomial-time many-one reduction (Theorem 3.4.14).

Quantified propositional formulas

We will establish the PSPACE-completeness of a generalization of the satisfiability problem for propositional formulas. This generalization deals with the following extended notion of propositional formula, where quantification over propositional variables is allowed.

Definition 4.1.16. We define a **quantified propositional formula** (for short, **qp-formula**) as a formula that can be derived by applying the following rules a finite number of times.

- v is a qp-formula, for each variable v.
- $\neg\phi$ is a qp-formula, when ϕ is a qp-formula.

- $\phi \vee \phi'$ is a qp-formula, when ϕ and ϕ' are qp-formulas.
- $\phi \wedge \phi'$ is a qp-formula, when ϕ and ϕ' are qp-formulas.
- $\exists v \phi$ is a qp-formula, when v is a variable and ϕ is a qp-formula.
- $\forall v \phi$ is a qp-formula, when v is a variable and ϕ is a qp-formula.
- (ϕ) is a qp-formula, when ϕ is a qp-formula.

To present qp-formulas, we use the following standard shorthand notations. When ϕ and ϕ' are qp-formulas, we use $\phi \rightarrow \phi'$ to denote the formula $(\neg \phi) \vee \phi'$, and we use $\phi \leftrightarrow \phi'$ to denote the formula $(\phi \rightarrow \phi') \wedge (\phi' \rightarrow \phi)$. When $Q \in \{\exists, \forall\}$ is a quantifier and $w_1, \dots, w_k$ is a sequence of variables, we use $Qw_1, \dots, w_k$ to denote $Qw_1 \dots Qw_k$. ◇

We generally use parenthesization to specify the order of evaluation in qp-formulas. We say that a qp-formula ψ **has the form** $\phi \wedge \phi'$ when there exist qp-formulas ϕ and ϕ' such that ψ is syntactically equal to $\phi \wedge \phi'$, and when evaluating ψ, each of ϕ and ϕ' are evaluated prior to considering the connective $\wedge$. We define in a similar fashion what it means to **have the form** $\phi \vee \phi'$, $\neg \phi$, $\exists v \phi$, and $\forall v \phi$. We say that a qp-formula ψ **has the form** (ϕ) simply when there exists a qp-formula ϕ such that ψ is syntactically equal to (ϕ).

When working with a usual propositional formula, we spoke of an assignment *satisfying* or *not satisfying* the formula when the assignment was defined on all variables appearing in the formula. In discussing satisfaction of a qp-formula ψ by an assignment, due to the potential presence of quantification, the assignment does not always need to be defined on all variables appearing in ψ; rather, it suffices that the assignment be defined on all *free variables* of ψ.

Definition 4.1.17. For each qp-formula ψ, we inductively define the set of **free variables** of ψ, denoted by free(ψ), as follows.

- free(v) = $\{v\}$, for each variable v.
- free(ψ) = free(ϕ), when ψ has the form $\neg \phi$.
- free(ψ) = free(ϕ) $\cup$ free(ϕ'), when ψ has the form $\phi \vee \phi'$ or $\phi \wedge \phi'$.
- free(ψ) – free(ϕ) $\setminus \{v\}$, when ψ has the form $\exists v \phi$ or $\forall v \phi$.
- free(ψ) = free(ϕ), when ψ has the form (ϕ). ◇

We can next define satisfaction of a qp-formula by an assignment.

Definition 4.1.18. Let ψ be a quantified propositional formula, and let $f \colon V \rightarrow \{0, 1\}$ be an assignment defined on each variable in free(ψ), that is, where free(ψ) $\subseteq V$. We define what it means for f to **satisfy** ψ, denoted $f \models \psi$, by the following rules.

- $f \models v$ iff $f(v) = 1$.
- $f \models \psi$ iff $f \models \phi$ does not hold, when ψ has the form $\neg \phi$.
- $f \models \psi$ iff $f \models \phi$ or $f \models \phi'$, when ψ has the form $\phi \vee \phi'$.
- $f \models \psi$ iff $f \models \phi$ and $f \models \phi'$, when ψ has the form $\phi \wedge \phi'$.

- $f \models \psi$ iff $f[v \mapsto 0] \models \phi$ or $f[v \mapsto 1] \models \phi$, when ψ has the form $\exists v \phi$.
- $f \models \psi$ iff $f[v \mapsto 0] \models \phi$ and $f[v \mapsto 1] \models \phi$, when ψ has the form $\forall v \phi$.   ◇

We define a **quantified propositional sentence** (for short, **qp-sentence**) as a quantified propositional formula ψ such that free(ψ) = $\emptyset$. We say that a qp-sentence ψ is **true** if there exists an assignment that satisfies ψ, and is **false** otherwise. It can be verified that, for a qp-sentence ψ, any assignment satisfies ψ if and only if any other assignment satisfies ψ; thus, ψ is satisfiable if and only if every assignment satisfies ψ.

Example 4.1.19. Consider a propositional formula ψ which makes no use of quantification, and let $u_1, \ldots, u_n$ denote the variables occurring in ψ. We have free(ψ) = $\{u_1, \ldots, u_n\}$. The question of whether ψ is satisfiable can be formulated as the question of whether the qp-sentence $\exists u_1 \ldots \exists u_n(\psi)$ is true: by the definitions, this qp-sentence is true if and only if there exists an assignment $f \colon \{u_1, \ldots, u_n\} \to \{0, 1\}$ that satisfies ψ.   ◇

Example 4.1.20. Let us denote assignments as sets of pairs, so for example, $\{(x, 0), (y, 1)\}$ denotes the assignment defined on $\{x, y\}$ that maps x to 0, and y to 1.

Let θ denote the propositional formula $(x \vee y) \wedge (\neg x \vee \neg y)$; we have free($\theta$) = $\{x, y\}$. The formula θ has two satisfying assignments defined on $\{x, y\}$, namely, $\{(x, 0), (y, 1)\}$ and $\{(x, 1), (y, 0)\}$. Thus, the qp-formula $\exists y(\theta)$, which has free($\exists y(\theta)$) = $\{x\}$, has two satisfying assignments defined on $\{x\}$, namely, $\{(x, 0)\}$ and $\{(x, 1)\}$. It follows that each of the qp-sentences

$$\forall x \exists y(\theta) \quad \text{and} \quad \exists x \exists y(\theta)$$

is true; each is satisfied by the empty assignment $\emptyset$ that is not defined on any variables. On the other hand, the qp-formula $\forall y(\theta)$, which has free($\forall y(\theta)$) = $\{x\}$, is seen to have no satisfying assignments. Thus, each of the qp-sentences

$$\exists x \forall y(\theta) \quad \text{and} \quad \forall x \forall y(\theta)$$

is false.

The formula θ' defined as $(x \vee y)$ has 3 satisfying assignments defined on $\{x, y\}$, namely, $\{(x, 0), (y, 1)\}$ $\{(x, 1), (y, 0)\}$, and $\{(x, 1), (y, 1)\}$. The qp-sentence $\forall y(\theta')$ is thus satisfied by $\{(x, 1)\}$, but not $\{(x, 0)\}$. Consequently, the qp-sentence $\exists x \forall y(\theta')$ is true, but the qp-sentence $\forall x \forall y(\theta')$ is false.   ◇

Completeness of quantified satisfiability

Define QSAT to be the language containing each true qp-sentence. We show that this language is PSPACE-complete; we begin by arguing that it is PSPACE.

Proposition 4.1.21. QSAT *is PSPACE.*

In this proof and in the sequel, we will say that a first quantity is **linear in** a second quantity if there exists a linear (degree 1) polynomial L such that, for any instances j and i of the first and second quantity, respectively, it holds that $j \leq L(i)$. We define **quadratic in** similarly, but with respect to quadratic (degree 2) polynomials; we also define **polynomial in** analogously, with respect to all polynomials.

Proof. We argue this proposition by first presenting an algorithm Satisfies(f, ψ) which is implementable by a polynomial-space DTM, as follows. The algorithm decides, given an assignment $f\colon V \to \{0,1\}$ and a qp-formula ψ such that free(ψ) $\subseteq V$, whether or not $f \models \psi$. The algorithm is defined recursively, following the rules given in Definition 4.1.18. For example, when ψ has the form $\phi \wedge \phi'$, the algorithm calls itself recursively on (f, ϕ) and (f, ϕ') in sequence and by reusing space, and accepts if and only if both of the recursive calls accepted. As another example, when ψ has the form $\exists v\phi$, the algorithm calls itself recursively on $(f[v \mapsto 0], \phi)$ and $(f[v \mapsto 1], \phi)$ in sequence and by reusing space, and accepts if and only if at least one of the recursive calls accepted. In each case, the algorithm calls itself recursively on a pair whose formula is strictly smaller than the formula ψ that it was given. Thus, when this algorithm is invoked on a pair (f, ψ), the number of nested recursive calls at any moment is bounded above by the length of ψ. Also, it can be seen that for any pair (g, ϕ) on which such a recursive call is made, the pair (g, ϕ) has a representation of size linear in the representation size of (f, ψ): whenever an invocation Satisfies(h, ψ) calls itself on a pair (h', ψ') where h' is different from h, it holds that h' has the form $h[v \mapsto b]$, where v is a variable such that $\psi = \exists v\psi'$ or $\psi = \forall v\psi'$, so an occurrence of the variable v has been removed in passing from ψ to ψ'. The algorithm thus admits an implementation that runs within space quadratic in the input size.

To decide the truth of a given qp-sentence ψ, one can simply check if the *empty assignment* not defined on any variable satisfies ψ. So, letting $\emptyset$ denote this empty assignment, one can simply invoke Satisfies($\emptyset, \psi$) to decide the truth of ψ. $\square$

Let us next focus on establishing PSPACE-hardness of the language QSAT. We will deal with space-bounded machines, and will work with representations of machine configurations. The following is a notion of space consumption for individual configurations.

Definition 4.1.22. When $p \geq 1$ is a value, we say that a configuration $[q, \tau, \ell]$ of a DTM or an NTM **consumes at most space** p when the head location ℓ satisfies $\ell \leq p$, and each location $i > p$ has $\tau(i) = \sqcup$. $\diamond$

So, a configuration that *consumes at most space* p can be described by the status of the first p tape cells: these cells contain all of the tape's non-blank symbols, and the head is located among them. A key property of this definition is the following.

Proposition 4.1.23. *Suppose that $S\colon \mathbb{N} \to \mathbb{N}$ is a function with $S(i) \geq i$ (for each $i \in \mathbb{N}$), and that M is a DTM or an NTM that runs within space S. When M is invoked on an input string of length n, each configuration consumes at most space $S(n)$.*

To argue this proposition, consider a computation of M on an input string of length n. First observe that, since M runs within space S, the head of M never ventures beyond the

$S(n)$th tape cell. Combining this observation with the assumption that $S(n) \geq n$, we obtain that all tape cells strictly beyond the $S(n)$th remain equal to the blank symbol $\sqcup$.

To prove the PSPACE-hardness of QSAT, we need to present, for each polynomial-space DTM M, a reduction from the language $L(M)$ to the language QSAT. Our reduction will map each string x to a qp-formula which (in effect) asserts that, starting from the initial configuration of M on x, the accepting configuration is reachable via a sequence of transitions. We will use the following definition, which facilitates discussing sequences of transitions where both the space and time usage are bounded.

Definition 4.1.24. Relative to a DTM or an NTM M, for each pair of values $p, t \in \mathbb{N}$, we define a binary relation $\vdash_{M,p}^{\leq t}$ on configurations of M, as follows. When γ and γ' are configurations of M, we define $\gamma \vdash_{M,p}^{\leq t} \gamma'$ to hold if and only if there exists a sequence of configurations $\gamma_0, \ldots, \gamma_k$, each consuming at most space p, such that $k \leq t$ and

$$\gamma = \gamma_0 \vdash_M \gamma_1 \vdash_M \cdots \vdash_M \gamma_k = \gamma'.$$

That is, $\gamma \vdash_{M,p}^{\leq t} \gamma'$ holds if and only if γ' is reachable from γ by taking a successor configuration up to t times, in such a way that all encountered configurations consume at most space p. ◇

Our reduction will construct a sequence of formulas where each answers the question of whether one configuration is reachable from another, within a certain amount of time (precisely, a certain number of transitions). These formulas are constructed in stages, using the following principle, which for each such question halves the amount of time that needs to be considered—at the expense of doubling the number of questions!

Proposition 4.1.25. *Suppose $p, t \in \mathbb{N}$ and that t is even. Let M be a DTM or an NTM; when γ and γ' are configurations of M, it holds that $\gamma \vdash_{M,p}^{\leq t} \gamma'$ if and only if there exists a configuration γ^- such that $\gamma \vdash_{M,p}^{\leq t/2} \gamma^-$ and $\gamma^- \vdash_{M,p}^{\leq t/2} \gamma'$.*

Proof. For the forward direction, let $\gamma = \gamma_0 \vdash_M \gamma_1 \vdash_M \cdots \vdash_M \gamma_k = \gamma'$ be a sequence witnessing $\gamma \vdash_{M,p}^{\leq t} \gamma'$, so that $k \leq t$; then, setting $\gamma^- = \gamma_{\lfloor \frac{k}{2} \rfloor}$, we obtain the needed conclusion. For the backward direction, take sequences witnessing $\gamma \vdash_{M,p}^{\leq t/2} \gamma^-$ and $\gamma^- \vdash_{M,p}^{\leq t/2} \gamma'$; concatenate them to witness $\gamma \vdash_{M,p}^{\leq t} \gamma'$. □

Having made the above preparations, we proceed to prove the hardness of QSAT.

Theorem 4.1.26. QSAT *is PSPACE-hard.*

The proof of this theorem argues that, when M is a DTM running within space S, where S is a polynomial, there is a reduction from $L(M)$ to QSAT. Given a string x of length n, the reduction outputs a formula that is true if and only if the DTM M can reach an accepting configuration from the initial configuration of M on x. The crux of the reduction's behavior is to construct a formula that characterizes reachability (that is, the relation $\vdash_M^*$) on the configurations (of M) that consume space at most $S(n)$. In order to construct this formula, the reduction computes a sequence $\phi^0, \phi^1, \phi^2, \ldots$ of qp-formulas where, for each formula ϕ^e, an assignment f to the free variables of ϕ^e can represent a pair (γ_y, γ_z) of configurations (of M); and such an assignment f satisfies ϕ^e if and only if its represented pair (γ_y, γ_z) is such that γ_z is reachable from γ_y within 2^e transitions (that is, $\gamma_y \vdash_{M,S(n)}^{\leq 2^e} \gamma_z$ holds). On a string of length n, a computation of M can last for at most $2^{S^+(n)}$ time steps, where S^+ is an appropriately defined polynomial proportional to S. Thus, the formula $\phi^{S^+(n)}$ will serve as the desired formula characterizing reachability.

The sequence $\phi^0, \phi^1, \phi^2, \ldots$ of qp-formulas is computed inductively: for each $i \geq 0$, the formula ϕ^{i+1} is constructed from ϕ^i, using the principle of Proposition 4.1.25. In essence, the formula ϕ^{i+1} characterizes reachability of a configuration γ_z from a configuration γ_y within 2^{i+1} transitions by asserting that there exists a configuration γ_u where γ_z is reachable from γ_u within 2^i transitions, and γ_u is reachable from γ_y within 2^i transitions—that is, if and only if ϕ^i holds on both (γ_y, γ_u) and (γ_u, γ_z). Expressing the existence of the configuration γ_u is achieved via existential quantification; expressing that the formula ϕ^i holds on both of the given pairs is achieved by using universal quantification, which allows the formula ϕ^{i+1} to contain just one occurrence of the formula ϕ^i. That the formula ϕ^i occurs just once in the formula ϕ^{i+1} is indispensable for controlling the sizes of the formulas $\phi^0, \phi^1, \phi^2, \ldots$; if each formula ϕ^i occurred twice in the formula ϕ^{i+1}, then the size of each formula ϕ^i would be exponential in i.

Proof. Let M be a polynomial-space DTM. Let Δ be an alphabet as described in the proof of Proposition 4.1.4, so that each configuration of M that consumes at most space p can be represented by a string of length p over Δ. Let $D > 1$ be a sufficiently large constant with $|\Delta| \leq 2^D$, so that each symbol in Δ can be represented by a bit sequence of length D.

Let $S \colon \mathbb{N} \to \mathbb{N}$ be a polynomial such that M runs within space S. Without loss of generality, we may assume that S is a polynomial where $S(i) \geq i$ for each $i \in \mathbb{N}$. Define $S^+ \colon \mathbb{N} \to \mathbb{N}$ as the polynomial $D \cdot S$. Then, for each $n \in \mathbb{N}$, whenever the DTM M is invoked on an input string of length n, each configuration consumes space at most $S(n)$ (by Proposition 4.1.23), and so can be represented by a bit sequence of length $S^+(n)$. On an input string of length n, the DTM M halts within $2^{S^+(n)}$ time steps: in a computation, at most $2^{S^+(n)}$ configurations can be encountered, and no configuration can be repeated, as M is halting.

We present a polynomial-time many-one reduction from $L(M)$ to QSAT. The reduction acts as follows, upon being given a string x of length n. The reduction first constructs, based on n, a sequence $(\phi^e(\mathbf{y^e}, \mathbf{z^e}))_{e=0,\ldots,S^+(n)}$ of qp-formulas. Here, $\mathbf{y^e} = y_1^e, \ldots, y_{S^+(n)}^e$ and $\mathbf{z^e} = z_1^e, \ldots, z_{S^+(n)}^e$ are variable sequences each having length $S^+(n)$, and we write $\phi^e(\mathbf{y^e}, \mathbf{z^e})$ to indicate that ϕ^e is a qp-formula whose free variables are among the variables in $\mathbf{y^e}, \mathbf{z^e}$. Since each of the sequences $\mathbf{y^e}, \mathbf{z^e}$ has length $S^+(n)$, an assignment to either of these sequences can represent any configuration that is reached when M is invoked on the string x. We will show that each formula ϕ^e characterizes the relation $\vdash_{M,S(n)}^{\leq 2^e}$. Precisely, we will show that each formula ϕ^e has the following key property: for any assignment f defined on all variables in $\mathbf{y^e}$ and $\mathbf{z^e}$, it holds that

$f \models \phi^e(\mathbf{y^e}, \mathbf{z^e})$ if and only if

$f(\mathbf{y^e})$ and $f(\mathbf{z^e})$ represent configurations γ_y and γ_z such that $\gamma_y \vdash_{M,S(n)}^{\leq 2^e} \gamma_z$.

The formulas (ϕ^e) are constructed inductively as follows:

- The formula $\phi^0(\mathbf{y^0}, \mathbf{z^0})$ is defined so that an assignment f satisfies it if and only if $f(\mathbf{y^0})$ and $f(\mathbf{z^0})$ represent configurations γ_y and γ_z such that $\gamma_y = \gamma_z$ or $\gamma_y \vdash_M \gamma_z$. Such a formula ϕ^0 can be constructed in time polynomial in n. While we do not engage here in a detailed presentation of such a formula ϕ^0, let us briefly describe one way to construct this formula. We can use the bit representation of configurations discussed in the proof of Theorem 3.6.15, and then directly use the formulas given there to construct a formula that holds on configuration representations γ_y, γ_z if and only if $\gamma_y \vdash_M \gamma_z$ holds; we can then form the disjunction of this formula with a formula that holds when $\gamma_y = \gamma_z$ (the latter formula is straightforwardly constructed).

- For each i with $0 \leq i < S^+(n)$, the formula ϕ^{i+1} is defined inductively from the formula ϕ^i; namely, we define

$\phi^{i+1}(\mathbf{y^{i+1}}, \mathbf{z^{i+1}}) =$

$\quad \exists \mathbf{u} \forall \mathbf{y^i} \forall \mathbf{z^i} \left(\left(((\mathbf{y^i}, \mathbf{z^i}) \leftrightarrow (\mathbf{y^{i+1}}, \mathbf{u})) \vee ((\mathbf{y^i}, \mathbf{z^i}) \leftrightarrow (\mathbf{u}, \mathbf{z^{i+1}})) \right) \to \phi^i(\mathbf{y^i}, \mathbf{z^i}) \right).$

Here, we understand $\mathbf{u}$ to be a variable sequence having length $S^+(n)$. And we view each of the pairs $(\mathbf{y^i}, \mathbf{z^i})$, $(\mathbf{y^{i+1}}, \mathbf{u})$, and $(\mathbf{u}, \mathbf{z^{i+1}})$ as a variable sequence having length $2S^+(n)$. When $\mathbf{v} = v_1, ..., v_k$ and $\mathbf{w} = w_1, ..., w_k$ are sequences of the same length, we understand $\mathbf{v} \leftrightarrow \mathbf{w}$ to be an abbreviation for $(v_1 \leftrightarrow w_1) \wedge \cdots \wedge (v_k \leftrightarrow w_k)$.

The subformula $((\mathbf{y^i}, \mathbf{z^i}) \leftrightarrow (\mathbf{y^{i+1}}, \mathbf{u})) \vee ((\mathbf{y^i}, \mathbf{z^i}) \leftrightarrow (\mathbf{u}, \mathbf{z^{i+1}}))$ appearing to the left of the implication has the effect of restricting the universal quantification $\forall \mathbf{y^i} \forall \mathbf{z^i}$ to the two pairs $(\mathbf{y^{i+1}}, \mathbf{u})$ and $(\mathbf{u}, \mathbf{z^{i+1}})$. Accordingly, the formula ϕ^{i+1} has the same satisfying assignments as the formula $\exists \mathbf{u}(\phi^i(\mathbf{y^{i+1}}, \mathbf{u}) \wedge \phi^i(\mathbf{u}, \mathbf{z^{i+1}}))$.

Let us verify, by induction, that each of the formulas (ϕ^e) has the key property. This is evident by construction for ϕ^0. Consider a formula ϕ^{i+1} as given by the inductive definition. Let f be an assignment defined on the variables in $\mathbf{y^{i+1}}$ and $\mathbf{z^{i+1}}$. As discussed, we have that

$\quad f \models \phi^{i+1}$ if and only if $f \models \exists \mathbf{u}(\phi^i(\mathbf{y^{i+1}}, \mathbf{u}) \wedge \phi^i(\mathbf{u}, \mathbf{z^{i+1}})).$

Thus, $f \models \phi^{i+1}$ if and only if there exist values $b_1, ..., b_{S^+(n)} \in \{0, 1\}$ such that the mapping $f' = f[u_1 \mapsto b_1, ..., u_{S^+(n)} \mapsto b_{S^+(n)}]$ satisfies $f' \models \phi^i(\mathbf{y^{i+1}}, \mathbf{u})$ and $f' \models \phi^i(\mathbf{u}, \mathbf{z^{i+1}})$. By induction, such a mapping f' exists if and only if $f(\mathbf{y^{i+1}})$ and $f(\mathbf{z^{i+1}})$ represent configurations γ_y and γ_z such that there exists a configuration γ_u where $\gamma_y \vdash_{M,S(n)}^{\leq 2^i} \gamma_u$ and $\gamma_u \vdash_{M,S(n)}^{\leq 2^i} \gamma_z$; equivalently, such that $\gamma_y \vdash_{M,S(n)}^{\leq 2^{i+1}} \gamma_z$ (recall Proposition 4.1.25).

The sequence (ϕ^e) of formulas can be constructed in polynomial time: there are a polynomial number of them, and for each i with $0 \leq i < S^+(n)$, the formula ϕ^{i+1} is longer than ϕ^i by an amount that is polynomial in n.

Let α_x be the initial configuration of the DTM M on input string x. Let $\psi_x(\mathbf{y}^{S^+(\mathbf{n})}, \mathbf{z}^{S^+(\mathbf{n})})$ be a formula that is satisfied when the variables $\mathbf{y}^{S^+(\mathbf{n})}$ are mapped to a representation of the configuration α_x, and the variables $\mathbf{z}^{S^+(\mathbf{n})}$ are mapped to a representation of an accepting configuration. Such a formula ψ_x can be constructed in time polynomial in n. One way to present the construction, under the bit representation used in Theorem 3.6.15's proof, is to imitate some instructions of the circuit constructed in this proof: the instructions of the row 1 gates can be used to handle the variables $\mathbf{y}^{S^+(\mathbf{n})}$, and the instruction of the output gate can be used to handle the variables $\mathbf{z}^{S^+(\mathbf{n})}$.

The formula $\exists \mathbf{y}^{S^+(\mathbf{n})} \exists \mathbf{z}^{S^+(\mathbf{n})} (\psi_x \wedge \phi^{S^+(n)})$ is the output of the reduction. This formula is evidently true if and only if there exists an accepting configuration β such that the relationship $\alpha_x \vdash_{M,S(n)}^{\leq 2^{S^+(n)}} \beta$ holds, which occurs if and only if M accepts x; recall that, when invoked on the string x, the DTM M halts within $2^{S^+(n)}$ time steps. $\qquad\square$

Combining Proposition 4.1.21 and Theorem 4.1.26, we obtain the following completeness result.

Theorem 4.1.27. QSAT *is PSPACE-complete.*

Remark 4.1.28. In the proof of Theorem 4.1.26, the polynomial-time computability of the formulas (ϕ^e) relies crucially on the inductive definition of ϕ^{i+1} containing ϕ^i just once—as suggested prior to the proof. As indicated in the proof, the formula ϕ^{i+1} behaves just as the formula $\exists \mathbf{u}(\phi^i(\mathbf{y}^{i+1}, \mathbf{u}) \wedge \phi^i(\mathbf{u}, \mathbf{z}^{i+1}))$ does; however, if the latter formula were used as the definition of ϕ^{i+1}, the size of each formula ϕ^{i+1} would be more than double the size of ϕ^i, prohibiting the polynomial-time computation of the formula sequence (ϕ^e). The use of universal quantification, in effect, obviates the need to perform this doubling. $\qquad\diamond$

Remark 4.1.29. Essentially as it stands, the proof of Theorem 4.1.26 shows that for each polynomial-space *nondeterministic* Turing machine M, the language $L(M)$ polynomial-time many-one reduces to QSAT. In conjunction with Theorem 4.1.15 and Proposition 4.1.21, this result implies the fact that for each polynomial-space NTM M, its language $L(M)$ is PSPACE. The fact implies that the nondeterministic mode of computation offers no benefit over the deterministic mode, under polynomial space bounds. Precisely, if we let $\mathcal{NPSPACE}$ denote the class containing each language $L(M)$ of a polynomial-space NTM M, we have $\mathcal{NPSPACE} \subseteq \mathcal{PSPACE}$! We will also derive this containment later (in Theorem 4.1.32); along with the observation that $\mathcal{PSPACE} \subseteq \mathcal{NPSPACE}$, it implies the complexity class equality $\mathcal{PSPACE} = \mathcal{NPSPACE}$. Due to this equality result, the class $\mathcal{NPSPACE}$ often is not explicitly defined or referred to. $\qquad\diamond$

4.1.4   Savitch's theorem

Savitch's theorem concerns the relative power of determinism and nondeterminism in the context of space-bounded computation. This theorem essentially states that any space-bounded NTM M can be simulated by a DTM whose space usage is a quadratic polynomial in that of M, and is thus just modestly higher than that of M.

Theorem 4.1.30 (Savitch's theorem). *Suppose that M is an NTM that runs within space $S: \mathbb{N} \to \mathbb{N}$, where, for each $i \in \mathbb{N}$, it holds that $S(i) \geq i$. There exist a quadratic polynomial Q and a DTM M' such that M' runs within space $Q \circ S$ and has $L(M') = L(M)$.*

This theorem reveals a sharp contrast between what is known about space and about time: the known simulations of NTMs by DTMs incur an exponential increase in the time usage (as discussed in Section 2.6.2). As we will show, Savitch's theorem readily implies that the language of any polynomial-space NTM is PSPACE.

In order to prove Savitch's theorem, starting from a halting NTM we need to design a DTM that, on an input string x, decides if there exists an accepting computation of the NTM on x, and does so without using much more space than the NTM does. We can reason that naively searching over the configurations of the NTM is unlikely to be a fruitful strategy for designing the DTM: at each time point of a computation, the NTM can nondeterministically branch; a computation of the NTM may run for a number of time steps that is exponential in the input string length; and accordingly, the number of configurations reachable from the NTM's initial configuration is thusly exponential.

To perform the search in a space-efficient fashion, we use a technique sometimes referred to as **middle-first search**, whereby to determine if one configuration γ can reach another configuration γ' within some amount of time (precisely, some number of transitions), we search for a configuration γ^- such that γ reaches γ^- in half the amount of time, and γ^- reaches γ' in half the amount of time. Each of these latter two reachability checks can be resolved in sequence and by reusing space. Applying this technique recursively, the search for an accepting computation that may be exponentially long can be carried out in a polynomial amount of space, since in each successive reachability check, the amount of time considered is halved. The resulting recursive algorithm alternates between searching *existentially* for a suitable middle configuration, and verifying *universally* that the configuration at hand passes both of the two reachability checks. (Conceptually, the same idea was used to prove the PSPACE-hardness of the language QSAT: the reduction constructed, in stages, a sequence of quantified propositional formulas, characterizing reachability for increasing time amounts;[30] using the same halving technique enabled control of the formulas' size. In both situations, Proposition 4.1.25 serves as a key principle.)

---

30. In fact, relative to a polynomial-space NTM, consider the algorithm that, given an input string x, applies the reduction of Theorem 4.1.26 to x and then invokes Proposition 4.1.21's polynomial-space DTM, which decides QSAT, on the reduction's result. This algorithm can be verified to behave essentially identically to the DTM provided by the proof of Savitch's theorem; it runs in polynomial space, and was suggested in Remark 4.1.29.

Let M be an NTM. Based on M, we can define an alphabet Δ such that each configuration of M that consumes at most space p can be represented by a length p string over Δ. (Such an alphabet is briefly described in the proof of Proposition 4.1.4; and we here use the notion of *consumes* from Definition 4.1.22.) In the following discussion, we work with such string representations of configurations; we will refer to them directly as *configurations*, and will apply (for example) the $\vdash_M$ relation to them.

Relative to the NTM M, we define an algorithm Reach(γ, γ', e) that takes as input two configurations $\gamma, \gamma' \in \Delta^p$ of M having the same length and a value $e \geq 0$.

Algorithm Reach(γ, γ', e).

- If $e = 0$, accept if either $\gamma = \gamma'$ or $\gamma \vdash_M \gamma'$ holds, and reject otherwise.
- Otherwise:
  - Loop over all configurations $\gamma^- \in \Delta^p$; for each such configuration γ^-, check, in sequence, if both Reach($\gamma, \gamma^-, e - 1$) and Reach($\gamma^-, \gamma', e - 1$) hold, and accept if so.
  - Reject.

Lemma 4.1.31. *Relative to an NTM M, let $\gamma, \gamma' \in \Delta^p$ be configurations having the same length p. For each $e \geq 0$, we have that* Reach(γ, γ', e) *accepts if and only if* $\gamma \vdash_{M,p}^{\leq 2^e} \gamma'$.

Proof. We prove this by induction on e. The case $e = 0$ is evident. When $e > 0$, the lemma follows from the fact that Reach(γ, γ', e) accepts if and only if there exists a length p configuration γ^- such that both Reach($\gamma, \gamma^-, e - 1$) and Reach($\gamma^-, \gamma', e - 1$) accept; the inductive hypothesis that the lemma holds for the value $e - 1$; and Proposition 4.1.25. □

We next proceed to the proof of Savitch's theorem. Before diving into the proof, let us highlight that this theorem makes no assumption about the computability of the bounding function $S\colon \mathbb{N} \to \mathbb{N}$. The DTM that we present, upon being given a string, first determines the amount of space used by the NTM on the string.

Proof of Theorem 4.1.30. We first describe the behavior of the DTM M', and then discuss this DTM's correctness and space consumption. Let Δ be the alphabet defined from the NTM M as described above. Let $D > 1$ be a sufficiently large constant so that $|\Delta| \leq 2^D$; then, for each $k \geq 0$, we have $|\Delta^k| \leq 2^{kD}$.

Given a string x of length n, the DTM M' performs a two-phase process in which it works with configurations of the NTM M. Let α_x denote the initial configuration of M on x, and for each $\ell \geq n$, let $\alpha_{x;\ell}$ denote the representation of α_x as a length ℓ string over Δ.

- In the first phase, the DTM determines the minimum value $p > 0$ such that every configuration of M that is reachable from α_x consumes at most space p. Here, we say that a configuration γ of M is *reachable* from α_x when $\alpha_x \vdash_M^* \gamma$. We have $p \geq n$, since the tape contents of α_x begins with n non-blank symbols. To determine the value p, the DTM does the following. For increasing values $\ell = n + 1, n + 2, \ldots,$ it checks whether or not there exists a configuration $\beta_\ell \in \Delta^\ell$, where the head is in the rightmost location ℓ, and where Reach($\alpha_{x;\ell}, \beta_\ell, \ell D$) accepts. For the first value ℓ where this check fails, the DTM assigns $p = \ell - 1$.

- In the second phase, the DTM loops over each accepting configuration $\beta_p \in \Delta^p$ of M, and checks whether Reach($\alpha_{x;p}, \beta_p, pD$) accepts. If there exists such an accepting configuration β where Reach($\alpha_{x;p}, \beta_p, pD$) accepts, the DTM accepts; otherwise, the DTM rejects.

The first phase correctly computes the desired minimum value p; we argue this by proving that the check passes for a value $\ell > n$ if and only if there exists a configuration β that is reachable from α_x and that does not consume at most space $\ell - 1$ (in other words, that really requires space ℓ). The forward direction is quite immediate: when one of the calls to the Reach algorithm accepts, by Lemma 4.1.31, a configuration β_ℓ as described in the first phase is reachable from $\alpha_{x;\ell}$; since β_ℓ has the head in the rightmost location, it does not consume at most space $\ell - 1$. For the backward direction, suppose that there exists a configuration β as specified. Then there exists a sequence of configurations

$$\alpha_x = \gamma_1 \vdash_M \gamma_2 \vdash_M \cdots \vdash_M \gamma_k$$

where γ_k is the first and only configuration in the sequence not using space at most $\ell - 1$, and no configuration repeats. We have that each configuration in the sequence can be represented by a length ℓ string; letting $\beta_\ell \in \Delta^\ell$ be the respective representation of γ_k, we have that the configuration $\beta_\ell \in \Delta^\ell$ has its head in the rightmost location ℓ. Since no configuration in the sequence repeats, we have $k \leq 2^{\ell D}$. Thus $\alpha_{x;\ell} \vdash_{M,\ell}^{\leq 2^{\ell D}} \beta_\ell$ holds, implying by Lemma 4.1.31 that Reach($\alpha_{x;\ell}, \beta_\ell, \ell D$) accepts, and so the check passes for the value ℓ.

We argue that the DTM accepts in the second phase if and only if the NTM M accepts x. For the forward direction, when the DTM accepts, one of the calls Reach($\alpha_{x;p}, \beta_p, pD$) accepts, implying by Lemma 4.1.31 that there exists an accepting configuration β where $\alpha_x \vdash_M^* \beta$, and hence that M accepts x. For the backward direction, suppose that the NTM M accepts x. Then there exists an accepting configuration β such that $\alpha_x \vdash_M^* \beta$. Each configuration that is reachable from α_x consumes at most space p, and there are at most 2^{pD} such configurations; thus, $\alpha_x \vdash_{M,p}^{\leq 2^{pD}} \beta$; letting $\beta_p \in \Delta^p$ denote the length p string representation of β, it follows from Lemma 4.1.31 that Reach($\alpha_{x;p}, \beta_p, pD$) accepts.

Let us analyze the space consumption of the DTM M' on the string x. Since p is the minimum value as described in the first phase, it holds by Proposition 4.1.23 (and the assumption that $S(i) \geq i$ for all $i \in \mathbb{N}$) that $p \leq S(n)$. Each existence check in the first phase can be performed by looping over all configurations in Δ^ℓ, and similarly the loop of the second phase can be performed by looping over all configurations in Δ^p. In each case, the same space can be used to enumerate each of the needed configurations. Thus in the two phases, the amount of space needed to set up the calls to Reach is at most linear in p: the first phase calls Reach on configurations of length up to $p + 1$, and the second phase calls Reach on configurations of length p. Each time one of the two phases makes a call to Reach, the third argument is at most $(p + 1)D$, and thus linear in p; since it decreases by 1 each time Reach calls itself recursively, the number of nested calls at any point in time is linear in p. The amount of information that each call needs to maintain is linear in the size of the configurations passed in, which as mentioned is at most linear in p. Thus, there exists a quadratic polynomial $Q: \mathbb{N} \to \mathbb{N}$ such that the amount of space used by the DTM M', on a string x of length n, is at most $Q(p)$; since $p \leq S(n)$, it holds that $Q(p) \leq Q(S(n))$. □

The following result is a consequence of Savitch's theorem (and was previously alluded to in Remark 4.1.29).

Theorem 4.1.32. *A language B is PSPACE if and only if there exists a polynomial-space NTM M such that L(M) = B.*

Proof. For the forward direction, we appeal to Proposition 2.6.11, which showed how to construct, from a DTM M^-, an NTM M having the same notion of successor configuration as M^-, that is, where $\vdash_{M^-}$ and $\vdash_M$ are equal. From this construction, it follows that for any polynomial-space DTM M^-, there is a polynomial-space NTM M such that $L(M) = L(M^-)$.

For the backward direction, suppose that M is a polynomial-time NTM. By Savitch's theorem (Theorem 4.1.30), there exists a polynomial-time DTM M' with $L(M') = L(M)$; thus, the language $L(M)$ is PSPACE. □

Remark 4.1.33. We previously showed that $\mathcal{NP} \subseteq \mathcal{PSPACE}$ (in Proposition 4.1.10). This containment can alternatively (but less directly!) be argued by relying on Savitch's theorem, as follows: each language B in $\mathcal{NP}$ is the language of a polynomial-time NTM M; the NTM M is polynomial-space by Proposition 4.1.3; thus, by the backward direction of Theorem 4.1.32, we have that the language $L(M) = B$ is in $\mathcal{PSPACE}$. Using the definition of $\mathcal{NPSPACE}$ from Remark 4.1.29, this argument amounts to justifying and combining the containments $\mathcal{NP} \subseteq \mathcal{NPSPACE}$ and $\mathcal{NPSPACE} \subseteq \mathcal{PSPACE}$. ◇

4.2 Hierarchy theorems

In this section, we establish *hierarchy theorems* which show that, for each of the resources of space and time, *one can do more, with more of the resource*. For example, we will prove a time hierarchy theorem essentially showing that, when $T: \mathbb{N} \to \mathbb{N}$ is a function satisfying mild well-behavedness conditions, there is a language that is decided by a DTM using a bit more than time T, but not decided by any DTM using time less than T; we will make precise what is meant by *more* and *less* in this context. These hierarchy theorems are notable in that, as we will see, they can be used to separate natural complexity classes of languages. Their success in doing so can be attributed to their comparing the situation of having more of a resource to that of having less of the *same* resource. In contrast to this form of situation, our ignorance in relating complexity classes becomes bluntly apparent when we are challenged to compare *modes* of computation, as in the question of whether $\mathbb{P} = \mathcal{NP}$—can nondeterministic computation do more than deterministic computation, under polynomial time bounds?—or to compare *different resources*, as in the question of whether $\mathbb{P} = \mathcal{PSPACE}$—can more be done under polynomial space bounds than under polynomial time bounds, by deterministic computation?

We introduce a couple of definitions that will allow us to formalize our hierarchy theorems. In rough form, our time hierarchy theorem posits that for certain well-behaved functions $T\colon \mathbb{N} \to \mathbb{N}$, there is a language that is decided by a DTM running in time slightly higher than T, but that is not decided by any DTM whose running time is *dominated* by T. Our space hierarchy theorem makes a similar assertion, but with *space* in place of *time*. Let us turn to define the notion of *domination* on functions.

Definition 4.2.1. A function $T\colon \mathbb{N} \to \mathbb{N}$ **dominates** a function $T'\colon \mathbb{N} \to \mathbb{N}$ when there exists a value $C \in \mathbb{N}$ such that, for each value $i \geq C$, it holds that $T'(i) < T(i)$; that is, the latter inequality holds for all but finitely many values in $\mathbb{N}$. ◇

We also need to qualify what it means for a function to be well-behaved.

Definition 4.2.2. A function $U\colon \mathbb{N} \to \mathbb{N}$ is **constructible** if there exists a polynomial P and a DTM M computing a function where, for all $n \in \mathbb{N}$, it holds that

- $g(1^n) = 1^{U(n)}$, where g denotes the function computed by M; and
- $\text{time}_M(1^n) \leq P(n + U(n))$. ◇

That is, $U\colon \mathbb{N} \to \mathbb{N}$ is constructible when there is a DTM that computes the mapping $n \mapsto U(n)$ in unary representation, and does so within time polynomial in $n + U(n)$; here, we allow a polynomial function of both the input size n as well as the output size $U(n)$, as the output size may be considerably larger than the input size (as occurs, for example, with the function $U(n) = 2^n$). Note that when the function U satisfies $U(n) \geq n$ (for each $n \in \mathbb{N}$), being bounded by a polynomial in $n + U(n)$ is equivalent to being bounded by a polynomial in $U(n)$.

Example 4.2.3. The identity function on $\mathbb{N}$, which maps each natural number to itself, is clearly constructible. Each constant function—that is, each function mapping all natural numbers to the same value—is also readily verified to be constructible. It can further be verified that the constructible functions are closed under addition and multiplication, so we can conclude that every polynomial is constructible. ◇

Example 4.2.4. When $U\colon \mathbb{N} \to \mathbb{N}$ is a constructible function, the function 2^U is also constructible. This is witnessed by a DTM M that, on a high level, performs the following. When given a string of the form 1^n, the DTM M first computes $1^{U(n)}$ by invoking a DTM witnessing the constructibility of U; then, the DTM M counts up to $1^{U(n)}$ in binary, looping over all binary strings of length $U(n)$, and recording an instance of the symbol 1 for each such binary string. The number of such binary strings is $2^{U(n)}$, and so the recorded string will be $1^{2^{U(n)}}$, which is the desired output. ◇

Time hierarchy

Our first hierarchy theorem concerns deterministic time-bounded computation, and is stated as follows.

Theorem 4.2.5 (Time hierarchy theorem). *Suppose that $T: \mathbb{N} \to \mathbb{N}$ is a constructible function where $T(n) \geq n$ (for each $n \in \mathbb{N}$). There exists a polynomial P and a language B such that*

- *there exists a DTM running within time $P \circ T$ whose language is B, but*
- *for any function $T': \mathbb{N} \to \mathbb{N}$ that is dominated by T, there exists no DTM running within time T' whose language is B.*

Let us preview the proof of this theorem. Our goal is to construct a language that is different from the language of each DTM in an ensemble—namely, each DTM that runs within time T', where T' is dominated as described. This goal recalls our previous aim (achieved in Section 2.4) of constructing a non-CE language, that is, a language that was different from the language of each DTM. However, the present theorem requires the constructed language to be the language of a time-restricted DTM, which we will call M_0. Due to the constructibility of the function T, the DTM M_0 can efficiently determine, on any given input string of length n, the amount of time $T(n)$ it is permitted (up to a polynomial). A first attempt at designing the DTM M_0 would be to allocate a string x_M to each DTM M, and then have the DTM M_0, on such an allocated string x_M, simulate the DTM M for as long as possible on x_M, and yield the outcome opposite to M's if M halts (rejecting if M accepts, and accepting if M rejects). However, there is an issue with this design strategy: even if a DTM M has a running time that is dominated in the stated sense, it may be that on the allocated string x_M, the described simulation does not halt: domination of T' by T provides that for sufficiently large values n, it holds that $T'(n) < T(n)$, but the length $|x_M|$ of the allocated string x_M might not be sufficiently large in this sense. To remedy this issue, instead of allocating a single string to each DTM M, we allocate *infinitely* many strings to each DTM M—namely, to a DTM M, we allocate each string of the form $\langle \ulcorner M \urcorner, y \rangle$. This ensures that, where necessary, the DTM M_0 has enough time to properly determine whether or not a DTM M accepts, on *at least*[31] one string $\langle \ulcorner M \urcorner, y \rangle$ allocated to M.

It is worth remarking that this design does not require the DTM M_0 to evaluate whether or not any given DTM M has a running time that is dominated (in the sense of the theorem statement). Given a pair $\langle \ulcorner M \urcorner, y \rangle$, the DTM M_0 simply simulates the DTM M on the pair for as long as it is permitted; it will succeed in seeing the outcome of the DTM M on one such pair wherever it needs to.

---

31. In fact, the DTM M_0 will have enough time to determine this on infinitely many of the strings allocated to M.

We introduce a result that encapsulates what is required for the DTM M_0 to perform time-bounded DTM simulations. Define TIME-BAP as the language that contains each triple $\langle \ulcorner M \urcorner, x, 1^u \rangle$ such that

- $\ulcorner M \urcorner$ is the encoding of a DTM M,
- x is a string over the alphabet $\Sigma = \{0, 1\}$,
- $u \in \mathbb{N}^+$,

and where *M accepts x within u time steps*; by this, it is meant that, when α_x denotes the initial configuration of M on x, there exists an accepting configuration β of M and a value $u' < u$ such that $\alpha_x \vdash_M^{u'} \beta$.

Proposition 4.2.6. *The language* TIME-BAP *is PTIME.*

To justify this proposition, a polynomial-time DTM whose language is TIME-BAP can be presented as follows. On a triple $\langle \ulcorner M \urcorner, x, 1^u \rangle$ of the described form, the DTM simply invokes a typical universal Turing machine, such as that presented in Section 2.3, on the pair $\langle \ulcorner M \urcorner, x \rangle$. The DTM allows the universal Turing machine to simulate M on x for up to u time steps; if the simulation is seen to accept or reject by then, then the DTM does the same, otherwise, the DTM rejects. That this DTM is polynomial-time can be argued simply by analyzing the time usage of such a typical universal Turing machine, in particular, by arguing that each simulation step can be carried out in time polynomial in the input pair; we omit a detailed analysis.

Proof of Theorem 4.2.5. We set B to be the language $L(M_0)$, where M_0 is the DTM defined as follows. On an input string x, the DTM M_0 performs the following steps.

1. Check if x is of the form $\langle \ulcorner M \urcorner, y \rangle$, where $\ulcorner M \urcorner$ is the encoding of a DTM M, and y is a string. If not, reject.

2. Compute, from x, the string $1^{|x|}$, and then using the constructibility of the function T, compute the string $1^{T(|x|)}$.

3. Decide if $\langle \ulcorner M \urcorner, x, 1^{T(|x|)} \rangle \in$ TIME-BAP holds; reject if so, and accept otherwise. Perform this decision by invoking the polynomial-time DTM whose existence is given by Proposition 4.2.6.

Let us consider the time used by the DTM M_0 on an input string x of length n. Step 1 can be done within time polynomial in n (recall Remark 3.2.11). Step 2 can be done within time polynomial in $n + T(n)$, by the definition of *constructible*. In step 3, the length of the triple is linear in $n + T(n)$, so by Proposition 4.2.6, this step can be done within time polynomial in $n + T(n)$. Overall, all steps can be done within time polynomial in $n + T(n)$, which, as $T(n) \geq n$, is within time polynomial in $T(n)$. We have thus shown that the time consumption of the DTM M_0 has the required form.

Suppose that M is a DTM that runs within time $T': \mathbb{N} \to \mathbb{N}$, and that T' is dominated by T; we show that $L(M) \neq B$. We show this by considering input strings of the form $\langle \ulcorner M \urcorner, y \rangle$. Since T dominates T', there exists a sufficiently large string y^+ where, when x^+ is set as the string $\langle \ulcorner M \urcorner, y^+ \rangle$, it holds that $T'(|x^+|) < T(|x^+|)$. From this inequality and the assumption that M runs within time T', we have that

$$M \text{ accepts } x^+ \quad \Leftrightarrow \quad \langle \ulcorner M \urcorner, x^+, 1^{T(|x^+|)} \rangle \in \mathsf{TIME\text{-}BAP}.$$

From the specification of the DTM M_0, we have

$$\langle \ulcorner M \urcorner, x^+, 1^{T(|x^+|)} \rangle \in \mathsf{TIME\text{-}BAP} \quad \Leftrightarrow \quad x^+ \notin L(M_0).$$

It thus follows that $x^+ \in L(M) \Leftrightarrow x^+ \notin L(M_0)$, and so we have $L(M) \neq B$, as desired. $\qquad\square$

Space hierarchy

We next present a hierarchy theorem for space. Define SPACE-BAP as the language that contains each triple $\langle \ulcorner M \urcorner, x, 1^u \rangle$ such that each part thereof is as described as in the definition of TIME-BAP, and where *M accepts x within space u*, by which is meant that, when α_x denotes the initial configuration of M on x, each configuration γ with $\alpha_x \vdash_M \gamma$ has a head location that is no more than u (equivalently, a head location that is within the first u tape locations). We have the following result on space-bounded DTM simulation.

Proposition 4.2.7. *The language* SPACE-BAP *is PSPACE.*

This proposition can be justified along the lines of the argument given for Proposition 4.2.6; we describe a polynomial-space DTM whose language is SPACE-BAP as follows. On a triple $\langle \ulcorner M \urcorner, x, 1^u \rangle$ of the specified form, the DTM invokes a typical universal Turing machine on the pair $\langle \ulcorner M \urcorner, x \rangle$, allowing the simulation of M on x to use up to u tape cells. If the simulation is seen to accept or reject, then the DTM does the same. If the simulation ever tries to use more than u tape cells, the DTM rejects. The simulated machine, however, may repeat configuration; in order to detect such a repetition, the DTM keeps track of the number of seen configurations, and if this number is ever detected to exceed the total number of configurations that use u tape cells, it rejects. (An upper bound on this total number can be computed as c^u, where $c > 1$ is the constant given by Proposition 4.1.4 and its proof.)

Our second hierarchy theorem concerns deterministic space-bounded computation, and is stated as follows.

Theorem 4.2.8 (Space hierarchy theorem). *Suppose that $S \colon \mathbb{N} \to \mathbb{N}$ is a constructible function where $S(n) \geq n$ (for each $n \in \mathbb{N}$). There exists a polynomial P and a language B such that*

- *there exists a DTM running within space $P \circ S$ whose language is B, but*
- *for any function $S' \colon \mathbb{N} \to \mathbb{N}$ that is dominated by S, there exists no DTM running within space S' whose language is B.*

A proof of Theorem 4.2.8 can be obtained by making minor adjustments to the proof of Theorem 4.2.5: essentially, one can replace each instance of *time* with *space*, and the language TIME-BAP with the language SPACE-BAP. While we omit giving a full proof of Theorem 4.2.8, let us give some details on how such a proof could go. Following the proof of Theorem 4.2.5, we define a DTM M_0' that performs the 3 steps performed by that proof's DTM M_0, but uses the function S in place of the function T, and uses the language SPACE-BAP in place of the language TIME-BAP in step 3. The analysis in the previous proof of the first 2 steps applies to the DTM M_0'; the first 2 steps of M_0' can be done within time polynomial in $S(n)$, and hence within space polynomial in $S(n)$. Via Proposition 4.2.7, step 3 of the DTM M_0' can be done within space polynomial in $S(n)$.

Ramifications

Let us discuss some ramifications of our hierarchy theorems. For each $k \geq 0$, we define the *k*-**exponential functions**, a set of functions from $\mathbb{N}$ to $\mathbb{N}$, inductively as follows.

- Define a 0-**exponential function** to be a polynomial.
- For each $k > 0$, define a k-**exponential function** to be a function of the form 2^G, where G is a $(k-1)$-exponential function.

So, a 1-exponential function has the form 2^P, where P is a polynomial, a 2-exponential function has the form $2^{(2^P)}$, where P is a polynomial, and so forth.

- Define k-$\mathcal{EXPTIME}$ to be the class containing each language B such that there exists a k-exponential function Q and a DTM M that runs within time Q and has $L(M) = B$.
- Define k-$\mathcal{EXPSPACE}$ to be the class containing each language B such that there exists a k-exponential function Q and a DTM M that runs within space Q and has $L(M) = B$.

We have 0-$\mathcal{EXPTIME} = \mathcal{P}$ and 0-$\mathcal{EXPSPACE} = \mathcal{PSPACE}$.

Consider the functions $U_1, U_2, \ldots$ defined as follows: U_1 is the 1-exponential function given by $U_1(n) = 2^n$, and for each $k > 1$, we define U_k as the k-exponential function $2^{U_{k-1}}$. The function U_1 is known to dominate each polynomial, from which it follows that (for each $k > 1$) the function U_k dominates every $(k-1)$-exponential function. It can also be verified that applying any polynomial to the function U_k results in a function bounded above by a k-exponential function. By applying our hierarchy theorems to this k-exponential function U_k, for each $k \geq 1$, we hence obtain the following.

Corollary 4.2.9. *For each $k \geq 1$, it holds that $(k-1)$-$\mathcal{EXPTIME} \subsetneq k$-$\mathcal{EXPTIME}$ and $(k-1)$-$\mathcal{EXPSPACE} \subsetneq k$-$\mathcal{EXPSPACE}$.*

The class 1-$\mathcal{EXPTIME}$ is typically denoted as $\mathcal{EXPTIME}$. Using this notation, Corollary 4.2.9 implies that $\mathcal{P} \subsetneq \mathcal{EXPTIME}$; that is, the class $\mathcal{EXPTIME}$ is strictly larger than the class $\mathcal{P}$. When one uses polynomial-time many-one reductions to define hardness for the class $\mathcal{EXPTIME}$, proving that a language is hard for $\mathcal{EXPTIME}$ thus implies *unconditionally* that the language is not in $\mathcal{P}$.

By appeal to Propositions 4.1.3 and 4.1.4, we have the containments

$$0\text{-}\mathcal{EXPTIME} \subseteq 0\text{-}\mathcal{EXPSPACE} \subseteq 1\text{-}\mathcal{EXPTIME} \subseteq 1\text{-}\mathcal{EXPSPACE} \subseteq \cdots.$$

Corollary 4.2.9 implies that, of any two consecutive containments given here, at least one must be proper; but none of the given containments has yet been proven proper! For example, taking the first two containments, we have

$$0\text{-}\mathcal{EXPTIME} \subseteq 0\text{-}\mathcal{EXPSPACE} \subseteq 1\text{-}\mathcal{EXPTIME},$$

or equivalently,

$$\mathcal{P} \subseteq \mathcal{PSPACE} \subseteq \mathcal{EXPTIME}.$$

Corollary 4.2.9 implies that $\mathcal{P} \subsetneq \mathcal{EXPTIME}$, so of the two containments $\mathcal{P} \subseteq \mathcal{PSPACE}$ and $\mathcal{PSPACE} \subseteq \mathcal{EXPTIME}$, one of them must be proper, although neither has been proven to be so.

Remark 4.2.10. In the statements of our hierarchy theorems (Theorems 4.2.5 and 4.2.8), there is a polynomial gap between the time or space usage of the DTM whose language is B, and the respective usage of each DTM shown not to have B as its language. By restricting further the definition of *constructibility* and by performing a close analysis of the DTM simulations behind Proposition 4.2.6 and Proposition 4.2.7, this gap can be tightened. We do not pursue such a tightening here. ◇

4.3 Fixed-parameter tractability

In this section, we present *fixed-parameter tractability*, a notion of computational tractability that allows for a more refined analysis of languages and problems than the notion of polynomial time. In order to motivate the notion of fixed-parameter tractability, let us reconsider the *clique* and *vertex cover* problems. For each of these problems, an instance consists of a pair (G, k) where G is a graph and k is a natural number, and the question is whether or not there exists a size k subset of the graph's vertex set satisfying a particular property, namely, the property of being a clique or a vertex cover, respectively. A naive algorithm for these problems would be to exhaustively consider all size k subsets of the given graph's vertex set; letting n denote the number of vertices, the number[32] of such subsets is proportional to n^k. In considering n^k as a running time,[33] the value of k appearing as the exponent of n is highly troublesome. If we consider this running time for increasing fixed values of k, that is, for $k = 1, 2, 3, \ldots$, we obtain the functions $n^1, n^2, n^3, \ldots$, which

---

32. The number of such subsets is equal to $\binom{n}{k}$; when $1 \leq k \leq n$, this quantity satisfies $\frac{n^k}{k^k} \leq \binom{n}{k} \leq n^k$, and for the purposes of our discussion, behaves as n^k does.

33. Note that the running time of the mentioned naive algorithm would be slightly higher than the number of size k subsets, since for each size k subset, the algorithm needs to check whether or not the subset satisfies the desired property. Our discussion aims to argue that this number of subsets already grows too quickly, and so we neglect a closer analysis of the naive algorithm.

quite rapidly become infeasible for use. This leads to a question: apart from presenting a polynomial-time algorithm, is there any hope for mitigating this exponential dependence on k?

Fortunately, there *is* an avenue for ameliorating this running time; it is exemplified by an algorithm for the vertex cover problem—to be presented—that runs within time $2^k \cdot P(n)$, where P is a polynomial.[34] While this algorithm's running time still exhibits an exponential dependence on k, the dependence on k is—in a sense—decoupled from the dependence on n. To grasp this, consider that for each fixed value of k, we have not only that $2^k \cdot P(n)$ is a polynomial in n, but that each such polynomial *has the same degree*: for the values $k = 1, 2, 3, \ldots$, the running time is given by the polynomials $2^1 \cdot P(n), 2^2 \cdot P(n), 2^3 \cdot P(n), \ldots$, each having the same degree, namely, the degree of P. This behavior critically contrasts with that of the naive algorithm's n^k running time: for the values $k = 1, 2, 3, \ldots$, the resulting functions $n^1, n^2, n^3, \ldots$ are each polynomials, but exhibit degrees that increase unboundedly as k does.

The notion of fixed-parameter tractability provides a general way to identify running times where, for each fixed value of a so-called *parameter*, the running time is a polynomial, and the resulting polynomials have degrees that are bounded and controlled in the presented sense. Whereas the notion of polynomial-time tractability is applied to languages, the notion of fixed-parameter tractability is applied to so-called *parameterized languages*, which are languages where each instance has an associated value referred to as the instance's *parameter*; a mapping from an instance to its parameter is referred to as a *parameterization*. A parameterized language is considered fixed-parameter tractable, essentially, when there is an algorithm whose running time is of the form $f(k) \cdot Q(n)$, where f is a function, k is the instance's parameter, Q is a polynomial, and n is the instance's size. Observe that here the parameter is confined to only levying a multiplicative effect on the running time; for each fixed value of k, the running time is a polynomial—and again, each such polynomial has the same degree. The vertex cover problem is fixed-parameter tractable, via the mentioned algorithm, when the parameter of an instance (G, k) is defined simply as the value k. Under this definition of parameter, however, the clique problem is not known to be fixed-parameter tractable; in fact, the assertion that it is not fixed-parameter tractable is a central hardness assumption in parameterized complexity theory.[35]

Fixed-parameter tractability is thus a relaxation of polynomial time, where an instance's parameter may multiplicatively increase a polynomial running time, without affecting the polynomial's degree. Fixed-parameter tractability is sometimes said to have a *two-dimensional* nature, as it measures running times both in terms of an instance's size as well as in terms of an instance's parameter. The notion of fixed-parameter tractability, in essence, allows one to identify problems where a seemingly unavoidable combinatorial

---

34. This algorithm is presented in Section 4.3.1; Corollary 4.3.6 states the result on the vertex cover problem.
35. This assumption and this theory are studied in Section 4.4.

explosion can be confined to a parameter, and thus to finely pinpoint sources of combinatorial hardness. One motivation behind fixed-parameter tractability is that, in many problems of interest, it is possible to exhibit a parameterization that tends to be small relative to overall instance size,[36] and so a non-polynomial dependence on an instance's parameter is tolerable, as long as the parameter exerts a limited influence on the overall running time.

Numerous graph-theoretic problems can be studied from the parameterized perspective. Another group of problems that are naturally analyzed using this perspective are *database query evaluation* problems, where an instance consists of a database query and a database, and the question is to decide whether or not the query evaluates to true on the database. In this context, it is natural to take the query as the parameter of an instance, as it frequently occurs that a database query is relatively small compared to the database on which it is evaluated; thus, as regards running time, a non-polynomial dependence on the query may be tolerable, so long as there is a well-behaved polynomial dependence on the database. More generally, there are many situations where one has a large data structure, and wants to decide if it satisfies various queries or properties of a relatively succinct makeup.

For many parameterized languages of interest, the parameter appears as part of an instance. However, there are natural and relevant parameterized languages where this is not the case. For example, there are graph-theoretic languages where each instance includes a graph, and it is of interest to take the parameter to be a structural measure of the graph. In this vein, one surface-level such measure is the maximum degree (over all vertices); more subtle measures include the *vertex cover number* of a graph (defined as the minimum size over all vertex covers), and the *treewidth* of a graph.[37]

Remark 4.3.1. Recall that polynomials were defined to always have natural number coefficients. On some occasions, we will use the straightforwardly verified property that, for any polynomial $P \colon \mathbb{N} \to \mathbb{N}$ and any values $a, b \in \mathbb{N}$, it holds that $P(ab) \leq P(a)P(b)$.   ◇

Remark 4.3.2. Over the remainder of this chapter, to promote readability, we typically do not distinguish between objects and their encodings, and omit the $\ulcorner \cdot \urcorner$ and $\langle \cdot, \cdot \rangle$ notations for specifying encodings (as was done in Section 3.8). So for example, when H is a hypergraph and k is a number, we write (H, k) instead of $\langle \ulcorner H \urcorner, \ulcorner k \urcorner \rangle$.   ◇

4.3.1 The hitting set problem

We begin our technical development by looking at algorithms for the *hitting set problem*, a generalization of the vertex cover problem; these algorithms yield fixed-parameter tractability results. Define a **hypergraph** to be a pair (V, E) where V is a finite set,

---

36. Such parameterizations often arise in conjunction with human-generated artifacts or human-related needs: as examples, consider the query in a database query evaluation scenario, the nesting depth of a computer program, or the number of people requested to form a committee.

37. The measure of *treewidth* is presented in Section 4.6.3.

and $E \subseteq \wp(V)$; the elements of E are referred to as **hyperedges** or **edges** of the hyper-graph. A **hitting set** of a hypergraph (V, E) is a subset $S \subseteq V$ such that, for each $e \in E$, it holds that $S \cap e \neq \emptyset$. That is, a hitting set of a hypergraph is a subset S of the hyper-graph's vertex set such that each hyperedge contains at least one vertex in S. Observe that each graph is a hypergraph (where each hyperedge has size 2), and that, for any graph, the notions of hitting set and vertex cover coincide.

Here, we study and present algorithms for the **hitting set problem** where an instance is a pair (H, k) consisting of a hypergraph H and a number $k \in \mathbb{N}$; the initial goal is to decide if H has a hitting set of size k, and a subsequent goal will be to enumerate representative hitting sets of size at most k.

Our first algorithm, which decides the existence of a hitting set, will make use of the following notion. When $H = (V, E)$ is a hypergraph and $u \in V$, we define H_{-u} to be the hypergraph (V_{-u}, E_{-u}), where $V_{-u} = V \setminus \{u\}$ and $E_{-u} = \{e \in E \mid u \notin e\}$. That is, H_{-u} is the hypergraph derived from H where the vertex u, and all edges containing it, are removed. The key property of this notion to be exploited is the following; it is straightforwardly verified.

Proposition 4.3.3. *Let $H = (V, E)$ be a hypergraph, and let $e \in E$ be a hyperedge of H. A set $S \subseteq V$ is a hitting set of H if and only if there exists $u \in e$ such that $u \in S$ and $S \setminus \{u\}$ is a hitting set of H_{-u}.*

The following is our first algorithm, which receives a pair (H, k) consisting of a hyper-graph $H = (V, E)$ and a number $k \in \mathbb{N}$. Putting aside boundary cases, the crux of its behavior is to arbitrarily pick a hyperedge $e \in E$ and, for each vertex $u \in e$, to call itself recursively on H_{-u}, inquiring if at least one such hypergraph H_{-u} has a hitting set of size one less than the hitting set size sought in H. Essentially, this behavior is justified by Proposition 4.3.3; although the hyperedge e is picked arbitrarily, *any* hitting set must contain a vertex in e.

Algorithm HS(H, k).

- If $E = \emptyset$: return true when $|V| \geq k$, and return false otherwise.
- If $k = 0$: return false.
- Otherwise:
  - Let e be any hyperedge in E.
  - Recursively call HS$(H_{-u}, k-1)$ on each $u \in e$; return true if at least one such call returns true, and return false otherwise.

We establish the correctness of this algorithm.

Theorem 4.3.4. *For each input (H, k), the algorithm HS returns true if and only if H has a size k hitting set.*

Proof. Let (V, E) denote the hypergraph H. We prove correctness of the algorithm by induction on $|E|$.

Suppose that $|E| = 0$. We have $E = \emptyset$; every subset of the vertex set is a hitting set, so there exists a hitting set of size k if and only if $|V| \geq k$, which holds if and only if the algorithm returns true.

Suppose that $|E| > 0$.

- When $k = 0$, there is no hitting set of size 0, as the empty set is not a hitting set, so the algorithm correctly returns false.
- When $k > 0$, let e be any hyperedge in E. It follows directly from Proposition 4.3.3 that H has a hitting set of size k if and only if there exists $u \in e$ such that H_{-u} has a hitting set of size $k - 1$. Thus, by induction, the algorithm returns true if and only if H has a hitting set of size k. $\qquad\square$

We next perform a time analysis of this algorithm. Our analysis will lead to tractability results for restricted versions of this language where the edge size is bounded. When $H = (V, E)$ is a hypergraph, we use $\mathrm{card}(H)$ to denote the maximum size of any edge in H, that is, we define $\mathrm{card}(H) = \max_{e \in E} |e|$.

Theorem 4.3.5. *There exists a DTM M implementing the algorithm HS and a polynomial P such that, on each instance (H, k), it holds that*

$$\mathrm{time}_M(H, k) \leq (2 \cdot \mathrm{card}(H)^k) \cdot P(n),$$

where n denotes the encoding size of (H, k).

In the following, we use the term *at most* to mean *less than or equal to*.

Proof. The algorithm HS can be implemented by a DTM M in a way that there is a polynomial $P \colon \mathbb{N} \to \mathbb{N}$ with the following property: for all instances (H', k') having encoding size at most n, the DTM uses at most $P(n)$ time steps, not including the time spent by the recursive calls.

Let $T(n, c, k)$ be the maximum running time on instances (H', k') having encoding size at most n, having $\mathrm{card}(H') \leq c$, and having $k' \leq k$. It suffices to prove that for each $c \geq 2$ and $k \geq 0$, the inequality $T(n, c, k) \leq (2c^k - 1)P(n)$ holds; this is proved by induction on k.

When $k = 0$, we have $T(n, c, k) \leq P(n) \leq (2c^0 - 1)P(n)$.

When $k > 0$, an invocation of $\mathrm{HS}(H', k')$, on an instance (H', k') as described, will perform at most c recursive calls, each on an instance of the form $(H'_{-u}, k' - 1)$. We have

$$T(n, c, k) \leq cT(n, c, k - 1) + P(n)$$
$$\leq c(2c^{k-1} - 1)P(n) + P(n)$$
$$= (2c^k - c + 1)P(n)$$
$$\leq (2c^k - 1)P(n). \qquad\square$$

Each graph G (having an edge) is a hypergraph with card$(G) = 2$. Viewing each instance (G, k) of the language VERTEX-COVER as an instance of the hitting set problem, we obtain the following consequence of the just-given theorem.

Corollary 4.3.6. *There exists a polynomial Q and a DTM that decides each instance (G, k) of the language* VERTEX-COVER *within time $2^k Q(n)$, where n is the encoding size of the instance.*

Remark 4.3.7. The algorithm HS exemplifies an algorithmic technique known as *bounded search trees.*This technique generally involves a recursive search where each invocation of the algorithm calls itself on instances simpler than the one passed in, and where the size of the resulting search tree can be bounded by a function of the original instance's parameter.   ◇

We next present an enumeration algorithm that, given an instance (H, k) of the hitting set problem, outputs all *minimal* hitting sets of H having size at most k. We here say that a hitting set S of a hypergraph H is **minimal** when no proper subset of S is a hitting set of H. Our algorithm will make use of the following fact, which is analogous to Proposition 4.3.3's forward direction.

Proposition 4.3.8. *Let $H = (V, E)$ be a hypergraph, and let $e \in E$ be an edge. If T is a minimal hitting set of H, then there exists a vertex $u \in e$ such that $u \in T$ and $T \setminus \{u\}$ is a minimal hitting set of H_{-u}.*

The following is our enumeration algorithm; it receives as input a hypergraph $H = (V, E)$ and a value $k \in \mathbb{N}$.

Algorithm EnumHS(H, k).

- If $E = \emptyset$: return $\{\emptyset\}$.
- If $k = 0$: return $\emptyset$.
- Otherwise:
  - Assign $\mathcal{S} := \emptyset$.
  - Pick e to be any hyperedge in E.
  - For each $u \in e$ and for each $S \in$ EnumHS$(H_{-u}, k - 1)$:
    If the set $S \cup \{u\}$ is a minimal hitting set of H, place it in $\mathcal{S}$.
  - Return $\mathcal{S}$.

Remark 4.3.9. We take it as understood that this algorithm checks whether a set T is a minimal hitting set of a hypergraph H by verifying both that T is a hitting set and that for each $v \in T$, the set $T \setminus \{v\}$ is not a hitting set.   ◇

We begin our analysis of this algorithm by establishing correctness.

Theorem 4.3.10. *Let S be the result returned by EnumHS(H, k); then, S is the set containing all minimal hitting sets of H having size at most k.*

Proof. We prove the theorem by induction on $|E|$.

Suppose that $|E| = 0$. Then $E = \emptyset$; the empty set $\emptyset$ is the unique minimal hitting set of H.

Suppose that $|E| > 0$. There is no hitting set of size 0, so when $k = 0$, the result $S = \emptyset$ is as the theorem describes. We next assume that $k > 0$. Let e be the picked hyperedge. Each set placed in S is a minimal hitting set, and has size at most k, since by induction the set returned by each recursive call to EnumHS$(H_{-u}, k-1)$ has size at most $k-1$. We need to show that an arbitrary minimal hitting set S' of H having size at most k is an element of S. By Proposition 4.3.8, such a set S' contains a vertex $u \in e$ and is equal to $S \cup \{u\}$ where S is a minimal hitting set of H_{-u} having size at most $k-1$. By induction, the set S is returned by EnumHS$(H_{-u}, k-1)$, and so S' is placed into S by the algorithm. $\square$

Having established correctness of the algorithm EnumHS, we can observe a bound on the *number* of minimal hitting sets.

Proposition 4.3.11. *Suppose that $c \geq 2$ and that (H, k) is an instance of the hitting set problem with $\mathrm{card}(H) \leq c$. The hypergraph H has at most c^k minimal hitting sets of size at most k.*

This proposition is straightforwardly verified by showing, by induction on k, that the size of the set returned by EnumHS(H, k) is at most c^k. We remark that the bound given here fails (in general) if one simply counts hitting sets, without the assumption of minimality: a hypergraph with n vertices and no edges has $\binom{n}{k}$ hitting sets of size k.

Finally, we present a time bound on the algorithm EnumHS.

Theorem 4.3.12. *Let $c \geq 2$. There exists a DTM implementing the algorithm EnumHS, a computable function $g: \Sigma^* \to \mathbb{N}$, and a polynomial R such that, on each instance (H, k) with $\mathrm{card}(H) \leq c$, it holds that*

$$\mathrm{time}_M(H, k) \leq g(k) \cdot R(n),$$

where n denotes the encoding size of (H, k).

Proof. As implied by Remark 4.3.9, it is possible to check in polynomial time whether a given set T is a minimal hitting set of a hypergraph. The algorithm EnumHS can be implemented by a DTM in a way that there is a polynomial Q' with the following property: for all instances (H', k') having encoding size at most n and with $k' \leq k$, the DTM uses at most $Q'(c^k n)$ time steps, omitting the time spent by the recursive calls. The factor c^k comes from the loop: each recursive call made on such an instance returns a set of size at most c^{k-1}, and the loop over each u in the picked hyperedge e incurs another factor of c. An analysis analogous to that of Theorem 4.3.5's proof thus holds, but with the function $Q(n, k) = Q'(c^k n)$ in place of $P(n)$. $\square$

4.3.2 Definitions and discussion

Just as the classical complexity theory seen in the previous chapter provides a taxonomy for classifying languages, as we saw in the previous chapter, parameterized complexity theory provides a taxonomy for classifying *parameterized languages*. We here present our definition framework for discussing parameterized languages and fixed-parameter tractability. Before we can formally define parameterized languages, however, some preparatory definitions are needed. We first define, with respect to a function $\kappa \colon \Sigma^* \to \Sigma^*$, the notion of a κ-*scaled polynomial*, which is the adjusted form of polynomial running time that we are interested in. A κ-*fpt-time DTM* is a DTM whose running time is bounded by a κ-scaled polynomial; here and in the sequel, **fpt** abbreviates *fixed-parameter tractable*.

Definition 4.3.13. Let $\kappa \colon \Sigma^* \to \Sigma^*$ be a function.

- A function $T \colon \Sigma^* \to \mathbb{N}$ is a κ-**scaled polynomial** if there exist a computable function $g \colon \Sigma^* \to \mathbb{N}$ and a polynomial $P \colon \mathbb{N} \to \mathbb{N}$ such that, for each $x \in \Sigma^*$, it holds that $T(x) = g(\kappa(x))P(|x|)$.

- A κ-**fpt-time DTM** is a halting DTM M for which there exists a κ-scaled polynomial $T \colon \Sigma^* \to \mathbb{N}$ such that (for each $x \in \Sigma^*$) it holds that $\text{time}_M(x) \leq T(x)$. ◇

Here and later, we associate each natural number n with its encoding $\ulcorner n \urcorner$, so a function $g \colon \Sigma^* \to \mathbb{N}$ is considered *computable* when the function sending each $x \in \Sigma^*$ to $\ulcorner g(x) \urcorner$ is. In the definition of κ-scaled polynomial, the requirement that the function g be computable is included as it confers robustness on the notion of fixed-parameter tractability, defined below; we will later see (in Section 4.3.3) two natural characterizations of this notion, which evidence this robustness.

We next give an example of a κ-fpt-time DTM—after a remark.

Remark 4.3.14 (The projection functions π_1 and π_2). We will work with a number of languages whose members are all pairs. In this context, we will want to use the functions that return the first and second entries of a pair, in the role of the function κ in Definition 4.3.13. Technically, however, such a function κ need be defined on all strings, not just those arising as pair encodings.

In such a context, we understand π_1 and π_2 to be the polynomial-time computable functions from Σ^* to Σ^* where, for all strings $x, y \in \Sigma^*$, it holds that

$$\pi_1(\langle x, y \rangle) = x \quad \text{and} \quad \pi_2(\langle x, y \rangle) = y,$$

and where, for each string $z \in \Sigma^*$ that is not a pair encoding, it holds that $\pi_1(z) = \pi_2(z) = \epsilon$. That is, the functions π_1, π_2 return the first and second entries of each pair, respectively, and return the empty string on non-pairs.

When dealing with languages consisting of pairs, the reader usually can safely neglect to think about strings that are not pairs; indeed, when we apply the functions π_1, π_2 to instances, it is intended that the strings sent to ϵ by these functions will be obviously outside of the languages at hand, and we will often omit these strings from our analyses. In general, we assume that each function definition is interpreted reasonably on non-instances. ◇

Example 4.3.15. To illustrate Definition 4.3.13, we can state that there exists a π_2-fpt-time DTM whose language is VERTEX-COVER. This follows from Corollary 4.3.6, whose DTM decides each instance $x = (G, k)$ of VERTEX-COVER within time $2^k Q(|x|) = 2^{\pi_2(x)} Q(|x|)$. Here, we measure the running time of an instance $x = (G, k)$ in terms of both $|x|$ and $\pi_2(x) = k$. This running time is of the form required by Definition 4.3.13, via taking $g(k) = 2^k$. ◇

Using the notion of κ-fpt-time DTM, we can next define the property of κ-fpt-computability on languages and functions.

Definition 4.3.16. Let $\kappa \colon \Sigma^* \to \Sigma^*$ be a function.

- A language B is κ-**fpt-computable** if there exists a κ-fpt-time DTM M with $B = L(M)$.
- A function $f \colon \Sigma^* \to \Sigma^*$ is κ-**fpt-computable** if there exists a κ-fpt-time DTM that computes it. ◇

Example 4.3.17. We saw in Example 4.3.15 that there is a π_2-fpt-time DTM whose language is VERTEX-COVER. To use the terminology of Definition 4.3.16, we can say that the language VERTEX-COVER is π_2-fpt-computable. ◇

The next proposition shows that, for any function κ, the κ-fpt-computable languages and functions include the PTIME languages and polynomial-time computable functions, respectively. We will sometimes invoke these facts tacitly in the sequel.

Proposition 4.3.18. *Let* $\kappa \colon \Sigma^* \to \Sigma^*$ *be any function. Each polynomial-time DTM is a κ-fpt-time DTM. Thus, each PTIME language is κ-fpt-computable, and likewise each polynomial-time computable function is κ-fpt-computable.*

Proof. Suppose that M is a polynomial-time DTM, and let P be a polynomial such that M runs within time P. For each string $x \in \Sigma^*$, we have time$_M(x) \leq P(|x|)$. The function $T \colon \Sigma^* \to \mathbb{N}$ defined by $T(x) = P(|x|)$ is a κ-scaled polynomial, via taking $g \colon \Sigma^* \to \mathbb{N}$ in the definition to be the constant function always equal to 1; thus, M is a κ-fpt-time DTM. The rest of the proposition follows from the relevant definitions. □

We can now define the key notion of a *parameterization*.

Definition 4.3.19. A **parameterization** is a function $\kappa \colon \Sigma^* \to \Sigma^*$ that is κ-fpt-computable. Relative to a parameterization κ, the **parameter** of a string $x \in \Sigma^*$ is the string $\kappa(x)$. ◇

Remark 4.3.20. Oftentimes, we will refer to the *parameter* of a string without naming the parameterization; when we do so, the parameterization will be clear from the context. ◇

Each polynomial-time computable function is a parameterization (by Proposition 4.3.18), including the functions π_1 and π_2 from Remark 4.3.14. Also, studied parameterizations are often polynomial-time computable; a typical situation where this occurs is when the parameter of an instance appears explicitly as part of each instance. On a first reading, one may conceive of the set of parameterizations as a mild (but meaningful) expansion of the set of polynomial-time computable functions. Our definition of *parameterization* encompasses functions that are not known to be polynomial-time computable, such as the vertex cover number, and the graph-theoretic measure of treewidth. At the same time, our definition of *parameterization* is stringent enough to ensure that, in designing a parameterized algorithm, the algorithm can compute and thus make use of the parameter of an instance.

To discuss an example parameterization, let $\tau \colon \Sigma^* \to \Sigma^*$ denote the function that maps each graph G to the minimum size over all vertex covers of G. We call this function the **vertex cover number**. This function is not known to be polynomial-time computable (if it were, the NP-complete language VERTEX-COVER could be readily shown to be PTIME), but is nonetheless a parameterization.

Theorem 4.3.21. *The vertex cover number τ is τ-fpt-computable, and is hence a parameterization.*

Proof. Consider the DTM M' that, given a graph $G = (V, E)$, invokes the DTM M of Corollary 4.3.6 on increasing values of k starting from 0, that is, for $k = 0, 1, 2, \ldots$, until the DTM M accepts; the value of k for which the DTM M accepts (G, k) is the output of the DTM M', and is evidently the desired value $\tau(G)$. We can estimate the time usage of M' as

$$2^0 Q(|(G, 0)|) + 2^1 Q(|(G, 1)|) + \cdots + 2^{\tau(G)} Q(|(G, \tau(G)|)).$$

This sum can be bounded above by $2 \cdot 2^{\tau(G)} Q(|(G, |V|)|)$, which can be seen as a computable function of $\tau(G)$ multiplied by a polynomial in $|G|$. $\square$

We next present the central notions of *parameterized language* and of *fixed-parameter tractability*.

Definition 4.3.22. A **parameterized language** is a pair (B, κ) consisting of a language B and a parameterization κ. $\diamond$

Definition 4.3.23. A parameterized language (B, κ) is **fixed-parameter tractable**, or **FPT**, if the language B is κ-fpt-computable. $\diamond$

Example 4.3.24. The pair (VERTEX-COVER, π_2) is a parameterized language: the function π_2 is polynomial-time computable and is hence a parameterization. This parameterized language is FPT: as stated in Example 4.3.17, the language VERTEX-COVER is π_2-fpt-computable. $\diamond$

The following proposition, which is a consequence of Proposition 4.3.18, supplies numerous examples of parameterized languages that are FPT.

Proposition 4.3.25. *Let B be any PTIME language, and let κ be any parameterization. The parameterized language (B, κ) is FPT.*

Due to the general principle given by Proposition 4.3.25, the quest for FPT results typically focuses on parameterized languages whose language component is not known to be PTIME. Indeed, recall that one motivation behind introducing fixed-parameter tractability was to seek positive results where they could not be identified under classical complexity theory.

Let us identify some further FPT results that follow from the algorithms given for the hitting set problem (in Section 4.3.1). Define the language

HITTING-SET = $\{(H, k) \mid H$ is a hypergraph having a size k hitting set$\}$.

For each $c \geq 2$:

- We define c-HITTING-SET as the language $\{(H, k) \in$ HITTING-SET $\mid$ card$(H) \leq c\}$.
- We define p-c-HITTING-SET as the parameterized language $(c$-HITTING-SET$, \pi_2)$; so, the parameter of an instance (H, k) is the value $\pi_2(H, k) = k$.

Theorem 4.3.26. *For each $c \geq 2$, the parameterized language p-c-HITTING-SET is FPT.*

Proof. This is immediate from Theorems 4.3.4 and 4.3.5: each instance of c-HITTING-SET has card$(H) \leq c$, and so Theorem 4.3.5's DTM runs within time $(2c^k) \cdot P(n)$. $\qquad\square$

Remark 4.3.27. Let γ denote the parameterization that maps each instance (H, k) of HITTING-SET to the pair (card$(H), k$); so here, the parameter of an instance holds the maximum edge size in addition to the value k. Theorem 4.3.5's running time bound in fact directly implies that the parameterized language (HITTING-SET$, \gamma$) is FPT. $\qquad\diamond$

We next present two basic properties of parameterizations and parameterized languages. The first property, which applies to any parameterization, holds that for any particular parameter k, the set of all strings having parameter k is PTIME; the second property holds that, for a parameterized language (B, κ) that is FPT, the same set restricted to strings inside the language B is also PTIME.

Proposition 4.3.28. *Let κ be a parameterization, and let $k \in \Sigma^*$ be a string. The language $\{x \in \Sigma^* \mid \kappa(x) = k\}$—that is, the set of all strings with parameter k, denoted here by $\Sigma^*_{\kappa=k}$— is a PTIME language.*

Proof. By the definition of parameterization, there exists a κ-fpt-time DTM M computing κ. Let $T(x) = g(\kappa(x))P(|x|)$ be a κ-scaled polynomial such that time$_M(x) \leq T(x)$ (for all $x \in \Sigma^*$). Set $C = g(k)$; on each string $x \in \Sigma^*_{\kappa=k}$, it holds that time$_M(x) \leq C \cdot P(|x|)$. Thus, the language $\Sigma^*_{\kappa=k}$ is the language of the polynomial-time DTM that, on any input string $x \in \Sigma^*$, runs M on x for up to $C \cdot P(|x|)$ time steps, and after that accepts if M outputs k within the allotted time, and rejects otherwise. $\qquad\square$

Proposition 4.3.29. *Let (B, κ) be a parameterized language that is FPT, and let $k \in \Sigma^*$ be a string. The language $\{x \in B \mid \kappa(x) = k\}$, denoted here by $B_{\kappa=k}$, is a PTIME language.*

Proof. Let M_B be a κ-fpt-time DTM with $B = L(M_B)$, and let $T'(x) = g'(\kappa(x))P'(|x|)$ be a κ-scaled polynomial such that $\text{time}_{M_B}(x) \leq T'(x)$ (for all $x \in \Sigma^*$). Set $D = g'(k)$.

Define M_k to be the DTM that behaves as follows, on an input string x: first, invoke the DTM given by Proposition 4.3.28, which decides whether or not $\kappa(x) = k$; reject if this does not hold, otherwise invoke the DTM M_B on the string x. The language of M_k is equal to $B_{\kappa=k}$: M_k accepts a string x if and only if $\kappa(x) = k$ and M_B accepts x. Also, M_k runs within polynomial time: the DTM of Proposition 4.3.28 runs within polynomial time, and the inequality $\text{time}_{M_B}(x) \leq T'(x) = D \cdot P'(|x|)$ holds on any string x with $\kappa(x) = k$. $\square$

Proposition 4.3.29 indicates that, in order for a parameterized language (B, κ) to be FPT, it is *necessary* for each of the languages $B_{\kappa=k}$ to be PTIME.

Remark 4.3.30. By an **instance** of a parameterized language (B, κ), we refer to an *instance* of the underlying language B. Often, a parameterized language (B, κ) is referred to as a *parameterized problem*, particularly when the language B is viewed as a decision problem. We will sometimes loosely refer to parameterized languages simply as *problems*. (Remark 3.8.1 discussed the usage of the terms *instance*, *problem*, and *decision problem* in classical complexity theory.) $\diamond$

One can find the notion of *parameterized language* defined in a number of ways in the literature; in Note 4.6.22, we compare our definition thereof with some of the alternatives.

4.3.3 Characterizations of fixed-parameter tractability

We present two fundamental characterizations of fixed-parameter tractability.

Characterization by compilation

Our first characterization shows that a parameterized language is FPT if and only if it is *para-PTIME*, meaning essentially that there is a computable way to transform each parameter k into a string $\pi(k)$ such that, when an input string x is presented along with the transformation $\pi(\kappa(x))$ of its parameter $\kappa(x)$, membership of x can be decided in polynomial time. The transformation from each parameter k to the string $\pi(k)$ is here conceived of as being separate from the process of deciding membership in the language, and the string $\pi(k)$ is referred to as the *compilation* of the parameter k. See Figure 4.3.1 for a diagram representation of this definition.

Definition 4.3.31. A parameterized language (B, κ) is **para-PTIME** if there exist a computable function $\pi \colon \Sigma^* \to \Sigma^*$ and a PTIME language C such that (for each $x \in \Sigma^*$)

$$x \in B \quad \Leftrightarrow \quad \langle x, \pi(\kappa(x))\rangle \in C. \qquad \diamond$$

Theorem 4.3.32. *A parameterized language (B, κ) is FPT if and only if it is para-PTIME.*

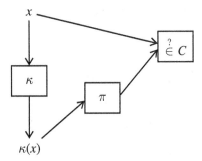

Figure 4.3.1. A schema indicating what it means for a parameterized language (B, κ) to be para-PTIME (Definition 4.3.31). The language B should be decided by the given schema, where the function π is required to be computable, and the language C is required to be PTIME.

The parameterized languages that are para-PTIME are sometimes referred to as being PTIME *after a precomputation on the parameter*. Intuitively speaking, in order for a parameterized language to be para-PTIME, its language must be PTIME when each instance is presented along with a piece of auxiliary information, which depends only on the instance's parameter.

Observe that the only computational notions that the definition of para-PTIME refers to are those of *computability* and *polynomial-time computability*; thus, in a sense, this characterization of FPT is purely in terms of computational notions introduced in previous chapters.

Observe also that the function π is required just to be computable; thus, when k is a parameter, the string $\pi(k)$ may be much longer than k itself. Indeed, the forward direction of this theorem's proof essentially involves taking a κ-fpt-time DTM for the parameterized language at hand, and defining, for each parameter k, the string $\pi(k)$ to be sufficiently long so that, when an input string x is presented with the string $\pi(\kappa(x))$, the DTM runs within polynomial time. The backward direction of this theorem's proof involves performing a time analysis.

Proof of Theorem 4.3.32. We begin with the backward direction. Suppose that (B, κ) is para-PTIME, and let C and π be as in the definition of para-PTIME. Let M_C be a polynomial-time DTM whose language is C and let P_C be a polynomial such that M_C runs within time P_C. As κ is a parameterization, there exists a κ-fpt-time DTM that computes $\kappa(x)$ from x; the time needed to compute $\pi(\kappa(x))$ from $\kappa(x)$ depends only on $\kappa(x)$, so there exists a κ-fpt-time DTM M_0 that computes $\pi(\kappa(x))$ from x. Consider the DTM M that, on an input string x, invokes M_0 to obtain $\pi(\kappa(x))$, and then passes control to the execution of M_C on $\langle x, \pi(\kappa(x)) \rangle$. From the definition of para-PTIME, it is clear that $L(M) = B$. To conclude that M is a κ-fpt-time DTM, we need to upper bound $\text{time}_{M_C}(\langle x, \pi(\kappa(x)) \rangle)$.

By the pair encoding that we presented, it holds that $|\langle x, \pi(\kappa(x))\rangle| = 2|x| + 2 + |\pi(\kappa(x))|$. We thus have

$$
\begin{aligned}
\text{time}_{M_C}\big(\langle x, \pi(\kappa(x))\rangle\big) &\leq P_C\big(2|x| + 2 + |\pi(\kappa(x))|\big) \\
&\leq P_C\big((|x| + 1) \cdot (|\pi(\kappa(x))| + 2)\big) \\
&\leq P_C\big(|\pi(\kappa(x))| + 2\big) \cdot P_C\big(|x| + 1\big).
\end{aligned}
$$

The last inequality is justified by Remark 4.3.1. The final expression is the product of a function of $\kappa(x)$ with a polynomial of $|x|$.

For the forward direction, let M_B be a κ-fpt-time DTM whose language is B; and let $g \colon \Sigma^* \to \mathbb{N}$ be a computable function and let P_B be a polynomial that together yield a κ-scaled polynomial witnessing that M_B is a κ-fpt-time DTM. Define the function $\pi \colon \Sigma^* \to \Sigma^*$ by $\pi(k) = 1^{g(k)}$; π is computable as a consequence of g being computable. Let M_C be a DTM that, when given as input a pair of the form $\langle x, 1^t \rangle$, runs M_B on x for up to $t \cdot P_B(|x|)$ time steps; and then accepts if M_B accepts x within this number of time steps, and rejects otherwise. On each pair $z = \langle x, 1^t \rangle$, the DTM M_C runs M_B for at most $t \cdot P_B(|x|) \leq |z| \cdot P_B(|z|)$ many time steps, and thus it is possible to implement M_C as a polynomial-time DTM. Set $C = L(M_C)$; we then have that C is a PTIME language. To conclude the proof, we confirm the condition in the definition of para-PTIME. For each string $x \in \Sigma^*$, we have

$$
\begin{aligned}
x \in B \quad &\Leftrightarrow \quad M_B \text{ accepts } x \\
&\Leftrightarrow \quad M_B \text{ accepts } x \text{ within } g(\kappa(x))P_B(|x|) \text{ time steps} \\
&\Leftrightarrow \quad \langle x, 1^{g(\kappa(x))} \rangle \in C \\
&\Leftrightarrow \quad \langle x, \pi(\kappa(x)) \rangle \in C. \qquad\qquad\qquad\qquad\qquad\qquad \square
\end{aligned}
$$

Let us mention that there are certain database query evaluation problems that are naturally shown to be FPT via the characterization given by Theorem 4.3.32. An instance of these problems requests the evaluation of a database query on a database; the database query is the parameter, and the compilation $\pi(k)$ of a database query k is an optimized rewriting of the query that allows for polynomial-time evaluation.

Characterization by kernelization

We next characterize fixed-parameter tractability via a type of preprocessing method,[38] called a *kernelization*, that converts each instance of a problem into a short form. Intuitively speaking, a kernelization efficiently processes manageable aspects of an instance,

---

38. While the function π of Definition 4.3.31 can be viewed as performing a brand of preprocessing, note that this function is applied only to parameters of instances.

simplifying it so that after it is done, what remains constitutes a hard inner core of the original instance. A kernelization is required to shrink each instance x to a size that is bounded above by a function of x's parameter.

Formally, a **kernelization** of a parameterized language (B, κ) is defined as a polynomial-time many-one reduction $\rho \colon \Sigma^* \to \Sigma^*$ from B to B such that there exists a computable function $h \colon \Sigma^* \to \mathbb{N}$ where (for each $x \in \Sigma^*$) it holds that $|\rho(x)| \leq h(\kappa(x))$. That is, a kernelization of a parameterized language is an efficient self-reduction of the underlying language whose output size is bounded above by a function of the input's parameter. The output $\rho(x)$ of a kernelization on a string x is sometimes referred to as the **kernel** of x. The following is our characterization.

Theorem 4.3.33. *A parameterized language (B, κ) is FPT if and only if there exists a kernelization of it and the language B is computable.*

Proving the backward direction is relatively straightforward: fixed-parameter tractability is witnessed by the algorithm that, on an input string x, first applies the kernelization to x, and then invokes a DTM deciding B on the kernelization's result.

The essential idea of the forward direction's proof is to define the kernelization ρ as the function computed by a DTM M_ρ that, given a string x, runs a κ-fpt-time DTM M with language B, for a sufficiently large amount of polynomial time. If M is seen to accept or reject x, then M_ρ outputs a fixed string inside or outside of B, respectively; otherwise, M_ρ outputs the string x itself. In the latter case, the running time of M exceeded the allocated polynomial time, and so the length $|x|$ is smaller than a function of x's parameter, as required by the definition of kernelization.

Proof. We first prove the backward direction. By assumption, the language B is computable; let M_B be a halting DTM whose language is B. Let ρ be a kernelization of (B, κ), let M_ρ be a polynomial-time DTM that computes ρ, and let P_ρ be a polynomial such that M_ρ runs within time P_ρ. Consider the DTM M that, on an input string x, first uses M_ρ to compute $\rho(x)$, and then passes control to the execution of M_B on $\rho(x)$. Let $h^+ \colon \Sigma^* \to \mathbb{N}$ be the function defined by

$$h^+(k) = \max \left\{ \mathrm{time}_{M_B}(y) \mid y \in \Sigma^*, |y| \leq h(k) \right\}.$$

For all $x \in \Sigma^*$, we have that $|\rho(x)| \leq h(\kappa(x))$ and hence that $\mathrm{time}_{M_B}(\rho(x)) \leq h^+(\kappa(x))$. We may thus observe that

$$\mathrm{time}_M(x) \leq P_\rho(|x|) + \mathrm{time}_{M_B}(\rho(x)) \leq P_\rho(|x|) + h^+(\kappa(x)) \leq \left(h^+(\kappa(x)) + 1 \right) \left(P_\rho(|x|) + 1 \right).$$

We conclude that M is a κ-fpt-time DTM whose language is B.

We next prove the forward direction. Observe that if B is trivial, it is computable, and we obtain a kernelization of (B, κ) by defining ρ as the constant function equal everywhere to ϵ, and by defining h as the constant function equal everywhere to 0. We thus assume in the sequel that B is nontrivial. By assumption, there exists a κ-fpt-time DTM M whose

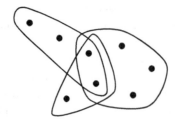

Figure 4.3.2. An example sunflower with 3 hyperedges. In a sunflower having at least 2 hyper-edges, each pair of hyperedges has a common intersection, which is the *core* of the sunflower. In this example sunflower, the core contains 2 vertices.

language is B; let g be a computable function and let P be a polynomial that together yield a κ-scaled polynomial witnessing that M is a κ-fpt-time DTM. As the DTM M is halting by definition, we have that the language B is computable. Fix y_0 and y_1 to be strings such that $y_0 \notin B$ and $y_1 \in B$; such strings exist by the assumption that B is nontrivial.

Define M_ρ to be the DTM that, on an input string $x \in \Sigma^*$, carries out the following. Run M on x for up to $|x| \cdot P(|x|)$ time steps, and then:

- If M rejects or accepts, within the allotted time, output y_0 or y_1, respectively.
- Otherwise, output x.

Let $\rho \colon \Sigma^* \to \Sigma^*$ be the function computed by M_ρ. It is evident that ρ is a polynomial-time many-one reduction from B to B. Define the function $h \colon \Sigma^* \to \mathbb{N}$ by $h(k) = \max\{|y_0|, |y_1|, g(k)\}$. We verify that ρ is a kernelization via h, by considering the behavior of M_ρ on an input string x:

- If M accepts or rejects within the allotted time, then $|\rho(x)| \le \max\{|y_0|, |y_1|\} \le h(\kappa(x))$.
- Otherwise, we may observe that $|x| \cdot P(|x|) < \text{time}_M(x) \le g(\kappa(x))P(|x|)$, which implies that $|x| \le g(\kappa(x))$; it thus holds that $|\rho(x)| = |x| \le g(\kappa(x)) \le h(\kappa(x))$.   □

An example kernelization

The presentation of a kernelization has become a basic tool for exhibiting FPT results. Let us give an example kernelization, which is for the parameterized language p-c-HITTING-SET. We begin by introducing the notion of a *sunflower* in a hypergraph and a result on the existence of sunflowers; the presentation of the kernelization will rely on these.

A *sunflower* in a hypergraph is a set of hyperedges where any two hyperedges therein have a common intersection. Formally, a **sunflower** in a hypergraph $H = (V, E)$ is a sub-set $F \subseteq E$ such that there exists $C \subseteq V$ having the property that for any two distinct elements $f, f' \in F$, it holds that $f \cap f' = C$; a set C having this property is said to be a

core of the sunflower F. See Figure 4.3.2 for an example of a sunflower. Note that when F is a sunflower with $|F| > 1$, it holds that $\bigcap_{f \in F} f$ is the unique core of F and is a subset of each $f \in F$; note also that, in a hypergraph, any subset of a sunflower is also a sunflower.

The relevance of sunflowers to hitting sets is given by the following lemma, which holds that, in determining whether a hypergraph has a hitting set of a certain size k, any sunflower (in the hypergraph) whose size exceeds k can be replaced with its core.

Lemma 4.3.34. *Suppose that $H = (V, E)$ is a hypergraph, $k \geq 1$, and F is a sunflower in H with $|F| > k$ and having core C. Let $H^- = (V, E^-)$ be the hypergraph with hyperedges $E^- = (E \setminus F) \cup \{C\}$; then,*

$$(H, k) \in \textsf{HITTING-SET} \quad \text{if and only if} \quad (H^-, k) \in \textsf{HITTING-SET}.$$

Proof. For the forward direction, when S is a size k hitting set of H, it must hold that $S \cap C$ is nonempty: if not, S would contain a vertex from each set of the form $f \setminus C$, where $f \in F$; but these sets are pairwise disjoint, implying $|S| \geq |F| > k$, a contradiction. For the backward direction, when S is a size k hitting set of H^-, it holds that $S \cap C$ is nonempty, from which it follows that, for any $f \in F$, the set $S \cap f$ is nonempty. $\qquad\qquad\square$

Example 4.3.35. Suppose one has a graph $G = (V, E)$ in hand; if a vertex $v \in V$ is picked, and F_v is defined as the set $\{e \in E \mid v \in e\}$ of edges where v appears, then F_v is a sunflower of which $\{v\}$ is a core, and whose size is the degree of v. Applying Lemma 4.3.34 to this sunflower, we obtain from the proof of this lemma's forward direction that if v has degree strictly above k (where $k \geq 1$), then any hitting set of G with size k must contain v. $\quad\Diamond$

The following lemma is a version of a classical combinatorial result known as the *Sunflower Lemma*, and will be the main engine powering our kernelization. This lemma essentially states that in a hypergraph with edge size bounded above by c, one finds a sunflower of size k so long as the hypergraph has sufficiently many edges, as a function of c and k.

Lemma 4.3.36. *For each $c \geq 1$, there exists a polynomial-time DTM M_c that, given as input a pair (H, k) where*

- $k \geq 1$, *and*
- $H = (V, E)$ *is a hypergraph with* $\mathrm{card}(H) \leq c$ *and* $|E| > c!(k-1)^c$,

outputs a size k sunflower in H.

Proof. We prove this by induction on c.

Suppose that $c = 1$. In this case, the set E is itself a sunflower in H, as any two distinct edges $e, e' \in E$ have $e \cap e' = \emptyset$. By the assumption on H, it holds that $|E| > k - 1$, so the DTM can simply output any size k subset of E.

Suppose that $c > 1$. The DTM greedily computes an inclusion-maximal set $D \subseteq E$ of pairwise disjoint hyperedges, by beginning with the empty set, and repeatedly adding hyperedges to the set so long as pairwise disjointness can be preserved, until no more hyperedges can be added. The resulting set D is a sunflower in H with the empty set $\emptyset$ as core. The DTM then proceeds as follows:

- If $|D| \geq k$, the DTM outputs any size k subset of D.
- If $|D| < k$, set $W = \bigcup_{d \in D} d$; it holds that $|W| \leq c(k-1)$. By the inclusion-maximality of D, each hyperedge $e \in E$ contains at least one element of W. Thus, there exists an element $w \in W$ that is contained in at least $\frac{|E|}{|W|} > \frac{c!(k-1)^c}{c(k-1)} = (c-1)!(k-1)^{c-1}$ many hyperedges of E. The DTM finds such an element w; sets $E' = \{e \setminus \{w\} \mid w \in e, e \in E\}$; and invokes the DTM M_{c-1}, on the hypergraph $H' = (V, E')$ and the value k, to obtain a size k sunflower F' in H'. The DTM then outputs $F = \{f' \cup \{w\} \mid f' \in F'\}$, which is a sunflower in H. □

We can now present the kernelization. Essentially, on an instance (H, k), it repeatedly finds a sunflower of size greater than k and replaces the sunflower with its core, which is justified by Lemma 4.3.34; when it can no longer do this, the number of hyperedges that it has must be bounded, via Lemma 4.3.36.

Theorem 4.3.37. *For each $c \geq 1$, there exists a kernelization of* p-c-HITTING-SET *that, when given a pair (H, k) where $k \geq 1$ and H is a hypergraph with card$(H) \leq c$, outputs a pair (H', k) where $H' = (V', E')$ is a hypergraph with card$(H) \leq c$ and $|E'| \leq c! k^c$.*

Proof. Each instance (H, k) of p-c-HITTING-SET with $k = 0$ can be readily resolved by a polynomial-time DTM. Thus, to show that there exists a kernelization of p-c-HITTING-SET, it suffices to define the kernelization on the pairs (H, k) described in the theorem statement, which is what we shall do.

Consider the DTM that, given a pair (H, k) as described, initially defines the **active** hypergraph H_a to be H, and iteratively checks if the active hypergraph $H_a = (V_a, E_a)$ has $|E_a| > c! k^c$; so long as it does, it invokes the DTM of Lemma 4.3.36 to obtain a sunflower F of size $k + 1$, and then replaces H_a with the reduced hypergraph H^- given by Lemma 4.3.34. After this procedure is done, the result is a hypergraph (V, E') where $|E'| \leq c! k^c$ and— by Lemma 4.3.34—has a size k hitting set if and only if the original hypergraph H does. Assuming that $|V| \geq k$, the existence of a size k hitting set in (V, E') is retained by removing vertices from V that do not occur in any hyperedge of E', so long as such a removal does not cause the number of vertices to decrease below k. By performing this removal, we obtain a hypergraph (V', E') where $|V'| \leq c \cdot c! k^c$, and hence where both $|V'|$ and $|E'|$ are bounded by functions of k, as desired. □

While the parameterized languages p-c-HITTING-SET were previously shown to be FPT (by Theorem 4.3.26), Theorem 4.3.37's kernelization of these parameterized languages yields, via Theorem 4.3.33, an alternative derivation of this fact.

4.4 Parameterized complexity

This section presents *parameterized complexity theory*, a complexity-theoretic framework which complements the notion of fixed-parameter tractability. This framework provides notions and tools that allow one to give evidence that a parameterized language is not fixed-parameter tractable—just as the framework of classical complexity theory, studied in the previous chapter, allowed one to give evidence that a language is not PTIME. Throughout this section, we make use of the functions π_1 and π_2 presented in Remark 4.3.14, and will discuss the following parameterized languages.

Definition 4.4.1. We define the following parameterized languages:

$$\text{p-VERTEX-COVER} = (\text{VERTEX-COVER}, \pi_2),$$
$$\text{p-INDEP-SET} = (\text{INDEP-SET}, \pi_2),$$
$$\text{p-CLIQUE} = (\text{CLIQUE}, \pi_2). \qquad \diamond$$

In each case of Definition 4.4.1, the parameterization π_2 sends a pair (G, k) to the value $\pi_2(G, k) = k$. This parameterization is often called the *standard parameterization* of the respective language: it provides the size of the object whose existence is under question. It is worth bearing in mind that it is not, by any means, the only parameterization that can be paired with these languages!

4.4.1 Reductions

We begin by presenting a parameterized version of many-one reducibility for comparing parameterized languages. A key property of the reduction notion to be presented is that the FPT parameterized languages are closed under it, that is, when an arbitrary parameterized language (B, κ) reduces to a parameterized language (B', κ') that is FPT, it holds that (B, κ) is FPT as well. In order to ensure this closure, the reduction should be a function where the process of computing the function and invoking a κ'-fpt-time DTM on the result can be performed by a κ-fpt-time DTM. We give a sufficient condition for a function to have this property; the following definition forms part of the sufficient condition.

Definition 4.4.2. Let κ, κ' be parameterizations. A function $f\colon \Sigma^* \to \Sigma^*$ is (κ, κ')-**parameter bounded** if there exists a computable function $s\colon \Sigma^* \to \wp_{\text{fin}}(\Sigma^*)$ where (for each $x \in \Sigma^*$) it holds that $\kappa'(f(x)) \in s(\kappa(x))$. $\qquad \diamond$

Recall that $\wp_{\text{fin}}(\Sigma^*)$ denotes the set whose elements are the finite subsets of Σ^*.

When $\gamma\colon \Sigma^* \to \Sigma^*$ is a function, define a γ-**slice** as a set having the form

$$\{x \in \Sigma^* \mid \gamma(x) = k\},$$

where $k \in \Sigma^*$. Under this terminology, when a function f is (κ, κ')-parameter bounded, the stipulation of Definition 4.4.2 that each set $s(k)$ is finite entails that the image of any κ-slice under f falls into finitely many κ'-slices. Let us remark that, for many of the reductions that we will present, the image of each κ-slice under f will in fact fall into a *single* κ'-slice.

The next lemma presents the promised sufficient condition in full.

Lemma 4.4.3. *Suppose that M is a (κ, κ')-fpt-time DTM that computes a (κ, κ')-parameter bounded function f, and that M′ is a κ'-fpt-time DTM. Let M^+ be the DTM that, on an input x, invokes M to compute f(x), and then invokes M′ on f(x); it holds that M^+ is a κ-fpt-time DTM.*

Proof. Let $g, g'\colon \Sigma^* \to \mathbb{N}$ be computable functions and let P, P' be polynomials such that, for all $x \in \Sigma^*$, it holds that

$$\mathrm{time}_M(x) \le g(\kappa(x))P(|x|) \quad \text{and} \quad \mathrm{time}_{M'}(x) \le g'(\kappa'(x))P'(|x|).$$

Let s be a function witnessing that f is (κ, κ')-parameter bounded. Define $g''\colon \Sigma^* \to \mathbb{N}$ to be the function defined by $g''(k) = \max \big\{ g'(k') \,\big|\, k' \in s(k) \big\}$, for all $k \in \Sigma^*$. From the computability of g' and s, it follows that g'' is computable.

Let $x \in \Sigma^*$, and set $y = f(x)$. We have $\kappa'(y) \in s(\kappa(x))$, and so $g'(\kappa'(y)) \le g''(\kappa(x))$. Thus,

$$\mathrm{time}_{M^+}(x) = \mathrm{time}_M(x) + \mathrm{time}_{M'}(y)$$

$$\le g(\kappa(x))P(|x|) + g'(\kappa'(y))P'(|y|)$$

$$\le g(\kappa(x))P(|x|) + g''(\kappa(x))P'(|g(\kappa(x))P(|x|)|)$$

$$\le g(\kappa(x))P(|x|) + g''(\kappa(x))P'(|g(\kappa(x))|)P'(P(|x|))$$

$$\le \big(g(\kappa(x)) + g''(\kappa(x))P'(|g(\kappa(x))|)\big)\big(P(|x|) + P'(P(|x|))\big).$$

In the second-to-last inequality, we make use of Remark 4.3.1. We conclude that the DTM M^+ is a κ-fpt-time DTM.   □

With this lemma in hand and as a basis, we give the notion of reduction to be used.

Definition 4.4.4. Let (B, κ), (B', κ') be parameterized languages. An **fpt-many-one reduction** from (B, κ) to (B', κ') is a κ-fpt-computable function $\rho\colon \Sigma^* \to \Sigma^*$ satisfying the following conditions:

- for each $x \in \Sigma^*$, it holds that $x \in B \Leftrightarrow \rho(x) \in B'$, and
- ρ is (κ, κ')-parameter bounded.

To indicate that there exists an fpt-many-one reduction from (B, κ) to (B', κ'), we write $(B, \kappa) \le_m^{\mathrm{fpt}} (B', \kappa')$ and we say that (B, κ) **fpt-many-one reduces** to (B', κ'). We refer to the first condition as the **correctness** of the function ρ, and to the second condition as the **parameter boundedness** of the function ρ.   ◇

Let us reconsider our first two examples of polynomial-time many-one reductions, and analyze whether they provide fpt-many-one reductions between the corresponding parameterized languages given in Definition 4.4.1.

Example 4.4.5. We saw a polynomial-time many-one reduction $\rho\colon \Sigma^* \to \Sigma^*$ from INDEP-SET to CLIQUE, in Proposition 3.4.7. This reduction maps each pair (G, k), where G is a graph and $k \in \mathbb{N}$, to the pair $(\overline{G}, k)$, where the graph G has been replaced with its complement $\overline{G}$.

This mapping ρ is a fpt-many-one reduction from p-INDEP-SET = (INDEP-SET, π_2) to p-CLIQUE = (CLIQUE, π_2); let us see why. Since ρ is polynomial-time computable, it is κ-fpt-computable for any function κ (recall Proposition 4.3.18). The correctness condition, which states that $x \in$ INDEP-SET $\Leftrightarrow \rho(x) \in$ CLIQUE, for each string x, is inherited from the correctness of ρ as a polynomial-time many-one reduction. Finally, we have that ρ is (π_2, π_2)-parameter bounded, via the function $s \colon \Sigma^* \to \wp_{\text{fin}}(\Sigma^*)$ defined by $s(k) = \{k\}$, as the reduction does not change the parameter of an instance. ◇

Example 4.4.6. We saw a poynomial-time many-one reduction $\rho : \Sigma^* \to \Sigma^*$ from INDEP-SET to VERTEX-COVER, in Proposition 3.4.10. This reduction maps each pair (G, k), where G is a graph with n vertices and $n \geq k$, to the pair $(G, n - k)$.

This mapping ρ is *not* an fpt-many-one reduction from p-INDEP-SET = (INDEP-SET, π_2) to p-VERTEX-COVER = (VERTEX-COVER, π_2). It maps an instance (G, k), which has parameter k, to the instance $(G, n - k)$, which has parameter $n - k$. Fix any natural number k; instances with parameter k, when mapped under ρ, can thus produce instances whose parameter is *any* natural number, since any natural number can be attained as $n - k$ for a value $n \geq k$. So, this mapping ρ is not (π_2, π_2)-parameter bounded: for any fixed natural number k, by varying the graph G, the parameter $\pi_2(\rho(G, k))$ of the instance $\rho(G, k)$ can take on an infinity of values, and thus it is not possible to define a finite set $s(k)$ that contains all possible values of this parameter. ◇

We now turn to identify some key properties of this reduction notion. First, we observe that the existence of a reduction is preserved under complementation, in the following sense.

Proposition 4.4.7. *Let (B, κ) and (B', κ') be parameterized languages such that $(B, \kappa) \leq_m^{\text{fpt}} (B', \kappa')$. Then it holds that $(\overline{B}, \kappa) \leq_m^{\text{fpt}} (\overline{B'}, \kappa')$.*

We next establish that the FPT parameterized languages are closed under reduction.

Theorem 4.4.8. *Suppose that (B, κ) and (B', κ') are parameterized languages such that $(B, \kappa) \leq_m^{\text{fpt}} (B', \kappa')$. If (B', κ') is FPT, then (B, κ) is FPT.*

Proof. Let ρ be a fpt-many-one reduction from (B, κ) to (B', κ'), and let M be a κ-fpt-time DTM that computes ρ. Let M' be a κ'-fpt-time DTM such that $B' = L(M')$. The machine M^+ obtained by applying Lemma 4.4.3 to M and M' is a κ-fpt-time DTM. The machine M^+ has $B = L(M^+)$: on an input x, it accepts if and only if $\rho(x) \in B'$, which holds if and only if $x \in B$, by the correctness of ρ. □

We observe that the relation $\leq_m^{\text{fpt}}$ is reflexive, due to the identity mapping being polynomial-time computable, and hence κ-fpt-computable, for any function κ.

Proposition 4.4.9. *For any parameterized language* (B, κ), *it holds that* $(B, \kappa) \leq_m^{\text{fpt}} (B, \kappa)$.

We next show that the relation $\leq_m^{\text{fpt}}$ is transitive; to do so, we again make use of Lemma 4.4.3.

Theorem 4.4.10. *Let* (B, κ), (B', κ'), *and* (B'', κ'') *be parameterized languages such that* $(B, \kappa) \leq_m^{\text{fpt}} (B', \kappa')$ *and* $(B', \kappa') \leq_m^{\text{fpt}} (B'', \kappa'')$. *Then it holds that* $(B, \kappa) \leq_m^{\text{fpt}} (B'', \kappa'')$.

Proof. Let ρ be a fpt-many-one reduction from (B, κ) to (B', κ'), and let σ be a fpt-many-one reduction from (B', κ') to (B'', κ''). We define $\tau \colon \Sigma^* \to \Sigma^*$ to be the composition of σ and ρ, that is, we define $\tau(x) = \sigma(\rho(x))$, for all $x \in \Sigma^*$. We show that τ is a fpt-many-one reduction from (B, κ) to (B'', κ''), by verifying each of the requisite properties:

- The function τ is κ-fpt-computable; this follows from applying Lemma 4.4.3 to a κ-fpt-time DTM that computes ρ, and a κ'-fpt-time DTM that computes σ.
- For all $x \in \Sigma^*$, it holds that $x \in B \Leftrightarrow \rho(x) \in B' \Leftrightarrow \sigma(\rho(x)) \in B'' \Leftrightarrow \tau(x) \in B''$.
- We verify that τ is (κ, κ'')-parameter bounded as follows. Let s_ρ witness that ρ is (κ, κ')-parameter bounded, and let s_σ witness that σ is (κ', κ'')-parameter bounded. We have $\kappa'(\rho(x)) \in s_\rho(\kappa(x))$ for all strings $x \in \Sigma^*$, and we have $\kappa''(\sigma(y)) \in s_\sigma(\kappa'(y))$ for all strings $y \in \Sigma^*$.

    Define $s_\tau \colon \Sigma^* \to \wp_{\text{fin}}(\Sigma^*)$ by $s_\tau(k) = \bigcup_{k' \in s_\rho(k)} s_\sigma(k')$, for each $k \in \Sigma^*$. Each set $s_\tau(k)$ is the finite union of finite sets, and is hence finite. We have that s_τ is computable, as a consequence of the computability of s_ρ and of s_σ.

    For any string $x \in \Sigma^*$, we have $\kappa''(\tau(x)) = \kappa''(\sigma(\rho(x)) \in s_\sigma(\kappa'(\rho(x))) \subseteq s_\tau(\kappa(x))$. $\square$

4.4.2 W[1] parameterized languages

The theory of NP-hardness and NP-completeness allowed us to relate and equate hypotheses about which languages were PTIME. The NP-completeness results that we saw revealed that the different languages treated were interreducible, and that their apparent intractability could be boiled down to and backed by the single hypothesis that $\mathbb{P} \neq \mathbb{NP}$. We here develop a theory of hardness and completeness for the class of *W[1] parameterized languages*, a class which, in the parameterized setting, plays a role similar to that of the NP languages in the classical setting. The class of W[1] parameterized languages is one of the initial classes in a hierarchy of classes known as the *W-hierarchy*.

We begin by defining the W[1] parameterized languages, via *weighted satisfiability problems*. An instance of one of these problems consists of a CNF-formula and a value $k \geq 0$, which is the parameter; the question is to decide whether the formula has a satisfying assignment with exactly k variables set to true. Thus, in faithfulness to the spirit of the problems p-VERTEX-COVER and p-CLIQUE, an instance here involves deciding if, from a given set, there is a selection of k elements satisfying a particular property.

When $f\colon V \to \{0, 1\}$ is an assignment to a finite set of variables V, define the **weight** of f as the number of variables set to 1, that is, as $|\{v \in V \mid f(v) = 1\}|$. When ϕ is a propositional formula, let $\mathrm{vars}(\phi)$ denote the set of all variables appearing in ϕ. Let $k \geq 0$; a CNF-formula ϕ is k-**satisfiable** if there exists an assignment $f\colon \mathrm{vars}(\phi) \to \{0, 1\}$ of weight k that satisfies ϕ. For each $d \geq 2$, define the language

WEIGHTED-d-CNF-SAT $= \{(\phi, k) \mid \phi$ is a k-satisfiable d-CNF-formula, and $k \in \mathbb{N}\}$,

and define the parameterized language

p-WEIGHTED-d-CNF-SAT $=$ (WEIGHTED-d-CNF-SAT, π_2).

Recall that a *d-CNF-formula* is a conjunction of clauses where each clause contains d or fewer literals.

Definition 4.4.11. A parameterized language (B, κ) is **W[1]** if there exists $d \geq 2$ such that

$$(B, \kappa) \leq_m^{\mathrm{fpt}} \text{p-WEIGHTED-}d\text{-CNF-SAT}. \qquad \diamond$$

Remark 4.4.12. In contrast to previously defined classes of languages and the class of the FPT parameterized languages, in Definition 4.4.11 we have defined a class of parameterized languages not via a computational model, but rather, by taking the closures, under reduction, of a sequence of parameterized languages. (In doing so, we nearly follow a definitional schema previously discussed in Remark 3.5.9.) Defining a class of parameterized languages as the closure (under reduction) of one or more parameterized languages is not at all uncommon in parameterized complexity theory. $\qquad \diamond$

Let us present a couple of basic properties of this definition. First, we have that the W[1] parameterized languages encompass the FPT ones: when a parameterized language (B, κ) is FPT, a κ-fpt-time DTM M with $B = L(M)$ can be readily modified to compute an fpt-many-one reduction from (B, κ) to any nontrivial language (along with a parameterization), and hence to the parameterized language p-WEIGHTED-2-CNF-SAT.

Proposition 4.4.13. *Each parameterized language that is FPT is W[1].*

Next, we have closure of the W[1] parameterized languages under reduction. This result will help us to establish that languages are W[1]; it can also be employed to give evidence that languages are not W[1].

Theorem 4.4.14. *Suppose that (A, γ) and (B, κ) are parameterized languages such that (B, κ) is W[1], and $(A, \gamma) \leq_m^{\mathrm{fpt}} (B, \kappa)$. Then, it holds that (A, γ) is W[1].*

Proof. By the hypothesis that (B, κ) is W[1], there exists $d \geq 2$ such that $(B, \kappa) \leq_m^{\mathrm{fpt}}$ p-WEIGHTED-d-CNF-SAT. We have $(A, \gamma) \leq_m^{\mathrm{fpt}} (B, \kappa)$ by hypothesis; by the transitivity of the relation $\leq_m^{\mathrm{fpt}}$ (Theorem 4.4.10), we obtain that $(A, \gamma) \leq_m^{\mathrm{fpt}}$ p-WEIGHTED-d-CNF-SAT, and hence that (A, γ) is W[1]. $\qquad \square$

Let us look at two examples showing parameterized languages to be W[1].

Example 4.4.15. Each of the parameterized languages p-c-HITTING-SET is FPT by Theorem 4.3.5, and hence is W[1] by Proposition 4.4.13. However, we here argue directly that, for each $c \geq 2$, the parameterized language p-c-HITTING-SET is W[1]. In particular, we explicitly present an fpt-many-one reduction from p-c-HITTING-SET to p-WEIGHTED-c-CNF-SAT. We define a mapping ρ on each instance (H, k) of p-c-HITTING-SET, where $H = (V, E)$ is a hypergraph, according to the following process. First, remove each vertex in H that does not occur in an edge; if this causes the number of vertices to fall strictly below k, then the original instance can be readily resolved, and ρ can be defined accordingly. Otherwise, produce the pair (ϕ, k), where ϕ is the CNF-formula $\bigwedge_{e \in E} \bigvee_{u \in e} u$. That is, ϕ is the CNF-formula whose variables are drawn from the vertex set V, and which has one clause for each hyperedge $e \in E$, equal to the disjunction over all vertices in e. Since each edge has size at most c, the CNF-formula ϕ is a c-CNF-formula.

This mapping ρ is polynomial-time computable and is thus π_2-fpt-computable (by Proposition 4.3.18); as it does not change the parameter of any instance when its output has the form (ϕ, k), it is (π_2, π_2)-parameter bounded. To confirm that it is an fpt-many-one reduction as claimed, it remains to argue correctness, that is, that $(H, k) \in c$-HITTING-SET if and only if $(\phi, k) \in$ WEIGHTED-c-CNF-SAT. Let U denote the set of variables appearing in ϕ, which equivalently is the set of vertices occurring in an edge of H. By the definition of ρ, we may assume $k \leq |U|$. Correctness follows from the straightforwardly verified observation that an assignment $f : U \to \{0, 1\}$ satisfies ϕ if and only if the vertices mapped to 1 by f constitute a hitting set of H.   ◇

Example 4.4.16. Let us argue that the parameterized language p-CLIQUE is W[1]. We present an fpt-many-one reduction from p-CLIQUE to p-WEIGHTED-2-CNF-SAT. Let ρ be the mapping that, given an instance (G^-, k) of p-CLIQUE, where G^- is a graph assumed to have a nonempty vertex set of size at least k, performs the following. It adds an isolated vertex[39] to the graph G^- to obtain the graph $G = (V, E)$ and produces the pair (ϕ, k), where ϕ is the 2-CNF-formula that has a clause $\neg u \vee \neg w$ for each vertex pair $\{u, w\}$ that is *not* an edge of G. That is, a clause appears in ϕ if and only if it has the form $\neg u \vee \neg w$, where $u, w \in V$ is a pair of vertices with $u \neq w$ and $\{u, w\} \notin E$.

As in the previous example, this mapping ρ is polynomial-time computable and is thus π_2-fpt-computable; as it does not change the parameter of any instance, it satisfies the parameter boundedness condition. To confirm that it is an fpt-many-one reduction, it remains to argue correctness, that is, that

$$(G^-, k) \in \text{CLIQUE} \quad \text{if and only if} \quad (\phi, k) \in \text{WEIGHTED-}c\text{-CNF-SAT}.$$

Since the graph G was obtained from G^- by adding an isolated vertex, we have that $(G^-, k) \in$ CLIQUE if and only if $(G, k) \in$ CLIQUE; and that every vertex of G appears

---

39. This added vertex serves to ensure that each vertex appears in the produced 2-CNF-formula.

in a clause along with the added isolated vertex, implying $V = \text{vars}(\phi)$. Correctness then follows from the straightforwardly verified observation that an assignment $f : V \to \{0, 1\}$ satisfies ϕ if and only if the vertices mapped to 1 by f constitute a clique of G. ◇

Observe that, to argue that each parameterized language p-c-HITTING-SET is W[1], we presented a reduction that produced CNF-formulas having only positive literals. On the other hand, to argue that the parameterized language p-CLIQUE is W[1], we presented a reduction that produced CNF-formulas having only negative literals. While in general any clause in an instance of p-WEIGHTED-d-CNF-SAT may contain both positive and negative literals, we will later give reductions implying that p-WEIGHTED-d-CNF-SAT reduces to p-CLIQUE; these reductions will make use of the algorithms for p-c-HITTING-SET presented in Section 4.3.1.

Let us now define notions of *hardness* and *completeness* relative to the W[1] parameterized languages.

Definition 4.4.17. A parameterized language (B, κ) is **W[1]-hard** if for each parameterized language (A, γ) that is W[1], it holds that $(A, \gamma) \leq_m^{\text{fpt}} (B, \kappa)$. ◇

Definition 4.4.18. A parameterized language (B, κ) is **W[1]-complete** if it is W[1] and it is W[1]-hard. ◇

We can tie the possibility of having a parameterized language that is both FPT and W[1]-hard to the FPT status of the entire class of W[1] parameterized languages, as follows.

Theorem 4.4.19. *Suppose that (B, κ) is a W[1]-hard parameterized language; if (B, κ) is FPT, then each W[1] parameterized language is FPT.*

Proof. Let (A, γ) be an arbitrary parameterized language that is W[1]. Since (B, κ) is W[1]-hard, it holds that $(A, \gamma) \leq_m^{\text{fpt}} (B, \kappa)$. By the assumption that (B, κ) is FPT and by Theorem 4.4.8, it follows that (A, γ) is FPT. □

Just as establishing a reduction from an NP-hard language was a way to establish additional NP-hardness results, we have that establishing a reduction from a W[1]-hard parameterized language is a way to establish additional W[1]-hardness results.

Proposition 4.4.20. *Suppose that (B, κ) is a W[1]-hard parameterized language, and that (C, λ) is a parameterized language such that $(B, \kappa) \leq_m^{\text{fpt}} (C, \lambda)$. Then, it holds that (C, λ) is W[1]-hard.*

Proof. Let (A, γ) be an arbitrary parameterized language that is W[1]. By the W[1]-hardness of (B, κ), we have that $(A, \gamma) \leq_m^{\text{fpt}} (B, \kappa)$. By the hypothesis that $(B, \kappa) \leq_m^{\text{fpt}} (C, \lambda)$ and the transitivity of $\leq_m^{\text{fpt}}$ (Theorem 4.4.10), we obtain that $(A, \gamma) \leq_m^{\text{fpt}} (C, \lambda)$. □

In the literature, the class of FPT parameterized languages and the class of W[1] parameterized languages are typically denoted with class notation; we here denote these classes by $\mathcal{FPT}$ and $\mathcal{W}[1]$, respectively. Utilizing this class notation, we can formulate Proposition 4.4.13 as the containment $\mathcal{FPT} \subseteq \mathcal{W}[1]$. And we can formulate Theorem 4.4.19 as stating that the existence of a parameterized language that is both W[1]-hard and FPT implies that $\mathcal{W}[1] \subseteq \mathcal{FPT}$. Let us remark here that the existence of a W[1]-complete parameterized language that is FPT is equivalent to $\mathcal{FPT} = \mathcal{W}[1]$.[40]

At the time of writing, the assumption that $\mathcal{FPT} \neq \mathcal{W}[1]$ is viewed as a valid working hypothesis. This assumption implies, via Theorem 4.4.19, that each W[1]-hard parameterized language is not FPT. Correspondingly, a W[1]-hardness result on a parameterized language is viewed as evidence that the parameterized language is not FPT. Observe that the hypothesis that $\mathcal{FPT} \neq \mathcal{W}[1]$ implies and is thus at least as strong as the hypothesis that $\mathcal{P} \neq \mathcal{NP}$: if $\mathcal{P} = \mathcal{NP}$, then each language WEIGHTED-d-CNF-SAT is a PTIME language, and thus each parameterized language p-WEIGHTED-d-CNF-SAT is FPT, implying by Theorem 4.4.8 that $\mathcal{FPT} = \mathcal{W}[1]$. At the time of writing, it is not known whether $\mathcal{P} \neq \mathcal{NP}$ implies $\mathcal{FPT} \neq \mathcal{W}[1]$. Parameterized complexity theory thus deals in distinctions that, apparently, are finer than those of classical complexity theory.

The class of W[1] problems is a member of a family of parameterized complexity classes called the *W-hierarchy*, which contains a class W[t] for each $t \geq 1$. These classes W[t] can be defined using weighted satisfiability problems on layered propositional formulas, where t restricts the number of layers; they can equivalently be defined using weighted satisfiability problems on circuits, using a circuit measure called *weft*.[41]

4.4.3 W[1]-completeness results

We here establish the W[1]-completeness of a number of parameterized languages, including p-CLIQUE. Our study of W[1]-completeness largely concerns various flavors of the so-called *homomorphism problem on relational structures*, where the question is to decide if there exists a homomorphism between a given pair of relational structures. Let us give the needed definitions; recall that, when k is a natural number, we use $[k]$ to denote the set $\{1, ..., k\}$.

A **relation** R over a set C is defined as a subset of a set C^r, where $r \in \mathbb{N}$; the **arity** of R, denoted by arity(R), is defined as this value r. Recall that C^r is the set containing each tuple having r entries, each drawn from C; such a tuple is also said to have **arity** r. We adhere to the convention that there is a unique tuple of arity 0, over any set. We say a relation R is **at most binary** if it holds that arity(R) ≤ 2.

A **relational structure** C is a tuple $(C; R_1^C, ..., R_k^C)$ consisting of a finite set C, called the **universe** of the structure, and a sequence of relations $R_1^C, ..., R_k^C$, each of which is over C. When notating a relational structure, as in $(C; R_1^C, ..., R_k^C)$, we separate the universe

40. This fact, Theorem 4.4.19, and Proposition 4.4.20 can all seen to be analogs of results from our treatment of NP-hardness and NP-completeness.
41. The standard parameterizations of the dominating set problem and the hitting set problem—that is, of the languages DOM-SET and HITTING-SET—are W[2]-complete.

from the relations using a semicolon, and generally notate each relation with a superscript indicating the structure to which the relation belongs. We sometimes refer to a relational structure simply as a *structure*.

Two relational structures $\mathbf{C} = (C; R_1^{\mathbf{C}}, \ldots, R_k^{\mathbf{C}})$ and $\mathbf{D} = (D; R_1^{\mathbf{D}}, \ldots, R_\ell^{\mathbf{D}})$ are **similar** when $k = \ell$, that is, they have the same number of relations, and for each $i \in [k]$, it holds that $\mathrm{arity}(R_i^{\mathbf{C}}) = \mathrm{arity}(R_i^{\mathbf{D}})$, that is, the arities of their respective relations match. When $\mathbf{C} = (C; R_1^{\mathbf{C}}, \ldots, R_k^{\mathbf{C}})$ and $\mathbf{D} = (D; R_1^{\mathbf{D}}, \ldots, R_k^{\mathbf{D}})$ are similar relational structures, a **homomorphism** from $\mathbf{C}$ to $\mathbf{D}$ is a mapping $h \colon C \to D$ such that, for each $i \in [k]$ and each tuple $(c_1, \ldots, c_r) \in R_i^{\mathbf{C}}$, it holds that $(h(c_1), \ldots, h(c_r)) \in R_i^{\mathbf{D}}$; here, r denotes the arity of $R_i^{\mathbf{C}}$. A homomorphism $h \colon C \to D$ from $\mathbf{C}$ to $\mathbf{D}$ is considered **injective** when the mapping $h \colon C \to D$ is injective.

The question of whether a graph contains a clique of some specified size can be formulated as the question of whether there is a homomorphism between two appropriately defined structures, as we discuss next.

Example 4.4.21 (Clique-searching formulated using homomorphisms). Let $G = (V, E)$ be a graph and let $k \in \mathbb{N}$. Based on G, we define a relational structure $\mathbf{G} = (V; F^{\mathbf{G}})$ where $F^{\mathbf{G}} = \left\{ (v, v') \mid \{v, v'\} \in E \right\}$. That is, we transform G into a relational structure by naturally representing its edge set as a symmetric binary relation. We define the relational structure $\mathbf{C}_k = ([k]; F^{\mathbf{C}_k})$ where $F^{\mathbf{C}_k} = \left\{ (i, j) \in [k]^2 \mid i \neq j \right\}$; this is the structure one obtains from applying the just-given transformation to the *k-clique graph* having vertex set $[k]$ and all possible edges on this vertex set.

We claim that the graph G contains a size k clique if and only if there exists a homomorphism $h \colon [k] \to V$ from $\mathbf{C}_k$ to $\mathbf{G}$. For the backward direction, suppose that h is a homomorphism from $\mathbf{C}_k$ to $\mathbf{G}$; we claim that the set $U = \{h(1), \ldots, h(k)\}$, that is, the image of h, is a size k clique of G. For any two distinct values $i, j \in [k]$, it holds that $(i, j) \in F^{\mathbf{C}_k}$, and so by definition of homomorphism, we have $(h(i), h(j)) \in F^{\mathbf{G}}$, from which it follows that $\{h(i), h(j)\} \in E$. Thus, $h(i)$ and $h(j)$ are distinct vertices forming an edge in G, establishing that the set U is a size k clique of G. This reasoning readily reverses to establish the forward direction: when $u_1, \ldots, u_k$ are vertices forming a size k clique in G, the mapping $h \colon [k] \to V$ defined by $h(i) = u_i$ is a homomorphism from $\mathbf{C}_k$ to $\mathbf{G}$.

This argumentation shows that any homomorphism h from $\mathbf{C}_k$ to $\mathbf{G}$ is injective, as two distinct values $i, j \in [k]$ must be mapped to two distinct values $h(i), h(j) \in V$. Thus, we also obtain that the graph G contains a size k clique if and only if there exists an injective homomorphism from $\mathbf{C}_k$ to $\mathbf{G}$. $\diamond$

As mentioned, one of our goals is to prove the W[1]-completeness of p-CLIQUE. To aid us, we define various homomorphism problems that will be shown to be equivalent (under fpt-many-one reductions) to p-CLIQUE, and will be convenient to reduce *to*.

Definition 4.4.22. We here define the languages HOM, INJ-HOM, and BIN-HOM. Each element of one of these languages is a pair $(\mathbf{C}, \mathbf{D})$ of similar relational structures, and these languages are defined by the following conditions:

- $(\mathbf{C}, \mathbf{D}) \in$ HOM $\Leftrightarrow$ there exists a homomorphism from $\mathbf{C}$ to $\mathbf{D}$,
- $(\mathbf{C}, \mathbf{D}) \in$ INJ-HOM $\Leftrightarrow$ there exists an injective homomorphism from $\mathbf{C}$ to $\mathbf{D}$,
- $(\mathbf{C}, \mathbf{D}) \in$ BIN-HOM $\Leftrightarrow$ $(\mathbf{C}, \mathbf{D}) \in$ HOM and each relation of the structures $\mathbf{C}, \mathbf{D}$ is at most binary. $\qquad\qquad\qquad\qquad\qquad\qquad\qquad\qquad\qquad\qquad$ $\diamond$

Definition 4.4.23. We define the following parameterized languages:

p-HOM = (HOM, π_1); p-INJ-HOM = (INJ-HOM, π_1); p-BIN-HOM = (BIN-HOM, π_1).

That is, for each of the languages in the previous definition, we define a parameterized language by pairing the language along with the first projection π_1. (This projection function was presented in Remark 4.3.14.) $\qquad\qquad\qquad\qquad\qquad\qquad\qquad\qquad\qquad$ $\diamond$

Theorem 4.4.24. *Each of the following parameterized languages fpt-many-one reduces to each of the others:* p-INJ-HOM, *p-HOM,* p-BIN-HOM, *p-CLIQUE.*

Proof. In order to establish the theorem, we give four mappings that we show to be fpt-many-one reductions. Each of them is readily verified to be polynomial-time computable and to satisfy the parameter boundedness condition, so in each case, we focus on verifying correctness.

We have p-CLIQUE $\leq_m^{\text{fpt}}$ p-INJ-HOM via the mapping given in Example 4.4.21; this mapping sends an instance (G, k) of CLIQUE to the pair $(\mathbf{C}_k, \mathbf{G})$ defined in the example. Correctness follows from the discussion in the example.

Having established this initial reduction, we next prove that each of the first three parameterized languages in the sequence fpt-many-one reduces to the one that comes after it; this suffices to establish the theorem, by the transitivity of fpt-many-one reducibility (Theorem 4.4.10).

p-INJ-HOM $\leq_m^{\text{fpt}}$ p-HOM: When E is a set, let us here use $\neq_E$ to denote the binary relation $\{(e, e') \in E^2 \mid e \neq e'\}$. Let $(\mathbf{C}, \mathbf{D})$ be an instance of INJ-HOM, where $\mathbf{C} = (C; R_1^{\mathbf{C}}, ..., R_k^{\mathbf{C}})$ and $\mathbf{D} = (D; R_1^{\mathbf{D}}, ..., R_k^{\mathbf{D}})$. The reduction creates the instance $(\mathbf{C}^+, \mathbf{D}^+)$ of p-HOM, defined as follows. The relational structure $\mathbf{C}^+$ is defined as $(C; R_1^{\mathbf{C}}, ..., R_k^{\mathbf{C}}, \neq_C)$, that is, $\mathbf{C}^+$ is equal to $\mathbf{C}$ expanded by the binary relation $\neq_C$. Similarly, the relational structure $\mathbf{D}^+$ is defined as $\mathbf{D} = (D; R_1^{\mathbf{D}}, ..., R_k^{\mathbf{D}}, \neq_D)$.

Observe that a mapping $h \colon C \to D$ is a homomorphism from $\mathbf{C}^+$ to $\mathbf{D}^+$ if and only if it is a homomorphism from $\mathbf{C}$ to $\mathbf{D}$ satisfying the additional property that, for $c, c' \in C$ with $c \neq c'$, it holds that $h(c) \neq h(c')$. Thus, a mapping $h \colon C \to D$ is a homomorphism from $\mathbf{C}^+$ to $\mathbf{D}^+$ if and only if it is an injective homomorphism from $\mathbf{C}$ to $\mathbf{D}$. It follows that $(\mathbf{C}, \mathbf{D}) \in$ INJ-HOM if and only if $(\mathbf{C}^+, \mathbf{D}^+) \in$ HOM.

p-HOM $\leq_m^{\text{fpt}}$ p-BIN-HOM: For each relational structure $\mathbf{E} = (E; R_1^{\mathbf{E}}, ..., R_\ell^{\mathbf{E}})$ whose relations each have arity 1 or greater, we define the *incidence structure* of $\mathbf{E}$ as the structure $\mathbf{E}^I$, defined as follows. The universe E^I of $\mathbf{E}^I$ is defined as $E \cup R_1^{\mathbf{E}} \cup \cdots R_\ell^{\mathbf{E}}$. We associate together elements of E and length 1 tuples over E, that is, when $e \in E$, we consider e

to be equal to (e). For each $i \in [\ell]$, let r_i denote the arity of $R_i^{\mathbf{E}}$. Define

$$\mathbf{E}^I = (E^I; R_{1,1}^{\mathbf{E}^I}, ..., R_{1,r_1}^{\mathbf{E}^I}, R_{2,1}^{\mathbf{E}^I}, ..., R_{2,r_2}^{\mathbf{E}^I}, ..., R_{\ell,1}^{\mathbf{E}^I}, ..., R_{\ell,r_\ell}^{\mathbf{E}^I}),$$

where for each $i \in [\ell]$ and $j \in [r_i]$, we define $R_{ij}^{\mathbf{E}^I}$ as the binary relation

$$\{((e_1, ..., e_{r_i}), e_j) \mid (e_1, ..., e_{r_i}) \in R_i^{\mathbf{E}}\}.$$

Let $(\mathbf{C}, \mathbf{D})$ be an instance of p-HOM, where $\mathbf{C} = (C; R_1^{\mathbf{C}}, ..., R_k^{\mathbf{C}})$ and $\mathbf{D} = (D; R_1^{\mathbf{D}}, ..., R_k^{\mathbf{D}})$. We may assume that each relation of these structures has arity 1 or greater.[42] The reduction produces the instance $(\mathbf{C}^I, \mathbf{D}^I)$ of p-BIN-HOM.

Suppose that $h \colon C \to D$ is a homomorphism from $\mathbf{C}$ to $\mathbf{D}$. Define $h^I \colon C^I \to D^I$ by $h^I((c_1, ..., c_r)) = (h(c_1), ..., h(c_r))$ for each tuple $(c_1, ..., c_r) \in C \cup R_1^{\mathbf{C}} \cup \cdots \cup R_k^{\mathbf{C}}$. We argue that h^I is a homomorphism from $\mathbf{C}^I$ to $\mathbf{D}^I$. Let $i \in [j], j \in [r_i]$ be arbitrary, and suppose $((c_1, ..., c_{r_i}), c_j) \in R_{i,j}^{\mathbf{C}^I}$. It follows from the definition of $R_{i,j}^{\mathbf{C}^I}$ that $(c_1, ..., c_{r_i}) \in R_i^{\mathbf{C}}$, from which we obtain that $(h(c_1), ..., h(c_{r_i})) \in R_i^{\mathbf{D}}$, and then that

$$(h^I((c_1, ..., c_{r_i})), h^I(c_j)) = ((h(c_1), ..., h(c_{r_i})), h(c_j)) \in R_i^{\mathbf{D}^I}.$$

Suppose that h^I is a homomorphism from $\mathbf{C}^I$ to $\mathbf{D}^I$. Define $g \colon C \to D$ by $g(c) = h^I(c)$ when $h^I(c) \in D$, and set $g(c)$ to an arbitrary element of D otherwise. Let $i \in [k]$ be arbitrary, and suppose that $(c_1, ..., c_{r_i}) \in R_i^{\mathbf{C}}$. Due to the definition of the relations $R_{i,j}^{\mathbf{C}^I}$ and $R_{i,j}^{\mathbf{D}^I}$, we obtain that $(h^I(c_1), ..., h^I(c_{r_i})) = h^I((c_1, ..., c_{r_i})) \in R_i^{\mathbf{D}}$, and also that each of $h^I(c_1), ..., h^I(c_{r_i})$ is an element of D. It follows that

$$(g(c_1), ..., g(c_{r_i})) = (h^I(c_1), ..., h^I(c_{r_i})) \in R_i^{\mathbf{D}}.$$

p-BIN-HOM $\leq_m^{\mathrm{fpt}}$ p-CLIQUE: We introduce the following notion. Let $\mathbf{C} = (C; R_1^{\mathbf{C}}, ..., R_k^{\mathbf{C}})$ and $\mathbf{D} = (D; R_1^{\mathbf{D}}, ..., R_k^{\mathbf{D}})$ be similar relational structures. Let $g \colon C' \to D$ be a mapping defined on a subset C' of C. The mapping g is a **partial homomorphism** from $\mathbf{C}$ to $\mathbf{D}$ if, for each $i \in [k]$ and each tuple $(c_1, ..., c_r) \in R_i^{\mathbf{C}}$ such that $\{c_1, ..., c_r\} \subseteq C'$, it holds that $(g(c_1), ..., g(c_r)) \in R_i^{\mathbf{D}}$. We will make use of the following straightforwardly verified facts concerning homomorphisms and partial homomorphisms from a structure $\mathbf{C}$ to a structure $\mathbf{D}$: a homomorphism is a partial homomorphism, and any restriction of a partial homomorphism is also a partial homomorphism.

Let $(\mathbf{C}, \mathbf{D})$ be an instance of BIN-HOM. Define $G_{\mathbf{C},\mathbf{D}}$ to be the graph (V, E) where $V = C \times D$ and, for $(c, d), (c', d') \in V$, it holds that $\{(c, d), (c', d')\} \in E$ if and only if $c \neq c'$ and the mapping $g \colon \{c, c'\} \to D$ defined by $g(c) = d$ and $g(c') = d'$ is a partial homomorphism. The produced instance of CLIQUE is $(G_{\mathbf{C},\mathbf{D}}, |C|)$.

---

42. When arity 0 relations are present, the reduction may do the following: check whether, for each $R_i^{\mathbf{C}}$ that is arity 0 and is nonempty, the corresponding relation $R_i^{\mathbf{D}}$ is nonempty. If this does not hold, then there is no homomorphism from $\mathbf{C}$ to $\mathbf{D}$; otherwise, the existence of a homomorphism is not affected by eliminating all arity 0 relations from each structure.

Suppose that there exists a homomorphism $h \colon C \to D$ from $\mathbf{C}$ to $\mathbf{D}$. We claim that the set $K = \{(c, h(c)) \mid c \in C\}$ is a clique of $G_{\mathbf{C},\mathbf{D}}$. For, let $(c, h(c)), (c', h(c'))$ be distinct elements in K; then, $c \neq c'$ and these two elements form an edge in E, since the restriction of the homomorphism h to $\{c, c'\}$ is a partial homomorphism. We thus have that K is a clique of size $|C|$ in $G_{\mathbf{C},\mathbf{D}}$.

Suppose that K is a clique in $G_{\mathbf{C},\mathbf{D}}$ of size $|C|$. Any two distinct elements $(c, d), (c', d')$ in K form an edge in E and thus have $c \neq c'$; so, each element $c \in C$ appears exactly once as the first entry of a pair in K. Thus, there exists a mapping $h \colon C \to D$ such that $K = \{(c, h(c)) \mid c \in C\}$. By the definition of E, one obtains a partial homomorphism whenever one restricts h to a subset of C having size 2, and hence whenever one restricts h to a subset of C having size less than or equal to 2. Let $R_i^{\mathbf{C}}$ be any relation of $\mathbf{C}$, and suppose that $(c_1, \ldots, c_r) \in R_i^{\mathbf{C}}$. The arity r of $R_i^{\mathbf{C}}$ is less than or equal to 2 by assumption, and thus the restriction of h to $\{c_1, \ldots, c_r\}$ is a partial homomorphism from $\mathbf{C}$ to $\mathbf{D}$. It follows that $(h(c_1), \ldots, h(c_r)) \in R_i^{\mathbf{D}}$, where $R_i^{\mathbf{D}}$ is the relation of $\mathbf{D}$ corresponding to $R_i^{\mathbf{C}}$. We thus have that h is a homomorphism from $\mathbf{C}$ to $\mathbf{D}$. □

We next define generalizations of the just-studied homomorphism problems that will be even easier to reduce to than the original problems. We subsequently show that, under reductions, the parameterized versions of these generalizations are equivalent to p-CLIQUE; by Theorem 4.4.24, they are hence equivalent to the original problems.

Definition 4.4.25. We here define the languages ∨-HOM, ∨-INJ-HOM, and ∨-BIN-HOM. Each element of one of these languages is a pair $(\mathcal{C}, \mathbf{D})$ where $\mathbf{D}$ is a relational structure and $\mathcal{C}$ is a finite set of relational structures, each of which is similar to $\mathbf{D}$; these languages are defined by the following conditions:

$$(\mathcal{C}, \mathbf{D}) \in \text{∨-HOM} \quad \Leftrightarrow \quad \text{there exists } \mathbf{C} \in \mathcal{C} \text{ such that } (\mathbf{C}, \mathbf{D}) \in \text{HOM},$$
$$(\mathcal{C}, \mathbf{D}) \in \text{∨-INJ-HOM} \quad \Leftrightarrow \quad \text{there exists } \mathbf{C} \in \mathcal{C} \text{ such that } (\mathbf{C}, \mathbf{D}) \in \text{INJ-HOM},$$
$$(\mathcal{C}, \mathbf{D}) \in \text{∨-BIN-HOM} \quad \Leftrightarrow \quad \text{there exists } \mathbf{C} \in \mathcal{C} \text{ such that } (\mathbf{C}, \mathbf{D}) \in \text{BIN-HOM}.$$

That is, for each of the languages B presented in Definition 4.4.22, we define the language ∨-B according to the rule

$$(\{\mathbf{C}_1, \ldots, \mathbf{C}_\ell\}, \mathbf{D}) \in \text{∨-}B \quad \Leftrightarrow \quad (\mathbf{C}_1, \mathbf{D}) \in B \vee \cdots \vee (\mathbf{C}_\ell, \mathbf{D}) \in B. \qquad \diamond$$

Definition 4.4.26. We define the following parameterized languages: p-∨-INJ-HOM = (∨-INJ-HOM, π_1); p-∨-HOM = (∨-HOM, π_1); p-∨-BIN-HOM = (∨-BIN-HOM, π_1). $\qquad \diamond$

Definition 4.4.26 is analogous to Definition 4.4.23.

Theorem 4.4.27. *Each of the following parameterized languages fpt-many-one reduces to each of the others:* p-∨-INJ-HOM, p-∨-HOM, p-∨-BIN-HOM, p-CLIQUE.

Proof. We give a sequence of reductions that implies the theorem statement by the transitivity of $\leq_m^{\text{fpt}}$ (Theorem 4.4.10). For each of the reductions that we give, polynomial-time computability and parameter boundedness is straightforward to verify, so we focus on showing correctness.

p-CLIQUE $\leq_m^{\text{fpt}}$ p-∨-INJ-HOM: The reduction sends an instance (G, k) of CLIQUE to the pair $(\{\mathbf{C}_k\}, \mathbf{G})$, where the structures $\mathbf{C}_k$ and $\mathbf{G}$ are as specified in Example 4.4.21; correctness follows from this example's discussion.

p-∨-INJ-HOM $\leq_m^{\text{fpt}}$ p-∨-HOM: The reduction we give is directly based on the corresponding reduction of Theorem 4.4.24. Let $(\{\mathbf{C}_1, ..., \mathbf{C}_m\}, \mathbf{D})$ be an instance of p-∨-INJ-HOM. Let $\mathbf{C}_1^+, ..., \mathbf{C}_m^+, \mathbf{D}^+$ be the structures defined from $\mathbf{C}_1, ..., \mathbf{C}_m, \mathbf{D}$ as given by the reduction showing p-INJ-HOM $\leq_m^{\text{fpt}}$ p-HOM, in the proof of Theorem 4.4.24. The created instance of p-∨-HOM is $(\{\mathbf{C}_1^+, ..., \mathbf{C}_m^+\}, \mathbf{D}^+)$. We have

$$(\{\mathbf{C}_1, ..., \mathbf{C}_m\}, \mathbf{D}) \in \vee\text{-INJ-HOM} \Leftrightarrow (\mathbf{C}_1, \mathbf{D}) \in \text{INJ-HOM} \vee \cdots \vee (\mathbf{C}_m, \mathbf{D}) \in \text{INJ-HOM}$$

$$\Leftrightarrow (\mathbf{C}_1^+, \mathbf{D}^+) \in \text{HOM} \vee \cdots \vee (\mathbf{C}_m^+, \mathbf{D}^+) \in \text{HOM}$$

$$\Leftrightarrow (\{\mathbf{C}_1^+, ..., \mathbf{C}_m^+\}, \mathbf{D}^+) \in \vee\text{-HOM}.$$

p-∨-HOM $\leq_m^{\text{fpt}}$ p-∨-BIN-HOM: The reduction we give is directly based on the corresponding reduction of Theorem 4.4.24. Let $(\{\mathbf{C}_1, ..., \mathbf{C}_m\}, \mathbf{D})$ be an instance of p-∨-HOM. Let $\mathbf{C}_1^l, ..., \mathbf{C}_m^l, \mathbf{D}^l$ be the structures defined from $\mathbf{C}_1, ..., \mathbf{C}_m, \mathbf{D}$ as given by the reduction that p-HOM $\leq_m^{\text{fpt}}$ p-BIN-HOM, in the proof of Theorem 4.4.24. We have

$$(\{\mathbf{C}_1, ..., \mathbf{C}_m\}, \mathbf{D}) \in \vee\text{-HOM} \Leftrightarrow (\mathbf{C}_1, \mathbf{D}) \in \text{HOM} \vee \cdots \vee (\mathbf{C}_m, \mathbf{D}) \in \text{HOM}$$

$$\Leftrightarrow (\mathbf{C}_1^l, \mathbf{D}^l) \in \text{BIN-HOM} \vee \cdots \vee (\mathbf{C}_m^l, \mathbf{D}^l) \in \text{BIN-HOM}$$

$$\Leftrightarrow (\{\mathbf{C}_1^l, ..., \mathbf{C}_m^l\}, \mathbf{D}^l) \in \vee\text{-BIN-HOM}.$$

p-∨-BIN-HOM $\leq_m^{\text{fpt}}$ p-CLIQUE: Let $(\{\mathbf{C}_1, ..., \mathbf{C}_m\}, \mathbf{D})$ be an instance of p-∨-BIN-HOM. Let X be the maximum universe size among the structures $\mathbf{C}_1, ..., \mathbf{C}_m$, that is, set $X = \max\{|C_1|, ..., |C_m|\}$. Starting from the structures $\mathbf{C}_1, ..., \mathbf{C}_m$, add new elements to these structures' universes (if necessary) so that each universe has size X, and then, in each structure, rename the elements (if necessary) so that the universes are pairwise disjoint; let $\mathbf{C}_1', ..., \mathbf{C}_m'$ be the resulting structures. Observe that each structure $\mathbf{C}_i$ admits a homomorphism to $\mathbf{D}$ if and only if the modified version $\mathbf{C}_i'$ does. We have $|C_1'| = \cdots = |C_m'| = X$, and that $C_1', ..., C_m'$ are pairwise disjoint. For each index $i = 1, ..., m$, let $G_i = (V_i, E_i)$ denote the graph $G_{\mathbf{C}_i', \mathbf{D}}$ defined as in the proof that p-BIN-HOM $\leq_m^{\text{fpt}}$ p-CLIQUE. We have (for each index i) that $V_i = C_i' \times D$, and thus that $V_1, ..., V_m$ are pairwise disjoint. Set $G = (V, E)$, where $V = \bigcup_{i=1}^m V_i$, and $E = \bigcup_{i=1}^m E_i$. The produced instance is (G, X).

If there exists a size X clique in one of the graphs G_i, then there exists a size X clique in G; this is evident from the definition of G. The converse also holds: if there exists a size X clique in G, then one of the graphs G_i must contain a size X clique, since any edge of G is contained in one of the sets V_i, and the sets V_i are pairwise disjoint. We therefore have

$$({\mathbf{C}_1, ..., \mathbf{C}_m}, \mathbf{D}) \in \vee\text{-BIN-HOM} \Leftrightarrow (\mathbf{C}_1, \mathbf{D}) \in \text{BIN-HOM} \vee \cdots \vee (\mathbf{C}_m, \mathbf{D}) \in \text{BIN-HOM}$$

$$\Leftrightarrow (\mathbf{C}_1', \mathbf{D}) \in \text{BIN-HOM} \vee \cdots \vee (\mathbf{C}_m', \mathbf{D}) \in \text{BIN-HOM}$$

$$\Leftrightarrow (G_1, X) \in \text{CLIQUE} \vee \cdots \vee (G_m, X) \in \text{CLIQUE}$$

$$\Leftrightarrow (G, X) \in \text{CLIQUE}. \qquad \square$$

The following theorem links the class of W[1] problems to the problems we have been studying, and implies the W[1]-completeness of p-$\vee$-INJ-HOM. Establishing this theorem will allow us to readily conclude the W[1]-completeness of all problems studied in the previous two theorems.

Theorem 4.4.28. *For each $d \geq 2$, the parameterized language* p-WEIGHTED-d-CNF-SAT *fpt-many-one reduces to the parameterized language* p-$\vee$-INJ-HOM.

In the following proof, for each set E and each value $r \in \mathbb{N}$, we use the notation $E^{\leq r}$ to denote the set $E^0 \cup \cdots \cup E^r$, that is, the set of tuples over E of arity less than or equal to r.

Proof. Fix a value $d \geq 2$. Let (ϕ, k) be an instance of p-WEIGHTED-d-CNF-SAT. Let $\mathcal{C}$ denote the set of clauses appearing in ϕ, and let V denote the set of variables appearing in ϕ. For each clause $C \in \mathcal{C}$, we use Pos(C) to denote the set of positive literals occurring in C, and Neg(C) to denote the set of negative literals occuring in C. We further introduce the following notions:

- For each tuple $(v_1, ..., v_r) \in V^{\leq d}$, define

$$\mathcal{C}(v_1, ..., v_r) = \{C \in \mathcal{C} \mid \{\neg v_1, ..., \neg v_r\} = \text{Neg}(C)\}.$$

- Say that a tuple $(v_1, ..., v_r) \in V^{\leq d}$ is **realized** if $\mathcal{C}(v_1, ..., v_r)$ is nonempty.
- For each realized tuple $(v_1, ..., v_r) \in V^{\leq d}$, define

$$P(v_1, ..., v_r) = \{\text{Pos}(C) \mid C \in \mathcal{C}(v_1, ..., v_r)\}.$$

We view each set $P(v_1, ..., v_r)$ as the edge set of a hypergraph with vertex set V, and thusly speak of hitting sets of $P(v_1, ..., v_r)$.

It can be seen that each clause falls into exactly one of the sets $\mathcal{C}(v_1, ..., v_r)$, and the clauses in a set $\mathcal{C}(v_1, ..., v_r)$ all share the same set of negative literals. Let us make an observation: when $(v_1, ..., v_r) \in V^{\leq d}$ is a realized tuple, an assignment $g \colon V \to \{0, 1\}$ satisfies all clauses in $\mathcal{C}(v_1, ..., v_r)$ if and only if it satisfies $\neg v_1 \vee \cdots \vee \neg v_r$ or $g^{-1}(1)$ is a hitting set of $P(v_1, ..., v_r)$. Essentially, this observation says that g satisfies all clauses in $\mathcal{C}(v_1, ..., v_r)$ precisely when one of the shared negative literals is satisfied, or when the positive portion Pos(C) of every clause C therein is satisfied.

The instance of p-∨-INJ-HOM computed by the reduction has the form $(\{\mathbf{A}_f \mid f \in F\}, \mathbf{B})$ where F is a set of functions, each $\mathbf{A}_f$ is a structure, and $\mathbf{B}$ is a structure. Let us give the definitions of these structures.

Definition of the structure B. For each realized tuple $\bar{v} = (v_1, \ldots, v_r)$, invoke the DTM of Theorem 4.3.12 to obtain an enumeration of all minimal hitting sets of $P(v_1, \ldots, v_r)$ having size less than or equal to k. If this enumeration is nonempty, then define $H_1^{\bar{v}}, \ldots, H_{d^k}^{\bar{v}} \in V^k$ as a list of the hitting sets in the enumeration, where repetitions are allowed; otherwise, consider each of $H_1^{\bar{v}}, \ldots, H_{d^k}^{\bar{v}}$ to be undefined. Here, a tuple $(v_1, \ldots, v_k)$ in V^k is considered to represent a hitting set U when $\{v_1, \ldots, v_k\} = U$. The DTM of Theorem 4.3.12 will return at most d^k minimal hitting sets, by Proposition 4.3.11; if it returns strictly fewer than d^k minimal hitting sets, we simply introduce repetitions so that the enumeration's size is exactly d^k, as specified.

The universe of $\mathbf{B}$ is defined as V. The relations of $\mathbf{B}$ are defined as follows:

- For each $r \in \{0, \ldots, d\}$, define $S_r^{\mathbf{B}}$ as $\{(v_1, \ldots, v_r) \in V^r \mid (v_1, \ldots, v_r) \text{ is not realized}\}$.
- For each $r \in \{0, \ldots, d\}$, $u \in [d^k]$, and $\ell \in [k]$, define $T_{r,u,\ell}^{\mathbf{B}}$ as

$$\{(v_1, \ldots, v_r, \pi_\ell(H_u^{(v_1, \ldots, v_r)})) \in V^{r+1} \mid (v_1, \ldots, v_r) \text{ is realized and } H_u^{(v_1, \ldots, v_r)} \text{ is defined}\}.$$

Here, π_ℓ denotes the projection function that, given a tuple, returns its ℓth entry. ◇

Definition of the structures $\mathbf{A}_f$. Fix A to be a k-element set, and let F denote the set of all functions $f \colon A^{\le d} \to (\{\bot\} \cup ([d^k] \times A^k))$. For each function $f \in F$, we define a structure $\mathbf{A}_f$, as follows. The universe of $\mathbf{A}_f$ is defined to be A.

The relations of $\mathbf{A}_f$ are defined as follows:

- For each $r \in \{0, \ldots, d\}$, define $S_r^{\mathbf{A}_f} = \{(a_1, \ldots, a_r) \in A^r \mid f(a_1, \ldots, a_r) = \bot\}$.
- For each $r \in \{0, \ldots, d\}$, $u \in [d^k]$, and $\ell \in [k]$, define $T_{r,u,\ell}^{\mathbf{A}_f}$ as the set containing each tuple $(a_1, \ldots, a_r, c) \in A^{r+1}$ such that $f(a_1, \ldots, a_r)$ is equal to a pair having the form $(u, (c_1, \ldots, c_k))$, where $c = c_\ell$. ◇

We justify the π_2-fpt-computability of this proposed reduction as follows. Concerning the computation of the structure $\mathbf{B}$, the number of tuples in $V^{\le d}$ is a polynomial in $|V|$ (since d has been fixed), and each time the mentioned DTM is invoked, it behaves as a π_2-fpt-time DTM. Concerning the computation of the structures $\mathbf{A}_f$, the size $|F|$ of F can be bounded above by a function of k; for each $f \in F$, the structure $\mathbf{A}_f$ can be constructed in polynomial time. The parameter boundedness of the proposed reduction follows from the observation that the structures $\{\mathbf{A}_f \mid f \in F\}$ are constructed solely based on the value k. In the rest of this proof, we thus focus on establishing correctness of the proposed reduction.

The conception behind the construction of the structures is as follows. An injective homomorphism h from A to V selects k elements of V, namely, the elements in the image $h(A)$ of h; thus, such an injective homomorphism induces a weight k assignment $g \colon V \to \{0, 1\}$, and vice versa. The structures are defined in a way that h is an injective homomorphism from one of the structures $\mathbf{A}_f$ to $\mathbf{B}$ if and only if g is a satisfying assignment of ϕ. The assignment g satisfies ϕ when, for each $(a_1, \ldots, a_r) \in A^{\leq d}$, either the tuple of variables $(h(a_1), \ldots, h(a_r))$ is not realized, or $h(A)$ is a hitting set of $P(h(a_1), \ldots, h(a_r))$. This is because each clause of ϕ is in a set $\mathcal{C}(v_1, \ldots, v_r)$ where $(v_1, \ldots, v_r)$ is realized; and, for any realized tuple $(v_1, \ldots, v_r)$, the following hold:

- If one of the negative literals $\neg v_1, \ldots, \neg v_r$ is satisfied by g, then all clauses in $\mathcal{C}(v_1, \ldots, v_r)$ are satisfied by g.
- If each of the negative literals $\neg v_1, \ldots, \neg v_r$ is falsified by g, which occurs when each v_i is in the image $h(A)$ of h, then for g to be a satisfying assignment, it must be that $h(A)$ is a hitting set of $P(v_1, \ldots, v_r)$.

The function f in effect asserts, for each tuple $(a_1, \ldots, a_r) \in A^{\leq d}$, either that the tuple is not realized—when $f(a_1, \ldots, a_r) = \bot$ holds—or, that the image of h contains the uth hitting set $H_u^{(h(a_1), \ldots, h(a_r))}$ of $P(h(a_1), \ldots, h(a_r))$—when $f(a_1, \ldots, a_r)$ has the form $(u, \cdot)$.

We show the following claim.

Let $g \colon V \to \{0, 1\}$ be an assignment and let $h \colon A \to V$ be an injective map having the property that $h(A) = g^{-1}(1)$. Then, g is a satisfying assignment of ϕ if and only if there exists $f \in F$ such that h is a homomorphism from $\mathbf{A}_f$ to $\mathbf{B}$.

Establishing this claim suffices to conclude the theorem. Why? When g is a weight k satisfying assignment of ϕ, one can define an injective map $h \colon A \to V$ with the given property, and thus there exists f such that h is an injective homomorphism from $\mathbf{A}_f$ to $\mathbf{B}$. Conversely, when there exists f such that h is an injective homomorphism from $\mathbf{A}_f$ to $\mathbf{B}$, then when g is defined to have the given property, we obtain that g is a weight k satisfying assignment of ϕ.

Let us prove the claim's forward direction. We define a function $f \in F$ by considering each tuple $(a_1, \ldots, a_r) \in A^{\leq d}$:

- When $(h(a_1), \ldots, h(a_r))$ is not realized, define $f(a_1, \ldots, a_r)$ as $\bot$.
- When $(h(a_1), \ldots, h(a_r))$ is realized, since each of the variables $h(a_1), \ldots, h(a_r)$ is assigned to 1 by g, it must hold that $h(A)$ is a hitting set of $P(h(a_1), \ldots, h(a_r))$. It is thus possible to select $u \in [d^k]$ such that the tuple $H_u^{(h(a_1), \ldots, h(a_r))}$ is defined and each entry thereof is an element of $g^{-1}(1) = h(A)$; let $c_1, \ldots, c_k \in A$ be values such that $H_u^{(h(a_1), \ldots, h(a_r))} = (h(c_1), \ldots, h(c_k))$, and define $f(a_1, \ldots, a_r) = (u, (c_1, \ldots, c_k))$.

We argue that h is a homomorphism from $\mathbf{A}_f$ to $\mathbf{B}$.

- Suppose that $(a_1, \ldots, a_r) \in S_r^{\mathbf{A}_f}$. Then, it holds that $f(a_1, \ldots, a_r) = \bot$ and, by the definition of f, the tuple $(h(a_1), \ldots, h(a_r))$ is not realized and is hence an element of $S_r^{\mathbf{B}}$.
- Suppose that a tuple $(a_1, \ldots, a_r, c_\ell)$ is in a relation $T_{r,u,\ell}^{\mathbf{A}_f}$. Then, the value c_ℓ can be completed to a sequence $c_1, \ldots, c_k$ where $f(a_1, \ldots, a_r) = (u, (c_1, \ldots, c_k))$; by the definition of f, we have that $(h(a_1), \ldots, h(a_r))$ is realized. As we have $H_u^{(h(a_1), \ldots, h(a_r))} =$

$(h(c_1), \ldots, h(c_k))$, it is immediate from the definition of $T^{\mathbf{B}}_{r,u,\ell}$ that this relation contains the tuple $(h(a_1), \ldots, h(a_r), h(c_\ell))$.

Let us prove the claim's backward direction. Let $f \in F$ be such that h is a homomorphism from $\mathbf{A}_f$ to $\mathbf{B}$. Let $(v_1, \ldots, v_r) \in V^{\leq d}$ be arbitrary. We argue that g satisfies all clauses in $\mathcal{C}(v_1, \ldots, v_r)$. We consider the following cases:

- If $(v_1, \ldots, v_r)$ is not realized, we have $\mathcal{C}(v_1, \ldots, v_r) = \emptyset$, and g trivially satisfies all clauses in this set.

- If $(v_1, \ldots, v_r)$ is realized and there exists a variable v_i in this tuple such that $g(v_i) = 0$, then g satisfies the literal $\neg v_i$ and hence all clauses in $\mathcal{C}(v_1, \ldots, v_r)$.

- If $(v_1, \ldots, v_r)$ is realized and g maps each variable in this tuple to 1, then there exists $(a_1, \ldots, a_r) \in A^r$ such that $h(a_1) = v_1, \ldots, h(a_r) = v_r$. Since $(h(a_1), \ldots, h(a_r)) \notin S^{\mathbf{B}}_r$, we have $(a_1, \ldots, a_r) \notin S^{\mathbf{A}_f}_r$, and $f(a_1, \ldots, a_r) \neq \perp$. Thus, $f(a_1, \ldots, a_r)$ has the form $(u, (c_1, \ldots, c_k))$. For each $\ell \in [k]$, we have $(a_1, \ldots, a_r, c_\ell) \in T^{\mathbf{A}_f}_{r,u,\ell}$, implying that $(h(a_1), \ldots, h(a_r), h(c_\ell)) \in T^{\mathbf{B}}_{r,u,\ell}$. From this, we conclude that $(h(c_1), \ldots, h(c_k)) = H^{(v_1, \ldots, v_r)}_u$, which in turn implies that $\{h(c_1), \ldots, h(c_k)\}$, and hence also $h(A) = g^{-1}(1)$, is a hitting set of $P(v_1, \ldots, v_r)$. $\square$

Theorem 4.4.29. *Each of the parameterized languages appearing in the statements of Theorems 4.4.24 and 4.4.27 is W[1]-complete. In particular, each of the parameterized languages* p-HOM, p-INJ-HOM, *and* p-CLIQUE *is W[1]-complete.*

Proof. We have that p-CLIQUE is W[1] by Example 4.4.16, implying by Theorem 4.4.8 and by Theorems 4.4.24 and 4.4.27 that each of the parameterized languages under consideration is W[1].

Each W[1] parameterized language fpt-many-one reduces to p-∨-INJ-HOM, by Theorem 4.4.28 and by the transitivity of fpt-many-one reducibility, shown in Theorem 4.4.10. Thus, we have that p-∨-INJ-HOM is W[1]-hard. By Proposition 4.4.20 and by Theorems 4.4.24 and 4.4.27, we obtain that each of the parameterized languages under consideration is W[1]-hard. $\square$

Remark 4.4.30. The homomorphism problem can be formulated using first-order logic, and this remark assumes basic familiarity with this logic. Here, we define a **conjunctive query** as a relational first-order sentence[43] having the form $\exists v_1 \ldots \exists v_n \psi$, where ψ is a conjunction of atomic formulas, each having the form $R(u_1, \ldots, u_k)$, where each variable u_i occurs in the sequence $v_1, \ldots, v_n$. Define **conjunctive query evaluation** to be the problem where an instance is a pair $(\phi, \mathbf{D})$ consisting of a conjunctive query ϕ and a structure $\mathbf{D}$ providing an interpretation $R^{\mathbf{D}}$ for each relation symbol R appearing in ϕ; the question is whether ϕ evaluates to true on $\mathbf{D}$ (in logical notation, whether $\mathbf{D} \models \phi$ holds). Let CQ-EVAL

---

43. It is also possible to consider conjunctive queries that are not sentences, but we do not do so here.

denote the language containing each such pair $(\phi, \mathbf{D})$ where ϕ is true on $\mathbf{D}$. The problem of conjunctive query evaluation is central in database theory, where conjunctive queries are viewed as a fundamental and frequently occurring class of *database queries*.

Let $\mathbf{C} = (C; R_1^{\mathbf{C}}, \ldots, R_k^{\mathbf{C}})$, be any relational structure, and denote C by $\{c_1, \ldots, c_n\}$; we can translate the structure $\mathbf{C}$ to the conjunctive query $\phi_{\mathbf{C}} = \exists c_1 \ldots \exists c_n \psi_{\mathbf{C}}$ where $\psi_{\mathbf{C}}$ is a conjunction containing, as a conjunct, each atomic formula $R_i(b_1, \ldots, b_k)$ such that $(b_1, \ldots, b_k) \in R_i^{\mathbf{C}}$. This translation has the straightforwardly verified and key property that, for any relational structure $\mathbf{D}$, it holds that $\mathbf{C}$ has a homomorphism to $\mathbf{D}$ if and only if $\phi_{\mathbf{C}}$ is true on $\mathbf{D}$. In effect, the sentence $\phi_{\mathbf{C}}$ asserts the existence of a homomorphism *from* $\mathbf{C}$. Recall that the homomorphism problem involves deciding, given two relational structures $(\mathbf{C}, \mathbf{D})$, whether $\mathbf{C}$ has a homomorphism to $\mathbf{D}$. An instance $(\mathbf{C}, \mathbf{D})$ of the homomorphism problem can thus be formulated as the instance $(\phi_{\mathbf{C}}, \mathbf{D})$ of conjunctive query evaluation, via the given translation. In the other direction, one can also readily reformulate an instance of conjunctive query evaluation as an instance of the homomorphism problem. Consider the problem of conjunctive query evaluation paired with the parameterization π_1 that returns the conjunctive query ϕ of an instance $(\phi, \mathbf{D})$; by Theorem 4.4.29, the corresponding parameterized language (CQ-EVAL, π_1) is W[1]-complete.

The homomorphism problem in fact appears throughout computer science in many guises. It can also be formulated as the *constraint satisfaction problem*, a problem which originated in the artificial intelligence literature, and which is discussed in Notes 4.6.52, 4.6.53, and 4.6.54. The discussed problems can be viewed very directly as formulations of each other, and results on one can often be naturally framed as results on the others.   ◇

4.5 Compilability theory

When trying to solve instances of a problem, if it is the case that multiple instances of relevance share a feature in common, it may be fruitful to *compile* this feature into a format that allows for more efficient solution, even if the compilation process is relatively expensive. For example, consider the problem of evaluating a database query on a database; if one is interested in a small set of queries that will be posed to numerous databases, it may be worthwhile to compile these queries into a format that allows for fast evaluation. Indeed, a relatively expensive compilation process may be worthwhile if its results are amortized by repeated use.

We saw that fixed-parameter tractability could be characterized by compilation: as shown in Section 4.3.3, a parameterized language (B, κ) is FPT if there is a computable function $\pi: \Sigma^* \to \Sigma^*$ such that when each input string x is presented along with the compilation $\pi(\kappa(x))$ of its parameter, membership of x in B can be decided in polynomial time. Here, the parameter $\kappa(x)$ of a string x is viewed as identifying a feature that is amenable to compilation.

A potential hindrance to using compilation in the described fashion is that *storing* compilations of the form $\pi(k)$, over various parameters k of interest, may be costly in terms

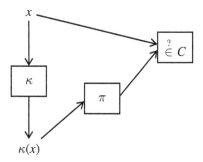

Figure 4.5.1. A schema indicating what it means for a parameterized language (B, κ) to be poly-comp-PTIME (Definition 4.5.3). The language B should be decided by the given schema, where the function π is required to be polynomial-length and computable, and the language C is required to be PTIME.

of space: a compilation $\pi(k)$ may, in general, be much larger than its respective parameter k. In this section, we present the basic ingredients of a theory of storage-efficient compilation: we model storage-efficient compilation by posing the requirement that the compilation function π be a *polynomial-length* function, which means that there is a polynomial bounding the length of $\pi(k)$ as a function of the length of k.

Basic notions

In the theory that we develop here, our intention is to model efficient computation modulo knowledge of a compilation function π; we thus put in effect the following assumption.

Assumption 4.5.1. Each parameterization is polynomial-time computable. ◇

We formally define the notion of a *polynomial-length* function as follows.

Definition 4.5.2. Let Σ_1, Σ_2 be alphabets. A function $\pi \colon \Sigma_1^* \to \Sigma_2^*$ is **polynomial-length** if there exists a polynomial P where, for each $x \in \Sigma_1^*$, it holds that $|\pi(x)| \leq P(|x|)$. ◇

The next definition captures those parameterized languages that admit polynomial-length compilations to a PTIME language; see Figure 4.5.1 for a diagram. This definition and the subsequent definitions will be seen to be restricted versions of definitions from parameterized complexity theory.

Definition 4.5.3. A parameterized language (B, κ) is **poly-comp-PTIME** if there exists a PTIME language C and a polynomial-length, computable function $\pi \colon \Sigma^* \to \Sigma^*$ such that (for each $x \in \Sigma^*$):

$$x \in B \quad \Leftrightarrow \quad \langle x, \pi(\kappa(x)) \rangle \in C.$$ ◇

Definition 4.5.3 is a restriction of the definition of para-PTIME (Definition 4.3.31): the requirement that π be polynomial-length has been added. Via Theorem 4.3.32, which

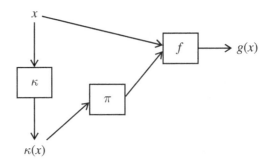

Figure 4.5.2. A schema indicating what it means for a function g to be κ-*poly-compilable* (Definition 4.5.5). The function g should be computed by the given schema, where the function π is required to be polynomial-length and computable, and the function f is required to be polynomial-time computable.

showed that being para-PTIME was the same as being FPT, we thus have the following fact.

Proposition 4.5.4. *Each parameterized language that is poly-comp-PTIME is also FPT.*

We next define a function version of poly-comp-PTIME; see Figure 4.5.2 for a diagram illustrating the definition.

Definition 4.5.5. Suppose that κ is a parameterization. A function $g\colon \Sigma^* \to \Sigma^*$ is κ-**poly-compilable** if there exists a polynomial-time computable function $f\colon \Sigma^* \to \Sigma^*$ and a polynomial-length, computable function $\pi\colon \Sigma^* \to \Sigma^*$ such that (for each $x \in \Sigma^*$)

$$g(x) = f(\langle x, \pi(\kappa(x))\rangle).$$ ◇

We have that the condition of being κ-poly-compilable is a restriction of that of being κ-fpt-computable.

Proposition 4.5.6. *Each function $g\colon \Sigma^* \to \Sigma^*$ that is κ-poly-compilable is a κ-fpt-computable function.*

Proposition 4.5.6 can be justified by the time analysis of the backward direction of Theorem 4.3.32's proof.

Poly-comp reducibility

We next turn to present a notion of reduction under which the poly-comp-PTIME parameterized languages are closed. This notion of reduction is a restricted version of fpt-many-one reduction. In order to present it, we identify the following restricted version of (κ, κ')-parameter boundedness.

Definition 4.5.7. Let κ, κ' be parameterizations. Say that a function $f: \Sigma^* \to \Sigma^*$ is **polynomially (κ, κ')-parameter bounded** if there exists a polynomial-length, computable function $s: \Sigma^* \to \wp_{\text{fin}}(\Sigma^*)$ where (for each $x \in \Sigma^*$) it holds that $\kappa'(f(x)) \in s(\kappa(x))$. $\quad\diamond$

This definition is a restriction of that of being (κ, κ')-*parameter bounded*; the requirement that the function s be *polynomial-length* has been added.

Here, when we speak of a function $s: \Sigma^* \to \wp_{\text{fin}}(\Sigma^*)$ being *polynomial-length* or *computable*, we assume that each finite subset of Σ^* is encoded by a representation where the elements in the subset are listed. Thus, when such a function s is *polynomial-length*, there is a polynomial that, as a function of $|k|$, upper bounds both the size of the set $s(k)$ and the length of each element in the set $s(k)$.

We can next present the reduction notion of our theory.

Definition 4.5.8. Let (B, κ), (B', κ') be parameterized languages. A **poly-comp reduction** from (B, κ) to (B', κ') is a κ-poly-compilable function $\rho: \Sigma^* \to \Sigma^*$ such that:

- for each $x \in \Sigma^*$, it holds that $x \in B \Leftrightarrow \rho(x) \in B'$, and
- ρ is polynomially (κ, κ')-parameter bounded.

To indicate that there exists a poly-comp reduction from (B, κ) to (B', κ'), we say that (B, κ) **poly-comp reduces** to (B', κ'). $\quad\diamond$

This definition of *poly-comp reduction* is different from the definition of *fpt-many-one reduction* in two respects: first, the mapping is required to be κ-poly-compilable in place of κ-fpt-computable; second, the mapping is required to be polynomially (κ, κ')-parameter bounded, as opposed to just (κ, κ')-parameter bounded. Each of these changes causes the definition of *poly-comp reduction* to be more restrictive than that of *fpt-many-one reduction*, and so we have the following fact.

Proposition 4.5.9. *When (B, κ) and (B', κ') are parameterized languages, a poly-comp reduction from (B, κ) to (B', κ') is an fpt-many-one reduction from (B, κ) to (B', κ').*

We next show two basic properties of poly-comp reducibility, namely, that the poly-comp-PTIME parameterized languages are closed under this reducibility, and that this reducibility is transitive. The following lemma[44] will aid us in establishing these properties; its setup is depicted in Figure 4.5.3.

Lemma 4.5.10. *Let (B, κ) and (B', κ') be parameterized languages. Suppose that $g: \Sigma^* \to \Sigma^*$ is a poly-comp reduction from (B, κ) to (B', κ'), and that $g': \Sigma^* \to \Sigma^*$ is a κ'-poly-compilable function. Then, the composition of g and g'—that is, the function $h: \Sigma^* \to \Sigma^*$ defined by $h(x) = g'(g(x))$—is a κ-poly-compilable function.*

---

44. Lemma 4.5.10 is this section's analog of Lemma 4.4.3.

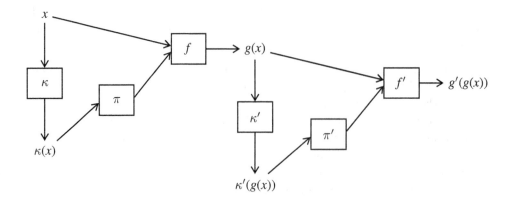

Figure 4.5.3. The setup of Lemma 4.5.10, which shows the following. Suppose that g is a poly-comp reduction from a parameterized language (B, κ) to a parameterized language (B', κ'). Then one obtains a κ-compilable function when composing the reduction g with a κ'-poly-compilable function g'.

Proof. Since g is a poly-comp reduction, it is polynomially (κ, κ')-bounded, and so there exists a polynomial-length, computable function $s \colon \Sigma^* \to \wp_{\text{fin}}(\Sigma^*)$ where, for each string x, it holds that $\kappa'(g(x)) \in s(\kappa(x))$. Since g is a κ-poly-compilable function and g' is a κ'-poly-compilable function, there exist polynomial-time computable functions f, f' and polynomial-length, computable functions π, π' such that

$$g(x) = f(\langle x, \pi(\kappa(x)) \rangle) \quad \text{and} \quad g(x') = f'(\langle x', \pi'(\kappa'(x')) \rangle).$$

Let $\pi^+ \colon \Sigma^* \to \Sigma^*$ be the function defined by $\pi^+(k) = \langle \pi(k), \{ \langle k', \pi'(k') \rangle \mid k' \in s(k) \} \rangle$. Intuitively speaking, for each string k, the string $\pi^+(k)$ holds all of the values of the functions π and π' that are needed to compute $h(x)$ on a string x with parameter k. Define $f^+ \colon \Sigma^* \to \Sigma^*$ as the function computed by the following algorithm:

- Check that the input string is a pair $\langle x, a \rangle$ such that a is a pair $\langle p, P' \rangle$ where P' is a set of pairs of strings. If this check fails, output ϵ.
- Assign $x' := f(\langle x, p \rangle)$.
- Assign $k' := \kappa'(x')$.
- If there exists a string p' such that $\langle k', p' \rangle \in P'$, fix p' as such a string. Otherwise, output ϵ.
- Output $f'(\langle x', p' \rangle)$.

The functions f and f' are each polynomial-time computable, and κ' is polynomial-time computable by Assumption 4.5.1; it follows that f^+ is polynomial-time computable. Also, given that π, π', and s are each polynomial-length and computable, it follows that π^+ is polynomial-length and computable.

We show that h is κ-poly-compilable via f^+ and π^+, that is, that $h(x) = f^+(\langle x, \pi^+(\kappa(x))\rangle)$. Let x be a string, and consider the algorithm's behavior when given the pair $\langle x, \pi^+(\kappa(x))\rangle$ as input. The value p is set equal to $\pi(\kappa(x))$. The algorithm sets x' as $f(\langle x, \pi(\kappa(x))\rangle)$, which is equal to $g(x)$; and it sets k' as $\kappa'(x')$. Since $k' = \kappa'(x') = \kappa'(g(x)) \in s(\kappa(x))$, due to the definition of π^+, the algorithm fixes the string p' as $\pi'(k')$. Thus, the result output by the algorithm is

$$f'(\langle x', p'\rangle) = f'(\langle g(x), \pi'(\kappa'(x'))\rangle)$$
$$= f'(\langle g(x), \pi'(\kappa'(g(x)))\rangle)$$
$$= g'(g(x))$$
$$= h(x). \qquad \square$$

Using the just-given lemma, we next show the closure of the poly-comp-PTIME parameterized languages under poly-comp reducibility.

Theorem 4.5.11. *Suppose that (B, κ) and (B', κ') are parameterized languages such that (B, κ) poly-comp reduces to (B', κ'). If (B', κ') is poly-comp-PTIME, then (B, κ) is poly-comp-PTIME.*

Proof. By hypothesis, (B', κ') is poly-comp-PTIME; thus, there exist a PTIME language C' and a polynomial-length, computable function $\pi \colon \Sigma^* \to \Sigma^*$ such that (for each $x' \in \Sigma^*$)

$$x' \in B' \quad \Leftrightarrow \quad \langle x', \pi(\kappa'(x'))\rangle \in C'.$$

Define $g' \colon \Sigma^* \to \Sigma^*$ as the function such that $g'(x') = \langle x', \pi(\kappa'(x'))\rangle$, for each $x' \in \Sigma^*$; we have that g' is κ'-poly-compilable, and is such that (for each $x' \in \Sigma^*$)

$$x' \in B' \quad \Leftrightarrow \quad g'(x') \in C'.$$

Let $g \colon \Sigma^* \to \Sigma^*$ be a poly-comp reduction from (B, κ) to (B', κ'). Applying Lemma 4.5.10 to g and g', we obtain that the composition h of g and g' is κ-poly-compilable. Thus, there exist a polynomial-time compilable function $f_h \colon \Sigma^* \to \Sigma^*$ and a polynomial-length, computable function $\pi_h \colon \Sigma^* \to \Sigma^*$ where (for each $x \subset \Sigma^*$) it holds that $h(x) = f_h(\langle x, \pi_h(\kappa(x))\rangle)$. Define $f_h^{-1}(C')$ as the language $\{z \mid f_h(z) \in C'\}$. The language $f_h^{-1}(C')$ is PTIME; one way to reason this is to observe that f_h is a polynomial-time many-one reduction from $f_h^{-1}(C')$ to C', and then to invoke the closure of the PTIME languages under polynomial-time many-one reductions (Theorem 3.4.14). We obtain that (B, κ) is poly-comp-PTIME via the PTIME language $f_h^{-1}(C')$ and the function π_h:

$$x \in B \quad \Leftrightarrow \quad g(x) \in B'$$
$$\Leftrightarrow \quad g'(g(x)) \in C'$$
$$\Leftrightarrow \quad h(x) \in C'$$

$$\Leftrightarrow \quad f_h(\langle x, \pi_h(\kappa(x))\rangle) \in C'$$

$$\Leftrightarrow \quad \langle x, \pi_h(\kappa(x))\rangle \in f_h^{-1}(C'). \qquad \square$$

We next establish transitivity of poly-comp reducibility.

Theorem 4.5.12. *Let* (B, κ), (B', κ'), *and* (B'', κ'') *be parameterized languages such that* (B, κ) *poly-comp reduces to* (B', κ') *and* (B', κ') *poly-comp reduces to* (B'', κ''). *Then it holds that* (B, κ) *poly-comp reduces to* (B'', κ'').

Proof. Let g be a poly-comp reduction from (B, κ) to (B', κ'), and let g' be a poly-comp reduction from (B', κ') to (B'', κ''). Lemma 4.5.10 yields that the composition h of g and g' is κ-poly-compilable. We verify that h is a poly-comp reduction from (B, κ) to (B'', κ'').

For each $x \in \Sigma^*$, we have:

$$x \in B \quad \Leftrightarrow \quad g(x) \in B'$$
$$\Leftrightarrow \quad g'(g(x)) \in B''$$
$$\Leftrightarrow \quad h(x) \in B''.$$

Let us argue that h is polynomially (κ, κ'')-bounded. Let $s\colon \Sigma^* \to \wp_{\mathrm{fin}}(\Sigma^*)$ witness that g is polynomially (κ, κ')-bounded, and let $s'\colon \Sigma^* \to \wp_{\mathrm{fin}}(\Sigma^*)$ witness that g' is polynomially (κ', κ'')-bounded. Then for each $x \in \Sigma^*$, we have

$$\kappa'(g(x)) \in s(\kappa(x)) \quad \text{and} \quad \kappa''(g'(g(x))) \in s'(\kappa'(g(x))).$$

Define $t\colon \Sigma^* \to \wp_{\mathrm{fin}}(\Sigma^*)$ as the function where, for each $k \in \Sigma^*$, it holds that

$$t(k) = \bigcup_{k' \in s(k)} s'(k').$$

We then have, for each $x \in \Sigma^*$, that

$$\kappa''(h(x)) = \kappa''(g'(g(x))) \in s'(\kappa'(g(x))) \subseteq t(\kappa(x)).$$

It is straightforward to verify that t is polynomial-length and computable. Thus, t witnesses that h is polynomially (κ, κ'')-bounded. $\qquad \square$

Establishing hardness

We here establish a means for evidencing that a parameterized language is not poly-comp-PTIME.

Let $\mathrm{len}\colon \Sigma^* \to \Sigma^*$ be the function defined by $\mathrm{len}(x) = 1^{|x|}$, that is, the function giving the length of each string in unary; this function is clearly polynomial-time computable, and we will use it as a parameterization. Let us introduce a relaxation of the class $\wp$ of PTIME languages, known as a *nonuniform* or *advice* version of $\wp$: essentially, a language is in this relaxed class if deciding membership of a string x can be performed efficiently when x is presented along with an *advice string* that depends only on x's length. Define

$\mathcal{P}$/poly as the class that contains a language B when there exists a language $C \in \mathcal{P}$ and a polynomial-length function $\pi \colon \{1\}^* \to \Sigma^*$ such that (for each $x \in \Sigma^*$)

$$x \in B \quad \Leftrightarrow \quad \langle x, \pi(\mathrm{len}(x)) \rangle \in C.$$

Remark 4.5.13. Our hardness results will be based on the hypothesis $\mathfrak{NP} \not\subseteq \mathcal{P}$/poly. This is an established complexity-theoretic hypothesis that is known to hold under a natural extension of the assumption $\mathfrak{NP} \not\subseteq \mathcal{P}$. ◇

The following observation is immediate from the definitions of poly-comp-PTIME and of $\mathcal{P}$/poly.

Proposition 4.5.14. *If B is a language such that (B, len) is poly-comp-PTIME, then it holds that $B \in \mathcal{P}$/poly.*

The following theorem provides examples of parameterized languages that are not poly-comp-PTIME, under the assumption that $\mathfrak{NP} \not\subseteq \mathcal{P}$/poly.

Theorem 4.5.15. *Suppose that D is an NP-hard or coNP-hard language. Then, the parameterized language (D, len) is not poly-comp-PTIME, unless $\mathfrak{NP} \subseteq \mathcal{P}$/poly.*

Proof. First, suppose that D is NP-hard and that (D, len) is poly-comp-PTIME; we argue that each language in $\mathfrak{NP}$ is in $\mathcal{P}$/poly. By Proposition 4.5.14 , we have that $D \in \mathcal{P}$/poly. Any language C in $\mathfrak{NP}$ has $C \leq_m^p D$, from which it follows that $C \in \mathcal{P}$/poly, since the class $\mathcal{P}$/poly is closed under polynomial-time many-one reductions (Exercise 4.6.19). We obtain that $\mathfrak{NP} \subseteq \mathcal{P}$/poly.

If we suppose that D is coNP-hard in place of being NP-hard, a similar argument shows that $\mathrm{co}\mathfrak{NP} \subseteq \mathcal{P}$/poly. But the class $\mathcal{P}$/poly is immediately verified to be closed under complementation, so the containment $\mathrm{co}\mathfrak{NP} \subseteq \mathcal{P}$/poly implies (and is indeed equivalent to) the containment $\mathfrak{NP} \subseteq \mathcal{P}$/poly. □

As a consequence of this theorem, we obtain the following principle for evidencing that a parameterized language is not poly-comp-PTIME.

Theorem 4.5.16. *Suppose that D is an NP-hard or coNP-hard language, and that the parameterized language (D, lcn) poly-comp reduces to a parameterized language (B, κ). Then, (B, κ) is not poly-comp-PTIME, unless $\mathfrak{NP} \subseteq \mathcal{P}$/poly.*

Proof. We argue that if (B, κ) is poly-comp-PTIME, then $\mathfrak{NP} \subseteq \mathcal{P}$/poly. If (B, κ) is poly-comp-PTIME, then (D, len) is also poly-comp-PTIME, by Theorem 4.5.11. From this, Theorem 4.5.15 implies that $\mathfrak{NP} \subseteq \mathcal{P}$/poly. □

4.5.1 An example hardness result

We use the established framework to present a negative compilability result on the problem of deciding, given a CNF-formula and a satisfying assignment, whether the satisfying assignment is *minimal*. The requisite definitions are as follows. Let us use $\leq$ to denote the usual total order on $\{0, 1\}$, where $0 \leq 1$. We extend this notation to pairs of propositional assignments $f, g: V \to \{0, 1\}$ defined on the same set V of variables by writing $f \leq g$ if and only if for each $v \in V$, it holds that $f(v) \leq g(v)$; and we write $f < g$ when $f \leq g$ and $f \neq g$. When ψ is a propositional formula and W is the set of variables appearing in ψ, a **minimal satisfying assignment** of ψ is a satisfying assignment $g : W \to \{0, 1\}$ where there is no satisfying assignment $f : W \to \{0, 1\}$ of ψ such that $f < g$, or equivalently, where for each satisfying assignment $f : W \to \{0, 1\}$ of ψ, it holds that $f \leq g$ implies $f = g$.

Define MIN-CNF-SAT as the language containing each pair (ψ, g) where ψ is a CNF-formula, and g is a minimal satisfying assignment of ψ. In the study of this language, the CNF-formula of an instance is sometimes conceived of as a knowledge base, and a natural question is whether or not each such knowledge base can be rewritten into a format that does not significantly increase length, but supports efficient answering of whether or not given satisfying assignments are minimal. Following these concerns, we study the parameterized language (MIN-CNF-SAT, π_1). This parameterized language is para-PTIME, via a compilation function that, given a CNF-formula, simply provides a listing of all of the formula's minimal satisfying assignments. We here unfortunately show this parameterized language's hardness in the setting of compilability: this parameterized language is not poly-comp-PTIME, unless $\mathcal{NP} \subseteq \mathcal{P}/\text{poly}$. The heart of the argumentation is a reduction from 3-CNF-UNSAT to MIN-CNF-SAT, which we give next.

The reduction will create instances of MIN-CNF-SAT whose formulas are drawn from a sequence $(\psi_n)_{n \geq 1}$ of CNF-formulas, defined as follows. For each $n \geq 1$, let V_n be the set $\{u_1, ..., u_n\}$ of variables, and let $\mathcal{C}_n$ be the set of all clauses over V_n having size 3 or less. It holds that $|\mathcal{C}_n| \leq (2n + 1)^3$, since we may represent each clause in $\mathcal{C}_n$ as a 3-tuple where each entry is either a variable, the negation of a variable, or absent. The variables occurring in ψ_n are those in the set W_n defined by

$$W_n = V_n \cup \{y\} \cup \left\{ d_C, d_C' \mid C \in \mathcal{C}_n \right\}.$$

That is, the set W_n includes each variable in V_n; an extra variable y; and a pair of variables, d_C and d_C', for each clause C in $\mathcal{C}_n$. We have $|W_n| = n + 1 + 2|\mathcal{C}_n|$. The formula ψ_n consists of three types of clauses:

(1) There is a clause $\neg y \vee u$ for each variable $u \in V_n$.

(2) There is a clause $d_C \vee d_C'$ for each clause $C \in \mathcal{C}_n$.

(3) There is a clause $\neg d_C \vee y \vee C$ for each clause $C \in \mathcal{C}_n$.

Theorem 4.5.17. *There exists a polynomial-time many-one reduction from* 3-CNF-UNSAT *to* MIN-CNF-SAT *where each 3-CNF-formula ϕ is mapped to an instance of the form $(\psi_n, \cdot)$, where n is the number of variables occurring in ϕ.*

Proof. Given a 3-CNF-formula ϕ with $n \geq 1$ variables, the reduction behaves as follows. By renaming the variables of ϕ (if necessary), it may be assumed that V_n is the set of variables occurring in ϕ. Define $g_\phi : W_n \to \{0, 1\}$ as the mapping where

- $g_\phi(u) = 1$ for each variable $u \in V_n$;
- $g_\phi(y) = 1$;
- $g_\phi(d_C) = 1$ for each clause C appearing in ϕ, and $g_\phi(d_C) = 0$ for each other clause $C \in \mathcal{C}_n$; and
- $g_\phi(d_C') = \neg g_\phi(d_C)$ for each clause $C \in \mathcal{C}_n$.

The reduction creates the instance (ψ_n, g_ϕ), and is straightforwardly verifiable to be polynomial-time computable.

We verify correctness of this reduction by proving that ϕ is satisfiable if and only if g_ϕ is not a minimum satisfying assignment of ψ_n.

For the forward direction, suppose that $f : V_n \to \{0, 1\}$ is a satisfying assignment of ϕ. Let $f^+ : W_n \to \{0, 1\}$ be the extension of f where $f^+(y) = 0$ and where $f^+(d_C) = g_\phi(d_C)$ and $f^+(d_C') = g_\phi(d_C')$ for each clause $C \in \mathcal{C}_n$. It is immediately verified that $f^+ < g_\phi$; it thus suffices to show that f^+ satisfies ψ_n. It is readily verified that f^+ satisfies all clauses of type (1) and (2) in ψ_n. Consider an arbitrary clause $\neg d_C \vee y \vee C$ of type (3) in ψ_n. This clause is clearly satisfied by f^+ when $f^+(d_C) = 0$, so assume that $f^+(d_C) = 1$. By the definitions of f^+ and g_ϕ, it holds that C occurs as a clause in ϕ. Since f satisfies ϕ, it holds that f satisfies C, implying that f^+ satisfies C and thus that f^+ satisfies $\neg d_C \vee y \vee C$.

For the backward direction, suppose that $g_\phi : W_n \to \{0, 1\}$ is not a minimal satisfying assignment of ψ_n. As is straightforwardly verified, g_ϕ is a satisfying assignment of ψ_n; thus, there exists a satisfying assignment $f : W_n \to \{0, 1\}$ of ψ_n such that $f < g_\phi$. Let us make two observations about f, accompanied with justifications.

(α) It holds that $f(d_C) = 1$ and $f(d_C') = 0$ for each clause C appearing in ϕ.

Justification: for such a clause C, due to $f \leq g_\phi$, we have $f(d_C') \leq g_\phi(d_C') = 0$ and thus $f(d_C') = 0$. If $f(d_C) = 1$ did not hold, it would be that $f(d_C) = 0$; but then, the type (2) clause $d_C \vee d_C'$ in ψ_n would be falsified by f, a contradiction.

(β) It holds that $f(y) = 0$.

Justification: if this did not hold, it would be that $f(y) = 1$; but then, since f satisfies all type (1) clauses in ψ_n, it would hold that $f(u) = 1$ for each variable $u \in V_n$; combined with (α), this would imply $f = g_\phi$, a contradiction.

With these two observations in place, we show that f is a satisfying assignment of ϕ. Let C be any clause appearing in ϕ. By the observations, we have $f(d_C) = 1$ and $f(y) = 0$; since f satisfies the clause $\neg d_C \vee y \vee C$ in ψ_n, it follows that f satisfies the clause C. $\qquad\square$

In what follows, let ν denote the function that, for each CNF-formula ϕ, returns 1^n, where n is the number of variables appearing in ϕ; that is, it returns this number of variables in unary representation. We will see in a moment that the just-given reduction can be viewed as a poly-comp reduction from the parameterized language (3-CNF-UNSAT, ν), whose hardness is implied by the following reduction.

Lemma 4.5.18. (3-CNF-UNSAT, len) *poly-comp reduces to* (3-CNF-UNSAT, ν).

Proof. Assuming a standard representation of CNF-formulas, each variable in a formula contributes at least 1 to the length of the formula's representation; so, for each CNF-formula ϕ, it holds that $|\nu(\phi)| \leq \|\text{len}(\phi)\|$. The identity mapping thus gives the desired a poly-comp reduction, where the function $s(1^\ell) = \{1^0, 1^1, ..., 1^\ell\}$ witnesses that this mapping is polynomially (len, ν)-parameter bounded. $\square$

Remark 4.5.19. It can be verified that the reduction of Lemma 4.5.18 can be reversed, that is, that $(\text{3-CNF-UNSAT}, \nu)$ poly-comp reduces to $(\text{3-CNF-UNSAT}, \text{len})$. $\diamond$

We next present our example non-compilability result, which relies strongly on the reduction of Theorem 4.5.17.

Theorem 4.5.20. $(\text{MIN-CNF-SAT}, \pi_1)$ *is not poly-comp-PTIME, unless* $\mathbb{NP} \subseteq \mathbb{P}/\text{poly}$.

Proof. First, we observe that the reduction of Theorem 4.5.17 is a poly-comp reduction from $(\text{3-CNF-UNSAT}, \nu)$ to $(\text{MIN-CNF-SAT}, \pi_1)$: this reduction is polynomial-time computable and hence ν-poly-compilable, and for any parameter value 1^n, each formula ϕ with $\nu(\phi) = 1^n$ is mapped to an instance with parameter value ψ_n. By Lemma 4.5.18 and the transitivity of poly-comp reducibility (Theorem 4.5.12), we obtain that there is a poly-comp reduction from $(\text{3-CNF-UNSAT}, \text{len})$ to $(\text{MIN-CNF-SAT}, \pi_1)$. As the language 3-CNF-UNSAT is coNP-hard (by Corollary 3.8.15), the present theorem follows from Theorem 4.5.16. $\square$

Finally, we note the following consequence of Theorem 4.5.17.

Corollary 4.5.21. MIN-CNF-SAT *is coNP-complete.*

Proof. The language MIN-CNF-SAT is straightforwardly verified to be coNP: relative to a CNF-formula ψ, non-minimality of a satisfying assignment g can be certified by a satisfying assignment f where $f < g$. The language 3-CNF-UNSAT is coNP-hard (by Corollary 3.8.15) and admits a polynomial-time many-one reduction to MIN-CNF-SAT by Theorem 4.5.17, implying the coNP-hardness of MIN-CNF-SAT. $\square$

4.6 Exercises and notes

This section consists of three parts: we present general exercises and notes, for the whole chapter, in Section 4.6.1. We then explore two topics in depth: *logarithmic space computation*, in Section 4.6.2, and *treewidth*, in Section 4.6.3; in the coverage of these topics, the notes are intended to be read in sequence.

4.6.1 General

Exercise 4.6.1: Logically equivalent qp-formulas. Let us say that two qp-formulas ϕ, ϕ' are **logically equivalent** if for every assignment $f: V \to \{0, 1\}$ defined on both $\text{free}(\phi)$ and free(ϕ') (that is, where free(ϕ) $\subseteq V$ and free(ϕ') $\subseteq V$), it holds that f satisfies ϕ if and only if f satisfies ϕ'.

1. Let $Q \in \{\forall, \exists\}$ be a quantifier, let u be a variable, and let ψ and ψ' be any qp-formulas such that $u \notin$ free(ψ'). Prove that the qp-formulas $Qu((\psi) \wedge (\psi'))$ and $(Qu(\psi)) \wedge (\psi')$ share the same set of free variables, and are logically equivalent to each other. (Note that these assertions can also be proved when the connective $\wedge$ is replaced with the connective $\vee$ in each of the formulas.)

2. Let ψ, ψ' be any two qp-formulas. Prove that the qp-formulas $\forall y((\psi) \wedge (\psi'))$ and $(\forall y(\psi)) \wedge (\forall y(\psi'))$ share the same set of free variables, and are logically equivalent to each other.

3. Let y be a variable, and let ψ be any qp-formula such that $y \notin$ free(ψ). Prove that the qp-formulas ψ, $\forall y((\psi) \vee y)$, and $\forall y((\psi) \vee \neg y)$ share the same set of free variables, and are logically equivalent to each other. $\diamond$

Note 4.6.2: Prenex qp-formulas. Let us introduce some notions associated with qp-formulas, which were presented in Section 4.1.3. Define a **quantifier prefix** to be a sequence of the form $Q_1 v_1 \ldots Q_k v_k$ where each Q_i is a quantifier in $\{\exists, \forall\}$, each v_i is a variable, and no variable occurs more than once. A qp-formula is *prenex* if all occurrences of quantification appear in the front of the formula. Precisely, a **prenex qp-formula** is a qp-formula ϕ that has the form $Q_1 v_1 \ldots Q_k v_k \psi$ where $Q_1 v_1 \ldots Q_k v_k$ is a quantifier prefix, and ψ is a qp-formula not containing any quantifiers; the formula ψ is referred to as the **quantifier-free part** of ϕ, and a variable v_i is said to be **existentially quantified** in ϕ if $Q_i = \exists$, and is said to be **universally quantified** in ϕ if $Q_i = \forall$. A **prenex qp-sentence** is a qp-formula that is prenex and is a qp-sentence.

A prenex qp-formula is Σ_0 if it does not contain any quantifiers, and is Π_0 if it does not contain any quantifiers. That is, a prenex qp-formula is Σ_0 and is Π_0 if its quantifier prefix is empty. For each $i > 0$, a prenex qp-formula is Σ_i if it has the form $\exists x_1 \ldots \exists x_\ell \theta$, where θ is a Π_{i-1} prenex qp-formula, and dually, a prenex qp-formula is Π_i if it has the form $\forall y_1 \ldots \forall y_\ell \theta$, where θ is a Σ_{i-1} prenex qp-formula. So in particular, a prenex qp-formula is Σ_1 if $\exists$ is the only quantifier used, and is Π_2 if its quantifier prefix has the form $\forall y_1 \ldots \forall y_\ell \exists x_1 \ldots \exists x_m$. $\diamond$

Exercise 4.6.3. Define 2-CNF-QSAT as the language containing each prenex qp-sentence that is true and whose quantifier-free part is a 2-CNF-formula. Prove that this language is PTIME. Hint: try to give an algorithm that eliminates quantifiers one by one. $\diamond$

Exercise 4.6.4. Define Π_2-$(1, 2)$-CNF-QSAT as the language containing each Π_2 prenex qp-sentence that is true and whose quantifier-free part is a 3-CNF-formula where each clause has at most 1 variable that is universally quantified, and at most 2 variables that are existentially quantified. Prove that this language is coNP-complete. $\diamond$

Exercise 4.6.5: Extended Horn clauses. When ϕ is a prenex qp-sentence whose quantifier-free part is a CNF-formula ψ, say that a clause C of ψ is an **extended Horn clause** if C contains at most one positive literal that is an existentially quantified variable. Equivalently, a clause C of ψ is an *extended Horn clause* if after removing the literals whose variables are universally quantified, the resulting clause is a Horn clause. Define an **extended qp-Horn-sentence** as a qp-sentence that is prenex and whose quantifier-free part is a CNF-formula where each clause is an extended Horn clause.

1. Define Π_2-∃HORN-CNF-QSAT as the language containing each Π_2 prenex qp-sentence that is true and is an extended qp-Horn-sentence. Prove that this language is coNP-complete.

2. Define Σ_3-∃HORN-CNF-QSAT as the language containing each Σ_3 prenex qp-sentence that is true and is an extended qp-Horn-sentence. Prove that this language is coNP.   ◇

Exercise 4.6.6: Extended 2-clauses. When ϕ is a prenex qp-sentence whose quantifier-free part is a CNF-formula ψ, say that a clause C of ψ is an **extended 2-clause** if C contains at most two occurrences of existentially quantified variables. Equivalently, a clause C of ψ is an *extended 2-clause* if after removing the literals whose variables are universally quantified, the resulting clause has 2 or fewer literals. Define an **extended qp-2-sentence** as a qp-sentence that is prenex and whose quantifier-free part is a CNF-formula where each clause is an extended 2-clause.

Define Σ_3-∃2-CNF-QSAT as the language containing each Σ_3 prenex qp-sentence that is true and is an extended qp-2-sentence. Prove that this language is coNP.   ◇

Note 4.6.7: Q-resolution. In this note, we present a proof system for certifying the falsity of prenex qp-sentences. Let ϕ be a prenex qp-sentence whose quantifier-free part is a CNF-formula. A **Q-resolution proof** for ϕ is a sequence $\Pi = D_1, \ldots, D_\ell$ of clauses, where each clause D_i is derived according to one of the following rules: **download**, **structural**, **∃-cut**, and **∀-elimination**. We describe these rules as follows.

- The *download* and *structural* rules are defined as they are for resolution, in Note 3.10.29.
- The *∃-cut* rule is also defined as in Note 3.10.29, but with the requirement that the variable x on which the cut is performed must be an existentially quantified variable.
- To present the *∀-elimination* rule, we first give a definition. Let C be a clause in a prenex qp-sentence; define a literal in C as **trailing** in C if its variable occurs strictly after the variable of any other literal in C, in the quantifier prefix of the sentence. That is, a literal in a clause is *trailing* if, among all variables occurring in the clause, the literal's variable is the last one to appear in the quantifier prefix, and only occurs once in the clause.

  The *∀-elimination* rule allows for the derivation of a clause D_i from a clause D_j appearing before D_i (that is, with $j < i$) when the following holds: D_j contains a trailing literal λ whose underlying variable is universally quantified, and D_i is equal to D_j but with the literal λ removed.   ◇

The notion of *Q-resolution proof* strictly generalizes that of *resolution proof*; when ϕ is a prenex qp-sentence containing only existential quantifiers and whose quantifier-free part ψ is a CNF-formula, it can be seen that the resolution proofs of ψ and the Q-resolution proofs of ϕ coincide.

Exercise 4.6.8. Let ϕ be a prenex qp-sentence whose quantifier-free part is a CNF-formula. Prove that ϕ is false if and only if there exists a Q-resolution proof for ϕ in which the empty clause appears. $\diamond$

Exercise 4.6.9: Bounded-occurrence qp-sentences. For each $k \geq 1$, define the language k-OCC-CNF-QSAT to contain each true prenex qp-sentence ϕ whose quantifier-free part is a CNF-formula where each variable *occurs k or fewer times*, that is, such that if one looks through the literals of ϕ's CNF-formula one by one, each variable is seen k or fewer times.

1. Prove that the language 2-OCC-CNF-QSAT is PTIME.
2. Prove that the language 3-OCC-CNF-QSAT is PSPACE-complete. $\diamond$

Exercise 4.6.10: Equivalence problems on qp-formulas. In this exercise, we consider equivalence problems on Σ_1 qp-formulas. Here, we use the notion of *logical equivalence* given in Exercise 4.6.1.

1. Define Σ_1-2-CNF-EQUIV as the language containing each pair (ϕ, ϕ') of Σ_1 qp-formulas that are logically equivalent and whose quantifier-free parts are 2-CNF-formulas.
2. Define Σ_1-HORN-CNF-EQUIV as the language containing each pair (ϕ, ϕ') of Σ_1 qp-formulas that are logically equivalent and whose quantifier-free parts are Horn-CNF-formulas.

For each of these languages, prove either that it is PTIME, or that it is coNP-complete. $\diamond$

Exercise 4.6.11: A game-theoretic view of qp-sentences. There is a game-theoretic way to view and reason about qp-formulas, which we describe for prenex qp-sentences. Let $Q_1 v_1 \ldots Q_k v_k \psi$ be a prenex qp-sentence, where ψ is the quantifier-free part of the sentence. This sentence can be presented as a game between two players, the $\exists$ *player* and the $\forall$-*player*; to play the game, the Q_1-player sets the variable v_1 to a value in $\{0, 1\}$, the Q_2-player sets the variable v_2 to a value in $\{0, 1\}$, and so on, until all of the variables $v_1, \ldots, v_k$ have been set. The $\exists$-player wins a play if the resulting assignment from $\{v_1, \ldots, v_k\}$ to $\{0, 1\}$ satisfies the quantifier-free part ψ. This game leads to a characterization of truth for qp-sentences: a qp-sentence is true if and only if the $\exists$-player has a winning strategy that permits them to always win, regardless of how the $\forall$-player acts. This exercise requests a proof of this characterization.

Relative to a prenex qp-sentence $Q_1 v_1 \ldots Q_k v_k \psi$, we introduce the following definitions. Let X denote the set of existentially quantified variables, let U denote the set of universally quantified variables, and for each $x \in X$, let $U_{<x}$ denote the set containing each universally

quantified variable appearing before x in the quantifier prefix (that is, to the left of x). Define an $\exists$-**strategy** as a family $(\sigma_x \colon \{0,1\}^{U_{<x}} \to \{0,1\})_{x \in X}$ of maps; here, $\{0,1\}^{U_{<x}}$ denotes the set of maps from $U_{<x}$ to $\{0,1\}$. Say that an $\exists$-strategy $(\sigma_x)_{x \in X}$ is **winning** when, for each mapping $f \colon U \to \{0,1\}$, the following holds: the extension $f^+ \colon (X \cup U) \to \{0,1\}$ of f defined by $f^+(x) = \sigma_x(f \upharpoonright U_{<x})$, for each $x \in X$, is a satisfying assignment of ψ. Here, we use $f \upharpoonright U_{<x}$ to denote the restriction of f to the set $U_{<x}$.

Prove that a prenex qp-sentence is true if and only if there exists a winning $\exists$-strategy relative to it.   ◇

Exercise 4.6.12: κ-added polynomials. Let $\kappa \colon \Sigma^* \to \Sigma^*$ be a function. Call a function $U \colon \Sigma^* \to \mathbb{N}$ a κ-**added polynomial** if there exist a computable function $h \colon \Sigma^* \to \mathbb{N}$ and a polynomial $Q \colon \mathbb{N} \to \mathbb{N}$ such that, for each $x \in \Sigma^*$, it holds that $U(x) = h(\kappa(x)) + Q(|x|)$.

Prove that each κ-scaled polynomial is bounded above by a κ-added polynomial and that each κ-added polynomial is bounded above by a κ-scaled polynomial. Here, for functions $T, T' \colon \Sigma^* \to \mathbb{N}$, we say that T is bounded above by T' when, for each $x \in \Sigma^*$, it holds that $T(x) \leq T'(x)$.

This exercise implies that, in Definition 4.3.13, the notion of κ-*fpt-time DTM* could have been equivalently defined with κ-*added polynomial* in place of κ-*scaled polynomial*.   ◇

Exercise 4.6.13: Closure properties of FPT parameterized languages. Prove the following results.

- Suppose that (B, κ) is an FPT parameterized language. Then, $(\overline{B}, \kappa)$ is an FPT parameterized language.
- Suppose that (B, κ) and (C, κ) are FPT parameterized languages having the same parameterization. Then, $(B \cap C, \kappa)$ and $(B \cup C, \kappa)$ are FPT parameterized languages.   ◇

Exercise 4.6.14: Parameterizations incorporating the maximum degree. Define λ to be the parameterization where, for each pair (G, k) consisting of a graph G and a number $k \in \mathbb{N}$, it holds that $\lambda(G, k)$ is equal to the pair $(k, \Delta(G))$, where $\Delta(G)$ is the maximum degree over all vertices of G.

1. Prove that the parameterized language (DOM-SET, λ) is FPT.
2. Prove that the parameterized language (INDEP-SET, λ) is FPT.   ◇

Exercise 4.6.15: Length-decreasing self-reductions. Suppose that B is a language, and that there exist a constant value $K \geq 0$ and a polynomial-time many-one reduction $\rho \colon \Sigma^* \to \Sigma^*$ from B to B where, for each string x with $|x| \geq K$, it holds that $|\rho(x)| < |x|$. So, the function ρ is a self-reduction of B, which decreases the length of each string that is sufficiently large. Prove that the language B is PTIME.   ◇

Exercise 4.6.16. Prove that there exists a polynomial-time many-one reduction ρ from the language 1-in-3-SAT to itself having the following property: for any instance T, when n denotes the number of variables appearing in T, it holds that $\rho(T)$ is an instance where the number of 3-tuples is $n + 1$ or less. This language was defined in Exercise 3.10.41. Hint: $a + b + c = 1$.   ◇

Exercise 4.6.17: Explicit parameters. Let (B, κ) be an arbitrary parameterized language, and define B^+ to be the language $\{(x, \kappa(x)) \mid x \in B\}$. Prove that the parameterized languages (B, κ) and (B^+, π_2) fpt-many-one reduce to each other.   ◇

Exercise 4.6.18. This exercise considers two restricted versions of conjunctive query evaluation (which was presented in Remark 4.4.30). For each $n \geq 2$, define ϕ_n to be the conjunctive query $\exists v_1 \ldots \exists v_n (\bigwedge F(v_i, v_j))$, where the conjunction is over all pairs of numbers $(i, j) \in [n] \times [n]$ with $i \neq j$. Here, we deal only with relational structures that interpret the single binary relation symbol F.

1. Let L_{999} denote the language containing each pair $(\phi_n, \mathbf{B})$ where $2 \leq n \leq 999$ holds and $\mathbf{B}$ is a relational structure on which ϕ_n is true. Prove either that this language is PTIME or that it is NP-complete.

2. Let R_{999} denote the language containing each pair $(\phi_n, \mathbf{B})$ where $n \geq 2$ holds, $\mathbf{B}$ is a relational structure on which ϕ_n is true, and the universe B of $\mathbf{B}$ has $|B| \leq 999$. Prove either that this language is PTIME or that it is NP-complete.   ◇

Exercise 4.6.19: Closure of $\mathcal{P}/\text{poly}$ under reductions. Prove that if B and C are languages such that $C \in \mathcal{P}/\text{poly}$ and the relationship $B \leq_m^p C$ holds, then $B \in \mathcal{P}/\text{poly}$. This establishes that the class $\mathcal{P}/\text{poly}$ is closed under polynomial-time many-one reductions.   ◇

Exercise 4.6.20: On being chopped-NP. Define a parameterized language (B, κ) to be **chopped-NP** if there exists a κ-poly-compilable function $g \colon \Sigma^* \to \Sigma^*$ such that the following hold: (1) there exists an NP language B' where (for each $x \in \Sigma^*$) it holds that $x \in B \Leftrightarrow g(x) \in B'$, and (2) there exists a polynomial $p \colon \mathbb{N} \to \mathbb{N}$ where (for each $x \in \Sigma^*$) it holds that $|g(x)| \leq p(|\kappa(x)|)$. Assuming that (B, κ) is a parameterized language and that κ is polynomial-time computable, prove that the following are equivalent:

1. The parameterized language (B, κ) is chopped-NP.

2. For every NP-complete language C, it holds that (B, κ) poly-comp reduces to (C, len).

3. There exists an NP-complete language C such that (B, κ) poly-comp reduces to (C, len).

4. There exists an NP language B' such that (B, κ) poly-comp reduces to (B', len).   ◇

Exercise 4.6.21: Unary existential positive queries. This exercise studies the complexity of evaluating a particular type of first-order sentence, and presupposes a basic familiarity with first-order logic. Define an **existential positive query** as a relational first-order sentence built from atomic formulas, conjunction, disjunction, and existential quantification. Say that an existential positive query is **unary** if each relation symbol appearing in it has arity 1, so that each atomic formula has the form $U(v)$, where U is a relation symbol and v

is a single variable. Define UNARY-EPQ-EVAL as the language containing each pair $(\phi, \mathbf{D})$ where ϕ is an unary existential positive query, $\mathbf{D}$ is a structure interpreting each relation symbol appearing in ϕ, and $\mathbf{D} \models \phi$.

1. Prove that the language UNARY-EPQ-EVAL is NP-complete.
2. Prove that the parameterized language (UNARY-EPQ-EVAL, π_1) is FPT.
3. Prove that the parameterized language (UNARY-EPQ-EVAL, π_1) is not poly-comp-PTIME, unless $\mathbb{NP} \subseteq \mathbb{P}/\text{poly}$. ◇

Note 4.6.22: On defining parameterized languages. The literature contains several variations on the definition of *parameterized language*; let us discuss them and the rationale behind our choice of definition.

One variation is to require each parameter to be a natural number. While this is not, by any means, a strong restriction (strings can be encoded as natural numbers, and vice versa), there are scenarios where this variation is arguably awkward to work with: in the setting of database query evaluation, for example, it is natural to take each instance's parameter to be the instance's query, which by default would customarily be presented as a string. In this setting, one can alternatively take each instance's parameter to be the *length* of the instance's query; this change of parameterization does not affect the property of being fixed-parameter tractable, but it does affect the presentation of reductions, as well as the discussion and analysis of *compilability* (as presented in Section 4.5).

Another variation requires that each parameterization be polynomial-time computable, or more strongly, that each instance contains its parameter explicitly. The author elected a formulation of parameterized language where the language and parameterization are separate, for a couple of reasons. First, the author believes that this facilitates the discussion of different parameterizations of the same language; after identifying a language of interest, one can orthogonally deal with and compare different parameterizations. Second, the author's view is that this formulation allows for smooth discussions of whether various functions should be considered parameterizations or not, independently of applying them to languages. As mentioned, the computational requirement we impose on parameterizations is formulated so as to allow, as parameterizations, certain graph measures not known to be polynomial-time computable, such as the vertex cover number and treewidth. At the same time, this requirement's generality is not overly liberal in that it allows for key characterizations of FPT to hold (as shown in Section 4.3.3).

The discussed variations, in any case, can be obtained as special cases of our definition. The author indeed preferred here to provide a general treatment, which can be specialized according to need. We mention that, in the given formulation, each parameterized language is equivalent—up to reductions preserving fixed-parameter tractability—to a parameterized language where each instance contains its parameter explicitly (refer to Exercise 4.6.17). ◇

4.6.2 Logarithmic space computation

By restricting the amount of space that a Turing machine can use to be *logarithmic* in the input string length, we obtain subsets of the class $\mathcal{P}$ and, indeed, a complexity theory within the class $\mathcal{P}$. Restricting the amount of allowed space below the input string length, however, is something of a delicate affair: the entire input string should be readable by a computation, but the amount of working space should be limited. In order to effect these criteria, we employ 2-tape Turing machines, presented in Section 2.7.1, as follows: the first tape, which contains the input string, can only be read from, and the second tape can both be written to and read from, but under the space restriction.

Precisely, we define a **logspace DTM** to be a halting 2-tape DTM where, on an input string of length n, no transition may change any symbol on the first tape, so that the first tape is in effect read-only; the first tape's head location never exceeds $n + 1$, so that the blank symbol following the input can be detected, but the machine cannot wander further on the first tape; and there exists a linear polynomial P such that the second tape's head location never exceeds $P(\log n)$. We define a **logspace NTM** as a halting 2-tape NTM satisfying the same requirements. (We remark that a logspace DTM or a logspace NTM can keep track of the first tape's head location by maintaining this location on its second tape.) Here, we view the logarithm as an operation on the natural numbers; the exact details do not matter much here due to our application of a linear polynomial, but this can be done concretely by defining, for each $m \in \mathbb{N}$, the value $\log m$ to be the minimum number $k \in \mathbb{N}$ such that $2^k \geq m$.

Define $\mathcal{L}$ as the class containing each language B such that there exists a logspace DTM M where $L(M) = B$; define $\mathcal{NL}$ as the class containing each language B such that there exists a logspace NTM M where $L(M) = B$. A 2-tape DTM can be naturally converted to a 2-tape NTM giving rise to the same computations (along the lines of, but extending, the conversion from a DTM to an NTM; see the justification of Proposition 2.6.11). We thus have the containment $\mathcal{L} \subseteq \mathcal{NL}$.

Note 4.6.23: From nondeterministic logarithmic space to digraph reachability. The notion of nondeterministic logarithmic space computability can be strongly intertwined with the problem of deciding, in a digraph, whether or not one marked vertex admits a walk to a second marked vertex. Let us formulate this problem as follows. Define DI-REACH to be the language containing each triple (G, s, t) such that G is a digraph obeying the following conditions: s and t are vertices of G, and t is *reachable* from s in that there exists a walk in G that starts at s and ends at t.

Whether or not a logspace NTM accepts an input can be formulated as an instance (G, s, t) of DI-REACH. Let M be a logspace NTM and let P be a linear polynomial obeying the requirement in the definition of *logspace NTM*. An input string x of length n can be translated to an instance (G, s, t) described as follows. To describe the vertex set of G, we restrict attention to the configurations of M having a particular form: we consider configurations where only the initial $P(\log n)$ cells of the second tape may hold nonblank symbols, the first head's location is at most $n + 1$, and the second head's location is at most $P(\log n)$. Each configuration reachable from the initial configuration of M on x has the described form, by the definition of *logspace NTM*. The vertex set of G consists of the target vertex t along with all configurations having the described form, but where the first tape's contents are not included—since these contents are never modified. The vertex s is defined as the initial configuration of M on x. The edge set of G contains an edge (γ, γ') between two configurations when $\gamma \vdash_M \gamma'$ holds, that is, when it is possible to transition from γ to γ'; this edge set also contains an edge (γ, t) from each accepting configuration γ to t. The existence of a walk from s to t evidently implies the existence of an accepting computation of M on x, and vice versa; thus, we have $x \in L(M)$ if and only if $(G, s, t) \in$ DI-REACH.

The size of the vertex set is the product of the number of possible locations of the NTM's first head, the number of possible locations of the NTM's second head, and the number of ways the relevant cells of the second tape can be set; this product is $(n + 1) \cdot P(\log n) \cdot |\Gamma|^{P(\log n)}$, where Γ denotes the tape alphabet of M. This number is readily seen to be bounded above by a polynomial in n. Indeed, for a fixed logspace NTM M, the translation from a string x to the described instance (G, s, t) is polynomial-time computable.

The language DI-REACH is PTIME, that is, it is in the class $\mathcal{P}$. One natural polynomial-time algorithm for deciding an instance (G, s, t) is to flag the vertex s, and then iteratively flag every vertex admitting an incoming edge from an already flagged vertex, until no more vertices can be flagged; then the set of flagged vertices are exactly those that are reachable from s in the sense of admitting a walk from s, and so (G, s, t) is in DI-REACH if and only if t is flagged.

Putting together this translation and the containment of DI-REACH in $\mathcal{P}$, we obtain the containment $\mathcal{NL} \subseteq \mathcal{P}$.   ◇

Note 4.6.24: Logarithmic space computation and parallel computation. One motivation for the study of logarithmic space computation is that each language in $\mathcal{NL}$ (and hence also each language in $\mathcal{L}$) can be solved in a small amount of *parallel time*. To qualify this notion, we use the circuit model of computation (as presented in Definition 3.6.13). Viewing the different gates in a circuit as individual computational units that can act concurrently, the value of a gate g can be determined as soon as the values of the gates appearing in the instruction of g have been determined. This view naturally leads to the following notions of *depth*.

- With respect to a circuit, we define the **depth** of each gate inductively. A gate has depth 1 if its instruction contains only inputs and sources; a gate has depth 2 if it does not have depth 1, but each gate in its instruction has depth at most 1, and so on: when $k > 1$, a gate has depth k if it does not have depth $k - 1$, but each gate in its instruction has depth at most $k - 1$.

- We define the **depth** of a circuit as the maximum depth over all of its gates.

In a parallel evaluation of a circuit, each gate at depth 1 can be evaluated in the first time step, followed by each gate at depth 2 in the second time step, and so on: circuit depth is a reasonable proxy for parallel computation time.

Let us briefly argue the claim that each language B in $\mathfrak{NL}$ is computed by a circuit family $(C_n)_{n \in \mathbb{N}}$ where the circuit C_n has depth proportional to $\log n$ (precisely, depth bounded above by $Q(\log n)$, for a linear polynomial Q). As we saw in Note 4.6.23, when we have a language $B \in \mathfrak{NL}$, for each string $x \in \Sigma^*$, we can form a triple (G, s, t) that is in DI-REACH if and only if $x \in B$. The vertex set V of G is common over all strings of the same length and, using the input string, the edge set can be determined by a circuit without incurring more than a constant amount of depth. The crux of the argument is to give a circuit for characterizing reachability in G, which tells, for any pair $u, v \in V$ of vertices, whether or not v is reachable from u in G. Let $A = (A_{uv})$ denote the adjacency matrix of the graph G, having an entry A_{uv} for each pair $u, v \in V$ of vertices, where A_{uv} is equal to 1 if $u = v$ or $\{u, v\}$ is an edge in G, and is equal to 0 otherwise. Assuming that each entry of this matrix is represented by a circuit gate, we can compute the square A^2 of this matrix according to the formula $(A^2)_{uv} = \bigvee_{x \in V}(A_{ux} \wedge A_{xv})$; this formula can be implemented as a circuit (via Proposition 3.6.9) and adds 2 to the depth of the circuit. By performing repeated squaring, the circuit can compute the matrices A^2, A^4, A^8, and so on, until it computes a matrix A^{2^ℓ} for a power 2^ℓ that is at least n. Each power A^m of the matrix A, where $m \geq 1$, has $(A^m)_{uv}$ equal to 1 if and only if there exists a walk from u to v using at most m edges. So, any matrix A^m with $m \geq n$ characterizes reachability in G, and such a matrix can be computed from A in depth proportional to $\log n$, establishing the claim. It can in fact be further verified that the resulting circuit family (C_n) is polynomial-time uniform. $\diamond$

Note 4.6.25: Solving digraph reachability using nondeterministic logarithmic space.

In Note 4.6.23, we saw that the question of whether a logspace NTM accepts an input could be translated to an instance of the language DI-REACH. Rotating the situation around, we can show that the language DI-REACH itself is solvable by a logspace NTM, and is in the class $\mathfrak{NL}$. Putting together these results leads to the suggestion that the language DI-REACH is in some sense *complete* for the class $\mathfrak{NL}$—a suggestion that we will formalize subsequently.

How can we solve DI-REACH with a logspace NTM? Consider an NTM that behaves as follows. Given an instance (G, s, t), where G is a graph with N vertices, the NTM maintains the vertex s on its second tape, and then iteratively performs the following, up to N times: it nondeterministically guesses a vertex v; if the maintained vertex has an edge to v, it replaces the maintained vertex with v, and otherwise, it rejects. If at any point during this process the vertex t becomes the maintained vertex, the NTM accepts; if the process terminates without encountering the vertex t, the NTM rejects. (To store a vertex, the NTM can store an index of the input string x; under our definition of the operation log, such an index can be stored using log |x| many bits. Also, note that a counter storing the number of performed iterations can be stored in log N space.)

Let us argue that this NTM has DI-REACH as its language; consider this NTM's behavior on an input instance (G, s, t). Whenever the maintained vertex is replaced, it is replaced with a vertex having an edge from the previous maintained vertex, so at any point in time, the maintained vertex can be reached from s via a walk. Thus, if the NTM ever accepts, the vertex t is reachable from the vertex s, and so the instance is in DI-REACH. On the other hand, if there exists a walk from s to t in G, then there exists such a walk with N or fewer vertices, and thus there is a sequence of nondeterminisic guesses that the NTM can make under which it traverses such a walk and accepts.

We conclude that DI-REACH $\in \mathcal{NL}$. ◇

Note 4.6.26: Logarithmic space reductions. In order to identify a meaningful sense in which DI-REACH is complete for the class $\mathcal{NL}$, we need to present a notion of reduction that has less power than the machines used to define this class—namely, logspace NTMs. (Otherwise, the reduction itself can in effect decide the language; this phenomenon was previously discussed in Remark 3.4.16.) The reductions that we will use are those computable by logspace DTMs, and indeed the completeness result obtained will imply that the open question of whether or not DI-REACH is in $\mathcal{L}$ is the same as the open question of whether $\mathcal{NL} \subseteq \mathcal{L}$ (equivalently, whether $\mathcal{NL} = \mathcal{L}$).

Our notion of reduction is a type of many-one reduction that is based on logspace DTMs; to define it, we have to specify what it means for a function to be computed by a logspace DTM. It is perhaps not obvious how to do this: a logspace DTM has a limited working space that is in general smaller than the input string, but we would like to use the logspace DTM model to compute functions whose output may be at least the size of the input. For example, it seems reasonable to request that the identity mapping is computable by a logspace DTM.

We proceed as follows. Let Σ be the alphabet $\{0, 1\}$. When $f: \Sigma^* \to \Sigma^*$ is a function, define G_f as the language containing each triple $(x, i, b) \in \Sigma^* \times \mathbb{N}^+ \times \Sigma$ such that the ith symbol of $f(x)$ is defined (that is, $i \leq |f(x)|$ holds) and is equal to b. Observe that the function f and the language G_f hold exactly the same information; the language G_f is an implicit representation of the function f. We define a function $f: \Sigma^* \to \Sigma^*$ to be **logspace computable** if it is polynomial-length (under Definition 4.5.2) and the language G_f is in $\mathcal{L}$. A **logspace many-one reduction** from a language B to a language C is a logspace computable function $\rho: \Sigma^* \to \Sigma^*$ such that, for each $x \in \Sigma^*$, the correctness condition $x \in B \Leftrightarrow \rho(x) \in C$ holds; to indicate that such a reduction exists, we write $B \leq_m^{\log} C$ and say that B **logspace many-one reduces** to C.

Exercise 4.6.28 requests proofs of some primary properties of these notions. ◇

Exercise 4.6.27. There is an alternative way to characterize what it means for a function to be logspace computable, which, relative to the definition in Note 4.6.26, is perhaps closer to our definition of polynomial-time computable function. This alternative characterization posits the existence of a 3-tape DTM that extends the notion of *logspace DTM* in that its third tape is a write-only tape that must contain the function's result upon halting. Define a **logspace transducer** to be a halting 3-tape DTM that uses its first 2 tapes as specified in the definition of *logspace DTM*, and only moves right on its third tape. We say that a logspace transducer M **computes** a function $f\colon \Sigma^* \to \Sigma^*$ when, for each string $x \in \Sigma^*$, the computation of M on x halts with the third tape's contents equal to $f(x)\sqcup\ldots$, that is, this computation results in the string $f(x)$ being written to the third tape.

Prove that a function $f\colon \Sigma^* \to \Sigma^*$ is logspace computable if and only if there exists a logspace transducer that computes it. ◇

Exercise 4.6.28. This exercise studies notions introduced in Note 4.6.26.

1. Prove that the composition of two logspace computable functions $f, g\colon \Sigma^* \to \Sigma^*$ is logspace computable.

2. Prove that any function that is logspace computable is also polynomial-time computable. This implies that, for any languages B and C, when $B \leq_m^{\log} C$ holds, $B \leq_m^p C$ holds as well.

3. Prove that the relation $\leq_m^{\log}$ is reflexive and transitive. That is, prove that for any language B, it holds that $B \leq_m^{\log} B$; and—for any languages A, B, and C—it holds that $A \leq_m^{\log} B$ and $B \leq_m^{\log} C$ imply $A \leq_m^{\log} C$.

4. Prove that the classes $\mathcal{L}$ and $\mathcal{NL}$ are closed under logspace many-one reduction. Here, we say that a class $\mathcal{C}$ is *closed* under logspace many-one reduction when the following holds: if B and C are languages where $B \leq_m^{\log} C$ and $C \in \mathcal{C}$, then $B \in \mathcal{C}$.

We remark that part 2 of this exercise, in conjunction with Theorem 3.4.14, implies that the classes $\mathcal{P}$, $\mathcal{NP}$, and $\mathrm{co}\mathcal{NP}$ are closed under logspace many-one reduction. ◇

Note 4.6.29: Completeness via logspace reductions. By the discussion so far, we have $\mathcal{L} \subseteq \mathcal{NL} \subseteq \mathcal{P}$. At the time of writing, it is not known whether any of the containments $\mathcal{L} \subseteq \mathcal{NL}$, $\mathcal{NL} \subseteq \mathcal{P}$, or $\mathcal{L} \subseteq \mathcal{P}$ are proper.

Using our notion of *logspace many-one reduction*, we can define meaningful notions of completeness for the classes $\mathcal{NL}$ and $\mathcal{P}$. Let us say that a language C is $\mathcal{NL}$-**complete** if, for each language $B \in \mathcal{NL}$, it holds that $B \leq_m^{\log} C$; analogously, a language C is $\mathcal{P}$-**complete** if, for each language $B \in \mathcal{P}$, it holds that $B \leq_m^{\log} C$. By the closure of $\mathcal{NL}$ and of $\mathcal{P}$ under logspace many-one reduction (see Exercise 4.6.28), it can be verified that for any $\mathcal{NL}$-complete language C, it holds that $C \in \mathcal{L}$ if and only if $\mathcal{NL} \subseteq \mathcal{L}$; the analogous property for $\mathcal{P}$, in place of $\mathcal{NL}$, also holds.

Note 4.6.23 explained that, for any logspace NTM M, there is a translation that takes any string x and produces a triple (G, s, t) that is in DI-REACH if and only if $x \in L(M)$.

This translation can be verified to be logspace computable; thus, it constitutes a logspace many-one reduction from $L(M)$ to DI-REACH. Since for any logspace NTM there exists such a reduction, it follows that the language DI-REACH is $\mathfrak{NL}$-complete.

What can we say about $\mathcal{P}$-completeness? We saw, in Theorem 3.6.15, that any language in $\mathcal{P}$ could be characterized by a circuit family having one circuit for each possible string length. Whereas the problem of deciding *satisfiability* of a circuit was shown to be complete for the class $\mathfrak{NP}$, the problem of determining the *value* output by a circuit is complete for the class $\mathcal{P}$. This can be formalized as follows. Define CIRCUIT-VALUE as the language containing each circuit having no inputs whose output gate evaluates to 1 (under Definition 3.6.3); for a circuit having no inputs, the only sources are $\underline{0}$ and $\underline{1}$. This language is $\mathcal{P}$-complete; let us explain why. Theorem 3.6.15 shows that each language $B \in \mathcal{P}$ is computed by a circuit family $(C_n)_{n \in \mathbb{N}}$ that is polynomial-time uniform in that there exists a polynomial-time computable function f having the following property: for each $n \in \mathbb{N}$, it holds that $f(1^n) = \ulcorner C_n \urcorner$. It can be verified that this function f is actually logspace computable. Consequently, for each polynomial-time DTM M, there exists a logspace many-one reduction from $L(M)$ to CIRCUIT-VALUE: given a string x of length n, the reduction returns the modification of the circuit C_n where its inputs $v_1, \ldots, v_n$ have been *instantiated* with the symbols of the string x (under Definition 3.6.8); the modified circuit has no inputs, and its output gate evidently evaluates to 1 if and only if $x \in L(M)$. ◇

Note 4.6.30: The Immerman-Szelepcsényi theorem. Neil Immerman and Róbert Szelepcsényi independently showed, in the late 1980s, that $\mathfrak{NL}$ is closed under complementation—a result that was highly surprising at the time! They showed not just the closure under complementation of $\mathfrak{NL}$, but also that of further complexity classes defined using space-bounded NTMs.

Let us briefly illustrate the proof technique used to achieve this result, known as *inductive counting*, by arguing the closure under complementation of $\mathfrak{NL}$. It suffices to show that the complement of the language DI-REACH is in $\mathfrak{NL}$; to do so, we present a logspace NTM for the problem of deciding, given a triple (G, s, t) where $G = (V, E)$ is a digraph and $s, t \in V$, whether t is *not* reachable from s. So, the logspace NTM that we present accepts such a triple if and only if t is *not* reachable from s.

For each $\ell \geq 1$, let V_ℓ denote the set of vertices that are reachable from s via a walk having length ℓ or less; here, we measure the length of a walk according to its length as a sequence, that is, the number of vertices it contains. The NTM computes, for increasing values of $\ell \geq 1$, the size $|V_\ell|$ of the set V_ℓ, denoted by r_ℓ. The values $r_1, r_2, \ldots$ are computed inductively: r_2 is computed from r_1, r_3 is computed from r_2, and so forth. Clearly, $V_1 = \{s\}$ and $r_1 = 1$.

Assuming that r_k has been determined, where $k \geq 1$, the NTM determines r_{k+1} in the following way. It first sets a counter variable r to 0. Then, for each vertex $v \in V$ of the graph, it performs the following procedure, which can be carried out by a logspace NTM:

1.   Assign a counter variable p to 0, and assign a flag variable g to 0.
2.   Loop over each vertex x of the graph and nondeterministically guess a walk from s to x having k or fewer vertices; if such a walk is found, increment p by 1, check if v is equal to x or has an incoming edge from x, and set the flag variable g to 1 if this check passes.
3.   If the counter variable p is not equal to r_k, reject.
4.   If the flag variable g is set to 1, increment r by 1.

Let us consider computations that carry out this procedure for each vertex $v \in V$. We argue that, for any such computation that survives without rejecting, the value r_{k+1} is correctly computed in the variable r, and also that there exists at least one such computation that survives without rejecting. First, we observe that there exists a computation that does not reject. Namely, consider a computation that, in each invocation of the procedure, finds a walk from s to x of the described type, whenever one exists; such a computation will have p equal to r_k after step 2 is completed, and so will not reject in step 3. We thus need to argue that, under the assumption that a computation completes the procedure for each vertex v without rejecting, the value r_{k+1} is correctly computed; let us put this assumption into effect. Each time the procedure was executed, for each vertex x that is reachable from s via a walk of length k or less, a walk from s to x was successfully found in step 2; otherwise, rejection would have occurred in step 3. Since V_{k+1} is the set of vertices that are either in V_k or admit an incoming edge from a vertex in V_k, after an execution of the procedure, the flag variable g is set to 1 if and only if the vertex v is in V_{k+1}. Thus, the value r_{k+1} is computed correctly in the variable r.

Let n denote $|V|$, the number of vertices in the graph. Each vertex that is reachable from s is reachable via a walk that does not repeat vertices, and hence via a walk of length n or less. Assuming that $n > 1$, in the determination of r_n from r_{n-1}, a variable $v \in V$ is not reachable from s if and only if, when the procedure is invoked, the flag variable is set to 0 after the procedure finishes. Thus, once the value r_{n-1} has been computed, the question of whether t is not reachable from s is answered properly by invoking the given procedure on the vertex t, and accepting if and only if the flag variable is set to 0 after the procedure finishes. ◇

Note 4.6.31: Graph reachability and logarithmic space. Via a proof that is well beyond our present scope, Omer Reingold proved in the 2000s that the *undirected* reachability problem is in $\mathcal{L}$. By this, we mean the problem deciding whether a *graph G*, with marked vertices s and t, contains a walk from s to t. ◇

Note 4.6.32. The theory of space complexity, at least as seen here, is something of a theory of graph reachability problems! This suggestion is reinforced in the next exercise. ◇

Exercise 4.6.33: Succinct digraph reachability. Prove that the following *succinct* version of the reachability problem in digraphs is PSPACE-complete. An instance consists of a triple (C, s, t) where s and t are strings over $\{0, 1\}$ of the same length n, and C is a circuit having $2n$ inputs. The question is whether there exists a walk from s to t in the digraph with vertex set $\{0, 1\}^n$ and whose edge set contains a pair $(u, v) \in \{0, 1\}^n \times \{0, 1\}^n$ if and only if the string uv satisfies C. ◇

4.6.3 Treewidth

Treewidth is a graph measure that—as is often said—indicates how *tree-like* a graph is, that is, how similar a graph is to a tree. The *treewidth* of a nonempty graph is a natural number; the lower the treewidth of a graph, the more tree-like it is considered to be. When a graph G has treewidth k, it by definition has a data structure called a *tree decomposition* which shows how to decompose it into sections called *bags*, each having at most $k + 1$ vertices of G, that together exhibit a tree structure. While treewidth is typically framed and presented as a measure on graphs, it is quite readily applicable to other objects, such as hypergraphs, relational structures, and certain logical formulas.

The measure of treewidth has been of great import in computer science. For many hard problems where the input consists of a graph, or another object on which treewidth is defined, polynomial-time tractability can be established when the problem is restricted to input objects having treewidth below a fixed bound; indeed, fixed-parameter tractability can often be proved on such hard problems when treewidth is used as the parameterization. Typically, algorithms evidencing these tractability results perform dynamic programming over tree decompositions.

In our discussion of treewidth, we depict vertices of graphs using solid dots.

Note 4.6.34: Definition of treewidth. We here formally define the notions of *tree decomposition* and *treewidth*; see Figure 4.6.1 for a first illustration.

Define a **path**, in a graph, as a walk where no vertex appears more than once. Define a **cycle**, in a graph, as a walk $v_1, \ldots, v_m$ that is closed in that $v_1 = v_m$, and where $v_1, \ldots, v_{m-1}$ is a path with $m - 1 \geq 3$; this inequality implies that a cycle must contain 3 or more distinct vertices, and thus prohibits a single edge from being considered a cycle. A graph is **acyclic** if it does not contain any cycles. A graph G is **connected** if for any two vertices $u, v \in V(G)$, there exists a walk from u to v in G. Relative to a graph G, a subset $S \subseteq V(G)$ is **connected** if for any two vertices $u, v \in S$, there exists a walk, consisting of vertices from S, from u to v in G. A **tree** is a graph that is acyclic and connected; we will freely use the fact that a graph G is a tree if and only if for any two vertices u, v of G, there exists a unique path from u to v (that is, beginning at u and ending at v). In what follows, when H is a graph, we use $V(H)$ and $E(H)$ to denote the vertex set and edge set of H, respectively.

A **tree decomposition** of a graph G is a pair $(T, (B_t)_{t \in V(T)})$ providing a tree T and a subset B_t of $V(G)$ for each vertex t of T, such that the following three properties hold.

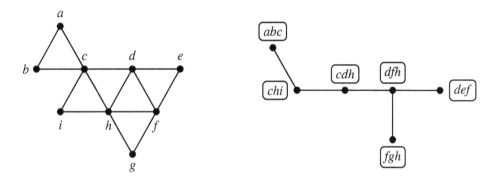

Figure 4.6.1. An example of a graph (on the left) and a tree decomposition of the graph (on the right). The graph on the left is not a tree: it contains a number of cycles, such as a, b, c, a. The tree decomposition consists of a tree where each vertex t has an associated bag B_t, which is a subset of the vertex set of the left graph. Here, the vertices of the tree are not labeled, but each vertex has its bag presented next to it. This tree decomposition only has bags of size 3, and so has width 2.

- **Vertex coverage:** For each vertex $v \in V(G)$, there exists $t \in V(T)$ such that $v \in B_t$.
- **Edge coverage:** For each edge $e \in E(G)$, there exists $t \in V(T)$ such that $e \subseteq B_t$.
- **Coherence:** For any two vertices $t, t' \in V(T)$, if a vertex $v \in V(G)$ is in both B_t and $B_{t'}$, then for any vertex t^- on the path (in T) from t to t', the vertex v is in B_{t^-}.

When $(T, (B_t)_{t \in V(T)})$ is a tree decomposition of a graph G, each subset B_t is referred to as a **bag**. The first two properties require that each vertex of G and each edge of G is contained in a bag. The coherence property is equivalent to requiring that, for each vertex $v \in V(G)$, the set of vertices $S_v = \{t \in V(T) \mid v \in B_t\}$ is connected with respect to T. (We can remark that this property of *coherence* is sometimes referred to as *connectivity*.)

The **width** of a tree decomposition $(T, (B_t)_{t \in V(T)})$ is defined as $(\max_{t \in V(T)} |B_t|) - 1$, that is, as its maximum bag size minus one.[45] The **treewidth** of a graph G is the minimum value w such that there exists a width w tree decomposition of G. Thus, exhibiting a width k tree decomposition of a graph demonstrates that the graph has treewidth k or less.

See Figures 4.6.1, 4.6.2, and 4.6.3 for examples of tree decompositions. ◇

Note 4.6.35. The most straightforward and coarsest way to present a tree decomposition of a graph G is to take a tree T with one vertex t, and define that vertex's bag B_t as $V(G)$, the entire vertex set of G; it is straightforwardly verified that this object satisfies the defining properties of a tree decomposition. This observation shows that any graph with n vertices has treewidth $n - 1$ or less. This upper bound is attainable: for each $n \geq 1$, an n-clique (that

---

45. The *minus one* in this definition is included so that each tree (with an edge) has treewidth 1.

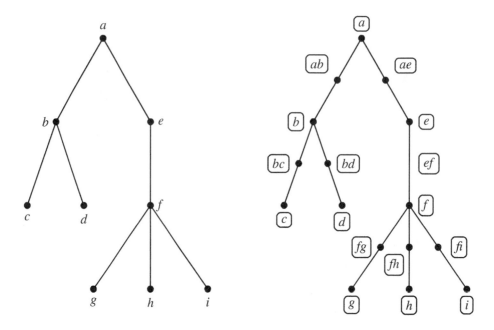

Figure 4.6.2. An example tree (on the left) and a tree decomposition of this tree (on the right). Here, the tree decomposition has been obtained from the left tree by subdividing each edge into two edges; then, the bag of each original vertex v is defined simply as $\{v\}$, and the bag of each vertex arising from subdividing an edge $\{u,v\}$ is defined as the edge itself. This method can be applied to any tree to obtain a tree decomposition; so long as the original tree contains an edge, the resulting tree decomposition has maximum bag size 2, and hence has width 1. Each tree containing an edge e thus has treewidth 1: any tree decomposition thereof must have a bag of size 2 or greater, since the edge e must be contained in a bag.

is, a graph on n vertices with all possible edges) has treewidth $n-1$; this fact follows from the just-given observation along with Exercise 4.6.36.   ◇

Exercise 4.6.36: Cliques and treewidth. Prove that when $G = (V, E)$ is a graph and a set $U \subseteq V$ is a clique in G, any tree decomposition of G must have a bag containing U as a subset. This fact implies that any graph with a clique of size $k \geq 1$ must have treewidth $k-1$ or greater.   ◇

Exercise 4.6.37. Suppose that $(T, (B_t)_{t \in V(T)})$ is a tree decomposition of a graph G, that u is a vertex of T occurring in just one edge $\{u, t\}$ of T, and that $B_u \subseteq B_t$. Let T' be the tree obtained from T by removing the vertex u and the edge $\{u, t\}$. Prove that $(T', (B_t)_{t \in V(T')})$ is a tree decomposition of G.   ◇

Exercise 4.6.38: From treewidth to coloring. Prove that, for each $k \geq 0$, any graph having treewidth k is $(k+1)$-colorable.   ◇

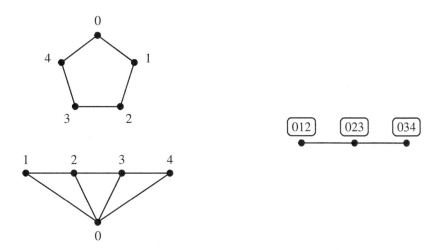

Figure 4.6.3. Each of the two graphs on the left has the object on the right as a width 2 tree decomposition. On the left, the bottom graph can be viewed as the top graph with two edges, $\{0, 2\}$ and $\{0, 3\}$, added; the top graph is a 5-*cycle*. (The notion of *k*-*cycle* was defined in Exercise 3.10.59.) Each *k*-cycle can be shown to have a tree decomposition of width 2, by generalizing the tree decomposition given here; in fact, it is known that the treewidth of each *k*-cycle is 2.

Exercise 4.6.39: Minors and treewidth. A graph $H = (V(H), E(H))$ is a **minor** of a graph $G = (V(G), E(G))$ if there exists a **minor map** from H to G, which is defined as a map $\mu\colon V(H) \to \wp(V(G))$ where

- for each $v \in V(H)$, it holds that $\mu(v)$ is a nonempty, connected subset of $V(G)$;
- the sets $\mu(v)$ are pairwise disjoint; and
- for each edge $\{x, y\} \in E(H)$, there exist $x' \in \mu(x), y' \in \mu(y)$ such that $\{x', y'\} \in E(G)$.

Let us remark that a *minor* of a graph G can alternatively be characterized as a graph that is obtainable from G by renaming the vertices and by performing the following operations any number of times: contracting an edge, deleting an edge, and deleting a vertex.

Prove that whenever G and H are graphs where H is a minor of G, the treewidth of H is less than or equal to the treewidth of G. ◇

Exercise 4.6.40: Cycles and treewidth. Prove that each graph containing a cycle has treewidth 2 or greater. This implies that each graph with treewidth 1 is acyclic. ◇

Note 4.6.41: Characterizing treewidth via elimination orderings. An **elimination ordering** of a graph G consists of an ordering $v_1, \ldots, v_n$ of the vertex set $V(G)$, and a set F whose elements are size 2 subsets of $V(G)$ with $F \supseteq E(G)$, having the property that (for all indices $i, j, k \in \{1, \ldots, n\}$) when $i \neq j$, $i < k$, $j < k$, $\{v_i, v_k\} \in F$, and $\{v_j, v_k\} \in F$, it holds that $\{v_i, v_j\} \in F$. Relative to an elimination ordering, let us say that a vertex v_j is a **lower neighbor** of a vertex v_k when $j < k$ and $\{v_j, v_k\} \in F$; then, the given property, which we shall call the **lower neighbor property**, states that any two distinct lower neighbors of any vertex v_k form an edge. Define the **width** of an elimination ordering to be the maximum number of lower neighbors, over each vertex; that is, as $\max_k \left| \{ j \mid j < k, \{v_j, v_k\} \in F \} \right|$, where the maximum is taken over all indices $k \in \{1, ..., n\}$.

Elimination orderings yield another characterization of treewidth: the treewidth of a graph is the minimum width over all elimination orderings of the graph. This fact follows from the next exercise, Exercise 4.6.42.

Given a graph G and an ordering $v_1, ..., v_n$ of its vertex set $V(G)$, there is a canonical, minimal, and natural way to find a set F of pairs which, when paired with the ordering, yields an elimination ordering: start with F equal to $E(G)$, and so long as the lower neighbor property is violated by F, take two lower neighbors of a vertex that are not joined by an edge, and add the pair containing them to F.   ◇

Exercise 4.6.42: Between tree decompositions and elimination orderings. Prove that (for any value w) a graph G has a tree decomposition of width w if and only if it has an elimination ordering of width w. Hints: to pass from an elimination ordering to a tree decomposition, one can form a bag for each vertex, which contains the vertex along with its lower neighbors; to pass from a tree decomposition $(T, (B_t)_{t \in V(T)})$ to an elimination ordering, try using induction on $|V(G)|$.   ◇

Note 4.6.43. Exercise 4.6.42 implies that the treewidth of a graph can be determined by computing, for every ordering of the graph's vertex set, the minimal set F that yields an elimination ordering when paired with the ordering (as described in Note 4.6.41), and taking the minimum width over all such resulting elimination orderings. Proving the forward direction of this exercise by creating one bag for each vertex also implies that, for any graph G with n vertices, there is a tree decomposition with n bags whose width is the treewidth of G. So, for many intents and purposes—such as that of determining the treewidth of a graph—one never has to consider tree decompositions where the number of bags (precisely, the number of vertices in the tree) exceeds the number of vertices in the graph being decomposed. (We next see, however, a form of tree decomposition called a *nice tree decomposition*; converting a tree decomposition to this form does incur an increase in the number of bags, in general.)   ◇

Note 4.6.44: Nice tree decompositions. The presentation of algorithms that operate on tree decompositions is often facilitated when each tree decomposition can be assumed to be in a particular format, known as a *nice tree decomposition*, and which we here present.

A **rooted tree** is a tree with a distinguished vertex called its **root**. A rooted tree has natural parent and child relations on its vertices, as well as natural ancestor and descendant

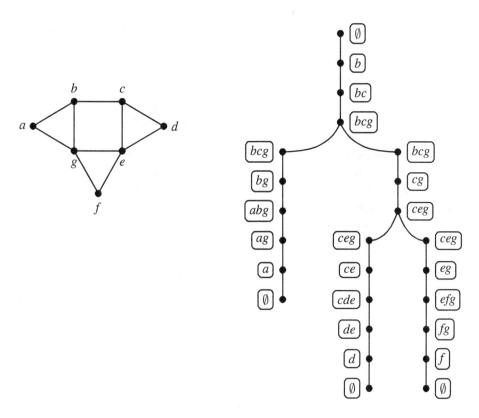

Figure 4.6.4. An example graph (on the left) and a nice tree decomposition of this graph (on the right). Following convention, the root of the tree is given at the top, as the highest vertex. Each edge in the right tree indicates a parent-child relationship: in looking at the two vertices in an edge, the higher vertex is the parent of the lower vertex, and the lower vertex is a child of the higher vertex.

relations; here, we consider a vertex of a rooted tree to be both an ancestor and a descendant of itself.

A **nice tree decomposition** $(T, (B_t)_{t \in V(T)})$ of a graph G is a tree decomposition where T is a rooted tree whose root r has $B_r = \emptyset$, and where each vertex of T is of one of the following four types:

- A **leaf vertex** t has no children and has $B_t = \emptyset$.
- An **introduce vertex** t has one child t' such that there exists a vertex $v \in V(G) \setminus B_{t'}$ where $B_t = B_{t'} \cup \{v\}$; the vertex v is referred to as being **introduced** by t.
- A **forget vertex** t has one child t' such that there exists a vertex $v \in B_{t'}$ where $B_t = B_{t'} \setminus \{v\}$; the vertex v is referred to as being **forgotten** by t.
- A **join vertex** t has two children t_1, t_2 such that $B_t = B_{t_1} = B_{t_2}$.

When a vertex t has one child t', the vertex t is either an introduce vertex or a forget vertex; in this case, the bags B_t, $B_{t'}$ differ by a single vertex, and the bag B_t introduces or forgets a vertex relative to $B_{t'}$, respectively.

An example of a nice tree decomposition is given in Figure 4.6.4.   ◇

Exercise 4.6.45. Argue that there exists a polynomial-time algorithm that, given a tree decomposition of a graph, outputs a nice tree decomposition of the graph.   ◇

Note 4.6.46: Bodlaender's theorem. Let tw denote the function which sends each graph to its treewidth; so, for each graph G, it holds that $\mathrm{tw}(G)$ is the treewidth of G. *Bodlaender's theorem*, published by Bodlaender in 1996, shows that there is a tw-fpt-time DTM that, when given any graph G as input, computes a tree decomposition of G having width $\mathrm{tw}(G)$. This result, whose proof is out of our scope, immediately implies that the function tw is a parameterization. Moreover, this result implies that when one attempts to establish fixed-parameter tractability by presenting a tw-fpt-time DTM for a language of graphs (or other objects to which the function tw can be applied), it can be assumed that each instance G is accompanied by a tree decomposition of G having width $\mathrm{tw}(G)$. In fact, it can be further assumed that this tree decomposition is nice, by Exercise 4.6.45.   ◇

Note 4.6.47: A game view of treewidth. There is an entertaining characterization of treewidth in terms of a so-called pursuit-evasion game, which we refer to as the k-**cops-and-robbers game** (or, as the k-**CR-game**, for short) and which is played by $k \geq 1$ cops and a robber, on a graph. In this game, the cops attempt to capture the robber, and the robber attempts to evade capture. The k cops can each travel in a helicopter, and begin the game by each landing on a vertex; the robber then must place themself on a vertex not occupied by a cop. From this starting position, some of the cops can then fly off in helicopters; they then land on vertices, but before doing so, the robber sees where the cops who flew off are about to land, and can quickly run to another vertex to avoid capture—so long as it runs along a path not containing any cop on the ground. Assuming that the robber eluded capture, some of the cops can again fly off in helicopters, and the robber can then run again; the cops and the robber alternate making moves in this fashion. The cops win if after some finite number of rounds, they capture the robber; the robber wins if they can indefinitely avoid capture. It is known that the treewidth plus one is equal to the minimum number of cops needed to capture the robber in this game; Exercise 4.6.48 requests a proof of one of the two inequalities needed to establish this equality.

We formalize the notion of a winning strategy for the robber as follows. Let G be a graph. In the k-CR-game on G, define a **position** to be a pair (C, x) where $C \subseteq V(G)$ is a set of vertices with $|C| \leq k$, indicating where the cops are stationed, and x is a vertex in $V(G) \setminus C$, indicating the location of the robber; define a **robber winning strategy** for this game to be a nonempty set $\mathcal{P}$ of positions where for each position $(C, x) \in \mathcal{P}$ and each subset $C' \subseteq V(G)$ with $|C'| \leq k$, there exists a vertex $x' \in V$ such that $(C', x') \in \mathcal{P}$ and there exists a path from x to x' in the graph $G \setminus (C \cap C')$. (Here, when $W \subseteq V(G)$ is a set of vertices, we use $G \setminus W$ to denote the graph with vertex set $V(G) \setminus W$ and whose edge set contains each edge in $E(G)$ not having a vertex in W.) ◇

Exercise 4.6.48. Let G be a graph, and let $k \geq 1$. Prove that if there exists a tree decomposition of G where each bag has size k or less (equivalently, if the treewidth of G is strictly less than k), then there does not exist a robber winning strategy for the k-CR-game. We note that the converse of this statement holds.

Hint: one way to proceed is as follows. Assume for a contradiction that there does exist a robber winning strategy $\mathcal{P}$. Let $(T, (B_t)_{t \in V(T)})$ be a tree decomposition of the described form. Arbitrarily select a root $r \in V(T)$ for the tree T, and have the cops start on the vertices B_r; let x_0 be a vertex such that $(B_r, x_0) \in \mathcal{P}$. In each position that we will consider, the cops will be located on the vertices B_t of a bag, and the robber will be locatable in a bag B_u where u is a descendant of t. From such a position $(B_t, x) \in \mathcal{P}$, let u be a descendant of t with $x \in B_u$, let t' be the child of t on the path from u to t, and let the cops move to the bag $B_{t'}$. Continue doing this until the cops have moved to the bag of a leaf of T, at which point the robber will be cornered and captured! ◇

Exercise 4.6.49: Brambles. The existence of a robber winning strategy in the k-CR-game can be conveniently characterized using the notion of a *bramble* of a graph. A **bramble** of a graph G is a set $F \subseteq \wp(V)$ where for each $f, f' \in F$, it holds that $f \cup f'$ is a connected subset of $V(G)$. In particular, each element f of a bramble (of a graph G) must itself be a connected subset of $V(G)$. The **order** of a bramble F of a graph G is the minimum value $m \geq 0$ such that there exists a size m hitting set of the hypergraph $(V(G), F)$.

Let G be a graph, and let $k \geq 1$. Prove that if there exists a bramble of G having order strictly greater than k, then there exists a robber winning strategy for the k-CR-game on G. We note that the converse of this statement holds, and so the maximum order of a bramble is equal to the minimum number of cops needed to defeat the robber. Hint: one way to obtain the desired robber winning strategy from a bramble F having the described order is to include, for each subset $C \subseteq V(G)$ with $|C| \leq k$, a position (C, x) where x is an element of a subset f in F having $C \cap f = \emptyset$. ◇

Note 4.6.50. Combining the results of Exercises 4.6.48 and 4.6.49, we obtain that the treewidth of a graph can be lower bounded by exhibiting a bramble of the graph. Concretely, let G be a graph and let $k \geq 1$; these results immediately imply that, when there exists a bramble of G having order strictly greater than k, the treewidth of G is k or more. ◇

Exercise 4.6.51: The treewidth of grid graphs. For each $k \geq 1$, the k-by-k **grid graph**, denoted by D_k, is defined as the graph with vertex set $\{1, ..., k\} \times \{1, ..., k\}$, and where two vertices $(i,j), (i',j')$ form an edge if and only if $|i-i'|+|j-j'| = 1$. Prove that, for each value $k \geq 2$, the treewidth of the grid graph D_k is k.

Hint: to prove that the treewidth of D_k is greater than or equal to k, use the fact identified in Note 4.6.50; one can consider the bramble consisting of the last column, the last row minus the last column, and all crosses in the subgrid obtained by deleting the last column and the last row.   ◇

Note 4.6.52: The constraint satisfaction problem. The **constraint satisfaction problem** (for short, **CSP**) is a general umbrella problem in which one seeks to decide if there exists an assignment, defined on a set of variables, that satisfies each constraint in a given collection.

Define a *constraint network* as a triple $(V, D, \mathcal{C})$ where V is a finite set of variables, D is a set called the **domain**, and $\mathcal{C}$ is a finite set of constraints, where each constraint is a pair $((v_1, ..., v_k), P)$ consisting of an arity $k \geq 0$ tuple of variables $(v_1, ..., v_k) \in V^k$ and a relation $P \subseteq D^k$ over the domain with matching arity; we will refer to k as the **arity** of the constraint. (Here, we will always assume that the domain D is a finite set, although there are many scenarios where it is natural to consider infinite domains.) Relative to a constraint network $(V, D, \mathcal{C})$, an **assignment** is a function $f \colon V \to D$ which assigns, to each variable, an element of the domain; it is said to **satisfy** a constraint $((v_1, ..., v_k), P)$ when $(f(v_1), ..., f(v_k)) \in P$, and is a **satisfying assignment** of a constraint network $(V, D, \mathcal{C})$ when it satisfies each constraint $C \in \mathcal{C}$. A constraint network that has a satisfying assignment is said to be **satisfiable**. We define the CSP as the problem where an instance consists of a constraint network, and the question is to decide whether or not the instance is satisfiable. We use CSP to denote the language containing each satisfiable constraint network.

Many problems from all throughout computer science can be viewed as cases of the CSP. Let us give some examples. When S is a set, let us use $=_S$ to denote the equality relation $\{(s, s) \mid s \in S\}$, and $\neq_S$ to denote the *not equals* relation $\{(s, s') \in S \times S \mid s \neq s'\}$.

- Let $G = (V, E)$ be a graph forming an instance of the k-colorability problem (that is, of the language k-COL). It can be viewed as an instance $(V, D, \mathcal{C})$ of the CSP, where the set of variables is the vertex set of the graph G; the domain D is the set $\{1, ..., k\}$ of colors; and the set $\mathcal{C}$ contains, for each edge $\{v, v'\} \in E$, a constraint $((v, v'), \neq_D)$ stating that v and v' are mapped to different colors. It can be verified that a mapping from V to D satisfies this CSP instance if and only if it is a k-coloring of the graph G.

- Let $G = (V, E)$ be a graph with n vertices that is an instance of the *Hamiltonian cycle problem* (that is, of the language HAM-CYCLE). It can be viewed as an instance $(W, V, \mathcal{C})$ of the CSP, where the set W of variables is $\{w_1, ..., w_{n+1}\}$, representing the sought cycle, and the domain is the vertex set of the graph. The set $\mathcal{C}$ contains, for each pair of consecutive variables, a constraint stating that they are sent to adjacent vertices, that is, a constraint $((w_i, w_{i+1}), \{(v, v') \mid \{v, v'\} \in E\})$ for each $i \in \{1, ..., n\}$; a constraint $((w_1, w_{n+1}), =_V)$ stating that w_1 and w_{n+1} are mapped to the same vertex; and a constraint $((w_i, w_j), \neq_V)$ for each pair $i, j \in \{1, ..., n\}$ of distinct indices stating that w_i and w_j are mapped to different vertices. It can be verified that a mapping $f \colon W \to V$ satisfies this CSP instance if and only if $f(w_1), ..., f(w_{n+1})$ is a Hamiltonian cycle of the graph G.

- Let $\phi = C_1 \wedge \cdots \wedge C_m$ be a CNF-formula that is an instance of the language CNF-SAT, where C_i denotes a clause. The formula ϕ can be viewed as an instance (V, D, C) of the CSP, where V is the set of variables occurring in ϕ, the domain D is the set $\{0, 1\}$ of propositional values, and C contains, for each clause C_i, a constraint $C_i' = ((v_1, ..., v_k), P)$ where $v_1, ..., v_k$ is a list of the variables occurring in C_i, and P contains a tuple $(d_1, ..., d_k) \in \{0, 1\}^k$ if and only if the mapping sending each v_i to d_i satisfies C_i. For example, a clause $x \vee \neg y \vee z$ would be translated to the constraint $((x, y, z), \{0, 1\}^3 \setminus \{(0, 1, 0)\})$. It can be seen that a mapping $f \colon V \to D$ satisfies the presented CSP instance if and only if it satisfies the original CNF-formula.

- Let $t^1, ..., t^m$ be a k-NAE-system that is an instance of k-NAE-SAT. It can be formulated as an instance (V, D, C) of the CSP, where V is the set of variables appearing in the system, the domain D is the set $\{0, 1\}$ of propositional values, and C contains, for each tuple $t = (v_1, ..., v_k)$ of the system, a constraint $((v_1, ..., v_k), \{0, 1\}^k \setminus \{(0, ..., 0), (1, ..., 1)\})$ stating that the tuple's variables should be assigned to values that are not all equal. It can be verified that a mapping $f \colon V \to D$ satisfies this CSP instance if and only if it is a satisfying assignment of the k-NAE-system. $\diamond$

Note 4.6.53: Between constraint satisfaction and homomorphisms. The constraint satisfaction problem can be viewed as a formulation of the *homomorphism problem* of deciding, given a pair $(\mathbf{A}, \mathbf{B})$ of similar relational structures, whether the first structure $\mathbf{A}$ admits a homomorphism to the second structure $\mathbf{B}$. This homomorphism problem was formalized and studied as the language HOM in Section 4.4.3.

To translate from an instance $(\mathbf{A}, \mathbf{B})$ of the homomorphism problem to a constraint network (V, D, C), denote $\mathbf{A}$ by $(A; R_1^{\mathbf{A}}, ..., R_k^{\mathbf{A}})$, and $\mathbf{B}$ by $(B; R_1^{\mathbf{B}}, ..., R_k^{\mathbf{B}})$; define $V = A$, $D = B$, and, for each tuple $(a_1, ..., a_\ell)$ in a relation $R_i^{\mathbf{A}}$ of $\mathbf{A}$, introduce a constraint $((a_1, ..., a_\ell), R_i^{\mathbf{B}})$, where the tuple is paired with the corresponding relation of $\mathbf{B}$. In the other direction, from an arbitrary constraint network (V, D, C), we can define an instance $(\mathbf{A}, \mathbf{B})$ of the homomorphism problem: the structure $\mathbf{B}$ has universe D, and its relations $R_1^{\mathbf{B}}, ..., R_k^{\mathbf{B}}$ are those relations that appear in a constraint of C; the structure $\mathbf{A}$ has universe V and a relation $R_i^{\mathbf{A}}$ contains each tuple $(a_1, ..., a_\ell)$ such that $((a_1, ..., a_\ell), R_i^{\mathbf{B}})$ occurs as a constraint in C. In both cases, it is straightforwardly verified that a mapping from V to D satisfies the constraint network (V, D, C) if and only if it is a homomorphism from $\mathbf{A}$ to $\mathbf{B}$.

We next present positive results on the constraint satisfaction problem; these results can be applied directly to the homomorphism problem, via the translation just given. $\diamond$

Note 4.6.54: Constraint satisfaction with tree decompositions. We can use the measure of treewidth to present tractable cases of the CSP. Define the **constraint graph** of a constraint network (V, D, C) as the graph (V, E) where for any two distinct vertices $v, v' \in V$, the edge $\{v, v'\}$ is included in E if there exists a constraint $C \in C$ where both v and v' occur. That is, the constraint graph of a constraint network is the graph whose vertices are the variables of the network, and each edge indicates co-occurrence in a constraint. Define a **tree decomposition** of a constraint network as a tree decomposition of the network's constraint graph, and correspondingly, define the **treewidth** of a constraint network as the treewidth of the network's constraint graph. Say that a bag of a tree decomposition **covers** a constraint if each variable of the constraint is contained in the bag. When $((v_1, ..., v_k), P)$ is a constraint of a constraint network, it holds that $\{v_1, ..., v_k\}$ is a clique of the network's constraint graph, and so by Exercise 4.6.36, for any tree decomposition of the constraint network and for any constraint (of the network), there exists a bag covering the constraint.

We present an algorithm that, when given a constraint network (V, D, C) along with a nice tree decomposition $(T, (B_t)_{t \in V(T)})$ thereof, determines satisfiability of the network in a bottom-up, recursive fashion. In particular, we show how to recursively compute, for each vertex t of T, the set S_t containing each assignment $f \colon B_t \to D$ that can be extended to an assignment $f_\downarrow \colon (\bigcup_u B_u) \to D$ satisfying each constraint covered by a bag B_u, where u is a descendant of t; the union here is over each descendant u of t. Since every constraint is covered by a bag of the tree decomposition, the network is then satisfiable if and only if the root vertex r of T has a set S_r that is not empty; since $B_r = \emptyset$ by definition of a nice tree decomposition, S_r is nonempty if and only if it is the set containing the empty assignment.

We show how to inductively compute each set S_t, and provide a brief justification that the computation is correct; we leave a full verification to the reader.

- For each leaf vertex t, let S_t be the set that contains the empty assignment if each arity 0 constraint is satisfiable, and let S_t be the empty set otherwise. This is correct, since the only constraints that are covered by B_t are arity 0 constraints.

- For each introduce vertex t with child t', let S_t be the set that contains an assignment $f \colon B_t \to D$ if f satisfies each constraint that is covered by B_t and f is an extension of an assignment $f' \colon B_{t'} \to D$ in $S_{t'}$. By induction, the assignment f' has an extension $f'_\downarrow$ as required; the needed extension $f_\downarrow$ of f can be defined by setting each variable outside of B_t according to $f'_\downarrow$. Note that the variable v introduced by t does not occur in any bag that is a descendant of t'; if it did, the coherence condition would be violated, since $v \in B_t$ and $v \notin B_{t'}$.

- For each forget vertex t with child t', let S_t be the set that contains an assignment $f \colon B_t \to D$ having an extension $f' \colon B_{t'} \to D$ in $S_{t'}$. This is correct, since by induction, the assignment f' has an extension $f'_\downarrow$ as required; since $B_t \subseteq B_{t'}$, this assignment $f'_\downarrow$ is an extension of f, and has the necessary properties.

- For each join vertex t with children t_1, t_2, let S_t be the set $S_{t_1} \cap S_{t_2}$. For each assignment $f \in S_t$, the needed extension $f_\downarrow$ can be obtained by combining the two extensions of f that exist due to $f \in S_{t_1}$ and $f \in S_{t_2}$; note that when u_1 is a descendant of t_1 and u_2 is a descendant of t_2, by coherence, any vertex in $B_{u_1} \cap B_{u_2}$ must be in B_t.

There exists a polynomial Q and a DTM implementing this algorithm such that, on each input x consisting of a constraint network and a nice tree decomposition, the DTM halts within $Q(|D|^{k+1}|x|)$ time steps, where D denotes the domain of the network and k denotes the width of the nice tree decomposition. In short, this is because the set S_t is computed for each vertex t of the tree decomposition, and each set S_t has up to $|D|^{k+1}$ many assignments, as each bag of the tree decomposition has size $k + 1$ or less. ◇

Note 4.6.55: More on constraint satisfaction. Let us observe two consequences of Note 4.6.54's algorithm and analysis.

1. First, when restricted to instances with bounded treewidth, the CSP is PTIME. To be precise, for each $w \geq 1$, define $\mathrm{CSP}_{\mathrm{tw} \leq w}$ to be the language containing each satisfiable constraint network whose treewidth is at most w. We claim the following.

   For each $w \geq 1$, the language $\mathrm{CSP}_{\mathrm{tw} \leq w}$ is PTIME.

   Let us explain why. Given a constraint network N, whether its treewidth is bounded above by w can be polynomial-time decided via Bodlaender's theorem, presented in Note 4.6.46. When the bound is obeyed, appealing to this theorem and Exercise 4.6.45 allows us to assume (up to polynomial-time computation) that the constraint network is accompanied by a nice tree decomposition whose width is at most w, so satisfiability can be decided by Note 4.6.54's algorithm within polynomial time, specifically, within time $Q(|D|^{w+1}|x|)$ where Q is a polynomial, and x is the constraint network along with the nice tree decomposition.

2. Second, when restricted to instances with bounded domain size, fixed-parameter tractability holds on the CSP paired with the parameterization of treewidth. Precisely, for each $d \geq 1$, define $\mathrm{CSP}_{\mathrm{dom} \leq d}$ to be the language containing each satisfiable constraint network whose domain's size is at most d, and let us use $\mathrm{tw}(N)$ to denote the treewidth of a constraint network N. We claim the following.

   For each $d \geq 1$, the parameterized language $(\mathrm{CSP}_{\mathrm{dom} \leq d}, \mathrm{tw})$ is FPT.

   Let us explain why. By Note 4.6.46 and Exercise 4.6.45, to present a tw-fpt-time algorithm for this parameterized language, we can assume that, from a constraint network N, a nice tree decomposition of width $\mathrm{tw}(N)$ has been computed. When Note 4.6.54's algorithm is invoked on the pair x consisting of the network N along with such a nice tree decomposition, the algorithm runs within time $Q(d^{\mathrm{tw}(N)+1}|x|)$, where Q is a polynomial; this running time is bounded above by $Q(d^{\mathrm{tw}(N)+1})Q(|x|)$. Hence, we have obtained a tw-fpt-time algorithm.

This result in turn has the following implications. For any problem whose instances can be formulated as constraint networks having bounded domain size, we obtain that the problem is FPT under the treewidth parameterization, applied to the corresponding constraint networks. Here are some examples:

- Let us define the parameterization tw on CNF-formulas and k-NAE-systems by viewing them as constraint networks, as described in Note 4.6.52, and then by taking the treewidth of the respective constraint networks, as in Note 4.6.54. We then have that (CNF-SAT, tw) is FPT, and also that (k-NAE-SAT, tw) is FPT, for each $k \geq 2$.

- For each problem k-COL, the formulation of a graph G as a constraint network is such that the network's constraint graph is equal to the graph G itself, so we obtain that (k-COL, tw) is FPT, for each $k \geq 3$; we understand tw to apply directly to an instance G of k-COL.

We remark that the translation from the Hamiltonian cycle problem, in Note 4.6.52, does not give way to an FPT result via the above algorithm: under the translation, each network's domain is the vertex set of the original graph, and is hence unbounded in size (and in any case, each network's constraint graph has a clique on the variables $\{w_1, ..., w_n\}$).   ◇

Note 4.6.56: Counting constraint satisfaction with tree decompositions. The algorithm of Note 4.6.54 decides, given a constraint network along with a nice tree decomposition, whether or not the network is satisfiable. In this note, we explain how this algorithm can be extended to an algorithm that *counts* the number of satisfying assignments of the constraint network.

Let $(V, D, \mathcal{C})$ be a constraint network, and let $(T, (B_t)_{t \in V(T)})$ be a nice tree decomposition thereof. The extended algorithm inductively computes, for each vertex t of T and each assignment $f \colon B_t \to D$, the *number* of extensions $f_{\downarrow} \colon (\bigcup_u B_u) \to D$ satisfying each constraint covered by a bag B_u, where u is a descendant of t; the union here is over each descendant u of t. For each vertex t of T and each assignment $f \colon B_t \to D$, we let $\#(t, f)$ denote this number of extensions. The number of satisfying assignments of the constraint network is then computed as $\#(r, \emptyset)$, where r is the root vertex of the tree T, and $\emptyset$ is the empty assignment; this number is the output of the algorithm.

Following Note 4.6.54, we explain how to inductively compute each value $\#(t, f)$, and provide a brief justification that the computation is correct.

- For each leaf vertex t, let $\emptyset$ be the empty assignment; define $\#(t, \emptyset)$ as 1 if each arity 0 constraint is satisfiable, and as 0 otherwise. This is correct, since the only constraints that are covered by B_t are arity 0 constraints.

- For each introduce vertex t with child t', and for each assignment $f \colon B_t \to D$, let f' denote the map from $B_{t'}$ to D that is a restriction of f, and define $\#(t, f)$ as $\#(t', f')$ if f satisfies each constraint covered by B_t, and as 0 otherwise. In the latter case, this is correct, since f itself does not satisfy a constraint covered by B_t. In the former case, each extension $f_\downarrow$ of f having the desired form is obtained by setting each variable outside of B_t according to an extension $f'_\downarrow$ of f' having the desired form, and there is a one-to-one correspondence between the sets of these extensions.

- For each forget vertex t with child t', and for each assignment $f: B_t \to D$, define $\#(t,f)$ as the sum $\sum_{f'} \#(t',f')$ over all extensions $f': B_{t'} \to D$ of f; since $B_{t'}$ contains one variable that B_t does not, there are $|D|$ many such extensions. Correctness follows from the fact that each extension $f_\downarrow$ of f having the desired form is an extension of exactly one mapping $f': B_{t'} \to D$ that extends f.

- For each join vertex t with children t_1, t_2, and for each assignment $f: B_t \to D$, define $\#(t,f)$ as $\#(t_1,f) \cdot \#(t_2,f)$. As suggested in Note 4.6.54, each extension $f_\downarrow$ of f having the desired form is obtained by combining two extensions of f that contribute to the counts $\#(t_1,f)$ and $\#(t_2,f)$; any two such extensions can be combined independently of each other.

As with the algorithm of Note 4.6.54, there exists a polynomial Q where the algorithm just described can be implemented to run within time $Q(|D|^{k+1}|x|)$, where x denotes the input, D denotes the domain of the network, and k denotes the width of the nice tree decomposition. In short, this is because, for each vertex t of the tree decomposition and for each assignment $f: B_t \to D$, the value $\#(t,f)$ is computed; for any vertex t, the number of such assignments $f: B_t \to D$ is $|D|^{k+1}$ or less.

In light of the present note, the two positive consequences of Note 4.6.54 presented in Note 4.6.55 extend to the counting version of the CSP, where the input is a constraint network, and the task is to compute the number of satisfying assignments of the constraint network. ◇

Exercise 4.6.57: Incidence width. Suppose that $\phi = C_1 \wedge \cdots \wedge C_m$ is a CNF-formula, where each C_i denotes a clause of ϕ; let V be the set of variables occurring in ϕ. Define the **incidence graph** of ϕ as the graph with vertex set $V \cup \{C_1, \ldots, C_m\}$ and whose edge set contains each pair of the form $\{v, C_i\}$ where v is a variable, C_i is a clause, and v appears in C_i. That is, the incidence graph of ϕ only contains edges between variables and clauses; a variable v and a clause C_i form an edge if and only if the variable v underlies one of the literals in the clause C_i. Define the **incidence width** of ϕ to be the treewidth of the incidence graph of ϕ. For each $w \geq 1$, define CNF-SAT$_{iw \leq w}$ to be the language containing each satisfiable CNF-formula whose incidence width is at most w. Prove that, for each $w \geq 1$, the language CNF-SAT$_{iw \leq w}$ is PTIME. ◇

Note 4.6.58: Graph deconstructions. We saw that the homomorphism problem, formalized as the language HOM, is the problem of deciding, given a pair $(\mathbf{A}, \mathbf{B})$ of similar relational structures, whether or not there exists a homomorphism from $\mathbf{A}$ to $\mathbf{B}$. Relative to such a pair $(\mathbf{A}, \mathbf{B})$, we refer to $\mathbf{A}$ as the *left-hand side* structure, and to $\mathbf{B}$ as the *right-hand side* structure. In the following exercises and notes, we show how to prove a complexity classification of certain cases of the homomorphism problem where the left-hand side structure is restricted; in this classification, the measure of treewidth will play a decisive role. Via the correspondence between the homomorphism problem and conjunctive query evaluation (described in Note 4.4.30), this result can be viewed as a classification of sets of conjunctive queries; via the correspondence between the homomorphism problem and constraint satisfaction (described in Note 4.6.53), it can also be viewed as a classification of cases of the constraint satisfaction problem. To present this classification, we study a variation of the notion of tree decomposition known as *graph deconstruction*. This variation allows us to decompose a graph G according to the structure of a second graph H which need not be a tree.

For each graph G, define $\mathsf{loop}(E(G))$ as the set $E(G) \cup \{\{v\} \mid v \in V(G)\}$, that is, as the set that contains each edge of G and also contains the singleton set $\{v\}$, for each vertex v of G. Let G and H be graphs. An H**-deconstruction of** G is a family $(B_h)_{h \in V(H)}$ providing a subset B_h of $V(G)$ for each vertex h of H, such that the following two properties hold.

- **Coverage:** For each set $S \in \mathsf{loop}(E(G))$, there exists a set $\{h, h'\} \in \mathsf{loop}(E(H))$ such that $S \subseteq B_h \cup B_{h'}$.
- **Connectivity:** For each vertex $g \in V(G)$, the set $\{h \in V(H) \mid g \in B_h\}$ is connected, in the graph H.

We refer to the subsets B_h as **bags**. Note that, in the definition of *coverage*, it is permitted that $h = h'$; so, *coverage* holds that each set $S \in \mathsf{loop}(E(G))$ is contained either in a single bag B_h, or in the union of two bags $B_h, B_{h'}$ where h and h' form an edge in H. The **width** of an H-deconstruction $(B_h)_{h \in V(H)}$ is defined as the maximum bag size, that is, as $\max_{h \in V(H)} |B_h|$.

As an example, for each graph G, there is a G-deconstruction of G having width 1: define the sets $(B_g)_{g \in V(G)}$ by $B_g = \{g\}$. In general, for graphs G and H, a low-width H-deconstruction of G can be conceived of as witnessing that the structure of G can be approximated well by H. ◇

Exercise 4.6.59. For each $k \geq 1$, let D_k denote the k-by-k grid graph (defined in Exercise 4.6.51). Show that, for any graph G having $k \geq 1$ vertices, there exists a D_k-deconstruction of G having width 2. ◇

Exercise 4.6.60. We next use the notion of graph deconstruction to relate sets of graphs. When forming sets of graphs, we assume that each graph's vertices are drawn from a fixed base set $\{v_1, v_2, \dots\}$. Let $\mathcal{G}$ and $\mathcal{H}$ be sets of graphs. We say that $\mathcal{G}$ **has** $\mathcal{H}$**-deconstructions of bounded width**, denoted $\mathcal{G} \preceq \mathcal{H}$, if there exists $k \geq 1$ such that, for each graph $G \in \mathcal{G}$, there exists a graph $H \in \mathcal{H}$ admitting an H-deconstruction of G having width k or less.

1. Prove that the relation $\preceq$ is reflexive and transitive.

2. For any set $\mathcal{G}$ of graphs, let $\mathcal{M}(\mathcal{G})$ denote the set containing each graph that is a minor of a graph in $\mathcal{G}$. Prove that, for any set $\mathcal{G}$ of graphs, it holds that $\mathcal{M}(\mathcal{G}) \preceq \mathcal{G}$.

3. Let $\mathcal{G}$ be a set of graphs. Say that $\mathcal{G}$ has **bounded treewidth** if there exists $\ell \geq 1$ such that, for each graph $G \in \mathcal{G}$, it holds that $\mathrm{tw}(G) \leq \ell$; say that $\mathcal{G}$ has **unbounded treewidth** otherwise. Let $\mathcal{T}$ denote the set of all trees. Prove that a set $\mathcal{G}$ of graphs has bounded treewidth if and only if $\mathcal{G} \preceq \mathcal{T}$. ◇

Note 4.6.61. Let $\mathcal{L}$ denote the set of all graphs. When a set $\mathcal{G}$ of graphs has unbounded treewidth, it holds that $\mathcal{L} \preceq \mathcal{G}$. Here is why. The *excluded grid theorem* of graph minor theory states that there is a function $w \colon \mathbb{N}^+ \to \mathbb{N}^+$ such that, for all $k \in \mathbb{N}^+$, the *k-by-k* grid graph is a minor of any graph G with $\mathrm{tw}(G) \geq w(k)$. This theorem implies that, when $\mathcal{G}$ is a set of graphs having unbounded treewidth, it holds that each grid graph is an element of $\mathcal{M}(\mathcal{G})$, modulo renaming of vertices. Invoking Exercise 4.6.59, we obtain $\mathcal{L} \preceq \mathcal{M}(\mathcal{G})$; it then follows from Exercise 4.6.60 that $\mathcal{L} \preceq \mathcal{M}(\mathcal{G}) \preceq \mathcal{G}$, and thus that $\mathcal{L} \preceq \mathcal{G}$. ◇

Exercise 4.6.62. In the cases of the homomorphism problem that we will study, the left-hand side structure will always be a structure G^* arising from a graph G in the following way. Let G be a graph, and let $v_1, \ldots, v_n$ denote its vertices; we define G^* as the relational structure $(V^{G^*}; E^{G^*}, U_{v_1}^{G^*}, \ldots, U_{v_n}^{G^*})$, where $V^{G^*} = V(G)$, $E^{G^*} = E(G)$, and $U_{v_i}^{G^*} = \{v_i\}$ for each vertex v_i. That is, G^* is the relational structure whose universe is the vertex set of G, and which has as relations the edge set of G along with a singleton set $\{v_i\}$ for each vertex v_i of G. When $(G^*, \mathbf{C})$ is an instance of the homomorphism problem with G^* as the left-hand side structure, a homomorphism from G^* to $\mathbf{C}$ is sometimes referred to as a *list homomorphism*: for each vertex v of G, the structure $\mathbf{C}$ must provide a unary relation $U_v^{\mathbf{C}}$ giving a list of allowed values for the vertex v; any homomorphism h from G^* to $\mathbf{C}$ must obey $h(v) \in U_v^{\mathbf{C}}$.

Prove that, for each value $k \geq 1$, there exists a polynomial-time algorithm that, given graphs G and H, an H-deconstruction of G having width k or less, and a structure $\mathbf{C}$ similar to G^*, outputs a structure $\mathbf{D}$ similar to H^* such that

$$(G^*, \mathbf{C}) \in \mathsf{HOM} \quad \Leftrightarrow \quad (H^*, \mathbf{D}) \in \mathsf{HOM}.$$

Hint: one way to proceed is to define the universe D of $\mathbf{D}$ as the set of all partial homomorphisms from G^* to $\mathbf{C}$ whose domain has size at most k, and to define, for each vertex $h \in V(H)$, the set $U_h^{\mathbf{D}}$ to contain each partial homomorphism from G^* to $\mathbf{C}$ whose domain is B_h. ◇

Note 4.6.63. The cases of the homomorphism problem that we will classify are defined as follows. For each computable set $\mathcal{G}$ of graphs, define $\mathcal{G}^*$-HOM as the language containing each pair $(G^*, \mathbf{C})$ where G is a graph in $\mathcal{G}$, it holds that $\mathbf{C}$ is a structure similar to G^*, and there exists a homomorphism from G^* to $\mathbf{C}$ (that is, $(G^*, \mathbf{C}) \in \mathsf{HOM}$). That is, $\mathcal{G}^*$-HOM is the restricted version of HOM where the left-hand side structure must be of the form G^*, for a graph $G \in \mathcal{G}$. Define $\mathcal{G}^*$-p-HOM as the parameterized language $(\mathcal{G}^*\text{-HOM}, \pi_1)$.

Suppose that $\mathcal{G}$ and $\mathcal{H}$ are computable sets of graphs such that $\mathcal{G} \preceq \mathcal{H}$; then, it holds that

$$\mathcal{G}^*\text{-p-HOM} \leq^{\text{fpt}}_m \mathcal{H}^*\text{-p-HOM}.$$

To argue this, set $k \geq 1$ to be a value witnessing $\mathcal{G} \preceq \mathcal{H}$; let us describe a procedure giving a reduction. Given a pair $(G^*, \mathbf{C})$ where G is a graph and $\mathbf{C}$ is a structure similar to G^*, the procedure first checks whether or not G is in $\mathcal{G}$. If not, the pair $(G^*, \mathbf{C})$ is not in $\mathcal{G}^*$-HOM, and the reduction can output a string not in $\mathcal{H}^*$-HOM. Otherwise, the reduction searches exhaustively for a graph $H \in \mathcal{H}$ admitting an H-deconstruction of G having width k or less; when such a graph H and an H-deconstruction $(B_h)_{h \in V(H)}$ is found, the algorithm of Exercise 4.6.62 is invoked to obtain an instance $(H^*, \mathbf{D})$ of $\mathcal{H}^*$-HOM, which is output by the reduction. Other than the invocation of Exercise 4.6.62's algorithm, the procedure's computation depends only on the parameter G^* of the instance $(G^*, \mathbf{C})$, and so by arguing as in the backward direction of Theorem 4.3.32's proof, this procedure is implementable by a π_1-fpt-time DTM.   ◇

Note 4.6.64: Classification of homomorphism problems. We can now establish a classification of the problems $\mathcal{G}^*$-p-HOM, where $\mathcal{G}$ ranges over all computable sets of graphs. This classification is a *dichotomy theorem*: it shows that each such problem is either tractable or intractable, under established complexity-theoretic assumptions. In particular, assuming that $\mathcal{G}$ is a computable set of graphs, we argue that the problem $\mathcal{G}^*$-p-HOM is FPT when $\mathcal{G}$ has bounded treewidth, and is W[1]-complete when $\mathcal{G}$ has unbounded treewidth.

- Suppose that $\mathcal{G}$ has bounded treewidth. Then, the problem $\mathcal{G}^*$-p-HOM is FPT, via the algorithm that, given a pair $(G^*, \mathbf{C})$ where G is a graph and $\mathbf{C}$ is a structure similar to G^*, does the following. The algorithm first checks whether or not G is in $\mathcal{G}$. If not, the algorithm rejects, and otherwise, the instance $(G^*, \mathbf{C})$ can be viewed as an instance of the constraint satisfaction problem, as described in Note 4.6.53, and decided by the first consequence of Note 4.6.55.

- Suppose that $\mathcal{G}$ has unbounded treewidth. Then, the problem $\mathcal{G}^*$-p-HOM is W[1]-complete; let us explain why. That this problem is W[1] follows from the fact that the problem p-HOM is W[1]. Let us argue W[1]-hardness. By Note 4.6.61, it holds that $\mathcal{L} \preceq \mathcal{G}$, where $\mathcal{L}$ denotes the set of all graphs; by Note 4.6.63, it in turn holds that $\mathcal{L}^*$-p-HOM $\leq^{\text{fpt}}_m \mathcal{G}^*$-p-HOM. Each instance (G, k) of the language CLIQUE can be readily formulated as an instance $(K^*, \mathbf{C})$ of the language HOM, where K is a clique of size k; it follows that p-CLIQUE $\leq^{\text{fpt}}_m \mathcal{L}^*$-p-HOM, and hence that p-CLIQUE $\leq^{\text{fpt}}_m \mathcal{G}^*$-p-HOM.

An intriguing feature of this dichotomy theorem is that the problems treated do not, in their definitions, make any explicit reference to the notion of treewidth; yet, treewidth arises naturally as the decisive measure for describing the dichotomy.   ◇

4.7 Bibliographic discussion

Early systematic studies on space as a computational resource include those published by Stearns, Hartmanis, and Lewis (1965) and by Lewis, Stearns, and Hartmanis (1965). The PSPACE-completeness of the language QSAT, which we gave as Theorem 4.1.27, was proved by Stockmeyer and Meyer (1973), who noted the similarity of the formula construction to the proof of Savitch's theorem. Theorem 4.1.30 was presented by Savitch (1970).

The time and space hierarchy theorems presented in Section 4.2 have their origins in articles by Hartmanis and Stearns (1965) and Stearns, Hartmanis, and Lewis (1965).

Downey and Fellows (1987, 1992, 1995a, 1995b) systematically introduced and studied fixed-parameter tractability and the accompanying framework of parameterized complexity theory; in particular, they presented notions of reduction for parameterized languages, the class W[1], and the theory of W[1]-completeness. Prior to these developments, the research literature did present algorithms with time analyses that can now be recognized as fixed-parameter tractability results. One example is provided by a *linear temporal logic* model-checking algorithm presented by Lichtenstein and Pnueli (1985); the authors describe the algorithm's running time as being "exponential in the size of the formula but linear in the size of the checked program." As another example, a book of Mehlhorn (1984, Chapter 6) presented an algorithm for the vertex cover problem; this algorithm can be recognized as a version of the first hitting set algorithm in Section 4.3.1. Our presentation of the hitting set algorithms in Section 4.3.1 is based on that of Flum and Grohe's book (2006).

The compilation characterization of fixed-parameter tractability, Theorem 4.3.32, appears in an article by Flum and Grohe (2003). The kernelization characterization of fixed-parameter tractability, Theorem 4.3.33, appears in the *Habilitationsschrift* of Niedermeier (2002). More information on kernelizations can be found in the books by Fomin, Lokshtanov, Saurabh, and Zehavi (2019); and by Cygan, Fomin, Kowalik, Lokshtanov, Marx, Pilipczuk, Pilipczuk, and Saurabh (2015). The example kernelization presented in Section 4.3.3 has become well known; it originates in a kernelization which was for the vertex cover problem, and which was presented in the book by Downey and Fellows (1999, Section 3.2), where it is credited to Sam Buss. The Sunflower Lemma, a version of which was presented as Lemma 4.3.36, is due to Erdös and Rado (1960).

Our treatment of W[1]-completeness theory in Section 4.4 draws from the book treatment thereof by Flum and Grohe (2006), and is based on the work of Downey, Fellows, and Regan (1996); and of Flum and Grohe (2005). General references for parameterized complexity theory and parameterized algorithms include the books by Downey and Fellows (2013); Flum and Grohe (2006); and Cygan, Fomin, Kowalik, Lokshtanov, Marx, Pilipczuk, Pilipczuk, and Saurabh (2015).

The framework of compilability theory presented in Section 4.5 is based on the framework given by Chen (2015). Theorems 4.5.17 and 4.5.20 are due to Gogic, Kautz,

Papadimitriou, and Selman (1995). Karp and Lipton (1982) showed that the hypothesis $\mathit{NP} \not\subseteq \mathit{P}/\mathrm{poly}$, discussed in Remark 4.5.13, holds under the assumption that the *polynomial hierarchy*, a family of complexity classes generalizing P and NP, does not collapse.

The notions of extended Horn clause and of extended Horn qp-sentence, in Exercise 4.6.5, are due to Kleine Büning, Karpinski, and Flögel (1995); this exercise's coNP containment result, as well as that of Exercise 4.6.6, appear in an article by Chen (2009). The Q-resolution proof system of Note 4.6.7 was introduced by Kleine Büning, Karpinski, and Flögel (1995). The equivalence problems on Σ_1 qp-sentences appearing in Exercise 4.6.10 were studied, in a general setting, by Bova, Chen, and Valeriote (2012, 2013). Exercise 4.6.16 is due to Jansen and Pieterse (2019). Exercise 4.6.21 is based on work of Berkholz and Chen (2019).

The Immerman-Szelepcsényi theorem, presented in Note 4.6.30, was proved independently by Immerman (1988) and Szelepcsényi (1988). The result that the reachability problem for undirected graphs is in L, presented in Note 4.6.31, was shown by Reingold (2008).

The modern study of treewidth is due to articles by Robertson and Seymour (1984, 1986), from an article sequence entitled *Graph minors*. Bodlaender's theorem, from Note 4.6.46, is due to Bodlaender (1996). The game-theoretic characterization of treewidth given in Note 4.6.47 and the associated theory are due to Seymour and Thomas (1993). A book treatment of treewidth and graph minor theory is offered by Diestel (2012). The algorithm for counting constraint satisfaction given in Note 4.6.56 was presented in an article of Díaz, Serna, and Thilikos (2002); Figure 4.6.4 is based on an example in this article. The notion of graph deconstruction and the accompanying theory, as presented in Note 4.6.58 and subsequently, is due to Chen and Müller (2017). The dichotomy theorem of Note 4.6.64 is a formulation of the dichotomy first proved by Grohe, Schwentick, and Segoufin (2001), and subsequently generalized by Grohe (2007).

References

Aaronson, Scott. 2013. "Why Philosophers Should Care About Computational Complexity." In *Computability: Turing, Gödel, Church, and Beyond,* edited by B. Jack Copeland, Carl J. Posy, and Oron Shagrir, 261–328. MIT Press.

Aaronson, Scott. 2016. "P =? NP." In *Open Problems in Mathematics,* edited by John Forbes Nash Jr. and Michael Th. Rassias, 1–122. Springer.

Agrawal, M., N. Kayal, and N. Saxena. 2004. "PRIMES in P." *Annals of Mathematics* 160 (2): 781–793.

Allender, Eric. 2009. "A Status Report on the P Versus NP Question." *Advances in Computers* 77:117–147.

Arora, Sanjeev, and Boaz Barak. 2009. *Computational Complexity—A Modern Approach.* Cambridge University Press.

Bar-Hillel, Yehoshua, M. Perles, and E. Shamir. 1961. "On Formal Properties of Simple Phrase Structure Grammars." *Zeitschrift für Phonetik, Sprachwissenschaft und Kommunikationsforschung* 14:143–172.

Berkholz, Christoph, and Hubie Chen. 2019. "Compiling Existential Positive Queries to Bounded-Variable Fragments." In *Proceedings of the 38th ACM SIGMOD-SIGACT-SIGAI Symposium on Principles of Database Systems, PODS 2019,* 353–364. ACM.

Bodlaender, Hans L. 1996. "A Linear-Time Algorithm for Finding Tree-Decompositions of Small Treewidth." *SIAM Journal on Computing* 25 (6): 1305–1317.

Bova, Simone, Hubie Chen, and Matthew Valeriote. 2012. "On the Expression Complexity of Equivalence and Isomorphism of Primitive Positive Formulas." *Theory of Computing Systems* 50 (2): 329–353.

Bova, Simone, Hubie Chen, and Matthew Valeriote. 2013. "Generic Expression Hardness Results for Primitive Positive Formula Comparison." *Information and Computation* 222:108–120.

Chen, Hubie. 2009. "Existentially Restricted Quantified Constraint Satisfaction." *Information and Computation* 207 (3): 369–388.

Chen, Hubie. 2015. "Parameter Compilation." In *10th International Symposium on Parameterized and Exact Computation, IPEC 2015,* 43:127–137. LIPIcs. Schloss Dagstuhl—Leibniz-Zentrum für Informatik.

Chen, Hubie. 2017. "The Tractability Frontier of Graph-Like First-Order Query Sets." *Journal of the ACM* 64 (4): 26:1–26:29.

Chen, Hubie. 2020. *Algebraic Global Gadgetry for Surjective Constraint Satisfaction.* ArXiv:2005.11307.

Chen, Hubie, and Víctor Dalmau. 2005. "Beyond Hypertree Width: Decomposition Methods Without Decompositions." In *Principles and Practice of Constraint Programming—CP 2005, 11th International Conference, CP 2005,* 3709:167–181. Lecture Notes in Computer Science. Springer.

Chen, Hubie, and Moritz Müller. 2017. "One Hierarchy Spawns Another: Graph Deconstructions and the Complexity Classification of Conjunctive Queries." *ACM Transactions on Computational Logic* 18 (4): 29:1–29:37.

Church, Alonzo. 1932. "A Set of Postulates for the Foundation of Logic." *Annals of Mathematics* 33 (2): 346–366.

Church, Alonzo. 1936a. "A Note on the Entscheidungsproblem." *Journal of Symbolic Logic* 1 (1): 40–41.

Church, Alonzo. 1936b. "An Unsolvable Problem of Elementary Number Theory." *American Journal of Mathematics* 58 (2): 345–363.

Church, Alonzo. 1941. *The Calculi of Lambda Conversion.* Princeton University Press.

Cobham, Alan. 1965. "The Intrinsic Computational Difficulty of Functions." In *Logic, Methodology and Philosophy of Science: Proceedings of the 1964 International Congress (Studies in Logic and the Foundations of Mathematics),* edited by Yehoshua Bar-Hillel, 24–30. North-Holland Publishing.

Cook, Stephen A. 1971. "The Complexity of Theorem-Proving Procedures." In *Symposium on Theory of Computing,* 151–158. ACM.

Cook, Stephen A., and Robert A. Reckhow. 1979. "The Relative Efficiency of Propositional Proof Systems." *Journal of Symbolic Logic* 44 (1): 36–50.

Cormen, Thomas H., Charles E. Leiserson, Ronald L. Rivest, and Clifford Stein. 2009. *Introduction to Algorithms, 3rd Edition.* MIT Press.

Cygan, Marek, Fedor V. Fomin, Lukasz Kowalik, Daniel Lokshtanov, Dániel Marx, Marcin Pilipczuk, Michal Pilipczuk, and Saket Saurabh. 2015. *Parameterized Algorithms.* Springer.

Dasgupta, Sanjoy, Christos H. Papadimitriou, and Umesh V. Vazirani. 2008. *Algorithms.* McGraw-Hill.

Davis, Martin. 2004. *The Undecidable: Basic Papers on Undecidable Propositions, Unsolvable Problems and Computable Functions.* Dover Publications.

Díaz, Josep, Maria J. Serna, and Dimitrios M. Thilikos. 2002. "Counting H-colorings of partial k-trees." *Theoretical Computer Science* 281 (1-2): 291–309.

Diestel, Reinhard. 2012. *Graph Theory, 4th Edition.* Vol. 173. Graduate Texts in Mathematics. Springer. ISBN: 978-3-642-14278-9.

Downey, Rodney G., and Michael R. Fellows. 1987. "Fixed-Parameter Tractability and Completeness." *Congressus Numerantium* 87:161–178.

Downey, Rodney G., and Michael R. Fellows. 1992. "Fixed-Parameter Intractability." In *Proceedings of the Seventh Annual Structure in Complexity Theory Conference,* 36–49. IEEE Computer Society.

Downey, Rodney G., and Michael R. Fellows. 1995a. "Fixed-Parameter Tractability and Completeness I: Basic Results." *SIAM Journal on Computing* 24 (4): 873–921.

Downey, Rodney G., and Michael R. Fellows. 1995b. "Fixed-Parameter Tractability and Completeness II: On Completeness for W[1]." *Theoretical Computer Science* 141 (1&2): 109–131.

Downey, Rodney G., and Michael R. Fellows. 1999. *Parameterized Complexity*. Monographs in Computer Science. Springer.

Downey, Rodney G., and Michael R. Fellows. 2013. *Fundamentals of Parameterized Complexity*. Texts in Computer Science. Springer.

Downey, Rodney G., Michael R. Fellows, and Kenneth W. Regan. 1996. "Descriptive complexity and the *W* hierarchy." In *Proof Complexity and Feasible Arithmetics, Proceedings of a DIMACS Workshop,* 39:119–134. DIMACS Series in Discrete Mathematics and Theoretical Computer Science. DIMACS/AMS.

Edmonds, Jack. 1965a. "Minimum Partition of a Matroid into Independent Subsets." *Journal of Research of the National Bureau of Standards* 69B:67–72.

Edmonds, Jack. 1965b. "Paths, Trees, and Flowers." *Canadian Journal of Mathematics* 17:449–467.

Erdös, P., and R. Rado. 1960. "Intersection Theorems for Systems of Sets." *Journal of the London Mathematical Society* s1-35 (1): 85–90.

Erickson, Jeff. 2019. *Algorithms*. Self-published, Jeff Erickson.

Flum, Jörg, and Martin Grohe. 2003. "Describing Parameterized Complexity Classes." *Information and Computation* 187 (2): 291–319.

Flum, Jörg, and Martin Grohe. 2005. "Model-Checking Problems as a Basis for Parameterized Intractability." *Logical Methods in Computer Science* 1 (1).

Flum, Jörg, and Martin Grohe. 2006. *Parameterized Complexity Theory*. Texts in Theoretical Computer Science. An EATCS Series. Springer.

Fomin, Fedor V., Daniel Lokshtanov, Saket Saurabh, and Meirav Zehavi. 2019. *Kernelization: Theory of Parameterized Preprocessing*. Cambridge University Press.

Fortnow, Lance, and Steven Homer. 2003. "A Short History of Computational Complexity." *Bulletin of the EATCS* 80:95–133.

Garey, M. R., and David S. Johnson. 1979. *Computers and Intractability: A Guide to the Theory of NP Completeness*. W. H. Freeman.

Ginsburg, Seymour, and G. F. Rose. 1963. "Operations Which Preserve Definability in Languages." *Journal of the ACM* 10 (2): 175–195.

Gödel, Kurt. 1931. "Über formal unentscheidbare Sätze der Principia Mathematica und verwandter Systeme." *Monatshefte für Mathematik und Physik* 38 (1): 173–198.

Gogic, Goran, Henry A. Kautz, Christos H. Papadimitriou, and Bart Selman. 1995. "The Comparative Linguistics of Knowledge Representation." In *Proceedings of the Fourteenth International Joint Conference on Artificial Intelligence, IJCAI 95,* 862–869. Morgan Kaufmann.

Goldreich, Oded. 2008. *Computational Complexity—A Conceptual Perspective*. Cambridge University Press.

Goldreich, Oded. 2010. *P, NP, and NP-Completeness: The Basics of Complexity Theory.* Cambridge University Press.

Grohe, Martin. 2007. "The Complexity of Homomorphism and Constraint Satisfaction Problems Seen from the Other Side." *Journal of the ACM* 54 (1): 1:1–1:24.

Grohe, Martin, Thomas Schwentick, and Luc Segoufin. 2001. "When is the Evaluation of Conjunctive Queries Tractable?" In *Proceedings on 33rd Annual ACM Symposium on Theory of Computing,* 657–666. ACM.

Hartmanis, J., and R. E. Stearns. 1965. "On the Computational Complexity of Algorithms." *Transactions of the American Mathematical Society* 117:285–305.

Hopcroft, John E. 1971. "An n Log n Algorithm for Minimizing States in a Finite Automaton." In *The Theory of Machines and Computation,* edited by Z. Kohavi, 189–196. Academic Press.

Hopcroft, John E., Rajeev Motwani, and Jeffrey D. Ullman. 2007. *Introduction to Automata Theory, Languages, and Computation, 3rd Edition.* Pearson International Edition. Addison-Wesley.

Huffman, David A. 1954. "The Synthesis of Sequential Switching Circuits." *Journal of the Franklin Institute* 257, no. 3 (March): 161–190, 275–303.

Immerman, Neil. 1988. "Nondeterministic Space Is Closed under Complementation." *SIAM Journal on Computing* 17 (5): 935–938.

Jansen, Bart M. P., and Astrid Pieterse. 2019. "Optimal Sparsification for Some Binary CSPs Using Low-Degree Polynomials." *ACM Transactions on Computation Theory* 11 (4): 28:1–28:26.

Johnson, David S., Christos H. Papadimitriou, and Mihalis Yannakakis. 1988. "On Generating All Maximal Independent Sets." *Information Processing Letters* 27 (3): 119–123.

Karp, R., and R. Lipton. 1982. "Turing Machines That Take Advice." *L'Enseignement Mathématique* 28:191–209.

Karp, Richard M. 1972. "Reducibility among Combinatorial Problems." In *Complexity of Computer Computations,* edited by Raymond E. Miller, James W. Thatcher, and Jean D. Bohlinger, 85–103. Springer US.

Kleene, S. C. 1935. "A Theory of Positive Integers in Formal Logic." *American Journal of Mathematics* 57:153–173, 219–244.

Kleene, S. C. 1956. "Representation of Events in Nerve Nets and Finite Automata." In *Automata Studies,* edited by Claude Shannon and John McCarthy, 3–41. Princeton University Press.

Kleinberg, Jon, and Éva Tardos. 2006. *Algorithm Design.* Addison Wesley.

Kleine Büning, Hans, Marek Karpinski, and Andreas Flögel. 1995. "Resolution for Quantified Boolean Formulas." *Information and Computation* 117 (1): 12–18.

Knuth, Donald E. 1974. "A Terminological Proposal." *SIGACT News* 6 (1): 12–18.

Kozen, Dexter. 1997. *Automata and Computability.* Undergraduate Texts in Computer Science. Springer.

Kozen, Dexter. 2006. *Theory of Computation.* Texts in Computer Science. Springer.

Ladner, Richard E. 1975. "On the Structure of Polynomial Time Reducibility." *Journal of the ACM* 22 (1): 155–171.

Levin, Leonid A. 1973. "Universal Search Problems." In Russian, *Problems of Information Transmission* 9 (3).

Lewis, Philip M., II, Richard Edwin Stearns, and Juris Hartmanis. 1965. "Memory Bounds for Recognition of Context-Free and Context-Sensitive Languages." In *6th Annual Symposium on Switching Circuit Theory and Logical Design, Ann Arbor, Michigan, USA, October 6-8, 1965,* 191–202.

Lichtenstein, Orna, and Amir Pnueli. 1985. "Checking That Finite State Concurrent Programs Satisfy Their Linear Specification." In *Conference Record of the Twelfth Annual ACM Symposium on Principles of Programming Languages,* 97–107. ACM Press.

McCulloch, Warren S., and Walter Pitts. 1943. "A Logical Calculus of the Ideas Immanent in Nervous Activity." *The Bulletin of Mathematical Biophysics* 5, no. 4 (December): 115–133. ISSN: 1522-9602.

Mealy, George H. 1955. "A Method for Synthesizing Sequential Circuits." *Bell System Technical Journal* 34 (5): 1045–1079.

Mehlhorn, Kurt. 1984. *Data Structures and Algorithms 2: Graph Algorithms and NP-Completeness.* Vol. 2. EATCS Monographs on Theoretical Computer Science. Springer.

Moore, Cristopher, and Stephan Mertens. 2011. *The Nature of Computation.* Oxford University Press.

Moore, Edward F. 1956. "Gedanken-Experiments on Sequential Machines." In *Automata Studies,* edited by Claude Shannon and John McCarthy, 129–153. Princeton University Press.

Myhill, J. 1957. *Finite Automata and the Representation of Events.* Technical note. WADD 57-624, Wright Patterson AFB.

Nerode, A. 1958. "Linear Automaton Transformations." *Proceedings of the American Mathematical Society* 9 (4): 541–544.

Niedermeier, Rolf. 2002. "Invitation to Fixed-Parameter Algorithms." Habilitationsschrift, Universität Tubingen.

Papadimitriou, Christos H. 1994. *Computational Complexity.* Addison-Wesley.

Post, Emil L. 1944. "Recursively Enumerable Sets of Positive Integers and Their Decision Problems." *Bulletin of the American Mathematical Society* 50:284–316.

Rabin, Michael O., and D. Scott. 1959. "Finite Automata and Their Decision Problems." *IBM Journal of Research and Development* 3 (2): 114–125.

Reingold, Omer. 2008. "Undirected Connectivity in log-Space." *Journal of the ACM* 55 (4): 17:1–17:24.

Rice, H. G. 1953. "Classes of Recursively Enumerable Sets and Their Decision Problems." *Transactions of the American Mathematical Society* 74 (2): 358–366.

Robertson, Neil, and P. D. Seymour. 1984. "Graph Minors. III. Planar Tree-Width." *Journal of Combinatorial Theory. Series B* 36, no. 1 (February): 49–64.

Robertson, Neil, and P. D. Seymour. 1986. "Graph Minors. II. Algorithmic Aspects of Tree-Width." *Journal of Algorithms* 7, no. 3 (September): 309–322.

Rogers, Hartley. 1987. *Theory of Recursive Functions and Effective Computability.* MIT Press.

Rutten, Jan J. M. M. 1998. "Automata and Coinduction (An Exercise in Coalgebra)." In *CONCUR '98: Concurrency Theory, 9th International Conference,* 1466:194–218. Lecture Notes in Computer Science. Springer.

Savitch, Walter J. 1970. "Relationships between Nondeterministic and Deterministic Tape Complexities." *Journal of Computer and System Sciences* 4 (2): 177–192.

Seymour, P. D., and Robin Thomas. 1993. "Graph Searching and a Min-Max Theorem for Tree-Width." *Journal of Combinatorial Theory. Series B* 58, no. 1 (May): 22–33.

Sipser, Michael. 1992. "The History and Status of the P versus NP Question." In *Proceedings of the 24th Annual ACM Symposium on Theory of Computing,* 603–618. ACM.

Sipser, Michael. 2013. *Introduction to the Theory of Computation.* Third. Course Technology.

Soare, Robert I. 2016. *Turing Computability—Theory and Applications.* Theory and Applications of Computability. Springer.

Stearns, Richard Edwin, Juris Hartmanis, and Philip M. Lewis II. 1965. "Hierarchies of Memory Limited Computations." In *6th Annual Symposium on Switching Circuit Theory and Logical Design,* 179–190. IEEE Computer Society.

Stockmeyer, Larry J., and Albert R. Meyer. 1973. "Word Problems Requiring Exponential Time: Preliminary Report." In *Proceedings of the 5th Annual ACM Symposium on Theory of Computing,* 1–9. ACM.

Szelepcsényi, Róbert. 1988. "The Method of Forced Enumeration for Nondeterministic Automata." *Acta Informatica* 26 (3): 279–284.

Trakhtenbrot, Boris A. 1984. "A Survey of Russian Approaches to Perebor (Brute-Force Search) Algorithms." *IEEE Annals of the History of Computing* 6 (4): 384–400.

Turing, Alan M. 1936. "On Computable Numbers, with an Application to the Entscheidungsproblem." *Proceedings of the London Mathematical Society* 2 (42): 230–265.

Valiant, Leslie G. 1979. "The Complexity of Computing the Permanent." *Theoretical Computer Science* 8.

Wigderson, Avi. 2007. "P, NP and Mathematics—A Computational Complexity Perspective." In *Proceedings of the International Congress of Mathematicians 2006,* 665–712. EMS Publishing House.

Wigderson, Avi. 2009. "Knowledge, Creativity and P versus NP." Available on the web at URL https://www.math.ias.edu/ avi/PUBLICATIONS/MYPAPERS/AW09/AW09.pdf.

Wigderson, Avi. 2019. *Mathematics and Computation: A Theory Revolutionizing Technology and Science.* Princeton University Press.

Zhuk, Dmitriy. 2021. "No-Rainbow Problem and the Surjective Constraint Satisfaction Problem." In *36th Annual ACM/IEEE Symposium on Logic in Computer Science, LICS 2021,* 1–7. IEEE.

Index